JANSON'S
BASIC HISTORY
of WESTERN
ART

Eighth Edition

JANSON'S
BASIC HISTORY *of* WESTERN ART

Eighth Edition

PENELOPE J. E. DAVIES

FRIMA FOX HOFRICHTER

JOSEPH JACOBS

ANN M. ROBERTS

DAVID L. SIMON

PEARSON

Prentice Hall

Upper Saddle River, N.J. 07458

Library of Congress Cataloging-in-Publication Data is available on request
from the Library of Congress

Editor-in-Chief: Sarah Touborg
Senior Editor: Helen Ronan
Editorial Assistant: Carla Worner
Director of Media & Assessment: Brian Hyland
Media Editor: Alison Lorber
VP, Director of Marketing: Tim Stookesberry
Executive Marketing Manager: Wendy Gordon
Senior Managing Editor: Mary Rottino
Production Liaison: Barbara Taylor-Laino
Production Assistant: Marlene Gassler
Senior Operations Supervisor: Brian K. Mackey
Operations Specialist: Cathleen Peterson
Senior Art Director: Pat Smythe
Pearson Imaging Center: Corin Skidds, Greg Harrison, Robert Uibelhoer,
Ron Walko, Shayle Keating, and Dennis Sheehan
Site Supervisor, Pearson Imaging Center: Joe Conti
Director, Image Resource Center: Melinda Patelli
Manager, Rights and Permissions: Zina Arabia
Manager, Visual Research: Beth Brenzel
Manager, Cover Visual Research and Permissions: Karen Sanatar
Image Permission Coordinator: Debbie Latronica
Cover Printer: Phoenix Color Corporation
Printer/Binder: R. R. Donnelley

Commissioning Editor, LKP: Kara Hattersley-Smith
Senior Editor, LKP: Melissa Danny
Picture Editors, LKP: Julia Ruxton, Evi Peroulaki
Production, LKP: Simon Walsh
Copy Editor: Elisabeth Ingles
Design: Newton Harris Design

Pearson Education Ltd   Pearson Education, Canada, Ltd
Pearson Education Australia PTY, Limited   Pearson Educación de Mexico, S.A. de C.V.
Pearson Education Singapore, Pte. Ltd   Pearson Education-Japan
Pearson Education North Asia Ltd   Pearson Education Malaysia, Pte. Ltd

This book was designed by
Laurence King Publishing Ltd, London
www.laurenceking.co.uk

Cover: Photograph © 1984 The Detroit Institute of Arts

Frontispiece: James Abbott McNeill Whistler. *Symphony in White No. II: The Little White Girl*. 1864. Oil on canvas, 30⅛ × 20⅛″
(76.7 × 51.3 cm). Tate Britain, London. Tate Gallery, London/Art Resource, NY

10 9 8 7 6 5 4 3 2
ISBN 0-13-603912-X
ISBN 978-0-13-603912-9

Contents in Brief

Contents

Preface

Welcome to the Eighth Edition of Janson's concise introduction to the Western tradition in art, officially renamed *Janson's Basic History of Western Art* to reflect its relationship to the book that introduced many generations of students to art history.

Janson's *"Basic"* has always offered readers a strong focus on Western art, an important consideration of technique and style, and a clear point of view. Although largely revamped, this new edition follows the original's lead in important ways: It is limited to the Western tradition, with the addition of material on Islamic art and its relationship to Western art. It keeps the focus of the discussion on the object, its manufacture, and its visual character. It considers the contribution of the artist as an important part of the analysis. This edition is organized along the lines established by Janson, with separate chapters on the Northern European Renaissance, the Italian Renaissance, Baroque art, and the High Renaissance, with stylistic divisions for key periods of the modern era. This edition also creates a narrative of how art has changed over time in the cultures that Europe has claimed as its patrimony and that Americans have claimed through their connection to Europe.

What's new in *Janson's Basic History of Western Art?*

"The history of art is too vast a field for anyone to encompass all of it with equal competence."
—H. W. JANSON, from the Preface to the first edition of *History of Art*

Janson's Basic History of Western Art, eighth edition, is the product of careful revision by a team of scholars with different specialties, bringing great depth to the discussions of works of art.

New Organization and Contextual Emphasis

Most of the chapters have been reorganized to integrate the media into chronological discussions instead of discussing them in isolation from one another, which reflected the more formalistic approach used in earlier editions. Even though connections are drawn among works of art, as Janson did, emphasis is placed on the patronage and function of works of art and the historical circumstances in which they were created. The authors explore how works of art have been used to shore up political or social power.

Interpreting Cultures

Western art history encompasses a great many distinct chronological and cultural periods, which the authors wish to treat as distinct entities. So, for example, Etruscan art is presented as evidence for Etruscan culture, not as a precursor of Roman or a follower of Greek art.

Women in the History of Art

Another important feature of this edition is the greater visibility of women, whom the authors discuss as artists, as patrons, and as an audience for works of art. Inspired by contemporary approaches to art history, they also address the representation of women as expressions of specific cultural notions of femininity or as symbols.

Objects, Media, and Techniques

Many new objects have been incorporated into this edition to reflect changes in the discipline. The mediums discussed have been expanded to include not only modern art forms such as installations and earth art, but also the so-called minor arts of earlier periods—such as tapestries and metalwork. Discussions in the *Materials and Techniques* boxes illuminate this dimension of art history.

The Images

Not only have new objects been introduced, but every reproduction in the book also has been refreshed and expertly examined for fidelity to the original. We have obtained new photographs directly from the holding institutions to ensure that we have the most accurate and authoritative illustrations. Every image that could be obtained in color has been acquired. To further assist both students and teachers, we have sought permission for electronic educational use so that instructors who adopt *Janson's Basic History of Western Art* will have access to an extraordinary archive of high quality (over 300 dpi) digital images for classroom use. (See below for more detail on the Prentice Hall Digital Art Library.)

Chapter by Chapter Revisions

The following list includes the major highlights of this new edition:

CHAPTER 1: PREHISTORIC ART

Lengthened to include more information on the various contexts in which works of art are found. Expands upon the methods scholars (both art historians and anthropologists) use to understand artwork. Offering a wider range of interpretations, the text clarifies why scholars reconstruct the prehistoric world as they do.

CHAPTER 2: ANCIENT NEAR EASTERN ART

Expanded and reorganized to isolate cultures flourishing contemporaneously in the ancient Near East.

CHAPTER 3: EGYPTIAN ART

Includes an updated discussion of the Egyptian worldview, and relates Egyptian artworks to that view.

CHAPTER 4: AEGEAN ART

Examines how we construct our knowledge of an ancient society through studying works of art and architecture.

CHAPTER 5: GREEK ART

The organization of this chapter is altered radically to adhere more closely to a chronological, rather than medium-based, sequence. Expands discussions of the architecture of the Athenian Akropolis and Hellenistic art as a whole.

CHAPTER 6: ETRUSCAN ART

Discussion of Etruscan art is altered in order to characterize it as a visual culture in its own right rather than as an extension of Greek art or a precursor of Roman art.

CHAPTER 7: ROMAN ART

Features a greatly expanded section on art of the Republic, and a greater discussion of architecture in general. The organization is also radically altered to follow a chronological, rather than medium-based, sequencing.

CHAPTER 8: EARLY CHRISTIAN, BYZANTINE, AND EARLY ISLAMIC ART

Includes a discussion of early Islamic art and discusses both that art and Early Christian art in the context of the development of new religions. Accentuates changes and political dimensions in Early Christian art that occurred when Christianity became an accepted religion of the Roman Empire. Architecture is discussed in greater depth, stressing how the buildings were experienced. The iconography (i.e., meaning) of the forms employed is examined. The chapter expands the discussion of icons and of the iconoclastic controversy.

CHAPTER 9: EARLY MEDIEVAL ART

Discusses Irish manuscripts more thoroughly in terms of form and meaning. Expands the discussion of Charlemagne's political and social goals and the use of art to further that agenda. Additional early medieval buildings are discussed. Islamic art is discussed in depth and the connections between Islamic art and the art of the European West is emphasized.

CHAPTER 10: ROMANESQUE ART

Includes a new discussion of early Romanesque sculpture and architecture (of the first half of the twelfth century), and expands art of the pilgrimage road. The monasteries of Cluny and Moissac are discussed and Cistercian architecture is introduced. Reorganization of chapter allows integration of the various mediums to promote understanding that, despite intrinsic differences, the works demonstrate common expressive and aesthetic aims. A new box highlights the relationship between Spanish Islamic Art and the Christian art of Western Europe.

CHAPTER 11: GOTHIC ART

Reconfigured to remove Italian art (now in Chapter 12) and some International Style monuments (now in Chapter 13). Treats development of Gothic architecture more cogently with new examples (e.g., the interiors of Notre-Dame of Laon and Sainte-Chapelle). German Gothic architecture is introduced. Reorganization of chapter allows integration of the various mediums.

CHAPTER 12: ART IN THIRTEENTH- AND FOURTEENTH-CENTURY ITALY

Separates the thirteenth-and fourteenth-century Italian situation from the rest of Europe to highlight its specific role as a bridge between medieval and Renaissance art. More emphasis on how objects functioned. New works include Giotto's *Ognissanti Madonna* and Andrea da Firenze's *Way of Salvation* in the Spanish Chapel. New section added on Milan in the fourteenth century.

CHAPTER 13: ARTISTIC INNOVATIONS IN FIFTEENTH-CENTURY NORTHERN EUROPE

Now placed before the Italian fifteenth-century chapter, the new structure of the chapter integrates works of art of a particular time and place to emphasize historical context. Updates discussions of key works, such as the *Merode Triptych* and the *Garden of Earthly Delights*. Separate section on the International Gothic treats Limbourg Brothers and Sluter. Treats printmaking and the printed book in detail.

CHAPTER 14: THE EARLY RENAISSANCE IN FIFTEENTH-CENTURY ITALY

Situates art in specific moments or geographic regions and discusses different mediums in relation to their context, rather than discussing them by medium. Emphasizes role of patronage and meaning for original audiences. Introduces new sections on art outside of Florence. Updates treatment of Donatello's *David* and Uccello's *Battle of San Romano* by considering their Medici connections. Fra Angelico's *Annunciation* at San Marco, Piero della Francesca's portraits for the court of Urbino, Mantegna's *Camera Picta* in Mantua and Bellini's *San Zaccaria Madonna* are included.

CHAPTER 15: THE HIGH RENAISSANCE IN ITALY 1495–1520

Explains why a group of six key artists continue to be treated in monographic fashion. Focuses on the period 1495–1520, removing late Michelangelo and Titian to Chapter 16. Leonardo's drawing of the *Vitruvian Man*, Michelangelo's Roman *Pietà* and Titian's *Pesaro Madonna* and *Man with a Glove* are added.

CHAPTER 16: THE LATE RENAISSANCE AND MANNERISM IN SIXTEENTH-CENTURY ITALY

Follows a geographic structure, starting with Florence under the Medici dukes, and then moves among the regions of Rome, northern Italy, and Venice. Stresses courtly and papal patronage, as well as the founding of the Accademia del Disegno in Florence. Integrates late Michelangelo and Titian into these discussions. New discussions included for Bronzino, Giulio Romano, Titian's *Venus of Urbino*, and the work of Lavinia Fontana.

CHAPTER 17: RENAISSANCE AND REFORMATION THROUGHOUT SIXTEENTH-CENTURY EUROPE

Describes works of art in five different geographical regions. Considers the spread of Italian Renaissance style and the development of local traditions, among discussions of the Reformation and other crises. Treats French patronage of Italian artists at Fontainebleau and the work of El Greco in Spain. Considers influence of Italian art in Germany and the impact of the Reformation on artists in Germany, England and the Netherlands. Includes new discussions of the *Isenheim Altarpiece* and Aertsen's *Meat Stall*.

CHAPTER 18: THE BAROQUE IN ITALY AND SPAIN

Examines Caravaggio's and Bernini's roles in the Counter-Reformation. Discusses religious orders and the papacy, and develops an understanding of the role of patronage, the poor, street people, and the full nature of seventeenth-century life. New works include Gaulli's (Baccicio's) ceiling fresco, *Triumph of the Name of Jesus*, Borromini's *Sant'Ivo*, Ribera's *The Club-Footed Boy* as well as the portrait of *Juan de Pareja* by Velázquez.

CHAPTER 19: THE BAROQUE IN THE NETHERLANDS

Examines political and religious differences and artistic connections in the Netherlands. Explores the importance of Rubens through an examination of his workshop. The concept of an open market is treated in a discussion of the Dutch landscape, the still life, and the genre painting of Northern Europe. New works in prints and drawings by Rembrandt are added, including his *The Hundred Guilder Print* and his drawing

of his wife Saskia upon their betrothal. New works by Frans Hals (*Married Couple in the Garden*), Terbrugghen's *Singing Lute Player* and Judith Leyster's *Self-Portrait* better establish the early development of Dutch painting in the first half of the century and examine the development of a woman artist in the Netherlands. Also newly included is Ruisdael's splendid landscape *Bleaching Grounds near Haarlem*.

CHAPTER 20: THE BAROQUE IN FRANCE AND ENGLAND

Considers concept of classicism in the paintings of Poussin and the architecture of Jones and Wren. New works include Poussin's *Death of Germanicus* and *Landscape with St. John on Patmos* and new, improved views of the Palace of Versailles. Also newly included is Rigaud's *Portrait of Louis XIV* of 1701.

CHAPTER 21: THE ROCOCO

Explores the Age of Louis XV using new examples by Watteau and Fragonard, including a *trios crayon* drawing by Watteau and the infamous painting of *The Swing* by Fragonard. Elisabeth Vigée-Lebrun's *Portrait of Marie-Antoinette with Her Children* is introduced and the dispersal of the Rococo style beyond France to England, Germany, Austria and Italy is examined.

CHAPTER 22: ART IN THE AGE OF THE ENLIGHTENMENT, 1750–1789

Rewritten to focus more on the time period from roughly 1750 to 1789 than on Neoclassicism in particular. Emphasizes Neoclassicism's reliance on logic, morality, and the Classical past, while also pointing to the burgeoning importance placed on emotion, the irrational, and the sublime. Includes works by Mengs, Piranesi, and Ledoux.

CHAPTER 23: ART IN THE AGE OF ROMANTICISM, 1789–1848

Defines Romanticism and emphasizes the importance of emotion, individual freedom, and personal experience. It examines imagination, genius, nature, and the exotic. Puts Romanticism into the context of the perceived failures of the Enlightenment and French Revolution. More strongly states the idea of nationalism as a Romantic theme.

CHAPTER 24: THE AGE OF POSITIVISM: REALISM, IMPRESSIONISM, AND THE PRE-RAPHAELITES, 1848–1885

Organizes around the concept of Positivism, the reliance on hard fact, and the dramatic social transformations that artists recorded. Introduces photography within the context of Positivism. Focuses on the use of iron in engineering and architecture, especially in the Crystal Palace and the Eiffel Tower. Associates Rodin with Symbolism. Includes Daumier and Millet in the discussion of Realism.

CHAPTER 25: PROGRESS AND ITS DISCONTENTS: POST-IMPRESSIONISM, SYMBOLISM, AND ART NOUVEAU, 1880–1905

Emphasizes historical context rather than the Modernist tradition. Stresses disturbing psychology of the period and its manifestation in art. Places Frank Lloyd Wright here and into the context of the Chicago School and Arts and Crafts Movement. Photography section now includes Käsebier's *Blessed Art Thou Among Women*, which is dealt with in a feminist context.

CHAPTER 26: TOWARDS ABSTRACTION: THE MODERNIST REVOLUTION, 1904–1914

Emphasizes the social forces that resulted in radical formal and stylistic developments between 1904 and 1914 that culminated in abstractionism.

CHAPTER 27: ART BETWEEN THE WARS

Structured around the impact of World War I and the need to create utopias and uncover higher realities, especially as seen in Surrealism.

CHAPTER 28: POSTWAR TO POSTMODERN, 1945–1980

Emphasizes the enormous impact that Robert Rauschenberg had on the period, and stresses how art moved beyond its traditional definition of painting and sculpture to embrace radically new mediums.

CHAPTER 29: THE POSTMODERN ERA: ART SINCE 1980

Presents the concept of Postmodernism in clear, simple terms. Emphasizes the period's pluralism and the view of art as having no limits.

Acknowledgments

The Islamic material in this text is in large part adapted from Walter Denny's chapter entitled "Islamic Art" in the seventh edition of *Janson's History of Art: The Western Tradition*. The authors were deeply grateful for this solid foundation upon which to build the newly incorporated Islamic coverage in this eighth edition of *Janson's Basic History of Western Art*. Any inaccuracies that may have crept in are the responsibility of the current authorship and are not a reflection of the original material.

A special thanks also to Marian Feldman, University of California at Berkeley, for her advice and information about the status of looted objects in Iraq.

The authors and Prentice Hall are grateful to the following academic reviewers who helped shape this new edition:

Julie Anderson, Pacific University
Mark Deka, Edinboro College
Tana Harvey, Fairleigh Dickinson University
Joanne Kuebler, Manhattan College
Brian McConnell, Florida Atlantic University
Jeremy Miller, Fashion Institute of Design of Merchandising, San Francisco
Elizabeth Mix, Butler University
Henry Navarro, Fashion Institute of Design of Merchandising, San Francisco
Nancy M. Reale, New York University
Kathy Reba, Molloy College
Carolyn Robertson, The Fashion Institute of Design and Merchandising, CA
Gwen Robertson, Humboldt State University
Elizabeth Russell, Fashion Institute of Design of Merchandising, Los Angeles
Keri Shurtliff, The Fashion Institute of Design and Merchandising, CA
David Soren, University of Arizona
Lois Walsh, Marist College

Faculty and Student Resources for Teaching and Learning with *Janson's Basic History of Western Art*

PEARSON/PRENTICE HALL is pleased to present an outstanding array of high quality resources for teaching and learning with *Janson's Basic History of Western Art*. Please contact your local Prentice Hall representative (use our rep locator at www.pearsonhighered.com) for more details on how to obtain these items, or send us an email at art.service@pearson.com.

Digital and Visual Resources

THE PRENTICE HALL DIGITAL ART LIBRARY. Instructors who adopt *Janson's Basic History of Western Art* are eligible to receive this unparalleled resource. Available on DVD, The *Prentice Hall Digital Art Library* contains every image in *Janson's Basic History of Western Art* in the highest resolution (over 300 dpi) and pixilation possible for optimal projection and easy download. Developed and endorsed by a panel of visual curators and instructors across the country, this resource features images in jpeg and in PowerPoint, an instant download function for easy import into any presentation software, along with a zoom and a save-detail feature, as well as a compare/contrast function, both of which are unique and were developed exclusively for Prentice Hall.

MY ARTKIT is a state-of-the-art interactive and instructive solution for use in art history courses. MyArtKit gives you and your students access to a wealth of resources all geared to meet the individual teaching and learning needs of your classroom. These include practice quizzes, flashcards for studying images and terms, guided tours of key works of art, timelines, maps, and more. For more information visit www.myartkit.com.

CLASSROOM RESPONSE SYSTEM (CRS) IN CLASS QUESTIONS. Get instant, classwide responses to beautifully illustrated chapter-specific questions during a lecture to gauge students' comprehension—and keep them engaged. Contact your local Pearson representative for details.

PEARSON TEST GENERATOR is a commercial-quality computerized test management program available for both Microsoft Windows and Macintosh environments.

Print Resources

UNDERSTANDING THE ART MUSEUM by Barbara Beall-Fofana. This handbook gives students essential museum-going guidance to help them make the most of their experience seeing art outside of the classroom. Case studies are incorporated into the text, and a list of major museums in the United States and key cities across the world is included. Available at a nominal cost when packaged with the text.

A SHORT GUIDE TO WRITING ABOUT ART by Sylvan Barnet. This best-selling text has guided tens of thousands of art students through the writing process. Students are shown how to analyze pictures (drawings, paintings, photographs), sculptures and architecture, and are prepared with the tools they need to present their ideas through effective writing. Available at a discount when purchased with the text.

INSTRUCTOR'S MANUAL AND TEST ITEM FILE is an invaluable professional resource and reference for new and experienced faculty, containing sample syllabi, hundreds of sample test questions, and guidance on incorporating media technology into your course.

The Prentice Hall Digital Art Library DVD

Instructors who adopt *Janson's Basic History of Western Art*, eighth edition, are eligible to receive this unparalleled resource. The Prentice Hall Digital Art Library contains every image in the book in the highest resolution and pixilation possible for optimal projection and one-click download.

Instant Download

This powerful resource offers the images in jpeg format and in customizable PowerPoint slides with an instant download function.

Save Detail

Save Detail functionality allows you to zoom in and save any detail of an image to your hard drive, which you can then import into PowerPoint or any other presentation software.

MyArtKit

MyArtKit provides a robust suite of teaching and learning resources including chapter quizzes with feedback, flashcards of images in the book, primary source documents, and many more dynamic activities. MyArtKit offers you and your students a unique, interactive experience that helps bring art to life. Visit www.myartkit.com.

e-Flashcards

Interactive e-Flashcards offer all the benefits of traditional flashcards in a student-friendly and printable online format. Each e-Flashcard is accompanied by a critical thinking question to help students further analyze the individual works of art.

Guided Tour

Interactive Guided Tours give students an in-depth look at selected works of art from the text. Zoom in for a close-up look at particular details of the object and its meanings. Guided Tours help students develop the skills to closely "read" an image.

Quizzes

Self-study quizzes with targeted feedback for each chapter allow students to review their knowledge of the material and concepts. Feedback directs students to the relevant section of the textbook.

Introduction

Who was Freelove Olney Scott? Her portrait shows us a refined-looking woman, born, we would guess, into an aristocratic family, used to servants and power. We have come to accept John Singleton Copley's portraits of colonial Bostonians, such as Mrs. Joseph Scott, as accurate depictions of his subjects and their lifestyles. But many, like Mrs. Scott, were not what they appear to be. Who was she? Let's take a closer look at the context in which the painting was made.

I-1 John Singleton Copley. *Mrs. Joseph Scott.* ca. 1765. Oil on canvas, 69½ × 39½" (176.5 × 100 cm). Collection of The Newark Museum, Newark, New Jersey. 48.508

Copley is recognized as the first great American painter. Working in Boston from about 1754 to 1774, he became the most sought-after portraitist of the period. Copley easily outstripped the meager competition, most of whom earned their living painting signs and coaches. After all, no successful British artist had any reason to come to America. The economically struggling colonies were not a strong market for art. Only occasionally was a portrait commissioned, and typically, artists were treated like craftsmen rather than intellectuals. Like most colonial portraitists, Copley was self-taught, learning his trade by looking at black-and-white prints of paintings by the European masters.

As we can see in *Mrs. Joseph Scott* (**fig. I-1**), Copley was a master at painting textures, all the more astonishing when we realize that he had no one to teach him the tricks of the painter's trade. His illusions are so convincing that we think we are looking at real silk, ribbons, lace, pearls, skin, hair, and marble. Copley's contemporaries also marveled at his sleight of hand. No other colonial painter attained such a level of realism.

But is Copley just a "face painter," as portraitists were derogatorily called at the time, capturing only the resemblance of his sitter and her expensive accoutrements? And is this painting just a means to replicate the likeness of an individual in an era before the advent of photography? The answer to both questions is a resounding "no." Copley's job was not just to make a faithful image of Mrs. Scott, but to portray her as a woman of impeccable character, limitless wealth, and aristocratic status. The flowers she holds are a symbol of fertility, faithfulness, and feminine grace, indicating that she is a good mother and wife, and a charming woman. Her expensive dress was imported from London, as was her necklace. Copley undoubtedly took her pose from one of the prints he had of British or French royalty.

Not only is Mrs. Scott's pose borrowed, but most likely her clothing is too, for her necklace appears on three other women in Copley portraits. In other words, it was a studio prop, and the dress may have been as well. In fact, except for Mrs. Scott's face, the entire painting is a fiction designed to aggrandize the wife of a newly wealthy Boston merchant, who made a fortune selling provisions to the occupying British army. The Scotts were *nouveaux riches* commoners, not titled aristocrats. By the middle of the eighteenth century, rich Bostonians wanted to distinguish themselves from others who were less successful. Now, after a century of trying to escape their British roots (from which many had fled to secure religious freedom), they sought to imitate the British aristocracy, even to the point of taking tea in the afternoon and keeping English Spaniels, a breed that in England only aristocrats were permitted to own.

Mr. Scott commissioned this painting of his wife, as well as a portrait of himself, not just to record their features, but to show off the family's wealth. These pictures were extremely expensive and therefore status symbols, much as a Mercedes or a diamond ring from Tiffany's is today. The portraits were displayed in the public spaces of the house where they could be readily seen by visitors. Most likely they hung on either side of the mantel in the living room, or in the entrance hall. They were not intended as intimate, affectionate resemblances destined for the bedroom. If patrons wanted cherished images of their loved ones, they would commission miniature portraits. These captured the likeness of the sitter in amazing detail and were often so small that they could be encased in a locket for a woman to wear on a chain around her neck, or a gentleman to place in the inner breast pocket of his coat, close to the heart.

Let's move forward almost 200 years to look at a second image of a woman, Andy Warhol's

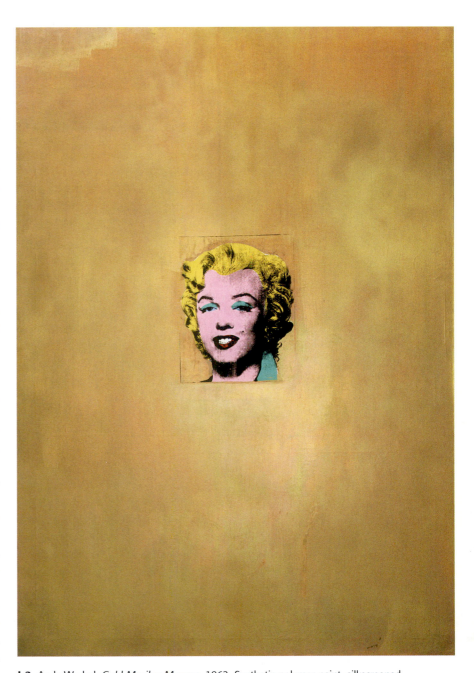

I-2 Andy Warhol. *Gold Marilyn Monroe*. 1962. Synthetic polymer paint, silkscreened, and oil on canvas, 6'11¼" × 4'7" (2.12 × 1.39 m). The Museum of Modern Art, New York. Gift of Philip Johnson. © 2008 Andy Warhol Foundation for the Visual Arts/ARS, New York/DACS, London

Gold Marilyn Monroe (**fig. I-2**) of 1962, and explore the surprising stories it contains. In a sense, the painting can be considered a portrait, because it portrays the famous 1950s film star and sex symbol. Unlike *Mrs. Joseph Scott*, however, the painting was not commissioned, and instead was made to be exhibited in a commercial art gallery, where it could be purchased by a private collector for display in a home. Of course, Warhol hoped that ultimately it would end up in a museum, something Copley never considered because they did not exist in his day. Because *Gold Marilyn Monroe* is not a commission, Warhol is not trying to flatter his subject. He is not even concerned about creating an illusionistic image; this image has no details and no sense of texture, as hair and flesh appear to be made of the same material—paint. Nor did Warhol painstakingly paint this picture. Instead he found a famous newspaper photograph of the film star and silkscreened it onto canvas, a process that involves first mechanically transferring the photograph onto a mesh screen and then pressing printing ink through the screen onto the canvas. He then surrounded Marilyn's head with a field of broadly brushed gold paint.

Warhol's painting is a pastiche of the public image of Monroe as propagated by the mass media. He even imitates the sloppy, gritty look and feel of color newspaper reproductions of the period, for the colors were often misregistered, not aligning properly with the image. The Marilyn we are looking at is the impersonal celebrity of the media, supposedly glamorous with her lush red lipstick and bright blond hair but instead appearing pathetically tacky because of the garish color (blond hair becomes bright yellow) and grimy black ink. Her personality is impenetrable, reduced to a public smile. The painting was prompted, in part, by Monroe's recent suicide. This was the real Marilyn—a depressed, miserable person. Warhol has brilliantly expressed the indifference of the mass media that glorifies celebrities by saturating a celebrity-thirsty public with their likenesses, but tells us nothing meaningful about them and shows no concern for them. Marilyn Monroe's image is about promoting a product, much as the jazzy packaging of Brillo soap pads or Campbell's soup cans is designed to sell a product without telling us anything about the product itself. The packaging is just camouflage. Warhol floats Marilyn's face in a sea of gold paint, imitating icons of Christ and the Virgin Mary that traditionally encase these religious figures in a spiritual aura of golden, heavenly light (see fig. 8.21). But Warhol's revered Marilyn is sadly dwarfed in her celestial gold, adding to the tragedy of this powerful portrait, which so trenchantly comments on the enormous gulf existing between public image and private reality.

Copley and Warhol worked in very different times, which tremendously affected the look and meaning of their portraits. Because art always serves a purpose, it is impossible for any artist to make a work that does not represent a point of view and tell a story, sometimes many stories. As we will see, great artists tell great and powerful stories. We will find that an important key to unraveling these stories is understanding the context in which the work was made.

The Power of Art and the Impact of Context

In a sense, art is a form of propaganda, for it represents an individual's or group's point of view, and this view is often presented as truth or fact. For centuries, art was used by the Church and the State to propagate the superiority of their powers. The *Alba Madonna* (see fig. I-16) was designed to proclaim the idealized, perfect state of existence attainable through Catholicism, and the Arch of Titus (**fig. I-3**) was erected to reinforce in the public's mind the military prowess and deification of the Roman emperor Titus. Even landscape paintings and still-lifes of fruit, dead game, and flowers are loaded with messages and are far from simple attempts to capture the splendor and many moods of nature or show off the painter's finesse at creating a convincing illusionistic image.

Epitomizing the power of art is its ability to evoke entire historical periods. Say the words ancient Egypt and most people conjure up images of the pyramids (**fig. I-4**), the Sphinx, and flat stiff figures lined up sideways across the face of sandstone (see fig. 3.9). Or look at the power

I-3 Arch of Titus, Forum Romanum. ca. 81 CE, as restored. Rome

of Grant Wood's famous 1930 painting *American Gothic* (**fig. I-5**), which has led us to believe that humorless, austere, hardworking farmers dominated the American hinterlands at the time. The painting has virtually become an emblem of rural America.

American Gothic has also become a source of much sarcastic humor for later generations, which adapted the famous pitchfork-bearing farmer and sour-faced daughter for all kinds of agendas unrelated to the artist's message. Works of art are often appropriated to serve purposes quite different from those initially intended, with context heavily influencing the meaning of a work. The reaction of some New Yorkers to *The Holy Virgin Mary* (**fig. I-6**) by Chris Ofili reflects the power of art to provoke and spark debate, even outrage. The work appeared in an exhibition titled *Sensation: Young British Artists from the Saatchi Collection*, presented at the Brooklyn Museum in late 1999. Ofili, who is British of African descent, made an enormous picture using dots of paint, glitter, map pins, and collaged images of genitalia from popular magazines to depict a black Virgin Mary. Instead of hanging on the wall, this enormous painting rested on two large wads of elephant dung, which had been a signature of the artist's large canvases since 1991. Elephant dung is held sacred in Zimbabwe, and for Ofili, a devout Catholic who periodically attends Mass, the picture was about the elemental sacredness of the Virgin. The so-called pornographic images were intended to suggest procreation.

I-5 Grant Wood. *American Gothic*. 1930. Oil on board, 30$\frac{11}{16}$ × 25$\frac{11}{16}$″ (78 × 65.3 cm). The Art Institute of Chicago. Friends of American Art Collection.

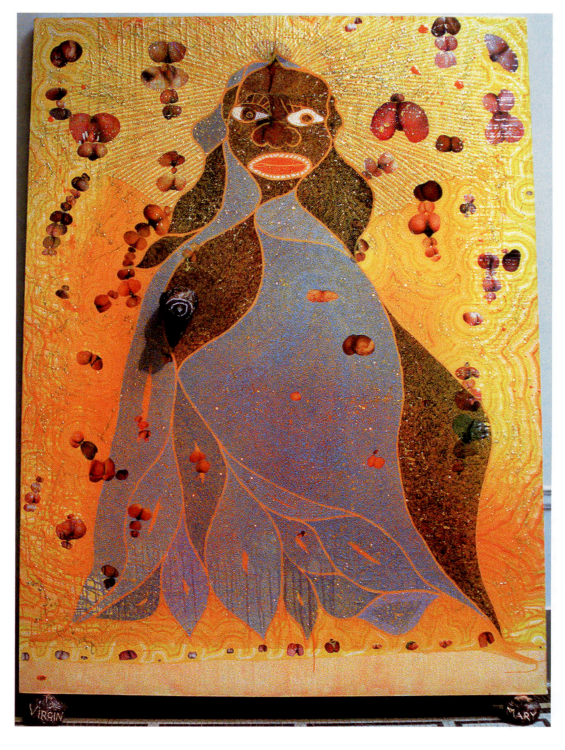

I-6 Chris Ofili. *The Holy Virgin Mary*. 1996. Paper collage, oil paint, glitter, polyester resin, map pins, and elephant dung on linen, 7'11" × 5'11⁵⁄₁₆" (2.44 × 1.83 m). The Saatchi Gallery, London

Many art historians, critics, and other viewers found the picture remarkably beautiful—glittering and shimmering with a delicate, ephemeral, otherworldly aura. Many Catholics, however, were repulsed by Ofili's homage to the Virgin. Instead of viewing the work through his eyes, they placed the painting within the context of their own experience and beliefs. Consequently, they interpreted the dung and so-called pornography (and probably even a black Virgin, although this was never mentioned) as sacrilegious. Within days of the opening of the exhibition, the painting had to be put behind a large Plexiglas barrier. One artist hurled horse manure at the façade of the Brooklyn Museum, claiming "I was expressing myself creatively"; a museum visitor sneaked behind the Plexiglas barrier and smeared the Virgin with white paint in order to hide her. But the greatest attack came from New York's mayor, Rudolph Giuliani, a Catholic, who was so outraged that he tried to eliminate city funding for the museum. Ultimately, he failed, but only after a lengthy lawsuit by the museum. The public outrage at Ofili's work is one instance in a long tradition that probably goes back to the beginning of image-making. Art has consistently provoked outrage, just as it has inspired pride, admiration, love, and respect, and the reason is simple: Art is never an empty container; rather, it is a vessel loaded with meaning, subject to multiple interpretations, and always representing someone's point of view.

Because the context for looking at art constantly changes, our interpretations and insights into art and entire periods evolve as well. For example, when the first edition of this book was published in 1971, women artists were not included, which was typical for textbooks of the time. America, like most of the world, was male-dominated and history was male-centric. Historically, women were expected to be wives and mothers, and to stay in the home and not have careers. They were not supposed to become artists, and the few known exceptions were not taken seriously by historians, who were mostly male. The feminist movement, beginning in the mid-1960s, overturned this restrictive perception of women. As a result, in the last 40 years, art historians—many of them women—have "rediscovered" countless women artists who had attained a degree of success in their day. Many of them were outstanding artists, held in high esteem during their lifetime, despite the enormous struggle to overcome powerful social and even family resistance against women becoming professional artists.

One of these lost women artists is the seventeenth-century Dutch painter Judith Leyster, a follower, if not a student, of Frans Hals. Over the centuries, all of Leyster's paintings were attributed to other artists, including Hals and Gerrit van Honthorst. Or they were labeled "artist unknown." At the end of the nineteenth century, however, she was rediscovered through an analysis of her signature, documents, and style, and her paintings were gradually restored to her name. It was only with the feminist movement that she was elevated from a minor figure to one of the more accomplished painters of her generation, one important enough to be included in basic histories of art. The feminist movement provided a new context for evaluating art, one that had an interest in rather than a denial of women's achievements and a study of issues relating to gender and how they appear in the arts.

A work like Leyster's ca. 1633 *Self-Portrait* (**fig. I-7**) is especially fascinating from this point of view. Because of its size and date, this may have been the painting the artist submitted as her presentation piece for admission into the local painters' guild, the Guild of St. Luke of Haarlem. Women were not encouraged to join the guild, which was a male preserve reinforcing the professional status of men. Nor did women artists generally take on students. Leyster bucked both restrictive traditions as she carved out a career for herself in a man's world. In her self-portrait, she presents herself as an artist, armed with many brushes, suggesting her deft control of the medium, which the presentation picture itself was meant to demonstrate. On the easel is a segment of a genre scene of which several variations are known. We must remember that at this time, artists rarely showed themselves working at their easels, toiling with their hands. They wanted to separate themselves from mere artisans and laborers, presenting themselves as belonging to a higher class. As a woman defying male expectations, however, Leyster needed to clearly declare that she was indeed an artist. But

I-7 Judith Leyster. *Self-Portrait*. ca. 1633. Oil on canvas, 29⅜ × 25⅝" (74.3 × 64.3 cm). National Gallery of Art. Gift of Mr. and Mrs. Robert Woods Bliss. 1949.6.4

she cleverly elevates her status by not dressing as an artist would when painting. Instead, she appears as her patrons do in their portraits, well-dressed and well-off. Her mouth is open, in what is called a "speaking likeness" portrait, giving her a casual but self-assured, animated quality, as she appears to converse on equal terms with a visitor, or with us. Leyster, along with Artemisia Gentileschi and Élisabeth Vigée-Lebrun, who also appear in this book, was included in a major 1976 exhibition titled *Women Artists 1550–1950*, which appeared in Los Angeles and Brooklyn, New York and played a major role in establishing the importance of women artists.

What is Art?

Ask most people without a background in art and art history, "What is art?," and they will respond with "an oil painting" or "a marble or bronze sculpture." Their criterion for quality is that it be beautiful, whatever that may be, although generally they define it as the degree to which a painting or sculpture is real-looking or adheres to their notion of naturalistic. Technical finesse or craft is viewed as the highest attribute of art-making, capable of inspiring awe and reverence. To debunk the myth that art is about technique and begin to get at what it is about, we return to Warhol's *Gold Marilyn Monroe*. The painting is rich with stories: we can talk about how it raises issues about the meaning of art, how it functions, and how it takes on value, both financial and aesthetic. Warhol even begs the question of the significance of technical finesse in art-making, an issue raised by the fact that in some respects he leads us to believe that he did not touch the painting himself! We have already seen how he appropriated someone else's photograph of Marilyn Monroe, not even taking his own. Warhol then instructed his assistants to make the screens for the printing process. They also prepared the canvas, screened the image with the colors Warhol selected, and may even have painted the gold to Warhol's specifications.

By using assistants to make his work, Warhol is telling us that art is not about the artist's technical finesse, but about communicating an idea using visual language, even if the idea does not require the artist to actually make the art. The measuring stick for quality in art is the quality of the statement being made, or its philosophy, as well as the quality of the technical means for making this statement. Looking at *Gold Marilyn Monroe* in the flesh at New York's Museum of Modern Art is a powerful experience. Standing in front of this six-foot-high canvas, we cannot help but feel the empty glory of America's most famous symbol of female sexuality and stardom. Because the artist's vision, and not his touch, is the relevant issue for the making of this particular work, it is of no consequence that Warhol leads us to believe that he never laid a hand to the canvas, except to sign the back. (Actually, Warhol was a workaholic, intensely involved even with the most mechanical of his works.) We will shortly see, however, that the artist's touch is often critical to the success of a work of art.

Warhol openly declared that his art was not about his technical ability when he called his midtown Manhattan studio "The Factory." He is telling us that art is a commodity, and he is manufacturing a product, even mass-producing his product. The Factory churned out over a thousand, if not thousands, of paintings and prints of Marilyn Monroe based on the same newspaper photograph. As far as the public knew, all Warhol did for the most part was sign them, his signature reinforcing the importance people place on the signature itself as being an essential part of the work (ironically, most Old Master paintings, dating to the fourteenth through the eighteenth centuries, are not signed).

Actually, artists for centuries used assistants to help make their pictures. Peter Paul Rubens, an Antwerp painter working in the first half of the seventeenth century and one of the most famous artists of his day, had an enormous workshop that cranked out many of his pictures, especially the large works. His assistants were often artists specializing in flowers, animals, or clothing, for example, and many went on to become successful in their own right. Rubens would design the painting, and assistants, trained in his style, would execute their individual parts. Rubens would then come in at the end and pull the painting together as needed. The price the client was willing to pay often determined how much Rubens himself participated in the actual painting of the picture, and many of his works were indeed made entirely by him. Rubens's brilliant, flashy brushwork was in many respects critical to the making of the picture. Not only was his handling of paint considered superior to that of his assistants, the very identity of his paintings, its very life, so to speak, was linked to his unique genius for applying paint to canvas, almost as much as it was to his dramatic compositions. His brushwork complemented his subject matter; it even reinforced it. The two went hand in hand, as we shall see later in the Introduction and in Chapter 19.

Warhol was not the first artist to make art that intentionally raised the issue of what is art and how does it function. This distinction belongs to the humorous and brilliant Parisian Marcel Duchamp. In 1919, Duchamp took a roughly 8- × 4-inch reproduction of Leonardo da Vinci's *Mona Lisa* in the Louvre Museum in Paris and drew a moustache and beard on the sitter's face (**fig. I-8**). Below, he wrote the letters L. H. O. O. Q., pronounced in French *elle a chaud au cul*, which translates, "She has hot pants." Duchamp was poking fun at the public's fascination with the mysterious smile on the Mona Lisa, which had intrigued everyone for centuries and eluded suitable explanation. Duchamp irreverently provided one: she is sexually aroused, and she is gay. With the childish gesture of affixing a moustache and beard to the Mona Lisa, Duchamp also attacked bourgeois reverence for Old Master painting and the age-old esteem of oil painting representing the pinnacle of art.

Art, Duchamp is saying, can be made by merely placing ink drawing on a mass-produced reproduction. It is not strictly oil on canvas or cast bronze or chiseled marble sculpture. Artists can use any imaginable medium in any way in order to express themselves. He is announcing that art is about ideas that are made visually, and not necessarily about craft. In this deceivingly whimsical work, which is rich with ideas, Duchamp is telling us that art is anything that someone wants to call art, which is not the same as saying it is good art. Furthermore, he is proclaiming that art can be small, since *L. H. O. O. Q.* is a fraction of the size of its source, the *Mona Lisa*. By appropriating Leonardo's famous picture and interpreting it very differently from traditional readings (see pages 332–333), Duchamp suggests that the meaning of art is not fixed forever by the artist, that it can change and be assigned by viewers, writers, collectors, and museum curators, who can use it for their own purposes. Lastly, and this is certainly one of Duchamp's many wonderful contributions to art, he is telling us that art can be fun; it can defy conventional notions of beauty, and while intellectually engaging us in a most serious manner, it can also provide us with a smile, if not a good laugh.

I-8 Marcel Duchamp. Replica of L. H. O. O. Q. (Mona Lisa) from Boite-en-valise. 1919. Rectified Readymade; pencil on a reproduction, 7 × 4⅞" (17.8 × 11 cm). The Philadelphia Museum of Art. Louise and Walter Arensberg Collection. © Succession Marcel Duchamp/ADAGP, Paris and DACS, London 2008

Art and Aesthetics

L. H. O. O. Q. also raises the issue of aesthetics, which is the study of theories surrounding art, including what is beauty, and the meaning and purpose of art. Duchamp selected the *Mona Lisa* for "vandalizing" for many reasons, but one of them had to be that many people considered it the greatest and therefore the most beautiful painting ever made. Certainly, it was one of the most famous paintings in the world, if not the most famous. In 1919 most of those who held such a view had probably never seen it and knew it only from reproductions, probably no better than the one Duchamp used in *L. H. O. O. Q.* And yet, they would describe the original painting as beautiful, but not Duchamp's comical version.

Duchamp called such altered found objects as *L. H. O. O. Q.* "assisted Readymades" (for another example, see *Fountain*, fig. 27.2), and he was adamant when he claimed that these works had no aesthetic value whatsoever. They were not to be considered beautiful, and they were selected because they were aesthetically neutral. What interested Duchamp were the ideas that these objects embodied once they were declared art.

Despite his claim, Duchamp's assisted Readymades can be perceived as beautiful, in ways, of course, that are quite different from Leonardo's *Mona Lisa*, but beautiful all the same. *L. H. O. O. Q.* has an aura about it, an aura of wit and ideas that are specific to Duchamp. As a result, this slightly altered cheap reproduction is transformed into a compelling work of art, in a way that is very different from Leonardo's. And so the qualities that attract us to it, which we can

describe as its beauty, could not be further from those of the *Mona Lisa*. Ultimately, beauty can be equated with quality.

Beauty is not just a pretty, colorful picture or a perfectly formed, harmonious nude marble figure. Beauty resides in content and how successfully the content is made visual. This book is intended to suggest the many complex ways that quality, and thus beauty, appears in art. Some of the greatest paintings depict horrific scenes that many people could never find acceptable, but they are nonetheless beautiful—scenes such as beheadings (see fig. 18.3), crucifixions (see fig. 17.4), death and despair (see figs. 23.7 and 23.8), emotional distress (see fig. 25.8), and the brutal massacre of innocent women and children (**fig. I-9**). Like Duchamp's *L. H. O. O. Q.*, these works

I-9 Pablo Picasso. Detail of *Guernica*. 1937. Oil on canvas, whole painting 11′6″ × 25′8″ (3.51 × 7.82 m). Museo Nacional Centro de Arte Reina Sofia, Madrid. On permanent loan from the Museo del Prado, Madrid. © Succession Picasso/DACS, London 2008

possess an aura that makes them powerful and riveting, despite the repulsiveness of the subject matter. They have quality, and to those who recognize and feel this quality, that makes these works beautiful. Others will continue to be repulsed and offended by them, or at best just be uninterested.

Illusionism and Meaning in Art

The Roman historian Pliny tells the story about the competition between the Greek painters Zeuxis and Parrhasius to see who could make the most illusionistic work. Zeuxis painted grapes so real that birds tried to eat them, but Parrhasius won the competition. He had painted a curtain covering a painting. So realistic was the work that Zeuxis asked him to pull back the curtain covering his painting only to discover that he was looking at the painting. The story of this competition is interesting, because despite a recurring emphasis on illusionism in art, the ability to create illusionistic effects and "fool the eye" is generally not what determines quality in art. As we discussed, quality in art comes from ideas and execution. Just being clever and fooling the eye is not enough.

A look at the sculpture of the twentieth-century artist Duane Hanson shows us how illusionism can be put in the service of meaning to create a powerful work of art. Hanson's 1995 sculpture, *Man on a Lawnmower* (**fig. I-10**), is a work that too often is appreciated only for its illusionistic qualities, while the real content goes unnoticed. Yet, it is the content, not the illusionism, that makes this sculpture so potent. Hanson began making his sculptures in the late 1960s. He cast his figures in polyester resin, and meticulously painted them. He then dressed them in real clothing, used real accessories (including wigs and artificial eyeballs), and placed them in real furniture. Most museum visitors are startled to discover that his sculptures are not real, and many people have tried to interact with his characters, which include museum guards, tourists, shoppers, house painters, and female sunbathers.

But Hanson's art is more than just about a visual sleight of hand. He is also a realist and a moralist, and his art is filled with tragic social content. By realist, we mean that his sculpture is not limited to attractive, beautiful, and ennobling objects and situations but instead focuses on the base, coarse, crude, disgusting,

I-10 Duane Hanson. *Man on a Lawnmower*. 1995. Bronze polychromed with mower, life-size. The Newark Museum, New Jersey, courtesy the O'Hara Gallery, New York. © Estate of Duane Hanson/VAGA, New York/DACS, London 2008

and unseemly. In *Man on a Lawnmower*, we see an overweight man clutching a diet soda. He dwarfs the shabby riding mower he sits on. His T-shirt, baseball hat, pants, and sneakers are soiled. He is common and ordinary, and the entire sculpture is remarkably prosaic.

Man on a Lawnmower is a sad work. We see disillusionment in the man's eyes as he blankly stares off into space. The diet soda he holds suggests that he is trying to lose weight but is losing the battle. Grass-cutting is another metaphor for a losing battle, as the grass is going to grow back. This work also represents the banality of human existence. What is life about? The monotony of cutting grass, Hanson is saying. In this last work, made when he knew he was dying of cancer, Hanson captured what he perceived to be the emptiness of human existence and contemporary life. The illusionism of the sculpture makes this aura of alienation and lack of spirituality all the more palpable. This man is us, and this is our life too. He embodies no poetry, nobility, or heroism. Our twentieth-century *Man on a Lawnmower* has no causes and beliefs to turn to as he confronts the down-to-earth reality of life and death.

Can a Mechanical Process Be Art?: Photography

The first edition of this book did not include photography, reflecting a prevailing attitude that photography, because it was largely a mechanical process, was not an art form. Now, three decades later, the artistic merit of photography seems self-evident. When it was invented in 1839, the art world largely dismissed it as a mechanical process with little artistic merit. Or it was perceived as not having sufficient aesthetic merit to be seen in the same lofty company with the twin peaks of art—painting and sculpture. It has struggled ever since to shed that stigma. Within the last 25 years, however, photography has been vindicated. Along with video and film, it has been elevated to an important medium used by today's artists. Pictures from the nineteenth and twentieth centuries that had interested only a handful of photography insiders suddenly became intensely sought after, with many museums rushing to establish photography departments and amass significant collections. In other words, it took well over 100 years for people to get beyond the stigma of the mechanical process to develop an eye for the quality and beauty of the medium.

We need only look at a 1972 photograph titled *Albuquerque* (**fig. I-11**) by Lee Friedlander to see how photography matches painting and sculpture in artistic merit. In *Albuquerque*, Friedlander portrays a modern America that is vacuous and lifeless, which he suggests is due to

technology. How does he do this? The picture has a haunting emptiness. It has no people, and it is filled with strange empty spaces of walkway and street appearing between the numerous objects that pop up everywhere. A hard, eerie geometry prevails, as seen in the strong verticals of the poles, buildings, hydrant, and wall. Cylinders, rectangles, and circles are everywhere. (Notice the many different rectangles on the background building, or the rectangles of the pavement bricks and the foreground wall.)

Despite the stillness and emptiness, the picture is busy and restless. The vertical poles and the strong vertical elements on the house and building establish a vibrant staccato rhythm. The energy of this rhythm is reinforced by the asymmetrical composition that has no focus or center, as well as by the powerful intersecting diagonals of the street and the foreground wall. (Note how the shadow of the fire hydrant runs parallel to the street.) Disturbing features appear throughout the composition. The street sign—which cannot be seen because it is cropped at the top of the print—casts a mysterious shadow on the wall. A pole visually cuts the dog in two, and the dog has been separated from his attribute, the fire hydrant, as well as from his absent owner. The fire hydrant, in turn, appears to be mounted incorrectly, because it sticks too far out of the ground. The car on the right has been brutally cropped, and a light pole seems to sprout strangely from its hood. The telephone pole in the center of the composition is crooked, as though it has been tilted by the force of the cropped car entering from outside the edge of the picture (of course, the car is parked and not moving). Why do we assume this empty, frenetic quality is human-made? Because the work is dominated by the human-made and by technology. We see telephone poles, electrical wires, cross-walk signs, an ugly machinelike modular apartment building, sleek automobiles, and a fire hydrant. Cropped in the lower left foreground is the steel cover to underground electrical wiring.

Everywhere, nature has been cemented over, and besides a few scraggly trees in the middle ground and distance, only the weeds surrounding the hydrant thrive. In this brilliant print, Friedlander captures his view of the essence of modern America: The way in which technology, a love of the artificial, and a fast, fragmented lifestyle are spawning alienation and a disconnection with nature and spirituality. As important, he is telling us that modernization is making

I-11 Lee Friedlander. *Albuquerque*. 1972. Gelatin silver print, 11 × 14″ (28 × 35.5 cm).
© Lee Friedlander

America homogeneous. The title tells us we are in Albuquerque, New Mexico, but without the title we are otherwise in Anywhere, U.S.A.

Friedlander did not just find this composition. He very carefully selected it and he very carefully made it. He not only needed the sun, he had to wait until it was in the right position (otherwise, the shadow of the fire hydrant would not align with the street). When framing the composition, he very meticulously incorporated a fragment of the utility cover in the left lower foreground, while axing a portion of the car on the right. Nor did the geometry of the picture just happen; he made it happen. Instead of a soft focus that would create an atmospheric, blurry picture, he used a deep focus that produces a sharp crisp image filled with detail, allowing, for example, the individual rectangular bricks in the pavement to be clearly seen. The strong white tones of the vertical rectangles of the apartment building, the foreground wall, and the utility box blocking the car on the left edge of the picture were probably carefully worked up in the darkroom, as was the rectangular columned doorway on the house. Friedlander has exposed the ugliness of modern America in this hard, cold, dry image, and because of the power of its message has created an extraordinarily beautiful work of art.

Can Architecture Communicate Ideas?

An art form that is basically abstract and dedicated to structuring space in a functional way might be seen as hardly able to carry a message. And yet it does, especially in the hands of great architects. We see Gianlorenzo Bernini doing it in 1657 when he was asked by Pope Alexander VII to design a large open space, or piazza, in front of Saint Peter's Cathedral in Rome. Bernini obliged, creating a space defined by a row of columns (a colonnade) resembling arms that appear to maternally embrace visitors, welcoming them into the bosom of the Church (**fig. I-12**). His form anthropomorphized the building by emphasizing its identification with the Virgin Mary. At the same time, the French architect Claude Perrault was commissioned to design the east façade of King Louis XIV's palace, the Louvre in Paris (**fig. I-13**). To proclaim Louis's grandeur, he made the ground floor, where the day-to-day business of the court was carried out, a squat podium. The second floor, where Louis lived, was much higher and served as the main floor. Perrault articulated this elevated second story with a design that recalled Roman temples, thus associating Louis XIV with Imperial Rome and worldly power.

I-12 Saint Peter's Cathedral. Nave and façade by Carlo Maderno, 1607–1615; colonnade by Gianlorenzo Bernini, designed 1657. Rome

I-13 Claude Perrault. East front of the Louvre. 1667–1670. Paris

In our own era, an enormously wealthy businessman, Solomon R. Guggenheim, indulged his passion for modern art by commissioning the architect Frank Lloyd Wright to design a museum in New York City. One of the boldest architectural statements of the mid-twentieth century, Wright's Solomon R. Guggenheim Museum is located on upper Fifth Avenue, overlooking Central Park (**fig. I-14**). The building, erected from 1956 to 1959, is radically different from the surrounding residential housing, thus immediately declaring that its function is different from theirs. As a matter of fact, the building is radically different from almost anything built up until that time. We can say that the exterior announces that it is a museum, because it looks as much like a gigantic sculpture as a functional structure.

Wright conceived the Guggenheim in 1945, and his goal was to create an organic structure that deviated from the conventional static rectangular box filled with conventional static rectangular rooms. Beginning in the early twentieth century, Wright designed houses that related to the landscape and nature, both in structure and material (fig. 25.18). The structure of his buildings, whether domestic or commercial, reflects the very structure of nature, which he saw as a continuous expansion. His buildings radiate out from a central core or wrap around a central void, but in either case, they are meant to expand or grow like a leaf or crystal, with one form opening up into another.

The Guggenheim is based on a natural form. It is designed around a spiral ramp (**fig. I-15**), which is meant to evoke a spiral shell. The structure also recalls a ceramic vase: it is closed at the bottom and open at the top, and as it rises it widens, until it is capped by a light-filled glass roof. When referring to the Guggenheim, Wright often cited an old Chinese aphorism, "The reality of the vase is the space inside," and for the most part, the exhibition space is one enormous room formed by the spiral viewing ramp. Wright wanted visitors to take the elevator to the top of the ramp, and then slowly amble down its three percent grade, gently pulled by gravity. Because the ramp was relatively narrow, viewers could not get too far back from the art and were forced to have an intimate relationship with it. At the same time, they could look back across the open space of the room to see where

I-14 Frank Lloyd Wright. The Solomon R. Guggenheim Museum. 1956–1959. New York.
David Heald © The Solomon R. Guggenheim Foundation, New York

they had gone, comparing the work in front of them to a segment of the exhibition presented on a sweeping, distant arc. Or they could look ahead as well, to get a preview of where they were going. The building has a sense of continuity and mobility that Wright viewed as an organic experience, and looking down from the upper reaches of the ramp, we can see the undulation of the concave and convex forms that reflect the subtle eternal movement of nature. Wright even placed a pool on the ground floor, facing the light entering from the skylight high above.

Regardless of their size, no other museum has succeeded in creating a sense of open space and continuous movement as Wright did in the Guggenheim. Nor does any other museum have the same sense of communal spirit; at the Guggenheim everyone is united in one big room (see fig. I-15).

The Language of Art

As we have discussed, art is the visual expression of ideas. It has a message and makes statements. Like any language, it has a vocabulary. When discussing the Friedlander photograph, Wright's architecture, Hanson's sculpture, and the Copley and Warhol paintings, we actually touched on this vocabulary, because it is nearly impossible to talk about the messages in these works without describing how the artists brought them about.

In the Friedlander photograph, for example, we discussed the artist's use of voids and harsh geometry, and how these devices had an impact on the way we viewed the print's presentation of modern technology. Friedlander used both representational motifs and abstract tools to tell his story. In painting, these abstract devices—line, color, composition, space, and form, for example—are also referred to as the formal qualities of the medium.

For most of the history of art, each period tends to share a similar vocabulary, or style. Each period has its own spirit, often called a *Zeitgeist*, meaning the spirit of the time, and it employs a similar language to convey a similar message. Within this *Zeitgeist*, there are regional variations, and within the regional variations, individual styles. But most art is contained within the broad period style that makes it instantly recognizable as being of its time.

We can see how this concept of style operates by comparing Raphael's *Alba Madonna* of ca. 1510 (see fig. I-16) with Peter Paul Rubens's *Raising of the Cross* of 1610–1611 (see fig. I-17). Made roughly 100 years apart, the Raphael painting reflects a fifteenth- and early sixteenth-century view of Catholicism, whereas the Rubens painting supports a new, more fervent and emotional approach that characterizes the seventeenth century. The former period is called the Renaissance, the latter the Baroque. What concerns us now, however, is not the labeling, but rather the different languages and messages of the two artists.

In *Alba Madonna* (**fig. I-16**), Raphael presents us with a harmonious view of the Catholic Church, as represented by John the Baptist, the Christ Child, and the Virgin Mary. The three figures are organized to form a stable pyramid with little sense of movement in this quiet scene. These sculpturesque monumental figures become frozen as they are aligned parallel to the picture plane. We can see this clearly in the crisp contour surrounding the group, but also in such passages as Christ's left arm and the Virgin's left shoulder and upper arm, as well as the outline of her headdress. Elements of the landscape follow the plane of the picture. Notice the buildings on the left, the earth immediately behind them, and the flat silhouette of the grouping of some of the trees. Despite this planarity, each figure is volumetric, that is, round and three-dimensional. Raphael draws the rounded outline of each figure, and then bathes it in a soft, dispersed light that gently models his forms, allowing shadow to make an arm or leg recede and light to pull it forward. Raphael's brushstrokes are virtually imperceptible as they create his sculpturesque

forms. Everything is solid, settled, and rational in this image. Even color has its assigned place, carefully contained in discreet areas to form solid building blocks of composition. Raphael has presented the Church as the embodiment of perfection—rock solid, rational, serene, harmonious, and comforting.

Rubens's *The Raising of the Cross* (**fig. I-17**) is anything but. His image is filled with dramatic movement as well as physical and emotional intensity. His composition is based on a pyramid as well. But now it is asymmetrical and unstable, pushed off to the left, creating unstable motion and action. Instead of running parallel to the picture plane, his composition moves in and out of the space. The plunging diagonal of the figure pulling up the cross in the lower right corner and Christ slanting backward set the tone for fierce spatial dynamics. This straining figure actually seems to be falling out of the composition into our space, drawing us into the scene. In contrast, Raphael's perfect heavenly world was hermetically sealed from us earthbound sinners by his planar composition. Rubens's crowd of figures is composed of rippling muscles and undulating contours. A blast of light enters from the right, dramatically highlighting Christ's torso and flickering throughout the image, causing our eye to jump from one light area to the next. Spots of strong color scattered here and there have the same effect. Although not obvious from our reproduction, Rubens's brushwork is bold and dramatic, causing the surface of the painting to ripple and be in constant flux. Nothing in this painting sits still.

Clearly, Rubens's sense of the world is quite different from Raphael's. As you will learn when studying the Baroque period, the political, social, scientific, and religious landscape changed enormously by the seventeenth century. Consequently, the language of art changed as well, reflecting fresh ways of perceiving the physical world, an increased religious fervor, and an unprecedented opulence that accompanied the rise of powerful monarchies. Throughout this book, we will be looking at how the language of art changes from one period to the next, as artists express changing views of the world. We shall also explore regional, nationalistic, and individual variations within each of these periods.

I-17 Peter Paul Rubens. *The Raising of the Cross.* 1610–1611. Center panel of a triptych, oil on panel, 15′1″ × 11′9⅝″ (4.57 × 3.6 m). Antwerp Cathedral, Belgium

Experiencing Art

You will be astonished when you see at first hand much of the art in this book. No matter how accurate the reproductions in this book—or any other—are, they are just stand-ins for the actual objects. We hope you will visit some of the museums where the originals are displayed. But keep in mind that looking at art, absorbing its full impact, takes time and repeated visits. Occasionally, you might do an in-depth reading of individual works. This would involve carefully perusing details and questioning why they are there. Ideally, the museum will help you understand the art. Often, there are introductory text panels that tell you why the art has been presented together, and labels for individual works provide further information. Major temporary exhibitions generally have a catalogue, which adds yet another layer of interpretation. But text panels, labels, and catalogues generally reflect one person's reading of the art, and there are usually many other ways to approach or think about it.

Although the museum is an effective way to look at art and certainly the most efficient, art museums are relatively new. Indeed, before the nineteenth century, art was not made to be viewed in museums. Ultimately, art is everywhere: in galleries, corporate lobbies and offices, places of worship, and private homes. It can be found in public spaces, from subway stations and bus stops to plazas to such civic buildings as libraries, performing arts centers, and city halls. University and college buildings are often filled with art, and the buildings themselves are art. The chair you are sitting in and the house and building where you are reading this book are also works of art, maybe not great art, but art all the same, as Duchamp told us. Even the clothes you are wearing are art. And everywhere you find art, it is telling you something and making a statement.

Art is not a luxury, as many people would have us believe, but an integral part of daily life. It has a major impact on us, even when we are not aware of it; we feel better about ourselves when we are in environments that are visually enriching and exciting. Most importantly, art stimulates us to think. Even when it provokes and outrages us, it broadens our experience by making us question our values, attitudes, and worldview. This book is an introduction to this fascinating field that is so intertwined with our lives. After reading it, you will find that the world will not look the same.

The Ancient World

ART HISTORY IS MORE THAN a stream of art objects created over time. It is closely tied to history itself, that is, the recorded evidence of human events. We must therefore consider the concept of history. History, we are often told, began with the invention of writing by the "historic" civilizations of Mesopotamia and Egypt some 5,000 years ago. Without writing, the growth we have known would have been impossible. However, the development of writing seems to have taken place over a period of several hundred years—roughly between 3300 and 3000 BCE, with Mesopotamia in the lead—after the new societies were past their first stage. Thus "history" was well under way by the time writing could be used to record events.

The invention of writing serves as a landmark, for the lack of written records is one of the key differences between prehistoric and historic societies. But as soon as we ask why this is so, we face some intriguing problems. First of all, how valid is the distinction between "prehistoric" and "historic"? Does it merely reflect a difference in our knowledge of the past? (Thanks to the invention of writing, we know a great deal more about history than about prehistory.) Or was there a real change in the way things happened, and in the kinds of things that happened, after "history" began? Obviously, prehistory

was far from uneventful. Yet the events of this period, decisive though they were, seem slow-paced and gradual when measured against the events of the last 5,000 years. The beginning of "history," then, means a sudden increase in the speed of events, a shift from low gear to high gear, as it were. It also means a change in the kinds of events. Historic societies literally make history. They not only bring forth "great individuals and great deeds" (one definition of history) by demanding human effort on a large scale, but they make these achievements memorable. And for an event to be memorable, it must be more than "worth remembering." It must also occur quickly enough to be grasped by human memory, not spread over many centuries. Taken together, memorable events have caused the ever-quickening pace of change during the past five millenniums, which begin with what we call the ancient world.

This period was preceded by a vast prehistoric era of which we know almost nothing until the last Ice Age in Europe began to recede, from about 40,000 to 8000 BCE. (There had been at least three previous ice ages, alternating with periods of subtropical warmth, at intervals of about 25,000 years.) At the time, the climate between the Alps and Scandinavia resembled that of present-day Siberia or Alaska. Huge herds of reindeer and other large plant-eating

animals roamed the plains and valleys, preyed upon by the ancestors of today's lions and tigers, as well as by our own ancestors. These people lived in caves or in the shelter of overhanging rocks. Many such sites have been found, mostly in Spain and in southern France. This phase of prehistory is known as the Old Stone Age, or Paleolithic era, because tools were made only from stone. Its way of life was adapted almost perfectly to the special conditions of the waning Ice Age, and it could not survive beyond them.

The Old Stone Age came to a close with what is termed the Neolithic Revolution, which ushered in the New Stone Age. And a revolution it was indeed, even though it was a period of transition that extended over several thousand years during the Mesolithic Age. It began in the "fertile crescent" of the Near East (an area covering what is now Turkey, Iraq, Iran, Jordan, Israel, Lebanon, and Syria) sometime about 12,000–8000 BCE, with the first successful attempts to domesticate animals and food grains. The Neolithic came later to Europe but then spread much more rapidly.

The cultivation of regular food sources was one of the most decisive achievements in human history. People in Paleolithic societies had led the unsettled life of the hunter and food-gatherer, reaping wherever nature sowed. They were at the mercy of forces that they could neither understand nor control. But having learned how to ensure a food supply through their own efforts, they settled down in permanent villages. A new discipline and order entered their lives. There is, then, a very basic difference between the Neolithic and the Paleolithic, despite the fact that at first both still depended on stone for tools and weapons. The new way of life brought forth a number of new crafts and inventions long before the appearance of metals. Among them were pottery, weaving, and spinning, as well as basic methods of construction in wood, brick, and stone. When metallurgy in the form of copper finally appeared in southeastern Europe around 4500 BCE, at the beginning of the so-called Eneolithic era, it was as a direct outgrowth of the technology gained from pottery. Thus it did not in itself constitute a major advance; nor, surprisingly enough, did it have an immediate impact.

The Neolithic Revolution placed us on a level at which we might well have remained indefinitely. The forces of nature would never again challenge men and women as they had Paleolithic peoples. In a few places, however, the balance between humans and nature was upset by a new threat, one posed not by nature but by people themselves. Evidence of that threat can be seen in the earliest Neolithic fortifications, built almost 9,000 years ago in the Near East.

What was the source of the human conflict that made these defenses necessary? Competition for grazing land among groups of herders or for arable soil among farming communities? The basic cause, we suspect, was that the Neolithic Revolution had been too successful. It had allowed population groups to grow beyond the available food supply. This situation might have been resolved in a number of ways. Constant warfare could have reduced the population. Or the people could have united in larger and more disciplined social units for the sake of group efforts—such as building fortifications—that no loosely organized society could achieve on its own.

We do not know the outcome of the struggle in the region. (Future excavations may tell us how far the urbanizing process extended.) But about 3,000 years later, similar conflicts, on a larger scale, arose in the Nile Valley and again in the plains of the Tigris and Euphrates rivers. The pressures that forced the people in these regions to abandon Neolithic village life may well have been the same. These conflicts created enough pressure to produce the first civilizations. To be civilized, after all, means to live as a citizen, a town dweller. (The word civilization derives from the Latin term for something pertaining to a city, civilis.) These new societies were organized into much larger units—cities and city-

states—that were far more complex and efficient than had ever existed before. First in Mesopotamia and Egypt, somewhat later in neighboring areas, and in the Indus Valley and along the Yellow River in China, people would henceforth live in a more dynamic world. Their ability to survive was challenged not by the forces of nature but by human forces: by tensions and conflicts arising either within society or as the result of competition between societies. Efforts to cope with such forces have proved to be a far greater challenge than the earlier struggle with nature. The problems and pressures faced by historic societies thus are very different from those faced by peoples in the Paleolithic and Neolithic eras.

These momentous changes also spurred the development of new technologies in what we term the Bronze Age and the Iron Age, which, like the Neolithic, are stages, not distinct eras. People first began to cast bronze, an alloy of copper and tin, in the Near East around 3500 BCE, at the same time that the earliest cities arose in Egypt and Mesopotamia. The smelting and forging of iron were invented about 2000–1500 BCE by the Hittites, an Indo-European-speaking people who settled in Cappadocia (today's east central Turkey), a high plateau with abundant copper and iron ore. Indeed, it was the competition for mineral resources that helped create the conflicts that beset civilizations everywhere.

ATLANTIC
OCEAN

IRELAND

ENGLAND

NORTH
SEA

Stonehenge
Thames R.

BRITTANY

Trier

Seine R.

Rhine R.

Loire R.

E U R O P E

FRANCE

GERMANY

Hohlenstein-Stadel

Willendorf

Vistula R.

Lake Constance

Lake Geneva

Lascaux

DORDOGNE

Altamira

Pech-Merle

Rhône R.

Chauvet

Po R.

DACIA

BALKANS

Danube R.

Cernavo

SPAIN

Segovia

ITALY

Florence

Arno R.

Perugia

Tiber R.

Vulci

Tarquinia

Veii

Cerveteri

Rome

Praeneste

Primaporta

Mt. Vesuvius

Naples

Boscoreale

ISCHIA

Herculaneum

Pompeii

Paestum

ADRIATIC SEA

MACEDONIA

Mt. Olympus

GREECE

Byzantium
(Constantinople)

SAMOTH

Troy

Pergam

LYDIA

LEMNOS

IONIA

TYRRHENIAN SEA

CORFU

Actium

Mt. Parnassus

Athens

IONIAN
SEA

AEGEAN SEA

SICILY

Mt. Etna

Syracuse

Carthage

CRETE

See inset

M E D I T E R R A N E A N
S E A

NORTH AFRICA

LIBYA

LIBYAN

AEGEAN
SEA

LYL

Mt. Parnassus
Delphi

CHIOS

IONIA

Olympia

Corinth

ATTICA

Athens

SAMOS

Ephesos

Mycenae

Salamis

Prie

PELOPONNESUS

AEGINA

CYCLADES

DELOS

Miletus

PAROS

Didyma

NAXOS

Halikarnasso

AMORGOS

Knid

THERA
(SANTORINI)

Akrotiri

SIPHNOS

MEDITERRANEAN
SEA

CRETE

Heraklion

Knossos

Mt. Ida

Mallia

Phaistos

0   50   100 Miles
0   50   100 Kilometers

Legend:

The Roman Empire
at the Time of Hadrian

0   250   500 Miles
0   250   500 Kilometers

N

THE ANCIENT WORLD

SCYTHIA

ARAL
SEA

Don R.

Volga R.

CASPIAN SEA

BLACK SEA

PARTHIA

Lake
Van

Lake Urmia

BACTRIA

Tigris R.

Dur Sharrukin

OLIA

CAPPADOCIA

E A R

MESOPOTAMIA

PERSIA

LURISTAN

Nimrud

ASSYRIA

Assur

Issos

Antioch

E A S T

Euphrates R.

AKKAD

Tel Asmar

ELAM

Persepolis

Babylon

BABYLONIA

Ancient coastline (?)

SYRIA

PHOENICIA

Jordan R.

SUMER

Uruk

Ur

Ain Ghazal

JORDAN

Persian Gulf

PALESTINE

MIDDLE EAST

DEAD SEA

ndria

Petra

iro

a

ra

Gulf of
Suez

ARABIA

Fayum

Mt. Sinai

ER EGYPT

RED SEA

Beni Hasan

El

na

Akhetaten

EASTERN DESERT

Deir
El-Bahri

Thebes
Luxor

Hierakonpolis

Aswan

UPPER   EGYPT

1 Prehistoric Art

*W*hen modern humans first encountered prehistoric cave paintings in the 1870s, they literally could not believe their eyes. Although the evidence indicated that the site at Altamira in Spain dated to around 13,000 BCE, the paintings found there had been executed with such skill and sensitivity that historians initially considered them forgeries (see fig 1.1). Since then, some 200 similar sites have been found all over the world. As recently as 1994, the discovery of a cave in southeastern France (see fig. 1.2) brought hundreds more paintings to light, pushing back the date of the first prehistoric paintings even further, to approximately 30,000 BCE. Carved objects have been discovered that are equally old.

These earliest forms of art raise more questions than they answer. Why did prehistoric humans expend time and energy to make art? What functions did these visual representations serve? What do the images mean? Art historians often use contemporaneous written texts to supplement their understandings of art; yet prehistoric art dates to a time before writing, for which works of art are among our only evidence. Art historians deploy scientific and anthropological tools in their attempts to interpret them. With new finds being reported with regularity, the study of prehistoric art continues to develop and refine its interpretations and conclusions.

Though fully modern humans have lived on the earth for over 100,000 years, the dates assigned to the earliest objects classed as "art" go back about 40,000 years; earlier humans crafted tools from stone and bone, but what inspired them to make detailed representations of forms found in nature? The skill with which the earliest objects are executed may have been the product of a lost period of experimentation in carving and painting techniques, making the practice of art much older than the surviving objects. Yet some scholars suppose that image-making and symbolic language result from a new brain structure associated with *homo sapiens sapiens*, when a sudden neurological mutation opened up the capacity for abstract thought. Indeed, art emerges at about the time that fully modern humans moved from Africa into Europe, Asia, and Australia, encountering—and eventually displacing—the earlier Neanderthals (*homo neanderthalensis*). Tens of thousands of works survive from this time before history, most of which were discovered in Europe. Many are breathtakingly accomplished. Whatever led to the ability to create art, its impact on the emergence of human culture was enormous, and these prehistoric works force us to reevaluate many of our assumptions about art and the creative process.

Paleolithic Art

For the era before the written word (prehistory), historians use the activity of toolmaking as the defining feature for measuring human time. They divide the broad span of prehistory into the Paleolithic or Old Stone Age (from the Greek *palaio-*, meaning "ancient," and *lithos*, meaning

Major Events in Prehistory

ca. 2,000,000 BCE	Earliest known toolmaking
ca. 70,000 –8000 BCE	Last Ice Age in Europe
ca. 40,000 –8000 BCE	Old Stone (Paleolithic) Age
ca. 40,000 BCE	Earliest known stone figures in Europe
ca. 28,000 BCE	Earliest known cave paintings
ca. 8000 –2300 BCE	New Stone (Neolithic) Age
ca. 8000 –1000 BCE	Plants and animals domesticated
ca. 4500 –1500 BCE	Megalithic tombs and monuments
ca. 3300 –3000 BCE	Earliest writing developed
ca. 3000 –1000 BCE	Bronze Age

Map 1.1 Prehistoric Europe

"stone"), the Mesolithic or Middle (*meso-*) Stone Age, and the Neolithic or New (*neo-*) Stone Age. The Paleolithic era spans from two million years ago to about 10,000 BCE. Within this range, scholars describe the oldest material as the Lower Paleolithic (ending about 100,000 years ago), since it lies at the lowest layer of an excavation. The Middle Paleolithic era dates from 100,000 years ago to about 40,000 years ago, and the most recent layers reveal the Upper Paleolithic (about 40,000 BCE to around 10,000 BCE). It is in the Upper Paleolithic that the earliest works of art emerge.

Upper Paleolithic painting, drawing, and sculpture appeared over a wide swath of Eurasia, Africa, and Australia between 10,000 and 40,000 years ago (see map 1.1). This period falls in the Pleistocene era, also known as the Ice Age, when glaciers covered much of the northern hemisphere.

Prehistoric paintings were first recognized in 1878 in a cave named Altamira, in Santillana del Mar in northern Spain. Accompanying her father, Count Don Marcelino Sanz de Sautuola, as he scoured the ground for flints and animal bones, 12-year-old Maria spied bison painted on the ceiling (**fig. 1.1**). There, and in other

❖ This 30,000-year-old image of an owl in the Chauvet cave was made by pressing a flat-ended tool of some kind into the soft limestone surface of the cave wall, a process called **incising**. Most prehistoric incising produced chiseled lines that are narrower than those of this owl, but the process is the same.

1.1 *Wounded Bison.* ca. 15,000–10,000 BCE. Altamira, Spain. Black manganese outlines with red ocher and shading

1.2 *Lions and Bison.* ca. 30,000–28,000 BCE. End Chamber, Chauvet Cave, Vallon-Pont-d'Arc, Ardèche Gorge, France

more recently discovered caves, painted and engraved images depict predominantly animals. The greatest variety known is in the vast cave complex of Chauvet, near Vallon-Pont-d'Arc in southeastern France. Here the 427 animal representations found to date depict 17 species, including lions, bears, and aurochs (prehistoric oxen), in black or red outlines (**fig. 1.2**), sometimes **polychromatic** (containing several colors). In rare instances, images depict human or partly human forms.

On first assessing the Altamira paintings, experts declared them too advanced to be authentic and dismissed them as a hoax. Indeed, though cave art may represent the dawn of art as we know it, it is often highly sophisticated. The bison of Altamira and other sites were painted from memory, and their forms demonstrate the painters' acute powers of observation and skill in translating memory into image. Standing at rest, bellowing or rolling on the ground, bison behave in these paintings as they do in the wild. Shading (**modeling**) expresses the volume of a bison's belly, and the forward contour of an animal's far leg is often rendered with a lighter hue to suggest distance.

Initially, scholars assigned relative dates to cave paintings according to their degree of **naturalism**, that is, how closely the image resembled the subject in nature. As naturalism was then considered the most advanced form of representation, the more naturalistic the image, the more evolved and, therefore, the more recent it was considered to be. Radiocarbon dating exposed flaws in this approach. Judged to be more recent in the overall sequence on account of their remarkable naturalism, some of the paintings at Chauvet proved to be among the earliest known, dating to about 32,000 years ago. Indeed, it is a mistake to assume that naturalism was a Paleolithic artist's—or any artist's—inevitable or only goal.

Interpreting Prehistoric Painting

As majestic as these paintings can be, they are also profoundly enigmatic. What purpose did they serve? The simplest view, that they were merely decorative—"art for art's sake"—is highly unlikely. Most of the existing paintings and

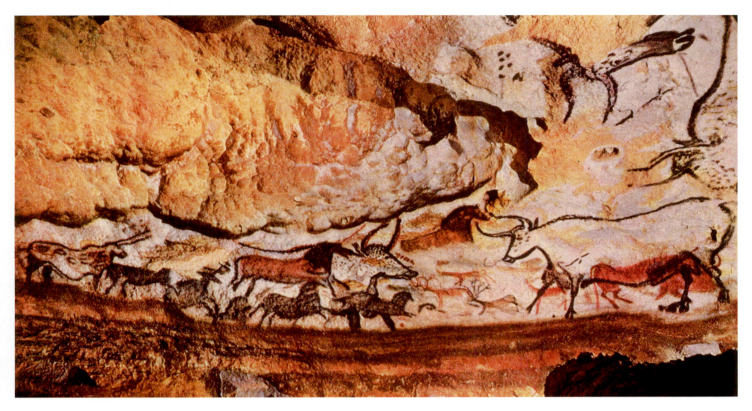

1.3 *Hall of the Bulls*. ca. 15,000–10,000 BCE. Lascaux Cave, Dordogne, France

engravings are readily accessible, and many more that embellished caves opening directly to the outside have probably perished. But some, as in the cave complex at Lascaux, in the Dordogne region of France, and elsewhere, lie deep inside extensive cave systems, remote from habitation and difficult to reach (**figs. 1.3, 1.4**). In these cases, the image's power may have resided in its making, rather than in its viewing: the act of creating it may have served some ritual or religious purpose.

Scholars next turned to approaches developed by ethnographers (anthropologists who study cultural behavior) to interpret cave paintings and engravings. Most often, the inspiration for these works was and is attributed to magico-religious motives. Thus early humans may have perceived an image as equivalent to the animal it represented; to create or possess the image was to exert power over its subject, which might result in a more successful hunt. Gouge marks on cave walls indicate that in some cases spears were cast at the images. Similarly, artists may have hoped to stimulate fertility in the wild—ensuring a continuous food supply—by depicting

1.4 Schematic plan of Lascaux Cave system (based on a diagram by the Service de l'Architecture, Paris)

1.5 *Spotted Horses and Human Hands.* Horses ca. 16,000 BCE; hands ca. 15,000 BCE. Limestone, approximate length 11′2″ (3.4 m). Pech-Merle Cave, Dordogne, France

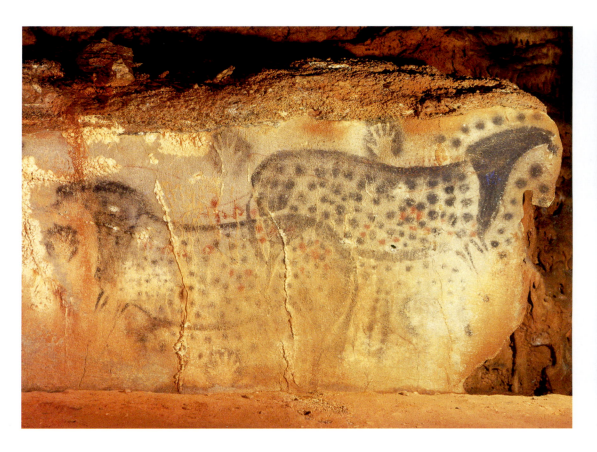

pregnant animals. A magico-religious interpretation might explain the choice to make animals appear lifelike, and to control them by fixing them within outlines.

More recent theories concerning shamanism—a belief in a parallel spirit world accessed through alternative states of consciousness—build upon these interpretations, arguing that an animal's "spirit" was evident where a bulge in the wall or ceiling suggested its shape, as with the *Spotted Horses* (**fig. 1.5**) at Pech-Merle in southwestern France. The artist's or shaman's power brought that spirit to the surface. Some scholars have cast the paintings as images for worship; others focus on a painting's physical context. This means examining relationships between figures to determine, in the absence of an artificial frame, a ground-line or a landscape, whether multiple animal images signify individual specimens or a herd, and whether these images represent a mythical past for early communities. It also means recognizing that a cave 15 feet deep is a very different space from another over a mile deep, and was possibly used for different purposes, and that paintings in different spaces may have functioned differently. It means factoring in experiential aspects of caves: a prehistoric viewer had to contend with a precarious path, eerie flickering lights, echoes, and the musty smells that permeate subterranean spaces, all of which

added texture to the viewing process. Most important, recent interpretations acknowledge that one explanation may not suffice for all times and places. For instance, even if sympathetic magic makes sense of some paintings, it hardly explains the art at Chauvet, where 72 percent of the animals represented were not hunted, judging by organic remains found in the cave.

Paleolithic Carving

Prehistoric artists also carved and modeled sculptures, in a variety of materials. At just under a foot high, a figure from Hohlenstein-Stadel in Germany (**fig. 1.6**) represents a standing creature, half human and half feline, crafted out of ivory. Although it is in a poor state of preservation, it is clear that the creation of this figure, with rudimentary stone tools, was an arduous business. It involved splitting the dried mammoth tusk, scraping it into shape, and using a sharp flint blade to incise such features as the striations on the arm and the muzzle. Strenuous polishing followed, using powdered hematite (an iron ore) as an abrasive. Exactly what the figure represents is unclear: perhaps a human dressed as an animal, possibly for hunting purposes. Some prehistorians have named these composite creatures shamans or "sorcerers," who could contact the spirit world through ritualistic behavior.

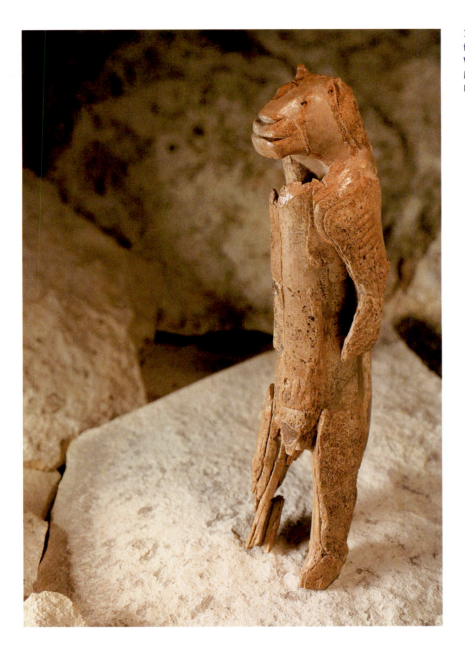

1.6 Hybrid figure with a human body and feline head, from Hohlenstein-Stadel (Baden-Württemberg), Germany. ca. 32,000 BCE. Mammoth ivory, height 11⅔″ (29.6 cm). Ulmer Museum

Women were frequent subjects in prehistoric sculpture, especially in the Gravettian period (which follows AURIGNACIAN), when they far outnumbered men as subject material. Discovered in 1908, the hand-sized limestone carving of the *Woman of Willendorf* from Austria dates from about 28,000–25,000 BCE (**fig. 1.7**), and still bears traces of ocher rubbed on to the carved surface. The artist reduced the female form to basic, abstract shapes instead of rendering it with the naturalism found in the representations of animals. Facial features are not a priority: Schematically rendered hair covers the entire head. Instead, emphasis rests on the figure's reproductive qualities: Diminutive arms sit on pendulous breasts, whose rounded forms are echoed in the bulging belly and copious buttocks. Genitalia are shown between large thighs. These

features suggest a fertility charm, yet the intention may have been to ensure a successful birth outcome rather than an increase in numbers of pregnancies. Perhaps she was a doll, or a venerable ancestor. In a period when food was scarce, a woman with these proportions may well have been exceptional.

The uncertainty of our interpretation of figures like the *Woman of Willendorf* has been further complicated by the terminology applied to them in the past. The *Woman of Willendorf*, like many other Paleolithic female figurines, was named a "Venus" figure. The term dates back to the discovery of the first female figurines in the mid-nineteenth century. Venus, the Roman version of the Greek goddess of love, Aphrodite, was portrayed as a nude female; nineteenth-century archaeologists saw these figures as similar in

The earliest Upper Paleolithic art dates to the AURIGNACIAN period. Among the best-known works are carved female statuettes such as the *Woman of Willendorf* (see fig. 1.7); some 130 of these have been found over a vast area from France to Siberia. The zenith of prehistoric art was reached during the Magdalenian era, the last period of the Upper Paleolithic. Its masterpieces are the magnificent cave paintings of animals in the Dordogne region of France, in the Pyrenees Mountains, and at Altamira in Spain.

1.7 *Woman of Willendorf.* ca. 28,000–25,000 BCE. Limestone, height 4⅜″ (11.1 cm). Naturhistorisches Museum, Vienna

function, if not in form, to the Roman goddess. Contemporary scholars are still debating their meaning, and avoid such anachronisms in terminology.

Neolithic Art

Around 10,000 BCE, the climate began to warm, and the ice that had covered almost a third of the globe began to recede, leaving Europe with more or less the geography it has today. New vegetation and changing animal populations caused human habits to mutate. Previously people had built small huts and used caves where the landscape allowed; in the Neolithic period, or New Stone Age, they began to build more substantial structures, choosing settlement places for favorable qualities, such as a water supply, rather than moving seasonally. Instead of hunting and gathering what nature supplied, they

domesticated animals and plants. This gradual change occurred at different times across the world; in some places, hunting and gathering are still the way of life.

Settled Societies and Neolithic Art

During the Neolithic period, technologies developed that suggest the beginnings of specialization. As the community could depend on a regular food supply, some members could devote time to acquiring special skills. These technologies included oven-fired pottery, weaving, and smelting of copper and lead.

In Europe, artists fashioned clay figurines, such as a woman and man from Cernavoda in Romania, of about 3500 BCE (**fig. 1.8**). Like the *Woman of Willendorf*, they are highly abstract, yet their forms are more linear than rounded: The woman's face is a flattened oval poised on a long, thick neck, and sharp edges articulate her corporeality—across her breasts, for instance, and at

1.8 Female and male figures, from Cernavoda, Romania. ca. 3500 BCE. Ceramic, height 4½″ (11.5 cm). National Museum of Antiquities, Bucharest

the fold of her pelvis. Elbowless arms meet where her hands rest on her raised knee, delineating a triangle and enclosing space within the sculptural form. This emphasizes the figurine's three-dimensionality, encouraging a viewer to look at it from several angles, moving around it or shifting it in the hand. The abstraction highlights the pose; yet, tempting as it may be to interpret it, perhaps as coquettishness, we should be cautious about reading meaning into it, since gestures can have dramatically different meanings from one culture to another. Found in a tomb, the couple may represent the deceased, or mourners; perhaps they were gifts that had a separate purpose before burial.

Architecture: Tombs and Rituals

Neolithic dwellings were mostly framed in wood, with walls of wattle (branches woven into a frame) and daub (mud or earth), and roofs of thatch, which rarely survive. In western and northern Europe, concerns about ceremonial burial and ritual inspired monumental architecture, using huge blocks of stone known as MEGALITHS. They were usually mounted in a **post-and-lintel** arrangement (two upright stones supporting a horizontal capstone).

Often, megaliths appear in circles, called **cromlechs**. The best-known megalithic structure is Stonehenge, on the Salisbury Plain in southern England (**figs. 1.9** and **1.10**). What now appears as a unified design is in fact the result of at least four phases of construction, beginning with a huge ditch defining a circle some 330 feet in diameter in the white chalk ground, and an embankment of over six feet in height running around the inside. A wide stone-lined avenue led from the circle to a pointed gray sandstone (sarsen) megalith, known today as the Heel Stone. By about 2100 BCE, Stonehenge had grown into a horseshoe-shaped arrangement of five sarsen triliths (two upright stones supporting a third, horizontal one), encircled by a ring of upright blocks capped with a lintel; between the rings was a circle of smaller bluestone blocks. Recent excavations exposed remains of a similar monument built of wood two miles away, as well as remnants of a village. Archaeologists believe the structures are related.

What Stonehenge—and its counterpart—signified to those who constructed them remains a tantalizing mystery. Many prehistorians believe that Stonehenge marked the passing of time. Given its monumentality, most also concur that

◆ MEGALITHS: Generally undressed or rough-hewn stones, menhirs are often found on hilltops from southern France to Scotland and are particularly common in Brittany, in northwestern France. Dolmens, the simplest form of megalithic tomb, have several large upright stones supporting a single massive capstone. About 50,000 of these survive from Spain to Sweden. Scholars have long debated how the 30- to 40-ton capstones were placed atop the standing stones.

menhirs

dolmen

1.9 Stonehenge (aerial view). ca. 2100 BCE. Diameter of circle 97′ (29.6 m). Salisbury Plain, Wiltshire, England

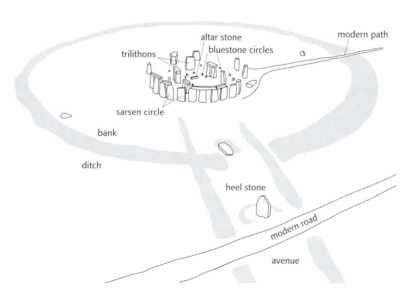

1.10 Diagram of original arrangement of stones at Stonehenge

it had a ritual function, perhaps associated with burial; its circular arrangement supports this conjecture, as circles are central to rituals in many societies. What is certain is that it represents tremendous manpower organization and engineering skill. The largest trilith soars 24 feet, supporting a lintel 15 feet long and 3 feet thick. The sarsen blocks weigh up to 50 tons apiece, and traveled 23 miles from the Marlborough Downs; the bluestones originated 200 miles away, in the Welsh Preseli Mountains. The blocks reveal evidence of meticulous stone-working. Holes hollowed out of the capstones fit snugly over projections on the uprights (forming a **mortise and tenon joint**), to make a stable structure. Moreover, upright megaliths taper upwards, with a central bulge, visually implying the weight they bear, and capturing an energy that enlivens the stones. The lintels are worked in two directions, their faces inclining outward by about 6 inches to appear vertical from the ground, while at the same time they curve around on the horizontal plane to make a smooth circle. This kind of refinement is usually associated with the Parthenon of Classical Athens (see fig. 5.17).

SUMMARY

Humans began to express themselves visually during the prehistoric age. With no written records to explain their intentions, however, prehistoric art raises many questions. Even so, by the end of the era, people had established techniques of painting, sculpting, and pottery-making, and begun to construct monumental works of architecture. They also developed a strong sense of the power of images and spaces: They recognized how to produce impressive shapes, such as those at Altamira and other caves, and how to alter space in sophisticated ways, as seen in the megaliths at Salisbury.

During the Paleolithic period, humans subsisted by hunting animals and gathering other available foods. Yet they found the time—and had the need—to make art. Paleolithic art survives mostly in two forms: paintings on cave walls, such as those at Lascaux, and smaller objects carved from bone or stone, such as the *Woman of Willendorf*. Its most frequent subject is the animal—most often those animals used for food. These renderings of animal forms are incredibly lively and naturalistic, though their function and meaning are not well understood. They may have been aids to hunting or a record of seasons or events.

During the Neolithic period, humans domesticated animals and raised plants for food, which led to a more settled way of life. Architecture was made from more permanent materials than those of Paleolithic dwellings. The formation of human communities resulted in increased specialization and new technologies, such as pottery-making. Sculpted and painted representations give evidence of developing religious practices and concern for the dead. Other innovations include large-scale stone structures for burial and other monuments, like Stonehenge, which many scholars see as tools for marking the passage of the seasons.

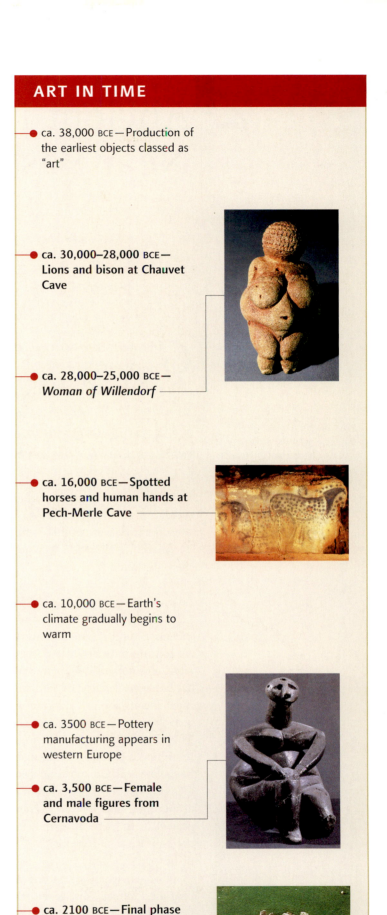

ART IN TIME

- ca. 38,000 BCE—Production of the earliest objects classed as "art"

- ca. 30,000–28,000 BCE—**Lions and bison at Chauvet Cave**

- ca. 28,000–25,000 BCE—**Woman of Willendorf**

- ca. 16,000 BCE—**Spotted horses and human hands at Pech-Merle Cave**

- ca. 10,000 BCE—Earth's climate gradually begins to warm

- ca. 3500 BCE—Pottery manufacturing appears in western Europe

- ca. 3,500 BCE—**Female and male figures from Cernavoda**

- ca. 2100 BCE—**Final phase of the construction at Stonehenge**

CHAPTER

2 | Ancient Near Eastern Art

Growing and storing crops and raising animals for food, the signature accomplishments of Neolithic peoples, would gradually change the course of civilization. In the fourth millennium BCE, large-scale urban communities of as many as 40,000 people began to emerge in Mesopotamia, the land between the Tigris and the Euphrates rivers. The establishment of cities had tremendous ramifications for the development of human life and for works of art.

◆ CUNEIFORM characters were made by pressing a stylus into damp clay. The stylus, usually fashioned from a reed, was shaped on both ends. One end was wedge-shaped; the other was pointed, rounded, or flat-tipped. The pointed end was used to draw lines and make punch marks. The tablets were then sun-dried or baked.

◆ This ca. 1750 BCE Babylonian deed of sale graphically shows the impressions made by the stylus in the soft clay. The British Museum, London.

Written, archaeological, and artistic evidence indicates that at the dawn of civilization Mesopotamia was covered with lush vegetation. By mastering irrigation techniques, populations there exploited the rivers and their tributaries to enrich the fertile soil even further. New technologies, including the wheel and the plow, and the casting of tools in copper and bronze, increased food production and facilitated trade. As communities flourished, they developed into city-states with distinct patterns of social organization. Specialization of labor and trade, and the mechanisms for the resolution of disputes, all required a central authority and government. The administration that developed in response to these needs probably generated what may have been the earliest writing system, known as CUNEIFORM. This system was used for accounting, and for the Sumerian *Epic of Gilgamesh* in the late third millennium BCE. With the invention of writing, we enter the realm of history.

The geography of Mesopotamia had other profound effects on developing civilizations. Unlike the narrow, fertile strip of the Nile Valley, protected by deserts on either side, where urban communities now also began to thrive, Mesopotamia is a wide trough with few natural defenses. The region was constantly traversed by people wanting to exploit its fertility. Indeed, throughout the history of the ancient Near East,

city-states were constantly warring with one another and were only sometimes united under a single ruler. Still, Mesopotamian visual culture retains a surprisingly constant character. Two dominant themes emerge: Art enabled and reflected political power; and Mesopotamians used visual narrative, exploring strategies for telling stories through art.

Sumerian Art

The first major civilization in MESOPOTAMIA was in the southern region of Sumer, near the junction of the Tigris and Euphrates rivers, where several city-states flourished from before 4000 BCE (see map 2.1) until about 2340 BCE. Who the Sumerians were is unknown, as their language is not related to any other known tongue. Along with architecture and writing, works of art in the form of sculpture, relief, and pottery inform us about Sumerian society.

For this people, life itself depended on appeasing the gods, who controlled natural forces and phenomena such as weather and water, the fertility of the land, and the heavenly bodies. Each city had a patron deity, to whom residents owed devotion and sustenance. The god's earthly steward was the city's ruler, who directed an administrative staff based in the temple. As the produce of the city's land belonged to

Map 2.1 The Ancient Near East

the god, the staff took charge of supplying farmers with seed, work animals, and tools. They built irrigation systems, and stored and distributed the harvest. Centralized food production meant that much of the population could specialize in other trades, donating a portion of the fruits of their labor to the temple. This system is called theocratic socialism.

Temple Architecture: Linking Heaven and Earth

The temple was the city's architectural focus. Good stone being scarce, Sumerians built predominantly with mud brick, covered with plaster. Their temples stood either at ground level or raised on a platform, which was gradually transformed into a squat, stepped pyramid known as a **ziggurat**. The names of some ziggurats—such as Babylon's Etemenanki ("House temple, bond between heaven and earth")—suggest that they may have been links or portals to the heavens, where priest and god could commune. Ziggurats functioned as the equivalents of mountains, which held a sacred status for Sumerians. A source of water, mountains were also a place of refuge during floods, and symbolized the Earth's generative power. Significantly, raised platforms made temples more visible. Mesopotamian texts indicate that the act of seeing was paramount: In seeing an object and finding it pleasing, a god

might act favorably toward those who made it. The desired response of a human audience, in turn, was wonder. Finally, there was probably a political dimension to the high platform: It emphasized and maintained the priests' status by expressing their separation from the rest of the community.

Around 3500 BCE, the city of Uruk (present-day Warka and biblical Erech) emerged as a center of Sumerian culture, flourishing from trade in its agricultural surplus. One of its temples, the "White Temple," named for its white-washed brick surfaces, was probably dedicated to the sky god Anu, chief of the Sumerian gods. It sits on a 40-foot mound constructed by filling in the ruins of older temples with brickwork, which suggests that the site itself was sacred (**figs. 2.1a** and **2.1b**). Recessed brickwork articulated its sloped sides. A system of stairs and ramps led counterclockwise around the mound, culminating at an entrance in the temple's long north side. This indirect approach is a characteristic feature of Mesopotamian temple architecture (in contrast to the direct axial approach favored in Egypt), and the winding ascent mirrored a visitor's metaphorical ascent into a divine realm. From three sides, members of the community could also witness the ceremonial ascent of priests and leaders who had exclusive access to the temple. Enough survives of the superstructure to

Major Civilizations in the Ancient Near East

ca. 4000 −2340 BCE	Sumerian
ca. 1792 −1595 BCE	Babylonian
ca. 1000–612 BCE	Assyrian
ca. 612–539 BCE	Neo-Babylonian
ca. 559–331 BCE	Persian

Apparently independent of one another, the earliest civilizations arose along four great rivers during the fourth millennium BCE. Egyptian civilization is found in the northeast corner of the continent of Africa, nourished by the Nile River. MESOPOTAMIA is the area encompassed by present-day Iraq and its immediate neighbors, drained by the Tigris and Euphrates rivers. In roughly what is Pakistan today, drained by the Indus River, were the Indus Valley or Harappa civilizations, and in west central China, civilizations arose along the Yellow River.

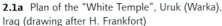

2.1a Plan of the "White Temple", Uruk (Warka), Iraq (drawing after H. Frankfort)

processional path

0	10	20	meters
0	20 40	60	feet

N

2.1b Remains of the "White Temple" on its ziggurat. ca. 3500–3000 BCE. Uruk (Warka), Iraq

indicate that thick buttressed walls surrounded a central, rectangular hall (a **cella**) housing a stepped altar. Along the long sides of the cella were smaller rooms serving as offices, priests' quarters, and storage areas, creating an overall tripartite layout typical of the earliest temples.

Sculpture

Within these temples, Sumerians often displayed sculptures to represent deities or worshipers.

TELL ASMAR A group of limestone, alabaster, and gypsum figures was excavated in the 1930s at a temple at Tell Asmar (**fig. 2.2**). Ranging in size from several inches to 2½ feet high, these figures

probably originally stood in the temple's cella. They were purposely buried near the altar along with other objects, perhaps when the temple was rebuilt or redecorated. Their identities are controversial: Some scholars have identified the two larger figures as cult statues of Abu, god of vegetation, and his consort. Most consider the entire group to represent worshipers, who dedicated them in hope of being perpetually present before the divinity. Some statues of this kind from elsewhere are even inscribed with the names of the dedicator and the god.

All but one of the figures in this group stand in a static pose, with hands clasped between chest and waist level. The style is decidedly abstract: On most of the standing male figures, horizontal or zigzag ridges define long hair and a full beard; the arms hang from wide shoulders; hands are clasped around a cup; narrow chests widen to broad waists; and the legs are cylindrical. The male figures wear fringed skirts hanging from a belt in a stiff cone shape, while the women have full-length drapery.

Both the poses and the costumes represent conventions of Sumerian art that later Mesopotamians adopted. Most distinctive are the faces, dominated by wide, almost round eyes, accentuated by dark inlays of lapis lazuli and shells set in bitumen, and by powerful eyebrows meeting over the bridge of the nose. It is tempting to read them through a lens tinted by Christian thought and to see the enlarged eyes as a window to the soul. However, such an interpretation misunderstands the specific cultural context of these images. Seeing was a major channel of communication with the gods, and the sculptures were probably responding to the god's awe-inspiring nature, with eyes wide open in admiration.

THE ROYAL CEMETERY AT UR At the Sumerian city of Ur (the present-day city of Muqaiyir and the birthplace of Abraham) in southern Mesopotamia, an extensive cemetery is preserved under the walls of Nebuchadnezzar II's later city. The cemetery contained some 1,840 burials dating between 2600 and 2000 BCE. Some were humble, but others were substantial subterranean structures and contained magnificent offerings, earning them the designation of "royal graves," even though scholars remain uncertain whether the deceased were royalty, priests, or members of another elite.

Visual Narratives

The so-called *Royal Standard of Ur*, of about 2600 BCE, found within the Royal Cemetery, offers a glimpse of the early development of visual narrative in Mesopotamia. It consists of four panels of red limestone, shell, and lapis lazuli inlay set in bitumen, originally attached to a wooden framework (**fig. 2.3**). The two principal sections show a military victory and a celebration or ritual feast, each unfolding in three superposed **registers**. Reading from the bottom, the "war" panel shows charioteers pulled by onagers (wild asses), riding over enemy bodies. In the middle register, infantry soldiers do battle and escort denuded prisoners of war. At the top, soldiers present the prisoners to a central figure, whose importance the artist signals through his position and through his larger size, a device known as **hieratic scale**; his head even breaks through the register's frame. In the "peace" panel, figures burdened with booty accompany onagers and, in the center, animals for a banquet, which is already under way in the top register. Seated figures raise their cups to the sound of music from a nearby harpist and singer; a larger figure toward the left of the scene is presumably a leader or king, perhaps the same figure as on the "war" side. Thus the panels tell a story, unfolding moment by moment as the eye follows the registers, guided by the figures' motion. Despite the action, however, the images have a static quality, emphasized by each figure's isolation; their descriptive forms (half frontal, half profile) rarely overlap. This gives the narrative an easy legibility, even from a distance. On excavating the *Royal Standard of Ur* in the 1920s, Leonard Woolley envisioned it held aloft on a pole as a military standard, and named it accordingly. In fact, it is unclear what it was used for;

2.3 *Royal Standard of Ur*, front and back sides. ca. 2600–2400 BCE. Wood inlaid with shell, limestone, and lapis lazuli, height 8″ (20.3 cm). The British Museum, London

it may have been the sounding-box for a stringed instrument, an object that was commonly found in burials.

Art of Akkad

Around 2350 BCE, Sumerian city-states began to fight over access to water and fertile land. Gradually their social organization was transformed, as local "stewards of the god" positioned themselves as ruling kings. The more ambitious tried to enlarge their domains through conquest. In many places, Semitic-speaking peoples from the northern region gradually assumed positions of power in the south. Although they adopted many features of Sumerian civilization, they were less bound to the tradition of the city-state. Sargon (meaning "true king") conquered Sumer, as well as northern Syria and Elam (to the northeast of Sumer), in about 2334 BCE (see map 2.1), basing himself in the city of Akkad (probably northwest of Sumer, near modern Baghdad). Sargon's ambitions were both imperial and dynastic; his goal was to unite the region in loyalty to his personal rule. Under his grandson, Naram-Sin, who ruled from 2254 to 2218 BCE, the Akkadian empire stretched from Sumer in the south to Elam in the east, and then to Syria in the west and Nineveh in the north.

Sculpture: Power

Under the Akkadians, the visual arts were increasingly used to establish and reflect the monarch's power, not for the last time in art history. A magnificent copper head found in a rubbish heap at Nineveh, dated between 2250 and 2200 BCE and sometimes identified as Naram-Sin himself (**fig. 2.4**), derives its extraordinary power from a number of factors. It was designed to be seen from the front, and this **frontality** makes it appear unchanging and eternal. The abstract treatment of beard and hair contrasts with the smooth flesh to give the head a memorable simplicity and a strong symmetry, which denote control and order. The intricate, precise patterning of hair and beard testify to the metalworker's expertise in hollow casting. Furthermore, at a time before metallurgy was widely understood, the use of cast metal for a portrait demonstrated the patron's control of a technology primarily associated with weaponry. Originally, the portrait would have had eyes inlaid with precious and semiprecious materials, as other surviving figures do. The damage to the head was probably incurred during the Medes' invasion of Nineveh in 612 BCE. The enemy gouged out its eyes and hacked off its ears, nose, and lower beard, as if attacking the person represented. Many cultures, even in our own day, practice such acts of ritualized vandalism as symbolic acts of violence or protest.

The themes of power and narrative combine in a 6½-foot **stele** (upright marker stone) erected in the Akkadian city of Sippar during the rule of Naram-Sin (**fig. 2.5**). The stele commemorates, in relief, Naram-Sin's victory over the Lullubi, people of the Zagros mountains in eastern Mesopotamia. This time the story is not narrated in registers; instead, ranks of soldiers, in composite view, climb the contours of a wooded mountain. Their ordered march contrasts with the enemy's chaotic rout. As the victorious soldiers

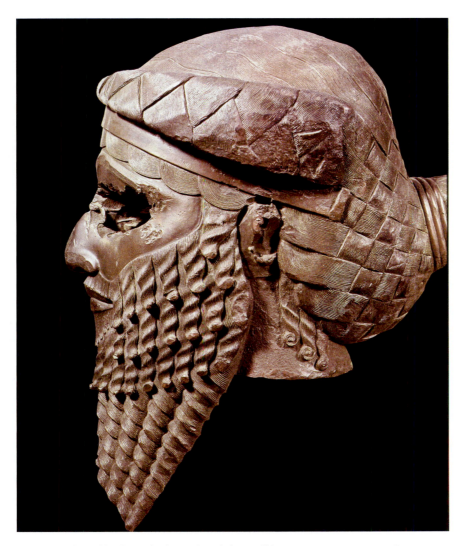

2.4 *Head of an Akkadian Ruler* from Nineveh (Kuyunjik), Iraq. ca. 2250–2200 BCE. Bronze, height 12″ (30.7 cm). Iraq Museum, Baghdad

2.5 Stele of Naram-Sin. ca. 2270 BCE. Red sandstone, height 6'6" (2 m). Musée du Louvre, Paris

that suggests proximity to the divine. His horned crown, formerly an exclusive accoutrement of the gods, marks him as the first Mesopotamian king to deify himself (an act that his people did not unanimously welcome). The bold musculature of his limbs and his powerful stance make him a heroic figure. Solar deities shine auspiciously overhead, as if witnessing his victory.

Neo-Sumerian Revival

The rule of the Akkadian kings came to an end when a mountain people, the Guti, gained control of the Mesopotamian Plain. The cities of Sumer rose up in retaliation and drove them out in 2112 BCE, under the leadership of King Urnammu of Ur, who united a realm that was to last a hundred years. As part of his renewal project, he returned to building on a magnificent scale.

Part of Urnammu's legacy is the Great Ziggurat at Ur of about 2100 BCE, dedicated to the Sumerian moon god Nanna (Sin in Akkadian) (**fig. 2.6**). Its 190- by 130-foot base soared to 50 feet in three stepped stages. The base was constructed of solid mud brick and faced with baked bricks set in bitumen, a tarry material used here as mortar. Although not structurally functional, thick **buttresses** (vertical supporting elements) articulate the walls, giving an impression of strength. Moreover, a multitude of upward lines adds a dynamic energy to the monument's appearance. Three staircases, now reconstructed, converged high up at the fortified gateway. Each 100 steps long, one was set perpendicular to the temple, the other two parallel to the base wall. From the gateway, a fourth staircase once rose to the temple proper, which does not survive. The stairways may have provided an imposing setting for ceremonial processions.

Babylonian Art

The late third and early second millennia BCE were a time of turmoil and warfare in Mesopotamia. The region was then unified for over 300 years under a Babylonian dynasty. During the reign of its most famous ruler, Hammurabi (r. 1792–1750 BCE), the city of Babylon assumed the dominant role formerly played by Akkad and Ur. Combining military prowess with respect for Sumerian tradition, Hammurabi cast

trample the fallen foe underfoot, the defeated beg for mercy or lie contorted in death. Above them, the king's large scale and central position make his identity clear. He stands isolated against the background, next to a mountain peak

2.6 Great Ziggurat of King Urnammu, Ur. ca. 2100 BCE. Muqaiyir, Iraq

himself as "the favorite shepherd" of the sun god Shamash, stating his mission "to cause justice to prevail in the land and to destroy the wicked and evil, so that the strong might not oppress the weak nor the weak the strong." Babylon retained its role as cultural center of Sumer for more than a thousand years after its political power had waned.

The Code of Hammurabi

Hammurabi is best known for his LAW CODE. It survives as one of the earliest written bodies of law, engraved on a black basalt stele reaching over seven feet in height (**fig. 2.7**). The largest portion of the text concerns commercial and property law, rulings on domestic issues, and questions of physical assault, detailing penalties to be inflicted on noncompliers.

At the top of the stele, Hammurabi is depicted in relief, standing with his arm raised in greeting before an enthroned Shamash, whose shoulders emanate sun rays. The sun god extends his hand, which holds the rope ring and the measuring rod of kingship; this single gesture unifies both the scene's composition and the implied purpose of the two protagonists. The image is a variant of the "introduction scene" found on cylinder seals, where a goddess leads a human individual with his hand raised in salute before a seated godlike figure who bestows his blessing. Hammurabi appears without the benefit—or need—of a divine intercessor, implying an especially close relationship with the sun god. Yet the smaller scale of Hammurabi compared with the seated god expresses his status as "shepherd" rather than god himself. The symmetrical composition and smooth surfaces result in a

The LAW CODE of Hammurabi contains 282 articles set down in 3,600 lines of cuneiform writing. Enforced throughout the empire, it aimed "to destroy the wicked and the evil, that the strong may not oppress the weak." It specifies penalties for crimes (including fines, beatings, maimings, and executions), as well as laws relating to family life, such as those covering divorce. The well-known phrase "an eye for an eye, a tooth for a tooth" is a quotation from the code, repeated in the Bible.

2.7 Upper part of stele inscribed with the Law Code of Hammurabi. ca. 1760 BCE. Diorite, height of stele approx. 7′ (2.1 m); height of relief 28″ (71 cm). Musée du Louvre, Paris legible image of divinely ordained power that is fully in line with Mesopotamian traditions.

Assyrian Art

Babylon fell around 1595 BCE to the Hittites, who had established themselves in Anatolia (modern Turkey), and departed leaving a weakened Babylonian state open to other invaders. By the end of the millennium, the Assyrians more or less controlled southern Mesopotamia. Their home was the city-state of Assur, named for the god Ashur, located on the upper course of the Tigris.

Art of Empire: Expressing Royal Power

Under a series of able rulers, the Assyrian realm expanded, in time covering not only Mesopotamia but surrounding regions as well. At its height, in the seventh century BCE, the empire stretched from the Sinai Peninsula to Armenia; even Egypt was successfully invaded about 670 BCE (see map 2.1). The Assyrians adapted the artistic achievements of the Sumerians and Babylonians to their own purpose, to create an art of empire: propagandistic and public, designed to proclaim and sustain the supremacy of the Assyrian civilization, particularly through representations of military power. Their architectural emphasis shifted primarily to royal palaces, which grew to unprecedented size and magnificence, loudly expressing a royal presence and domination.

The palace complex of Sargon II (r. 721–705 BCE) at Dur Sharrukin (present-day Khorsabad, Iraq) comprised about 30 courtyards and 200 rooms, and this impressive scale was accompanied by monumental imagery. At the gateways stood huge, awe-inspiring guardian figures known as **lamassu**, in the shape of winged, human-headed bulls (**fig. 2.8**). The illustration here shows the lamassu of Khorsabad during excavation in the 1840s. The massive creatures are almost carved in the round, yet the addition of a fifth leg, visible from the side, reveals that the sculptor conceived of them as relief sculptures on two sides of the stone block, so that the figures are legible both frontally and in profile. Carved out of the limestone, they are, in a sense, one with the building. With their tall, horned headdresses and deep-set eyes, and with the powerful muscularity of their legs and bodies set off by the delicate patterning of the beard and feathers, they towered over an approaching visitor,

2.8 Gate of the Citadel of Sargon II, Dur Sharrukin (photo taken during excavation). 742–706 BCE. Khorsabad, Iraq

2.9 *Lion Hunt* relief, from reign of Ashurbanipal. ca. 645 BCE. Gypsum, height 3'7" (109.22 cm). The British Museum, London

embodying the king's fearful authority. The Assyrians may have believed the hybrid creatures had the power to ward off evil spirits.

Once inside a royal palace, a visitor would confront another distinctive feature of Assyrian architecture: the upright gypsum slabs called **orthostats** with which the builders lined the lower walls. Structurally, the slabs protected the mud brick from moisture and wear, but they served a communicative purpose as well. On their surfaces, narrative images in low relief, painted in places for emphasis, glorified the king with depictions of lion hunts and military conquests (with inscriptions giving supplementary information). Actions take place in a continuous band, propelling a viewer from scene to scene. As in Egypt, royal lion hunts were staged events within palace grounds. Earlier Mesopotamian rulers hunted lions to protect their subjects, but by the time of the Assyrians, the activity had become more symbolic than real, ritually showcasing the king's strength and serving as a metaphor for military prowess. One of the best-known sections of Assyrian relief comes from the North Palace of Ashurbanipal (r. 668–627 BCE) at Nineveh, dating to roughly 645 BCE (**fig. 2.9**). The king races forward in his chariot with bow drawn, leaving wounded and dead lions in his wake. As attendants plunge spears into its

chest, a wounded lion hurls itself at the chariot, its body flat out in a clean diagonal line, its claws spread and mouth open in what appears to be pain combined with desperate ferocity. Clearly, the sculptor ennobled the victims of the hunt, contrasting the limp bodies of the slain animals with the taut leaping lion and the powerful energy of the king's party. Yet we should not conclude that the artist necessarily intended to evoke sympathy for the beasts, or to comment on the cruelty of a staged hunt; it is more likely that by ennobling the lions the sculptor glorified their vanquisher, the king, even more.

Late Babylonian Art

The Assyrian empire came to an end in 612 BCE, when Nineveh fell to the Medes (an INDO-EUROPEAN-speaking people from western Iran) and the resurgent Babylonians. Under the Chaldean dynasty, the ancient city of Babylon had a final brief flowering between 612 and 539 BCE, before it was conquered by the Persians.

The royal palace at Babylon was on almost the same scale as Assyrian palaces, with five huge courtyards surrounded by numerous reception suites. For its decoration, the Late Babylonians adopted the use of baked and

INDO-EUROPEAN describes the world's largest language group, or linguistic family. It takes its name from the area where the original language arose sometime before 2000 BCE—that encompassed by Europe and India and the lands in between. The term denotes only a linguistic group, not ethnic or cultural divisions. Not all peoples living in this area speak an Indo-European language. Vocabulary and grammar structure are the common elements. The subfamilies include Anatolian, Baltic, Celtic, Germanic (which contains English), Italic, Greek, Slavic, Indo-Iranian, and several other smaller language groups.

◆ The Hanging Gardens of Babylon were classified by the ancients as one of the Seven Wonders of the World. The others were the Pyramid of Khufu at Giza (see fig. 3.5), the Mausoleum at Halikarnassos (see fig. 5.22), the Colossus of Rhodes (a statue of the sun god Helios), the Temple of Artemis at Ephesos, the statue of Olympian Zeus by Pheidias, and the Pharos (lighthouse) at Alexandria.

2.10 Ishtar Gate (restored), from Babylon, Iraq. ca. 575 BCE. Glazed brick 48′4″ × 51′6⅛″ × 14′3⅝″ (14.73 × 15.70 × 4.36 m). Staatliche Museen zu Berlin, Preussischer Kulturbesitz, Vorderasiatisches Museum

glazed brick, molded into individual shapes. Glazing brick involved putting a film of glass over the brick's surface. Its coloristic effect appears on the courtyard façade of the Throne Room and the Processional Way leading to the Ishtar Gate and the gate itself, now reassembled in Berlin (**fig. 2.10**). Against a deep blue background, a procession of bulls, dragons, and other animals sacred to the gods of Babylon, set off in molded brick, is contained within a framework of brightly colored ornamental bands. Unlike the massive muscularity of the lamassu, their forms are light and agile-looking, arrested in a processional stride that slowly accompanies the ceremonial parades leading to the gate's arched opening.

Iranian Art

Alongside the successive cultures of Mesopotamia, a variety of other civilizations developed in areas beyond the Tigris and Euphrates. Some of them invaded or conquered contemporaneous city-states in Mesopotamia. Others, such as the sea-going Phoenicians on the Mediterranean coast to the west, traded with the people of Mesopotamia and in so doing spread its visual forms to Africa and Europe.

The Persian Empire: Cosmopolitan Heirs to the Mesopotamian Tradition

During the mid-sixth century BCE, the entire Near East came to be dominated by the small kingdom of Parsa to the east of lower Mesopotamia. Under the Achaemenid ruler Cyrus the Great (r. 559–530/29 BCE), the Persians (or Iranians) overthrew the king of the Medes, then conquered major parts of Asia Minor and Babylon. Cyrus assumed the title "King of Babylon," along with the broader ambitions of Mesopotamian rulers.

The empire he founded continued to expand under his successors. Egypt fell in 525 BCE, while Greece narrowly escaped Persian domination in the early fifth century BCE. At its height, under Darius I (r. 521–486 BCE) and his son Xerxes (r. 485–465 BCE), the Persian empire in its territorial reach far outstripped the Egyptian and Assyrian empires combined. Its huge domain endured for two centuries, during which it developed an efficient administration and monumental art forms.

Persian religious beliefs were related to the prophecies of ZOROASTER (Zarathustra) and were based on the dualism of good and evil, embodied in Ahuramazda (Light) and Ahriman (Darkness). The cult of Ahuramazda focused its rituals on fire altars in the open air; consequently, Persian kings did not construct religious architecture. Instead they concentrated their attention and resources on royal palaces, at once vast and impressive.

PERSEPOLIS The most ambitious of these palaces, at Parsa or Persepolis, was begun by Darius I in 518 BCE, and enlarged by subsequent rulers (**fig. 2.11**). Set on a plateau in the Zagros highlands, it consisted of a great number of rooms, halls, and courts laid out in a grid plan; the whole was fortified and raised on a platform. The palace is a synthesis of materials and design traditions from all parts of the far-flung empire, a clear statement of internationalism. Darius boasts in his inscriptions that its timber came from Lebanon (cedar), Gandhara and Carmania (yaka wood), and its bricks from Babylon. To work these materials, the Achaemenid dynasty brought in craftsmen from all over the empire, who then returned to their respective homes taking this international style with them.

ZOROASTER was a prophet and religious teacher born about 628 BCE in northwestern Persia. His name derives from the Persian Zarathustra, meaning "camel driver." Interestingly, the sixth century BCE saw the birth of three other great religions: Daoism (China), Confucianism (China), and Buddhism (India)—each because of the appearance of a great religious teacher.

0   20   50   70   100 meters
0   100   200   300 feet

2.11 Plan of Palace of Darius and Xerxes, Persepolis. 518–460 BCE. Solid triangles show the processional route taken by Persian and Mede notables; open triangles indicate the way taken by heads of delegations and their suites

2.12 East stairway of the Audience Hall of Darius and Xerxes. ca. 500 BCE. Persepolis, Iran

Reliefs embellishing the platform of the huge audience hall, or *apadana*, and its double stairway proclaim the theme of harmony and integration across the multicultural empire, in marked contrast to the military narratives of the Assyrians (**fig. 2.12**). Long rows of marching figures, sometimes shown in registers one above another, represent the empire's 23 subject nations, as well as royal guards and Persian dignitaries. Each of the nations' representatives wears indigenous dress and brings a regional gift as tribute to the Persian king. Colored stone and metals applied to the relief once added richness to the wealth of carved detail. The relief is remarkably shallow, yet by keeping the figures' roundness to the edge of their bodies (so that they cast a shadow), and by cutting the background away to a level field, the sculptors have created the impression of greater depth. Most of the figures are depicted in true profile, even though some figures turn their heads back to address those who follow. The repetition of the walking human form contributes a powerful dynamic quality that guides a visitor's path through the enormous space. The repetition also lends the reliefs an eternal quality, as if preserving the action in perpetual time. This would be especially fitting if, as some scholars believe, the relief represents the recurring celebration of the New Year Festival.

The Achaemenid synthesis of traditions at Persepolis demonstrates the longevity and flexibility of the Near Eastern language of rulership. On a grand scale, the palace provides a dramatic and powerful setting for imperial court ritual.

SUMMARY

During the last four millennia BCE, numerous civilizations rose and fell in the fertile lands of Mesopotamia and the neighboring lands in western Asia. Yet, their art forms remained extraordinarily similar. Artists and architects were hired to express the authority of gods and rulers; in doing so, they played a vital role in maintaining that authority. They produced monuments like magnificent temples and palaces, reliefs and free-standing sculpture, often on a dizzying scale. They also explored sophisticated strategies for narrative, and for guiding a visitor's movement through space. Mesopotamian art is deeply informed by the constant movement of peoples, objects, and ideas.

The art and artifacts of Sumer provided a model of visual communication that later groups entering Mesopotamia adapted to their own needs. Ziggurats offered imposing platforms for religious structures and rituals. Surviving sculptures demonstrate a refined but abstract approach to representing the figure. The expensive materials used in grave goods for elites express the level of resources they controlled as well as their power. Sumerian objects such as the Standard of Ur also reveal an interest in telling stories visually.

Akkadian rulers altered Sumerian imagery to create their own language of power; figural representations harked back to Sumerian precedents but expressed the authoritarian nature of Akkadian kingship. One of the most impressive surviving works is the magnificent copper portrait head found at Nineveh.

As the third millennium BCE came to an end, the cities of Sumer returned to the Sumerian language and blended their old artistic traditions with those of the Akkadian traditions. Building great ziggurats like that at Ur to local gods was an act of piety and of power.

After a period of war and turmoil, the Babylonians unified the region, centered in the city of Babylon. The most famous ruler of this period was Hammurabi, who combined military prowess with a respect for Sumerian tradition. He is best known for his Law Code, which is one of the earliest surviving written bodies of law, preserved on a stele.

Assyria conquered southern Mesopotamia by the end of the first millennium BCE and expanded to stretch from the Sinai Peninsula to Armenia. The theme of Assyrian art is the ruler's power, and both walled cities and sprawling palaces reflect its military culture. Large guardian figures, lamassu, protected the palaces, while numerous reliefs on the walls recounted the king's victories and virtues.

Before it was conquered by the Persians, the city of Babylon had a brief reflowering. The royal palace built at this time was decorated with colorful glazed bricks, decorated with a procession of hundreds of sacred animals.

East of Mesopotamia, ancient Iran became a gateway for migrating tribes, and its art reflects these intersections. Under Cyrus the Great, the Persians or Iranians came to dominate their neighbors and eventually—during the reigns of Darius and Xerxes—the entire Near East. One remarkable artistic achievement of the ancient Iranians was the grand palace at Persepolis.

ART IN TIME

- ca. 3500 BCE—The Sumerian city of Uruk emerges

- ca. 2900 BCE—Mesopotamians begin using cuneiform writing

- ca. 2600 BCE—The Sumerian *Royal Standard of Ur*

- ca. 2100 BCE—The Great Ziggurat at Ur built, commissioned by King Urnammu

- ca. 1792–1750 BCE—Babylon ruled by Hammurabi

- ca. 668–627 BCE—Assyrian construction of the North Palace of Ashurbanipal

- ca. 604–562 BCE—Reign of the Late Babylonian ruler Nebuchadnezzar II

- ca. 575 BCE—Babylonian construction of the Ishtar Gate

- ca. 559–530/529 BCE—Rule of Cyrus the Great, who leads the Persians to overthrow the Medes

- ca. 518—Construction of the Persian palace at Persepolis begins

- 331 BCE—Alexander the Great defeats the Persians

3 Egyptian Art

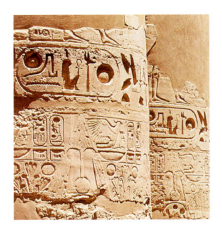

Speaking Of

king, kingship, kingdom, dynasty, and pharaoh

Egyptian kings were believed to combine divine and mortal qualities and thus to be quasi-divine. Kingship passed from father to son or to near kin. Dynasties were groupings of kings linked by kinship and were first devised in the early third century BCE by the priest Manetho, who designated clusters of dynasties into Kingdoms and "Intermediate Periods." Three main kingdoms — the Old, Middle, and New — comprise clusters through the Twentieth Dynasty. Manetho recognized 30 dynasties to 343 BCE, after which ancient Egypt continued another 750 years until the division of the Roman Empire in 395 CE. The word "pharaoh" has been used synonymously with "king" by modern writers. It derives from the Egyptian term for "royal palace"; the Egyptians employed it to mean "king" beginning only in the Eighteenth Dynasty.

*E*gypt has long fascinated the West. The ancient Greeks and the Romans knew and admired Egypt, and their esteem was taken up by Renaissance collectors and scholars. Napoleon's incursions into Egypt in the late eighteenth century brought artifacts and knowledge back to France and stimulated interest throughout Europe. European-sponsored excavations have been going on in Egypt since the nineteenth century, sometimes, as with the discovery in 1922 of the tomb of King Tutankhamun, with spectacular results.

One reason that ancient Egypt enthralls us is the exceptional quality and monumental character of its works of art. Most surviving works come from tombs, which were built to assure an afterlife for the deceased. Works of art contained within them were intended to accompany the deceased into eternity. Thus, Egyptian art is an art of permanence. Artists did not strive for change or originality, but adhered instead to traditional formulations that expressed specific ideas. Continuity of form and subject is therefore a characteristic of ancient Egyptian art.

Egyptian artists made art mainly for the elite patrons of a society that was extremely hierarchical. Contemporary with the Egyptian development of writing around 3000 BCE was the emergence of a political and religious system that placed a god-king (called a pharaoh from the New Kingdom on) in charge of the physical and spiritual well-being of the land and its people. Many of the best-known and most evocative works of Egyptian art were made for these powerful rulers, and express the multifaceted ways that the king was envisioned: as a human manifestation of the gods, as a god in his own right, as a beneficent ruler, and as an emblem of life itself. Royal projects for the afterlife dominated the landscape and provided models for elite burials.

Egyptian geography also played an important role in the development of art forms. Established along the course of the Nile River in North Africa and protected by the surrounding desert, or "red land," Egypt comprised two regions. Upper Egypt, in the south, includes the Nile Valley between present-day Aswan and the point where the river fans out into the Delta, near present-day Cairo. Lower Egypt, in the north, consists mainly of the vast Delta, from ancient Memphis to the Mediterranean. The river floods annually, inundating the land on either side. As it recedes, the water leaves a dark strip of soil fertilized by silt. The Egyptians called this rich soil the "black land." It was irrigated and farmed and regularly produced surplus food, allowing Egyptians to diversify and develop a complex culture.

Egypt's agrarian society depended on the Nile's flooding to survive. The king had to assure continuity of life through intercession with the gods, who often represented natural forces. The chief deity was the sun, worshiped as Ra-Horakhty. In matters concerning the afterlife, the deities Osiris, his consort Isis, and their son Horus played key roles. Gods took many forms: Ra might appear as a falcon-headed man; Osiris—who was killed and resurrected—as a mummy. The king himself was called the son of Ra and the human embodiment of Horus. As an equal to the gods, he controlled the land, the future, and the afterlife. A large priesthood, an administrative bureaucracy, and a strong military assisted him.

Predynastic and Early Dynastic Art

The origins of Egyptian culture stretch back into the Neolithic period. By at least 5000 BCE, humans were growing crops and domesticating animals in the Nile Valley. Settlements there were gradually transformed into urban centers. According to tradition, the first king of the first dynasty founded the city of Memphis, at the mouth of the Delta (see map 3.1), uniting Upper and Lower Egypt. The division of Egypt into two regions was consistent with the Egyptian worldview. They saw the world as a set of dualities in opposition: Upper and Lower Egypt, the red land of the desert and the black land of cultivation, Osiris (the god of civilization) opposed to Seth (the god of chaos). The king had to balance the forces of chaos and order, by bringing *ma'at* (harmony or order) to the world. Recognizing this worldview has led some scholars to reconsider the traditional explanation that Upper and Lower Egypt were independent regions unified by King Narmer. Instead, they argue that this division was an imaginative construction of the past.

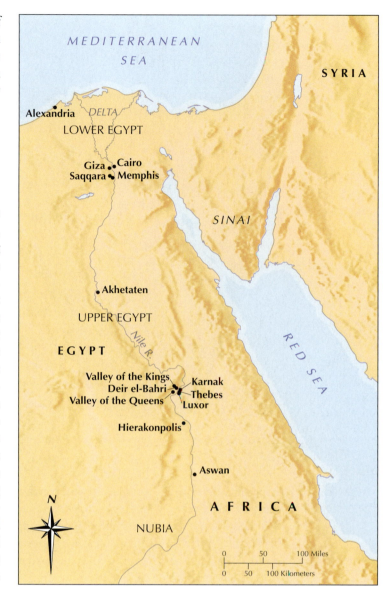

Map 3.1 Ancient Egypt

The Palette of King Narmer

The concept of the king as unifier was expressed in the *Palette of King Narmer* (**fig. 3.1**), dated around 3150–3125 BCE. The Palette is a stone tablet with a central depression for grinding protective paint, which was applied around the eyes. Its size—more than two feet high—implies that it was not for ordinary use, but was probably reserved for a ceremony to grind makeup for a cult statue. This ritual function may explain its findspot in the temple of Hierakonpolis, where it had been buried along with other offerings to Horus.

The Palette is carved on both sides in registers (rows) in shallow relief. At the top of each side, in the center, Narmer's name is written in HIEROGLYPHS, within an abstract rendering of the king's palace. Hieroglyphs were a writing system that the Egyptians developed at about the same time as the Mesopotamians were

inventing cuneiform. On either side of the hieroglyphs, heads of cows represent the sky goddess, locating the king in the sky. On one side of the Palette (shown on the left), Narmer holds a fallen enemy by the hair, as he raises his mace—an emblem of kingship—with the other. The king is shown in the composite view that will be the hallmark of Egyptian two-dimensional art: With a frontal view of eye, shoulders, and arms, but a profile of head and legs. He wears the white crown of Upper Egypt and from his belt hangs the tail of a bull, a symbol of power that Egyptian kings would wear as part of their ceremonial dress for 3,000 years. The large scale of his figure compared with others immediately establishes his authority. For his part, the enemy, like the two defeated enemies in the bottom register, is stripped of clothing as an act of humiliation. Behind the king, and

3.1 *Palette of King Narmer* (both sides), from Hierakonpolis. ca. 3150–3125 BCE. Slate, height 25″ (63.5 cm). Egyptian Museum, Cairo

HIEROGLYPHS were named by the Greeks, who saw them as sacred writings, from *hieros* (sacred), and *glyphs* (carving). The Egyptians themselves called them "god's words," and used them in religious and administrative contexts as ideographs and as phonetic signs. In this Twelfth Dynasty amulet, the stylized papyrus clump on the left is an ideograph for "around" or "behind." The *ankh* in the center is a symbol for life, and the *sa* on the right is a symbol of protection. The basket (*nebet*) means variously "all," "lord," or "master." Thus, this ideographic amulet is read as "All life and protection are around [the master, king, lord]."

amulet

The phonetic reading of this hieroglyph is, from top to bottom: *sha* (for the stand of lotus), *ba* (Egyptian for "ram"), *ka* (upraised arms meaning "spirit" or "soul"). Because the signs are enclosed by the lozenge-like rope, called a cartouche, we know that this hieroglyph means "King Shabaka."

cartouche

standing on his own ground-line, is an attendant carrying his sandals. Hieroglyphs identify both the sandal-carrier and the enemy. To the right of Narmer appears a falcon resting on a papyrus stand, which grows from a human-headed strip of land; the falcon holds a rope tethered to the face.

On the other side of the Palette (on the right in fig. 3.1), Narmer appears in the highest register, now wearing the red crown of Lower Egypt. Flanked by the sandal-carrier and a long-haired figure, he follows four standard-bearers to inspect the decapitated bodies of prisoners, arranged with their heads between their legs. In the larger central register, two animals, each roped in by a male figure, twist their long necks to frame a circle. The symmetrical motif may represent *ma'at*. In the lowest register, a bull representing the king attacks a city and tramples down the enemy. The Palette is significant because it communicates its message by combining several different types of signs into one object. Some of these signs—the king, attendants, and prisoners—are literal representations. Others are symbolic representations, such as the depiction of the king as a bull, denoting his strength. Pictographs, small symbols based on abstract representations of concepts, encode

further information: In the falcon and papyrus group, the falcon represents Horus, whom the Egyptians believed the king incarnated, while the human-headed papyrus stand represents Lower Egypt, where papyrus grew abundantly. A possible interpretation is that this pictograph expresses Narmer's control of that region. Finally, the artist included identifying texts in the form of hieroglyphs. Together, these different signs on the Palette drive home important messages about the nature of Egyptian kingship: The king embodied the unified Upper and Lower Egypt, and though human, he occupied a divine office, as shown by the placement of his name in the sky, the realm of Horus.

The Old Kingdom: A Golden Age

The image of kingship offered by the *Palette of King Narmer* is one that transcends earthly power, representing the king as a divinity as well as a ruler. The kings of the Old Kingdom (Dynasty Three to Dynasty Six, ca. 2649–2150 BCE) found more monumental ways to express this notion. Their dynasties and their works of art would be emulated for two millennia.

Old Kingdom Funerary Complexes

During the Old Kingdom, buildings that housed the day-to-day activities of the living were constructed mainly of perishable materials, and little survives. The bulk of archaeological evidence comes instead from tombs. The majority of the population were probably buried in shallow desert graves, but the elite had the resources to build elaborate funerary monuments. The survival of these tombs is no accident; they were purposely constructed to endure.

These structures had several important functions. As in many cultures, tombs served the living by giving the deceased a permanent marker in the landscape. They indicated the status of the dead and perpetuated their memory. These monuments also served a critical function in ensuring the preservation of a deceased individual's life force, or *ka*. Egyptians considered that the *ka* survived after death, and so required a place to reside for eternity. This is why embalmers went to such lengths to preserve the body through mummification. The mummified body, usually placed within a **sarcophagus** (a stone coffin), was interred in a burial chamber, often surrounded by chambers for funerary equipment. Should the embalmers' efforts fail and the body decay, a statue placed within the burial chamber could serve as a surrogate home for the *ka*. Egyptians also equipped their tombs with objects of daily life for the *ka* to enjoy.

THE FUNERARY COMPLEX OF KING DJOSER
The first known major funerary complex is that of the Third Dynasty King Djoser (Netjerikhet), at Saqqara (**fig. 3.2** and see fig. 3.4), who ruled between 2630 and 2611 BCE. On the west side of the Nile, Saqqara was the **necropolis**, or city of the dead, of the capital city of Memphis in Lower Egypt. Encircling the entire complex is a rectangular enclosure wall of stone 33 feet high, stretching over a mile in length. Dominating it is a stepped pyramid, seen in fig. 3.2 and in a transverse section in fig. 3.4. Originally a 26-foot high **mastaba** (a bench tomb), it rose to its towering 204-foot high form over the course of years as progressively diminishing layers of masonry were added, resulting in a staircase, perhaps the

3.2 Imhotep. Step Pyramid and Funerary Complex of King Djoser. Third Dynasty. ca. 2681–2662 BCE. Saqqara

3.3 Papyrus-shaped half-columns, North Palace, Funerary Complex of King Djoser. Saqqara

papyrus-bud column   open-flower papyrus column

means by which the king could ascend to the gods. The treads of the "steps" incline downwards and the uprights outwards, giving the structure an impressively stable appearance. A chamber excavated about 90 feet into the rock beneath the pyramid contained the burial, accompanied by other chambers for provisions. North of the pyramid was a labyrinthine funerary temple, where offering rituals were performed for the dead king.

The buildings in the burial complex mimic the palace architecture inhabited by the living king. A large court to the south of the pyramid may have housed rituals for receiving tribute or asserting royal dominion. The smaller court to its east, flanked by shrines of Upper and Lower Egypt, may have been the site of the *sed* festival, which celebrated the king's 30-year jubilee and rejuvenated his power. Both sets of rituals were thought to be enacted by the dead king. Unlike the structures in a palace, many of the buildings in the funerary complex are nonfunctional: For instance, of 14 gateways indicated in the niched enclosure wall, which evokes a palace façade, only one allows entrance; the rest are false doors. Furthermore, while palaces were built of perishable materials—primarily mud brick—the funerary complex, constructed entirely in limestone,

was built to last. Masons dressed the limestone blocks of the enclosure wall to resemble the niched façades of mud-brick architecture. Additionally, the reconstructed façade of a shrine echoes the form of an Upper Egyptian tent building, with tall poles supporting a mat roof that billows in the wind. Engaged COLUMNS imitate the PAPYRUS stems or bundled reeds that Egyptian builders used to support mud-brick walls, with capitals shaped to resemble blossoms (**fig. 3.3**).

Many elements of the complex served as permanent settings for the dead king to enact rituals of kingship perpetually—rituals that maintained order among the living. The king's presence in the complex was assured by the installation of a life-sized seated statue of him in a *serdab* (an enclosed room without an entrance) to the east of the funerary temple. Two holes in the *serdab*'s front wall enabled his *ka*, residing in the statue, to observe rituals in his honor and draw sustenance from offerings of food and incense. The complex was oriented north–south, and the king's statue looked out toward the circumpolar stars in the northern sky. Within the precinct, his *ka* would remain eternally alive and vigilant.

Inscriptions on fragments of statues found within the complex preserve the name of the

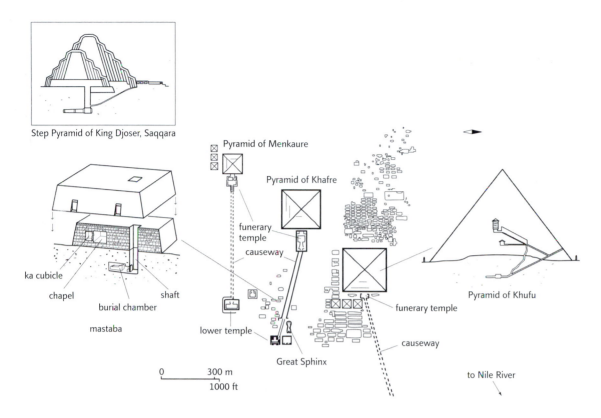

Step Pyramid of King Djoser, Saqqara

Pyramid of Menkaure

Pyramid of Khafre

funerary temple

causeway

Pyramid of Khufu

ka cubicle

chapel

shaft

burial chamber

funerary temple

mastaba

lower temple

causeway

Great Sphinx

to Nile River

0   300 m
1000 ft

3.4 Plan of necropolis at Giza with sections of Pyramid of Khufu and mastaba, and with inset of Step Pyramid of Djoser at Saqqara

mastermind behind its construction, a high official in Djoser's court named Imhotep, who is often identified as the first named architect in history. High priest of the sun god Ra, Imhotep was credited with advancing Egyptian culture through his wisdom and knowledge of astronomy, architecture, and medicine, and he was so highly regarded, within his own time and beyond, that he was deified.

The Pyramids at Giza: Reflecting a New Royal Role

Other kings followed Djoser's lead, but during the Fourth Dynasty, ca. 2575–2465 BCE, funerary architecture changed dramatically. To the modern eye, the most obvious change is the shift from a step pyramid to a smooth-sided one.

The best-known pyramids are the three Great Pyramids at Giza (**figs. 3.4** and **3.5**), built in commemoration of Khufu (the first and largest pyramid), Khafra (a somewhat smaller one), and Menkaure (the smallest). Throughout the ages since their construction, the pyramids have continued to impress. Their grandeur derives both from their sheer monumentality (Khafra's covers 13 acres at the base, and still rises to a height of about 450 feet) and from their extraordinary simplicity. On a square plan, their four surfaces,

shaped as equilateral triangles, taper up from the desert toward the sky. At any time of day, one side will hold the sun's full glare, while another is cast into shadow. Before Islamic builders plundered their stone, each pyramid was dressed with white limestone, preserved only on the pinnacle of the Pyramid of Khafra; at the tip, moreover, each was covered with a thin layer of gold. The entrance to each pyramid was on its north face, and somewhere within the solid stone mass a burial chamber was concealed in the hope of foiling tomb-robbers. Encircling each pyramid was an enclosure wall, and clustered all around were smaller pyramids and mastabas for members of the royal family and high officials.

Like Djoser's complex at Saqqara and most subsequent royal burials, Fourth Dynasty burials were located on the Nile's west bank, the side of the setting sun, across from the habitations of the living on the east bank. Yet, unlike Djoser's complex, with its compact form laid out on a north–south axis, those at Giza were set out on an extended east–west axis. At the start of the funeral ceremony, the body was transported across the Nile to the valley temple, connected to the river by a canal. A causeway, running west from the valley temple into the desert for about a third of a mile, led to the funerary temple,

3.5 The Pyramids of Menkaure, ca. 2533–2515 BCE, Khafra, ca. 2570–2544 BCE, and Khufu, ca. 2601–2528 BCE. Giza

3.6 The Great Sphinx. ca. 2570–2544 BCE. Sandstone, height 65′ (19.8 m). Giza

adjoining the pyramid's east face, where the dead king's body was brought for embalming, and where the living perpetuated the cult for his *ka*. Next to the valley temple of Khafra stands the Great Sphinx, carved from an outcropping of rock left after quarrying stone (**fig. 3.6**). Damage inflicted under Islamic rule has obscured details of the face, and the top of the head is missing, but scholars believe that a portrait of Khafra (or possibly Khufu) was combined with the body (and thus strength) of a lion. Its huge scale also expresses the king's power.

The change from the stepped form of funerary architecture suggests a shift in the way Egyptians perceived their ruler. The smooth-sided pyramid was the shape of the *ben-ben*, the sacred stone in Heliopolis, center of the sun cult. This may indicate that these tombs emphasized the solar aspect of the king's person; indeed, the change coincides more or less with the king's adoption of the title "son of Ra" (the sun god). The change in orientation for the complexes also meant that the king's funerary temple did not face the northern stars, as before, but the rising sun in the east, signifying eternity through its daily rising and setting. The complex at Giza contains no buildings for reenacting rituals of kingship, suggesting that the perpetual performance of these rituals was no longer the dead king's task. Now, his role was to rise to the sun god on the sun's rays, perhaps symbolized by the pyramid's sloping sides, and to accompany him on his endless cycle of regeneration.

Representing the Human Figure

Indentations in the paving of the hall in the valley temple of Khafra show that a series of 23 seated statues of the king once lined its walls. Archaeologists discovered one of these almost intact and six in poorer condition, interred in the temple floor. The best-preserved statue represents the seated king in a rigidly upright and frontal pose (**fig. 3.7**), which allowed him to watch—and thus, in a sense, take part in—rituals enacted in his honor; frontality gave him presence. Behind him, the falcon Horus spreads his wings protectively around his head. Like the *Palette of King Narmer*, this sculpture neatly expresses the qualities of kingship. Horus declares the king to be his earthly manifestation and protégé, and the king's muscular form indicates his power. The smooth agelessness of his face bespeaks his eternal nature, while the sculpture's compact form gives it a solidity that suggests permanence. Intertwined plants—papyrus and perhaps sedge—carved between the legs of his chair are indigenous to Lower and Upper

Carved sculpture is subtractive in the sense that the sculptor begins with a block of raw material, such as stone, that is larger than the finished sculpture and carves away what is not needed for the form of the final piece. This drawing was copied from a wall painting decorating the tomb of Rekhmire in Western Thebes (ca. 1500–1300 BCE).

3.7 *Sculpture of Khafra*, from Giza. ca. 2500 BCE. Diorite, height 66″ (167.7 cm). Egyptian Museum, Cairo

3.8 *Sculpture of Seated Scribe*, from Saqqara. ca. 2400 BCE. Limestone, height 21″ (53.3 cm). Musée du Louvre, Paris

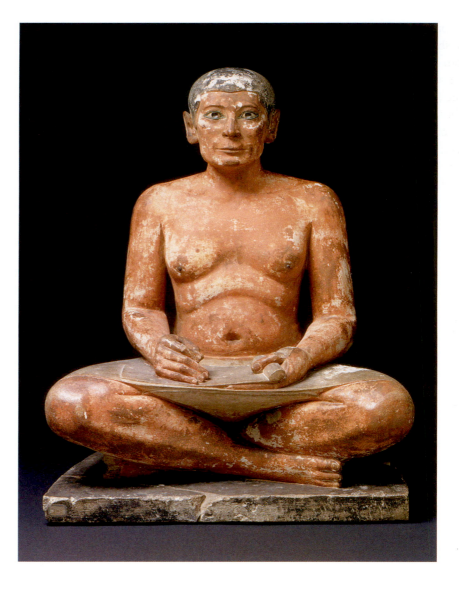

The Egyptian CANON: In royal and elite sculpture in the round, and in relief and painting, body proportions are consistent enough for scholars to believe that artists used guidelines for designing the human image. Traces of such guidelines are still visible on reliefs and paintings. The system of guidelines began in the Fifth Dynasty with a grid of one vertical line, running through the body at the point of the ear, and as many as seven horizontal lines dividing the body according to a standard module. Over time, the guidelines changed, but the principle of this "canon" remained: Although body part measurements could change from person to person, the relationship between parts stayed constant. With that relationship established, an artist who knew the measurement of a single body part could depict a human portrait at any scale, taking the proportions of other essential forms from copybooks.

Egypt, indicating the territorial reach of royal authority. Even the material used to carve his image expresses the king's control of distant lands. The stone, diorite, was brought from the deserts of Nubia. A hard stone, it lends itself to fine detail and a high polish.

Egyptian artists used a defined CANON of proportions when depicting the human figure. Within that canon, elite males were depicted by two kinds of ideal images, each representing a different life stage. One is a youthful, physically fit image, like Khafra or Hesyra. The other is a mature image, often indicated by a paunch, rolls of fat, or slack muscles, and signs of age on the face. A painted limestone figure of a scribe, perhaps named Kay, from his mastaba at Saqqara, is an example of the second type (**fig. 3.8**). The scribe is rigidly upright and frontal, like Khafra, but his body shows signs of slackening, in the sallow cheeks, sagging jaw, and loose stomach. Since Egyptian society was mostly illiterate, a scribe occupied an elevated position; indeed, the

figure, seated on the floor, is depicted in the act of writing, the skill in which his status resided. The image reinforces his social status: It shows an official who has succeeded in his career, eats well, and relies on subordinates to work on his behalf.

These conventions of pose and appearance applied only to the highest echelons of society—royalty and courtiers. By contrast, the lower the status of the beings represented, the more relaxed and naturalistic their pose. Once the conventions were established, ignoring them could result in a change of meaning for a figure, even a change of status, from king or official to servant or captive. The correlation between rank and degree of naturalism is neatly encapsulated in fine low-relief paintings in the tomb chapel of Ti, a high official during the Fifth Dynasty, at Saqqara (**fig. 3.9**). In the section illustrated here, Ti stands on a boat in a thicket of papyrus, observing a hippopotamus hunt. He stands in the traditional composite view, legs and head in profile, torso and eye frontal, while hunters, shown on a smaller scale, attack their prey from a second boat in a variety of active poses that more closely reflect nature. Zigzagging blue lines beneath the boats denote the river, where hippopotami and fish—on the lowest rung of the natural world—swim about in naturalistic poses. Similarly, nesting birds and predatory foxes freely inhabit the papyrus blossoms overhead.

The Middle Kingdom: Reasserting Tradition Through the Arts

The central government of the Old Kingdom disintegrated with the death of the Sixth Dynasty King Pepy II in around 2152 BCE. This led to the turbulent First Intermediate Period, lasting over a century, when local or regional overlords fostered antagonisms between Upper and Lower Egypt. The two regions were reunited in the Eleventh Dynasty, as King Nebhepetra Mentuhotep or Mentuhotep II (ca. 2061–2010 BCE) reasserted regal authority over all of Egypt. The Eleventh and Twelfth Dynasties make up the Middle Kingdom (ca. 2040–1640 BCE), and much of the art of the period deliberately echoed Old Kingdom forms, especially in the funerary realm, to assert a link to the golden days of the past. Sculptures of members of the royal family, however, show breaks with tradition.

Royal Portraiture: Changing Expressions and Proportions

A fragmentary quartzite sculpture of Senwosret III (r. 1878–1841 BCE) suggests a change in conventional depictions of royalty (**fig. 3.10**). Rather than sculpting a smooth-skinned, idealized face, untouched by time, the artist depicted a king with signs of age: A creased brow, drooping eyelids, and lines beneath the eyes. Scholars have described the image as "introspective," and read it against the background of Senwosret's difficult campaign of military expansion in Nubia to the south, seeing the imperfections as visible signs of the king's stress. Facial expressions or signs of age, however, signify quite different things to different societies, and it is equally likely that the tight-lipped expression reflects a new face of regal authority, projecting firm resolve. The aged face tended to be combined with a youthful, powerful body.

3.9 *Ti Watching a Hippopotamus Hunt.* ca. 2510–2460 BCE. Painted limestone relief, height approx. 45" (114.3 cm). Tomb of Ti, Saqqara

Most figures were represented like the long-haired woman: Eyes and shoulders seen frontally and everything else rendered in profile. Figures that are drawn more naturalistically—like the short-haired woman—depict enemies, commoners, and slaves.

3.10 *Sculpture of Senwosret III* (fragment). ca. 1850 BCE. Quartzite, height 6½" (16.5 cm). The Metropolitan Museum of Art, New York. Purchase, Edward S. Harkness Gift, 1926 26.7.1394

As the central authority weakened after about 1785 BCE, local governors usurped power. During the Twelfth Dynasty, immigrants from Palestine known as the Hyksos (from the Egyptian for "rulers of foreign lands") moved into the Nile Delta, gaining control of the area and forcing the king to retreat southward to Thebes. This era is known as the Second Intermediate Period.

The New Kingdom: Restored Glory

The Hyksos were expelled from Egypt by Ahmose (1550–1525 BCE), first king of the Eighteenth Dynasty. The 500 years after their expulsion, the Eighteenth, Nineteenth, and Twentieth Dynasties, are designated the New Kingdom, a time of renewed territorial expansion and prosperity for Egypt, and a time when the arts flourished. Tremendous architectural projects were carried out along the full length of the Nile,

centering on the region of Thebes (modern Luxor). Of these projects, many secular buildings, including palaces and forts, were made of mud brick and have perished. Stone tombs and temples, however, retain a small measure of their former glory.

Royal Burials in the Valley of the Kings

A major difference between the Old Kingdom and the New is clear from the change in burial practices. Having witnessed the loss of order that allowed royal burials to be robbed, Eighteenth Dynasty kings abandoned the practice of marking their tombs with pyramids. Instead, tombs were excavated out of the rock face in the Valley of the Kings west of Thebes, with their entrances concealed after burial. Rituals of the funerary cult took place away from the tomb, over a rocky outcropping to the east, at a temple on the edge of the land under cultivation.

HATSHEPSUT'S TEMPLE The best-preserved example of a New Kingdom funerary temple is that of the female king HATSHEPSUT, built by her architect Senenmut (ca. 1478–1458 BCE) (**fig. 3.11**). Hatshepsut was the chief wife—and half-sister—of Thutmose II. On his death in 1479 BCE, power passed to Thutmose III, his young son by a minor wife. Designated regent for the young king, Hatshepsut ruled with him as female king until her death in 1458 BCE, claiming that her father, Thutmose I, had intended her as his successor.

Nestled in the cliff side at Deir el-Bahri, Hatshepsut's temple was built beside the spectacular Eleventh Dynasty temple of Mentuhotep II, who had reunited Egypt during the Middle Kingdom. The architects who designed Hatshepsut's temple may have modeled some of its features after this earlier temple, with its terraces extending into the cliff face, topped with a pyramid or a mastaba. Once joined by a causeway to a valley temple beside the Nile, Hatshepsut's temple is a striking response to its setting. Its ascending white limestone courts, linked by wide ramps on a central axis, echo the desert's strong horizontal ground-line and the cliff top above. A multitude of vertical lines, meanwhile, created by the alternating bright light and shadows of the colonnades, harmonizes with the fissures of the cliff. With its clean contours, the royal structure imposes order on the less regularized forms of nature, just as the king's role was to impose order on chaos. Trees lined the way leading up to the temple entrance, with paired sphinxes

3.11 Temple of Hatshepsut. ca. 1478–1458 BCE. Deir el-Bahri

facing each other. At the furthest reach of the temple, cut into the rock, a principal sanctuary was dedicated to Amun-Ra, god of the evening sun. Throughout the complex, painted relief sculptures brought the walls to life, depicting battles, a royal expedition to the land of Punt in search of myrrh trees for the terraces, and scenes of Thutmose I legitimizing his daughter's unusual rule. Sculptures of the king and deities abounded.

Sometime after Hatshepsut's death, Thutmose III constructed his own temple between his mother's and Mentuhotep's, with the purpose of eclipsing Hatshepsut's. He designated his temple as the destination of the boat carrying the statue of Amun in the Festival of the Wadi, held at Deir el-Bahri. One result of his efforts was the destruction of many images of Hatshepsut and

the replacement of her name with his in some of the inscriptions; but, nonetheless, Hatshepshut's temple remains a monument to her memory.

Temples to the Gods

Besides building funerary temples for themselves, Eighteenth Dynasty kings expended resources on temples to the gods, such as the Theban divine triad: Amun, his consort Mut, and their son Khons. At Karnak and nearby Luxor, successive kings constructed two vast temple complexes to honor the triad, and on special festivals the gods' images were conveyed on divine boats along waterways between the temples.

THE TEMPLE OF AMUN-RA At the temple of Amun-Ra at Karnak, a vast wall encircled the temple buildings. Entering the complex, a visitor

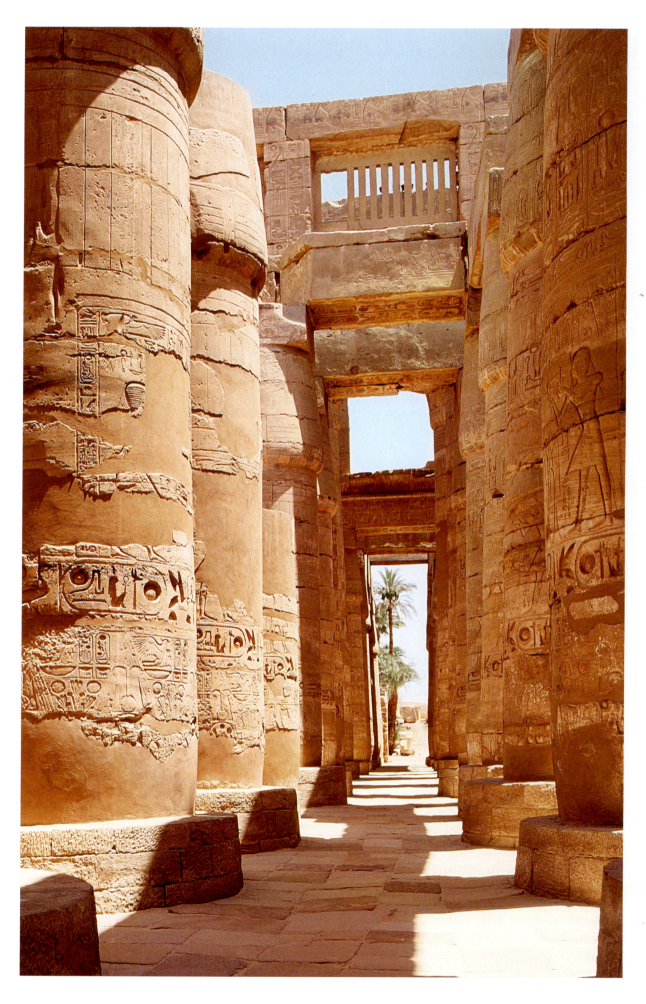

3.12 Hypostyle Hall of Temple of Amun-Ra. ca. 1290–1224 BCE. Karnak, Thebes walked through massive **pylons** or gateways built as monuments to individual kings. As a ceremonial procession moved within the buildings, the pylons marked its progress deeper and deeper into sacred space. A vast **hypostyle** hall (a building with a roof supported by columns) was the farthest point of access for all but priests and royalty (**fig. 3.12**). Here, a visitor would be awed by the forest of columns, their sheer mass rendering the human form almost insignificant. They were closely spaced to support a ceiling of stone lintels. Unlike wooden lintels, these had to be short to prevent them from breaking under their own weight. The architect nonetheless made the columns far heavier than they needed to be, with the effect that a viewer senses the overwhelming presence of stone all around, heavy, solid, and permanent. Beyond the hall, a sacred lake allowed the king and priests to purify themselves before entering the temple proper. They proceeded through smaller halls, sun-drenched courts, and processional ways decorated with **obelisks**, tall stone markers topped by pyramid-shaped points, as well as through chapels where they would pause to enact ceremonies. Every day the priests would cleanse and robe the images of the gods, and offer sacred meals to nourish them. These rituals were conducted by the king and the priests away from the public eye, gaining power for being shrouded in mystery.

Essential to the temple's ritual functioning was its metaphorical value, symbolizing the world at its inception. The columns of the hypostyle hall represented marsh plants in stylized form: Their capitals emulated the shape of both papyrus flowers and buds, so that the building evoked the watery swamp of chaos out of which the mound of creation emerged. The temple was thus the king's exhortation in stone to the gods to maintain cosmic order.

Akhenaten and the Amarna Style

Another Eighteenth Dynasty ruler, Amenhotep III, fostered devotion to the sun god during his reign (1391–1353 BCE). In temple complexes at Karnak and elsewhere, the king built open-air courtyards where the sun could be worshiped in its manifestation as a disk (or Aten) in the sky—not as the traditional falcon-headed figure. Devotion to Aten grew stronger in the reign of his son, Amenhotep IV, who stressed the sun's

life-giving force. The young king's attempts to introduce this new cult at traditional religious centers, such as Thebes, were thwarted by a powerful conservative priesthood, enraged by his monotheistic vision of Aten. In response, he founded a city devoted entirely to Aten on the Nile's east bank in central Egypt. He named his city Akhetaten, meaning horizon of Aten (now known as Amarna), and changed his own name to Akhenaten, meaning "beneficial to Aten." His new cult and fledgling city lasted only as long as its founder; after his death the city was razed to the ground. Still, archaeological remains suggest that Akhenaten built temples in the contemporary style, using massive pylons and obelisks, as at Karnak, but with an emphasis on open-air courts beneath the sun's glare.

The Amarna Style

Sculptures of Akhenaten and his family break with long-established conventions for depicting royal subjects. In numerous representations, the figure of Akhenaten exhibits radically different proportions from those of previous kings. This is clear on a sunken relief scene on an altar stele, the kind that Egyptians would have erected in small shrines in their homes and gardens (**fig. 3.13**). Beneath the disk of the sun, its life-giving beams are shown as lines radiating downward with hands at their terminals. The king and his consort Nefertiti sit facing each other on stools. Attenuated reed columns suggest that the scene is set within a garden pavilion, which is stocked with wine jars. The king has narrow shoulders lacking in musculature, a marked pot belly, wide hips, and generous thighs. His large lips, distinctive nose and chin, and narrow eyes make his face readily recognizable. Scholars have found these unusual portraits puzzling. Some dismiss them as caricatures, yet such expensive and prominent images must have had the king's approval. There have also been attempts to diagnose a medical condition from these representations; the king's features have been read as symptoms of Frolich's Syndrome, a hormonal deficiency that produces androgynous (both male and female) characteristics. A more likely explanation is that his "feminized" appearance was intended to capture the androgynous fertile character of Aten as life-giver. The style was not restricted to the king's image, but influenced portrayals of court officials and others as well.

Group representations of Akhenaten with his family are remarkable for an apparent intimacy among the figures. He and Nefertiti hold three

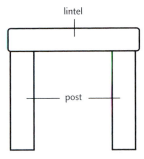

A simple space-spanning construction device is the post-and-lintel combination. The wider the distance spanned (and the less the "give" of the spanning material), the closer the uprights (posts) have to be. Egyptians used stone columns for posts; the weight of the rigid stone lintels forced the builders to place the columns close together.

lintel

post

3.13 *Akhenaten and His Family.* ca. 1355 BCE. Limestone, 12¾ × 15⅓″ (32.5 × 39 cm). Staatliche Museen zu Berlin, Preussischer Kulturbesitz, Ägyptisches Museum

lively daughters, who clamber onto their laps and nestle in their arms, uniting the composition with animated gestures that reach across the relief, in marked contrast to the static scenes of other times. The deliberate emphasis on the daughters' childishness marks a change: In the past, children had been represented by a hieroglyphic pictograph of an adult in miniature, sucking a finger. The emphasis on children epitomizes the regeneration that the royal couple represent, and especially the king as manifestation of the sun god Aten.

PORTRAITS OF NEFERTITI As with Akhenaten's images, early depictions of Nefertiti emphasize her reproductive capacity by contrasting a slender waist with large thighs and buttocks. Sculptures from the second half of Akhenaten's reign, however, are less extreme. At Amarna archaeologists discovered the studio of the king's chief sculptor, in which were sculptures at every stage of production: Heads and limbs of quartzite and jasper, and torsos of royal statues to which they could be affixed. Plaster casts were found, modeled from clay or wax studies taken from life. The most famous of the sculptures is a bust of Nefertiti, plastered over a limestone core and painted—a master sculpture, perhaps, from which other images could be copied (**fig. 3.14**). The left eye lacks the inlay of the right, showing that the bust remained unfinished, but its extraordinary elegance derives from a command of geometry that is at once precise—the face is completely symmetrical—and subtle. This piece and another similar head were abandoned in the workshop when the sculptor moved from Amarna to Memphis after Akhenaten's death in 1335 BCE.

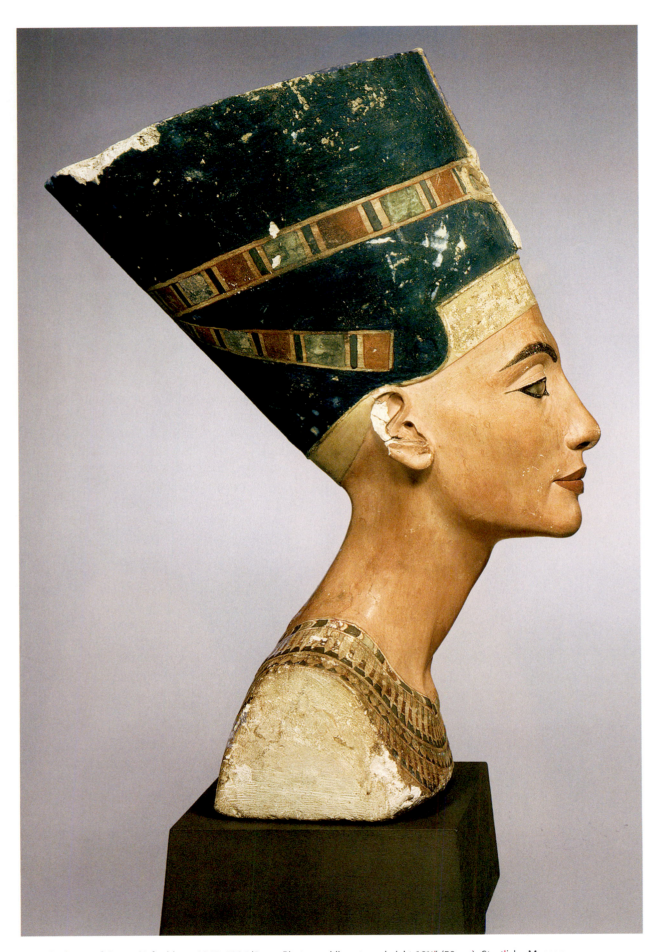

3.14 *Sculpture of Queen Nefertiti.* ca. 1348–1336/5 BCE. Plaster and limestone, height 19⅔″ (50 cm). Staatliche Museen zu Berlin, Preussischer Kulturbesitz, Ägyptisches Museum

Tutankhamun and the Aftermath of Amarna

Shortly after Akhenaten's death, a young king ascended the throne. Married to Akhenaten's daughter, and perhaps even one of Akhenaten's sons, Tutankhaten was only nine or ten when he became king. Possibly under the influence of the priests of Amun, he restored the royal residence to Memphis and resurrected the orthodox religion of Egypt that Akhenaten had neglected. He changed his name to Tutankhamun to reflect the restoration of the king's association with Amun. His sudden death at the age of 19 has inspired numerous theories about murder and conspiracy, but recent scientific studies of his mummy point to natural causes.

Tutankhamun's greatest fame results not from his life, but from the discovery of his tomb in 1922 by the British archaeologist Howard Carter. Although it had been robbed twice, much of the tomb was untouched. With its stairway, corridor, and four chambers, the tomb is uncharacteristically small for a royal burial, leading scholars to suppose that a non-royal tomb might have been hastily co-opted for the king at the time of his unexpectedly early death. All the same, the offerings buried with him lacked nothing in volume or quality. The tomb contents included funerary equipment, such as coffins, statues, and masks, as well as items used during his lifetime such as furniture, clothing, and chariots. The king's mummified corpse was preserved in three coffins, the innermost of which (**fig. 3.15**), is of gold and weighs over 250 pounds. Even more impressive is the exquisite workmanship of its cover, with its rich play of colored inlays against polished gold surfaces.

The process of restoring the old religion was continued by Tutankhamun's short-lived successor, the aged Ay. He married Tutankhamun's widow, perhaps to preserve, rather than usurp, the throne. The restoration of the old religion was completed under Horemheb, who had been head of the army under Tutankhamun and became the last king of the Eighteenth Dynasty. He set out to erase all traces of the Amarna revolution, repairing shattered images of the gods and rebuilding their temples; but the effects of Akhenaten's rule could be felt in Egyptian art for some time to come.

3.15 Cover of the coffin of Tutankhamun. Eighteenth Dynasty (ca. 1567–1320 BCE). Gold and precious stones, height 72″ (182.9 cm). Egyptian Museum, Cairo

SUMMARY

Ancient Egypt flourished along the Nile River in North Africa. Its society was extremely hierarchical, and artists produced paintings, sculptures, and other objects for elite patrons, including the all-powerful god-kings and their families. Exceptional technique and monumentality are common characteristics of Egyptian art, which quickly developed a conservative tradition of form and subject. Religious beliefs and rituals stressed the importance of the afterlife, and many of the Egyptian art objects produced over thousands of years were made for the elaborate tombs of the ruling class.

The Old Kingdom endured for five centuries, and its rulers commissioned works of art that would be emulated for the following two millennia. Artists followed a formula for representing idealized human figures according to an evolving set of conventions. And since Egyptians believed that the *ka*, or life force, of an individual lived on in the grave, artists went to great lengths to provide for it for eternity. Among the most significant achievements of the Old Kingdom are the burial complex of Djoser at Saqqara and the three massive pyramids built at Giza, each representing the ruler's immense religious and political power.

The Middle Kingdom lasted roughly 400 years. During this time artists deliberately echoed Old Kingdom forms, especially in the funerary realm, but one innovation of the Middle Kingdom was a more naturalistic expression on royal images such as the head of Senwosret.

Lasting roughly five centuries, the New Kingdom followed the expulsion of the Hyksos from Egypt. It was an era of renewed territorial expansion and tremendous prosperity, and the arts flourished. Major building projects were carried out along much of the Nile, especially around Thebes (present-day Luxor). Monumental funerary complexes were built for rulers, including the magnificent and well-preserved temple of Hatshepsut. Kings spent considerable sums on structures dedicated to the gods, too, such as the massive temple of Amun-Ra at Karnak.

King Akhenaten established a new city devoted to the sun-god Aten at Akhetaten (now called Amarna). Refuting traditional religious cults, Akhenaten intended the cult of Aten to be monotheistic, which enraged the priests of the other religious cults. The new cult and its city were razed after Akhenaten's death, though portraits of the king, his wife Nefertiti, and their family survive. These works break with long-established conventions of portraiture and include rare examples of apparent intimacy among the figures. Akhenaten was succeeded by short-lived kings, including Tutankhamun, whose tomb—when discovered in 1922—was found to house a staggering volume of exquisite treasures including his coffin lid.

ART IN TIME

- ca. 5000 BCE — Human settlements along the Nile Valley

- **ca. 3000 BCE — The ancient Egyptian *Palette of King Narmer***

- ca. 2900 BCE — Mesopotamians begin using cuneiform writing

- 2630–2611 BCE — Rule of King Djoser; entombment at Saqqara

- **ca. 2575–2465 BCE — Ancient Egypt's Fourth Dynasty; construction of the three Great Pyramids at Giza**

- ca. 2100 BCE — Final phase of construction at Stonehenge

- **ca. 1870s–1840s BCE — Naturalistic sculpture of King Senwosret III**

- 1792–1750 BCE — Babylon ruled by Hammurabi

- **ca. 1458 BCE — King (*sic*) Hatshepsut dies; her tomb was designed by Senenmut**

- ca. 1353–1335 BCE — Rule of King Akhenaten; new religious center at Amarna

- **ca. 1348–1336/5 BCE — Plaster and limestone portrait bust of Akhenaten's wife, Nefertiti**

CHAPTER

4 | Aegean Art

*T*he Mediterranean was one of the primary highways that connected the cultures of antiquity. With North Africa on the south, Asia on the east and Europe on the west and north, this body of water brought disparate cultures into contact for both trade and conflict. The Greeks named one branch of the Mediterranean, between Greece and Turkey, the Aegean Sea (see map 4.1), and on islands and peninsulas there several closely related but distinct cultures developed in the third and second millennia BCE. The Cycladic culture emerged on the islands forming an irregular circle between the Greek mainland and the island of Crete. The British archaeologist Sir Arthur Evans named the culture on Crete Minoan, for the legendary King Minos. That on the mainland is called Helladic, from the Greek Hellas, name of a legendary ancestor.

Until the second half of the nineteenth century, Aegean civilization was known principally from the Homeric poems the *Iliad* and the *Odyssey*. Prompted by these stories, Heinrich Schliemann, a German archaeologist, excavated sites in Asia Minor and Greece during the 1870s, looking for Homer's Troy. Following his lead, Arthur Evans began excavations in Crete in 1900. Since then, a great deal of archaeological evidence has come to light, some consistent with, but much contradicting, these narratives. Although writing exists from Minoan and Mycenaean contexts, scholars can decipher little of it. Consequently, we understand less about Aegean civilization than we do about the cultures of Egypt or the ancient Near East. Nevertheless, the fact that Greek myths and legends look back to these cultures testifies to their importance in the development of later Greek culture.

Evidence of human habitation throughout the Aegean dates from as early as the Paleolithic period, though settlements spread and grew mainly in the Neolithic and Early Bronze Ages. Scholars divide the Aegean Bronze Age into three phases: Early (ca. 3000–2000 BCE), Middle

(ca. 2000–1600 BCE), and Late (ca. 1600–1100 BCE), each of which is subdivided into phases I, II, and III. Archaeologists often prefer these relative dates to absolute ones, because Aegean chronology is so controversial. A mass destruction of Aegean sites, from an unknown cause, led to significant depopulation in about 1200 BCE, and by 1100 BCE the Aegean Bronze Age had ended.

Early Cycladic Art

Information about the culture of the Cyclades comes entirely from the archaeological record, which indicates that wealth accumulated there early in the Bronze Age as trade developed. Funerary practice reflects this prosperity. At the beginning of the Early Bronze Age, around 2800 BCE, the islanders started to bury their dead in stone-lined pits known as cist graves. Some of these graves contained offerings of weapons, jewelry, and pottery, and some included striking figures, usually female, carved from the local white marble. The Early Cycladic II example illustrated here represents the prevalent

Major Periods of Aegean Art	
ca. 2800 –1600 BCE	Cycladic
ca. 3000 –1450 BCE	Minoan
ca. 1700 –1100 BCE.	Mycenaean
ca. 3000 –2000 BCE.	Early Aegean Bronze Age
ca. 2000 –1600 BCE.	Middle Aegean Bronze Age
ca. 1600 –1100 BCE.	Late Aegean Bronze Age
ca. 1600 –1200 BCE.	Late Helladic period

Map 4.1 The Bronze Age Aegean

type (**fig. 4.1**). The figure is nude, with arms folded across the waist, and toes extended. The flat body is straight-backed, while a long, thick neck supports a shield-shaped face at an angle. The artist used abrasives, probably emery from the island of Naxos, to distinguish details on the figure, such as a ridgelike nose, pointed breasts, a triangular pubic area, and toes. Traces of pigments on some figures indicate that other details were painted on, including eyes, hair, jewelry, and body markings similar to tattoos. Their sizes vary, but their form is consistent enough for scholars to speak of a governing canon of proportions, as for Egyptian sculptures.

For many years, archaeologists called these figures "idols," and pictured them playing a central role in a religion focusing on a mother goddess. More recently scholars have offered at least two explanations for their functions. Perhaps they were manufactured purely for funerary purposes, representing servants or surrogates for human sacrifices, or even for the deceased. Alternatively, they may have functioned in daily life,

possibly within household shrines, before being buried. Although most have been found in a reclining position, they may also have been propped upright. The largest figures (reaching five feet long) may have been cult statues. Some examples show signs of repair with wire, which indicates that they were used before being deposited in graves.

It is most likely that no single explanation applies to all of them. The greatest obstacle to determining their function is our lack of knowledge about their **provenance**, that is, where and how they were found and their subsequent history. The simplicity and clear geometry of the figures appeals to a twentieth- and twenty-first-century aesthetic that favors understated and unadorned geometric forms. Those qualities and the luscious white marble used to form them have led to their widespread appearance on the art market, often without any record of archaeological context. To have a clearer sense of how to interpret these figures, archaeologists need to know their findspots, whether in a burial or in living quarters.

4.1 Figure, Cyclades. ca. 2500 BCE. Marble, height 15¾" (40 cm). Nicholas P. Goulandris Foundation, Museum of Cycladic Arts, Athens. N.P. Goulandris Collection, No. 206

Minoan Art

The island of Crete, south of the Cyclades, and about 400 miles northwest of Egypt, stretches over 124 miles from east to west, divided by mountain ranges, and with few large areas of flat, arable land (see map 4.1). Consequently, early communities were small and scattered. The island's geography, then, along with continuous migration, encouraged diversity and independence among the population. The major flowering of Minoan art occurred about 2000 BCE, when Crete's urban civilizations constructed great "palaces" at Knossos, Phaistos, and Mallia. At this time, the first Aegean script, known as Linear A, appeared. Scholars call this the First Palace period, comprising Middle Minoan I and II. All three centers were heavily damaged, probably by an earthquake, in about 1700 BCE, and a short time later the Minoans built new and larger structures on the same sites. This phase constitutes the Second Palace period, which includes Middle Minoan III, and Late Minoan IA and IB.

An earthquake demolished these centers, too, in about 1450 BCE. After that, the palaces at Phaistos and Mallia were abandoned, but the Mycenaeans, who gained control of the island, occupied Knossos.

The Palace at Knossos

The buildings of the Second Palace period are our chief source of information for Minoan architecture. The largest is the structure at Knossos, which Evans dubbed the Palace of MINOS (**figs. 4.2** and **4.3**). In fact, Knossos may have been the most powerful Cretan center of the Middle and Late Bronze Age. The palace consisted of courts, halls, workshops, storerooms, and perhaps residential quarters, linked by corridors, staircases, and porticoes. Interior spaces were lit and ventilated by light wells.

Evans reconceived and reconstructed much of the palace in concrete. Originally, walls were framed with timbers and constructed of rubble masonry or mud brick. Some were of **ashlar masonry** (cut and dressed stone), which gave

The legendary MINOS was the son of Zeus and Europa and the husband of Pasiphaë, who bore the Minotaur as a punishment after her husband had disobeyed the god Poseidon. Greek historians also speak of a King Minos as the strongest, most prosperous ruler in the Mediterranean and the first to control the area with a powerful navy.

theatral area

North entrance

East entrance

corridor access to magazines

temple repositories

throne room

staircase

main shrine

pillar crypt

grand staircase

lapidary's workshop

West entrance

altars

Hall of the Double Axes

bathroom

storeroom

Corridor of the Procession

South entrance

staircase

lavatory

Queen's Hall

| 0 | 10 | 20 | 30 | meters |
| 0 | 20 40 | 60 80 | 100 | feet |

4.2 Plan of the Palace Complex. Knossos, Crete

4.3 Reconstruction of the Palace Complex. Knossos, Crete them a more ornamental appearance. Columns, often made of wood with a stone base, supported the porticoes. Their form was unusual: A smooth shaft, often oval in cross-section, tapered downward from a generous cushionlike capital. Wall paintings suggest that capitals were painted black and shafts red or white.

At first glance, the palace's plan (see fig. 4.2) looks haphazard, which probably explains why later Greek legend referred to it as the LABYRINTH, home of the MINOTAUR. The mazelike arrangement may have been part of a defensive strategy; certainly no exterior fortifications protected the palace from attack, and entrances were not emphasized. Nevertheless, the design does have an underlying logic. Its core is a central court, onto which important rooms opened. The court divides the plan on an approximately north–south axis. On the west, a corridor running north–south separates narrow storerooms from rooms of less uniform shapes close to the court; the latter rooms may have performed a ceremonial role. The palace appears to grow outwards from the court, and using flat (rather than pitched) roofs would have greatly facilitated the building of additions. Compared to Near Eastern palaces, such as the palace at Persepolis (see fig. 2.11), the overall effect at Knossos is modest; individual units are relatively small and the ceilings low. Still, some of the interior walls were richly decorated. We should also remember that much of what remains belongs to subterranean or ground-floor levels, and archaeologists have long believed that grander rooms once existed on an upper level.

Exactly how the palaces of Crete functioned, and who lived in them, is debated. Evans described the complex as a "palace" (assigning royal names to various rooms), and the term stuck, regardless of its accuracy. Evans conceived of the complex as an elite residence for several reasons. He was reacting partly to discoveries on the Mycenaean mainland, described subsequently, and partly to the presence of a grand Throne Room. But the social and political realities of Evans's own homeland may have been even more influential: He would have been familiar with the palaces occupied by the extensive royal family of late Victorian England. In fact, excavation of the complex at Knossos suggests that many different activities went on there. Extensive storage areas suggest that the palace was a center of manufacturing, administration, and commerce. Additionally, ceremonial spaces, such as the great court, and small shrines with religious paraphernalia imply that political and ritual activities took place there too. There is no reason to believe that the Minoans segregated these activities as neatly as we often do today. Moreover, we have no evidence suggesting that the functions of the various palaces were identical, or that they remained constant over time.

Wall Paintings: Representing Rituals and Nature

Grand rooms within Minoan palaces were decorated with paintings. Most of them were found in extremely fragmentary condition, so what we see today is the result of extensive restoration, which may not always be reliable. Vibrant mineral colors characterize the frescoes, applied to wet or dry plaster in broad washes without shading; wide bands of geometric patterns serve as frames. Many Minoan paintings depict nature. A painting restored to a wall in the room Evans called the Queen's Megaron in Knossos' east wing (**fig. 4.4**) shows sinuous blue and yellow dolphins swimming against a blue-streaked cream background, cavorting with small fish. Multilobed green forms represent plants or rocks. Curving, organic elements throughout the composition animate the painting. The many images of marine creatures in Minoan art probably reflect a keen awareness of and respect for the sea.

PAINTED LANDSCAPES IN A SEASIDE TOWN   In the middle of the second millennium BCE, a volcano erupted on the Cycladic island of Thera (present-day Santorini), about 60 miles north of Crete. The eruption covered the town of Akrotiri in a deep layer of volcanic ash and pumice. Beginning in 1967, excavations uncovered houses dating from the Middle Minoan III phase (approximately 1670–1620 BCE) preserved up to a height of two stories. On their walls was an extraordinary series of paintings, including a rocky landscape known as the *Spring Fresco* (**fig. 4.5**). The craggy terrain undulates dramatically, its dark outline filled with rich washes of red, blue, and ocher—colors that were probably present in the island's volcanic soils—with swirling black lines adding texture. Sprouting from its surface, trios of lilies flower vivid red, while swallows dart between them, painted in a few graceful black strokes.

Minoan Pottery and Faience

By the Middle and Late Minoan periods, pottery was manufactured on the wheel, and, like the

4.4 The Queen's Megaron, from Knossos, Crete. ca. 1700–1300 BCE. Archaeological Museum, Iráklion, Crete

4.5 *Spring Fresco*, from Akrotiri, Thera. ca. 1600–1500 BCE. National Archaeological Museum, Athens

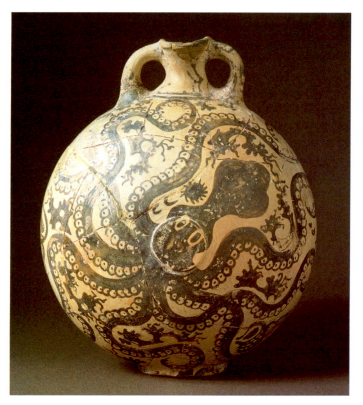

4.6 *Octopus Vase*, stirrup jar from Palaikastro, Crete. ca. 1500–1450 BCE. Clay, height 11″ (28 cm). Archaeological Museum, Iráklion, Crete

wall paintings, its decoration was inspired by the natural world. Lively organic forms enhanced the vases' curving shapes. In the Late Minoan IB phase, marine motifs became prevalent. A vivid example is a jar decorated with a wide-eyed black octopus with swirling tentacles, contrasted against the eggshell-colored clay (**fig. 4.6**). Clumps of algae float between the tentacles. The sea creature's rounded contours emphasize the jar's swollen belly, while the curves of its tentacles echo its curved handles. Beneath the spout, the end of a tentacle curls to define a circle of the same size as the jar's opening.

Religious life on Minoan Crete centered on natural places deemed sacred, such as caves and mountain-tops. No temples or large cult statues have been discovered. Archaeologists at Knossos did find two small-scale **faience** (colored glass) statuettes from the Middle Minoan III phase (about 1650 BCE). One shows a female figure raising a snake in each hand and wearing a headdress topped by a feline creature (**fig. 4.7**). She wears a

4.7 *Snake Goddess*, from the Palace Complex, Knossos. ca. 1650 BCE. Faience, height 11⅝″ (29.5 cm). Archaeological Museum, Iráklion, Crete

4.8 *The Toreador Fresco*, from the Palace Complex, Knossos. ca. 1550–1450 BCE (restored). Height including upper border approx. 24½" (62.3 cm). Archaeological Museum, Iráklion, Crete

flounced skirt and bares her breasts. In some ancient religions, snakes are associated with earth deities and male fertility, just as the bared breasts of this statuette suggest fecundity. Moreover, the statuettes were found in pits known as the Temple Repositories, sunk in the floor of a room on the west side of the central court, which has led scholars to associate them with a mother goddess. Alternatively, they could have represented ritual attendants.

Late Minoan Art

It is unclear what brought Minoan civilization to an end. Some scholars argue that the volcanic eruption on the island of Thera may have hastened its decline. Recent discoveries and dating of the ash from this eruption, however, indicate that the Cretan culture survived this natural disaster, though perhaps in a weakened state. About 1450 BCE (Late Minoan II), the palaces were taken over by invaders from the Greek mainland, whom archaeologists call Mycenaeans. They established themselves in the palace at Knossos until around 1375 BCE, when Knossos was destroyed and the Mycenaeans abandoned most of the island's sites. While they were in control, however, artists at Knossos worked in Minoan styles.

The fragmentary *Toreador Fresco* dates from the Mycenaean occupation (Late Minoan II–IIIA), and appears to have decorated an upper room in the northeast part of the palace (**fig. 4.8**). Against a blue background, a white-skinned figure clad in a kilt clasps the horns of a huge, curvaceous bull, painted at a full gallop. Behind the bull, a white-skinned figure stands on tiptoe with arms outstretched, while above the animal's back, a dark-skinned figure performs a backward somersault. The figures have long limbs and small waists, yet they are painted in true profile. The painting's washes of color and animated though stylized poses demonstrate the continuity of Minoan practice into the Late period.

Scholars continue to debate the meaning of this painting. Although most agree that such bull-leaping performances had a ritual function, its purpose and the identity of the participants are not clear. Following a widespread Mediterranean convention for distinguishing gender by skin tone, Evans identified the light-skinned figures as female and the darker one as male. Others have seen all three figures as sequential representations of one person, taking part in a coming-of-age initiation ceremony in which boys emerge masculine from their earlier "feminine" guise.

Mycenaean Art

The TROJAN WAR was a half-legendary conflict fought between a number of the Greek city-states and Troy, a city on the northwest coast of Asia Minor (modern Turkey). Homer's epic poem the *Iliad* describes events that took place during the last year of the war, and the *Odyssey* recounts the ten-year homeward voyage of one of the Greek kings, Odysseus (Roman Ulysses), after the conflict. These poems—part history and part myth—developed gradually within the oral tradition of Greek poetry for centuries before there was a written Greek language and were passed down from one generation of poets to another.

By the time the Mycenaeans conquered Crete in about 1450 BCE, they had been building cities on the Greek mainland since the start of the Late Helladic period ca. 1600. They probably made early contact with Minoan Crete, which exerted important influences on their own culture. Archaeologists place the height of the culture between about 1500 and 1200 BCE (Late Helladic III). The most imposing remains are citadels at sites that Homer named: Mycenae, Pylos, and Tiryns. The culture takes its name from the first of these, the legendary home of King Agamemnon, who led the Greek forces in Homer's TROJAN WAR.

Architecture: Citadels

At the beginning of the Second Palace period on Crete, growing settlements throughout the Greek mainland, including that at Mycenae (**fig. 4.9**), centered around large structures known as citadels (when fortified) or palaces. In some of them, archaeologists unearthed clay tablets inscribed with a second early writing system. Dubbed Linear B because of its linear character and because it drew, in part, from Minoan Linear A, the system was decoded by Michael Ventris in 1952. The tablets proved to have been inventories and archival documents, in a language now considered an early form of Greek. The inhabitants of these Late Bronze Age sites, therefore, were the precursors of what we refer to as the ancient Greeks.

The Linear B tablets refer to a *wanax* ("lord" or "king"), suggesting something of a Mycenaean social order. Mycenaean citadels and palaces may have incorporated royal residences, centered on a **megaron**, a large rectangular audience hall. Many of them were enclosed by imposing exterior walls, often expanded and improved in several building phases, and constructed so as to exploit the site's topography. They were built of large irregularly shaped (or polygonal) stone blocks, and in places reached 20 feet thick. At entrances or other highly visible places, the stones might be saw-cut and dressed, or smoothed with a hammer. Centuries later, the massiveness of these walls so awed the Greeks that they declared them the work of the Cyclopes, a mythical race of one-eyed giants. Even today, the walls are termed "Cyclopean." The walls, and tunnels leading to wells for water during a siege, have led scholars to regard the

4.9 Aerial view of Mycenae, Greece. ca. 1600–1200 BCE

❖ Corbeling as a space-spanning device relies on the downward pressure of overlapped layers of stone to lock in the projecting ends.

corbel arch

corbel vault

4.10 The Lion Gate, Mycenae, Greece. ca. 1250 BCE

Mycenaeans as quite different from the Minoans, with a culture focused on warfare. An essential character difference is implied between nature-loving Minoans and warmongering Mycenaeans. We should note, however, that the fortifications date to after the destruction of Minoan centers, so the Mycenaeans may have been responding to a new set of political and social circumstances.

At Mycenae, when the city walls were enlarged, the Lion Gate of about 1250 BCE was built as a principal entrance (**fig. 4.10**). Two massive stone posts support a huge lintel to form the opening. Above the lintel, a **corbel** arch directs the weight of the heavy wall to the strong posts below it: Each course of masonry projects slightly beyond the course below it, until the span is covered when the walls meet. The corbel thus relieves the weight resting on the vast stone lintel, which itself weighs 25 tons; it is known as a relieving triangle. To seal the resulting gap, a triangular limestone slab was inserted above the lintel, carved with a pair of huge animals, probably lionesses (though they may be sphinxes or griffins). They stand in a **heraldic pose** (mirror images of each other), with their front paws on altars of a Minoan style, and flanking a tapering Minoan-style column. Dowel holes in their necks suggest that their heads were added in wood or a different stone. At almost 10 feet high, this relief is the first large-scale sculpture known on the

Greek mainland. The lionesses function as guardians, and their tense, muscular bodies and symmetrical design suggest an influence from the Near East. Mycenaeans ventured all over the Mediterranean, including Egypt and Anatolia, and Hittite records suggest contact with a people who may have been Mycenaean.

Mycenaean Tombs and Their Contents

At the end of the Middle Helladic period at Mycenae ca. 1600, the ruling elite began to bury their dead in deep rectangular shafts, marking them at ground level with stone stelai. The burials were distributed in two groups (known as Grave Circles A and B), which later generations set off and monumentalized with a low circular wall. As time passed, the elite built more dramatic tombs, in a round form known as a *tholos*. Over 100 *tholoi* are known on the mainland.

One of the best-preserved and largest of these tombs is at Mycenae. Dubbed the "Treasury of ATREUS," it dates to about 1250 BCE (Late Helladic III B). A great pathway, or *dromos*, lined with ashlar masonry, led to a large circular chamber excavated into sloping ground and then built up from ground level with a corbel vault: Courses of ashlar (square-cut stone) blocks protruding inwards beyond one another up to a capstone (**fig. 4.11**), resulting in a beehive profile for the roof. Earth covered the structure, helping

Reconstruction of façade of "Treasury of Atreus," Mycenae, Greece. ca. 1300–1250 BCE

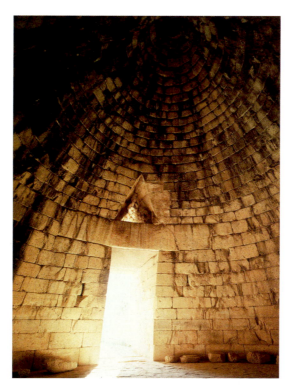

4.11 Interior of "Treasury of Atreus," Mycenae, Greece. ca. 1300–1250 BCE

to stabilize the layers of stone and creating a small hill, which was encircled with stones. The vault rose 43 feet over a space 48 feet in diameter. Such a large unsupported span would not be seen again until the Pantheon of Roman

times. Gilded rosettes may once have decorated the ashlar blocks of the vault to resemble a starry sky. To one side of the main room, a small rectangular chamber contained subsidiary burials.

METALWORK Like the Great Pyramids of Egypt, these monumental *tholoi* exalted the dead by drawing attention to themselves. As a result, they also attracted robbers throughout the ages, and the grave goods that once filled them have long been dispersed. Many of the earlier shaft graves also contained lavish goods, ranging from luxurious clothing and furniture to weaponry. On excavating Grave Circle A, Schliemann discovered five extraordinary male death masks of hammered gold. Although far from naturalistic, each displays a distinct treatment of physiognomy: Some faces are bearded while others are clean-shaven. This suggests that the masks were individualized to correspond to the deceased's appearance. On finding the example illustrated in **fig. 4.12** in 1876, Schliemann told the press, "I have gazed into the face of Agamemnon." Since modern archaeology places the mask between 1600 and 1500 BCE, and the Trojan War—if it happened—would date to about 1300–1200 BCE, this could not be a mask of Agamemnon. But it may represent a Mycenaean king of some stature, given the expense of the materials.

4.12 *Mask of Agamemnon*, from a shaft grave in Circle A, Mycenae. ca. 1600–1500 BCE. Gold, height 12″ (30 cm). National Archaeological Museum, Athens

SUMMARY

The Mediterranean Sea was a highway that brought the various civilizations of antiquity into contact with one another for both trade and war. During the third and second millennia BCE, several closely related but distinct cultures developed on the islands and peninsulas in and adjacent to the Aegean Sea. These include the Cycladic culture, named for islands north of Crete; the Minoan culture, which constructed and decorated so-called palaces on Crete; and the Mycenaean culture, which left behind remarkable citadels and grave goods on the Greek mainland. The distinct art forms produced by each of these groups provide insights into the practices and ideals of ancient Aegean peoples.

The most characteristic art forms of the Cycladic islands of the third millennium BCE are carved marble figures of women. Although both the meaning and the functions of these sculptures are obscure, the clean geometry and smooth surfaces of their abstracted forms hold great appeal for modern viewers.

Despite over a hundred years of archaeological research on Crete and other sites in the Aegean, Minoan culture remains mysterious. The large and complex palaces, such as that at Knossos, dominated the landscape of Crete and probably served as administrative and ritual centers as well as residences. These structures were adorned with numerous frescoes and wall paintings and other decorative elements that represent, among other things, the natural world in lively, animated forms. Minoan pottery, which demonstrates organic and dynamic compositions, exhibits a high degree of craftsmanship.

The Mycenaeans were named for the fortified settlement of Mycenae in the Peloponnesian region of mainland Greece. Their citadels—with huge walls, massive fortifications and defensive layouts—suggest a culture concerned with defense, if these people were not overtly warlike themselves. Nevertheless, the luxurious objects placed in Mycenaean burial sites, such as the gold masks from the Shaft Graves at Mycenae, and the lavish adornment of their palaces reveal that they were open to influences from around the Mediterranean. Minoan, Egyptian, and Mesopotamian elements all contributed to Mycenean art.

ART IN TIME

- ca. 2500 BCE—White marble Cycladic figurines

- ca. 2575–2465 BCE—Ancient Egypt's Fourth Dynasty; construction of the three Great Pyramids at Giza

- ca. 1792–1750 BCE—Babylon ruled by Hammurabi

- ca. 1700–1300 BCE—Minoan construction of the Second Palace at Knossos

- ca. 1628—Volcanic eruption on Thera

- ca. 1500–1450 BCE—*Octopus Vase*, an example of Minoan "marine style" pottery

- ca. 1450 BCE—Earthquake demolishes Knossos and other Minoan centers; Mycenaeans invade Crete

- ca. 1600–1500 BCE—Mycenaean death masks of hammered gold

- ca. 1500–1200 BCE—Height of Mycenaean culture

- ca. 1250 BCE—Construction of the Lion Gate at Mycenae

*G*reek architecture, sculpture, and civilization are immediately recognizable as the ancestors of Western civilization, despite their debts to earlier art. A Greek temple reminds us of government buildings, banks, and college campuses, and a Greek statue recalls statues of our own day. This is neither coincidental nor inevitable. Western civilization has carefully constructed itself in the image of the Greek and Roman worlds. For an art historian trying to understand the visual culture of those worlds, this presents a special challenge: It is tempting to believe that something familiar on the surface holds the same significance for us as it did for the Greeks or the Romans, but scholars have discovered time and time again that this is a dangerous fallacy.

Another complication in studying Greek art arises because there are three separate, and sometimes conflicting, sources of information on the subject. First, there are the works themselves—reliable, but only a small fraction of what once existed. Secondly, there are Roman copies of Greek originals, especially sculptures. These works tell us something about important pieces that would otherwise be lost to us, but pose their own problems. Without the original, we cannot determine how faithful the copy is, and sometimes multiple copies present several versions of one original. Moreover, a Roman copyist's notion of a copy was quite different from ours: A copy was not necessarily intended as a strict imitation, but allowed for adapting the work according to the taste or skill of the copyist or the patron's wishes.

The third source of information about Greek works is literature. The Greeks were the first Western people to write at length about their artists. Roman writers incorporated Greek accounts into their own; many of these have survived, although often in fragmentary condition. These written sources offer a glimpse of what the Greeks considered their most important artistic achievements, and help us to identify celebrated artists and monuments. The literature deals largely with works that have not survived, while surviving Greek works that strike us as great masterpieces are not mentioned. Weaving these strands of information into a coherent picture of Greek art has been the difficult task of archaeologists and art historians for several centuries.

The flowering of ancient Greek art was just one manifestation of a wide-ranging exploration of humanistic and religious issues. Artists, writers, and philosophers struggled with common questions, still preserved in a huge body of works. Their inquiries cut to the core of human existence, and form the backbone of much of Western philosophy. For the most part, they accepted a pantheon of gods, whom they worshiped in human form. Yet they debated the nature of those gods, and the relationship between divinities and humankind.

Major Periods of Greek Art

ca. 900–725 BCE	Geometric
ca. 725–650 BCE	Orientalizing
ca. 650–480 BCE	Archaic
ca. 480–400 BCE	Classical
ca. 400–325 BCE	Late Classical
ca. 325–30 BCE	Hellenistic

Map 5.1 The Ancient Greek World

Greek thinkers conceived of many aspects of life in dualistic terms. Order (*cosmos*, in Greek) was opposed to disorder (*chaos*), and both poles permeated existence. Civilization, which was, by definition, Greek, stood in opposition to an uncivilized world beyond Greek borders; all non-Greeks were "barbarians," named for the non-sensical sound of their languages to Greek ears ("bar-bar-bar-bar"). Reason, too, had its opposite: The irrational, mirrored in light and darkness, in man and woman. In their literature and in their art, the ancient Greeks addressed the tension between these polar opposites.

The Emergence of Greek Art: The Geometric Style

The first Greek-speaking groups came to Greece about 2000 BCE, bringing a culture that soon encompassed most of mainland Greece, as well as the Aegean islands. By the first millennium BCE they had colonized the west coast of Asia Minor and Cyprus (see map 5.1). Despite cultural differences between Greeks of different regions, they had a strong sense of kinship, based

on language and common beliefs. From the mid-eighth through the mid-sixth centuries BCE, the Greeks expanded in a wave of colonization across the Mediterranean and as far as the Black Sea. They founded settlements in Sicily and southern Italy, collectively known as Magna Graecia, and in North Africa.

After the collapse of Mycenaean civilization (see chapter 4), art became largely nonfigural (that is, abstract) for several centuries. In the eighth century BCE, the oldest Greek style that we know in the arts developed, called today the Geometric.

Geometric Style Pottery

The earliest Greek vase-painters decorated their wares with abstract designs, such as triangles, "checkerboards," and concentric circles. Toward 800 BCE, at about the time the alphabet was introduced (under Near Eastern influence) and contemporaneous with *The Iliad* and *The Odyssey*, human and animal figures began to appear within the geometric framework. In the most elaborate examples these figures interacted in narrative scenes. The vase shown here, from a cemetery near the later Dipylon gate in Athens,

◆◆ Used almost continuously throughout Western art, the Greek vocabulary of ornamental motifs is vast, highly adaptable, and very durable.

guilloche

palmette

rosette

acanthus

meander

egg-and-dart

Some common Greek vessel forms

As quickly as pottery became an art form, Greek potters developed an extensive, if fairly standardized, repertoire of vessel shapes. Each type was well adapted to its function. As a result, each shape presented unique challenges to the painter, and some became specialists at decorating certain types of vases. Larger pots often attracted the most ambitious craftsmen because they provided a more generous field on which to work. Making and decorating vases were complex processes, usually performed by different artisans. From the middle of the sixth century BCE, many of the finest vessels bear signatures of the artists who made them, indicating the pride that potters and painters took in their work. In many cases, vase painters had such distinctive styles that scholars can recognize their work even without a signature, and use modern names to identify them. Dozens of vases might survive by the same hand, allowing a single painter's development to be traced over many years.

amphora

krater

hydria

lekythos

oinochoe

kylix

5.1 Late Geometric belly-handled amphora by the Dipylon Master, from the Dipylon Cemetery, Athens. ca. 750 BCE. Height 51″ (1.55 m). National Archaeological Museum, Athens

dates to around 750 BCE (**fig. 5.1**). Known as the Dipylon Vase, it was one of a group of unusually large vessels used as grave monuments. Holes in its base allowed liquid offerings (libations) to filter down to the dead. In earlier centuries, Athenians had placed the ashes of their dead inside vases, choosing the vase's shape according to the sex of the deceased. A woman's remains were buried in a belly-handled amphora, a type of vase commonly used for storing wine or oil; a man's ashes were placed in a neck-amphora. A krater, a large bowl-like vessel normally used for mixing wine with water, had also been used as a burial marker since the early first millennium. The shape and monumentality of the example illustrated here show that the deceased was a woman of considerable means.

The amphora is a masterpiece of the potter's craft. At over five feet tall, it was too large to be thrown in one piece. Instead, the potter built it up in sections, joined with a clay slip (clay mixed with water or another liquid). A careful proportional scheme governed the vessel's form: Its width measures half of its height and the neck measures half the height of the body. The artist placed the handles so as to emphasize the widest point of the body. Most of the decoration is given over to geometric patterns dominated by a meander pattern, also known as a maze or Greek key pattern, a band of rectangular scrolls, punctuated with bands of lustrous black paint at the neck, shoulder, and base. The geometric design reflects the proportional system of the vase's shape. Single meander patterns run in bands toward the top and bottom of the neck; the triple meander encircling the neck at the center emphasizes its length. The double and single meanders on the amphora's body appear stocky by contrast, complementing the body's rounder form. On the neck, deer graze, one after the other, in an identical pattern circling the vase. At the base of the neck, they recline, with their heads turned back over their bodies, like an animate version of the meander pattern, which moves ever forward while turning back upon itself.

In the center of the amphora, framed between its handles, is a narrative scene. The deceased lies on a bier, beneath a checkered shroud. Standing figures flank her with their arms raised above their heads in lamentation; four additional figures kneel or sit beneath the bier. The painter uses solid black geometric forms to construct human bodies. A triangle represents the torso, and the raised arms extend the triangle beyond the shoulders. The scene represents the *prothesis*, part of the Athenian funerary ritual when the deceased lay in state and public mourning took place. A lavish funeral was an occasion to display wealth and status, and crowds of mourners were so desirable that families would hire professional mourners for the event. Thus the depiction of a funeral on the vase is not simply journalistic reportage but a visual record of the deceased person's high standing in society.

Archaeologists have found Geometric pottery in Italy and the Near East as well as in Greece. This wide distribution is a sign of the important role of not only the Greeks but also the Phoenicians, North Syrians, and other Near Eastern peoples as agents of diffusion all around the Mediterranean. What is more, from the second half of the eighth century onward, inscriptions on these vases show that the Greeks had already adapted the Phoenician alphabet to their own use.

5.2 Griffin-head *protome* from a bronze tripod-cauldron, from Kameiros, Rhodes. ca. 650 BCE. Cast bronze, 12.6″ (0.32 m) high. The British Museum, London

The Orientalizing Style: Horizons Expand

Between about 725 and 650 BCE, a new style of art emerged in Greece that reflects strong influences from the Near East and Egypt. Scholars know this as the Orientalizing period. This absorption of Eastern motifs and ideas, including hybrid creatures such as griffins and sphinxes, led to a vital period of experimentation.

During the Geometric period, the Greeks had sometimes set up bronze tripod cauldrons in sanctuaries as dedications to the gods. The gesture was an act of piety, and a display of wealth, and some of the tripod cauldrons reached monumental proportions. From the early seventh century BCE, a new type of monumental vessel was introduced—the Orientalizing cauldron. Around the edge of the bowl, bronze-workers might attach *protomes*, images of sirens (winged female creatures), and griffins—fantasy creatures known in the Near East. The cast *protome* shown here, from the island of Rhodes, is a magnificently ominous creature, standing watch over the dedication (**fig. 5.2**). The boldly upright ears and the vertical knob on the head contrast starkly with the strong curves of the neck, head, eyes, and mouth, while its menacing tongue is silhouetted in countercurve against the beak. The straight lines appear to animate the curves, so that the dangerous hybrid seems about to spring.

Archaic Art: Art of the City-State

During the course of the seventh and sixth centuries BCE, the art of which is termed ARCHAIC, "early," the Greeks appear to have refined their notion of a *polis*, or city-state. Once merely a citadel, the place of refuge in troubled times, the city came to represent a community and an identity. CITY-STATES, as they are known, were governed in various ways, including, in Athens, democracy. With the changing ideal of the city-state came a change in its physical appearance.

The Rise of Monumental Temple Architecture

At some point in the seventh century BCE, Greek architects began to design temples in stone rather than wood. The earliest were probably built at Corinth, in a style known as Doric, named for the region where it originated. From there the idea spread to the mainland, then rapidly throughout the Hellenic (or Greek, from Hellas, meaning Greece) world. The Ionic style developed on the Aegean islands and the coast of Asia Minor. The Corinthian style did not develop until the late fifth century BCE (see page 101). Greeks recognized the importance of this revolution at the time: Architects wrote treatises on architecture—the first we know of—and the fame they achieved through their work has lasted to this day (see below, Temple Plans: Reading Architectural Drawings).

The essential components of Doric and Ionic temples are similar, though they vary according to the building's size or regional preferences (**fig. 5.3**). The nucleus of the building—its very reason for existing—is its main chamber, its **cella** or *naos*. This chamber housed an image of the god to whom the temple was dedicated. Often, interior columns lined the cella and helped to support the roof, as well as visually framing the cult statue. Approaching the cella is a porch or *pronaos*, and in some cases a second porch stood behind the cella, making the design more symmetrical and providing space for religious paraphernalia. In large temples, a colonnade or **peristyle** surrounds the cella and porches, and the building is known as a **peripteral temple**. The largest temples of Ionian Greece had a double colonnade.

The peristyle added more than grandeur: It offered worshipers shelter from the elements.

Temple Plans: Reading Architectural Drawings

ARCHITECTS AND architectural historians use three types of drawings to design and study buildings: Ground plans, sections, and elevations. Together, these three views furnish a basic visual description of the building.

A plan, or **ground plan**, depicts a building as if it were sliced horizontally about three feet above the ground. It usually shows solid parts in a darker tone than openings (doors and windows) and open spaces. Lines may indicate changes of level, such as steps. This plan shows a typical Doric temple. It allows us to understand how the main parts of the temple (colonnade, porches, rooms, and so on) relate to each other, and to trace the path of a typical visitor through its interior.

The second type of architectural drawing, the **elevation**, shows one exterior side seen straight on, with the parts drawn to scale. This elevation is of the front (façade) of the Doric temple seen in the plan above. It gives us basic information about its height, scale, and style.

The third type of architectural drawing, the **section**, reveals the inside of a structure as if it were sliced clean through from side to side or end to end. It shows us the vertical arrangement of the building's interior, indicates the levels and heights of its rooms and other spaces, and reveals technical details such as the construction of foundations, floors, walls, ceilings, and roofs. This section cuts through the middle of the Doric temple seen in the plan and elevation above.

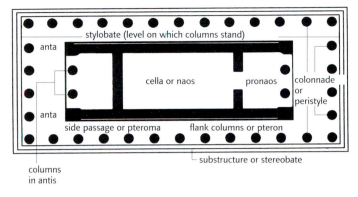

stylobate (level on which columns stand)

anta

cella or naos   pronaos

colonnade
or
peristyle

anta

side passage or pteroma   flank columns or pteron

substructure or stereobate

columns
in antis

5.3 Ground plan of a typical Greek peripteral temple (after Grinnell)

Being neither entirely exterior nor entirely interior space, it also functioned as a transitional zone, between the profane world outside and the sanctity of the cella. Some temples were set in sacred groves, where the columns, with their strong vertical form, integrated the temple with its environment. Echoed inside the cella, the columns also integrated the exterior and interior of the building. Most Greek temples are oriented so that the entrance faces east, toward the rising sun. East of the temple is usually the altar, the indispensable installation for the performance of ritual: It was there that Greeks performed sacrifices, standing before the cult statue and the community of the Greek *polis*.

Differences between the Doric and Ionic styles are apparent in elevation. Many of the terms that the Greeks used for the parts of their buildings, shown in **fig. 5.4**, are still in common usage. The building proper rests on an elevated

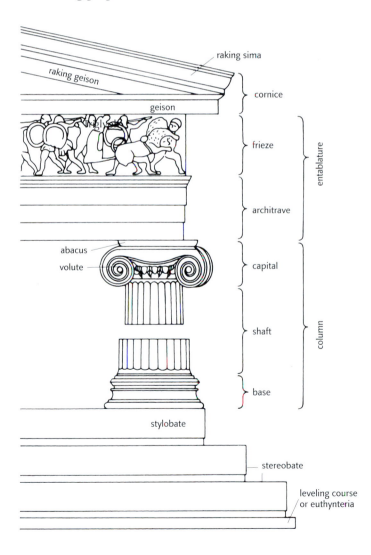

5.4 Doric and Ionic styles in elevation

platform, normally approached by three steps, known as the **stereobate** and **stylobate**. A **Doric column** consists of the shaft, usually marked by shallow vertical grooves, known as flutes, and the capital, made up of the flaring, cushionlike **echinus** and a square tablet called the **abacus**. The entablature includes all the horizontal elements that rest on the columns: The architrave (a row of stone blocks directly supported by the columns); the frieze, made up of alternating triple-grooved **triglyphs** and smooth or sculpted metopes; and a projecting horizontal cornice, or *geison*. The architrave in turn supports the triangular **pediment** and the roof elements.

Ionic temples tend to rest on a leveling course, or *euthynteria*, as well as three steps. An

Ionic column has an ornate base. Its shaft is more slender than the Doric, less tapered, and the capital incorporates a double scroll or volute. The Ionic column lacks the muscular quality of its mainland cousin. Instead, it evokes a growing plant, and this it shares with its Egyptian predecessors, though it may not have come directly from Egypt. Above the architrave, the frieze is a continuous, unbroken strip.

Whether Doric or Ionic, the temple was built of stone blocks fitted together without mortar, requiring precise shaping to achieve smooth joints. Where necessary, metal dowels or clamps fastened the blocks together. With rare exceptions, columns were made up of sections, called drums, and then fluted after the entire column

The Greek Gods and Goddesses

ALL EARLY CIVILIZATIONS and preliterate cultures had creation myths to explain the origin of the universe and humanity's place in it. Over time, these myths evolved into complex cycles that represent a comprehensive attempt to understand the world. The Greek gods and goddesses, though immortal, behaved in very human ways. They quarreled, and had children with each other's spouses and often with mortals as well. Sometimes their own children threatened and even overthrew them. The principal Greek gods and goddesses, with their Roman counterparts in parentheses, are given below.

ZEUS (Jupiter): Son of Kronos and Rhea; god of sky and weather, and king of the Olympian deities. After killing Kronos, Zeus married his sister HERA (Juno) and divided the universe by lot with his brothers: POSEIDON (Neptune) was allotted the sea, and HADES (Pluto) was allotted the Underworld, which he ruled with his queen PERSEPHONE (Proserpina).

Zeus and Hera had several children:

ARES (Mars), the god of war

HEBE, the goddess of youth

HEPHAISTOS (Vulcan), the lame god of metalwork and the forge

Zeus also had numerous children through his love affairs with other goddesses and with mortal women, including:

ATHENA (Minerva), goddess of crafts, including war, and thus of intelligence and wisdom. A protector of heroes, she became the patron goddess of Athens, an honor she won in a contest

with Poseidon. Her gift to the city was an olive tree, which she caused to sprout on the Akropolis.

APHRODITE (Venus), the goddess of love, beauty, and female fertility. She married Hephaistos, but had many affairs. Her children were HARMONIA, EROS, and ANTEROS (with Ares), HERMAPHRODITOS (with Hermes), PRIAPOS (with Dionysos), and AENEAS (with the Trojan prince Anchises).

APOLLON (Apollo), with his twin sister ARTEMIS, god of the stringed lyre and bow, who therefore both presided over the civilized pursuits of music and poetry, and shot down transgressors; a paragon of male beauty, he was also the god of prophecy and medicine.

ARTEMIS (Diana), with her twin brother, APOLLO, virgin goddess of the hunt and the protector of young girls. She was also sometimes considered a moon goddess and identified with SELENE.

DIONYSOS (Bacchus), the god of altered states, particularly that induced by wine. Opposite in temperament to Apollo, Dionysos was raised on Mount Nysa, where he invented winemaking; he married the princess Ariadne after the hero Theseus abandoned her on Naxos. His followers, the goatish satyrs and their female companions, the nymphs and humans who were known as maenads (bacchantes), were given to orgiastic excess. Yet there was another, more temperate side to Dionysos character. As the god of fertility, he was also a god of vegetation, as well as of peace, hospitality, and the theater.

HERMES (Mercury), the messenger of the gods, conductor of souls to Hades, and the god of travelers and commerce.

5.5 The Temple of Hera I ("Basilica"), ca. 550 BCE, and the Temple of Hera II ("Temple of Poseidon"), ca. 500 BCE. Paestum, southern Italy

was assembled. The roof was made of terracotta tiles over wooden rafters, and wooden beams were used for the ceiling.

Just how either style came to emerge in Greece, and why they came together into succinct systems so quickly, are still puzzling questions. Remains of the oldest surviving temples show that the main features of the Doric style were already well established soon after 600 BCE. Though it is possible that the temple's central unit, the cella and porch, derived from the plan of the Mycenaean megaron (see fig. 4.2), the notion that temples should be stone and have large numbers of columns was an Egyptian one. In fact, scholars believe that the rise of monumental stone architecture and sculpture must have been based on careful, on-the-spot study of Egyptian works and the techniques used to produce them. The opportunity for just such a study was available to Greek merchants living in trading camps in the western Nile delta, by permission of the Egyptian king Psammetichus I (r. 664–610 BCE).

Some scholars see Doric architecture as a petrification (or turning to stone) of existing wooden forms, so that stone form follows wooden function. Accordingly, triglyphs once masked the ends of wooden beams, and metopes evolved from boards that filled gaps between the triglyphs to guard against weather. Some derivations are more convincing than others. The vertical subdivisions of triglyphs hardly seem to reflect the forms of three half-round logs, as scholars suggest. The question of how far function can explain stylistic features faces the architectural historian repeatedly.

DORIC TEMPLES AT PAESTUM The early evolution of Doric temples is evident in two unusually well preserved examples in the southern Italian *polis* of Paestum, where a Greek colony flourished during the Archaic period. Both temples honor the goddess Hera, wife of Zeus (see left, Cultural Context: The Greek Gods and Goddesses); the Temple of Hera II, however, was built almost a century after the Temple of Hera I, the so-called Basilica (**fig. 5.5**). The differences in their proportions are striking. The Temple of Hera I (on the left, fig. 5.5) appears low and sprawling—and not just because so much of the entablature is missing—whereas the Temple of Hera II looks tall and compact. This is partly because the temple of Hera I is enneastyle (with nine columns across the front and rear), while the later temple is only hexastyle (six columns). Yet it is also the result of changes to the outline

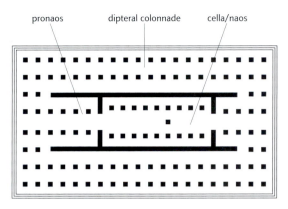

pronaos   dipteral colonnade   cella/naos

5.6 Restored plan of the Temple of Artemis at Ephesos, Turkey. ca. 560 BCE

of the columns. On both temples, the column shafts bulge outward slightly about a third of the way up, receding again at about two thirds of their height. This swelling effect, known as **entasis**, is much stronger on the earlier Temple of Hera I. It gives the impression that the columns bulge with the strain of supporting the superstructure and that the slender tops, although aided by the widely flaring, cushionlike capitals, can barely withstand the weight. The device adds an extraordinary vitality to the building—a sense of compressed energy waiting to be released.

EARLY IONIC TEMPLES The Ionic style first appeared about a half-century after the Doric in Ionian Greece, where cities erected vast, ornate temples in open rivalry with one another. Little survives of these early buildings. The Temple of Artemis at Ephesos (**fig. 5.6**) gained tremendous fame in antiquity, numbering among the seven wonders of the ancient world. The first monumental building to be constructed mostly of marble, the temple was dipteral, with two rows of columns surrounding it. Along with the vegetal capitals, this feature emphasized the forestlike quality of the building. These huge Ionic buildings had clear symbolic value: They represented their city's bid for regional leadership.

Stone Sculpture

According to literary sources, Greeks carved simple wooden sculptures of their gods in the eighth century BCE, but none of them survive. In about 650 BCE, sculptors, like architects, made the transition to working in stone, and so began one of the great traditions of Greek art.

KORE* AND *KOUROS Early Greek statues clearly show affinities with the techniques and proportional systems used by Egyptian sculptors. Two

5.7 *Kouros* (Youth). ca. 600–590 BCE. Marble, height 6'1½" (1.88 m). The Metropolitan Museum of Art, New York. Fletcher Fund, 1932. 32.11.1

are illustrated here, one a life-size nude male youth of about 600 BCE (**fig. 5.7**), known as the New York Kouros because it is displayed in the Metropolitan Museum of Art. The other is a female figure (**fig. 5.8**) of about 520 BCE, found on the Athenian Akropolis, but probably from Chios, an island of Ionian Greece. Like their Egyptian forerunners (see fig. 3.7), the statues are rigidly frontal, and conceived as four distinct sides, reflecting the form of the block from which they were carved. The Greek youth stands with his left leg forward, and his arms by his sides. His shoulders, hips, and knees are all level. Like Khafra, he is slim and broad-shouldered, his hair stylized and resembling a wig, like that of his Egyptian counterpart. Still, there are significant differences. First, the Greek sculptures are truly free-standing, separated from the back slab that supports Egyptian stone figures. In fact, they are the earliest large stone images of the human figure in the history of art that can stand on their own. Moreover, Greek sculptures incorporated empty space (between the legs, for instance), whereas Egyptian figures remained embedded in stone, with the spaces between forms partly filled. Early Greek sculptures are also more stylized than their Egyptian forebears. This is most evident in the large staring eyes, emphasized by arching eyebrows, the smiling features, known as the Archaic smile, and in the linear treatment of the anatomy: The male youth's pectoral muscles and ribcage appear to have been etched onto the surface of the stone, rather than modeled like Khafra's. Unlike Khafra, the Greek youth is nude. By contrast, the female sculpture is draped, wearing a light Ionian *chiton* under the heavier *himation*. The layers of the garment loop around the body in soft curves, and the play of richly differentiated folds, pleats, and textures is almost an end in itself; here much of the color that played an important role in such works survives. These conventions reflect the fact that public nudity in ancient Greece was acceptable for males, but not for females.

Dozens of Archaic sculptures of this kind survive throughout the Greek world. Some were discovered in sanctuaries and cemeteries, but most were found in reused contexts, which complicates any attempt to understand their function. Scholars describe them by the Greek terms for maiden (**kore**, plural *korai*) and youth (**kouros**, plural *kouroi*). These terms gloss over the difficulty of identifying them more precisely. Some are inscribed, with the names of artists or with dedications to deities, chiefly Apollo. These,

5.8 *Kore*, from Chios (?). ca. 520 BCE. Marble, height 21⅞" (55.3 cm). Akropolis Museum, Athens

then, were votive offerings. But in most cases we do not know whether they represent the donor, a deity, or a person deemed divinely favored, such as an athletic victor. Those placed on graves may have represented the deceased. No clear effort was made to individualize the statues as portraits, so they can represent the dead only in a general sense. It might make most sense to think of the figures as ideals of physical perfection and vitality shared by mortals and immortals alike, given meaning by their physical context. What is clear is that only the wealthy could afford to erect them, since many were over life-size and carved from high-quality marble. Indeed, the very stylistic cohesion of the sculptures may reveal their social function: By erecting a sculpture of this kind, a wealthy patron declared his or her status and claimed membership of ruling elite circles.

Architectural Sculpture: The Building Comes Alive

Soon after the Greeks began to build temples in stone, they started to decorate them with sculpture, which helped to articulate their sections and to bring them to life. Traces of pigment show that these sculptures were normally vividly painted—an image that is startlingly at odds with our conception of ancient sculpture as pristine white marble. Sculpture typically adorned the triangle between the ceiling and the roof, known as the pediment. Free-standing sculptures known as **acroteria** sometimes stood above the corners and center of the pediment, softening

the severity of its outline. Greek sculptors also decorated the frieze. In Doric temples, they would often decorate the metopes with figural scenes. In Ionic temples, the frieze was a continuous band of painted or sculpted decoration. Moreover, in Ionic buildings, female statues or **caryatids** might be substituted for columns to support the roof of a porch.

THE SIPHNIAN TREASURY, DELPHI These Ionic features came together in a treasury built at Delphi shortly before 525 BCE by the people of the Ionian island of Siphnos. Although the TREASURY OF THE SIPHNIANS no longer stands, archaeologists can reconstruct it from what survives. Supporting the architrave of the porch were two caryatids. Above the architrave was a magnificent sculptural frieze, part of which depicts the mythical battle of the Greek gods against the giants, who had challenged divine authority. At the far left of **fig. 5.9**, two lions pull the chariot of the mother goddess Cybele, and tear apart an anguished giant. In front of them, Apollo and Artemis advance together, shooting arrows, once added in metal, into a phalanx of giants. Stripped of his armor, a dead giant lies at their feet. The tale is a cautionary one, warning mortals not to aim higher than their natural place in the order of things. Though the subject is mythical, its depiction offers detail on contemporary weaponry and military tactics.

Astonishingly, the relief is only a few inches deep. Within that shallow space, the sculptors (more than one hand is discernible) created

5.9 *Battle of the Gods and Giants*, from the north frieze of the Treasury of the Siphnians, Delphi. ca. 530 BCE. Marble, height 26″ (66 cm). Archaeological Museum, Delphi

several planes. The arms and legs of those nearest a viewer are carved in the round. In the second and third layers, the forms become shallower, yet even those farthest from a viewer do not merge into the background. The resulting relationships between figures give a dramatic sense of the turmoil of battle and an intensity of action not seen before in narrative reliefs.

The protagonists fill the sculptural field from top to bottom, enhancing the frieze's power. This is a dominant characteristic of Archaic and Classical Greek art, and sculptors soon sought ways to fill the pediment, too, while retaining a unity of scale. Taking their cue, perhaps, from friezes such as that found on the Siphnian Treasury, they introduced a variety of poses, and made great strides in depicting the human body in naturalistic motion. This is well illustrated in the pediments of the Temple of Aphaia at Aegina, an island in the Saronic Gulf visible from Attica.

PEDIMENTS OF THE TEMPLE OF APHAIA The Persians probably destroyed the Temple of Aphaia's original east pediment when they took the island in 490 BCE. The Aeginetans commissioned the present one after defeating them at the battle of Salamis in 480 BCE. It depicts the first sack of Troy, by Herakles (see below, Cultural Context: Greek Heroes and Civic Values) and Telamon, king of Salamis. The west pediment, which dates from about 510–500 BCE, depicts the second siege of Troy (recounted in *The Iliad*) by Agamemnon, who was related to

Reconstruction drawing of the Treasury of the Siphnians. Sanctuary of Apollo at Delphi. ca. 525 BCE.

The TREASURY OF THE SIPHNIANS is one of 20 treasuries built by various Greek cities within the walls of the sacred precinct at Delphi, the god Apollo's main sanctuary. These small, rectangular buildings, fronted with two columns and often decorated with sculpture, were commissioned by cities as receptacles for their more precious offerings to the god. The other major buildings inside the sacred precincts were altars and temples. In the late sixth century BCE, when this treasury was built, Siphnos, one of the Cyclades islands, was extremely rich from its gold and silver mines.

Herakles. The pairing of subjects commemorates the important role played by the heroes of Aegina in both battles—and, by extension, at Salamis, where their navy helped win the day. The elevation of historical events to a universal plane through allegory was typical of Greek art.

By introducing a wide range of action poses for the figures, the designer could fill the pediment while maintaining uniformity of scale. By comparing a fallen warrior from the west pediment (**fig. 5.10**) with its counterpart from the later east pediment (**fig. 5.11**) we see some of the extraordinary advances sculptors made toward naturalism during the decades that separate them. As they sink to the ground in death, both

Greek Heroes and Civic Values

THE EPIC POETRY OF HOMER and the works of the great Classical playwrights focus on the world of the heroes. Some of these heroes were probably historical figures, but all were believed to be descendants of the gods, who often had children by mortal women. Thus PERSEUS was the son of Zeus by Danaë and HERAKLES his son by Alkmene. Such a lineage helped to explain the hero's extraordinary prowess. This prowess or *arete* could, in excess, lead to overweening pride (*hubris*), and then to often catastrophic error (*hamartia*). The results were the subject of many Classical tragedies.

Arete came to be identified with personal and civic virtues, such as modesty, selflessness, and piety, and eventually with

moral virtue. The ethical ideal of a self-knowledge (*sophrosyne*) that led to a measured self-restraint, to moderation in all things, was policed by Apollo, the god of rationality and civilization. His temple at Delphi bore the slogan "nothing to excess."

The greatest of all Greek heroes was HERAKLES (Hercules to the Romans), who became the only mortal ever to ascend to Mount Olympos upon his death. His most important exploits were the Twelve Labors. Undertaken over 12 years at the command of King Eurystheus of Tiryns, they were acts of atonement for killing his wife and children after he was driven mad by Hera (Zeus's wife), who hated him.

5.10 *Dying Warrior*, from the west pediment of the Temple of Aphaia. ca. 500–490 BCE. Marble, length 5′2½″ (1.59 m). Staatliche Antikensammlungen und Glyptothek, Munich

figures present a clever solution to filling the awkward corner space. Yet while the earlier figure props himself up on one arm, only a precariously balanced shield supports the later warrior, whose weight seems to pull him irresistibly to the ground. In both, the dying warrior's body is contorted in the agonies of death: The earlier sculptor crosses the warrior's legs in an awkward pose, while the later sculptor twists the body from the waist, so that the left shoulder moves into a new plane. Although the later warrior's anatomy does not fully respond to his pose (note, for instance, how little the pectorals stretch to accommodate the strenuous motion of

the right arm), his body is more modeled and organic than the earlier warrior's. He also breaks from the head-on stare of his predecessor, turning his gaze to the ground. The effect suggests introspection: The inscrutable smiling mask of the earlier warrior yields to the suffering and emotion of a warrior in his final moments. Depictions of suffering, and how humans respond to it, are among the most dramatic developments of late Archaic art.

Vase Painting: Art of the Symposium

A new Archaic style developed in vase painting, as workshops in Athens and other centers

5.11 *Dying Warrior*, from the east pediment of the Temple of Aphaia. ca. 480 BCE. Marble, length 6′ (1.83 m). Staatliche Antikensammlungen und Glyptothek, Munich

5.12 *Achilles and Ajax Playing Dice.* Black-figured amphora signed by Exekias as painter and potter. ca. 540–530 BCE. Height 2′ (61 cm). Vatican Museums

produced fine wares painted with scenes from mythology, legend, and everyday life. The vases illustrated here held wine, but were not for everyday use. The Greeks generally poured wine from plainer, unadorned vases, reserving decorated vessels for important occasions like the symposium (*symposion*), an exclusive drinking party. Men and courtesans reclined on couches around the edges of a room, and a master of ceremonies filled their cups from a large painted mixing bowl (a krater) in the middle of the room. Music, poetry, storytelling, and word games accompanied the festivities. Often the event ended in lovemaking, which is frequently depicted on drinking cups. Yet there was also a serious side to symposia, as described by Plato and Xenophon, centering on debates about politics, ethics, and morality. The great issues that the Greeks pondered in their philosophy, literature, and theater—the nature of virtue, or the value of an individual man's life, to name a few—were mirrored in, and prompted by, the images with which they surrounded themselves.

Toward the end of the seventh century BCE, Attic vase painters began to work in the BLACK-FIGURED technique: They painted the entire design in black silhouette against the reddish clay, and then incised the internal details into the design with a needle. White and purple were added over the black to make chosen areas stand out. The technique lent itself to a two-dimensional and highly decorative effect. A fine example of the black-figured technique is an Athenian amphora signed by Exekias as potter and painter, dating to the third quarter of the sixth century BCE (**fig. 5.12**). The painting shows the Homeric heroes Achilles and Ajax playing dice, in an episode that exists in no surviving literary sources. The figures lean on their spears; their shields are stacked behind them against the inside of a campaign tent. The black silhouettes create a rhythmical composition, symmetrical around the table in the center. Within the black paint, Exekias incised a wealth of detail, focusing upon the warriors' cloaks; their intricately woven texture contrasts with the lustrous blackness of their weapons.

The development of BLACK-FIGURED vase painting marks the beginning of an aggressive export industry, the main consumers of which were the Etruscans (see chapter 6). Vast numbers of black-figured vases were found in Etruscan tombs. Thus, although in terms of conception these vases (and later red-figured vessels) represent a major chapter in Greek (and specifically Athenian) art, if we think about their actual use, painted vases can be considered a major component of Etruscan culture, both visual and funerary.

5.13 Euthymides. *Dancing Revelers*. Red-figured amphora. ca. 510–500 BCE. Height 2′ (61 cm). Museum Antiker Kleinkunst, Munich

The extraordinary power of this scene derives from the tension within it. The warriors have stolen a moment of relaxation during a fierce war; even so, poised on the edge of their stools, one heel raised as if to spring into action, they are edgy. An inscription on the right reads "three," as if Ajax is calling out his throw. Achilles, who in his helmet slightly dominates the scene, answers with "four," making him the winner. Yet many Greek viewers would have understood the irony of the scene, for when they return to battle, Achilles will die, and Ajax will bear his friend's body back to the Greek camp, before falling on his own sword in despair. Indeed, Exekias himself would paint representations of the heroes' tragic deaths. This amphora is the first known representation of the gaming scene, which subsequently became popular, suggesting that vase paintings did not exist in artistic

isolation; painters responded to one another's work in a close and often clever dialogue.

Despite its decorative potential, the silhouette-like black-figured technique limited artists to incision for detail, leading them to develop the reverse procedure of leaving figures red and filling in the background. This **red-figured** technique replaced the older method between 520 and 500 BCE. The effects of the change are already discernible on an amphora of about 510–500 BCE, signed by Euthymides (**fig. 5.13**). No longer is the scene so dependent on profiles. The painter's new freedom with the brush translates into a freedom of movement in the dancing revelers. They cavort in a range of poses, twisting their bodies and showing off Euthymides' confidence in rendering human anatomy. The shoulder blades of the central figure, for instance, one higher than the other, reflect the motion of his raised arm. The turning poses allow Euthymides to tackle foreshortening, as he portrays the different planes of the body (the turning shoulders, for instance) on one surface. This was an age of intensive and self-conscious experimentation; indeed, so pleased was Euthymides with his painting that he inscribed a challenge to a fellow painter, "As never Euphronios."

The Classical Age

A new era was ushered in by crisis at the beginning of the fifth century BCE. When Athens supported a number of Ionian cities in rebellion against their Persian overlords, the Persians, led by Darius I, invaded the Greek mainland. At the Battle of Marathon in 490, a contingent of about 10,000 Athenians, with a battalion from nearby Plataea, repulsed a force of about 90,000 Persians. Ten years later, an even larger force of Persians returned under Darius' son, Xerxes I. They took control of Athens, burning and pillaging temples and statues. The Greeks fought them at Salamis and Plataea in 480–479, finally defeating them. These battles were defining moments for the Greeks, who first faced destruction in their cities, and then emerged triumphant after the horrors of invasion. At least in Athens, Persian destruction of public monuments is visible in the archaeological record, and, for archaeologists and art historians, signals the end of the Archaic period and the emergence of the Classical era.

The struggle against the Persians tested the recently established Athenian democracy. Athens emerged as the leader of a defensive alliance, which evolved quickly into a political and economic empire that facilitated numerous architectural and artistic projects. Scholars describe the period stretching from the end of the Persian Wars to the death of Alexander the Great in the late fourth century as the Classical Age. This was the time when Aristophanes, Aeschylus, Sophocles, and Euripides were penning comedies and tragedies for performance at religious festivals, and thinkers such as Socrates, Plato, and Aristotle engaged in their philosophical quests.

Classical Sculpture

Among the many statues excavated from the debris following the Persian sack of the Akropolis in 480 BCE, one *kouros* stands apart (**fig. 5.14**). Sometimes attributed to the Athenian sculptor Kritios, the work is known as the *Kritios Boy*. Archaeologists date it to shortly before the Persian attack on account of its findspot, and it differs significantly from the Archaic *kouros* discussed above (see fig. 5.6), not least because it is the first known statue that stands in the full sense of the word. Although the earlier figure is upright—instead of reclining or sitting—his stance is an arrested walk, with the body's weight resting evenly on both legs, in a pose that is unnaturalistic and rigid. Like earlier *kouroi*, the *Kritios Boy* has one leg forward, yet an important change has occurred. The sculptor has shifted the youth's weight, creating a calculated asymmetry in the two sides of his body. The knee of the forward leg is lower than the other, the right hip is thrust down and in, and the left hip up and out. The axis of the body is not a straight vertical line, but a reversed S-curve. Taken together, these small departures from symmetry indicate that the youth's weight rests mainly on the left leg, while the right leg acts as a prop to help balance the body.

The *Kritios Boy* not only stands; he stands at ease. The artist has masterfully observed the balanced asymmetry of this relaxed stance, which is known as **contrapposto** (Italian for "counterpoise"). The leg that carries the weight is called the engaged leg, the other, the free leg. With this simple observation came a recognition that, if one part of the body is engaged in a task, other parts respond. Bending the free knee results in a swiveling of the pelvis, a compensating curvature of the spine, and an adjusting tilt of the shoulders. This unified approach to the body enabled artists to represent movement with a new naturalism. Indeed, even though the *Kritios*

5.14 *Kritios Boy*. ca. 480 BCE. Marble, height 46″ (116.7 cm). Akropolis Museum, Athens

The Indirect Lost-Wax Process

THE *ZEUS* (fig. 5.15) is one of the earliest surviving Greek statues that was made by the indirect lost-wax process. This technique enables sculptors to create spatially freer forms than is possible in stone. Projecting limbs are made separately and soldered onto the torso, and need not be supported by unsightly struts. Compare, for example, the freely outstretched arms of the *Zeus* with the strut extending from hip to drapery on the *Aphrodite of Knidos* (fig. 5.25).

The Egyptians, Minoans, and early Greeks had often made statuettes of solid bronze using the direct lost-wax process. The technique was simple. The sculptor modeled his figure in wax; covered it with clay to form a mold; melted away the wax; melted copper and tin in the ratio of nine parts to one in a crucible; and poured this alloy into the space left by the "lost wax" in the clay mold. Yet because figures made in this way were solid, the method had severe limitations. A solid-cast, life-size statue would have been prohibitively expensive, incredibly heavy, and prone to developing unsightly bubbles and cracks as the alloy cooled. So from the eighth through the sixth centuries BCE the Greeks developed the indirect lost-wax method, which allowed statues to be cast hollow and at any scale.

First, the sculptor shaped a core of clay into the basic form of the intended metal statue. He then covered the clay core with a layer of wax to the thickness of the final metal casting, and carved the details of the statue carefully in the wax. The figure was then separated into its component parts—head, torso, limbs, and so on. For each part, a heavy outer layer of clay was applied over the wax and secured to the inner core with metal pegs. The package was then heated to melt the wax, which ran out. Molten metal—usually bronze, but sometimes silver or gold—was then poured into the space left by this "lost wax." When the molten metal cooled, the outer and inner molds were broken away, leaving a metal casting—the statue's head, torso, arm, or whatever. The sculptor then soldered these individual sections together to create the statue. He completed the work by polishing the surface, chiseling details such as strands of hair and skin folds, and inlaying features such as eyes, teeth, lips, nipples, and dress patterns in ivory, stone, glass, copper, or precious metal.

Canon

Kanon (canon) in ancient Greek meant "rule" or "measure." In art history, the canon has come to mean the large body of artworks that scholars and connoisseurs have judged through the centuries to be the central, most defining works of the Western tradition. That canon is constantly shifting, and books like this one play a role in defining it. The term also means a normative or ideal ratio of proportions, usually based on a unit of measure (see p. 54 margin note). This is why Polykleitos called the treatise that he wrote to accompany his *Doryphoros* (see fig. 5.15) the *Kanon*. "Canon" also describes the central and normative works in the fields of music, religion, and law; the central section of the Mass in the Catholic Church; and is used in cultural fields that parallel art history, such as literature.

Boy is at rest, his muscles suggest motion, and the sculpture has life; he seems capable of action. All the same, the artist recognized that strict adherence to nature would not always yield the desired result. So, as in the later Parthenon, refinements are at work. The sculptor exaggerated the line of muscles over the pelvis to create a greater unity between thighs and torso, and a more fluid transition from front to back. This emphasized the sculpture's three-dimensionality, and encouraged a viewer to move around it.

The innovative movement in the musculature gives a viewer the sense, for the first time, that muscles lie beneath the surface of the marble skin, and that a skeleton articulates the whole as a real organism. A new treatment of the flesh and the marble's surface adds to this impression. The flesh has a sensuousness, a softness that is alien to earlier *kouroi*, and the sculptor worked the surface of the marble to a gentle polish. Gone, also, is the Archaic smile, presumably as a result of close observation of a human face. The face has a soft fleshiness to it, especially marked around the chin, which is characteristic of early Classical sculpture. The head is turned slightly away from the front, removing the direct gaze of earlier *kouroi* and casting the figure into his own world of thought.

The *Kritios Boy* marks a critical point in Greek art. One of the changes it engendered was a whole-hearted exploration of the representation of movement, another hallmark of early Classical sculpture. A magnificent nude bronze dating to about 460–450 BCE, recovered from the sea near the Greek coast, illustrates this well (**fig. 5.15**). At almost 7 feet tall, it depicts a spread-eagled male figure in the act of throwing (see Materials and Techniques: The Indirect Lost-Wax Process). Scholars identify it as Zeus casting a thunderbolt, or Poseidon, god of the sea, hurling his trident. In a single figure, the sculptor captures and contrasts vigorous action and firm stability. The result is a work of outright grandeur, revealing the god's awe-inspiring power. The piece shows off not only the artist's powers of observation and understanding of bodies in motion, but also an extraordinary knowledge of the strengths of bronze, which allowed the god's arms to stretch out without support.

5.15 *Zeus or Poseidon*. ca. 460–450 BCE. Bronze, height 6'10" (2.08 m). National Archaeological Museum, Athens. Ministry of Culture Archaeological Receipts Fund. 15161

THE *DORYPHOROS*: IDEALS OF PROPORTION AND HARMONY Within half a century of the innovations witnessed in the *Kritios Boy*, sculptors were avidly exploring the body's articulation. One of those sculptors was Polykleitos of Argos, whose most famous work, the *Doryphoros* (*Spear Bearer*) (**fig. 5.16**), is known to us through numerous Roman copies. In this sculpture, the *contrapposto* is much more emphatic than in the *Kritios Boy*. The artist seems to delight in the possibilities it offers, examining how the anatomy on the two sides of the body responds to the pose.

The "working" left arm balances the "engaged" right leg in the forward position, and the relaxed right arm balances the "free" left leg. Yet, in the sculpture, Polykleitos did more than study anatomy. He explored principles of commensurability, *symmetria*, proposing an ideal system of proportions, not just for the individual elements of the body but for their relation to one another and to the body as a whole. He also addressed *rhythmos* (composition and movement). According to one ancient writer, the *Doryphoros* came to be known as his *kanon*. Where Egyptian artists

5.16 *Doryphoros* (*Spear Bearer*). Roman copy after an original of ca. 450–440 BCE by Polykleitos. Marble, height 6′6″ (2 m). Museo Archeologico Nazionale, Naples

had earlier aimed to establish guidelines for depiction based on proportion, for Polykleitos the search for an ideal system of proportions was more than an artist's aid: It was rooted in a philosophical quest for illumination, and based in a belief that harmony (*harmonia*)—in the universe, as in music and in all things—could be expressed in mathematical terms. Only slightly later than this sculpture, Plato would root his doctrine of ideal forms in numbers, and acknowledge that beauty was commonly based on proportion. Philosophers even referred to works of art to illustrate their theories. Beauty was more than an idle conceit for Classical Athenians; it also had a moral dimension. Pose and expression reflected character and feeling, which revealed the inner person and, with it, *arete* (excellence or virtue). Thus contemplation of harmonious proportions could be equated with the contemplation of virtue.

Architecture and Sculpture on the Athenian Akropolis

The Athenian Akropolis, the hilltop citadel, had been a fortified site since Mycenaean times, around 1250 BCE (**fig. 5.17**). During the Archaic period, it housed at least one sizeable temple dedicated to the city's patron goddess, Athena, as well as several smaller temples or treasuries and statues. For over 30 years after the Persian sack of 480 BCE, the Athenians left the sacred monuments in ruins, as a solemn reminder of the Persians' ruthlessness. In the mid-fifth century BCE, however, this changed with the emergence of PERIKLES into political life. Perikles' ambitions for Athens included making the city—with a population of about 150,000—the envy of the Mediterranean world. His projects, which the democratic assembly approved, began with the Akropolis site. The structures there have come to exemplify Classical Greek art at its height. In these monuments, artists continued to grapple with ways of creating visual harmony through mathematical ratios between the parts of the work.

THE PARTHENON The dominant temple on the Akropolis, and the only one to be completed before the Peloponnesian War, is the Parthenon (**fig. 5.18**), a structure conceived to play a focal role in the cult of Athena. There is no evidence that it was used directly for cult practices; there is no altar to the east, and the chief center of cult practice remained on the site of the Erechtheion, north of the Parthenon. Built of gleaming white

5.17 Plan of the Akropolis at Athens in 400 BCE (after A. W. Lawrence)

marble from nearby Mount Pentelikon, the Parthenon stands on a prominent site on the southern flank of the Akropolis. It dominates the city and the surrounding countryside, a brilliant landmark against the backdrop of mountains to the north, east, and west. Contemporary building records, and a biography of Perikles written by Plutarch, show that two architects, Iktinos and Kallikrates, oversaw its construction between 447 and 432 BCE.

Regardless of one's preference for Archaic or Classical proportions, when read against the architectural vocabulary of Classical Greece the Parthenon is an extraordinarily sophisticated building. Its parts are fully integrated, so that its spaces do not seem to be separated, but to melt into one another. Likewise, its architecture and sculpture are so intertwined that discussion of the two cannot be disentangled. The temple stood near the culminating point of a grand procession that would wind its way through the city and onto the Akropolis during the annual Panathenaic festival in Athena's honor, and as magnificent as it was to observe from a distance, it was also a building to experience. Imitating the grandiose temples of Archaic Ionia, the

Parthenon featured an octastyle (eight-column) arrangement of its narrow ends. This was unusually wide, offering a generous embrace and enough space for an interior arrangement of a U-shaped colonnade and an enormous statue of Athena by the famed sculptor Pheidias. Like all peripteral temples, the encircling colonnade gave the impression that the temple could be approached from all sides. A porch of six columns mediated entry to the cella, and to the *opisthonaos* (rear room) of the building. The porches are unusually shallow. This allowed light into the cella, which otherwise came in through two large windows on either side of the main entrance. In its combination of a well-lit interior and the rational articulation of the interior space with a colonnade, the Parthenon initiates a new interest in the embellishment of interior space.

Compared with the Temple of Hera II at Paestum (see fig. 5.5, right), the Parthenon appears far less massive, despite its greater size. One of the reasons for this is a lightening of proportions since the Archaic period. The columns are more slender, their tapering and entasis less pronounced, and the capitals are less flaring. Practical necessity partly determined the

The preeminent politician of Classical Greece was the Athenian PERIKLES (c. 495–429 BCE; often Latinized to Pericles). During his 33-year ascendancy, from 462 to 429 BCE, Athens became the center of a wealthy empire, a highly progressive democratic society, and a vibrant hub of art and architecture.

5.18 Iktinos and Kallikrates. The Parthenon (view from the west). 447–432 BCE. Akropolis, Athens

diameter of the columns. For convenience and economy, the architects reused many drums from an earlier Parthenon, still unfinished at the time of the Persian sack of Athens. Yet how the columns related to the rest of the building was a matter for new design. Their spacing, for instance, is wider than in earlier buildings. The entablature is lower in relation to their height and to the temple's width, and the cornice projects less. The load carried by the columns seems to have decreased, and as a result the supports appear able to fulfill their task with a new ease.

The governing principle behind the design was a ratio of $9 : 4$ or $2x + 1 : x$. Thus, for instance, the eight (x) columns across the façades are answered by seventeen ($2x + 1$) columns along the sides. Additionally, the ratio of the spacing between each column to the diameter at the lowest point of the column was $9 : 4$. It was not just a matter of design convenience, but an attempt to produce harmony through numerical relationships. The formula was used pervasively throughout the Parthenon, though never dogmatically, always allowing for minor adjustments.

Despite the relative precision that the formula dictated, intentional departures from the geometric regularity of the design were built into the Parthenon (and other temples). For

instance, the columns are not vertical, but lean in toward the cella (the corner columns in two directions). The stepped platform on which the temple rests is not fully horizontal, but bows upward, so that the center of the long sides is about four inches higher than the corners. This curvature is reflected up through the temple's entablature, and every column capital is slightly distorted to fit the bowed architrave. That these irregularities were intentional is beyond doubt, as masons tailor-made individual blocks to accommodate them. Why they were desirable is less clear.

When these irregularities were first introduced into temple architecture, some 100 years earlier, they may have been intended to solve drainage problems. Yet in the Parthenon, they are so exaggerated that scholars consider them to be corrections of optical illusions. For instance, when viewed from a distance, straight horizontals appear to sag, but if the horizontals curve upward, they look straight. When seen close up, a long straight line seems to curve like the horizon; by exaggerating the curve, the architects could make the temple appear even larger than it was. These two apparently contradictory theories could work in tandem, since different optical distortions would prevail depending on a viewer's vantage point. What is certain is that these refinements give the temple a highly dynamic quality. Rather than sitting quietly on its platform, the swelling forms give the building energy, as if it were about to burst out of its own skin; through the refinements, the temple comes alive.

The Parthenon is often viewed as the embodiment of Classical Doric architecture. Although this may be the impression from the outside, it is far from true. At architrave level within the peristyle, a continuous sculpted frieze runs around all sides of the building, in a variation of the Ionic style (see fig. 5.4). Moreover, while most of the temple's columns are Doric, four tall, slender columns in the rear room were Ionic. Even if Doric is the dominant style, Ionic is clearly present, for a reason that may have had as much to do with politics as with design. In pre-Classical times, the only Ionic structures on the Greek mainland had been small treasuries built by eastern Greek states at Delphi in their regional styles, such as the Siphnian Treasury. When Athenian architects used the Ionic style, Perikles may have been making a deliberate symbolic gesture, attempting to unite the disparate regions of Greece in an international style.

THE PARTHENON SCULPTURES The largest group of surviving Classical sculptures comes from the Parthenon, which had a more extensive decorative program than any previous temple. The sculptures have a vivid and often unfortunate

history. The temple was converted into a church, probably in the sixth century CE, and much of the decoration on the east side was destroyed or vandalized. In 1687, Venetian cannon fire ignited ammunition stored by Turkish forces in the temple. The west pediment figures survived the explosion, but not the war's aftermath. A crane used to remove the sculptures, so that the Venetian commander could take them back to Venice, dropped the figures, shattering them. Over 100 years later, Lord Elgin, British ambassador to Constantinople, bought and removed what he could of the temple's decoration and shipped it to England. In 1816, needing money, he sold the figures to an ambivalent British Museum, where the Elgin Marbles, as they are known, are housed today. They stand at the heart of a heated debate on the repatriation of national treasures. Other fragments of the Parthenon's sculptural decoration are on display in museums throughout Europe.

Thirteen years before the explosion in the Parthenon, an artist named Jacques Carrey executed drawings of the surviving sculptures, which have become invaluable resources for understanding the decorative program. Primarily from these drawings and from literary sources, we know that the west pediment portrayed the divine struggle between Athena and Poseidon for Athens. The east pediment represented the birth of Athena from the head of Zeus, in the presence of other deities. The

5.19 *Three Goddesses*, from the east pediment of the Parthenon. ca. 438–432 BCE. Marble, over life-size. The British Museum, London

pediment figures are strikingly impressive. Like the architecture into which they are embedded, their forms are strong and solid, yet their implied power contrasts with their languid poses and gains strength from the contrast. A closely knit group of three female deities, usually identified as Hestia, Dione, and Aphrodite (**fig. 5.19**), is a masterpiece of swirling drapery, which disguises the sheer bulk of the marble. The garments cling to their bodies as if wet, both concealing and revealing them. Yet the drapery does not follow the lines of the body so much as struggle with them, twisting around the legs in massive folds. The effect is extraordinary: Although a viewer can see the deities only from a frontal vantage point, as if the figures were two-dimensional, the curves of the deeply cut folds echo their forms in section (i.e., along a plane made by an imaginary vertical slice from front to back), and thereby broadcast their three-dimensionality. The sculptor could better express nature through the appearance of truth than through truth itself.

This optical device is a sculptural equivalent of the deliberate distortions in the temple's architecture.

The pediments and metopes were visible from a distance, but to see the frieze, a viewer had to come closer and walk parallel to the building. In a continuous sculpted band, some 525 feet long, the frieze depicts a procession, moving from west to east, propelling the viewer around the building. Horsemen jostle with musicians, water carriers, and sacrificial beasts, overlapping to create the illusion of a crowd, even though the relief is only inches deep. Frenzied animals emphasize the calm demeanor of the figures (**fig. 5.20**), who have the ideal proportions of the *Doryphoros*. According to the traditional view, the frieze depicts the Panathenaic procession, part of the annual festival celebrated on a grander scale every four years. The figures and their groupings are typical of the participants in these processions, and the frieze represents an idealized event, rather than a specific moment. Some

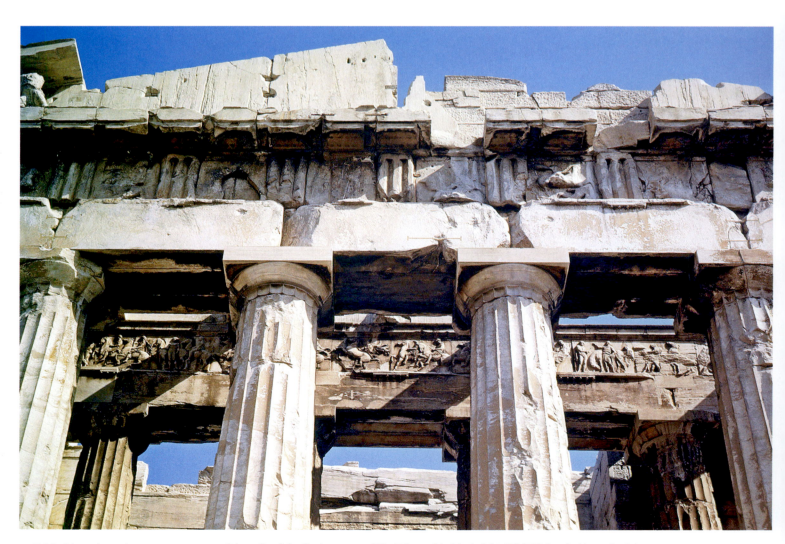

5.20 Frieze above the western entrance of the cella of the Parthenon. ca. 440–432 BCE. Marble, height 43″ (109.3 cm). Akropolis, Athens

5.21 Mnesikles. The Propylaea (view from the west), 437–432 BCE. Akropolis, Athens

scholars have suggested that this "heroicized" representation honors the 192 Athenians slain at the Battle of Marathon, on the basis that the frieze may originally have had a like number of equestrian figures. If this view is correct and the frieze represents the Panathenaic procession, it is remarkable in that it exalts mortal Athenians by depicting them in a space usually reserved for divine and mythological scenes.

THE PROPYLAEA During the year that the Parthenon was dedicated, 437 BCE, Perikles commissioned another costly project: The monumental gate at the western end of the Akropolis, called the Propylaea (see fig. 5.17). Mnesikles was the architect in charge, and he completed the main section in five years; the remainder was abandoned with the onset of the PELO-PONNESIAN WAR. The entire structure was built of marble and included refinements similar to those used in the Parthenon. Mnesikles ably

adapted elements of a Doric temple to a totally different task, and to an irregular and steeply rising site. Conceived on two levels, the design transforms a rough passage among rocks into a magnificent entrance to the sacred precinct. Only the eastern porch (or façade) is in fair condition today. It resembles a Classical Doric temple front, except for the wide opening between the third and fourth columns, which allowed traffic to pass onto the Akropolis; this feature appears often in Ionian architecture. Flanking the western porch (**fig. 5.21**) were two wings, of unequal size because of constraints imposed by the terrain. The larger one to the north contained a picture gallery (*pinakotheke*), the first known instance of a public room specially designed for the display of paintings. Placed along the central passageway through the Propylaea were two rows of slender Ionic columns, echoing the Ionic columns in the Parthenon.

By the end of the fifth century BCE, Athens' supremacy was on the wane. Conflict between Athens and the Peloponnesian cities of Corinth and Sparta had begun in about 460 BCE, and gradually escalated into the great PELOPONNESIAN WAR of 431–404 BCE, which Athens lost. During the fourth century, the Greek city-states were constantly at odds with one another.

The Late Classical Period

By the end of the fifth century BCE, Athens' supremacy was on the wane. The Peloponnesian War of 431–404 BCE had taken its toll, and during the fourth century the Greek city-states were constantly at odds with one another. In 338 BCE, Philip II, who had acceded to power in the kingdom of Macedon, to the north, exploited Greek disunity by invading Greece, and decisively defeated the Athenians and Thebans at the Battle of Chaironeia in central Greece.

Late Classical Architecture: Civic and Sacred

Two noteworthy changes in monumental architecture occurred in the late fifth and fourth centuries. One was a shift in emphasis: As well as constructing temples, architects explored a wide range of building types. Many of these types—stoas (colonnaded porticoes), meeting houses for the governing council, and the like—had long existed, but now took on grander form. Theaters, for instance, became more formalized. They had long been part of the religious landscape of Greek cities, since choral performances and, later, plays were central to sacred festivals of Dionysos. The basic prerequisites for a theater were a hillside, on which an audience could sit (the *cavea*), and a level area for the performance (the *orchestra*).

THE THEATER AT EPIDAUROS These essentials gradually took on architectural form, leading to the magnificent stone theater in the sanctuary of the healing god Asklepios at Epidauros (**fig. 5.22**). The theater was constructed in the early third century BCE, and the upper tier was not completed until the second century. Row upon row of stone seats lined the sloping hillside, covering slightly more than a semicircle. To facilitate circulation, seats were grouped in wedgelike sections (*cunei*), separated by staircases; a wide horizontal corridor divides the upper and lower sections. Performances took place in the level circle at the center, behind which a stage building (*skene*) served as a backdrop and contained utility rooms for storage and dressing. This form is familiar to theatergoers even today, a testament to its success. Because it was open to the sky, no roof supports obstructed viewing of the performance, and many of the seats offered spectacular

5.22 Theater at Epidauros. Early third to second centuries BCE

views across the landscape. Yet perhaps the most astonishing feature of the theater is its extraordinary acoustics, which can still be experienced: Its funnel shape carries the slightest whisper audibly up to the highest points of the auditorium.

THE MAUSOLEUM AT HALIKARNASSOS In Halikarnassos (present-day Bodrum, in southwest Turkey; see map 5.1), this tendency toward monumentalization resulted in a vast tomb built for King Mausolos by his wife and sister Artemisia. Mausolos ruled Caria from 377 to 353 BCE as *satrap* (governor) for the Persians. Such was the renown of this sepulcher in antiquity that it was counted among the seven wonders of the ancient world, and by Roman imperial times its title, the Mausoleum, had become the term used to describe any monumental tomb. Designed by Pytheos of Priene, the tomb stood reasonably intact until the thirteenth century CE, when an earthquake brought down the upper sections. In the late fifteenth and early sixteenth centuries, the Knights of St. John used the remains as a source of stone to refortify their castle. Still later, in 1857, the British archaeologist Charles Newton removed many sculptural fragments to the British Museum. Danish excavations continue to yield information at the site. Coupled with literary evidence, archaeological data permits reconstructions, though none has met with universal approval. One hypothesis appears in **fig. 5.23**. The tomb was rectangular in plan, and soared 140 feet high in at least three sections, covered with sculpture: A high podium, an Ionic colonnade, and a pyramidal roof, where steps climbed to a platform supporting a statue of Mausolos or one of his ancestors in a chariot.

The grouping of these elements within a single monument is further evidence of a growing diversity in architecture. They may also have had a propagandistic function. The Mausoleum celebrated Mausolos as hero-founder of Halikarnassos. It combined the monumental tomb-building tradition of this region, Lycia, with a Greek peristyle and sculpture, and an Egyptian pyramid. It may therefore have expressed Carian supremacy in the region and the symbiosis of Greek and non-Greek civilizations that might be achieved through the founding of an empire headed by Halikarnassos.

CORINTHIAN CAPITAL The other major change in architecture that took place in the late fifth century BCE was the development of the

5.23 Reconstruction drawing of the Mausoleum at Halikarnassos. ca. 359–351 BCE (from H. Colvin)

CORINTHIAN capital as an elaborate substitute for the Ionic. VITRUVIUS ascribed its invention to the metalworker Kallimachos. Its shape is an inverted bell covered with the shoots and leaves of an acanthus plant, which seem to sprout from the top of the column shaft. At first, Corinthian capitals were used only in temple interiors, perhaps because of the conservative nature of Greek architecture, or because of the perceived sanctity of its vegetal forms. It was not until the second century BCE that Corinthian columns appeared on the exteriors of buildings.

Late Classical Sculpture

The classical style associated with Pheidias, with its apparent confidence in the transcendence of the Athenian city-state, did not survive the devastating defeat of Athens in the Peloponnesian War. At the end of the fifth century, a shift in mood is visible in sculpture, which seems to reflect a new—and less optimistic—view of man's place in the universe.

Scholars have attempted to match surviving sculptures with several of the fourth-century sculptors named in literary sources. Among

Marcus VITRUVIUS Pollio (active 46–27 BCE) was a Roman architect, whose lasting fame rests on the fact that his ten-book treatise on classical architecture, *De architectura*, is the only such work to survive from antiquity. Based heavily on Greek architectural treatises, it is our most important written source of information about Greek architecture. From the fifteenth century to the present, architects have pored over translations of Vitruvius to learn about classical principles of proportion, the Greek styles, and other matters of architectural theory and practice—often interpreting them with wide latitude. Our readings of his text have been mediated through early modern commentators and illustrators, who wrote of Doric and Ionic "orders" rather than "types," which is a better translation of Vitruvius' "*genera*." The distinction is important: "Order" suggests an immutable quality, a rigid building code, when in fact we find a subtle but rich variation in surviving Greek architecture.

corona
dentils
cornice
frieze
architrave
entablature
abacus
acanthus
astragal
capital
shaft
column
base

them was Skopas of Paros, one of four masters chosen to work on the Mausoleum of Halikarnassos, according to PLINY THE ELDER. He is best known for the way he infused emotion into the faces of those he depicted. A fragmentary head of Herakles or his son Telephos from a pediment of the Temple of Athena Alea at Tegea of about 340 BCE is either by Skopas, or an artist deeply influenced by his work (**fig. 5.24**). The smooth planes and fleshy treatment of the face are characteristic of Classical art. What is new is how the sculptor cuts the marble away sharply over the eyes toward the bridge of the nose to create a dark shadow. At the outer edge, the eyelid bulges out to overhang the eye. This simple change charges the face with a depth of emotion not seen before, enhanced by the slightly parted lips and the sharp turn of the head.

PRAXITELES If the Greeks were less confident of their place in the late Classical period, they were also less certain of their relationship to fate and the gods. This is reflected in the work of Praxiteles, working at roughly the same time as Skopas. He executed a number of marble statues of divinities. Where fifth-century artists had stressed the gods' majesty, Praxiteles gave them a

5.24 *Head of Herakles* or *Telephos*, from the west pediment of the Temple of Athena Alea, Tegea. ca. 340 BCE. Marble, height 1′½″ (31.75 cm). Stolen from the Archaeological Museum, Tegea, Greece

youthful sensuousness that might, perhaps, suggest their wilful capriciousness toward humans. Most famous is his sculpture of Aphrodite, of about 340–330 BCE (**fig. 5.25**). Pliny records that the people of Kos commissioned a nude statue of Aphrodite from Praxiteles, but rejected it in favor of a draped version. The inhabitants of Knidos purchased the nude statue, and profited from the risk: Visitors came from far and wide to see her. Perhaps it was her nudity that drew so much attention: She was the first nude monumental statue of a goddess in the Greek world. Yet even if artists had previously reserved female nudity principally for representations of slaves or courtesans, the clinging drapery of the fifth century had exposed almost as much of the female anatomy as it concealed. Her appeal may have resided just as much in the blatant eroticism of her image. Aphrodite is seen as she is about to bathe or as she is rising from her bath. With her right hand, she covers her genitals in a gesture of modesty, while grasping for a robe with her left. Her head is slightly turned, so she does not engage a viewer's gaze directly, but a viewer is made complicit with the sculpture, willingly or not, by having inappropriately witnessed the goddess in her nudity. Perhaps, in her capriciousness, Aphrodite intended to be surprised as she bathed; the uncertainty for a viewer augments the erotic quality of the image. By some accounts, the Knidians displayed Praxiteles' sculpture in a circular shrine with entrances at front and back, so that visitors could view her from all sides.

The Age of Alexander and the Hellenistic Period

In 336 BCE, Philip II of Macedon died, and his kingdom passed to his son ALEXANDER THE GREAT. He embarked upon a great campaign of conquest, conquering Egypt and the Persians before continuing to Mesopotamia, and into present-day Afghanistan. He died young in 323 BCE, having founded over 70 cities. His conquests dramatically changed the face of the Greek world, expanding it into unknown areas and creating new political alignments. The years following his death were fraught with struggles among members of his family and his generals, as each tried to establish himself as Alexander's successor. By about 275 BCE, Alexander's lands had coalesced into three main kingdoms, which dominated the Mediterranean until the Romans

5.25 *Aphrodite of Knidos.* Roman copy after an original of ca. 340–330 BCE by Praxiteles. Marble, height 6′8″ (2 m). Musei Vaticani, Rome

Philip II (382–336 BCE), king of
Macedon—modern Macedonia—
was a military genius who, by the
time of his assassination, had
humbled the major powers of
mainland Greece and had cajoled
all the Greek states except Sparta
into an anti-Persian alliance. His
son, ALEXANDER THE GREAT
(356–323 BCE), was already an
accomplished general at the age of
18 and succeeded his father two
years later. He invaded Persia in
334 and within ten years created
an empire that stretched to the
Indus Valley. He founded many
cities in the conquered territories
that all bore his own name. He
died suddenly in his capital,
Babylon, when he was just 33.
His empire disintegrated into
several independent kingdoms
after his death.

gradually assumed control. Ptolemy founded a dynasty in Egypt that reigned until Octavian, later the Roman emperor Augustus, defeated Cleopatra VII in 31 BCE. In the east, the Seleucids captured Babylon in 312 BCE. From Syria they ruled a kingdom which, at its largest, extended from present-day western Turkey to Afghanistan. They lost control of a small pocket of territory around Pergamon to the Attalids, who bequeathed their city to the Romans in 133 BCE. In 64 BCE, the Seleucid kingdom came under Roman control. Most coveted was Alexander's ancestral Macedon, controlled by the Antigonids from 276 BCE until the Roman conquest in 168 BCE. Within these kingdoms, powerful cities grew—among them, Alexandria and Pergamon—with teeming populations drawn from all over the new Greek world. They vied for cultural preeminence, and art played a large part in the rivalry. Hellenistic culture was dramatically different from that of Classical times. The expansion of Greek dominance meant that Greek cultural institutions prevailed over a vast territory; yet those institutions commingled with the strong cultural traditions of the indigenous peoples to create a rich and diverse society.

Architecture: The Scholarly Tradition and Theatricality

Within the cultural centers of the Hellenistic world, academies emerged, fostering avid debate among scholars in many fields. They engaged, among other things, in a close analysis of the arts, and developed canons by which they could judge works of literature, art, and architecture. In architecture this led, predictably, to a heightened interest in systems of proportions, recorded in architectural treatises. Vitruvius asserts that a leading protagonist in this

movement was Pytheos (**fig. 5.26**), one of the architects of the Mausoleum of Halikarnassos (see fig. 5.22). Pytheos worked in the Ionic style, as seen in his temple to Athena at Priene, dedicated in 334 BCE. The temple's colonnade had six columns by 11 and a grid of squares, each six by six feet, that dictated the proportions of all of its elements. Proportions controlled the elevation as well: For instance, the columns were 43 feet high and the entablature was seven feet high—for a total of 50 feet, half the external length of the cella. Unlike the Parthenon and elsewhere, here there were no deviations from the rule, and no refinements. The temple is a work of the intellect, the product of a didactic tradition, rather than a compromise between theory and practice. In fact, Vitruvius faults Pytheos precisely for his inability to differentiate between the two.

While this scholarly tradition flourished, the relaxation of architectural guidelines and the combination of architectural types from the late Classical period heralded another development. This was a new penchant for dramatic siting, impressive vistas, and surprise revelations. Scholars have termed this movement theatricality, and it balanced and complemented the scholarly tradition. As the glory of Athens declined, the Athenians and other Greeks came to think of themselves less as members of a city-state and more as individuals; architecture, in turn, began to cater more and more to a personal experience, often manipulating visitors toward a meaningful revelation.

THE TEMPLE OF APOLLO AT DIDYMA Begun in about 300 BCE and still unfinished by the end of the Roman period, the Temple of Apollo at Didyma is a good example of architectural

5.26 Pytheos. Plan of the Temple of Athena. 334 BCE. Priene, Turkey

5.27 Paionios of Ephesos and Daphnis of Miletos. Temple of Apollo. Begun 313 BCE. Didyma, Turkey

theatricality (**figs. 5.27** and **5.28**). The huge temple was built on the site and to the scale of an Archaic temple destroyed by the Persians in 494 BCE. Its ground plan and design appear to have been established by the renowned Hellenistic architects Paionios of Ephesos and Daphnis of Miletos.

The temple stood in a grove of sacred trees and from the outside appeared similar to other large-scale Ionic buildings. A visitor would expect the temple's interior to repeat the format of canonical Greek temples such as the Parthenon, but, in fact, the architects constantly defied these expectations, as visitors were led to dramatic vistas, perhaps intended to heighten the religious experience.

5.28 Plan of Temple of Apollo by Paionios of Ephesos and Daphnis of Miletos. Begun 313 BCE. Didyma, Turkey

Placed on a high stylobate, seven massive steps above ground level, the temple was surrounded by two rows of tall columns. Although it appeared to be accessible from all sides, the steps were too high for comfortable climbing. Instead, visitors used a set of shallower steps at the front, entering the porch through vast columns, designed to mimic the surrounding forest of trees. As expected, an opening led to the cella, but this cella stood approximately five feet off the ground, making access impossible. On this platform, scholars believe, the oracular priestess uttered prophecies to those standing below in the porch. Those wishing to enter further into the building moved to the right or left of this elevated opening, where dark barrel-vaulted tunnels led downward. For a Greek visitor, a barrel-vaulted tunnel suggested a cave, or a dark interior, yet these passages led to a vast open courtyard drenched with sunshine: A revelation, it must have seemed, after the confinement of the tunnels.

At the end of this courtyard was the shrine itself, a small and simple Ionic building dedicated to Apollo. Turning back from the shrine, the visitor faced a wide, steep staircase leading up to a pair of towering engaged (i.e., partly merged with the wall) Corinthian columns. These may have signaled that the room beyond them was the innermost sanctuary of the priestess. Little is known of the proceedings inside Greek temples, yet the processional quality of this inner staircase and the large scale of the courtyard suggest that large crowds of worshipers may have gathered there to witness rituals. Also unknown is the function of the small staircases leading off from the sanctuary and up to the roof that covered the colonnades. Building inscriptions describe them as "labyrinths," and their ceiling is carved with a painted meander pattern, the Egyptian hieroglyph for a maze. Maintenance needs may explain their existence, but a role in a revelatory drama in honor of Apollo could do so just as well. As a whole, the temple manipulated visitors along unexpected paths, and offered constant surprises. This theatricality was a feature of a number of other buildings of this time.

The Temple of Apollo is remarkable for another reason besides the surprise experience it offered. Inside the courtyard under a strong raking light, archaeologists unexpectedly discovered diagrams incised (so lightly that they were barely visible) upon its walls. These etchings revealed scale drawings of the building's design, ranging from capital decoration to column entasis. They provide a rare insight into the design process in Greek building, which is otherwise poorly understood. The diagrams suggest that a building's design was drawn onto its existing surfaces as it rose, and then polished off as those surfaces were finished. This temple's chance incompletion preserved the design drawings in place.

Hellenistic Sculpture: Expression and Movement

Fourth-century sculptors had led the way in expressing emotion and exploring three-dimensional movement, and Hellenistic artists made further strides in these directions. Both result in heightened drama and viewer involvement. That said, one can make only broad generalizations about Hellenistic sculpture, as it is notoriously difficult to date and to attribute to a firm place of origin.

PORTRAITURE A chief development at this point was portraiture. One of the catalysts for this change was Alexander the Great himself. Recognizing the power of a consistent visual image, he retained the great fourth-century artist Lysippos as exclusive sculptor of his portraits. No surviving original preserves Lysippos' touch, but scholars consider the so-called "Azara herm" to be relatively faithful to its model (**fig. 5.29**). To be sure, the face has an idealized quality: Its planes are smooth, especially around the brow. Yet individuality comes through in the unruly hair, raised at the front in Alexander's characteristic cowlick (or *anastole*), and in the twist of the head, which takes the portrait out of a timeless realm and animates it with action. Moreover, the general does not engage with a viewer, but has a distant gaze. These characteristics would come to be emblematic of Alexander, and Hellenistic and Roman generals would adopt them as attributes in their own portraiture. With this portrait, the individual comes to inhabit the sculpture.

Like architects, Hellenistic sculptors engaged the audience in the experience of their work, and favored dramatic subjects infused with emotion. The *Dying Trumpeter*, preserved in a Roman copy, is an early example (**fig. 5.30**). The sculpture probably belonged on one of two statue bases found in the Sanctuary of Athena on the Akropolis of Pergamon, and it commemorated Attalos I's defeat of the Gauls (a CELTIC people) in about 233 BCE. Gone is the Classical tradition of referring to the enemy through mythological analogy. Instead, the sculptor identifies the

The CELTIC tribes first appeared in the second millennium BCE in southwestern Germany and eastern France (called Gaul by the Romans), and eventually ranged over a wide territory. They spoke Indo-European dialects, were skilled in the art of smelting iron, and raided and conquered other peoples in Europe and Asia Minor well into the third century BCE. They dominated Iron Age culture in Europe until displaced by the Germans in the east and subdued by the Romans in the west. Greek and Roman writers noted that Celtic warriors were tall, light-skinned, well muscled, and ferocious; the front ranks often fought naked (see fig. 5.30).

enemy as a Gaul through his bushy hair and moustache, and by the torque, or braided gold band, that he wears around his neck. Gone, too, is any suggestion of the inferiority of the vanquished. The Gaul dies nobly, sinking to the ground or struggling to prop himself up, as blood pours from a wound in his chest. His body is powerful, his strength palpable. He faces his agonies alone, mindless of any viewer. A viewer, in turn, is drawn in by the privateness of the moment, and drawn around the sculpture by the pyramidal composition and the foreshortening witnessed from every angle. The *Dying Trumpeter* was probably one sculpture in a group, but the victor, always present in Classical battle scenes, was absent. The monument celebrates the conqueror's valor by exalting the enemy he overcame; the greater the enemy, the greater the victory. Pliny records a famous sculpture by Epigonos of a trumpet player, and this Roman copy may reflect that work.

5.29 Lysippos. *Portrait of Alexander the Great*, the "Azara herm." Marble, height 27″ (68 cm). Roman copy after an original of the late fourth century BCE. Musée du Louvre, Paris

5.30 Epigonos of Pergamon (?). *Dying Trumpeter*. Perhaps a Roman copy after a bronze original of ca. 230–220 BCE, from Pergamon, Turkey. Marble, life-size. Museo Capitolino, Rome

DRAMATIC VICTORY MONUMENTS Sculptures decorating the Great Altar of Zeus at Pergamon exemplify the highly emotional, dramatic style at its height (**figs. 5.31** and **5.32**). The monument dates to about 180 BCE, when Eumenes II built it on a terrace on the Pergamene Akropolis to commemorate territorial victories over Pontos and Bithynia and the establishment of a grand victory festival, the *Nikephoria*. The altar stood high on a podium within a large enclosure surrounded by an Ionic colonnade, approached by a wide staircase; it has now been reconstructed in Berlin. The enclosure's boldest feature is a frieze encircling the base, which extends over 400 feet in length and is over seven feet in height. Its subject, the battle of the gods and giants, was a frequently used theme in architectural sculpture. Here, as before, it worked allegorically, symbolizing Eumenes' victories. Never before, however, had the subject been treated so extensively or so dramatically. About 84 figures crowd the composition, interspersed with animals. This was no mean feat: The sculptors must have relied upon research by scholars working in the Pergamene library to identify protagonists for this great battle. They may also have assisted with creating a balanced and meaningful composition, for

despite the chaotic appearance of the mêlée, guiding principles lurk behind it. Scholars struggle to understand the principles fully, even though inscriptions preserve some of the gods' names above the frieze and the giants' names beneath. On the eastern frieze, facing the sanctuary's Propylon and the rising sun, were the Olympian gods, with Athena, patron goddess of Pergamon, positioned most prominently. On the south, in full sunlight, were heavenly beings such as Helios; on the shadowy north were divinities of the night. Deities of the earth and sea were on the west. Compositional parallels unified the four sides. The frieze is direct evidence of the Hellenistic scholarly tradition at work.

On the other hand, the frieze is deeply imbued with Hellenistic theatricality. The figures are carved so deeply, and in places so forcefully undercut, that they are almost in the round. On the staircase, they seem to spill out onto the steps and climb alongside an ascending visitor. The high relief creates a vivid interplay of light and dark. Muscular bodies rush at each other, overlapping and entwined (see fig. 5.30). The giants' snaky extremities twist and curl, echoed in their deeply drilled tendrils of ropelike hair. Wings beat and garments blow furiously in the

5.31 The west front of the Great Altar of Zeus at Pergamon (restored). ca. 180 BCE. Marble, height 31′8⅓″ (9.66 m). Staatliche Museen zu Berlin, Preussischer Kulturbesitz, Antikensammlung

5.32 *Athena and Alkyoneus*, from the east side of the Great Frieze of the Great Altar of Zeus at Pergamon. ca. 180 BCE. Marble, height 7′6″ (2.29 m). Staatliche Museen zu Berlin, Preussischer Kulturbesitz, Antikensammlung

wind or twist and wind around those they clothe, not to reveal the anatomy beneath but to create motion; both have a life of their own and a texture that contrasts with the smoothness of the giants' flesh. The giants agonize in the torment of their defeat, their brows creased in pain, their eyes deepset in an exaggerated style reminiscent of Skopas. A writhing motion pervades the entire design, and links the figures in a single continuous rhythm. This rhythm, and the quiet classicism of the gods' faces, so starkly opposed to those of the giants, create a unity that keeps the violence of the struggle from exploding its architectural frame—but only just. For the first time in the long tradition of its depiction, a viewer has a visceral sense of what an awesome cosmic crisis this battle would be.

HELLENISTIC REALISM Scholars use the term "baroque" to describe the extreme emotions and extravagant gestures that characterize the Great Altar of Zeus. The term was first used to describe seventeenth-century CE art, and scholars of Hellenistic art borrowed it on recognizing similarities between the two styles. With its extraordinarily dramatic qualities, the Hellenistic baroque style has tended to eclipse the many other contemporary movements in sculpture. One of these other movements is a penchant for works depicting unidealized and realistic everyday life. Their genre is known as Hellenistic realism, and a sculpture of a drunken old woman illustrates it well (**fig. 5.33**). Known from Roman copies, this piece has at times been ascribed to Myron of Thebes, who may have worked at Pergamon. The evidence is slim, and the figure may be a better fit with the cultural context of Alexandria, where realism seems to have been particularly prevalent. The woman is crouched on the ground, clasping a wine bottle, her head

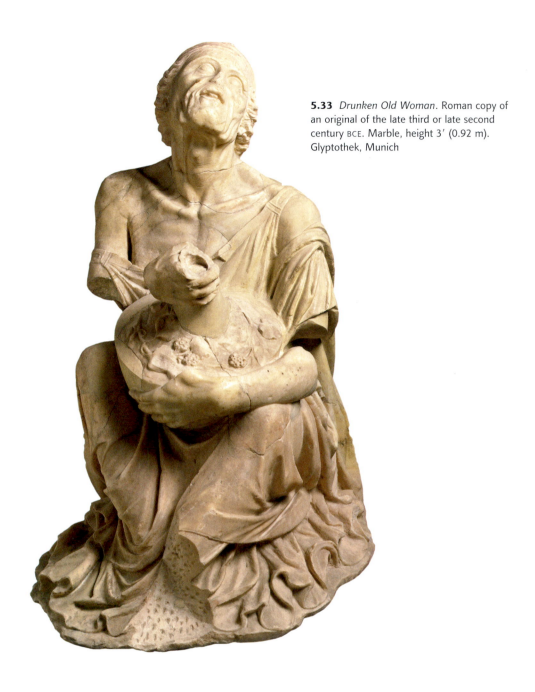

5.33 *Drunken Old Woman*. Roman copy of an original of the late third or late second century BCE. Marble, height 3′ (0.92 m). Glyptothek, Munich

flung far back. Wrinkles cover her face, and the skin on her exposed shoulder and chest sags with age. Her garment flows around her, forming a solid pyramid out of which she seems to rise. She wears a buckled tunic, which identifies her as a member of an affluent social class. Other sculptures of this kind focus on the ravaging effects of a rustic life on the poor—an old shepherdess, for instance; yet in this sculpture, the artist explores drunkenness and old age. Without further insights into the cultural context for the image, it is hard to know if the sculptor intended to offer a sympathetic view of his subject, exalting her nobility, or to engage in a hard social commentary.

Hellenistic Painting

It was in the fourth century BCE that Greek wall painting came into its own. Pliny names a number of leading artists, but no surviving painting can be attributed to them in confirmation. All the same, paintings are preserved in Macedonian tombs, several of which have come to light; more are regularly discovered in northern Greece (in the region of Macedonia). They offer a tantalizing glimpse of what painters could accomplish. Discovered recently, in 1976, these tombs are of great importance because they contain the only relatively complete Greek wall paintings to have been found. The section shown here illustrates the abduction of Persephone (**fig. 5.34**), and comes from a small tomb at Vergina, dating to about 340–330 BCE. The subject is appropriate to the funereal setting. Pluto, ruler of the underworld, abducts Persephone to be his queen. Thanks to Zeus' intervention, Persephone would be allowed to return to the world of the living for six months of every year. Here, the artist has chosen the moment when Pluto seizes Persephone and pulls her into his speeding chariot, her handmaiden rearing back in fright and horror. This is the dramatic moment, before Persephone knows that Zeus will find a compromise, when her futile struggle seems the only possible escape from the underworld. The painting captures all of the drama of the myth. Persephone flings her body backward, while the chariot rushes onward with her captor; their bodies cross as a sign of their conflict. The chariot plunges toward a viewer, its wheel sharply foreshortened. Masterful brushwork animates the scene. With swift flourishes, the artist sends hair and drapery flying, and lends plasticity to the figures' garments. Hatchwork rounds out the bodies' flesh, as on the arms and shoulders. The colors are brilliant washes, with shading for texture. Literary sources attribute the discovery of shading (the modulation of volume by means of contrasting light and shade), known as *skiagraphia*, to a painter named Apollodorus, who was using the technique perhaps as early as the fifth century BCE. They also associate spatial perspective with Agatharchos, creator of stage scenery during the heyday of Athenian drama. The exploration and perfection of both devices during the course of the fourth century illustrate the fascination with illusionism at this time.

Roman copies and imitations also provide a sense of what Greek wall painting might have

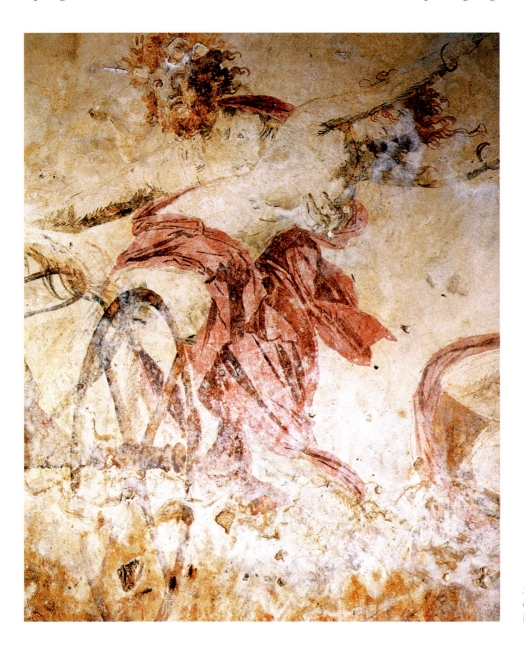

5.34 *The Abduction of Persephone.* ca. 340–330 BCE Detail of a wall painting in Tomb I, Vergina, Macedonia

5.35 *The Battle of Issos* or *Battle of Alexander and the Persians*. Mosaic copy from Pompeii, ca. 100 BCE, of a Hellenistic painting of ca. 315 BCE. 8'11" × 16'9½" (2.7 × 5.1 m). Museo Archeologico Nazionale, Naples

looked like. According to Pliny, at the end of the fourth century BCE, Philoxenos of Eretria painted Alexander the Great's victory over Darius III at Issos. This subject is shown in an exceptionally masterful floor mosaic from a Pompeian house of about 100 BCE (**fig. 5.35**). The scene depicts Darius and the fleeing Persians on the right and, in the badly damaged left-hand portion, the figure of Alexander. It is likely that this is a close copy of a Hellenistic painting from the late fourth century BCE. The picture follows the four-color scheme (yellow, red, black, and white) that is known to have been widely used at that time. The crowding, the air of frantic excitement, the powerfully modeled and foreshortened forms, and the precise shadows place the scene in the fourth century, as does the minimal treatment of landscape, suggested by a single barren tree to the left of center.

SUMMARY

Greek culture emerged by about the eighth century BCE. Centered in mainland Greece, the Aegean Islands, and Crete—and extending into southern Italy, northern Africa, and coastal Asia Minor—the Greeks were united by a shared language and common beliefs. The first known practitioners of analytical thought, they struggled with philosophical questions that endure today. Throughout more than seven centuries, wars, trade, and travel continually shaped Greek culture and art.

About the eighth century BCE, the Greeks began developing a repertoire of pottery forms and painted decoration in the oldest known Greek style: Geometric. Characteristic rectilinear meanders and geometric patterns cover the *Dipylon Vase*, and images of animals and humans add a narrative quality.

Between 725 and 650 BCE, Greek city-states grew prosperous, and sought luxury commodities from trade partners. Artists assimilated Eastern influences, experimenting with new techniques and developing an Orientalizing style.

As democracy emerged in Athens, the great traditions of monumental stone sculpture and temple architecture appeared. Sculptors and builders experimented with proportional systems and adorned structures with larger than life-size figures. The Temples of Hera at Paestum and the Temple of Artemis at Ephesos show the development of the Doric and Ionic styles, and large-scale sculpture enlivened the Temple of Aphaia. Increasingly naturalistic and free-standing figures are testaments to a preoccupation with ideals of physical perfection and freedom of movement. Vase painting saw the development of the black-figured and red-figured techniques.

Out of the destruction of the fifth-century Persian War, Athens rebuilt itself into a political and economic empire. Under the statesman Perikles, the arts flourished. Sculptors made great strides in the naturalistic representation of the human form, seen in the *contrapposto* stance of the *Kritios Boy*. The brilliance of the Parthenon, on the sacred Akropolis, reflects the splendor of the Classical city, with its refined proportions and extraordinary sculpture.

Noteworthy during the period following the invasion of Greece by Philip II of Macedon in 338 BCE was the elaboration of a wider range of existing architectural types, and the development of the Corinthian capital. Sculpture reflects the uncertain mood of the age. The works of Praxiteles convey the capriciousness of the gods toward humans.

The vast kingdom Alexander took control of in 336 BCE expanded Greek influence. Rivalries after his death in 323 BCE resulted in three kingdoms, each with powerful cities and diverse societies. With the dissolution of city-states, Greeks increasingly saw themselves as individuals, and the arts reflect this.

Building designs, such as the Temple of Apollo at Didyma, offered a more personal experience via unexpected paths, breathtaking panoramas, and dramatic theatricality. Hellenistic sculpture and painting also favored heightened drama and increased viewer involvement, with emotional subjects and dramatic realism.

ART IN TIME

- ca. eighth century BCE—Homer writes *The Iliad* and *The Odyssey*

- ca. 750 BCE *Dipylon Vase*

- mid-seventh century BCE—Black-figured vase-painting technique develops

- ca. 650 BCE—Greeks establish trading posts in Egypt

- seventh century BCE—Doric and Ionic styles develop

- ca. 500 BCE—Red-figured vase-painting technique becomes popular

- 490 BCE—Greeks defeat the Persians at the Battle of Marathon

- ca. 480 BCE—*Kritios Boy*

- ca. 447 BCE—Perikles orders construction of Parthenon

- 431–404 BCE—Peloponnesian War

- 387 BCE—Plato founds the Academy in Athens

- 336–323 BCE—Reign of Alexander the Great

- ca. 300 BCE—Construction begins on the Temple of Apollo, Didyma

*E*arly Etruscan culture, known as Villanovan, appeared on the Italian peninsula in the tenth century BCE. Who the Etruscans were remains a mystery; even in antiquity, writers disputed their origins. The Greek historian Herodotus believed that they had left their homeland of Lydia in Asia Minor in about 1200 BCE, and settled in what are now the Italian regions of Tuscany, Umbria, and Lazio (see map 6.1). Recent DNA sampling may support his view. Others claimed they were indigenous. Wherever they came from, the Etruscans had strong cultural links with Asia Minor and the ancient Near East. In fact, their visual culture is a rich blend of distinctly Etruscan traits with influences from the east and from Greece. They were sailors and merchants who traveled throughout the Mediterranean, amassing wealth from the mining of metals, and since from the eighth century BCE Greek city-states had established colonies in Italy, contact between the two cultures was inevitable. Toward the end of the eighth century they began to use the Greek alphabet, and this makes it possible to read their inscriptions, which survive in the thousands; but since their language is unrelated to any other, we cannot always understand them.

Periods of Etruscan Art

ca. 700–600 BCE	Orientalizing Period
ca. 600–480 BCE	Archaic Period
ca. 480–300 BCE	Classical Period
ca. 300 BCE	Etruscan culture is slowly absorbed into Roman culture

The Etruscans reached the height of their power in the seventh and sixth centuries BCE, coinciding with the Archaic age in Greece. Their cities rivaled those of the Greeks; their fleet dominated the western Mediterranean and protected a vast commercial network that competed with the Greeks and Phoenicians; and their territory extended from the lower Po River Valley as far as Naples. But, like the Greeks, the Etruscans never formed a unified nation. They remained a loose federation of individual city-states, united by a common language and religion, but given to conflict and slow to unite against a common enemy. This may have been one cause of their gradual downfall. In 474 BCE, the Etruscan fleet was defeated by the navy of its archrival, Syracuse.

And during the later fifth and fourth centuries BCE, one Etruscan city after another fell to the Romans. By 270 BCE, all the Etruscan city-states had lost their independence to Rome, although many continued to prosper, if we are to judge by the splendor of their tombs during this period.

Most of our information about Etruscan culture comes from art, and especially from the monumental tombs. These structures inform us about Etruscan building practices, and some are painted with scenes that offer a glimpse of Etruscan life. The objects found in the tombs attest to the reputation of the Etruscans as fine sculptors and metalworkers. Large numbers of Attic painted vases found in them also demonstrate close trade ties with Greece.

Map 6.1 Etruscan Italy

Funerary Art

As with burials elsewhere in prehistoric Europe, early Italian burials were modest. At the beginning of the seventh century BCE, Etruscans began to bury their dead in family groups. Funerary customs became more elaborate, and the tombs of the wealthy were gradually transformed into monumental structures.

Tombs and Their Contents

Etruscan tombs were grouped outside towns to create a city of the dead, or necropolis. In the necropolis near Cerveteri, many *tumuli* or tomb mounds were constructed over the course of several centuries until about 100 BCE (**fig. 6.1**). The local volcanic rock, known as tufa, is easy to cut and hardens after prolonged exposure to air. Those who built the *tumuli* excavated into

6.1 Aerial view of part of Banditaccia Cemetery. Seventh to second centuries BCE. Cerveteri, Italy

About 700 BCE Etruscans began to build tombs of stone. These imitated the interiors of dwellings, and were covered by great conical mounds of earth. Cinerary urns, which had formerly been simple pottery vessels, gradually took on human shape (see below). The frequent depictions of funerary meals in Etruscan art as well as the gold and other precious objects found in the tombs are evidence of a CULT OF THE DEAD.

bedrock, cutting away a path and burial chambers. They used excavated stone to build a retaining wall around the tomb chambers, and piled up soil above it. Often several *dromoi* (pathways) led to independent networks of chambers within one mound. The layout of the burial chambers varies, and scholars have supposed that these dwellings of the dead evoked the plans of contemporary houses, often complete with chairs or beds carved out of the rock as furnishing. This is impossible to confirm, given the scant evidence for Etruscan residences.

Further north, at Tarquinia, tombs consist of chambers sunk into the earth with a steep underground *dromos* or entrance corridor. Vibrant paintings cover the walls, executed while the plaster was wet. A painting in the Tomb of Hunting and Fishing, of about 530–520 BCE (**fig. 6.2**), depicts a marine panorama. Fishermen cast lines

from a boat, as brightly colored dolphins leap through waves. A sling-shot artist on a rocky promontory aims at large birds in bright red, blue, and yellow that swoop through the sky. Unlike Greek landscape scenes, where humans dominate their surroundings, here the figures are just one part of a larger scheme. The exuberance of the colors and gestures, too, is characteristically Etruscan. All the same, here as in most tombs, the treatment of drapery and anatomy reveals that Etruscan tomb painters were influenced by Greek art.

The artist seems to have conceived of the scene as a view from a tent or hut, defined by bands of color at cornice level and roofed with a tapestry. Hanging from the cornice are garlands of the kind probably used during funerary rituals. In many tombs, the gable is filled with images of animals—leopards, sometimes, or fantastic hybrids—perhaps used as guardian figures to ward off evil. Above this scene, a man and woman recline at a banquet, with musicians and servants. In contrast to Greek drinking parties (*symposia*), which were reserved for men and courtesans, Etruscan banquet scenes include respectable women reclining together with men.

The purpose of these paintings is unclear. They may record and perpetuate activities enjoyed by the deceased, or rituals observed at the funeral (the games, in fact, are probably the forerunners of Roman gladiatorial contests). Or, like Egyptian tomb paintings, they may have been part of a CULT OF THE DEAD, providing for the afterlife. As enigmatic as they are, these paintings constitute a large part of our evidence for Etruscan belief systems. In a few tombs, the paintings seem to reflect Greek myths, but in a sense these paintings compound the problem, since we cannot be sure whether the Etruscans intended the same meaning as Greek artists intended.

In Cerveteri, two monumental sarcophagi of the Archaic period were found, molded in terracotta in two separate halves. One of them, dating to about 520 BCE, is shown here (**fig. 6.3**). The lid is shaped like a couch, and reclining side by side on top are full-length sculptures of a man and woman, presumably a married couple. A wineskin (a canteen made from an animal skin) cushions the woman's left elbow, and the man has his arm around her shoulders. Both figures once held objects in their hands—a cup or an *alabastron* (a perfume container), perhaps, or an egg, symbol of eternity. Despite the abstract forms and rigid poses of the ARCHAIC style, the soft material allows the sculptor to model rounded forms and capture an extraordinary directness and vivacity. The entire work was once painted in bright colors.

Given the close relationship between Etruscan and Greek art forms, scholars define the stylistic periods of Etruscan art with terms that are similar to those of Greek art: ARCHAIC, Classical and Hellenistic.

6.2 Tomb of Hunting and Fishing. ca. 530–520 BCE. Tarquinia, Italy

6.3 Sarcophagus, from Cerveteri. ca. 520 BCE. Terracotta, length 6′7″ (2 m). Museo Nazionale di Villa Giulia, Rome

During the latter part of the fourth century BCE, the Romans conquered many Etruscan cities. In some tombs of this later period, ominous demons of death appear, painted green and blue, and a change in mood, from optimistic to somber, characterizes funerary art. On a stone cinerary container made soon after 400 BCE, a man and woman sit at either end of a couch (**fig. 6.4**). The woman's wings identify her not as the young man's wife but as a demon from the world of the dead, and the scroll in her left hand may record his fate. He wears his mantle pulled down around his waist, in the Etruscan style. The two figures create a balanced composition, but their separation marks a new mood of melancholy associated with death, which each individual must face alone. Still, wealthy Etruscans continued to bury their dead together in family tombs, and the familial context for cinerary urns like this one must have gone some way toward mitigating the isolation of death.

Architecture

According to Roman writers, the Etruscans were masters of engineering, town planning, and surveying. Almost certainly, the Romans learned from them, especially in water management (drainage systems and aqueducts) and bridge building. How much they learned is hard to determine. Since it was built predominantly of wood or mud brick, little Etruscan and early

6.4 *Youth and Female Demon.* Cinerary container. Early fourth century BCE. Stone (*pietra fetida*), length 47″ (119.4 cm). Museo Archeologico Nazionale, Florence

6.5 Reconstruction of an Etruscan temple, as described by Vitruvius. Museo delle Antichità Etrusche e Italiche, Università di Roma "La Sapienza"

Roman architecture survives. Additionally, many Etruscan towns lie beneath existing Italian towns, and any permanent materials used in their building have often been reused.

Temples, too, like other structures, were built of mud brick and wood (**fig. 6.5**), and only the stone foundations have survived. Early temples consisted of modest rectangular cellas (rooms for holding cult figures). Later ones were influenced by the innovative design of the Temple of Jupiter Optimus Maximus on the Capitoline Hill in Rome, ruled at the time by Etruscan kings (see fig. 7.1). They are characterized by a tall podium, with steps on the front. The steps lead to a deep porch, supported by rows of columns, and to the cella beyond, which was often subdivided into three compartments. The roof, made of terracotta tiles, hung well over the walls in wide eaves, to shield the mud bricks from rain.

Sculpture

Etruscan temples were highly ornate. Where Greeks used marble to adorn their temples, the decoration on Etruscan ones usually consisted of brightly painted terracotta plaques that covered the architrave and the edges of the roof, as a protection from damp. After about 400 BCE, Etruscan artists sometimes designed large-scale terracotta groups to fill the pediment above the porch. The most dramatic use of sculpture was on the ridgepole—the horizontal beam at the crest of a gabled roof. Terracotta sculptures at this height depicted not only single figures but narratives. One of the most famous surviving examples comes from Veii, a site some 14 miles north of Rome. Roman texts and archaeological evidence indicate that Veii was an important sculptural center by the end of the sixth century BCE.

Dynamism in Terracotta and Bronze

The late sixth-century temple at Veii was probably devoted to the gods Menrva, Aritimi, and Turan. Four life-sized terracotta statues crowned the ridge of the roof. They formed a dynamic group representing the contest of Hercle (Hercules) and Aplu (Apollo) for the sacred hind (female deer) in the presence of other deities. The best-preserved of the figures is Aplu (**fig. 6.6**). He wears a mantle with curved hem, later known

6.6 *Apollo* (*Aplu*), from Veii. ca. 510 BCE. Terracotta, height 5′9″ (1.75 m). Museo Nazionale di Villa Giulia, Rome

6.7 *She-Wolf*. ca. 500 BCE. Bronze, height 33½″ (85 cm). Museo Capitolino, Rome

to Romans as a toga. The drapery falls in ornamental patterns and exposes his massive body, with its sinewy, muscular legs. The stylistic similarity to contemporary Greek *kouros* and *kore* figures signals the influence of Greek sculpture. But this god moves in a hurried, purposeful stride that has no equivalent in free-standing Greek statues of the same date. Terracotta allowed freedom for the artist to experiment in MODELED SCULPTURE with various poses, and this has a purely Etruscan energy. These works have been attributed to a famous Etruscan sculptor, Vulca of Veii, known from Latin literary sources.

The sculptors also demonstrated extraordinary skill as bronze casters. One of the most renowned works of Etruscan sculpture is the bronze *She-Wolf* now housed in the Capitoline Museum in Rome (**fig. 6.7**). It almost certainly

dates from the fifth century BCE, and, judging by its workmanship, was made by an Etruscan artist (although one recent hypothesis argues that it is medieval because, like church bells, it was cast in one piece, not built up out of several independently cast pieces). The stylized, patterned treatment of the wolf's mane and hackles sets off the smoothly modeled muscularity of her body, tensed for attack. Simple lines add to her power: The straight back and neck contrast with the sharp turn of the head toward a viewer, highlighting her ferocity. So polished is the metal's surface that it almost seems wet; her fangs seem to glisten. The early history and subject matter of this statue are unknown, but the twin babies Romulus and Remus beneath her were added between 1471 and 1473 CE, probably by the Renaissance sculptor Antonio Pollaiuolo.

SUMMARY

Etruscan culture appeared on the Italian peninsula around 1000 BCE. The ancient Etruscans were skilled sailors and merchants whose wealth was founded on the exploitation of available copper, iron, and silver deposits. Most of their surviving artifacts come from their tombs.

The Etruscans began to bury their dead in family groups early in the seventh century BCE. Over time, tomb construction for the wealthy became more monumental, as seen in the tumulus tombs at the necropolis of Cerveteri, carved and constructed out of local volcanic rock. Many included spectacular grave goods, and some were decorated with vibrant wall paintings, as in the Tomb of Hunting and Fishing in Tarquinia. Sometimes they housed funerary objects, such as the terracotta sarcophagi from Cerveteri depicting reclining figures, or a later cinerary urn with a youth and a demon on its cover.

As it was built of wood, packed earth and mud brick, little Etruscan architecture is still standing. Of their temples, only the stone foundations remain, which reveal their plan. They were embellished with brightly painted terracotta plaques and groupings of sculpted figures, such as the statue of Aplu from Veii. As well as working in terracotta, sculptors were skilled in bronze casting, as the bronze *She-Wolf* in the Capitoline Museum bears witness.

ART IN TIME

- ca. 1000 BCE — Appearance of Etruscan culture on the Italian peninsula

- ca. 600s–500s BCE — The height of Etruscan power

- ca. 530–520 BCE — Tomb of Hunting and Fishing at Cerveteri

- ca. 520 BCE — Etruscan terracotta sarcophagi from Cerveteri

- ca. 518 BCE — Construction of the Persian palace at Persepolis begins

- ca. 510 BCE — The Etruscan Temple at Veii

- ca. 500 BCE — Etruscan bronze *She-Wolf* sculpture

- ca. 450–440 BCE — *Doryphoros* of Polykleitos

- Early fourth century — Youth and female, cinerary container

- 331 BCE — Defeat of the Persians by Alexander the Great

- by 270 BCE — All Etruscan city-states under the dominion of Rome

7 Roman Art

*O*f all the civilizations of the ancient world, the most accessible to modern scholars is that of ancient Rome. A vast literary legacy reveals a great deal about Roman culture, and the Romans built countless monuments throughout their empire, which are extraordinarily well preserved. Yet there are few questions more difficult to address than "What is Roman art?"

Much of Roman public art draws heavily on Greek styles. In the nineteenth and early twentieth centuries, art connoisseurs exalted Greek Classicism as the height of stylistic achievement, and considered Roman art derivative, the last chapter, so to speak, of Greek art history. This view changed radically in the ensuing years, especially as connoisseurship began to give way to other branches of art history. Scholars now focus, for instance, on the roles of a work of art in its social and political contexts. Moreover, Greek styles were by no means the only ones available in the Roman world. Works of art created in the provinces or by the non-elite have their own style, as do those of late antiquity. There were also phases of distinct "Egyptomania" in Rome.

Roman art was the art of both Republic and Empire, the art of a small city that became a vast power. It is an art created by Roman artists, but not exclusively; the greatest architect of Trajan's time may have been from Damascus. Perhaps the most useful way to think of Roman art is as one of syncretism—an art that brings diverse elements together to produce something entirely new, with a powerful message-bearing potential. Syncretism, in art as in politics and religion, was a profoundly Roman attitude, and was probably the secret to Rome's extraordinary expansion. Roman civilization incorporated other cultures and integrated them into its own, leading to a remarkably diverse world.

Early Rome and the Republic

According to legend, Romulus founded Rome in 753/52 BCE, in the region known as Latium, on a site near the Tiber River. However, archaeological evidence shows that people had lived there since about 1000 BCE. From the eighth to the sixth centuries BCE, a series of kings built the first defensive wall around the settlement, drained and filled the swampy plain of the FORUM, and built a vast temple on the CAPITOLINE Hill, making an urban center out of what had been a mere group of villages. The kings established many of Rome's lasting institutions, such as priesthoods and techniques of warfare. In about 509 BCE, the Roman elite expelled the last king, and gradually established a Republic, with an unwritten constitution.

Under the Republic, a group of elected magistrates, with an advisory Senate, managed the affairs of the growing state. Rome gradually took control of the Italian peninsula (see map 7.1), absorbing Etruscan cities to the north and Greek colonies to the south. After extensive wars with the Phoenicians of North Africa, Rome razed their city of Carthage in 146 BCE. During the second century Greece and Asia Minor also came under Roman domination, leading to a dramatic influx of Greek art and culture into Rome.

From about 133 BCE to 31 BCE, factional politics led to the breakdown of the constitution and

The FORUM was a square or rectangular market and meeting place in the heart of cities and towns built under Roman rule. The first Roman forum was laid out in a marshy valley between two of Rome's seven hills: The Palatine and the CAPITOLINE (Capitol). The Capitoline was the highest of the hills and was the religious center of the city from earliest times.

The Roman Republic and Empire

Roman Republic	510–31 BCE
Roman Empire	31 BCE–395 CE
Western Empire	395–476 CE
Eastern (Byzantine) Empire	395–1453

Map 7.1 The Ancient Roman World

to civil war. Julius Caesar became perpetual dictator in 46 BCE, a position that other senators could not tolerate; two years later, they assassinated him. In 27 BCE, the Senate named his heir Octavian as Augustus Caesar, and he became *princeps*, or first citizen. History recognizes him as the first Roman emperor from that date. During the course of the Republic, and continuing into the Empire, magistrates and emperors commissioned works of architecture and sculpture to embellish the city as well as to enhance their own prospects. Designs were strongly influenced by conquests abroad and by the development of new building technologies in Rome.

Architecture: The Concrete Revolution

It is probably fair to say that Roman architecture has had a more lasting impact than any other

ancient tradition on Western building through the ages. It is an architecture of power, mediated through the solidity of its forms, and through the experience of those forms. Roman builders were indebted to Greek traditions, especially in their use of the Doric, Ionic, and Corinthian styles, yet the resultant buildings were decidedly Roman.

The Temple of Jupiter Optimus Maximus on the Capitoline Hill was the first truly monumental building of Rome (**fig. 7.1**), begun under the late sixth-century BCE kings, Tarquinius the Ancient and Tarquinius the Proud. Its scale was new to the Italian peninsula, evoking the massive Ionic temples of eastern Greece. It stood on a high masonry platform, with steps leading up to the façade. Six wooden columns marked the front, and six columns flanked each side. Two

Cella of Juno   rear rooms   Cella of Minerva

Cella of Jupiter

presumed foundation walls

porch

01 6 10   20   30 meters

0   20   40   60   80   100 feet

N

7.1 Restored plan of Temple of Jupiter Optimus Maximus, Capitoline Hill, Rome. Dedicated ca. 509 BCE

rows of columns supported the roof over a deep porch. Later Roman historians tell us that an Etruscan artist, Vulca of Veii, crafted a vast terra-cotta *acroterion* for the peak of the pediment, representing Jupiter in a four-horse chariot. Three parallel cellas with mud brick walls accommodated cult statues of Jupiter, Juno, and Minerva, and recent excavations suggest that two additional rooms were arranged across the rear. Greek influence is evident in the rectilinear forms, the use of columns, and a gabled roof; yet the high podium and the emphatic frontal access set it apart. These features would characterize most Roman temples in centuries to come, as seen in the remarkably well-preserved temple to the harbor god Portunus, near the Tiber, often misnamed the Temple of Fortuna Virilis (**fig. 7.2**).

Roman architects quickly combined the rectilinear forms so characteristic of Greek architecture with the curved form of the **arch** (see box overleaf). The development of concrete, however, was the catalyst for the most dramatic changes in Roman architecture. Concrete is a mixture of mortar and pieces of aggregate such as tufa, limestone, or brick. On adding *pozzolana*

7.2 Temple of Portunus. ca. 80–70 BCE. Rome

7.3 Sanctuary of Fortuna Primigenia. Late second century BCE. Praeneste (Palestrina), Italy

sand to the mortar, Roman builders discovered a material of remarkable durability, and they used it with growing confidence from the second century BCE onward. They concealed it with facings of stone, brick, and plaster, the style of which changed with the passing years, and therefore provides archaeologists with an invaluable tool for dating Roman buildings. The advantages of concrete were quickly evident: It was strong and cheap, and could be worked by relatively unskilled laborers. It was also extraordinarily adaptable. By constructing wooden frameworks into which the concrete would be poured, builders could mold it to shapes that would have been prohibitively time-consuming, if not outright impossible to make using cut stone, wood, or mud brick. In a sense, the history of Roman architecture is a dialogue between the traditional rectilinear forms of the Greek and early Italic post-and-lintel traditions on the one hand, and the freedoms afforded by this malleable material on the other.

SANCTUARY OF FORTUNA PRIMIGENIA   East of Rome, in the foothills of the Apennines, the town of Palestrina (ancient Praeneste) is home to a masterpiece of concrete construction (**figs. 7.3** and **7.4**). The sanctuary to the goddess Fortuna Primigenia, dated to the late second century BCE, was an oracular center where priests interpreted divine will by drawing lots. Here, architects used concrete to mold structures over the entire surface of a hillside and to craft spaces that controlled and heightened a visitor's experience. At the bottom stood a temple, a basilica, and a senate house. The upper terraces rose in a

7.4 Axonometric reconstruction of the Sanctuary of Fortuna Primigenia, Praeneste, Italy

grand crescendo around a central axis, established by a series of statue niches and staircases. A visitor climbed lateral staircases to the third terrace, where steep ramps, roofed with sloping

Arches

ARCHES were constructed of stone or brick over a temporary wooden scaffold, called centering. Roman arches are semicircular, as opposed to later Gothic arches, which are pointed. In building the arch, the last stone laid is the keystone, which locks in the other arch stones (**voussoirs**) before the centering can be removed. The outside curve of the arch is the extrados, the inside curve the intrados.

Built on the principle of the semicircular arch, the **barrel vault** may be thought of as a continuous arch. This vaulting is very heavy and exerts enormous pressure (thrust) both outward and downward. Barrel vaulting, therefore, is usually supported by heavy walls and/or buttresses.

Also called the square vault, the **groin vault** was much favored in Roman architecture. The area enclosed within the four corner piers is called a bay.

arch

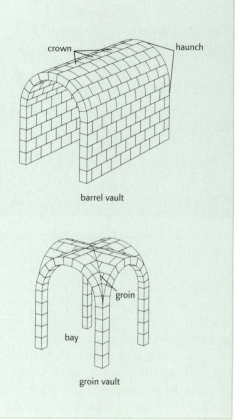

barrel vault

groin vault

barrel vaults, led upward. A bright shaft of daylight beckoned from the end of the ramp, where a landing provided the first of several glorious views across the countryside.

On the fourth level, colonnaded *exedrae* (semicircular recesses) framed the altars. Barrel vaults roofed the colonnades, forming a half-circle horizontally and vertically (annular barrel vaults). The curved forms of the *exedrae* animate the straight lines, since columns set in a semi-circle shift their relationship to the environment with every step a visitor takes. A wide central staircase leads upward to the next level, where souvenirs and votive objects were probably on sale in small shops. After the confinement of the ramps, its exposed steps give a sense of vulnerability. The next terrace was a huge open court, surrounded on three sides by double colonnades. The visitor continued to a small theater topped by a double annular colonnade. Here religious performances took place against the magnificent backdrop of the countryside beyond, and in full sight of the goddess, whose circular temple crowned the complex. Its diminutive size drew grandeur from the vast scale of the whole—all accomplished with concrete. The hugely versatile material plays easily with the landscape, transforming nature to heighten a visitor's religious experience.

Sculpture

The Republican period saw the beginning of a rich tradition of relief and free-standing sculpture in the Roman world, often created in the service of politics.

RELIEF SCULPTURE Like architecture, sculpture often commemorated specific events, as it did in the ancient Near East (see fig. 2.9). Greek sculpture disguised historical events in mythical clothing—a combat of gods and giants, for instance (see fig. 5.8). The Romans, by contrast, represented actual events, developing a form of sculpture known as historical relief—although many were not historically accurate. The reliefs shown in **fig. 7.5** probably decorated a base for a statuary group, which scholars place near the route used for triumphal processions through Rome. One long section shows a census, a ceremony during which individuals recorded their property with the state to establish qualification for military service. On the left side, soldiers and civilians line

7.5 Sculptural reliefs from statue base, showing sea *thiasos* and census. Late second to early first century BCE. Marble. Musée du Louvre, Paris, and Glyptothek, Staatliche Antikensammlungen, Munich

up to be entered into the census. Two large figures flanking an altar represent a statue of Mars, god of war, and the officiating censor, who probably commissioned the monument. Attendants escort a bull, a sheep, and a pig to sacrifice at an altar.

On the same monument, the remaining reliefs depict a *thiasos* (procession) across the sea for the marriage of the sea-god Neptune and the sea-nymph Amphitrite. But these reliefs are in an entirely different style. The swirling motion of the marriage procession and its Hellenistic forms contrast dramatically with the static composition of the census relief and the stocky proportions of its figures. Moreover, the panels are carved out of different marbles. Scholars suppose that the sea-*thiasos* sections were not original to this context, but were brought as spoils from Greece to grace a triumphal monument—proof, as it were, of conquest. The census relief, by contrast, was carved in Rome to complement the *thiasos*. Together, the reliefs may represent the patron's proud achievements.

PORTRAIT SCULPTURE   Literary sources reveal that the Senate and People of Rome honored political or military figures by putting their statues on display, often in the Roman Forum, the civic heart of the city. The custom began in the early Republic and continued until the end of the Empire. Many of the early PORTRAITS were bronze and have perished, melted down for coinage or weaponry. The majority were stone and date to the end of the second century and the first century BCE. Most represent men at an advanced age (**fig. 7.6**). Wrinkles cover their faces, etching crags into their cheeks and brows. Distinguishing marks—such as warts, or a hooked nose—are played up rather than smoothed over. In the example illustrated here, remnants of a veil suggest that the subject was represented as a priest. Although there is no way of knowing what the sitter looked like, the images appear overly realistic, so that scholars term the style **veristic**, from the Latin *verus*, meaning "true." For a twenty-first-century viewer, these images appear anything but

Where Romans found the impetus to produce likenesses is a mystery that scholars have been curious to solve. Some trace it to a Greek custom of placing votive statues of important individuals in sacred precincts, and indeed some Roman PORTRAITS were executed in a Hellenic style. For others, its roots lie in an Italic practice of storing ancestral masks in the home to provide a kind of visual genealogy, in a society where a good pedigree was the most reliable stepping-stone to political success.

7.6 Veristic male portrait. Early first century BCE. Marble, life-size. Musei Vaticani, Rome

Major Roman Emperors

Augustus	27 BCE–14 CE (in power from 31 BCE)
Vespasian	69–79
Trajan	98–117
Hadrian	117–138
Marcus Aurelius	161–180
Septimius Severus	193–211
Caracalla	211–217
Diocletian	284–305
Constantine	307–337

idealized. Yet it is worth bearing in mind that each culture constructs its own ideals. To Romans, responsibility and experience came with seniority, and most magistracies had minimum age requirements. An image marked by age therefore conveyed the requisite qualities for winning votes for political office (see box below).

The Early Empire

When the Senate declared Octavian as Augustus Caesar in 27 BCE, he proclaimed that the Republic was restored. In fact, AUGUSTUS reintroduced monarchy to Rome, and it would endure through several dynasties until the gradual transfer of imperial power to Constantinople

Roman Values

ORIGINALLY A NATION of farmers, the Romans prided themselves on their connection to the land and to rural values. The ideal Roman was exemplified by Cincinnatus, a patrician and consul in 460 BCE, who immediately returned to his farm when his term ended. Two years later, after a military disaster, the Senate recalled him from the plough and appointed him dictator; within two weeks he raised an army, defeated the enemy, triumphed, resigned his office, and returned to his plough again. This stern devotion to duty (*fides*), steadfastness (*constantia*), dignity (*dignitas*), austerity, modesty, and courage—all summed up by the Latin word *gravitas* (weightiness of character, gravity, seriousness)—is emphasized in the portraiture of the Roman republican elite (see fig. 7.6).

(beginning in about 330 CE). The birth of the Roman Empire brought a period of relative stability to the Mediterranean region. Roman domination continued to spread, and at its largest extent in the time of Trajan (98–117 CE) the empire stretched through most of Europe, as far north as northern England, through much of the Middle East including Armenia and Assyria, and throughout coastal North Africa. Roman institutions—political, social, and religious—mingled with indigenous ones, leading to a degree of homogenization across much of the Roman world. Increasingly, the emperor and his family became the principal patrons of public art and architecture in Rome. Often, these public monuments stressed the legitimacy of the imperial family.

Portrait Sculpture

By the time Augustus effectively became emperor, he was no more than 36. With its stress on maturity, the veristic style so characteristic of Republican portraiture might have served to underline the unconstitutional nature of his authority in Rome. He turned instead to a more Hellenizing style. Until his death in his late seventies, his portraits depict him as an ageless youth, as seen in the statue from the house of his wife Livia at Primaporta (**fig. 7.7**).

The statue appears to combine references to previous works of art and historical events in an effort to strengthen Augustus' claim to authority. The *contrapposto* stance, and the smooth features of his face, are reminiscent of Polykleitos' *Doryphoros* (see fig. 5.16). The resemblance is so strong that scholars assume that Augustus turned deliberately to this well-known image. There was good reason for this kind of imitation: The Classical Greek style evoked the apogee of Athenian culture, casting Augustan Rome as Greece's successor (and conqueror) in cultural supremacy. Even Augustus' hair is similar to that of the *Doryphoros*—except, that is, at the front, where the locks part slightly over the center of the brow, a subtle reference to the youthful general Alexander the Great, whose cowlick was such a distinctive feature of his portraits (see fig. 5.29). Next to Augustus' right ankle, the reinforcing strut is shaped as a cupid playfully riding a dolphin. Most Romans would have recognized that Cupid, or Eros, the son of Venus, symbolized Augustus' claim of descent from the goddess of love through his Trojan ancestor Aeneas. The dolphin evoked the sea, and the site off the coast of western Greece where Augustus had

7.7 *Augustus of Primaporta.* Possibly Roman copy of a statue of ca. 20 CE. Marble, height 6′8″ (2.03 m). Musei Vaticani, Braccio Nuovo, Rome

prevailed over Mark Antony and Cleopatra at the Battle of Actium in 31 BCE. By associating Augustus with historical or divine figures, these references projected an image of earthly and divinely ordained power.

The iconography of Augustus' breastplate serves a similar purpose by calling attention to an important diplomatic victory in 20 BCE, when the Parthians returned standards that they had captured, to Roman shame, in 53 BCE. This event took on momentous proportions in Augustan propaganda. Tiberius, Augustus' eventual successor, or the god Mars, is depicted accepting the standards from a Parthian soldier, possibly Phraates IV, the Parthian king. Gods and terrestrial personifications frame the scene, giving it a cosmic and eternal significance.

The Primaporta Augustus offers a good example of a tendency in Roman art to express a message through references to earlier works. Naturally, not all Romans would have understood all the references in any work, but the frequency of visual "quotations" suggests that the Romans, like many other ancient peoples, were visually astute. In fact, the history of Roman portraiture, as with many other branches of Roman art, is one of constant association with, or conscious turning away from, past images. Portraits of Augustus' dynastic successors, for instance, look very much like the first emperor from whom they drew their authority, even

though they were rarely (or at best distantly) related by blood.

Vast numbers of imperial portraits are in existence. On the whole, they fall into a number of types, suggesting that there was a master portrait, often executed for a specific occasion, that would be copied for dissemination within and outside of Rome; sculptors would copy these copies, in turn, leading to a ripple effect around the Empire. Unidentified nonimperial portraits also survive in great numbers, and scholars date them on the basis of similarities with those of members of the imperial family. When dealing with female portraits, hairstyles are especially useful, since they changed relatively rapidly. Domitia Longina, wife of the emperor Domitian, wore her hair in a towering style built around a framework (**fig. 7.8**). Her coiffure was a masterpiece in itself, and its representation in sculpture reflected her status, as well as affording the sculptor an opportunity to explore contrasts of texture between skin and hair, and to drill

7.8 *Portrait of Domitia Longina.* Late first century CE. Marble, height 2′ (0.608 m). Courtesy of San Antonio Museum of Art, San Antonio, Texas. Gift of Gilbert M. Denman, Jr.

Emperor MARCUS AURELIUS (121–180 CE; see fig. 7.9), a scholar and philosopher, was constantly forced to repress rebellions and incursions by "barbarian" peoples such as the Britons, Moors, Germans, and Parthians. His writings, known today as his *Meditations*, are imbued with STOIC philosophy. Stoicism expressed the ideas of the fourth-century Greek philosopher Zeno. Emotions were considered false and deceiving; impassive detachment was its highest virtue. Sacrifice and hardship were to be endured for the sake of moral principle.

deep into the marble for a strong play of light and shadow.

Beginning in the second half of the second century CE, Roman portraits gradually take on a more abstract quality. It is especially marked in the treatment of the eyes, whose heavy lids lend them a remote quality. This is perceptible in a spectacular gilded bronze portrait of MARCUS AURELIUS, which survived the melting pot in the medieval period because Christians misidentified it as Constantine the Great, champion of Christianity (**fig. 7.9**). With one arm outstretched in a gesture of mercy, the emperor sits astride a spirited horse, whose raised front leg once rested on a conquered barbarian. Like the majority of second- and third-century CE male portraits, Marcus Aurelius is bearded.

7.10 *Ara Pacis Augustae*, west façade. 13–9 BCE. Marble, width of altar approx. 35′ (10.7 m). Museum of the Ara Pacis, Rome

Relief Sculpture

The Republican practice of commissioning narrative reliefs to record specific events continued well into the Empire. They were mounted on public buildings and monuments, such as the *Ara Pacis Augustae*, or Altar of Augustan Peace (**fig. 7.10**), and the later Arch of Titus.

ARA PACIS AUGUSTAE The Senate and People of Rome vowed the MONUMENTAL ALTAR in Augustus' honor in 13 BCE and dedicated it in 9 BCE. It stood inside an open-air marble enclosure, which was richly sculpted over its entire surface. On the east and west sides, flanking two entrances, relief panels represent personifications or gods, and figures from Rome's

7.11 *Ara Pacis Augustae*, Imperial Procession south frieze. 13–9 BCE. Marble, height 63″ (1.6 m). Museum of the Ara Pacis, Rome

legendary past. On the west end, a fragmentary panel shows the twin boys Romulus and Remus, legendary founders of Rome. Abandoned as babies, they were suckled by a she-wolf, until they were found and adopted by the shepherd Faustulus, also shown in the panel. In a second relief, Aeneas (or perhaps, according to a recent interpretation, Numa, second king of Rome) sacrifices at a roughly hewn altar. At the east end, a relief depicting the goddess Roma seated on her weapons balances a panel with a female figure (the goddess Venus or Ceres, perhaps, or Peace, Italia, or Mother Earth) who embodies the notion of peace. Together, the panels express the message of peace that Augustus was intent on promoting, in contrast with the bleakness of the preceding civil wars. The same message was implicit in the acanthus relief that encircles the enclosure in a lower register. Vegetation unfurls in rich abundance, populated with creatures such as lizards and frogs.

On the north and south sides, the upper register contains continuous procession friezes that portray members of the imperial family interspersed with the college of priests and senators (**fig. 7.11**). The friezes seem to record a particular event—a sacrifice, perhaps, or the moment of the altar's dedication. The friezes are fragmentary, and most of Augustus' body is missing. His action would probably have revealed the occasion. Still, the friezes are significant for a number of reasons. In their resemblance to the Greek Parthenon frieze (see fig. 5.19) they bear witness, once again, to the preference for Greek styles in the age of Augustus. They also include a number of women from the imperial family, including Livia, and small children. One scholar has convincingly argued that their inclusion represents the importance of family and dynasty, as well as a reference to moral legislation that the emperor enacted to curb adultery and promote childbirth among the elite.

COLUMN OF TRAJAN The exploration of narrative strategies comes into full bloom in the Column of Trajan (**fig. 7.12**). The column was erected between 106 and 113 CE in a small court to the west of Trajan's Forum. Soaring about 150 Roman feet high, it supported a gilded statue of the emperor, lost in medieval times. Winding up through its shaft was a spiral staircase leading to a viewing platform, from which a visitor could see Trajan's extraordinary building accomplishments. Free-standing columns had been used as commemorative monuments in Greece from

7.12 Column of Trajan. 106–113 CE. Marble, height 125′ (38 m). Rome

Hellenistic times, but the sheer scale of Trajan's Column, and its role as a belvedere, made it nothing short of a world wonder. Its design is often credited to Apollodorus, who served as Trajan's military architect. However, art historians have tended to focus not on the engineering feat it represents, but on the 656-foot-long continuous narrative relief that winds counterclockwise around the shaft, celebrating the emperor's victorious campaigns against the Dacians (in present-day Romania).

The narrative begins with the Roman army crossing the Danube to reach Dacian territory (**fig. 7.13**). The river appears as a large personification. A second band shows Trajan speaking to his soldiers, and soldiers building fortifications. In the third, soldiers construct a camp and bridge as the cavalry sets out on a reconnaissance mission; and in the fourth, foot soldiers cross a stream while the emperor addresses his troops in front of a Dacian fortress. These scenes are a fair sampling of events shown on the column. Among

the more than 150 episodes, combat occurs rarely. The geographic, logistic, and political aspects of the campaign receive more attention.

Individual scenes are not distinctly separate from one another. Trees and buildings suggest divisions, but the scenes still merge into a continuous whole, with the chief figures, such as Trajan, appearing multiple times. Visual continuity is thus preserved without sacrificing the coherence of each scene. Although Assyrian and Egyptian artists created visual narratives of military conquests, this relief is by far the most ambitious composition so far in terms of the number of figures and the density of the narrative. Understanding it is a complicated matter. Continuous illustrated scrolls make a likely inspiration for the composition, except that none survive from the time before the column's construction. More problematic is how a viewer was supposed to read the narrative. In order to follow its sequence, one has to keep turning around the column. Above the fourth or fifth turn, details

7.13 Lower portion of the Column of Trajan. 106–113 CE. Marble, height of relief band approx. 50″ (127 cm). Rome

7.14 Forum of Trajan, Rome. Reconstruction by Gilbert Gorski

become hard to make out, even if the addition of paint would have made the sculpture more vivid. It might have been possible to view the upper spirals from balconies on surrounding buildings, but an encircling motion would still have been required. These problems have led scholars to propose strategies for reading the narrative. They have long noted that the relief is formulaic; that is, a limited number of stock scenes are repeated again and again. These include, for instance, sacrifice scenes, the emperor addressing his troops, or soldiers constructing forts and dismantling enemy cities. Though not identical, the scenes are similar enough to be recognized at a distance, making the upper spirals more legible. The designer may also have aligned important and representative scenes on the cardinal axes of the column, to make an abbreviated version of the whole visible from a single standpoint. Yet there is always the possibility that the designer intended viewers to have to turn around the column in order to read its narrative. After Trajan's death in 117 CE, the column's base served as a burial chamber for his ashes, and an encircling motion would be entirely consistent with a widespread Roman funerary ritual in which visitors walked around tombs to protect the dead buried within, to confine spirits to the grave, and to pay perpetual homage to the deceased.

Architecture

During the Empire, emperors commissioned monumental structures designed to curry favor with the populace. Beginning with Julius Caesar, several of them built large forums as backdrops to civic and religious functions. The largest of all of them was Trajan's, financed with the spoils of his Dacian wars. Recent reconstructions of the complex give some impression of its former magnificence (**fig. 7.14**). Porticoes lined the long sides of a large open plaza. Beyond a basilica at its far end, two libraries and a temple defined a small courtyard, where Trajan's Column stood (see fig. 7.12). Colored marbles were used in great abundance, and sculpture filled the complex. In the portico attics, for instance, were statues of captive Dacians carved from exotic stone. The Forum's message is clear: The Dacian Wars brought Rome great benefit. As in so many societies, the ruling elite hoped to dispel the starker realities of war through visual propaganda.

COLOSSEUM   As well as constructing a magnificent forum in the name of peace, Vespasian was the first to construct a permanent amphitheater in Rome for the gladiatorial games that were so central to Roman entertainment (**fig. 7.15a**). Earlier gladiatorial shows had taken place in the Roman Forum, with temporary wooden

7.15a Colosseum. 72–80 CE. Rome

bleachers for spectators. Vespasian died before completing the Colosseum, and his son Titus inaugurated it in 80 CE with over 100 days of games, at a cost of over 9,000 animal lives. In terms of sheer mass, it was one of the largest single buildings anywhere: It stood 159 feet high, 616 feet 9 inches long, and 511 feet 11 inches wide, and could hold 45,000 to 50,000 spectators. Concrete, faced with travertine, was the secret of its success. In plan, 80 radial barrel-vaulted wedges ringed an oval arena. Each barrel vault buttressed the next, making the ring remarkably stable (**fig. 7.15b**). The wedges sloped down toward the ringside to support seating, and accommodated within the wedges were countless stairways and corridors, designed to ensure the smooth flow of traffic to and from seating areas. During the hottest days, sailors stationed nearby could rig huge canvas sheets to shade the seating areas. The exterior reflects the structure's interior organization. Eighty arched entrances led into the building, framed with engaged Tuscan columns (which resemble Doric columns but have simple bases). On the second story, Ionic columns framed a second set of arches. At the third level were engaged Corinthian columns, and Corinthian pilasters flanked blind arcades in the fourth.

PANTHEON Of all the masterpieces Roman architects accomplished with concrete, the Pantheon is perhaps the most remarkable (**fig. 7.16**). As its name suggests, the temple honored all the gods. This was a Hellenistic concept, and it included living and deceased members of the ruling family among the gods. Augustus' right-hand man, Agrippa, had built the first Pantheon

7.15b Colosseum, sectional view

Transverse section of the Pantheon

on the site. A fire in 80 CE destroyed this temple, and a reconstruction perished after a lightning strike. The existing Pantheon, with a substantially different design, was probably begun under Trajan; it was completed under Hadrian in about 125 CE. Still, Agrippa's name remained in the inscription as an act of piety. It is one of the best-preserved pagan temples of Rome, thanks to its transformation into a church in the early seventh century CE.

The Pantheon's surroundings have changed sufficiently through the ages to alter a visitor's experience of the building profoundly (**fig. 7.17**). In Roman times, it stood, raised on a podium, at the south end of a large rectangular court. Porticoes framed the three remaining sides of the court and extended on the south up to the sides of the temple's pedimented porch, hiding the circular drum from view. A visitor approaching the

7.17 Pantheon, Rome. Schematic drawing

broad octastyle façade would have been struck by the forest of massive monolithic gray and pink granite columns soaring upward; but in most other respects the temple's form would have been familiar, evoking expectations of a rectangular cella beyond the huge bronze doors. Yet a surprise was in store. On stepping across the threshold, all a visitor could perceive was a glowing shaft of light, slicing through the shadows from high overhead (**fig. 7.18**). As the eyes grew accustomed to the darkness, a vast circular hall took form, with seven large niches at ground level. Engaged pilasters and bronze grilles decorated an attic level, and high above soared an enormous dome, pierced with a 27-foot hole or **oculus** open to the sky. Dome and drum are of equal height, and the total interior height, 143 feet, is also the dome's diameter. Many ancient viewers would have associated the resultant sphere with eternity and perfection, and the dome's surface, once emblazoned with bronze rosettes in its coffers (recessed panels), must have evoked a starry night sky.

For a visitor entering the space, there was no obvious cue to point out where to go, except toward the light at the center. In fact, the dome's coffers only make sense perspectively from directly beneath the oculus. Once a visitor reached the center, molded space and applied decoration combined to provide a stunning effect. Beginning in the Renaissance, scholars have faulted the Pantheon's architect for neglecting to align the ribs between the dome coffers with the pilasters in the attic zone and the ground-floor columns. Yet, the absence of continuous vertical lines from top to bottom means that, visually speaking, the dome is not anchored. The optical effect is that it hovers unfettered above the visitor—who feels, paradoxically, both sheltered and exposed. The dome seems to be in perpetual motion, spinning overhead in the same way as the heavens it imitates. An all-but-imperceptible rise in the floor at the center exaggerates this sensation, which can incite an unnerving feeling similar to vertigo. A visitor's instinct, in response, is to take refuge in the safety of the curved wall. The building is all experience, and photographs do it no justice. This is the place, so literary sources relate, where Hadrian preferred to hold court, greeting foreign embassies and adjudicating disputes. The temple's form cast the emperor in the authoritative position of controller of his revolving universe. He must have appeared like a divine revelation before his guest, who was already awed and completely manipulated by the building that enclosed them.

The Pantheon is the extraordinary result of an increased confidence in the potential and strength of concrete. The architect calibrated the aggregate as the building rose, from travertine to tufa, then brick, and finally pumice, to reduce its weight. The dome's weight is concentrated on eight wide pillars between the interior alcoves,

7.18 Pantheon. Interior. Rome

7.19 Aqueduct. First or early second century CE. Segovia, Spain

rather than resting uniformly on the drum. The alcoves, in turn, with their screens of columns, visually reduce the solidity of the walls, and colored marbles on the interior surfaces add energy to the whole. As in Trajan's Forum, the marbles were symbolic. They underlined the vast reach of imperial authority, assuming trade with or control over Egypt (gray and rose-pink granite, porphyry), Phrygia (Phrygian purple and white stone), the island of Teos (Lucullan red and black stone), and Chemtou in Tunisia (Numidian yellow stone).

Art and Architecture in the Provinces

The spread of Rome's authority had a profound impact on artistic and architectural production over a wide geographical reach. Since history is typically recorded by those in power, it is often hard to assess the reactions of local peoples to foreign control. To be sure, Roman rule brought some benefits. Roman engineers had mastered the art of moving water efficiently, and the new Roman aqueducts that sprang up in urban centers around the empire must have improved local

standards of living immeasurably. A striking aqueduct still stands at Segovia in Spain, dating to the first or early second century CE (**fig. 7.19**). It brought water from Riofrío, about 10½ miles away, which flowed for most of its length through an underground channel. Near the town, however, architects erected a massive bridge for it stretching 2,666 feet long and up to 98 feet high to span a valley. One hundred and eighteen arches support the water channel, built in two registers at the highest point. Like most provincial builders, the architects used a local stone, in this case a granite, assembled without mortar and left unfinished to give an air of strength. Despite the obvious advantages the aqueduct provided, it also illustrates how Roman architecture could effect dominion. The arches—a quintessentially Roman form—march relentlessly across the terrain, symbolically conquering it with their step.

The Romans carried their way of life and their style with them across the empire, constructing theaters and amphitheaters, and temples to accommodate their rituals. Indigenous building traditions combined with Roman styles to powerful new effect. This appears to be the case with the extraordinary rock-cut façade

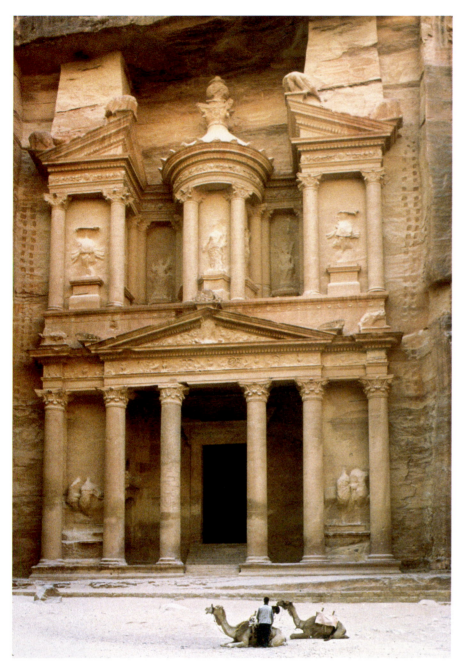

7.20 El Khasneh. Probably early second century CE. Petra, Jordan

decorated with floral designs and a pediment. In a second story, lateral columns support a broken pediment. Between them is a *tholos* with a conical roof, surmounted by an ornamental finial. In more recent times, locals imagined that pirates had stored treasure in the finial, lending the monument its name; bullet holes show how they tried to knock it to the ground.

The façade is a striking amalgamation of a Nabataean concept with Roman decorative features—the Corinthian column capitals, for instance, and the vegetal designs. The architectural elements are not structural, and this allows for a quality of freedom and fantasy in the design, not unlike the fantasy vistas of wall paintings. This playful treatment of once-structural elements became popular in the provinces and in Rome in the second century CE, and scholars sometimes describe it as a baroque phase, for its similarities to Italian baroque architecture. The monument's function may have changed for Roman usage as well: Relief sculptures between the columns seem to represent figures from the cult of Isis, suggesting that it was a temple. In some cases, inscriptions and other written documents indicate who commissioned monuments in the provinces; the patron might be local, a Roman official, or even the emperor himself. More often, as in this case, there is no such evidence, which makes it hard to determine meaning in a choice of style.

The greatest body of painting to survive from the Roman world is wall painting. Yet the sands of Fayum, in Lower Egypt, have preserved a magnificent group of painted portraits, once covering the faces of the embalmed, mummified bodies of the dead (**fig. 7.21**). The earliest of them appear to date from the second century CE. Artists painted them on wooden panels in a technique known as **encaustic**, which involves suspending pigments in hot wax. The mixture can be opaque and creamy, like oil paint, or thin and translucent. The medium is durable, and the panels retain an extraordinary freshness; the wax also gives them a luster that brings them vividly to life. At their best, these portraits have a haunting immediacy, largely the result of the need to work quickly before the hot wax set. The woman pictured here wears a deep crimson tunic and a wealth of jewelry. Rows of black circles denote the ringlets of her hair, bound with a golden diadem. Her appearance is Roman, yet the portrait itself speaks of her local identity, since she was buried in the Egyptian, not the Roman, fashion.

known as El Khasneh, or the Treasury, at the site of Petra in present-day Jordan (**fig. 7.20**). This façade is the first sight to greet a visitor who wanders through the long, twisting gorge known as the Siq, leading to the town center. The Nabataeans, a nomadic people who settled this area before the Romans took control in 106 CE, would bury their wealthy dead in tombs cut out of the pink sandstone cliffs, and some scholars have seen El Khasneh as one of their monuments. Most agree, however, that it belongs to the Trajanic or Hadrianic period. Carved from the living rock, the monument resembles a temple façade, with six columns beneath an architrave

Domestic Art and Architecture

The Romans are one of the few ancient peoples to leave abundant evidence of domestic architecture and its decoration. The burial of the cities of Pompeii and Herculaneum after the eruption of Vesuvius in 79 CE preserved an invaluable legacy for the archaeologist; and such was the durability of Roman domestic construction that houses survive elsewhere as well, as far afield as Morocco and Jordan. Their unusually good state of preservation has meant that houses buried by Vesuvius have dominated scholarly discussion, as they will here; yet although Roman houses around the empire have many qualities in common, they also differ from one region

to the next, to cater, for instance, to local climates. In any given region, there were also discrepancies between the dwellings of the very rich and the very poor. One should be cautious, therefore, about the concept of a "typical" Roman house.

Scholars describe elite Roman houses by their Latin name, *domus*, known from Vitruvius and other ancient writing. Their most distinctive feature is an ***atrium***, a square or oblong central hall lit by an opening in the roof, answered by a shallow pool, or *impluvium*, in the ground to collect rainwater. This kind of house may owe its origin, in part, to elite Etruscan residences. The atrium was where Romans kept ancestral portraits. Its airy quality confers an element of

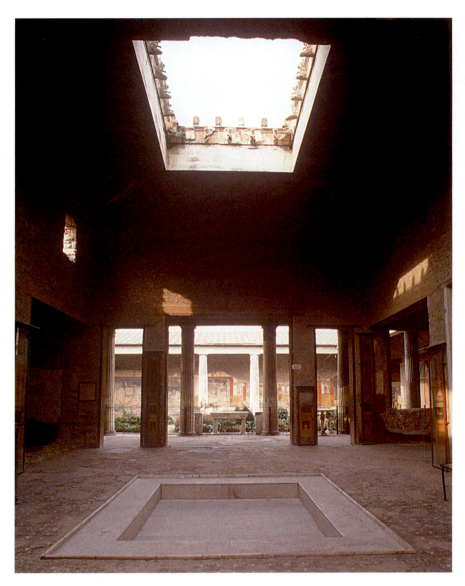

7.22 Atrium of the House of the Vettii. Second century BCE–79 CE. Pompeii

grandeur upon the house, visible here in the House of the Vettii (**fig. 7.22**). Other rooms, such as bedrooms (*cubicula*), are grouped around the atrium, which often leads on to a ***tablinum***, the principal reception room, where family records were kept. Beyond the tablinum is a garden, surrounded by a colonnade (the ***peristyle***). Additional rooms might be attached at the back of the house. Walls facing the street did not typically have windows, but one should not be misled into believing that Roman houses were particularly private. Rooms flanking the entryway were frequently used as shops, and the front door often stood open. Roman society was based on a client–patron relationship, and clients routinely visited their patrons in their homes.

Roman domestic painting survives in great abundance, mainly from Pompeii and Herculaneum, and from Rome and its environs. Basing his analysis partly on Vitruvius' discussion of painting, the late nineteenth-century German art historian August Mau distinguished four phases of Pompeian wall painting (see box opposite), dating from the end of the second century BCE to the late first century CE. The styles are not canonical, but have proved useful as general guidelines. In the First Style, dating to the late second century BCE, artists used paint and stucco to imitate expensive colored marble paneling. Starting about 100 BCE, Second Style painters opened up the flat expanse of the wall by including architectural features and figures, sometimes to suggest a fantasy realm beyond the room. In a room in the Villa of the Mysteries outside Pompeii, dating from about 60 to 50 BCE, the lower part of the wall, beneath the dado, and the upper section above the cornice level are painted in rich mottled colors to resemble exotic stone (**fig. 7.23**). In

Wall Painting, Mural, and Fresco

WALL painting is a very broad descriptive term for painting in any medium on a wall-like surface, from those in caves and rock-cut tombs to those on modern buildings. A mural is a painted image made on or attached to a particular wall, such as the painting cycle in the Villa of the Mysteries (see fig. 7.24). Fresco is a specific wall-painting technique favored in Italy from Roman times through the eighteenth century. In true (*buon*) fresco, the artist paints with water-based colored pigments directly onto fresh, still-damp plaster, working in small sections and producing a stable, long-lasting image. Dry (*secco*) fresco, in which the pigments are painted on dry plaster, is far less durable than true fresco and was used mostly for details.

1. The First, or Incrustation, Style: The wall is painted (and molded in stucco) to imitate masonry blocks, no figured scenes. Second century BCE

2. The Second, or Architectural, Style: Characteristically featuring illusionistic architectural vistas. ca. 100–15 BCE

3. The Third, or Ornate, Style: The vistas here give way to a delicate decorative scheme, concentrating on formal ornament. ca. 15 BCE–50 CE

4. The Fourth, or Intricate, Style: A more extravagant painterly style, parading the whole range of decorative idioms. ca. 50 CE

7.23 *Scenes of Dionysiac Mystery Cult*, Second Style wall painting from the Villa of the Mysteries. ca. 60–50 BCE. Pompeii

7.24 Fourth Style wall painting, Ixion Room, House of the Vettii. 63–79 CE. Pompeii between, figures interact as if on a narrow ledge set against a deep red background, articulated by upright strips of black resembling stylized columns. The figures are engaged in rites associated with the Dionysiac mysteries, one of the so-called mystery religions originating in Greece. The scene may represent an initiation into womanhood or marriage, conducted in the presence of Dionysos and Ariadne with SATYRS and SILENI. The solidity and bold modeling of the near life-sized figures, and their calm but varied poses, lend a quiet power and vivid drama to the room.

The Third Style dominated wall decoration from about 20 BCE until at least the middle of the first century CE. In this phase, artists abandoned illusionism in favor of solid planes of intense colors like black and red, often articulated with attenuated architectural features and imitation panel paintings. The Fourth Style, which prevailed at the time of the eruption of Vesuvius, united aspects of all three preceding styles to create an extravagant effect. The Ixion Room in the House of the Vettii (**fig. 7.24**) combines imitation marble paneling, framed mythological scenes set into the wall, and fantastic architectural vistas receding into space.

Like the Ixion painting, many Roman paintings were of Greek themes. The few painters' names that are recorded show that at least some of them were of Greek origin. There are also sufficient instances of paintings (or elements of paintings) closely resembling one another to indicate that artists used copybooks; in some cases, they may have been working from a Greek original, adapting the image freely to their own purposes. Given the evident innovation in Roman painting in general, there is no reason to suppose that Roman artists were not fully capable of creating their own compositions and narratives when they chose. In recent years, scholarship has focused on ways in which painting ensembles affected experience or dictated movement throughout a house and expressed the owner's status. In fact, an ancient genre of literature, known as *ekphrasis*, is a learned exposition on the subject of real or imagined paintings. These writings led scholars to believe that homeowners sometimes conceived paintings as conversation pieces for their guests, who might discuss them as they dined. Designing a painting program, then, took on a new level of importance for what it might subtly disclose about the patron's aspirations.

The Late Empire

Portrait Sculpture

During Marcus Aurelius' reign, incursions at the empire's German and Danubian borders were a constant threat. Succeeding him in 180 CE, his son Commodus was assassinated in 192 CE. After a brief respite from turmoil under the Severan dynasty, Rome entered a half-century of civil war, when a long succession of emperors came to power and quickly fell through violence. Imperial portraits of this time share a harsh, soldierly quality, intended to appeal to the military, where the power lay. Beards and hair are cropped short, with individual strands often etched with a quick chip of the chisel that scholars term negative carving (**fig. 7.25**). The twist of the head, the furrowed brow and the generally careworn features present the army with a man of action as their leader.

Imperial authority was restored in the reign of Diocletian (r. 284–305 CE). His approach was

In Greek mythology, SATYRS were phallic, goatish beings of the woods and hills. Although similar to satyrs, SILENI were older, usually bald, and always bearded.

7.25 *Portrait of Philip the Arab*. 244–249 CE. Marble, life-size. Musei Vaticani, Braccio Nuovo, Città del Vaticano, Rome

7.26 *Portrait of Constantine the Great.* Early fourth century CE. Marble, height 8′ (2.4 m). Museo del Palazzo dei Conservatori, Rome

to impose rigid order on all aspects of civil as well as military life, and to divide authority among four rulers, known as the tetrarchs. In the early fourth century, Constantine the Great rose to sole power, overcoming his chief rival, Maxentius, at the Battle of Milvian Bridge in Rome in 312. The colossal head of **fig. 7.26** is one fragment of a vast seated portrait that once occupied an apse in a huge BASILICA (see figs. 7.29 and 7.30). The head alone is eight feet tall. Its domi-

nant feature is the disproportionately large eyes. Deeply carved, they gaze into a faraway distance; combined with the stiff frontality of the face, they give the image an abstract and iconic quality. Some scholars associate changes like these with a new spirituality in the later Empire, exemplified by Constantine's adherence to Christianity. Perhaps the eyes gaze at something beyond this world; perhaps they are a window to the soul. At the same time, the full cap of hair, and the absence of a beard, appear to be direct references to Trajan and Augustus, great emperors of the past whose achievements still gave the office its authority.

Relief Sculpture

In 315 CE, the Senate and People of Rome dedicated the triple-bayed Arch of Constantine near the Colosseum to celebrate Constantine's ten-year anniversary and conquest of Maxentius (**fig. 7.27**). It is one of the largest imperial arches. What makes it most unusual is that little of the sculptural relief covering its surface was designed for this monument. Free-standing Dacian captives on the attic originated in the Trajanic period, as did the Great Trajanic Frieze on the ends of the attic and inside the central bay. Eight hunting and sacrifice *tondi* (circular reliefs) above the lateral bays once belonged to a Hadrianic monument, and eight panels on the attic may have decorated an arch to Marcus Aurelius. When the arch was constructed, sculptors recarved the heads of earlier emperors to resemble Constantine and his co-emperor Licinius. A modern restoration replaced some of them with heads of Trajan.

Scholars describe sculptural and architectural borrowings of this kind by the modern term ***spolia***, derived from the Latin *spolium*, meaning "hide stripped from an animal," a term primarily used for spoils taken in war. The *spolia* raise all manner of questions—such as how Romans perceived the stripping of one monument in favor of another, and what became of the original monument, presuming that it was still standing. In a renowned assault on late antique sculpture in the 1950s, the art historian Bernard Berenson condemned the use of *spolia* as evidence of a pervasive decline in form, which he attributed to a mass exodus of craftsmen and artists from Rome. Other scholars see the *spolia* as part of a legitimizing ideology, suggesting that they expressed qualities of "emperorness." By revisiting the reputations and successes of "good" rulers of the past, Constantine may have hoped to harness the reputations that they had earned during their lifetimes. He had every reason to legitimize his authority: Maxentius had been a formidable opponent, and Constantine, as the first openly Christian emperor, risked alienating a pagan Senate. If this interpretation is correct, it is not far from readings of the

7.27 Arch of Constantine. 312–315 CE. Rome

7.28 Constantinian relief from Arch of Constantine. Rome

Republican statue base, partly made up of Greek reliefs, as seen in figure 7.5.

To complement the borrowed pieces, Constantinian artists carved bases for the columns that flank the bays, a continuous relief to encircle the arch just above the lateral bays, and roundels for the sides of the arch. The section of frieze illustrated here depicts Constantine speaking to the Senate and people of Rome from the speaker's platform or **rostrum** in the Forum, after his entry into Rome in 312 CE (**fig. 7.28**). Figures crowd the scene. Their heads are disproportionately large, their bodies stocky, and their poses unnaturally rigid. Lines carved on the flat surface render anatomical details in place of modeling. Berenson judged the style of the Constantinian reliefs just as harshly as the act of spoliation. Yet their abstract quality makes them unusually legible from a distance, which is how they would have been seen. A careful order governs the composition, with the emperor occupying the center and shown fully frontal; other figures turn and focus attention on him. Buildings

in the background are sufficiently distinct to make the setting recognizable even today as the Roman Forum. The artists chose to emphasize the message-bearing potential of the reliefs over any attempt at illusionism or naturalism.

Architecture

By the time of the late Empire, architects in Rome had more or less abandoned the straightforward use of post-and-lintel construction. Their interests appear to have focused instead on exploring the interior spaces made possible by concrete. Column, architrave, and pediment took on decorative roles, superimposed on vaulted brick-and-concrete cores. When Maxentius commissioned a basilica, the architects looked to the massive uninterrupted spaces of BATH BUILDINGS for inspiration. The Basilica of Maxentius (**figs. 7.29** and **7.30**) was probably the largest roofed interior in Rome. It was divided into three aisles, of which only the north one still stands. Transverse barrel vaults covered the lateral aisles, and the wider, taller central aisle was covered with three massive

Public bathing facilities existed in other ancient civilizations, but none compared with those built by the Romans. Their thermae ranged from the great imperial BATH BUILDINGS in the capital to smaller local examples. Each had a *frigidarium* (cold bath), *tepidarium* (warm bath), and *caldarium* (hot bath), as well as a *natatio* (swimming pool) and small "plunge baths." The imperial baths built by Caracalla and Diocletian were massive complexes with richly decorated interiors.

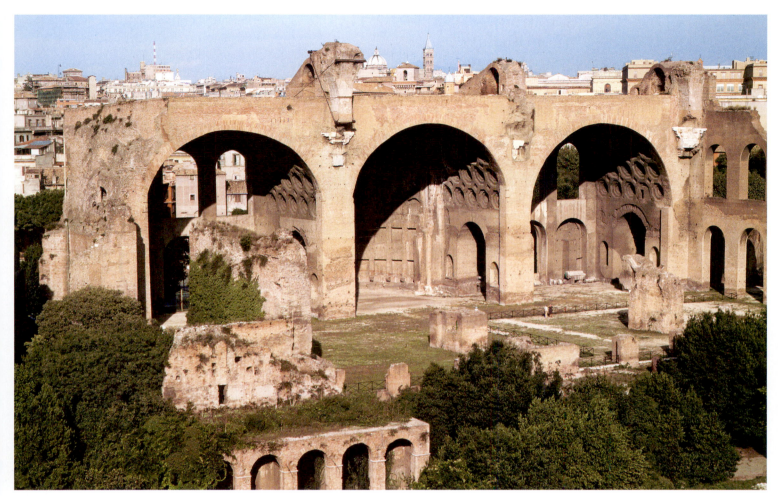

7.29 Basilica of Maxentius, renamed Basilica of Constantine. Begun ca. 307 CE. Rome

7.30 Basilica of Maxentius, renamed Basilica of Constantine. Reconstruction (after Huelsen)

groin vaults. Since a groin vault concentrates its weight and thrust at the four corners, the upper walls of the nave (central aisle) could be pierced by a large clerestory. As a result, the interior of the basilica must have had a light and airy quality despite its enormous size. The building had two entrances: Through a transverse vestibule at the east end, and through a stepped doorway on the south, leading from the Roman Forum. Apses faced each of the entrances. On overcoming Maxentius, Constantine expropriated the basilica, giving it his own name and placing his colossal portrait in the western apse (see fig. 7.26). Expropriations of this kind were not uncommon in Rome, and show how critical it was to have a physical presence in the city.

Late Roman Architecture in the Provinces

Developments in late Roman architecture appear to go hand-in-hand with the profound changes that the emperor Diocletian made to society. When Diocletian divided authority between the tetrarchs, each of them established a capital in a different region of the Empire and embellished it with appropriate grandeur. Constantius Chlorus, father of Constantine the Great, made his seat at Trier, in present-day Germany. There he, too, constructed a basilica, which now functions as a church (**figs. 7.31** and **7.32**). In its design, the Classical forms have dissolved entirely, leaving vast abstract expanses in solid and void. The great mass of its walls is broken by elongated arches, serving as visual buttresses framing the windows, beneath which were balconies. As vast as the interior was, the architect directed his skill toward achieving the illusion of even greater dimensions. The windows in the apse are significantly smaller than those in the side walls, and the apse ceiling is lower than the ceiling over the main hall. Both devices have the effect of making the apse look as if it recedes farther into the distance than it actually does. Not only did this make the building appear grander, but the apse was where the emperor—or his image—would hold sway, and the altered dimensions would have had the effect of making him appear significantly larger than life. The vocabulary of Roman building had changed, in other words, but it was still an architecture of power.

7.31 Basilica of Constantius Chlorus. Early fourth century CE. Trier, Germany

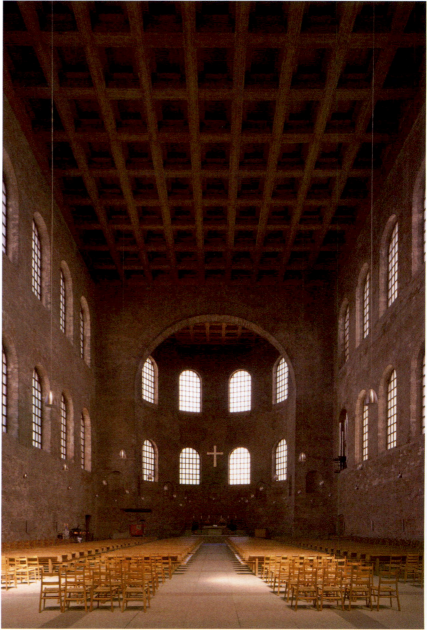

7.32 Interior of Basilica of Constantius Chlorus. Early fourth century CE. Trier, Germany

SUMMARY

During the course of about a millennium, Rome grew from a small city to the capital of a massive and culturally diverse empire. Those years witnessed major developments in architecture, due as much to changes in technology as to political motivations. In the provinces, architecture brought some improvements in standards of living, but also helped to secure Roman control, exerting a constant Roman presence far from the center of administration. Painting and sculpture abounded within public and private buildings—sculpture often carrying a strong political message, its style chosen to best reinforce its content.

Roman builders were indebted to Greek predecessors, especially in the use of the Doric, Ionic, and Corinthian styles. Their architects, however, used forms—such as the arch—that made their buildings decisively Roman. Concrete as a building material was exploited fully by the Romans, and its use allowed them to create remarkable spaces, as seen in the Sanctuary of Fortuna Primigenia. Political leaders used architecture, as well as sculpture, to express and justify their power and to commemorate specific events.

During the age of Augustus, Roman portrait sculpture turned from the earlier veristic style of the Republic to a more classicizing style associated with ancient Greece. The practice of commissioning narrative reliefs to record specific events remained popular, as seen in the Column of Trajan. Early imperial masterpieces of concrete construction include the Colosseum and the Pantheon, both in Rome.

As ancient Rome's authority spread over a wide geographical reach, it had a great impact on the art, architecture, and daily life of those regions. Roman rule brought practical benefits, such as aqueducts to move water. It also introduced a way of life that included frequent public entertainments and Roman religious practices, both of which are reflected in the theaters, amphitheaters, and temples constructed from one end of the empire to the other.

When the eruption of Mount Vesuvius buried the cities of Pompeii and Herculaneum, it preserved a wealth of houses, wall paintings, mosaics, and everyday objects. This invaluable legacy reveals that art played a powerful role in the home as well as in more public places, projecting an image of its patron for others to see.

Not long after the death of Marcus Aurelius, the Roman Empire entered a period of instability that lasted almost 100 years, until the reign of the emperor Diocletian. In late antiquity, an abstract style came to dominate sculpture and architecture, as seen in the colossal portrait of Constantine the Great, possibly due to an increased interest in spirituality, and to changing concepts of rulership.

During the Tetrarchy, the four emperors ruled the Empire from four capitals outside of Rome, and furnished these cities with new public buildings, such as Constantius Chlorus' basilica in Trier, Germany.

ART IN TIME

- ca. 509 BCE—The Romans turn against the monarchy, expelling the last king

- ca. 509 BCE—Dedication of the Temple of Jupiter Optimus Maximus

- 100s BCE—Greece and Asia Minor controlled by Rome

- 60–50 BCE—Paintings from the Villa of the Mysteries, outside Pompeii

- 46 BCE—Julius Caesar becomes perpetual dictator of Rome

- 27 BCE—Octavian named Augustus Caesar by the Roman Senate

- 9 BCE—Dedication of the *Ara Pacis Augustae*, the Altar of Augustan Peace

- 79 CE—Vesuvius erupts

- early 100s CE—Aqueduct built at Segovia, Spain

- 100s CE—The earliest painted portraits from the Fayum, Lower Egypt

- ca. 115–125 CE— Construction of the Pantheon in Rome

- fourth century CE— Constantine the Great

- 315 CE—Dedication of the Arch of Constantine in Rome

PART 2
The Middle Ages

THE LABELS WE USE for historical periods tend to be like the nicknames of people: Once established, they are almost impossible to change, even though they may no longer be apt. Those who coined the term "Middle Ages" thought of the thousand years or more from the fourth to the fifteenth centuries as an empty interval between classical Antiquity and its rebirth during the Renaissance in Italy. Since then, our view of the Middle Ages and of medieval art has changed greatly. (The term "medieval" is derived from the Latin med[ium] aev[um], thus a synonym for the Middle Ages.) The chronological limits of the period are somewhat fluid, but for many historians, the conversion of Constantine the Great in 312 CE marks the beginning of the Middle Ages, while the Renaissance in the 1400s marks its end. The sheer breadth of its chronological span suggests the durability of its art forms, which are in fact multi-faceted and varied. We now recognize this long period, not so much as one that marks a division between two greater eras, but as one of major cultural change and creative activity.

How did these dramatic artistic changes come about? In 324 CE Constantine the Great made a fateful decision, the consequences of which are still felt today. He resolved to move the capital of the Roman Empire to the strategically located Greek town of Byzantium, which came to be known as Constantinople (and today as Istanbul). Six years later, after a major building campaign, the transfer was officially completed. In taking this step, the emperor acknowledged the growing strategic and economic importance of the eastern provinces. The new capital also symbolized the new Christian basis of the Roman state, since it was in the heart of the most thoroughly Christianized region of the empire, far from Rome, whose senatorial elite continued to be practitioners of pagan religions.

Constantine could hardly have foreseen that shifting the seat of imperial power would result in splitting the empire. Yet, less than 75 years later, in 395, the division of the realm into the Eastern and Western empires was complete. Eventually that separation led to a religious split as well. The differences between Eastern and Western Christianity went very deep. Roman Catholicism maintained its independence from State authority and became an international institution, reflecting its character as the Universal Church. The Orthodox Church, on the other hand, was based on the union of spiritual and secular authority in the person of the emperor, who appointed the patriarch.

The two empires faced different political circumstances. The Eastern Empire was more secure, while the Western Roman Empire soon fell prey to invading Germanic tribes: Visigoths, Vandals, Franks, Ostrogoths, and Lombards. Once they had settled in their new lands, these invaders accepted the framework of late Roman Christian civilization.

But Christianity was not the only "new" religion to affect the development of medieval art. The religion of Islam, based on the teachings of its founder, the Prophet Muhammad, was significant for the rapidity with which it spread throughout the Roman world. The African and Near Eastern parts of the empire were overrun by conquering Arab Islamic armies and by 732, only a century after the death of Muhammad, Arab armies had absorbed Spain and threatened to conquer southwestern France as well. The Eastern Empire, with its domain reduced to the Balkan Peninsula, including Greece, held on until the year 1453, when the Islamic Turks conquered Constantinople itself. It is from this date that the city is known by its modern name of Istanbul. Islam created a new civilization stretching as far east as the Indus Valley (now in Pakistan).

Islamic art, learning and crafts were to have great influence on the European Middle Ages, from **arabesque** ornament, the manufacture of paper, and Arabic numerals to the transmission of Greek philosophy and science through the studies and writings of Arab scholars. (The English language records this debt in words such as algebra.) In recognition of the significant impact of Islamic culture, Islamic art is discussed in this book in the context of the art which was affected by it, but in itself it is not the central focus of our more Western-oriented studies.

It should be clear from the preceding account that the medieval world was set in motion by a series of severe turmoils that present a continually shifting picture. Not even the Frankish kingdom in northern Europe, ruled by the powerful Merovingian and Carolingian dynasties, was able to impose lasting order. As the only international organization of any sort,

Christianity was of critical importance in promoting a measure of stability.

The rapid spread of Christianity, like that of Islam, cannot be explained simply in institutional terms, for the Church did not perfectly embody Christian ideals. Christianity and Islam must have been extremely persuasive, in spiritual as well as in moral terms, to the masses of people who heard their messages. There is no other way to explain the rapid conversion of these religions.

Church and State gradually discovered that they could not live without each other. What was needed was an alliance between a strong secular power and a united Church. This link was forged when the Catholic Church, that is, the Roman Church, turned for support to the Germanic North. There the leadership of Charlemagne and his descendants—the Carolingian dynasty—made the Frankish kingdom the leading power during the second half of the eighth century. Charlemagne conquered most of Europe, from the North Sea to Spain and as far south as Lombardy in Italy. When Pope Leo III appealed to him for help, Charlemagne went to Rome, where on Christmas Day in the year 800, the pope bestowed on him the title of emperor— something that Charlemagne neither sought nor wanted.

In placing himself and all of Western Christianity under the protection of the king of the Franks and Lombards, Leo did not merely solemnize the new order of things. He also tried to assert his authority over the newly created Catholic emperor. He claimed that the emperor's legitimacy depended on the pope.

However, Charlemagne did not subordinate himself to the pope; rather, an interdependence of spiritual and political authority, of Church and State, was established. Although the emperor was crowned in Rome, he did not live there. Charlemagne built his capital at the center of his power, in Aachen, located in what is now north Germany and close to France, Belgium and the Netherlands.

The center of gravity of European civilization thus shifted north of the Alps, to what had been the northern boundaries of the Roman world. This shift led to dramatic cultural interchanges, which to some extent became defining features of subsequent medieval art, that is, from the period of Germanic tribal migration through the Romanesque and Gothic periods. Artistic methods, materials and traditions were brought with migration and were combined with those customs that predominated in the regions where tribes settled, in many cases areas that had been Romanized during the height of imperial expansion. Rome would continue to be a meaningful, if shifting, construct for the developing Middle Ages.

While the early medieval dream of a unified imperial Europe to rival the height of the Roman Empire faded, new authoritative structures provided real and continued political and social stability in the Romanesque and Gothic periods. These were manifested politically through a feudal system and ecclesiastically through both a monastic system and strong bishoprics.

Although one should not undervalue the political dimensions of medieval

art, the Middle Ages is generally epitomized as an era of faith and its art as an expression of piety and devotion. It is no mere coincidence that our discussion of medieval art begins with the Early Christian period, includes the art of Islam, and ends with the creation of immense Gothic cathedrals. Even as new towns were founded and old ones fortified and strengthened, religious institutions remained the fundamental patron of the arts throughout the Middle Ages. Certainly there was a shift inward, toward spiritualized representation, yet it would be an oversimplification to distinguish medieval from ancient art only by the medieval concentration on spiritual values. After all, the art of the ancient world also included a religious dimension, for the gods of Greece and Rome were virtually omnipresent in their art. However, whereas the ancients expressed the physical presence of their gods in naturalistic sculpture and paintings, Early Christian artists explored a different vision. In the service of their new faith, these artists concentrated on symbolic representation, using physical means to express a spiritual essence.

But the change in artistic purpose was not exclusively a result of changes in religion, since, as our discussion of later Roman art has shown, the movement toward increasing stylization and abstraction also appeared in pagan contexts: Witness the theories of Plotinus and the sculpture of Constantine and the Tetrarchs (see fig. 7.26). Medieval art must be seen as a result of wide-ranging and shifting cultural conditions.

ATLANTIC
OCEAN

NORTH
SEA

BALTIC

NORWAY
SWEDEN

SCANDINAVIA

SCOTLAND

Lindisfarne

DENMARK

BRITISH ISLES

Durham

Corvey

IRELAND

N

ENGLAND

Gloucester

Sutton Hoo
London

THE
NETHERLANDS

Utrecht

SAXONY

Hildesheim

Elbe R.

Salisbury

Canterbury

FLANDERS

Thames R.

Corbie

Laon

Bayeux

Caen

NORMANDY

ÎLE-DE-FRANCE

St-Denis

Chartres

Paris

Cologne
Limbourg

Aachen

RHINELAND

Bingen

Verdun

Metz

Reims

GERMANY

Naumburg

POL

Rhine R.

Meuse R.

HOLY

ROMAN

Nuremberg

BOHEMIA

Strasbourg

EMPIRE

Bay

of

Biscay

FRANCE

Poitiers

St Savin-
sur-Gartempe

Loire R.

Seine R.

BURGUNDY

Fontenay

Cîteaux

Autun

Schwäbisch Gmünd

Lake Constance

St. Gall

Munich

Lindau

Vienna

Cluny

Clairvaux

SWITZERLAND

Reichenau

HU

Santiago
de Compostela

Lake
Geneva

A

L

P

S

LOMBARDY

Rhône R.

Milan

Garonne R.

Moissac

PYRENEES

Po R.

Padua

Venice

Toulouse

Duero R.

Ebro R.

PROVENCE

Pisa

Arno R.

Ravenna

Florence

CROAT

Tajo R.

SPAIN

TUSCANY

Tiber R.

ADRIATIC SEA

IBERIAN

ITALY

PENINSULA

Córdoba

Rome

Guadalquivir R.

APULIA

Granada

TYRRHENIAN SEA

ION

S

MEDITERRANEAN

SICILY

NORTH AFRICA

Kairouan

	The Byzantine Empire
	c. 1025 A.D.

0   250   500 Miles
0   250   500 Kilometers

THE MIDDLE AGES

RUSSIA

Don R.

Volga R.

Dnieper R.

CASPIAN SEA

BLACK SEA

Danube R.

ARMENIA

Lake Van

Lake Urmia

Nerezi

Byzantium
(Constantinople)

CEDONIA

Halys R.

CAPPADOCIA

Salonica
ssalonika)

Mt. Athos

TURKEY

NEAR

Tigris R.

MESOPOTAMIA

REECE

AEGEAN
SEA

ANATOLIA

E A S T

Mt. Parnassus

Daphne

Athens

IONIA

Samarra

Baghdad

Euphrates R.

SYRIA

CRETE

SEA

Jordan R.

Jerusalem

8

Early Christian, Byzantine, and Early Islamic Art

❖ The CHI RHO sign, a monogram of Christ, is composed of the first two letters of Christ's name in Greek, *Christos*: Chi (χ) and rho (ρ). The monogram is often referred to as the Chrismon or the Christogram.

A spiritual crisis developed within the Roman Empire during the third century CE. Traditional value systems, including officially sanctioned religion, no longer satisfied a society weakened by inept, militaristic, or opportunistic rulers, and by threats to the borders of the empire from migrating tribes that the Romans considered barbarian. The Late Roman Empire was home to a vast melting pot of creeds—among them the ancient faith of Judaism alongside Christianity, Mithraism, Manichaeism, and Gnosticism, to name a few. These competing faiths shared several features, including an emphasis on divine revelation through a chief prophet or messiah and the hope of salvation. Additionally, they shared a belief in a cosmic struggle of good against evil, a ritual of initiation or purification (such as baptism), and, except for Judaism, the duty to seek converts. The last faith of this type to develop was Islam, which took form in the early seventh century on the Arabian peninsula and continues to dominate the Near East to this day.

Of these religions, Christianity—centering on the life and teachings of Jesus of Nazareth—became the most widespread and influential in Western Europe during the Middle Ages. It spread first to Greek-speaking communities, notably to Alexandria, in Egypt, then reached the Latin-speaking world by the end of the second century. The Gospels of Matthew, Mark, Luke, and John, our principal source of information about Jesus' life, were probably written in the late first century, some decades after Jesus' death (see Cultural Context: The Life of Jesus, pages 158–159). The Gospels present him as a historical person and as the Son of God and Messiah or the "Anointed One." The eloquence and significance of Christ's teachings, the miracles attributed to him, and his innate goodness were considered signs of his divinity. The Roman authorities, viewing Jesus' teaching as subversive, had him arrested, tried, and ultimately punished and executed by crucifixion. By 300 CE, nearly 20 percent of the Roman empire was Christian, though the new faith continued to have little standing until the conversion of Constantine the Great in 312.

In that year, Constantine was battling his fellow Tetrarch, Maxentius, for control of the Western Empire. Constantine claimed to have had a dream in which Christ himself, by a sign (reputedly the CHI RHO), assured him of his victory over Maxentius, which took place at the Milvian Bridge in Rome in 312. This is the triumph commemorated by the Arch of Constantine (see fig. 7.27). After this, Constantine accepted the Christian faith and, having consolidated imperial power, promoted Christianity throughout the empire. He claimed that his political authority was granted by God, and placed himself at the head of the Church as well as of the state. His choice to accept and promote Christianity was a turning point in history, as it resulted in the union of Christianity with the

Map 8.1 The Early Christian, Byzantine, and early Islamic worlds

legacy of the empire. Constantine's resolve to locate a new capital in Byzantium resulted in the division of Rome into two halves: An Eastern Empire, of which Constantinople was the capital, and a Western Empire centered at Rome. Imperial might and wealth were concentrated in Constantinople, enriching and protecting the Eastern Empire. In the West, imperial authority was less effective in the face of new challenges, as non-Roman groups first invaded and then settled in Europe.

Into the vacuum of power left by the decline of imperial institutions in the West stepped the bishop of Rome. Deriving his authority from St. Peter, the pope, as the bishop of Rome became known, claimed to be the head of the universal Christian Church, although his Eastern counterpart, the patriarch of Constantinople, disputed this claim. Differences in doctrine and liturgy continued to develop until eventually the division of Christendom into a Western or Catholic Church and an Eastern or Orthodox Church

became all but final. The Great Schism, or final break, between the two churches occurred in the eleventh century.

The religious separation of East and West profoundly affected the development of Christian art in the Late Roman Empire. "Early Christian" does not, strictly speaking, designate a style. It refers, rather, to any work of art produced by or for Christians during the time prior to the splitting off of the Eastern Church from the Western Church, that is, roughly during the first five centuries after the birth of Jesus. "Byzantine," on the other hand, designates not only the art of the Eastern Roman Empire but also its specific culture and style, which was linked to the imperial court of Constantinople.

Although Early Christian art has its origins in Rome, its forms differ from those of the classical world. Early Christian art refined the increasingly stylized and abstracted art forms of the Late Roman Empire into a visual language that

The Life of Jesus

IN THE CHRISTIAN RELIGION, events in the life of Jesus, from his birth through his ascension to heaven, are traditionally grouped in cycles, each with numerous episodes. The scenes most frequently depicted in European art are presented here.

Incarnation Cycle and The Childhood of Jesus

These episodes concern Jesus' conception, birth, infancy, and youth.

ANNUNCIATION. The archangel Gabriel tells Mary that she will bear God's son. The Holy Spirit, shown usually as a dove, represents the Incarnation, the miraculous conception.

VISITATION. The pregnant Mary visits her older cousin Elizabeth, who is to bear John the Baptist and who is the first to recognize the divine nature of the baby Mary is carrying.

NATIVITY. At the birth of Jesus, the Holy Family—Mary, her husband, Joseph, and the child—is usually depicted in a stable or, in Byzantine representations, in a cave.

ANNUNCIATION TO THE SHEPHERDS and ADORATION OF THE SHEPHERDS. An angel announces the birth of Jesus to shepherds in a field at night. The shepherds then go to the birthplace to pay homage to the child.

ADORATION OF THE MAGI. The Magi (also called the Three Kings), wise men from the East, follow a bright star for 12 days until they find the Holy Family and present their gifts to Jesus.

PRESENTATION IN THE TEMPLE. Mary and Joseph take the infant Jesus to the Temple in Jerusalem, where Simeon, a devout man, and Anna, a prophetess, foresee Jesus' messianic (savior's) mission and martyr's death.

MASSACRE OF THE INNOCENTS and FLIGHT INTO EGYPT. King Herod orders all children under the age of two in and around Bethlehem to be killed in order to preclude his being murdered by a rival newborn king spoken of in a prophecy. The Holy Family flees to Egypt.

Public Ministry Cycle

BAPTISM. John the Baptist baptizes Jesus in the Jordan River, recognizing Jesus' incarnation as the Son of God. This marks the beginning of Jesus' ministry.

CALLING OF MATTHEW. A tax collector, Matthew, becomes Jesus' first disciple (apostle) when Jesus calls to him, "Follow me."

JESUS WALKING ON THE WATER. During a storm, Jesus walks on the water of the Sea of Galilee to reach his apostles in a boat.

RAISING OF LAZARUS. Jesus brings his friend Lazarus back to life four days after Lazarus's death and burial.

DELIVERY OF THE KEYS TO PETER. Jesus names the apostle Peter his successor by giving him the keys to the Kingdom of Heaven.

TRANSFIGURATION. As Jesus' closest disciples watch, God transforms Jesus into a dazzling vision and proclaims him to be his own son.

CLEANSING THE TEMPLE. Enraged, Jesus clears the Temple in Jerusalem of money changers and animal traders.

Passion Cycle

The Passion (from passio, Latin for "suffering") cycle relates Jesus' death, resurrection from the dead, and ascension to heaven.

could express both profoundly spiritual and unmistakably secular power.

The last of the great faiths to arise, Islam, an Arabic word denoting submission to God's will, is now the predominant religion of a vast area of the world extending across Africa, Europe, and Asia. Many different ethnicities, cultures, languages, and forms of social and political organization marked, and still mark, Islamic culture. Muslims (meaning those who submit) believe that Muhammad (ca. 570–632), who came from the city of Mecca in the western Arabian peninsula, was chosen by God (in Arabic, Allah) to serve as God's Messenger, or Prophet, to humanity. Muhammad is said to have received the Word of God as a series of poetical recitations. These

were brought to him by the archangel Jibra'il (Gabriel). Muhammad memorized and recited these poetic verses, and taught them to his followers. Organized into *sura* (chapters) and finally written down after Muhammad's death, these prayers, stories, exhortations, and commandments constitute the Qur'an, Islam's sacred book. The Qur'an, together with official collections of *hadith* (remembrances) of the exemplary life of Muhammad as the Messenger, form the basis of Islamic religious practice and law (see Cultural Context: Islam: Beliefs and Practices, page 185).

While the Prophet quickly gained adherents, those in authority in Mecca were threatened by the challenges posed by the new faith to their

ENTRY INTO JERUSALEM. Welcomed by crowds as the Messiah, Jesus triumphantly rides an ass into the city of Jerusalem.

LAST SUPPER. At the Passover seder, Jesus tells his disciples of his impending death and lays the foundation for the Christian rite of the Eucharist: The taking of bread and wine in remembrance of Christ. (Strictly speaking, Jesus is called Jesus until he leaves his earthly physical form, after which he is called Christ.)

JESUS WASHING THE DISCIPLES' FEET. Following the Last Supper, Jesus washes the feet of his disciples to demonstrate humility.

AGONY IN THE GARDEN. In Gethsemane, the disciples sleep while Jesus wrestles with his mortal dread of suffering and dying.

BETRAYAL (ARREST). The disciple Judas Iscariot takes money to identify Jesus to Roman soldiers. Jesus is arrested.

DENIAL OF PETER. As Jesus predicted, Peter, waiting outside the high priest's palace, denies knowing Jesus three times as Jesus is being questioned by the high priest, Caiaphas.

JESUS BEFORE PILATE. Jesus is questioned by the Roman governor Pontius Pilate regarding whether he calls himself King of the Jews. Jesus does not answer. Pilate reluctantly condemns him.

FLAGELLATION (SCOURGING). Jesus is whipped by Roman soldiers.

JESUS CROWNED WITH THORNS (THE MOCKING OF CHRIST). Pilate's soldiers mock Jesus by dressing him in robes, crowning him with thorns, and calling him King of the Jews.

CARRYING OF THE CROSS (ROAD TO CALVARY). Jesus carries the wooden cross on which he will be executed from Pilate's house to the hill of Golgotha, "the place of the skull."

CRUCIFIXION. Jesus is nailed to the Cross by his hands and feet, and dies after great physical suffering.

DESCENT FROM THE CROSS (DEPOSITION). Jesus' followers lower his body from the Cross and wrap it for burial. Also present are the Virgin, the apostle John, and in some accounts Mary Magdalen.

LAMENTATION (PIETÀ or VESPERBILD). The grief-stricken followers gather around Jesus' body. In the *Pietà*, his body lies in the lap of the Virgin.

ENTOMBMENT. The Virgin and others place the wrapped body in a sarcophagus or in a rock tomb.

DESCENT INTO LIMBO (HARROWING OF HELL or ANASTASIS in the Orthodox Church). Christ descends to hell, or limbo, to free deserving souls who have not heard the Christian message—the prophets of the Old Testament, the kings of Israel, and Adam and Eve.

RESURRECTION. Christ rises from the dead on the third day after his entombment.

THE MARYS AT THE TOMB. As terrified soldiers look on, Christ's female followers (the Virgin Mary, Mary Magdalen, and Mary, mother of the apostle James) discover the empty tomb.

NOLI ME TANGERE, Supper at Emmaus, and the Doubting of Thomas. In three episodes during the 40 days between his resurrection and ascent into heaven, Christ tells Mary Magdalen not to touch him (*Noli me tangere*), shares a supper with his disciples at Emmaus, and invites the apostle Thomas to touch the lance wound in his side.

ASCENSION. As his disciples watch, Christ is taken into heaven from the Mount of Olives.

political and economic power. In 622 Muhammad was forced to leave Mecca with a few of his followers, moving to the city of Medina some 190 miles to the north. The Prophet's house in Medina, constructed in the form of an open square, became the prototype for countless mosques in subsequent centuries.

Upon the death of the Prophet in 632, he was succeeded by four caliphs, referred to as the "successors." They are recognized by Sunni Muslims, who make up some 90 percent of the faith. Shi'ite Muslims believed that only descendants of Muhammad could legitimately lead the Islamic community. They took their name from the term *shi'at'Ali* (the party of 'Ali), Muhammad's son-in-law and father of the Prophet's grandsons, Hasan and Husein. Upon Ali's death, a new dynasty, the Umayyad dynasty, was established, and its influence spread west from its capital in Damascus, Syria, as far as Córdoba, in southern Spain.

Early Christian Art

Christian Art before Constantine

We do not know when or where the first Christian works of art were produced. None of the surviving paintings or sculptures can be dated earlier than about 200 CE. In fact, we know little about Christian art before the reign of Constantine the Great.

8.1 Painted ceiling. Fourth century CE. Catacomb of Santissimi Pietro e Marcellino, Rome

THE ART OF THE CATACOMBS The painted decoration of the Roman catacombs, underground burial places, is the only sizeable body of material we have from which to study the earliest Christian art. The burial rite and the safeguarding of the tomb were of vital concern to early Christians, whose faith rested on salvation, the hope of eternal life in paradise.

The ceiling of one of the more elaborate chambers in the catacomb of Santissimi Pietro e Marcellino (**fig. 8.1**), in Rome, is decorated in a style that is at once formal and uncomplicated. Fixed borders control the overall organization; a central medallion or circle contains the figure of a shepherd, who is flanked by sheep and carries a lamb across his shoulders. The circle is connected to four **lunettes** (semicircular spaces), and in the four corners are single figures with outstretched, raised arms, known as **orants** (worshipers), represented in what had long been the standard pose of prayer. The style of painting reflects Roman murals, both in the landscape settings and in the use of linear devices to divide the scenes into compartments (see the

Ixion Room of the House of the Vettii, fig. 7.24). But the representations seem sketchier, less grounded in natural observation than their Roman relatives.

Catacombs would have been used only occasionally beyond the actual circumstance of burial, perhaps for a commemorative celebration. This is one reason why the wall paintings do not show much detail and care of execution. Another reason for this sketchiness is that their primary value is symbolic. Consistent with the biblical prohibition against image making, as specified in the Second Commandment of the Old Testament, Christ is generally not represented in the catacombs, except by metaphor. The shepherd with a sheep on his shoulder is a potent allusion to Christ, since in a number of biblical accounts Christ refers to himself as the Good Shepherd, concerned for the well-being of his flock and willing to sacrifice himself in order to guarantee the salvation of those who follow him (Luke 15: 4–6; John 10: 1–18). This Good Shepherd metaphor also builds on Old Testament references, as in Psalm 23:

The Lord is my shepherd, I shall not want.
He makes me lie down in green pastures;
he leads me beside still waters;
he restores my soul....
Surely goodness and mercy shall follow me
all the days of my life,
and I shall dwell in the house of the Lord
for ever.

The Old Testament correlation reflects the fact that many of the converts to the new faith were Jewish.

The four lunettes around the Good Shepherd form a cycle dedicated to the Old Testament prophet Jonah. Here too, the symbolic references to Christian beliefs about Christ are clear: Just as it is a principle of faith that Jonah spent three days within the belly of the whale, so Christ is supposed to have spent three days in the tomb, and just as Jonah was released with unharmed body, so Christ was resurrected from his tomb in physical wholeness. Recent converts would probably have felt comfortable knowing that didactic aspects of their old faith could find a sympathetic response in the new religion. Jonah's story is presented as a **prefiguration** (foreseeing) of events in Christ's life, thus assigning the Old Testament story the role of prophecy and the New Testament one its fulfillment.

The painted ceiling in Santissimi Pietro e Marcellino also borrows imagery from classical sources. The Good Shepherd himself is a reminder of pagan symbols of charity in the form of ancient sculptures of men carrying sacrificial animals on their shoulders. So, as with their Jewish counterparts, former practitioners of pagan religions who had converted to Christianity would also have been familiar with some of the images and ideas expressed in Early Christian art.

Both the Good Shepherd and Jonah are associated with messages of comfort, reminding us that Early Christian art develops during the turmoil of Rome's decline, a time of political, social, and economic instability. The allure of the new religion must have been profound indeed, suggesting that things of this world were of less significance than those of a future world, which offered the hope of eternal peace.

THE HOUSE CHURCH We have little archaeological evidence of the places where Early Christians gathered. Literary accounts, including biblical references, suggest that Christians met regularly to celebrate their shared belief in Christ

as the Son of God and Savior and to observe some type of Eucharist, or spiritual union, with him by the partaking of consecrated bread and wine (representing Christ's flesh and blood). The Eucharist commemorates the Last Supper, at which Jesus and his disciples enjoyed a final communal meal. Such gatherings of Christians probably originally took place in private homes and were only later replaced by public spaces designed specifically for Christian worship. In Rome itself we know of 25 private houses—and undoubtedly there were more—reserved as places of Christian worship, although most of them were destroyed by the later building of churches on their sites.

Christian Art after the Official Recognition of Christianity

The building of churches on the sites of what once were private houses used for Christian worship reflects a change in the nature of Christianity during the fourth century from an alternative religion to the official religion endorsed by the emperor Constantine. Almost overnight, an impressive architectural setting had to be created for the new official faith, so that the Church might be visible to all. Constantine himself devoted the full resources of his office to this task.

THE CHRISTIAN BASILICA The most important Constantinian church structures were a type of **basilica**, and this form provided the basic model for the development of church architecture in Western Europe. The Early Christian basilica owes its essential features to imperial basilicas (see page 146). Like them, it is characterized by a long **nave** flanked by side aisles and lit by **clerestory** windows, with an **apse** (though only at one end) and a trussed wooden roof. The Roman basilica was a suitable model, since it combined the spacious interior needed to accommodate a large number of people with (perhaps most important) the imperial associations that proclaimed the privileged status of Christianity. As its largely civil functions were quite different from its new uses as a house of worship, it had to be redesigned to acknowledge these changes. Therefore, the longitudinal plan of the basilica was given a new focus: The **altar** was placed in front of the semicircular apse, normally at the eastern end of the nave. The significance of the altar's placement in the east, where the sun rises, reminds us that Christianity inherited many attributes of divinities from

SPEAKING OF

pagans, infidels, heathens, and heretics

To early Christians and Muslims, all believers in polytheistic religions were called infidels, or unbelievers. In Early Christian Rome and during the Middle Ages, unbelievers were known either as pagans ("unenlightened ones," from the Latin *paganus*, "country dweller") or heathens (those who were not Christian, Jewish, or Muslim). Although, strictly speaking, the words pagan and heathen are synonyms, the former is often—including in this book—reserved for classical antiquity, the latter for northern Europe. Heretics, by contrast, are the faithful who hold opinions contrary to orthodox doctrine.

8.2 Jacopo Grimaldi. *Interior of Old St. Peter's, Rome.* 1619. Drawing, MS: Barbarini Lat. 2733 fols. 104v–105r. Vatican Library, Rome

Plan and reconstruction of Old Saint Peter's

other religions. In this case, Christ shares an imagery with the Roman god Apollo, in his manifestation as sun god.

The greatest Constantinian church was Old Saint Peter's Basilica in Rome. It was torn down and replaced by the present Saint Peter's Basilica, in the Vatican, during the sixteenth and seventeenth centuries, but its appearance is preserved in a seventeenth-century album of copies of earlier drawings (**fig. 8.2**), and there are literary descriptions as well. Together these sources give us a clear idea of the original plan for the church. Begun as early as 319 and finished by 329, Old Saint Peter's was built on the Vatican Hill next to a pagan burial ground. It stood directly over the grave of St. Peter, which was marked by a shrine covered with a *baldacchino*, a canopy that designates a place of honor. The location of St. Peter's burial spot was the focus of the church, and because of site restrictions, its apse was at the west end of the church, an unusual feature. Rituals were conducted from a portable altar placed before the shrine, using gold and silver implements donated by the emperor himself.

To enter the church the congregation first crossed a colonnaded court, the atrium, which was added toward the end of the fourth century; this feature derived from the Roman basilica. Congregants then passed through the **narthex**,

an entrance hall, into the church itself. The steady rhythm of the nave colonnade would have pulled them toward the **triumphal arch**, which framed the shrine of St. Peter and the apse beyond. The shrine stood at the junction of the nave and the **transept**, a separate space placed perpendicular to the nave and aisles. Spaces at the end of the transept, marked off by columns, might have served to prepare items used during church rites and to hold offerings brought by the faithful.

The main focus of Christian liturgy, a body of rites prescribed for public worship, was, and is, the Mass, which includes the sacrament of Communion, the symbolic reenactment on the altar of Jesus' sacrifice (see Cultural Context: The Liturgy of the Mass). The Early Christian basilica encouraged attention to the altar, making it the focal point of the church by placing it opposite the entrance and at the end of a long nave. Even beyond this general emphasis on the altar, Old Saint Peter's gave special prominence to the altar zone through this church's special, additional function as a **martyrium**, a building that housed sacred relics or the remains of a holy person.

CENTRAL-PLAN STRUCTURES Buildings of round or polygonal shape capped by a dome entered the tradition of Christian architecture in Constantine's time. Roman emperors had built

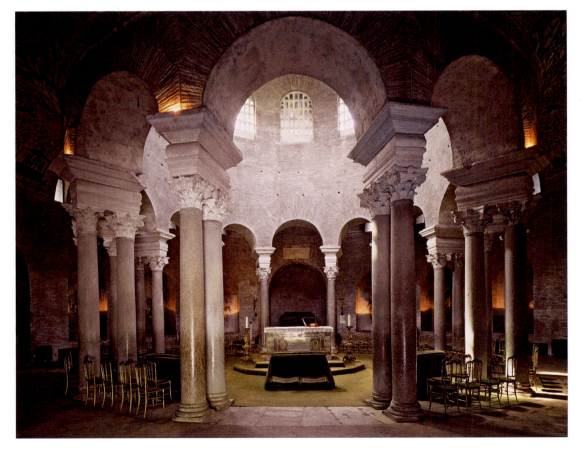

The Liturgy of the Mass

THE CENTRAL RITE of many Christian churches is the EUCHARIST or COMMUNION service, a ritual meal that reenacts Jesus' Last Supper. Bread and wine are consecrated and consumed in memory of Christ. Catholics hold that the bread and wine actually became the body and blood of Christ through transubstantiation. In the Catholic Church and in a few Protestant churches as well, this service is known as the MASS (from the Latin words *Ite, missa est*— "Go, [the congregation] is dismissed," at the end of the Latin service). The Mass was first codified by Pope Gregory the Great around 600 CE.

Each Mass consists of the "ordinary"—those prayers and hymns that are the same in all Masses—and the "proper," the parts that vary, depending on the occasion. The "proper" of the Mass consists of prayers, two readings from the New Testament (one from the Epistles and one from the Gospels); a homily, or sermon, on these texts; and hymns, all chosen specifically for the day. There are also Masses for special occasions, such as the Requiem Mass for the dead and the Nuptial Mass for weddings.

similar structures to serve as monumental tombs or mausoleums. Not surprisingly, therefore, the Early Christian **central-plan** building was often associated with funerary functions. Santa Costanza, in Rome, the mausoleum of Constantine's daughter Constantia (**fig. 8.3**), was built over a catacomb; it was originally attached to the now-ruined basilican church of Saint Agnes Outside the Walls. The focus of the building is on the central space, illuminated by clerestory windows, over which rises a dome supported by 12 pairs of columns. Four of the arches of this colonnade stand slightly higher than the others and suggest a cross inscribed within a circle. The significance of the cross in a funerary context results from its association with Christ, who, though martyred on a cross, rose victorious over death. The Cross was meaningful to all Christians

Ground plan of Santa Costanza

8.3 Interior (view through ambulatory into rotunda), Santa Costanza, Rome. ca. 350 CE but particularly to the family of Constantine, whose personal conversion was a result of his vision of it, which had signaled his victory at the Battle of the Milvian Bridge in 312. The sarcophagus of Constantia was originally placed under the eastern, more elevated arch. Encircling the building is an **ambulatory**, a ring-shaped aisle, covered by a barrel vault (see page 126).

ARCHITECTURAL DECORATION: WALL MOSAICS
The rapid growth of large-scale Christian architecture had a revolutionary effect on Early Christian pictorial art. All of a sudden, huge wall surfaces had to be covered with images worthy of their monumental framework. Out of this need emerged a great new art form, the Early Christian wall mosaic, which to a large extent replaced the older and cheaper medium of mural painting. The challenge of inventing a body of Christian imagery produced an extraordinary creative outpouring. Great pictorial cycles of subjects selected from the Old and New Testaments were spread over the nave walls, the triumphal arch, and the apse. These cycles must have drawn on sources that reflected the whole range of Graeco-Roman painting as well as the artistic traditions that had surely developed in the Christian communities of North Africa and the Near East.

The pictorial embellishment of fourth-century churches is largely fragmentary or known only from literary accounts; it is in fifth-century churches that we can see the full development of mosaic decoration. Central among the Early Christian churches in which a full mosaic program survives is the basilica of Santa Maria Maggiore in Rome. Built between 432 and 440, this was the first church dedicated to Mary, begun only a year after she was declared the *Theotokos* (Greek for "the bearer of God") by the Council of Ephesus.

The exterior brick walls of the building were always much simpler than the rich interior. Having left the everyday world behind, the visitor would encounter a shimmering realm of light and color where precious marble surfaces and glittering mosaics evoked the spiritual splendor of the Kingdom of God. To some extent the building is analogous to the ideal Christian, simple in external body and glorious in inner spirit, an analogy certainly not missed by Early Christians. Roman mural painting used illusionistic devices to suggest a reality beyond the surface of the wall (see fig. 7.23), whereas Early Christian mosaics used the glitter of gold tesserae to create a luminous realm filled with celestial beings, symbols, or narrative action. Thus, Early Christian mosaics transform the illusionistic tradition

8.4 Interior of Santa Maria Maggiore, Rome. ca. 442–440 CE

of ancient painting with the new Christian message.

The apse of Santa Maria Maggiore is a later replacement, but the general outline of the original building and much of the mosaic decoration survive (**fig. 8.4**). These mosaics include the triumphal arch decoration and more than half of the 42 mosaic panels that were placed above the classically inspired entablature of the nave colonnade. These panels were framed by pilasters and colonnettes. Sadly, much of this architectural decoration is now missing.

The panels above the nave colonnade illustrate scenes from the Old Testament. They combine narration with a concern for structured symmetry. For instance, in the left half of *The Parting of Lot and Abraham* (**fig. 8.5**), Abraham, his son Isaac, and the rest of his family depart for the land of Canaan. On the right, Lot and his clan, including his two small daughters, turn toward the city of Sodom. The artist who designed this scene from Genesis 13 faced the same task as the ancient Roman sculptors of the Column of Trajan (see fig. 7.12). He needed to condense complex actions into a form that could be read at a distance. In fact, he employed many of the same shorthand devices, such as the formulas for house, tree, and city, and the device of showing a crowd of people as a cluster of heads, rather like a bunch of grapes.

In the Trajanic reliefs, these devices were used only to the extent that they allowed the artist to portray actual historical events. The mosaics in Santa Maria Maggiore, by contrast, depict the history of human salvation, beginning with the Old Testament scenes along the nave and ending with the life of Jesus as the Messiah on the triumphal arch. For those who read the Bible literally, the scheme is not only a historical cycle but also a symbolic program that presents a higher reality—the Word of God. Hence the artist was not concerned with the details of historical narrative. Glances and gestures were more important than realistic movement or three-dimensional form. In *The Parting of Lot and Abraham*, the symmetrical composition, with its gap in the center, makes clear the significance of this parting. Abraham represents the way of righteousness, while Sodom, which was destroyed by the Lord, signifies the way of evil. Beneath *The Parting of Lot and Abraham* is a classically inspired but thoroughly transformed landscape, its shepherds placed on a green ground, while their sheep, as if on little islands, float in gold surroundings.

8.5 *The Parting of Lot and Abraham* and *Shepherds in a Landscape*. Mosaic. ca. 432–440 CE. Santa Maria Maggiore, Rome

The extensive and complex wall mosaics of Early Christian art are essentially without precedent. The color scale of Roman mosaics (see fig. 5.35), although rich in gradations, lacked brilliance, since it was limited to the kinds of colored marble found in nature. Early Christian mosaics, by contrast, consist of tesserae made of colored glass, which the Romans had known but never fully exploited. These glass tesserae offered colors, including gold, of far greater range and intensity than marble tesserae. Moreover, the shiny, somewhat irregular faces of the glass pieces, each set slightly askew from its neighbor, act as tiny reflectors, so that the overall effect is like a glittering, immaterial screen rather than a solid, continuous surface.

What were the visual sources of the mosaic compositions at Santa Maria Maggiore and other churches like it? These were certainly not the first depictions of scenes from the Bible (see Cultural Context: Versions of the Bible, overleaf). For

Versions of the Bible

THE WORD "BIBLE" is derived from the Greek word for "books," because it was originally a compilation of a number of sacred texts. Over time, the books of the Bible came to be regarded as a unit, and thus the Bible is now generally considered a single book.

There is considerable disagreement between Christians and Jews, and among various Christian and Jewish sects, over which books should be considered canonical—that is, accepted as legitimate parts of the biblical canon, the standard list of authentic texts. However, every version of the Bible includes the Hebrew TORAH, or the Law (also called the PENTATEUCH, or Books of Moses), as the first five books. Also universally accepted by both Jews and Christians are the books known as the Prophets (which include texts of Jewish history as well as prophecy). There are also a number of other books known simply as the Writings, which include history, poetry (the Psalms and the Song of Songs), prophecy, and even folktales, some universally accepted, some accepted by one group, and some accepted by virtually no one. Books of doubtful authenticity are known as APOCRYPHAL BOOKS, or simply Apocrypha, from a Greek word meaning "obscure." The Jewish Bible or Hebrew Canon—the books that are accepted as authentic Jewish scripture—was agreed upon by Jewish scholars sometime before the beginning of the Christian era.

The Christian Bible is divided into two major sections, the OLD TESTAMENT and the NEW TESTAMENT. The Old Testament contains many, but not all, of the Jewish scriptures, whereas the New Testament, originally written in Greek, is specifically Christian. It contains four GOSPELS—each written in the first century CE by one of the Early Christian disciples known as the four EVANGELISTS, Mark, Matthew, Luke, and John. The Gospels tell, from slightly different points of view, the story of the life and teachings of Jesus of Nazareth. They are followed by the EPISTLES, letters written by Paul and a few other Christian missionaries to various congregations of the Church. The final book is the APOCALYPSE, by John the Divine, also called the Book of Revelation, which foretells the end of the world.

Jerome (342–420), the foremost scholar of the early Church, selected the books considered canonical for the Christian Bible from a large body of Early Christian writings. It was because of his energetic advocacy that the Church accepted the Hebrew scriptures as representing the Word of God as much as the Christian texts, and therefore worthy to be included in the Bible. Jerome then translated the books he had chosen from Hebrew and Greek into Latin, the spoken language of Italy in his time. This Latin translation of the Bible was—and is—known as the VULGATE because it was written in the vernacular (Latin *vulgaris*) language. The Vulgate remained the Church's primary text for the Bible for more than a thousand years. It was regarded with such reverence that in the fourteenth century, when early humanists first translated it into the vernacular languages of their time, they were sometimes suspected of heresy for doing so. The writings rejected for inclusion in the New Testament by Jerome are known as Christian Apocrypha. Although not canonical, some of these books, such as the Life of Mary and the Gospel of James, were nevertheless used by artists and playwrights during the Middle Ages as sources for stories to illustrate and dramatize.

certain subjects, such as the Last Supper, models could have been found among the catacomb murals, but others, such as the story of Joshua, may have come from illustrated manuscripts, to which, since they were portable, art historians have assigned an important role as models.

ILLUSTRATED BOOKS Because Christianity was based on the Word of God as revealed in the Bible, early Christians, who referred to themselves as "people of the Book," sponsored duplication of sacred texts on a large scale. What did the earliest Bible illustrations look like? Because books are frail things, we have only indirect evidence of their history in the ancient world. It begins in Egypt with scrolls made from the papyrus plant, which is like paper but more brittle. Not until the second century BCE, in late Hellenistic times, did a better material become available. This was **parchment** (bleached animal hide) or **vellum** (a finer type of parchment), both of which last far longer than papyrus. They were strong enough to be creased without breaking and thus made possible the kind of bound book we know today, technically called a **codex**, which appeared sometime in the late first century CE.

Between the second and the fourth centuries CE, the vellum codex gradually replaced the papyrus roll. This change had an important effect on book illustration. Scroll illustrations seem to have been mostly line drawings, since layers of pigment would soon have cracked and come off during rolling and unrolling. Although parchment and vellum were less fragile than papyrus, they too were fragile mediums. Nevertheless, the codex permitted the use of rich colors, including gold. Hence it could make book illustration—or, as we usually say, manuscript **illumination**—the small-scale counterpart of murals, mosaics, and panel pictures. Some questions are still unanswered. When, where, and how quickly did book illumination develop? Were most of the subjects biblical, mythological, or historical? How much of a carryover was there from scroll to codex?

One of the earliest surviving books to illustrate the Bible is an early fifth-century fragment, the so-called *Quedlinburg Itala* (**fig. 8.6**). The fragment is from an illustrated Book of Kings (one of the 39 books of the Old Testament), which is calculated to have originally contained some 60 illustrations, each image probably comprising multiple scenes. On the **folio** (manuscript leaf) reproduced here, four scenes depict Saul's meeting with Samuel after the defeat of Amalekites (I Samuel 15:13–33), each scene framed so as to accentuate the overall unity of the composition. The misty landscape, architectural elements, and sky-blue and pink background are reminiscent of the antique Roman tradition of atmospheric illusionism.

Visible under the flaking paint in this badly damaged fragment are written instructions to the artist, part of which read, "You make the prophet speaking facing King Saul sacrificing." Apparently the artist was left free to interpret pictorially these written instructions, suggesting the lack of an illustrated model.

Particularly intriguing is the fact that the artist of the Quedlinburg fragment worked together in a Roman **scriptorium** (a workshop for copying and illustrating manuscripts) with an artist who illustrated Vergil's *Aeneid* and *Georgics*, the so-called *Vatican Vergil*, named after the collection in which it is housed today. We might well ask if this is evidence of non-Christian artists working for Christian patrons and to what extent pagan motifs might have been carried over to Christian subjects, or perhaps even the other way around. Perhaps not surprisingly, the Quedlinburg fragment and the other manuscripts produced in the same scriptorium are closely linked in style to the mosaics of the contemporaneous Santa Maria Maggiore.

SCULPTURE As we have seen, the increase in standing of Christianity had a profound effect on artistic production, moving Christian art from a modest and private sphere to a public and official

8.6 Scenes from the I Samuel Ch.15, *Quedlinburg Itala*. ca. 425–450 CE. Tempera on vellum, 12 × 18″ (30.5 × 45.8 cm). Staatliche Bibliothek, Berlin

arena. As Early Christian architecture and its decoration began to demonstrate increasing monumentality as a result of its dependence on Roman imperial traditions, so too Early Christian sculpture became more impressive. This is apparent in a fine Early Christian stone coffin, the *Sarcophagus of Junius Bassus* (**fig. 8.7**).

The richly carved sarcophagus was made for a prefect of Rome who died in 359 at age 42 and who, an inscription tells us, had been "newly baptized." The front, divided by columns into ten compartments, contains a mixture of Old and New Testament scenes. In the upper register we see (from left to right) the Sacrifice of Isaac, St. Peter Taken Prisoner, Christ Enthroned between Saints Peter and Paul, and Jesus before Pontius Pilate (this last scene composed of two compartments). In the lower register are the Suffering of Job, the Temptation of Adam and Eve, Jesus' Entry into Jerusalem, Daniel in the Lions' Den, and St. Paul Led to his Martyrdom.

Clearly the status of Christianity has changed when a major state official proclaims, both in

8.7 *Sarcophagus of Junius Bassus.* ca. 359 CE. Marble, 3'10½" × 8' (1.2 × 2.4 m). Museo Storico del Capitolino di San Pietro, Rome

inscription and through representation, his belief in Christianity. The depictions of Peter and Paul, the veritable official saints of the city of Rome—each saint is commemorated by a major basilica in the city—can be related to Junius Bassus' role as a high-ranking government official. Authoritative as well is Christ's place in the central scenes. In the top register, he is enthroned with his feet treading on a personification of Coelus, the Roman pagan god of the heavens, as he dispenses the law to his disciples. Thus, Christ appropriates the emperor's role as lawgiver. Below this compartment, he enters Jerusalem in triumph. As compared to the earliest Christian representations, such as in the catacomb of Santissimi Pietro e Marcellino (see fig. 8.1), Christ is now depicted directly, not through allusion alone, and his imperial nature is accentuated. Daniel in the Lions' Den, the Sacrifice of Isaac, and Adam and Eve are subjects that appeared in earlier representations in catacombs. Daniel's salvation is a type for Christ as well as for all Christians who hope for divine salvation; Abraham's willingness to sacrifice his beloved son Isaac parallels God's sacrifice of his only begotten son and

at the same time speaks of salvation by divine grace; Adam and Eve refer to the Original Sin that led to Christ's sacrificial death and his resurrection. Thus old methods of explication are combined with new manifestations of Christianity's important role in society, particularly by stressing Christ's imperial nature.

The style of the sarcophagus also relies on imperial convention. This is most evident in the elements of classicism that are expressed, such as the placement within deep, space-filled niches of figures that recall the dignity of Greek and Roman sculpture. Other classicizing features include the way that the figures seem capable of distributing weight, the draperies that reveal the bodies beneath them, and the narrative clarity. However, beneath this veneer of classicism we recognize doll-like bodies with large heads and a passive air in scenes that would otherwise seem to call for dramatic action. It is as if the events and figures are no longer intended to tell their own story but to call to mind a larger symbolic meaning that unites them.

The reliance on classicizing forms on the *Sarcophagus of Junius Bassus* reminds us that Early

Christian art appears throughout the Mediterranean basin in what we think of as the classical world. During the first five centuries after Jesus' death, the art of the entire area was more or less unified in content and style. Increasing political and religious divisions in the region, however, began to affect artistic production, so that it is appropriate to recognize the appearance, or, perhaps better stated, the growth of another branch of Christian art that we label Byzantine.

Byzantine Art

Early Byzantine Art

There is no clear-cut geographical or chronological line between Early Christian and Byzantine art. West Roman and East Roman—or as some scholars prefer to call them, Western and Eastern Christian—traits are difficult to separate before the sixth century. Until that time, both geographical areas contributed to the development of Early Christian art. As the Western Empire declined, however, cultural leadership tended to shift to the eastern part. This process was completed during the reign of Justinian, who ruled the Eastern Empire from 527 to 565. Under the patronage of Justinian, Constantinople became the artistic as well as the political capital of the empire. Justinian himself was a man of strongly Latin orientation, and he almost succeeded in reuniting Constantine's domain. The monuments he sponsored have a grandeur justifying the claim that his era was a Golden Age, as some have labeled it.

Ironically, the greatest number of early Byzantine monuments survives today not in Constantinople, where much has been destroyed, but on Italian soil, in Ravenna. That town had become the capital of the West Roman emperors at the beginning of the fifth century; when Rome was sacked by the Visigoths in 410, the capital of the Western Empire was moved farther north, first to Milan, then finally to Ravenna. At the end of the century Ravenna was taken by Theodoric, king of the Ostrogoths, whose tastes were patterned after those of Constantinople, where he had lived for some time. The Ostrogothic rule of Ravenna ended in 540, when the Byzantine general Belisarius conquered the city for Justinian. Ravenna became an exarchate, or provincial capital, the main stronghold of Byzantine rule in Italy. Thus, Ravenna serves as a kind of microcosm of the transformation and divisions of the later Roman Empire.

SAN VITALE The most important building of the early Byzantine period, begun in 526 under Ostrogothic rule, was the church of San Vitale. Built chiefly during the 540s and completed in 547, it represents a Byzantine building of a type derived mainly from Constantinople, the Byzantine capital. The octagonal plan with a circular core ringed by an ambulatory (**fig. 8.8**) is a descendant of buildings such as Santa Costanza in Rome (see fig. 8.3), compared to which, San Vitale is both larger in scale and significantly richer in spatial effect (**fig. 8.9**). In particular, below the clerestory, the nave wall turns into a series of semicircular niches that penetrate the ambulatory and thus link that surrounding aisle to the nave in a new and intricate way (**fig. 8.10**). The movement around the center space is thus enlivened so that the decorated surfaces seem to

Ground plan of San Vitale, Ravenna, Italy

8.8 Section of San Vitale. 526–547 CE. Ravenna, Italy

8.9 Exterior, San Vitale, Ravenna, Italy

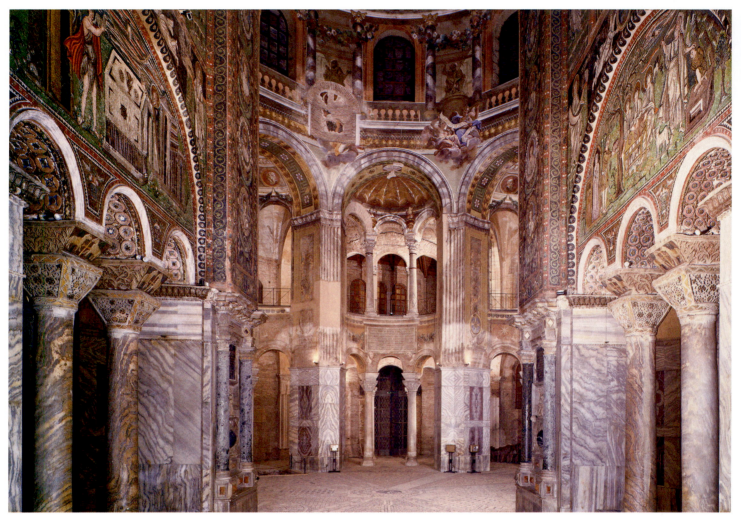

8.10 Interior (view from the apse), San Vitale, Ravenna, Italy

pulsate. The aisle itself has a second story, the galleries, which may have been reserved for women. This reflects a practice in a number of Eastern religions, including some forms of Judaism, in which it is current even today. Large windows on every level are made possible by a new economy in the construction of the vaulting—hollow clay tubes allowing for a lighter structure—and the interior is flooded with light.

The plan of San Vitale shows only remnants of the longitudinal axis of the Early Christian basilica: Toward the east, a cross-vaulted compartment for the altar, backed by an apse; and on the other side, a narthex. How did it happen that the East favored a type of church building (as distinct from mausoleums) so different from the basilica and—from the Western point of view—so ill adapted to Christian ritual? After all, had not the design of the basilica been backed by the authority of Constantine himself? Scholars have suggested a number of reasons: Practical, religious, and political. All of them may be relevant, but none is fully persuasive. In any event, from

the time of Justinian, domed, central-plan churches dominated the world of Orthodox Christianity as thoroughly as the basilican plan dominated the architecture of the medieval West.

At San Vitale the odd, nonaligned placement of the narthex, which has never been fully explained, might be a key to helping us understand how the building functioned. Some have suggested that the narthex is turned to be parallel to an atrium, the axis of which was determined by site limitations. Others see it as a conscious design feature that accentuates the transition between the exterior and interior of the church. Whatever the reason, in order to enter the building visitors were forced to change axis, shifting to the right or left in order to align themselves with the main apse. The alteration of the journey into the building is unsettling, almost disorienting, an effect heightened by passing from the lighted area of the narthex to the shaded ambulatory, and then into the high and luminous domed center space. The passage from

8.11 *Emperor Justinian and His Attendants.* ca. 547 CE. Mosaic. San Vitale, Ravenna, Italy

8.12 *Empress Theodora and Her Attendants.* ca. 547 CE. Mosaic. San Vitale, Ravenna, Italy

physical to spiritual realms so essential to worship is manifest as a separation between the external world and the internal space of the building.

The complexity of the interior architecture is matched by its lavish decoration. San Vitale's link with the Byzantine court can be seen in two prominent mosaics flanking the altar (**figs. 8.11** and **8.12**). They depict Justinian and his empress, Theodora, accompanied by officials, the local clergy, and ladies-in-waiting, about to enter the church, as if it were a palace chapel. In these large panels, the design of which probably came from an imperial workshop, we find an ideal of beauty that is very different from the squat, large-headed figures seen in the art of the fourth and fifth centuries. The figures are tall and slim, with tiny feet and small almond-shaped faces dominated by huge eyes. They seem capable only of making ceremonial gestures and displaying magnificent costumes. There is no hint of movement or change. The dimensions of time and earthly space, suggested by a green ground, give way to an eternal present in the form of a golden, otherworldly setting. Hence the solemn, frontal images seem to belong as much to a celestial court as to a secular one. The quality of soaring slenderness that endows the figures with an air of mute exaltation is shared by the mysterious interior space that they inhabit.

The union of political and spiritual authority expressed in the mosaics of San Vitale reflects the "divine kingship" of the Byzantine emperor and honors the royal couple as donors of the church. It is as though the mosaic figures are in fact participating in the liturgy, even though the empress and emperor are actually thousands of miles away. The embroidery on the hem of Theodora's mantle shows the three Magi carrying their gifts to Mary and the newborn King, and like them the imperial couple bring offerings. Justinian brings bread and Theodora a chalice, undoubtedly references to the Eucharist. The emperor is flanked by 12 companions, the imperial equivalent of the 12 apostles. Moreover, Justinian is portrayed in a manner that recalls Constantine, the first Christian emperor: The shield with Christ's monogram equates Justinian's conquest of Ravenna with the divinely inspired Constantinian triumph that ultimately led to the founding of Constantinople, the court to which Justinian was heir.

HAGIA SOPHIA Among the surviving monuments of Justinian's reign in Constantinople, the most important by far is Hagia Sophia (the Church of the Holy Wisdom) (**figs. 8.13** and **8.14**). The first church on that site was commissioned by Constantine but destroyed in 532 during rioting that almost deposed the emperor; he immediately rebuilt the church, a sign of the continuity of his imperial authority. Completed in only five years, Hagia Sophia achieved such fame that the names of the architects, too, were remembered: Anthemius of Tralles, an expert in geometry and the theory of statics and kinetics; and Isidorus of Miletus, who taught physics and wrote on vaulting techniques. The dome collapsed in the earthquake of 558, and a new, taller one was built from a design by Isidorus' nephew. After the Turkish conquest in 1453, the church became a mosque. At that time the Turks added four minarets and extra buttresses to the exterior (see fig. 8.14), as well as large medallions with Islamic invocations on the interior (**fig. 8.15**). In

8.13 Anthemius of Tralles and Isidorus of Miletus. Plan of Hagia Sophia, Istanbul. 532–537 CE. (after V. Sybel)

8.14 Exterior, Hagia Sophia, Istanbul

8.15 Interior, Hagia Sophia, Istanbul

the twentieth century, after the building was turned into a museum, some of the mosaic decoration that was largely hidden under whitewash was uncovered.

Hagia Sophia has the longitudinal axis of an Early Christian basilica, but the central feature of the nave is a vast, squarish space crowned by a huge dome. At either end are half-domes, arranged so that the nave takes the form of a great ellipse. Attached to the half-domes are semicircular apses with open **arcades**, series of arches, similar to those in San Vitale. One might say, then, that the dome of Hagia Sophia has been placed over a central space and, at the same time, inserted between the two halves of a divided central-plan church. The dome rests on four arches that carry its weight to the piers, large, upright architectural supports, at the corners of the square. Thus the brilliant gold-mosaic walls below these arches, pierced with windows, have no weight-bearing function at all and act as mere curtains. The transition from the square formed by the arches to the circular rim of the dome is achieved by spherical triangles called **pendentives**. Hence we speak of the entire unit as a dome on pendentives. This device, along with a new technique for building domes using thin bricks embedded in mortar, permits the construction of taller, lighter, and more economical domes than the older method of placing the dome on a round or polygonal base as, for example, in the Pantheon (see fig. 7.16).

Where or when the dome on pendentives was invented we do not know. Hagia Sophia is the earliest example we have of its use on a monumental scale, and it had a lasting impact. It became a basic feature of Byzantine architecture and, later, of Western architecture as well. Its massive exterior, firmly planted upon the earth like a great mound, rises by stages to a height of 184 feet—41 feet taller than the Pantheon—and therefore its dome, though its diameter is somewhat smaller (112 feet), stands out far more boldly in its urban setting.

Once we are inside Hagia Sophia (see fig. 8.15), all sense of weight disappears. Nothing remains but a space that inflates, like so many sails, the apses, the pendentives, and the dome itself. Here the architectural aesthetic we saw taking shape in Early Christian architecture has achieved a new, magnificent dimension. Even more than before, light plays a key role. The dome seems to float—"like the radiant heavens," according to a contemporary description—

because it rests upon a closely spaced row of windows; light, both real and reflected, virtually separates the dome from the arches on which it rests. So many openings pierce the nave walls that the effect is akin to the transparency of lace curtains. The purpose of all this is clear. As Procopius, the court historian to Justinian, wrote: "Whenever one enters this church to pray, he understands at once that it is not by any human power or skill, but by the influence of God, that this work has been so finely turned. And so his mind is lifted up toward God and exalted, feeling that He cannot be far away, but must especially love to dwell in this place that He has chosen." We can sense the new aesthetic even in ornamental details such as moldings and capitals. The scrolls, acanthus leaves, and similar decorations are motifs derived from classical architecture, but their effect here is radically different. The heavily patterned butterfly-marble facing of the piers denies their substantiality, and instead of actively cushioning the impact of heavy weight on the shaft of the column, the capital has become like an openwork basket of starched lace, the delicate surface pattern of which belies the strength and solidity of the stone.

The guiding principle of Graeco-Roman architecture had been to express a balance of opposing forces, rather like the balance within the *contrapposto* of a Classical statue. The result was a muscular display of active and passive members. In comparison, the material structure of Byzantine architecture, and to some extent of Early Christian architecture as well, is subservient to the creation of immaterial space. Walls and vaults seem like weightless shells, their actual thickness and solidity hidden rather than emphasized. And the glitter of the mosaics must have completed the illusion of unreality, fitting the spirit of these interiors to perfection.

SCULPTURE Beyond architectural decorations and some sarcophagi, early Byzantine sculpture consists mainly of reliefs in ivory and silver, which survive in considerable numbers. An ivory relief of *The Archangel Michael* (**fig. 8.16**), from the time of Justinian, looks back to earlier classical ivories. It may have been paired with a missing panel showing Justinian, who, it has been suggested, commissioned it. The inscription above has the prayer "Receive these gifts, and having learned the cause …," which would probably have continued on the missing leaf with a plea to forgive the owner's sins, apparently a reference to the emperor's humility. In any event,

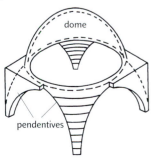

◆ Pendentives are the curved triangular sections that arc up from the corners of a square area to form a rounded base from which a dome springs. Such a construction is called a "pendentive dome" or "dome on pendentives."

8.16 *The Archangel Michael,* leaf of a diptych. Early sixth century CE. Ivory, 17 × 5½″ (43.3 × 14 cm). The British Museum, London

this ivory must have been carved around 520–530 by an imperial workshop in Constantinople.

The majestic archangel is a descendant of the winged Victories and deities of Graeco-Roman art, down to the rich drapery revealing lithe limbs (see figs. 5.19 and 5.32). Here classicism has become an eloquent vehicle for Christian content. The power the angel heralds is not of this world, nor does he inhabit an earthly space. The niche he occupies has lost all three-dimensional reality. His relationship to it is purely symbolic and ornamental, so that, given the position of the feet on the steps, he seems to hover rather than stand. From the ankles down he seems to be situated between the columns, while his arms and wings are in front of them. It is this disembodied quality, conveyed through harmonious forms, that makes the archangel Michael's presence so compelling. The paradox of a believable figure represented naturalistically but existing within an ambiguous, indeed impossible, setting connects this work with other products of Justinian's court, such as those buildings where solid structures serve to create ephemeral spaces.

ILLUSTRATED BOOKS Illustrated books of the early Byzantine period also contain echoes of Graeco-Roman style adapted to religious narrative. The most important example, the *Vienna Genesis* (**fig. 8.17**), containing a Greek text of the first book of the Bible, has a richness similar to the mosaics we have seen. White highlights and fluttering drapery that clings to the bodies animate the scene. The book was written in silver (now tarnished black) and decorated with brilliantly colored miniatures on dyed purple vellum, a color reserved for the imperial court. Although some scholars have suggested that an imperial scriptorium in Constantinople produced the manuscript, recent research points to Syria as the more likely source because there are parallels to manuscripts produced there and to some mosaics that survive there as well.

Our page shows a number of scenes from the story of Jacob. In the center foreground Jacob wrestles with the angel and then receives the angel's blessing. Hence the picture does not show just a single event but a whole sequence. The scenes take place along a U-shaped path, so that progression in space becomes progression in time. This method, known as **continuous narration**, goes back as far as ancient Egypt and Mesopotamia. Its appearance in miniatures such as this may reflect earlier illustrations made in scroll rather than book form, although this hypothesis has been highly contested. The picture certainly looks like a frieze turned back upon itself. For manuscript illustration, continuous narrative makes the most economical use of

8.17 *Jacob Wrestling the Angel.* Page from the *Vienna Genesis.* Early sixth century CE. Tempera and silver on dyed vellum, 13¼ × 9½" (33.6 × 24.1 cm). Österreichische Nationalbibliothek, Vienna

space. The painter can pack a maximum number of scenes into a small area, and the picture as a running account can be read like lines of text, rather than as a window that requires a frame.

ICONS The religious **icon** (from the Greek word *eikon*, meaning "image") provided another focus for representation at the time of Justinian. Icons generally showed Christ, the Enthroned Madonna, or saints and were objects of personal as well as public veneration. From the beginning they were considered portraits, for such pictures had developed in Early Christian times out of Graeco-Roman portrait panels. The issue that

they might be considered idols led to arguments about their appropriateness and their power. These discussions related to the contemporaneous debates on the dual nature of Christ as God and man, at once both spiritual and physical. One of the chief arguments in favor of image production was the claim that Christ had appeared with the Virgin to St. Luke and permitted him to paint their portrait together, and that other portraits of Christ or of the Virgin had miraculously appeared on earth by divine command. These "true" sacred images were considered to have been the sources for the later ones made by human artists, permitting a chain of copies and copies of copies, which has often made it difficult for art historians to date them.

Icons functioned as living images to instruct and inspire the worshiper. Because the actual figure—be it Christ, Mary, a saint, or an angel—was thought to reside in the image, icons were believed to be able to intercede on behalf of the faithful. They were reputed to have miraculous healing properties, and some were carried into battle or placed over city gates, effectively offering totemic protection to their communities. In describing an icon of the archangel Michael, the sixth-century poet Agathias writes: "The wax remarkably has represented the invisible. ... The viewer can directly venerate the archangel [and] trembles as if in his actual presence. The eyes encourage deep thoughts; through art and its colors the innermost prayer of the viewer is passed to the image."

Little is known about the origins of icons, since most early examples were intentionally destroyed by those who believed they led to idolatry; hence their scarcity. The irony of this is particularly poignant, since early icons were painted in **encaustic**, the medium in which pigment is suspended in hot wax, chosen for its durability.

Many of the surviving early examples come from the Monastery of Saint Catherine at Mount Sinai, Egypt, the isolated desert location of which aided the survival of numerous objects. A *Christ Icon* (**fig. 8.18**), generally dated to sometime in the sixth century but with later repainting, is magnificent for its freshness of color and vibrancy of brushstroke. Its link with Graeco-Roman portraiture is clear not only from the use of encaustic but also from the gradations of light and shade in Christ's face and on his neck, reminiscent of the treatment of the woman in the Roman Fayum portrait, also in encaustic (see fig. 7.21). The combination of a frontal, unflinching gaze, establishing a direct bond with the viewer, with the lively and lifelike modeling of the face suggests the kind of dichotomy between the spiritual and the physical that we have seen in so much early Byzantine art. That dichotomy is accentuated here by the enormous gold halo hovering over an architectural background. It is as if the walls retreat into the background in response to the halo and in order to allow space for Christ.

The Iconoclastic Controversy

After the time of Justinian, the development of Byzantine art—not only painting but sculpture and architecture as well—was disrupted by the Iconoclastic Controversy. The conflict, which began with an edict promulgated by the Byzantine emperor Leo III in 726 prohibiting religious images, raged for more than a hundred years between two hostile groups. The image destroyers, called iconoclasts, led by the emperor and

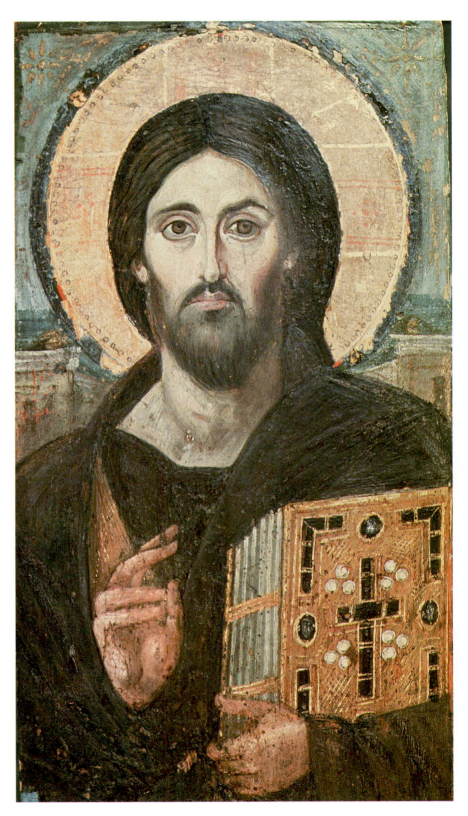

8.18 *Christ Icon.* Sixth century CE. Encaustic on panel, 34 × 17⅞" (84 × 45.5 cm). Monastery of Saint Catherine, Mount Sinai, Egypt

supported mainly in the eastern provinces, insisted on a literal interpretation of the biblical ban against graven images because their use encouraged idolatry. They wanted to restrict religious art to abstract symbols and plant or animal forms. Their opponents, the iconophiles, were led by the monks and were particularly centered in the western provinces, where the imperial edict remained ineffective for the most part. The strongest argument in favor of icons claimed that because Christ and his image are inseparable, the honor given to the image is transferred to him.

The roots of the argument went very deep. Theologically, they involved the basic issue of the relationship of the human and the divine in the person of Christ. Moreover, there was resentment that, for many, icons had come to replace the Eucharist as the focus of lay devotion. Socially and politically, the conflict was a power struggle between Church and State, organizations in theory united in the figure of the emperor. The conflict came during a low point in Byzantine power, when the empire had been greatly diminished by the rise of Islam. Iconoclasm, it was argued, was justified by Leo's victories over the Arabs, who were themselves, ironically, iconoclasts. The controversy caused an irreparable break between Catholicism and the Orthodox faith.

If the edict barring images had been enforced throughout the empire, it might well have dealt Byzantine religious art a fatal blow. It did succeed in greatly reducing the production of sacred images, but failed to wipe it out entirely, so there was a fairly rapid recovery after the victory of the iconophiles in 843.

Middle Byzantine Art

While we know little for certain about how the Byzantine artistic tradition managed to survive from the early eighth to the mid-ninth century, iconoclasm seems to have brought about a renewed interest in secular art, which was not affected by the ban. This may help to explain the astonishing appearance of antique motifs in the art of the Middle Byzantine period, sometimes referred to as the Second Golden Age. Hence there was a fairly rapid recovery after the victory of the iconophiles. A revival of Byzantine artistic traditions, as well as of classical learning and literature, followed the years of iconoclasm and lasted from the late ninth to the eleventh century. This revival, spearheaded by Basil I the Macedonian, was underscored by the reopening of the university in Constantinople. Scholars have referred to this period as a renaissance, crediting much of its vigor to Constantine VII. Emperor in name only for most of his life, he devoted his energies instead to art and scholarship.

ILLUSTRATED BOOKS *David Composing the Psalms* (**fig. 8.19**) is one of eight full-page scenes in the mid-tenth century *Paris Psalter*. Illustrating the biblical King David's life, these scenes introduce the Psalms, which David was thought to have composed. Not only do we find a landscape that recalls Pompeian murals, but the figures, too, clearly derive from Roman models. David himself could well be mistaken for Orpheus charming the beasts with his music. His companions

8.19 *David Composing the Psalms*, from the *Paris Psalter*. ca. 950 CE. Tempera on vellum, 14⅛ × 10¼" (36 × 26 cm). Bibliothèque Nationale, Paris are even more surprising, since they are allegorical figures that have nothing to do with the Bible. The young woman next to David is the personification of Melody, the one coyly hiding behind a pillar is the mountain nymph Echo, and the male figure with a tree trunk personifies the mountains of Bethlehem.

Once again style promotes meaning in the way consciously classical forms herald the revival of image making after iconoclasm. But despite the revivalist aspects, the late date of the picture is evident from certain qualities of style, such as the crowded composition of space-consuming figures and the abstract zigzag pattern of the drapery covering Melody's legs. In truth, one might well ask to what extent and how, despite iconoclasm, antique methods and forms survived—that is, how much of what we see is the result of continuities rather than revivals.

ARCHITECTURE AND ITS DECORATION Byzantine architecture never produced another structure to match the scale of Hagia Sophia. The churches built after the Iconoclastic Controversy were initially modest in scale and usually built for communities of monks, perhaps reflecting the fact that monks had been important in arguing against iconoclasm; later monasteries erected in Constantinople under imperial patronage were much larger and served social purposes as schools and hospitals. The monastic Church of the Dormition (meaning the "falling asleep" of Mary) at Daphni, in Greece, follows the usual Middle Byzantine plan of a Greek cross contained within a square, but with a narthex added on one side and an apse on the other. The central feature is a dome on a cylinder, or **drum**. The drum raises the dome high above the rest of the building and demonstrates a preference for elongated proportions. The impact of this verticality, however, strikes us fully only when we enter the church. As we raise our glance toward the luminous pool of space beneath the dome, it is as if we are drawn around and upward (**fig. 8.20**). The suspended dome of Hagia Sophia is clearly the conceptual precedent for this form.

The mosaics inside the church at Daphni are some of the finest works of the Second Golden Age. They show a classicism that merges harmoniously with the spiritualized ideal of human

Plan of the Church of the Dormition, Daphni

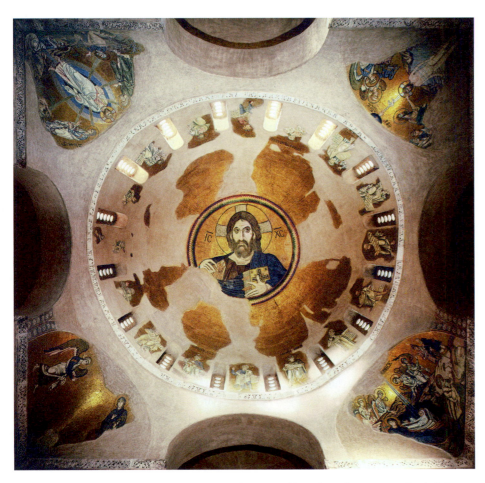

8.20 Christ Pantocrator, dome mosaics, Church of the Dormition. Eleventh century CE. Daphni, Greece

8.21 *The Crucifixion.* Late eleventh-century mosaic. Church of the Dormition. Daphni, Greece

beauty evident in the art of Justinian's reign. For instance, the classical qualities of *The Crucifixion* mosaic (**fig. 8.21**) are deeply felt, yet they are also completely Christian. There is no attempt to create a realistic spatial setting, but the composition has a balance and clarity that are truly monumental. Classical, too, are the heroic nudity of Christ and the statuesque dignity of the two flanking figures, which make them seem extraordinarily organic and graceful compared to the stiff poses in the Justinian and Theodora mosaics at San Vitale (see figs. 8.11 and 8.12).

The most important aspect of the classical heritage in Middle Byzantine depiction, however, is emotional rather than physical. This is evident in the new interest in depicting the crucified Christ, that is, the Christ of the Passion. In the Daphni *Crucifixion* mosaic, Christ is flanked by the Virgin and St. John. The gestures and facial expressions of all three figures convey a restrained and noble suffering. We cannot say

when and where this human interpretation of the Savior first appeared, but it seems to have developed in the wake of the Iconoclastic Controversy. There are, to be sure, a few earlier examples of it, but none of them appeals to the emotions of the viewer so powerfully as the Daphni *Crucifixion*.

Alongside the new emphasis on the Christ of the Passion, the Second Golden Age gave importance to the image of Christ the Pantocrator, an oversize, awesome (though heavily restored) mosaic image of which stares down from the center of the dome at Daphni against a gold background (see fig. 8.20). The Pantocrator is Christ as both Judge and Ruler of the Universe, the All-Holder who contains everything. The type descends from images of the bearded Zeus. The bearded face of Jesus first appears during the sixth century, and we have already seen an early example in the icon from Mount Sinai (see fig. 8.18). Once again tradition and innovation mark Middle Byzantine achievements.

Late Byzantine Art

In 1204 Byzantium suffered an almost fatal defeat when the armies of the Fourth Crusade, instead of warring against the Turks, captured and sacked the city of Constantinople. For more than 50 years, the core of the Eastern Empire remained in Western hands. Byzantium, however, survived this catastrophe. In 1261 it regained its independence, which lasted until the Turkish conquest in 1453. The fourteenth century saw a last flowering of Byzantine painting under a series of enlightened rulers.

ICONS The Crusades decisively changed the course of Byzantine art through bringing it into contact with the West. The impact is apparent in the *Madonna Enthroned* (**fig. 8.22**), which unites elements of East and West, so that its authorship has been much debated. Because icons were objects of veneration, and because they embodied sacredness, they had to conform to strict rules, with fixed patterns repeated over and over again. As a result, most icons are noteworthy more for exacting craftsmanship than artistic inventiveness. Although painted at the end of the thirteenth century, our example reflects a much earlier type. There are echoes of Middle Byzantine style in the graceful pose, the play of drapery folds, and the tender melancholy of the Virgin's face. But these elements have become abstract, reflecting a new taste and style in Late Byzantine art. The highlights on the drapery that resemble sunbursts are not a new development, yet they seem more rigid and stylized than in Middle Byzantine examples. Faces are carefully modeled, with gentle highlights and suave shading. The linear treatment of drapery in combination with the soft shading of hands and faces continues the long-established Byzantine pattern of playing off naturalistic and anti-naturalistic aspects against each other in the same work.

The total effect is neither flat nor spatial, but transparent—so that the shapes look as if they were lit from behind. Indeed, the gold background and highlights are so brilliant that even the shadows never seem wholly opaque. This all-pervading radiance, we will recall, first appears in earlier mosaics (see, for example, figs. 8.11, 8.12, 8.20, and 8.21). Panels such as the *Madonna Enthroned* may therefore be viewed as the aesthetic equivalent of mosaics and not simply as the descendants of the panel-painting tradition. In fact, some of the most precious Byzantine icons are miniature mosaics attached to panels, and our artist may have been trained as a mosaicist rather than as a painter.

Although many details relate this icon to Byzantine works, particularly from Constantinople, there is growing evidence that it was produced by a Western artist in emulation of Byzantine style. For example, the manner in which the Enthroned Virgin presents the Christ Child is Byzantine, while the blessing gesture of Christ is Western. The red background of the angels in medallions is a feature found not in Byzantium, but in the West. An origin in Cyprus, then ruled by the French, has been suggested, but where this work might have been painted remains a very open question. Whatever its origin, the *Madonna Enthroned* points to a profound shift in the relation between the two traditions: After 600 years of borrowing from Byzantium, Western art has begun to contribute something in return.

MOSAICS AND MURAL PAINTING The finest surviving cycles of Late Byzantine mosaics and paintings are found in Istanbul's Kariye Camii, the former Church of the Savior in the Chora Monastery. (*Kariye* is the Turkish adaptation of the ancient Greek word *chora*, which refers to the countryside, that is, outside the city walls; *camii* denotes a mosque, to which the building was converted after the Turkish conquest.) These particular mosaics and paintings represent the climax of the humanism that emerged in Middle

8.22 *Madonna Enthroned.* Late thirteenth century. Tempera on panel, 32⅛ × 19⅜″ (81.9 × 49.3 cm). National Gallery of Art, Washington, D.C., Andrew Mellon Collection. 1937.1.1

Byzantine art. Theodore Metochites, a scholar and poet who was prime minister to the emperor Andronicus II, restored the church and paid for its decorations at the beginning of the fourteenth century.

The wall paintings in the mortuary chapel attached to Kariye Camii are especially impressive. Some have suggested that because of the empire's greatly reduced resources, murals often took the place of mosaics, but at Kariye Camii they are of equal value and may even have been

8.23 *Anastasis.* ca. 1310–1320 CE. Fresco. Kariye Camii (Church of the Savior in the Chora Monastery), Istanbul

designed by the same artist. The main scene depicts the traditional Byzantine image of the *Anastasis* (**fig. 8.23**), the event just before the Resurrection, which Western Christians call the Descent into Limbo or the Harrowing of Hell, clearly a fitting subject for the funerary setting. Surrounded by a **mandorla**, a radiant almond shape, Christ has vanquished Satan and battered down the gates of Hell. (Note the bound Satan at his feet, in the midst of a profusion of hardware; the two kings to the left are David and Solomon.) The central group of Christ raising Adam and Eve from the dead has tremendous dramatic force; Christ moves with extraordinary physical energy, tearing Adam and Eve from their graves, so that they appear to fly through the air—a magnificently expressive image of divine triumph.

Such dynamism had been unknown in the Early Byzantine tradition, although the emotional force of Middle Byzantine painting might well have prepared the way for the vivacity of the Kariyi Camii representations. Coming in the fourteenth century, this Late Byzantine style shows that 800 years after Justinian, when the Anastasis first appeared as a subject, Byzantine art still had all its creative powers. Thus, despite the diverse uses it served, its long chronological spread, and the different cultures and wide geographic areas it spanned, Byzantine art continued to preserve long-established traditions. Indeed, its durability verges on the immutable.

Islamic Art

Islam, the religion, is a significant element in Islamic culture, but Islamic art is far more than a religious art; it includes secular elements and elements frowned upon, if not actually forbidden, by some Islamic theologians. With all of its individual styles of time and place, and with the various sectarian differences within Islam, Islamic art has certain unifying themes. The first of these is reverence for the Word—the Qur'an—and for the language of the Word—Arabic—as reflected in the art of beautiful writing. A second theme is the development of artistic expression independent of the human figure. Given the mistrust of figural images in many Islamic religious traditions, we see in Islamic art sophisticated and complex vocabularies of vegetal, floral, and geometric designs used in conjunction with fine calligraphy. A third theme is the equality of genres. To understand and appreciate Islamic art we need to discard the notion of the primacy of (figural) painting and (figural) sculpture in the European tradition. In the Islamic world, the arts of ceramics, metalware, weaving, and carving in precious materials rank with other media in an artistic spectrum devoid of the formal hierarchy that in the West led to a distinction between "fine arts" and "decorative arts." In this sense, looking at Islamic art can be both enlightening and liberating.

Islamic art first appears as a series of appropriations of preexisting Graeco-Roman, Byzantine Christian, and Sasanian (the dynasty that ruled in Persia from 224 to 636 CE) forms. These were molded into a new synthesis to serve the needs of the new Islamic religion and the desires and political goals of Islamic princes. The appropriation and adaptation of preexisting forms in the service of the emerging Islamic culture is particularly apparent in architecture.

Architecture

The new religion required certain types of distinctive buildings, such as a place for community prayers that was visually identified with the new faith. The new Islamic rulers required dwellings appropriate to their power and wealth. Eventually the faith required commemorative buildings that memorialized great rulers, holy men, or historic events. Ultimately, Islamic architecture developed a rich variety of forms and genres, and a distinctive repertoire of decoration that became emblematic of the faith itself.

DOME OF THE ROCK The earliest major Islamic building to have survived into our time, the Dome of the Rock in Jerusalem (**fig. 8.24**), is a case in point. After the Arabian cities of Mecca and Medina, Jerusalem was the holiest Islamic site. For the first Muslims, the Temple Mount in Jerusalem marked the place where God tested Ibrahim's faith by demanding the sacrifice of his first-born son Ismail. From the same site, according to later Islamic legend, the Prophet was taken by Gabriel on a *mi'raj* (spiritual journey) to experience both Heaven and Hell, Muhammad being

8.24 The Dome of the Rock. ca. 690 CE and later. Jerusalem

8.25 Interior, Dome of the Rock, Jerusalem

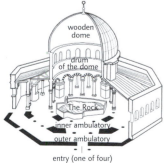

Cutaway drawing of the Dome of the Rock

the only mortal allowed to see these places before death.

It is far from coincidence that the Dome of the Rock is built on Mount Moriah in Jerusalem, a place that originally was the site of the First (Solomon's) and Second (Herod's) Temples, the geographic center of the Jewish faith. It is also far from coincidence that the domed silhouette and ringlike plan of the Dome of the Rock echo the form of the Holy Sepulchre, just a few hundred yards to the west, which marked the burial place of Christ. The Holy Sepulchre, a Constantinian foundation, was rebuilt by the Byzantines in the sixth century. The Dome of the Rock was constructed by artists and crafts-people, many of whom were undoubtedly local Christians or new converts to Islam, probably under orders from the Muslim caliph (from the Arabic *khalifa*, meaning "successor") Abd al-Malik sometime around the year 690.

Islam: Beliefs and Practices

SLAM WAS DEFINED by Muhammad as the culmination of a prophetic tradition that began with God's covenant with Ibrahim (Abraham). The Qur'an prominently mentions many of the major figures of the Hebrew Bible such as Ibrahim, Musa (Moses), and Sulayman (Solomon), as well as the prophet 'Isa (Jesus) and his mother Maryam (Mary). Islamic belief is fundamentally very simple: To become a Muslim, one repeats with conviction the phrase, "There is no God but God; Muhammad is the Messenger of God." This Affirmation of Faith is the first of the so-called Five Pillars of Islam. The others are prayer (the five daily prayers and the major weekly prayer at noon on Friday, the Muslim Day of Congregation), fasting (abstention from food and drink during daylight hours during the lunar month of Ramadan), pilgrimage (in Arabic, *hajj*, a journey to Mecca during the lunar month of Dhu'l Hijja), and charity (institutionalized as a formal system of tithing, intended to benefit the sick and needy of the Islamic community).

In addition, Islam proclaimed three other tenets that were to have a major impact on art. The first was the protected status of the "People of the Book"—Jews and Christians—in Muslim society, as ordained by God in the Qur'an. The second, based on several anecdotes from the Prophet's life, is a profound mistrust of certain images—pictures and statues of humans and animals—as potentially idolatrous, a point of view Islam shares with Judaism, and which influences the history of Christian art as well. The third, held in common with Judaism and contrasting markedly with the Christianity of that time, was a high regard for literacy and the individual's reading and study of scripture, coupled through most of Islamic history

with a reverence for the written alphabet—in the case of Islam, the Arabic alphabet, which in early Islam used an angular form of script known as *kufic* (see illustration). The beauty of the script, with its contrasting thin and thick lines, written from right to left in an almost rhythmic visual cadence, was deemed appropriate for the poetic words of God himself. These three factors, taken in the general context of Islamic belief and early Islamic political history, were to have a profound effect on the molding of the Islamic artistic tradition.

Page with Kufic script from an Abbasid Qur'an, probably from Tunisia. Ninth century. Ink, color, gold and silver on dyed blue vellum, 11¼ × 14¾" (28.6 × 37.5 cm). Courtesy of the Arthur M. Sackler Museum. Harvard University Museums, Cambridge, MA, Francis Burr Memorial Fund 1967.23

Erected on a holy place that was also one of the highest points in the city, it eloquently proclaimed that Jerusalem was under the control of Islam.

A closer look at the building shows the nature of early Islamic appropriation of Roman and Christian forms, as well as the impact of the Prophet's views on the visual arts. The ground plan of the building, with its two ambulatories around the central bare rock, ideal for organizing visits of large numbers of pilgrims to the shrine, recalls not only the Holy Sepulcher but also late Roman and Early Christian central-plan domed structures, such as Santa Costanza in Rome (see fig. 8.3). The dome of the shrine itself was a well-established symbol for the vault of heaven,

especially appropriate given the ultimate goal of Muhammad's mystical and spiritual journey. The columns and capitals, recycled from classical monuments, convey an impression of tradition and permanence, wealth and power, to Muslim and non-Muslim alike.

The original mosaic decoration (**fig. 8.25**) consisted of Arabic script, repeating geometric motifs, and highly stylized vegetal and floral elements. Eventually, these design elements would form a distinctively Islamic repertoire of decoration: One was Arabic script, used in the many religious inscriptions. Another was a vocabulary of scrolling vines, leaves, and flowers distantly based on nature, and a third a repertoire of repeating geometric patterns. Both of these were

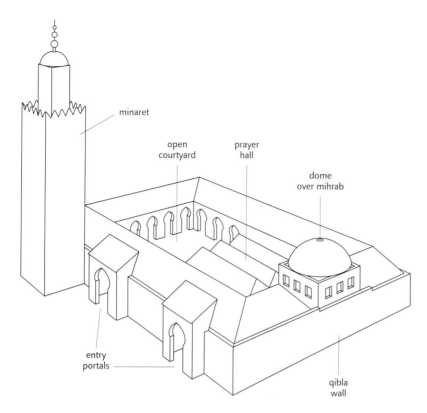

8.26 Schematic of a generic Arab hypostyle mosque

minaret

open courtyard

prayer hall

dome over mihrab

entry portals

qibla wall

staples of late classical and Sasanian art. A fourth set of motifs consisted of jewels and jeweled objects, symbols of royalty. But in marked contrast to the Graeco-Roman and Christian religious art traditions, nowhere in the Dome of the Rock do the forms of humans or animals appear. The inscriptions in the Dome of the Rock, taken from the Qur'an, were carefully chosen to underline the importance of the building itself, its symbolic location in a city holy to Jews and Christians as well as Muslims, and its place within a religion and society that saw itself as the culmination of the two earlier scriptural traditions, and which accorded tolerance towards and acceptance of both Christians and Jews (see Cultural Context: Islam: Beliefs and Practices).

THE HYPOSTYLE MOSQUE Of all of the pillars of Islam, the religious duty of prayer proved the most important in the development of Islamic architecture. In major cities such as Damascus, the Arab Umayyad caliphs of early Islam either built or converted from preexisting structures the first great buildings for Muslim public worship, called **mosques** in English (from the Arabic *masjid*, meaning "place of prostration"). These first mosques, designed to contain the entire male population of a city during the noonday prayer on Friday, recall the form of the Prophet's

house in Medina, with a rectangular courtyard, usually surrounded by covered arcades, and a larger hypostyle (many-columned) hall on the *qibla*, the side facing Mecca. The architecture emphasized the equality of all Muslims before God and the absence in Islam of ordained clergy. Unlike Early Christian basilican churches, such as Old Saint Peter's (see fig. 8.2), there is little axiality in the early Arab mosques—no long straight pathway leading to an architectural focus visible throughout the structure. With prayer occurring directly between each worshiper and God, and no ordained clergy or canonized saints to provide intercession, the interior space of the early mosque was essentially determined by practicality, not by ceremony. Thus there was no place for music or processions; many doors were placed for maximum convenience of the daily coming and going of worshipers; and a large centralized or axial space, so important for the drama of the Christian Mass, was deemed unnecessary. A simple *minbar* (pulpit) served for the delivery of sermons after the Friday noon prayer, and an empty *mihrab* (niche) in the *qibla* wall was added to indicate the direction of Mecca (**fig. 8.26**). Mats of grass or rushes, and later woolen carpets, often covered the floors. These provided a clean place for the standing, bowing, kneeling, and prostration, with the brief touching of the forehead to the ground, while reciting prayers, that constitute the essence of Islamic worship. Oil lamps provided illumination for the dawn and late evening prayers. Pools or fountains in the courtyard allowed for the ceremonial washing of hands and feet required before prayers. In later times, a tower, known in English as a **minaret**, advertised the presence of the mosque and served as a place from which to broadcast the call to prayer given five times a day by a *muezzin*, an individual usually selected for the beauty and power of his voice.

Islamic art shares with Early Christian art the capacity to find forms, whether by invention or appropriation, that satisfy new religious needs. And, as was the case with Early Christian and Byzantine artists, Islamic artists engaged in a form of syncretism, the process whereby a new artistic tradition emerges as a creative combination of previously existing artistic ideas under the impetus of a new ideology. Islamic art, like the first Christian art, developed out of a mixture of various preexisting artistic ideas adapted to serve the needs of religious and then royal or noble patrons.

SUMMARY

A weakened Roman Empire faced threats along its borders and during this time of turmoil many people sought solace in a variety of new religions. Principal among them was Christianity. It enjoyed special status during the rule of Constantine, a Christian convert who created a new capital for the Roman Empire at Constantinople. Eventually this move led to a split of the empire into separate Western and Eastern regions.

Although early centers of the Christian faith included cities along the eastern Mediterranean, the greatest concentration of surviving works is found in Rome. These include painted decorations from the catacombs, the underground burial places of early Christians. After the conversion of the emperor Constantine, many new and impressive Christian structures were built. Particularly significant was the transformation of the Roman basilica form so that it was suitable for Christian worship, as can be seen in Old Saint Peter's Basilica. Also important is the development of central-plan buildings. Although often relying on Roman artistic forms and subjects, Early Christian artists used them for new purposes that were in keeping with the values and goals of the new religion.

During Justinian's rule, Constantinople became the artistic and political capital of the Byzantine or Eastern Empire. The grand monuments of this time, such as Hagia Sophia, are a reflection of what some have called a Golden Age. Many outstanding works also survive in Ravenna, such as the church of San Vitale, which is decorated with a famed series of mosaics. A sense of tradition played a strong role in the development of Byzantine art, and even works from later centuries—whether icons, illustrated books, or small-scale reliefs—reflect a concern for continuity as much as for change.

Another "new" religion, Islam, also spread through the Mediterranean region. Because of its vast geographical and chronological scope, Islamic art cannot be defined simply, but it does have certain unifying themes. These include the development of artistic expression independent of the human figure, which leads Islamic artists to use sophisticated vocabularies of vegetal, floral, and geometric designs, as seen on the interior of the Dome of the Rock. Islamic art began as a series of appropriations of Graeco-Roman, Byzantine Christian, and Sasanian forms. The new religion of Islam required distinctive buildings, such as places for community prayers, that led to a rich variety of architecture emblematic of the faith itself.

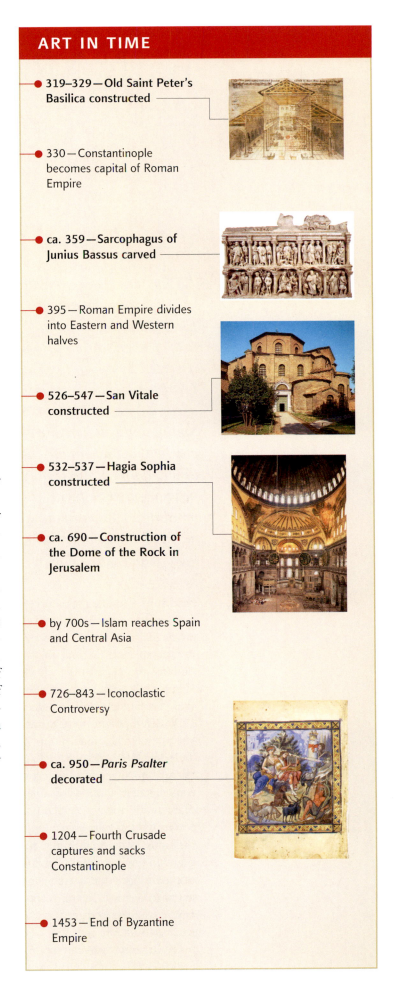

ART IN TIME

- 319–329—Old Saint Peter's Basilica constructed
- 330—Constantinople becomes capital of Roman Empire
- ca. 359—Sarcophagus of Junius Bassus carved
- 395—Roman Empire divides into Eastern and Western halves
- 526–547—San Vitale constructed
- 532–537—Hagia Sophia constructed
- ca. 690—Construction of the Dome of the Rock in Jerusalem
- by 700s—Islam reaches Spain and Central Asia
- 726–843—Iconoclastic Controversy
- ca. 950—*Paris Psalter* decorated
- 1204—Fourth Crusade captures and sacks Constantinople
- 1453—End of Byzantine Empire

9 Early Medieval Art

*T*he term "early medieval" is something of a catchall phrase used to describe the art of a number of cultures and a variety of regions in Western Europe between the Fall of Rome (476 CE) and the eleventh century (see map 9.1). The collapse of Roman institutions was in part the result of the power asserted by migrating Germanic peoples (including Franks, Visigoths, Ostrogoths, and Saxons), who moved westward into and through Europe and eventually established permanent settlements both north of the Alps and in Italy, Spain, and southern France. These were clearly tumultuous times, as invaders clashed and eventually mixed with local inhabitants, including the Celts, the descendants of the Iron Age peoples of Europe. As the invaders established permanent settlements, they adopted many customs traditional to the areas they inhabited. Overlaid on this mix of customs were Roman traditions, including those of Christianity, which in many cases had been adopted by indigenous local tribes when they were conquered by Rome.

The Church emerged as a force vitally important for European unification; even so, loyalty to family and clan continued to govern social and political alliances. Strong chiefs assumed leadership and established tribal allegiances and methods of exchange, both economic and political. These social structures would eventually result in the development throughout Europe of a system of political organization known as feudalism. Such social and political alignments led to a succession of ruling dynasties governed by strong leaders who were able to increase the areas under their dominion. These dynasties (principally the Carolingian and Ottonian) were ambitious to reestablish a centralized authority, absent in Europe after the fall of Rome. The attempt to provide a stable political structure was based, if not in the reality of the Roman Empire, then at least in the ideals embodied in its legacy.

Christianity was not the only religion to develop significant political sway during the early Middle Ages. By 750, the Muslim Umayyad dynasty, based in Roman Syria, had been supplanted by the Abbasid dynasty, centered in Mesopotamia. Here the new caliphs built their capital, called Baghdad, on the Tigris River, and later a vast palace city to the north of Baghdad at Samarra. The original Round City of Baghdad, the site of which lies under the present-day city, was largely abandoned and destroyed long before the Mongols sacked the city in 1258, but its powerful memory lived on in Arabic poetry and prose literature. Samarra's impressive mud-brick ruins still stretch for miles along the Tigris, although they were greatly damaged during the civil unrest that followed the American invasion of Iraq in 2003. Under Abbasid rule over the newly extensive Islamic empire the building of mosques in newly conquered areas, including North Africa and Western Europe, particularly Spain, proceeded apace.

The art of the early medieval period is a vibrant and vital mix, the result of significant

Map 9.1 Europe in the Early Middle Ages

cultural interchanges. Artistic methods, materials, and traditions, brought with migration, were combined with those customs that predominated in the regions where tribes settled and where new religions were established. Thus, out of an amalgam of diverse and conflicting forces, and as new social and cultural entities developed, an art emerged that is as varied as it is exciting.

Anglo-Saxon Art

The widespread migrations of peoples transformed Europe. In 376 CE, the Huns, who had advanced beyond the Black Sea from Central Asia, became a serious threat to Europe. They pushed the Germanic Visigoths westward into the Roman Empire from the Danube. Then in 451, under Attila (d. 453), they invaded Gaul, present-day France and Germany, and its resident Celts. Also in the fifth century, the Angles and Saxons from today's Denmark and northern Germany invaded the British Isles, which had been colonized for centuries by Celts. Many of these Germanic tribes founded virtual kingdoms: The Visigoths in Spain, the Burgundians and Franks in Gaul, the Ostrogoths and Lombards in Italy. The Vikings controlled Scandinavia and ventured afar, a result of their skill as sailors.

The Germanic peoples brought with them art forms that were portable: Weaving, metalwork, jewelry, and woodcarvings. Artistic production in these media required training and skilled execution, and metalwork in particular had intrinsic value, since it was often made of gold or silver and inlaid with precious stones (see Metalwork box overleaf). Metalworkers had high social status, a measure of respect for their labor and for the value of the objects they produced. In some Germanic folk legends metalworkers have abilities so remarkable that they are described as magical. Numerous small-scale objects reflect the vitality of artistic forms produced by these migrating peoples, demonstrating an aesthetic that is quite different from the tradition deriving from Greece and Rome, yet equally rich in myth and imagery.

The Animal Style

The artistic tradition of the Germanic peoples, referred to by some scholars as the animal style because of its heavy use of stylized animal-like forms, merged with the intricate ornamental metalwork of the Celts, producing a unique combination of abstract and organic shapes, of formal discipline and imaginative freedom.

SHIP BURIAL, SUTTON HOO, ENGLAND An Anglo-Saxon SHIP BURIAL in England follows the age-old tradition of burying important people with their personal effects. This custom may reflect a concern for the afterlife, or it may simply be a way to honor the dead. The double ship burial at Sutton Hoo (hoo is Anglo-Saxon for "headland" or "promontory") is of a seventh-century Anglian king (generally thought to be

King Raedwald, who died around 625). Military gear, silver and enamelware, official royal regalia, gold coins, and objects of personal adornment are all part of the entombment. Scholars have long noted that the Anglo-Saxon poem *Beowulf*, so concerned with displays of royal responsibility and obligation, includes a description of a ship fitted out for a funeral that is reminiscent of the Sutton Hoo burial. The funeral is that of Beowulf's father, King Scyld:

They stretched their beloved lord in his boat,
laid out by the mast, amidships,
the great ring-giver. Far-fetched treasures
were piled upon him, and precious gear.
I never heard before of a ship so well furbished
with battle tackle, bladed weapons
and coats of mail. The massed treasure
was loaded on top of him: it would travel far
on out into the ocean's sway.
—*Beowulf. A New Verse Translation*, translated by Seamus Heaney. New York: Farrar, Straus & Giroux, 2000

Although *Beowulf* describes events that predate the Sutton Hoo find by at least a century, the poem was probably not composed until a century or more after that burial. So, while *Beowulf*

Metalwork

METAL WAS a precious commodity in the Middle Ages. Even in the ancient world patterns of interchange and colonization can be related to exploration for desirable metals. In earlier chapters we have seen that the Greek settlements in Italy and the Roman settlements in Spain were partly the result of a quest for metals to use and trade. The most commonly employed in the early Middle Ages were gold, silver, copper, iron, and bronze. The many ways in which metals could be worked was undoubtedly one of their most compelling attractions. They could be flattened, drawn thin, or made into an openwork filigree design; they could

be cast, engraved, punched, stamped, and decorated with colored stones, glass, or enamels.

A large buckle from the Sutton Hoo ship burial contains nearly a pound of gold, although it is only one among many gold pieces found in the burial site. That so much early medieval metalwork from gravesites is gold reflects the value attached to it. In addition, gold is not harmed by contact with either earth or water (whereas silver and other metals are subject to progressive decay when exposed to the elements). Although gold had been mined in Europe since Roman times, the most common method of obtaining it was by collecting nuggets or small grains from

rivers and streams (called placer or alluvial gold). The Rhine, Tiber, Po, Rhône, and Garonne rivers, along which the Germanic tribes settled, were major sources of this type of gold, which medieval writers refer to as "sand" gold.

The Sutton Hoo purse lid (fig. 9.1) is notable for its *cloisonné* decoration. *Cloisonné* is an ancient technique, used as early as the second millennium BCE in the eastern Mediterranean. Individual metal strips or *cloisons* (French for "partitions") are attached by their edge to a baseplate to form little walls that make cells enclosing glass or gems. The Sutton Hoo jewelry includes more than 4,000 individual garnets.

9.1 Purse cover, from the Sutton Hoo ship burial. First half of seventh century. Gold with garnets and enamels, length 8″ (20.3 cm). The British Museum, London. Courtesy of the Trustees

should not be taken as a documentary account, it does suggest a royal context within which to appreciate the Sutton Hoo site.

A gold, enamel, and garnet purse cover (**fig. 9.1**) was found at Sutton Hoo. Its original ivory or bone background does not survive and has been replaced. Each of four pairs of symmetrical motifs has its own distinctive character, an indication that they were assembled from different sources. One, the standing man between facing animals in the lower row, has a very long history indeed, first appearing in Mesopotamian art more than 3,200 years earlier. The eagles pouncing on ducks motif brings to mind similar pairings of carnivore and victim in ancient bronzes. The upper design, at the center, is of more recent origin. It consists of fighting animals whose tails, legs, and jaws are elongated into bands that form a complex interweaving pattern. The fourth design, on the top left and right, uses interlacing bands as an ornamental device. The combination of these bands with the animal style, as shown here, seems to have been invented not long before the purse cover was made.

The Sutton Hoo objects are significant for the way they illustrate the transmission of motifs and techniques through the migration of various peoples. They show evidence of cultural interchange with Germanic peoples, combined with evidence of Scandinavian roots, but there are other noteworthy connections as well. King

Raedwald was reputed to have made offerings to Christ, as well as to his ancestral pagan gods. A number of the objects discovered at Sutton Hoo make specific reference to Christianity, including silver bowls decorated with a cross, undoubtedly the result of trade with the Mediterranean.

The chief medium of the animal style was clearly metalwork, in a variety of materials and techniques. Such articles, small, durable, and often of exquisitely refined craftsmanship, were eagerly sought after, which accounts for the rapid diffusion of the animal-style repertoire of forms. These forms spread not only geographically but also from one material to another, migrating from metal into wood, stone, and even paint. They were used to convey a variety of messages, some clearly pagan and others Christian.

Hiberno-Saxon Art

During the early Middle Ages, the Irish (called Hibernians after the Roman name for Ireland, Hibernia) were the spiritual and cultural leaders of Western Europe. They had never been part of the Roman Empire; thus the missionaries who carried Christianity to them from England in the fifth century found a Celtic society that was barbarian by Roman standards. But the Irish readily accepted Christianity, which brought them into contact with Mediterranean civilization. They adapted what they had received in ways that reflected their unique circumstances.

Because the institutional framework of the Roman Church was essentially urban, it did not suit the rural Irish way of life. Irish Christians preferred to follow the example of the desert saints of Egypt and the Near East, who had sought spiritual perfection in the solitude of the wilderness, where groups of them founded the earliest monasteries. Thus, Irish monasteries were established in isolated, secluded areas, even on islands off the mainland, and such places required complete self-sufficiency. By the fifth century, monasticism had spread from its Near Eastern origins north into Italy, across the Continent and throughout western Britain and Ireland.

Manuscripts

Irish monasteries soon became centers of learning and the arts, with much energy spent copying literary and religious texts. They also sent monks abroad to preach to nonbelievers and to found monasteries in northern Britain and Europe, from present-day France to Austria. Each monastery's scriptorium became an artistic center for developing its style. Pictures illustrating biblical events held little interest for the Irish monks, but they devoted great effort to decorative embellishment. The finest of these manuscripts belong to the Hiberno-Saxon style—a style that combines Christian with Celtic and Germanic elements and that flourished in the monasteries of Ireland as well as those founded

9.2 *Symbol of St. Matthew*, from the *Book of Durrow*. ca. 680 CE. Tempera on vellum, 9⅝ × 6⅛″ (24.7 × 15.7 cm). Trinity College, Dublin

by Irish monks in Saxon England. These Irish monks helped speed the conversion to Christianity of Europe north of the Alps. Throughout Europe they made the monastery a cultural center and thus influenced medieval civilization for several hundred years.

In order to spread the message concerning Christ, the kingdom of God, and salvation—called the Gospel—the Irish monasteries had to produce by hand copies of the Bible and other Christian books in large numbers. Every manuscript copy was looked upon as a sacred object containing the Word of God, and its beauty needed to reflect the importance of its contents. Irish monks must have been familiar with Early Christian illuminated manuscripts, but here, too, they developed an independent tradition instead of simply copying the older manuscripts. The earliest Hiberno-Saxon illuminators retained only the symbols of the four evangelists from the imagery in Early Christian manuscripts, perhaps because these symbols could be readily translated into their ornamental style. The four symbols—the man or angel (St. Matthew), the lion (St. Mark), the ox (St. Luke), and the eagle (St. John)—derive from the Old Testament Book of Ezekiel (1:5–14) and the Apocalypse of St. John the Evangelist (4:6–8) and were assigned to the four evangelists by St. Jerome and other early commentators.

The illustration of the *Symbol of St. Matthew* in the *Book of Durrow* (**fig. 9.2**) shows how ornamental pattern can animate a figure even while accentuating its surface decoration. The body of the figure, composed of framed sections of checkerboard pattern, recalls the ornamental quality of the Sutton Hoo purse cover (see fig. 9.1). The addition of a head, which confronts us directly, and feet, turned to the side, transform the decorative motifs into a human figure. Active, elaborate patterns, previously seen in metalwork, are here employed to demonstrate that St. Matthew's message is precious. Irish scribes and artists were revered for their abilities and achievements. A medieval account relates how, after his death, an Irish scribe's talented hands were preserved as relics capable of performing miracles.

THE LINDISFARNE GOSPELS Thanks to a later colophon (a note at the end of a manuscript), we know a great deal about the origin of the Lindisfarne Gospels, produced in Northumbria, England, including the names of the translator (Aldred) and the scribe (Bishop Eadfrith), who presumably painted the illuminations as well. Given the high regard in which Irish scribes and artists were held, it is not surprising that a bishop is credited with writing and decorating this manuscript. In Irish monasteries monks were divided into three categories: Juniors (pupils and novice monks), working brothers (engaged in manual labor), and seniors (the most experienced monks), who were responsible for copying sacred books.

The Lindisfarne Cross page (**fig. 9.3**) is a creation of breathtaking complexity. Working with the precision of a jeweler, the miniaturist poured into the geometric frame animal interlace so dense and yet so full of movement that the fighting beasts on the Sutton Hoo purse cover (see fig. 9.1) seem simple in comparison. In order to achieve this effect, the artist had to work within a severe discipline as though he were following specific rules. The smallest motifs and the largest patterns were worked out in advance of painting. Ruler and compass were used to mark the page with a network of grid lines and with points, both drawn and pricked. In applying paint, the artist followed his drawing exactly. No mark is allowed to interfere with either the rigid balance of individual features or the overall design. The scholar Françoise Henry has suggested that artists conceived of their work as "a sort of sacred riddle" composed of abstract forms to be sorted out and deciphered. Organic and geometric shapes had to be kept separate. Within the animal compartments, every line had to turn out to be part of an animal's body. Other rules concerned symmetry, mirror-image effects, and repetitions of shapes and colors. Only by intense observation can we enter into the spirit of this mazelike world. It is as if these biting and clawing monsters are subdued by the power of the Cross, converted to Christian purpose just as were the Celtic tribes themselves.

It has been traditional for scholars to refer to the need to decorate all surfaces, evident both in manuscripts and metalwork, as an expression of *horror vacui*, a fear of empty space. But this designation imposes our contemporary values on a culture alien to them. Unlike the Greeks and Romans, who used spatial illusionism to animate their art, Germanic and Celtic artists used intricate patterns to enliven the surface of their precious objects. Although the designs seem confusing and claustrophobic to us, there is, as we have seen, a consistent and intentional tightness in the way the patterns hold together. The richness and intricacy of the illustration compel

9.3 Cross page, from the *Lindisfarne Gospels*. ca. 700. Tempera on vellum, 13½ × 9¼″ (34.3 × 23.5 cm). The British Library, London concentration, establishing a direct connection between the viewer and the image in much the same way as does the fixed, direct gaze of the holy figure in an Early Byzantine icon (see fig. 8.18). In each work, icon and manuscript illumination, the power of the image is so strong that the viewer virtually enters into its realm, forgetting the world outside its frame.

Carolingian Art

During the late eighth century a new empire developed out of the collection of German tribes and kingdoms that had come to dominate northern continental Europe. This empire, which united most of Europe from the North Sea to Spain and as far south as Lombardy in northern Italy, was founded by CHARLEMAGNE, who ruled as king of the Franks from 768. Pope Leo III bestowed on him the title of emperor of Rome in Saint Peter's Basilica on Christmas Day in the year 800, pronouncing him successor to Constantine, the first Christian emperor. Although Charlemagne was able to resist the pope's attempts to assert his authority over the newly created Catholic empire, there was now an interdependence of spiritual and political authority, of Church and State, that would define the history of Western Europe for many centuries.

The emperors were crowned in Rome, but they did not live there. Charlemagne built his capital at the center of his power, in Aachen (Aix-la-Chapelle), located in what is now Germany and close to present-day France, Belgium, and the Netherlands. The period dominated by Charlemagne and his successors, roughly from 768 to 877, is labeled Carolingian (derived from Charlemagne's Latin name, Carolus Magnus, meaning "Charles the Great"). Among Charlemagne's goals were to better the administration of his realm and foster the teaching of Christian truths. He summoned the best minds to his court, including Alcuin of York, the most learned scholar of the day, to restore ancient Roman learning and to establish a system of schools at every cathedral and monastery. The emperor took an active hand in this renewal, which went well beyond a mere interest in the old books to include political objectives. He modeled his rule after the Roman Empire under Constantine and Justinian—rather than their pagan predecessors—and proclaimed a *renovatio imperii romani*, a "renewal of imperial Rome," his efforts aided by the pope who had crowned him Holy Roman Emperor. The artists working for Charlemagne and other Carolingian rulers consciously sought to emulate Rome; by combining their admiration for antiquity with native northern European features, they produced original works of art of the highest quality.

Sculpture

A bronze *Equestrian Statue of a Carolingian Ruler* (**fig. 9.4**), once thought to be Charlemagne himself but now generally assigned to his grandson Charles the Bald, conveys the political objectives of the Carolingian dynasty. The ruler, wearing imperial robes, sits as triumphantly on his steed

CHARLEMAGNE (742–814), king of the Franks, conquered the Saxons and the Lombards and fought the Arabs in Spain before being crowned Emperor of the West in 800 by Pope Leo III. Besides his accomplishments in the fields of art, architecture, and education, he vigorously promoted agriculture, manufacture, and commerce. After his death, he was declared "blessed" by the Church and even became a figure of legend, appearing, for instance, in the Chanson de Roland.

9.4 *Equestrian Statue of a Carolingian Ruler* (Charles the Bald?). Ninth century. Bronze, height 9½" (24.4 cm). Musée du Louvre, Paris

as if he were on a throne. In his hand is an orb signifying his domination of the world. The statue is probably modeled on a now lost antique Roman equestrian statue of Theodoric, which Charlemagne had brought from Ravenna for the courtyard of his imperial palace. There are other possible sources, including the bronze equestrian statue of Marcus Aurelius (see fig. 7.9), mistakenly thought to represent Constantine, the first Christian Emperor, and thus also an appropriate model for the ambitious Carolingian rulers.

The Carolingian statue is not a slavish copy of its antique model. Compared to the statue of Marcus Aurelius, it is simpler, less cluttered with detail, yet it still communicates the significant message that the Carolingian rulers were heirs to the Roman imperial throne. What is most striking is the difference in size: Marcus Aurelius stands more than 11 feet high, while the Carolingian figure does not reach ten inches. Yet the

diminutive statue expresses as much majesty and dignity as the more monumental example. Given the metalwork tradition of the Franks, the miniaturization is not only appropriate, but might in itself suggest value. Unfortunately, we do not know the audience for the work or how it was used, though portability could have been a factor in its smallness.

Illuminated Books

Charlemagne's interest in promoting learning and culture required the production of large numbers of books by his SCRIPTORIA. He established an "academy" at his court and encouraged the collecting and copying of many works of ancient Roman literature. In fact, the oldest surviving texts of many classical Latin authors are found in Carolingian manuscripts that were long considered of Roman origin. This very page is printed in letters the shapes of which

9.5 *St. Matthew*, from the *Gospel Book of Charlemagne* (*Coronation Gospels*). 800–810. Ink and colors on vellum, 13 × 10″ (33 × 25.4 cm). Kunsthistorisches Museum, Vienna

derive from the script in Carolingian manuscripts. The fact that these letters are known today as Roman rather than Carolingian is the result of this confusion.

THE *GOSPEL BOOK OF CHARLEMAGNE* The *Gospel Book of Charlemagne* (also known as the *Coronation Gospels*, because later German emperors swore on it during their coronations) is said to have been found in Charlemagne's tomb and is thought to have been produced at his court. Looking at the page with St. Matthew (**fig. 9.5**), we can hardly believe that such a work could have been executed in northern Europe, and little more than one hundred years after the *Book of Durrow* (see fig. 9.2). Were it not for the large golden HALO, the evangelist might almost be mistaken for the portrait of a classical author. Since the artist shows himself so fully conversant with the Roman tradition of painting and since

his manner of painting is so clearly Mediterranean, some scholars claim that he must have come from Byzantium or Italy. This classicism is evident throughout the work, from the painterly modeling of the forms to the acanthus ornament on the wide frame, which makes the picture seem like a window.

THE *GOSPEL BOOK OF ARCHBISHOP EBBO OF REIMS* Less reflective of classical models, but equally reliant on them, is a miniature painted some three decades later for the *Gospel Book of Archbishop Ebbo of Reims* (**fig. 9.6**). The subject is once again St. Matthew, and the pose is similar to that in the *Gospel Book of Charlemagne* (see fig. 9.5), but this picture is filled with a vibrant energy that sets everything into motion. The thickly painted drapery swirls about the figure, the hills heave upward, and the architecture and vegetation seem tossed about by a whirlwind.

◆ The HALO (or nimbus) represents light radiating around the head of a saint or divinity. The aureole is light around the body, and the glory is all the light—both halo and aureole. The mandorla is the almond-shaped form that encloses the image of a saint; it is also symbolic of the radiant light of holiness.

9.6 *St. Matthew*, from the *Gospel Book of Archbishop Ebbo of Reims*. Second quarter of ninth century. Ink, gold, and colors on vellum, 10¼ × 8¾″ (26 × 22.2 cm). Bibliothèque Municipale, Épernay, France

9.7 Front cover of binding, *Lindau Gospels*. ca. 870. Gold and jewels, 13 × 9⅞" (35 × 26.7 cm). The Pierpont Morgan Library, New York

◆ These five types of crosses are among those most often seen in Western art, though many variants exist.

Latin cross

Greek cross

Papal cross

Tau, Egyptian, or St. Anthony's cross

Celtic cross

Even the acanthus pattern on the frame assumes a strange, flamelike character. The evangelist has been transformed from a Roman author setting down his thoughts into a man seized with the frenzy of divine inspiration, a vehicle for recording the Word of God. The way the artist communicates this energy, particularly through the expressive use of flickering line, employing his brush as if it were a pen, recalls the endless interlaced movement in the ornamentation of Hiberno-Saxon manuscripts (see figs. 9.2 and 9.3).

THE *LINDAU GOSPELS* COVER The style of the Reims School is also apparent in the reliefs on the front cover of the *Lindau Gospels* (**fig. 9.7**). Given the Carolingian investment in preserving and embellishing the written word, the cover was a fittingly sumptuous protection for a book. This masterpiece of the goldsmith's art, dating from the third quarter of the ninth century, shows how splendidly the Germanic metal-work tradition was adapted to the Carolingian revival of the Roman Empire. The clusters of semiprecious stones are not mounted directly on the gold ground but raised on claw feet or arcaded turrets (towerlike projections), so that light can penetrate from beneath to bring out their full brilliance. The crucified Christ betrays no hint of pain or death. He seems to stand rather than to hang, his arms spread out in a solemn gesture.

Architecture

Although relatively few Carolingian buildings survive, excavations demonstrate a significant increase in building activity during the Carolingian period, a reflection of the security and prosperity enjoyed during Charlemagne's reign. As was the case with his painters, Charlemagne's architects sought to revive the splendor of the Roman Empire, by erecting buildings whose models were largely from Rome and Ravenna, both of which Charlemagne knew. While Rome had been the capital of the empire, Ravenna had been a Christian imperial outpost, thus a worthy prototype for what Charlemagne hoped to create in his own land.

PALACE CHAPEL OF CHARLEMAGNE, AACHEN

Toward the end of the eighth century, Charlemagne erected the imperial palace at Aachen. Prior to this time, Charlemagne's court was itinerant, moving from place to place as the political situation required. To signify Charlemagne's position as a Christian ruler, architects modeled his palace complex on Constantine's Lateran Palace in Rome. Charlemagne's palace included a basilica, called the Royal Hall, which was linked to the palace chapel (**fig. 9.8**). The plan for the palace chapel was probably inspired by the church of San Vitale in Ravenna, which the emperor saw at first hand (see figs. 8.8–8.10). It was designed by Odo of Metz, probably the earliest architect north of the Alps known to us by name. Einhard, Charlemagne's trusted adviser and biographer, supervised the project.

The debt to San Vitale is especially clear in cross-section. The chapel design is by no means a mere echo of San Vitale but a vigorous reinterpretation of it. Piers and vaults are impressively massive compared with San Vitale, while the geometric clarity of the spatial units is very different from the fluid space of the earlier structure. To construct such a building on northern soil was a difficult undertaking. Columns and bronze gratings were imported from Italy, and expert stonemasons must have been hard to find. The columns are placed within the arches

9.8 Odo of Metz. Interior of the palace chapel of Charlemagne. 792–805 CE. Aachen, Germany

of the upper story, where they are structurally unnecessary, but where they accentuate a sense of support and create opportunities to offer Roman details. San Vitale had been designed to be ambiguous, to produce an otherworldly interior space. Aachen, by comparison, is sturdy and sober. The soft, bulging curvilinear forms of San Vitale's arcades are replaced with clear-cut piers at Aachen. They make manifest their ability to support the heavy weight of Aachen's dome, while the dome at San Vitale seems light, appearing to hover above the interior space of the building.

Equally important is Odo's scheme for the western entrance, now largely obscured by later additions and rebuilding. At San Vitale, the entrance consists of a broad, semidetached

Section of palace chapel of Charlemagne

narthex with twin stair turrets, placed at an odd angle to the main axis of the church. At Aachen, these elements are molded into a tall, compact unit, in line with the main axis and attached to the chapel itself. This monumental structure, known as a westwork (from the German *Westwerk*), makes one of its first appearances here.

Charlemagne placed his throne in the tribune (the gallery of the westwork), behind the great opening above the entrance. From here the emperor could emerge into the view of people assembled in the atrium below. The throne faced an altar dedicated to Christ, who seemed to bless the emperor from above in the dome mosaic. Thus, although contemporary documents say very little about its function, the westwork seems to have served initially as a royal compartment or chapel.

ABBEY CHURCH, CORVEY The best-preserved surviving example of a Carolingian westwork is the Abbey Church at Corvey, Germany (**fig. 9.9**), built between 873 and 885. Except for the upper stories, which date from around 1146, the westwork retains much of its original appearance. It

9.9 Westwork, Abbey Church. Late ninth century, with later additions. Corvey, Germany

is impressive not only because of its height but also because of its expansive surfaces, which emphasize the clear geometry and powerful masses of the exterior. The westwork provided a suitably regal entrance, which may well be its greatest significance. But it had functional benefits too. Many westworks contained chapels housing numerous relics, and on feast days, and in particular at Easter, the community positioned itself there for the beginning of an elaborate processional liturgy. Thus, to some extent the westwork functioned as a separate commemorative building. At Corvey musical notation scratched on the walls of the gallery reminds us that the boys' choir would have been positioned here, its voices spreading upward as well as throughout the church.

In the end, the stability and grandeur the Carolingians hoped to express through their building programs did not reflect the reality of their political situation. Upon the death of Charlemagne's son, Louis I, in 840, a bitter struggle arose among his sons for the empire built by their grandfather. The brothers eventually signed a treaty in 843 dividing the empire into western, central, and eastern parts: Charles the Bald became the West Frankish King, founding the French Carolingian dynasty in what became modern France; Louis the German became the East Frankish King, ruling an area roughly that of today's Germany; and Lothair I became the Holy Roman Emperor, ruling the middle area running from the Netherlands through Lorraine (named for him) and down to Italy. The distribution of the Carolingian domain among Louis's heirs weakened the empire, brought a halt to Carolingian cultural efforts, and eventually exposed continental Europe to attack by the Muslims from the south, the Slavs and Magyars from the east, and the Vikings from the north. The Vikings invaded northwestern France, and through a land grant from Charles the Bald occupied the area now known as Normandy (named for the "Norsemen").

Although political stability ultimately eluded Charlemagne's heirs, the artists of the Carolingian period had been able to create an enduring art that combined the northern reliance on decoration—on surface, pattern, and line—with the Mediterranean concern for solidity and monumentality. Carolingian art was to serve as a worthy model for emulation by artists and patrons when the revival of Charlemagne's vision of a united and stable Europe would reappear during the next centuries.

Ottonian Art

When the last East Frankish monarch died in 911, the center of political power became consolidated in the eastern portion of the former Carolingian empire, under German kings of Saxon descent. Beginning with Henry I, these kings pushed back invaders, reestablished an effective central government, improved trade and the economy, and began a new dynasty, called Ottonian after its three principal rulers: Otto I, Otto II, and Otto III. During the Ottonian period, which lasted from 919 to 1024, Germany was the leading nation of Europe politically and artistically. German achievements in both areas began as revivals of Carolingian traditions but soon developed an original character.

The greatest of the Ottonian kings, Otto I, revived the imperial ambitions of Charlemagne. After marrying the widow of a Lombard king in 951, he extended his rule over most of what is now northern Italy. Then, in 962, he was crowned emperor by Pope John XII, at whose request he conquered Rome. The emperor later deposed this pope for conspiring against him.

Architecture

Among the most pressing concerns of the Ottonian emperors was the reform of the Church, which had become corrupt and mismanaged. They achieved this by establishing closer alliances with the papacy and by fostering monastic reforms, which they supported by sponsoring many new religious buildings. The renewal of impressive building programs effectively revived the architectural ambitions of their Carolingian predecessors, at the same time conveying and furthering the Ottonians' aspirations to restore the imperial glory of Christian Rome.

SAINT MICHAEL'S, HILDESHEIM The most ambitious patron of architecture and art in the Ottonian age was Bernward, who became bishop of Hildesheim after having been court chaplain. Bernward was also tutor of Otto III during the regency of his mother the Empress Theophano, wife of Otto II and a Byzantine princess in her own right. Bernward's chief monument is the Benedictine Abbey Church of Saint Michael at Hildesheim. The plan of this monastic church, with its two choirs and side entrances, derives from Carolingian monastic building types. However, in Saint Michael's the symmetry is carried much further. There are two identical transepts, each with a tower, where the transept and the

9.10 Interior, with view toward the apse (after restoration of 1950–1960), Abbey Church of Saint Michael. 1001–1033. Hildesheim, Germany

Reconstructed plan of Abbey Church of Saint Michael, Hildesheim

nave cross, and a pair of stair turrets at the end of each transept. But the supports of the nave arcade, instead of being uniform, consist of pairs of columns separated by square piers (**fig. 9.10**). This alternating system divides the arcade into three equal units, each with three openings. These units are equal in length to the width of the transepts, which are similarly divided into three compartments. Thus, a modular system governs the division of spaces. Saint Michael's was severely damaged during the Second World War, but the restored interior, with its great expanse of wall space between the arcade and

clerestory, retains the majestic feeling of the original design. (The capitals of the columns date from the twelfth century; the painted wooden ceiling from the thirteenth.)

Metalwork

The Ottonian emperors' reliance on Church authority to strengthen their own governmental rule encouraged them not only to build new churches but also to provide sumptuous works of art to decorate them. The works they and their cohorts sponsored were richly appointed and executed in expensive, often precious materials.

BRONZE DOORS OF BISHOP BERNWARD, HILDESHEIM For Saint Michael's at Hildesheim, Bernward commissioned a pair of extensively sculptured bronze doors (**fig. 9.11**), which were finished in 1015, the year the crypt was consecrated. According to his biographer, Thangmar of Heidelberg, Bernward excelled in the arts and "distinguished himself remarkably in the science of metalwork and the whole art of building." He must therefore have been closely involved in the project. The idea for the doors may have come to him as a result of his visit to Rome, where he could have seen ancient Roman (and perhaps Byzantine) doors of bronze or wood. He would also certainly have been aware of the bronze doors that Charlemagne had commissioned for his palace chapel at Aachen.

The doors at Hildesheim are considered by many scholars to be the first monumental sculptures created by the lost-wax process since antiquity (see page 92). Each door was cast as one piece and measures over 16 feet high. They are also the first doors since the Early Christian period to have been decorated with stories. Our detail (**fig. 9.12**) shows God accusing and judging Adam and Eve after they have committed the Original Sin of eating the forbidden fruit in the Garden of Eden. (This story is known as the Temptation and Fall.) Below it, in inlaid letters notable for their classical Roman character, is part of the inscription, with the date and Bernward's name. The inscription was added around 1035, when the doors were moved from the monastery of Saint Michael and attached to the westwork of Hildesheim Cathedral, where they would have been seen by a larger public than in the monastic setting of Saint Michael's. The new, prominent setting indicates how valued they were in their own time.

The composition most probably derives from a manuscript illumination, since there are very similar scenes in medieval Bibles. Yet this is no mere imitation. The story is conveyed with splendid directness and expressive force. The accusing finger of the Lord, seen against a great void, is the focal point of the drama. It points to a cringing Adam, who passes the blame to Eve, who in turn passes it to the serpent at her feet.

The subjects on the left door are taken from the Old Testament and those on the right from the New Testament (see fig. 9.11). The Old Testament stories are presented chronologically from top to bottom, while the New Testament scenes move in reverse order, from bottom to top, suggesting that the message of the Christian

9.11 Doors of Bishop Bernward, Hildesheim Cathedral (originally made for Abbey Church of Saint Michael, Hildesheim). 1015. Bronze, height approx. 16′ (4.8 m). Hildesheim, Germany

9.12 *Accusation and Judgment of Adam and Eve*, from the doors of Bishop Bernward. 1015. Bronze, approx. 23 × 43″ (58.3 × 109.3 cm). Hildesheim, Germany

Bible is uplifting. When read as horizontal pairs, the panels deliver a message of the origin and redemption of sin through a system of typology, whereby Old Testament stories prefigure New Testament ones. For example, the Temptation and Fall is opposite the Crucifixion. In the center of the left panel of this pair of scenes is the tree whose fruit led to the Original Sin; in the center of the right panel is the cross on which Jesus was crucified, which medieval Christians believed was made from the wood of the tree from Eden and was therefore the instrument for redemption from the sin of that original act. Compositional similarities between the two scenes stress their typological relationship: In the left panel Adam and Eve's hands flanking the cross-shaped tree establish a visual parallel to the spears the soldiers use to pierce Christ's body on the right panel.

Ivories and Manuscripts: Conveyors of Imperial Grandeur

The right of the Ottonian monarchs to call themselves Roman emperors was challenged by Byzantine rulers, who continued to claim that title as their own even though the division of the Roman Empire into Eastern and Western empires was complete by the end of the fourth century. When Otto II married the Byzantine princess Theophano, he was able to use the full title of Holy Roman Emperor with impunity. While early Ottonian illuminators faithfully replicated features of Carolingian manuscripts for the court school, later Ottonian manuscripts, as well as ivories, blend Carolingian and Byzantine elements into a new style of extraordinary scope and power. Byzantine artists working for the court provided an impetus for new ways of presenting both religious and imperial images. Ottonian manuscripts indicate an increasing interest on the part of artists and patrons in narrative cycles of Jesus' life, which is the period's most important contribution to the field of iconography.

THE *GOSPEL BOOK OF OTTO III* Produced for the son of Otto II and Theophano, the *Gospel Book of Otto III* (**fig. 9.13**) communicates an imperial grandeur that is impressive indeed. The emperor displays the imperial regalia—a crown, an eagle scepter, and a cross-inscribed orb—while his throne is decorated with imperial lions. Representatives of the two domains that he controls—the military and the ecclesiastical—flank him, reminiscent of Justinian's placement in the center of the same domains in the San Vitale mosaic (see fig. 8.11). On the facing folio, the four geographical parts of the realm—Slavinia, Germania, Gallia, and Roma—offer homage. Their stances recall traditional representations of the Magi offering gifts to Christ, such as the scene decorating Theodora's robe in the mosaic at San Vitale in Ravenna (see fig. 8.12).

The manuscript is dated around 1000, not long after Otto III was crowned king of Germany at Aachen in 986 and Holy Roman Emperor at Rome in 993. The way Otto is represented visually in the manuscript thus parallels historical facts; he is presented here as rightful and worthy heir to Roman and Byzantine emperors as well as to Charlemagne, and his imperial dignity is enhanced by association with Christ, a reverse of the case of Early Christian depictions, in which Christ is ennobled in the fashion of a Roman emperor (see fig. 8.7). The soft pastel hues of the background recall the illusionism of Graeco-Roman landscapes and the *Quedlinburg*

Itala fragment (see fig. 8.5). Such a style shows that the artist was probably aware of Roman, as well as Byzantine, manners of representation.

The *Gospel Book of Otto III* contains one of the most extensive sets of illustrations of the life of Christ. The scene of *Jesus Washing the Feet of St. Peter* (**fig. 9.14**) once again contains strong echoes of ancient painting, transmitted through Byzantine art. The architectural frame around Jesus is a late descendant of the kind of architectural perspectives used in Roman wall painting (see figs. 7.23 and 7.24), and the intense gold background reminds us of Byzantine painting and mosaics, which the Ottonian artist has put to new use (see fig. 8.21). What had previously been an architectural vista now becomes the Heavenly City, the House of the Lord, filled with golden celestial space in contrast with the atmospheric earthly space outside.

The figures have also been transformed. In ancient art this composition, in which a standing figure extends an arm to a seated, supplicating figure and is watched by onlookers and assisted by others, was used to depict a doctor treating a patient. Here the emphasis has shifted from physical to spiritual action. Not only do glances and gestures convey this new kind of action, but

9.13 *Otto III Receiving the Homage of the Four Parts of the Empire* and *Otto III Between Church and State*, from the *Gospel Book of Otto III.* ca. 1000. Tempera on vellum. Each folio 13 × 9⅜" (33 × 23.8 cm). Staatsbibliothek, Munich

9.14 *Jesus Washing the Feet of St. Peter*, from the *Gospel Book of Otto III*. ca. 1000. Tempera on vellum, 13 × 9⅜″ (33 × 23.8 cm). Staatsbibliothek, Munich

so too does scale. Jesus and his apostle Peter, the most animated figures, are larger than the rest, and Jesus' "active" arm is longer than his "passive" one. The blending of classical and Byzantine elements results in a new style of expressive abstraction.

Sculpture

Large-scale and free-standing sculpture was rare in the early Middle Ages, in part because of the lingering fear of idol worship and because the general interest in producing portable objects virtually precluded its production. However, during the Ottonian period the scale of sculpture increased (witness Bernward's doors for Saint Michael's at Hildesheim), and even many small-scale works demonstrate an imposing monumentality.

THE *GERO CRUCIFIX* The *Gero Crucifix* (**fig. 9.15**), named for Archbishop Gero of Cologne, who commissioned it around 970, is an example of a large-scale work—it is in fact life-size—with a monumental presence, indicative of the major transformation that Ottonian sculptors were able to achieve even when dealing with traditional subjects. How this happens is evident if we compare the *Gero Crucifix* with the Christ on the cover of the *Lindau Gospels* (see fig. 9.7). The two works are separated by little more than a hundred years but show marked contrast. The *Gero Crucifix* presents a sculptural image of the crucified Christ that is new to Western art, an image filled with deep feeling for Christ's suffering. Made of painted and gilded oak, it is carved in powerfully rounded forms. Particularly striking is the forward bulge of the heavy body, which

9.15 *Gero Crucifix*. ca. 970. Painted and gilded wood, height 6'2" (1.88 m). Cathedral. Cologne, Germany

emphasizes the physical strain on the arms and shoulders, making the pain seem almost unbearable. The face, with its deeply incised, angular features, is a mask of agony from which all life has fled.

How did the Ottonian sculptor arrive at this bold conception? The *Gero Crucifix* was clearly influenced by Middle Byzantine art, which had created the compassionate view of Christ on the Cross in other media (see fig. 8.21). Yet, that source alone is not enough to explain the results. It remained for the Ottonian artist to translate the Byzantine image into large-scale sculptural terms and to replace its gentle pathos with expressive realism. Even though there were some clerics who rekindled the deep-rooted fear of idolatry, they could not restrain the newly found emphasis on the humanity of Christ or the increasing interest in relics. In fact, there is a space in the back of the head of the Gero Christ to hold the Host (the bread or wafer taken during that part of the Mass referred to as Communion), transforming the sculpture into a reliquary (a container to enshrine holy remnants or relics). The marked movement toward monumentality of the *Gero Crucifix* heralds new aesthetic aims that will dominate eleventh-century sculpture throughout Europe.

The Development of Islamic Style

At the time that Charlemagne, his ancestors and descendants lived and governed, extensive building campaigns were undertaken by the Abbasid rulers in the greatly expanded areas where, largely through conquest, Islam became the dominant religion.

Religious Architecture

Chief among the new structures were the large Abbasid congregational mosques that both practically and symbolically served as religious gathering places for prayers, sermons, and religious education. Large examples, many now in ruins, were built all over Iraq, and in Egypt and elsewhere. An archetypal example is the largely ninth-century congregational mosque at Kairouan, a city established under the Abbasids in what is now Tunisia.

GREAT MOSQUE OF KAIROUAN Based, like all major Arab mosques, on the house of the Prophet in Medina and the four-square Mediterranean courtyard house, examples of which today still surround the structure, the Great Mosque of Kairouan consists of a rectangular courtyard surrounded by covered halls, a large hypostyle prayer hall, and a towering minaret (**fig. 9.16**). Two domes mark the area: In front of the *mihrab* and in the middle of the prayer hall facing the court. This aside, the multitude of entrances on three sides of the building, built in order to facilitate entry and exit for the five daily prayers, frees the building from the domination of a central axis for processions of clergy; it is thus the very opposite of the early Christian basilican church (see fig. 8.2), organized for priestly and theatrical ritual. The simplicity of the mosque reflects the simplicity of Islamic prayer, the essential lack of hierarchy among worshipers, and the absence of an ordained clergy in Islam. Each worshiper prays directly to God using a simple ritual formula usually completed in a few minutes. Artistic attention was lavished on the *mihrab*, of carved marble and ceramic tiles, and the *minbar* or pulpit, elaborately carved of Indian teak. In the Kairouan mosque, a carved wooden screen, primarily a product of security rather than ritual needs, encloses a small area near the *mihrab* called the *maqsura*, where the ruler could pray alone.

GREAT MOSQUE OF CÓRDOBA Even farther to the west, in Spain, where the sole surviving

9.16 Aerial view of the Great Mosque of Kairouan, Tunisia. Eighth century and later

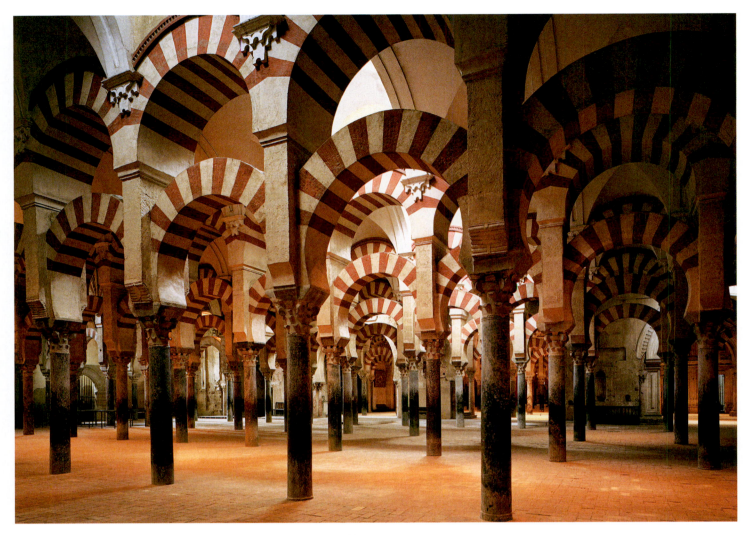

9.17 Interior of prayer hall, Great Mosque of Córdoba. Eighth century and later

prince of the exterminated Umayyad house founded an independent state after 750, a brilliant center of Islamic culture developed in the city of Córdoba, in the southern part of Spain, referred to as al-Andalus (now Andalusia). By the tenth century, the Great Mosque of Córdoba, after a series of embellishments and enlargements, had become one of the most beautiful Islamic houses of worship. A typical Arab hypostyle hall, the Córdoba mosque in its interior became after several expansions a virtual forest of columns (**fig. 9.17**). Its characteristic "horseshoe" arcades are composed of arches using alternating red and white voussoirs. This type of voussoir undoubtedly reflects Roman preedents and was clearly of interest to Christian architects, as demonstrated by its use in the palace chapel in Aachen (see fig. 9.8) and Saint Michael's at Hildesheim (see fig. 9.10). The superimposition of one set of arches above another on elongated imposts creates an impression of almost limitless space—this space is,

however, composed of relatively small architectural elements repeated again and again. Compared with a Christian structure like Hagia Sophia (see fig. 8.15) or Old Saint Peter's (see fig. 8.2), Córdoba has an equally large interior area, but there is no centralized space for the sacred theater of the Christian rite. The mosque interior, including the *maqsura* area around the *mihrab*, was lavishly decorated with mosaic and carved stone. Tenth-century marble grilles (**fig. 9.18**) on the *qibla* wall present early examples of what we sometimes call geometric arabesque: The artist carves out of marble what is essentially a single straplike line that intertwines, creating a characteristic openwork screen of stars and polygons. In the beauty of such artistic geometry many Muslims see a reflection of God's creative hand in the universe, not unlike the way Christian believers evaluated the elaborate patterns of Hiberno-Saxon manuscript illuminations such as those in the *Lindisfarne Gospels* (see fig. 9.3).

9.18 Carved stone grille on *qibla* wall of Great Mosque of Córdoba. Mid-tenth century

In addition to providing a community prayer hall, the institutional operations of the great Islamic mosques such as the Great Mosque of Córdoba also often incorporated schools and universities, public baths, hospitals and medical schools, soup kitchens for the poor, hostels for travelers and merchants, public clocks (knowing the correct time was essential for the variable timing of the five daily prayers), public toilets, and fountains serving as the public water supply for the immediate area. Endowments known as *waqf*, based on the income from rental properties, supported the many functions of mosques. *Waqf* were also established for social-service institutions and for shrines that were founded independently of mosques. Artistic votive gifts made to such institutions, such as Qur'an manuscripts, lamps, beautiful wooden furniture, carpets, and other objects, were in theory protected in perpetuity, becoming part of the *waqf* itself. As a consequence, such institutions often became great magnets for

9.19 Ivory casket of al-Mughira, from Córdoba, ca. 960. Height 6″ (15 cm), diameter 3″ (8 cm). Musée du Louvre, Paris

works of art, accumulating over time important libraries and collections of beautiful furnishings.

Luxury Arts

On the outskirts of Córdoba the Umayyads built another huge Islamic palace city, known as Medina al-Zahra. A ruin today, the palace complex once included royal workshops for luxury objects such as silk textiles and carved ivory, used as symbols of royal wealth and power and given as royal ceremonial gifts. A small, domed pyxis (ivory box) made there for a tenth-century Umayyad prince (**fig. 9.19**) incorporates in its decoration a microcosm of Islamic royal imagery and symbolism, including depictions of falconry and hunting, sports, and court musicians, set amid lush carved vegetal ornament and a kufic inscription frieze. Such lavish objects had a symbolic importance far beyond their practical use as containers for jewelry or cosmetics. Their complex, many-layered iconography and their importance and symbolism as royal gifts continue to be studied by scholars today. Despite, or perhaps because of, their Islamic origins, these luxury objects were greatly appreciated by Christians, and many of them made their way into princely collections and church treasuries.

In the eleventh century, Berber armies serving the Almoravid dynasty from North Africa razed Medina al-Zahra to its foundations; they and their successors, the Almohads, built significant monuments in the Maghreb (present-day Morocco and northwestern Africa) and in al-Andalus. But the growing and continual pressure of the Christian conquest from the north saw a dramatic decline in Muslim power in Spain. By the fourteenth century, the Almohad capital of Seville had fallen to the kings of Castile; Muslims working under Christian rule, known as Mudejares, continued Islamic artistic traditions under Christian patronage.

Islamic Art and the Persian Inheritance

As we have seen, in the central and western Islamic lands, from Spain to the western Mediterranean shore, Islamic arts developed within the geography and culture of the Graeco-Roman tradition; in the east, however, the situation was in many respects quite different. In Mesopotamia and Iran, the Arab Muslim conquerors encountered the cultural sphere of the Sasanians, heirs to over a thousand years of Per-

sian civilization with an impressive tradition of art and architecture. This tradition included royal imagery of ceremonial pomp, warfare, and the royal sport of hunting (see fig. 2.9), as well as large and impressive palace buildings.

Architecture

In the eastern Islamic world, following pre-Islamic architectural practice, brick rather than stone was the most common construction material. In place of cylindrical columns, massive brick piers often provided vertical structural support in buildings, and heavy vaults rather than tiled wooden-beam roofs were often chosen to cover interior spaces. Islamic architecture in Mesopotamia, Iran, and Central Asia reflects the available materials, earlier cultural traditions, and even the climate of those regions in distinctive ways. It also provides a curious blending of secular and religious buildings; just as the open arcaded courtyard helps to define both mosque and palace in the Islamic west, another form, known as the *iwan*, came to define both royal and religious structures in the east.

THE FOUR-*IWAN* MOSQUE One of the first large vaulted brick structures with one open side, known as an *iwan*, was constructed by the Sasanian ruler Shapur I as an audience hall for his royal palace at Ctesiphon in Mesopotamia. The form seems originally to have symbolized royal authority in Iran, and under Islam it eventually was incorporated into a new type of prayer structure, the four-*iwan* mosque (**fig. 9.20**), by

9.20 Cutaway of a generic Persian four-*iwan* mosque

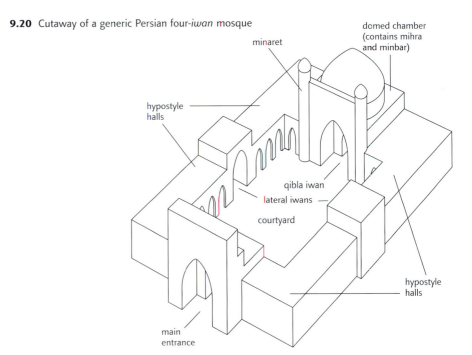

domed chamber (contains mihra and minbar)

minaret

hypostyle halls

qibla iwan

lateral iwans

courtyard

hypostyle halls

main entrance

9.21 *Mina'i* dish with story of Bahram Gur and Azadeh, from Iran. ca. 1200. Polychrome overglaze enamels on white composite body. Diameter 8½″ (22.2 cm), width 3¹³⁄₁₆″ (9.7 cm). The Metropolitan Museum of Art, New York. Purchase, Rogers Fund and gift of the Schiff Foundation, 1957 57.36.13

placing one massive brick recess in the middle of each of the sides of the rectangular courtyard. From the twelfth century onward the four-*iwan* courtyard was a standard feature of both mosques and religious schools of a type known as *madrasa* throughout Iran and Islamic Central Asia. In most of Iran, as in Mesopotamia, brick was the preferred building material, and the vaults of Iranian mosques were supported by heavy brick piers.

Figural Art Forms in Iran

The Iranian part of the Islamic world had inherited a rich tradition of material culture, and the successive rulers of Iran, whether themselves Arab, Persian, Turkish, or Mongol in ancestry, fell under the seductive spell of the Persian heritage, which they combined with their Islamic beliefs and traditions. From the prosperous cities of tenth- and eleventh-century Iran there have survived beautiful ceramic wares decorated with

maxims, good wishes, or prayers in beautiful calligraphy with figural and vegetal decoration, as well as some exceptional silk textiles and metal objects. The Seljuk Turkish invaders, who ruled Iran from the mid-eleventh century onward, not only built great mosques and tomb structures, but also ruled over a prosperous urban culture that among other things produced one of the richest known traditions of decorated ceramics. Using figural images of all kinds in a multitude of sophisticated techniques, including the use of a metallic pigment known as luster fired over the glaze, and polychrome enamel decoration known as *mina'i*, these ceramic wares incorporated for middle-class patrons a very diverse repertoire of scenes from Persian romances and mythology, themes from sufism (the Islamic mystical religious tradition), and Islamic royal images of hunting and other courtly pleasures. A favorite story finding its way into ceramics, metalwork, and book illustration was that of the royal hunter Bahram Gur and his skeptical sweetheart, the harpist Azadeh. A *mina'i* plate shows two episodes of continuous narrative, with Azadeh on the camel with her royal lover, and then pushed off the beast after making a remark belittling the hero's marksmanship (**fig. 9.21**). To what do we owe this burst of figural art in seeming contradiction to strict Islamic dogma? Practical rather than dogmatic, Iranians under the Seljuks apparently believed that figural images did not necessarily have to be identified with polytheism or idolatry, but could capably serve both secular and religious purposes without morally corrupting the viewer.

Out of the period of turmoil, marked by the decline of the Roman Empire and the appearance in Europe of new tribal groups, some willing to adopt the prevailing religion of Christianity and others eager to impose the religion of Islam, Europe coalesced into a group of states whose borders, though neither fixed nor constant, came to resemble those of the modern continent. What was to change was the diminution of the presence of Islam in western Europe, a result of the expulsion of the Muslim inhabitants of Spain from that country at the end of the fifteenth century. The art that developed during the early medieval period provided artistic modes and formal arrangements that would define the art of the remaining Middle Ages, that is, through the fourteenth century, and beyond.

SUMMARY

Western Europe was home to a number of cultures after the Fall of Rome. Migrations and invasions were common, and groups frequently clashed and mixed with one another. Overlaid on this mix were Roman traditions, among them Christianity. Over time, the Church became an important force in European unification, and strong political leaders led a succession of ruling dynasties, including the Carolingian and the Ottonian. Among the widespread migrations across Europe in the 300s and 400s were those of the Germanic peoples, whose art, including metalwork and jewelry, was portable. Their skillfully executed objects, such as the Sutton Hoo purse cover, were often made of gold or silver and included precious stones.

Also important for the development of Western art was the intrusion into Europe, mostly by way of Spain and beginning in the eighth century, of Islamic artistic forms and decorative motifs. Islamic monuments, such as the Great Mosque of Córdoba, made a profound impression on European artists and patrons.

During the early Middle Ages, Irish monasteries became centers of learning and the arts, with special attention devoted to copying and decorating literary and religious texts. The finest of these manuscripts belong to the Hiberno-Saxon style, which combines Christian, Celtic, and Germanic elements.

A new empire developed in Europe in the late 700s. It was founded by Charlemagne and was referred to as the Carolingian empire. Artists who worked for Charlemagne and his successors during this Carolingian period combined admiration for antiquity with native northern European features. High-quality works of the time include bronze sculptures and illuminated books as well as an increasing number of architectural projects.

After the last Carolingian monarch died, German kings of Saxon descent consolidated political power in the eastern portion of the empire. These rulers pushed back invaders, reestablished an effective central government, and began a new dynasty: The Ottonian. A pressing concern of these leaders was Church reform. Impressive building programs of the time include the Benedictine Abbey Church of Saint Michael at Hildesheim. Ottonian artists produced ivories and manuscripts that blended Carolingian and Byzantine elements, and they showed an increased interest in large-scale sculpture.

Islamic patrons were also concerned with the building of monumental structures. Of special significance is the Great Mosque of Kairouan, in north Africa. Farther to the west—in an independent state founded by an Umayyad survivor—Córdoba, Spain, became a brilliant center of Islamic culture and home to another great mosque.

In eastern Islamic lands, Arab Muslim conquerors encountered the Sasanians, heirs to the cultural traditions of Persian civilization. Combining these traditions with their own Islamic beliefs and traditions led to the construction of large and impressive complexes such as the four-*iwan* mosque. A prosperous urban culture arose that produced one of the richest known traditions of decorated ceramics.

ART IN TIME

- 400s—Angles and Saxons invade British Isles

- 476—The Fall of Rome

- **First half of 600s—Double ship burial at Sutton Hoo, England: Purse cover**

- **ca. 700—*Lindisfarne Gospels* produced**

- 787—Earliest recorded Viking raid of British Isles

- 750—Abbasid dynasty supplants Umayyad dynasty

- **Second half of 700s—Construction begins on Great Mosque at Córdoba, Spain**

- 792–805—Palace chapel of Charlemagne constructed in Aachen

- **800–810—Gospel Book of Charlemagne painted**

- 843—Charlemagne's three grandsons divide his empire

- 962—Otto I crowned as Holy Roman Emperor

- **1015—Bernward bronze doors completed for Saint Michael's at Hildesheim, Germany**

10 Romanesque Art

*R*omanesque means, literally, "in the Roman manner." We use this stylistic term today to identify the art of much of the eleventh and twelfth centuries. The borrowing of details or specific features from the antique past does not distinguish Romanesque art from the art of other post-classical periods, for Early Christian, Byzantine, Carolingian, and Islamic art also relied heavily on Rome for their formal and expressive languages. However, in Romanesque art, the aesthetic integrity and grandeur of the Roman model survive in a more vital and compelling form than in any previous period of art history. Yet Rome was not the period's only inspiration: Romanesque artists tapped sources in Carolingian and Ottonian art, and were influenced by Early Christian, Byzantine, Germano-Celtic, and Islamic traditions as well.*

Romanesque art sprang up all over Western Europe at about the same time and in a variety of regional styles that are nevertheless closely related. What welded this variety into a coherent style was not any single force but several factors. For one thing, Christianity was close to triumph almost everywhere in Europe. Most of the northern tribes had entered the Catholic fold, and in 1031 the caliphate of Córdoba had broken up into many small Muslim states, opening the way for Christian conquest of the Iberian peninsula.

Another significant factor was the growing spirit of religious enthusiasm. The year 1000—the millennium—had come and gone without the apocalyptic end of the world that many had predicted from their reading of the Book of Revelation in the Bible. Chapter 20 of this New Testament book, written about 50 years after Christ's death, prophesies that the Second Coming, when Christ will return to earth and end the world as we know it, was to occur after 1,000 years. Scholars have suggested that many people, fearing the dreaded end of days, reacted to the approach of the year 1000 with terror and to its smooth passing with great relief and, in some

quarters, a heightened spirituality. This was demonstrated by the large number of people making pilgrimages to sacred sites, by repeated Christian crusades against the Muslims in what was called the Holy Land, and by an increase in the number and size of monasteries, which also reflected the general growth in population and an increase in prosperity.

Equally important was the reopening of the Mediterranean trade routes by the navies of Venice, Genoa, Amalfi, Pisa, and Rimini (see map 10.1). The revival of trade and travel linked Europe commercially and culturally, stimulating the flowering of urban life. At the end of the early medieval period, Europe was still largely an agricultural society. A decentralized political and social system, known today as *feudalism,* had developed, mainly in France and Germany, where it had deep historical roots. In this system, landowning lords granted some of their property to knights (originally, these were cavalry officers). In return for these fiefs, or feuds, as the land parcels were called, the knights gave military and other service to their lords, to whom they were linked through a complex

Map 10.1 Europe in the Romanesque period

system of personal bonds—termed vassalage—that extended all the way to the king. A large class of generally downtrodden, virtually powerless peasants (serfs) worked the land itself. Towns that had shrunk in size during the migrations and invasions of the early Middle Ages started to regain their former importance and new towns sprang up everywhere, achieving independence via charters that enumerated a town's privileges and immunities in return for a feudal lord's guarantee of protection.

These social changes were also made possible by technological advances in agriculture. For the first time since the fall of Rome, farmers could grow more food than they needed for themselves. In many ways, then, Western Europe between 1050 and 1200 became a great deal more "Roman-esque" than it had been since the sixth century. It recaptured some of the trade patterns, the urban quality, and the military strength of ancient imperial times. To be sure, there was no central political authority, for

Europe was still divided into small units ruled by powerful families. Even the king of France controlled not much more than the area around Paris. However, some monasteries came to rival the wealth and power of kings, and the central spiritual authority of the pope acted as a unifying force throughout Europe.

This brief historical account underscores the number of institutions, organizations and systems that helped to create European stability. Monasticism, feudalism, urbanism, commerce, pilgrimage, crusade, papacy, and the royal court all played their roles by setting into motion internationalizing forces that affected the transmission of artistic forms. Population growth and the increase in the number of new settlements stimulated building activity, much of it for Christian use. The development of better tools, such as saws to cut stone, resulted in improved masonry techniques. Many new constructions were made of well-cut, straight-edged blocks of stone and were monumental, built on a scale that rivaled the achievements of Rome. The heavy walls created solid and durable structures that convey a sense of enclosure and security, and the stone vaults covering these buildings enhanced their stability. These vaults, as well as the proliferation of architectural sculpture, consciously emulated the Roman manner of construction and design.

First Expressions of Romanesque Style

Although Romanesque art quickly spread throughout Europe, it first appeared in a zone running from Lombardy in northern Italy through southern France and into northeastern Spain, the region of Catalonia. Even today, stone-vaulted buildings decorated with wall arcades and architectural sculpture, which are characteristic features of this early phase, survive in great numbers in these regions.

Architecture

The most striking feature of Romanesque art is the astonishing increase in building activity. An eleventh-century monk, Raoul Glaber, conveys the enthusiasm for building during the period:

> "Just before the third year after the millennium, throughout the whole world, but most especially in Italy and Gaul, men began to reconstruct churches... But it seemed as though each Christian community were aiming to surpass all others in the splendor of construction. It was as if the whole world were shaking itself free, shrugging off the burden of the past, and cladding itself everywhere in a white mantle of churches."

J. France, *The Five Books of the Histories.* Oxford, 1989.

10.1 Nave and choir (looking east), Sant Vincenç. ca. 1029–1040. Cardona, Spain

These churches were not only more numerous than those of the early Middle Ages, they were also larger, more richly ornamented, and more "Roman-looking." Their naves had stone vaults instead of wooden roofs, and their exteriors were decorated with both architectural ornament and sculpture.

CHURCH OF SANT VINCENÇ, CARDONA An excellent example of an early phase of Romanesque architecture is the collegiate church of Sant Vincenç (**fig. 10.1**), built within the walled confines of the castle at Cardona on the southern flank of the Catalan Pyrenees. The church, begun in 1029 and consecrated in 1040, is straightforward in both plan and elevation. A barrel-vaulted nave creates a continuous space marked off by transverse arches, which run across the width of the nave. These transverse arches divide the nave into units of space called **bays**. The domed bay in front of the chancel, the part of the church containing the altar and seats for the clergy and choir, focuses attention on the ceremonial heart of the building. Blind niches in the chancel walls establish a rhythmic variety that is accentuated in the nave by the staggered cadence of massive **compound piers**, solid masonry supports with rectangular projections attached to their four faces. The projections reflect the different structural elements that combine to support the building. One projection rises the full height of the nave to support the transverse arch, another forms the arch that extends across the side aisle, and two others connect to the arches of the nave arcade. The compound pier is, in fact, a major architectural innovation of the Romanesque period.

The clarity of articulation of the architectural details at Sant Vincenç endows the building with a heightened sense of unity and harmony. Limited light and robust stone construction create an interior at once sheltering and inspiring; the sober arrangement of simple yet powerful forms is masterfully realized.

Monumental Stone Sculpture

The revival of monumental stone sculpture in the Romanesque era is as significant as the architectural achievements of the period. Free-standing statues had all but disappeared from Western art after the fifth century, and stone relief survived only as architectural ornament or surface decoration, while three-dimensional sculpture was rare. Thus, the only sculptural tradition that continued through the early medieval period was that of sculpture-in-miniature: Small reliefs and occasional statuettes in metal or ivory. In works such as the bronze doors of Bishop Bernward (see fig. 9.11), Ottonian art had enlarged the small scale of this tradition but had not changed its spirit. Moreover, its truly large-scale sculptural efforts, such as the *Gero Crucifix* (see fig. 9.15), were limited almost entirely to wood.

LINTEL AT SAINT-GENIS-DES-FONTAINES The marble lintel at Saint-Genis-des-Fontaines, on the French side of the Pyrenees, is dated by inscription to between 1020 and 1021 (**fig. 10.2**). It spans the doorway of the church and is one

10.2 Lintel of west portal, Saint-Genis-des-Fontaines, France. 1020–1021. Approx. 2 × 7′ (61 × 213.4 cm)

Christian PILGRIMAGES began as early as the second century with journeys to Jerusalem. The pilgrim would travel to a sacred site to ask for help, to give thanks, or simply to express devotion. In medieval times, there were many pilgrimage destinations, the most popular being Rome, the Holy Land, and Santiago de Compostela in Spain. (The latter is where the remains of the apostle St. James are believed to have been buried.) Geoffrey Chaucer's classic *The Canterbury Tales* is an account of a pilgrimage to the tomb of St. Thomas Becket in Kent, England.

Between 1095 and 1291, seven different armies were raised in Europe to undertake campaigns, called CRUSADES, to the Holy Land in the name of "freeing" Jerusalem from Muslim control. In fact, the Church's broad call was for war against all of its perceived opponents: Political, heretical, and schismatic. In responding to the call, however, the nobles who volunteered themselves and their loyal soldiers believed they were accumulating merit by waging a "holy war" to reclaim the lands where Jesus had lived. The Crusades combined aspects of the pilgrimage as well, with Crusaders making stops at holy sites along the way to their various destinations in Syria, Palestine, and Egypt.

of the earliest examples of Romanesque figurative sculpture. The inscription cites the leaders of two stabilizing institutions of the period, *Rotberto Rege* (King Robert) and *Willelmus Aba* (Abbot William), the former a feudal lord and the latter the leader of a monastery. The central motif, Christ in Majesty supported by angels, is flanked by six apostles; each apostle holds a book and stands under an arcade. Christ's mandorla (see page 197) is formed by two intersecting circles. One symbolizes the earth and the other the heavens, the two realms over which he presides.

The Saint-Genis lintel is modest in size, about two feet high by seven feet long. The reliance on line to indicate facial features, drapery folds, and ornamental decoration is reminiscent of early medieval manuscript illumination and reaches as far back as the Hiberno-Saxon period. The carving, with flat surfaces marked by incision, resembles that of the minor arts, particularly ivories and metalwork. This can be verified by comparing some of the patterns (for example, the beading around the arches) with metalwork techniques (see fig. 9.1). The correlation explains where carvers might have found their sources of inspiration after centuries during which stone sculpture had been virtually abandoned.

Mature Romanesque

Early Romanesque experiments in sturdy construction, which relied on the skills of masons and sculptors, led to buildings that employed both more sculpture and increasingly sophisticated vaulting techniques. Sculptural decoration was arranged into complicated and didactic iconographic programs.

Pilgrimage Churches and Their Art

Among the most significant social phenomena of eleventh- and twelfth-century Europe was the increased ability of people of all classes to travel. While some journeys were a result of expanded trade, others, such as a crusade or pilgrimage, were ostensibly for religious purposes. Individual pilgrims made journeys to holy places for different reasons, but most shared the hope that they would find special powers or dispensations as a result of their journey. PILGRIMAGE was not a Romanesque invention. As early as the late fourth century, Egeria, a Spanish pilgrim to Jerusalem, chronicled her visit to the locations central to Christ's life. Special, often miraculous powers associated with these holy sites were transferred to relics, those body parts of holy persons or objects that had come in contact with Christ, his close followers, or other holy figures.

Partly as a result of the Muslim conquest of the Holy Land, travel there was difficult during the Middle Ages. This led, on the one hand, to the zeal for CRUSADE and, on the other, to the veneration of places within Europe that had important relics or that had been the site of special events. Rome, in particular, became a popular pilgrimage site, beneficiary of the aura of sanctity surrounding Saints Peter and Paul, both of whom lived and were buried there (see page 162). So did Santiago de Compostela on the Iberian peninsula.

SANTIAGO DE COMPOSTELA The tomb of St. James at Santiago de Compostela in northwest Spain (see map 10.2) marked the most westerly point of Christianity at the time. According to tradition, the apostle James (*Santiago* in Spanish) had preached Christianity on the Iberian peninsula and his body returned there in dramatic circumstances after his death. Reports of the tomb's miraculous power attracted large numbers of pilgrims from all over Europe. Many had to brave a difficult sea journey or an exhausting crossing of the Pyrenees Mountains in order to reach Compostela. In some years during the twelfth century tens of thousands made the journey, the difficulty of which added to its allure. Since much of Spain was under Muslim control, pilgrims considered the trip to Santiago equivalent to a journey to the Muslim-held Holy Land.

Map 10.2 The pilgrimage routes to Santiago de Compostela, Spain

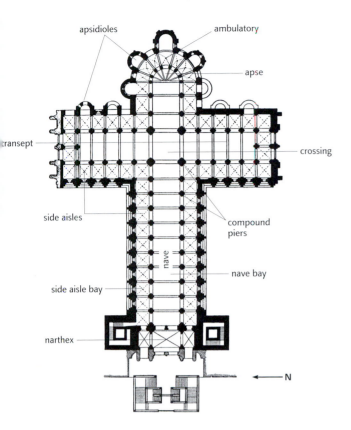

10.3 Plan of Cathedral of Santiago de Compostela, Spain (after Dehio)

10.4 Nave, Cathedral of Santiago de Compostela, Spain. ca. 1075–1120

The Cathedral of Santiago de Compostela had much to offer those brave hearts sufficiently fortunate to reach their goal. The plan of the church (**fig. 10.3**) includes side aisles that run uninterruptedly around the church and form an ambulatory, a passage around the apse. Visitors used these aisles to circumambulate the church, even when the religious offices were being celebrated in the nave and crossing. **Apsidioles**, or small apselike chapels, arranged along the eastern walls of the transepts and around the apse, provided multiple opportunities to display the relics that pilgrims had come to venerate. As they approached the nave from the west entrance and walked through the building, the pilgrims were conscious of marching step by step toward their goals in the apses, altars, and reliquaries at the east end of the church.

Passage through the cathedral was thus a microcosm of the longer journey the pilgrim had taken on the open road, and the cathedral might readily be called a **pilgrimage plan** church. Although not all pilgrimage churches have this same plan, a group of great churches of varying sizes and details, using the same plan as

Santiago de Compostela, were built along the roads leading to it.

The plan of Santiago de Compostela is composed of multiple modular units. It recalls the system of architectural composition based on additive components that was employed during the early Middle Ages (see page 202). The bays of the nave and the transept are half the size of the square crossing, and the square bays of the side aisles are in turn a quarter the size of the crossing and thus half the size of the nave bays. The building's interior (**fig. 10.4**) mirrors the clarity of its plan. As at Sant Vincenç at Cardona (see fig. 10.1), the four **colonnettes**, small attached columns, of the compound piers reflect the building's structural elements. In the nave of Santiago de Compostela vaults, arches, engaged

Seen in section, the physics of the Cathedral of Santiago de Compostela are quite apparent. The walls of the nave and the aisles transfer the weight downward through the piers and outward to the lowest side walls, where it is buttressed.

10.5 The Chasse of Champagnat. Reliquary casket with symbols of the four Evangelists. ca. 1150. Champlevé enamel on gilt and engraved copper, 4⅞ × 7⁷⁄₁₆ × 3⅜" (12.4 × 18.9 × 8.5 cm). The Metropolitan Museum of Art, New York. Gift of J. Pierpont Morgan, 1917 17.190.685

columns, and pilasters (flat shafts in shallow relief) are all firmly knit together into a coherent order that recaptures the vocabulary and syntax of ancient Roman architecture to a remarkable degree.

So as not to weaken the barrel vaults at their springing, precisely where they would need the most support, Santiago de Compostela was built without a clerestory (the row of windows in the upper part of the wall). Diffused light, subtle and atmospheric, filters into the nave through the side aisles and the galleries above. The galleries provide for an elegantly elaborated interior, as the famous *Pilgrim's Guide*, written around 1130, makes clear:

> In truth, in this church no fissure or fault is found; it is admirably constructed, grand, spacious, bright, of proper magnitude, harmonious in width, length and height, of admirable and ineffable workmanship, built in two storys, just like a royal palace. For indeed, whoever visits the naves of the gallery, if he goes up sad, after having seen the perfect beauty of this temple, he will be made happy and joyful.

> Paula Gerson, Annie Shaver Crandell, Alison Stones and Jeanne Krochalis, *Pilgrim's Guide to Santiago de Compostela: A Critical Edition*, II. London, 1998, pp. 69–71.

The synthesis of emotional and spiritual response described in the *Pilgrim's Guide* results

from the Romanesque builders' ability to fuse structure and aesthetics. In both detail and execution Santiago de Compostela emulates the nobility and dignity of Roman architecture.

RELIQUARIES A twelfth-century casket, today in the Metropolitan Museum of Art in New York (**fig. 10.5**), is typical of the kinds of decorated reliquaries (containers for holy relics) that pilgrims saw on their journeys to Compostela and Rome. This one was probably made in Limoges, a major stop on the road to Compostela and a center of enamel production, where there was a large church built on the pilgrimage plan. The material and the bold areas of flat color, evident in both the foliage and the symbols of the four evangelists, relate this work to the tradition of migration and early medieval metalwork (see fig. 9.1). The method of manufacture is *champlevé*, which was derived from the *cloisonné* technique (see page 190). Instead of having cells formed from thin strips of metal attached to a support, as with *cloisonné*, the metal surface of *champlevé* is gouged out to create compartments that contain the colored enamel. The preciousness of the enamel on the gilt copper of this reliquary and its lavish decoration suit its exceptional and holy contents, thought to be relics of St. Martial, identified by inscription on the other side of the box, since the casket comes from a church dedicated to him in Champagnat, about 60 miles from Limoges.

SCULPTURE AT SAINT-SERNIN Santiago de Compostela, like many of the other churches along the pilgrimage road, has stone sculptures decorating its interior and its portals. At Saint-Sernin at Toulouse, which is on the pilgrimage road that passes through southern France, some of the same sculptors who worked at Santiago de Compostela also carved sculpture. A series of large marble plaques, currently placed in the ambulatory of Saint-Sernin, date to the years immediately preceding 1100. Six of these plaques depict angels and apostles, while one represents a seated *Christ in Majesty* (**fig. 10.6**). Although their original location is not certain, the plaques probably decorated the zone around the altar and shrine of Saint-Sernin, thus embellishing an area deemed particularly holy by pilgrims.

The shallow relief and many decorative effects of the Christ plaque recall earlier metalwork and ivory objects (see fig. 9.7). The extensive use of double lines, some creating raised sections, some impressed ones, enhances the figure's volumetric presence. The treatment brings to mind manuscript illumination, particularly Carolingian and Ottonian examples, but also Byzantine ones. The emphasis on volume of the figure of Christ, somewhat more than half life-size, hints at what may have been the main inspiration behind the revival of large-scale sculpture. A stone-carved image, being solid and three-dimensional, is far more "real" than a painted one. To a cleric steeped in abstract theology, this might seem irrelevant or even dangerous, but for unsophisticated lay worshipers, by contrast, imposing sculpture must have had great appeal.

Cluniac Architecture and Sculpture

During the time when the sculptural decoration of Saint-Sernin was executed, that church was under the auspices of monks from the great Benedictine monastery of Cluny (see Cultural Context: Monasticism and Christian Monastic Orders). Cluny was responsible for a network of dependencies; its "daughter" houses, spread across Europe, numbered more than 1,400. This is evidence of the order's influence and growth. The Cluniac order could determine papal elections and call for crusades against the Muslims. The rise and spread of various monastic orders was significant for the development of Romanesque art, but none was more important than Cluny.

ABBEY CHURCH OF CLUNY The rapid growth of the Cluniac order can also be seen in the fact that its original basilica church of about 910 was

10.6 *Christ in Majesty* (*Maiestas Domini*). ca. 1096. Marble, height 50" (127 cm). Saint-Sernin, Toulouse

replaced with an ample one that itself was replaced only about 75 years later, in 1088, by the largest Romanesque church ever built, the third abbey church of Cluny (**fig. 10.7**). Unfortunately Cluny III, as it is known, was destroyed after the French Revolution, and only the south transept (the one to the right in the plan), and the octagonal tower remain from what was once the most impressive massing of towers in all of Europe. The auspicious use of towers in Carolingian buildings (see fig. 9.9) here reached its culmination. The apsidioles, apses, and towers at the east end of Cluny created a monumental gathering of ever higher forms.

Monasticism and Christian Monastic Orders

PEOPLE OF many times, places, and religious faiths have renounced the world and devoted themselves entirely to a spiritual way of life. Some have chosen to live alone as hermits, often in isolated places, where they have led harsh, ascetic existences. Others have come together in religious communities known as MONASTERIES to share their faith and religious observance. Among the Jews of the first century BCE, there were both hermits, or ANCHORITES (John the Baptist was one of these), and a kind of monasticism practiced by a sect known as the Essenes. Both forms are found in Christianity throughout most of its history as well. Their basis can be found in the scriptures. On the one hand, Jesus urged his followers to give up all earthly possessions as the road to salvation. On the other, the book of Acts in the Bible records that the disciples came together in their faith after the Crucifixion.

The earliest form of a devoted religious calling practiced by Christians was the hermit's life. It was chosen by a number of pious men and women who lived alone in the Egyptian desert in the second and third centuries CE. This way of life was to remain fundamental to the Eastern Church, especially in Syria. But early on, communities emerged when colonies of disciples—both men and women—gathered around the most revered of the hermits, such as St. Anthony (fourth century), who achieved such fame as a holy man that he was pursued by people asking him to act as a divine intercessor on their behalf.

Monasteries soon came to assume great importance in early Christian life. (They included communities for women, which are often called convents or nunneries.) The earliest known monastery was founded by Pachomius along the Nile about 320 and blossomed into a community of nine monasteries and two nunneries by the time of his death a quarter-century later. Similar ones quickly followed in Syria, where monachism (monasticism) flourished until the 638 conquest by the Arabs.

Eastern monasticism was founded by Basil the Great (ca. 330–379), bishop of Caesarea in Asia Minor. Basil's rule established the basic characteristics of Christian monasticism: Poverty, chastity, and humility. It emphasized prayer, scriptural reading, and work, not only within the monastery but also for the good of laypeople in the world beyond its walls; as a result, monasticism now assumed a social role.

The most important figure in Western monasticism was Benedict of Nursia (ca. 480–ca. 553), the founder of the abbey at Monte Cassino in southern Italy. His rule, which was patterned after Basil's, divided the monk's day into periods of private prayer, communal ritual, and labor; it also required a moderate form of communal life, which was strictly governed. This was the beginning of the BENEDICTINE order, the first of the great monastic orders (or societies) of the Western church. The

Benedictines thrived with the strong support of Pope Gregory the Great, himself a former monk, who codified the Western liturgy and the forms of Gregorian chant.

Because of their organization and continuity, monasteries were considered ideal seats of learning and administration under the Frankish kings of the eighth century. They were supported even more strongly by Charlemagne and his heirs, who gave them land, money, and royal protection. As a result, they became rich and powerful, even exercising influence on international affairs. Although they had considerable independence at first, the various orders eventually gave their loyalty to Gregory. They thereby became a major source of power for the papacy in return for its protection. Through these ties, Church and State over time became linked institutionally to their mutual benefit, thereby promoting greater stability. Besides the Benedictines, the other important monastic orders of the West included the Cluniacs, the Cistercians, the Carthusians, the Franciscans, and the Dominicans.

The CLUNIAC order (named after its original monastery at Cluny, in France) was founded as a renewal of the original Benedictine rule in 909 by Berno of Baume. CISTERCIAN monasteries were deliberately located in remote places, where the monks would come into minimal contact with the outside world, and the rules of daily life were particularly strict. In keeping with this austerity, the order developed an architecture recognizable by its geometric simplicity and lack of ornamentation (see pages 228 and 229).

The CARTHUSIAN order was founded by Bruno, an Italian monk, in 1084. Carthusians are in effect hermits, each monk or nun living alone in a separate cell, vowed to silence and devoted to prayer and meditation. Because of the extreme austerity and piety of this order, several powerful dukes in the fourteenth and fifteenth centuries established Carthusian houses (charterhouses; French, *chartreuses*), so that the monks could pray perpetually for the souls of the dukes after they died.

The FRANCISCAN order was founded in 1209 by St. Francis of Assisi (ca. 1181–1226) as a preaching community. Francis, who was perhaps the most saintly character since Early Christian times, insisted on a life of complete poverty, not only for the members personally but for the order as a whole. Franciscan monks and nuns were originally MENDICANTS—that is, they begged for a living. This rule was revised in the fourteenth century.

The DOMINICAN order was established in 1220 by St. Dominic (ca. 1170–1221), a Spanish monk who had been a member of the Cistercians. Besides preaching, the Dominicans devoted themselves to the study of theology. They were considered the most intellectual of the religious orders in the late Middle Ages and the Early Renaissance.

10.7 Gunzo and others. Plan of Monastery of Cluny (Cluny III), France (after Conant). ca. 1088–1130. Darkened areas represent the actual scant remains

latrine

court

latrine

great infirmary hall

chapter house

south transept

cemetery

cemetery chapel

Lady Chapel II

infirmary cloister

dormitory above

Cluny III

Cluny II

latrine

cloister

refectory II

novices' cloister

novitiate

0   10   60 meters
0   50   200 feet

atrium

cellar

bakery

court

portico

lay monk's kitchen

old guest house

south gate

pantries

stable

unfinished in 1157

hospice

thirteenth-century augmentation

hospice   stable

main gate II

latrine

The proportions of Cluny III were based on ratios of "perfect" numbers and on musical harmonies, reminding us of the importance of music to the medieval church. Monks chanted their prayers in the church eight times a day and Gunzo, one of the architects of Cluny III, was noted for his musicianship. A benefit of stone-vaulted buildings was their acoustic resonance; this feature might well have encouraged the widespread use of stone vaulting or at least made the heavy financial investment acceptable to the community. Even today it is a moving experience to hear Gregorian chants sung beneath the vaults of a Romanesque church.

The interior of Cluny III (**fig. 10.8**) was as elegant as it was huge, its vaults reaching 100 feet. Below the clerestory, and in place of a

10.8 Reconstruction of Abbey Church, Cluny

gallery, is a **triforium**, a series of three-arched openings (one set per bay); it creates a space within the wall that lightens it both physically and visually. The clerestory and triforium are connected by pilaster strips with Corinthian capitals, reminiscent of Roman architectural decoration. What is not Roman is the use of slightly pointed arches in the nave arcade, a device thought to derive from contact with Islamic culture. By eliminating the center part of the rounded arch, which responds the most to the pull of gravity, the two halves of a pointed arch brace each other. Because the pointed arch exerts less outward pressure than the semicircular arch, not only can it be made steeper, but the walls can be pierced and made lighter.

PRIORY OF MOISSAC The priory of Saint-Pierre at Moissac, located on the pilgrimage road close to Toulouse and also under the direction of Cluny, was another important center of Romanesque art. The cloister, adjacent to the church and reserved for use by its monks, was formed by four covered passageways arranged around an open garden (**fig. 10.9**). Protected from the elements, the monks could practice

their spiritual exercises here. Seventy-six sculptured capitals decorate this private zone. While they include both Old Testament and New Testament stories, many are decorated with foliage, birds, animals, and monstrous creatures.

Although the Romanesque period is far removed chronologically from the Early Christian aversion to image making, even during this period there were those who objected to the corruptive powers of visual representation. In truth, it is hard to correlate the worldly achievements of a monastery such as those at Moissac or Cluny—the wealth they acquired and the political clout they exercised—with the values to which monks traditionally aspired, which were based on the renunciation of earthly pleasures in favor of the pursuit of spiritual ideals. The pictorial representation of Christian themes was often justified by a famous saying: *Quod legentibus scriptura, hoc idiotis … pictura.* Translated freely, it means that painting conveys the Word of God to the unlettered.

If the Moissac monks had a profusion of sculpture to engage them, so too did pilgrims and layfolk visiting the monastery's church of Saint-Pierre. Its elaborately sculptured portal

10.9 Cloister, Priory of Saint-Pierre. ca. 1100. Moissac, France

(**fig. 10.10**) was executed almost a generation after the cloister was finished. Christ in Majesty takes center stage in the **tympanum**, the semicircular lunette above the lintel of the portal. He is shown during his Second Coming, when he returns to earth after the apocalyptic end of days, as described in the book of Revelation (4:1–8), in order to judge mortals as saved or damned. In accord with the biblical account, Christ is attended by four beasts, which accompany two angels and 24 elders, while wavy lines beneath their feet represent "the sea of glass like crystal." The elders, relatively small compared with the other figures, and many of them gesticulating, can barely contain their excitement in the face of the remarkable vision. Abstraction and activity characterize the style of carving, in which quivering lines, borders of meandering ribbon patterns, and fluttering drapery offset a hierarchy of scale and pose. The use of abstraction in the service of religious zeal has parallels in earlier medieval art, for example the manuscript illuminations of the *Ebbo Gospels* (see fig. 9.6). At Moissac, however, the presentation is on a monumental and public scale.

Other parts of the Moissac portal are also treated sculpturally. Both the **trumeau** (the center post supporting the lintel) and the **jambs** (the sides of the doorway) have scalloped outlines (see fig. 10.10), modeled on a popular Islamic device (see fig. 9.17). By borrowing forms from the art of Islam at Moissac and other churches, Christians were expressing their admiration and regard for Arab artistic achievements. At the same time, such acts of appropriation could also express the Christian ambition to dominate the Muslim enemy (see Cultural Context: Spanish Islamic Art and Europe in the Middle Ages). The pilgrimage to Santiago was a similar manifestation of anti-Islamic feeling.

The scalloped outlines framing the doorway activate and dramatize the experience of entering the church. Human and animal forms are treated with flexibility; for instance, the spidery prophet on the side of the trumeau seems perfectly adapted to his precarious perch, even as he struggles to free himself from the stone (**fig. 10.11**). With legs crossed in a graceful movement, he turns his head toward the interior of the church as he unfurls his scroll. The crossed lions that form a symmetrical zigzag on the face of the trumeau animate the shaft in the same way that the interlacing beasts of Irish miniatures (from which they are descended) enliven the spaces they inhabit.

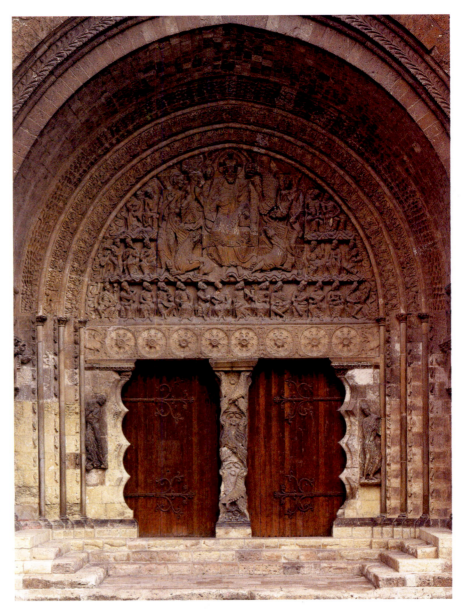

10.10 South portal with *Second Coming of Christ* on tympanum, Church of Saint-Pierre, Moissac, France. ca. 1115–1130

10.11 Trumeau and jambs, south portal, Church of Saint-Pierre, Moissac, France

Spanish Islamic Art and Europe in the Middle Ages

I N 711 THE COMBINED Arab and Berber forces of the Muslim commander Tariq ibn Ziyad crossed the straits of Gibraltar, and by 716 most of Spain was in Muslim hands. Under the rule of the Umayyad dynasty (751–1017), Córdoba became the capital of a prosperous, tolerant, and powerful Muslim kingdom in Spain (see page 209), in which Christians and Jews played important roles in cultural life. During the eleventh and twelfth centuries, in the aftermath of the fall of the Umayyads, successive Berber invasions from North Africa brought new Muslim dynastic patrons into Spain, who oversaw splendid new artistic production. But they also suffered a series of military defeats at the hands of the strengthening Christian powers in the north. Of the several small Islamic kingdoms that formed in the twilight of Muslim rule in Spain, one in particular, that of the Nasrids, ruling in Granada from 1230 to 1492, saw a last glorious flowering of the arts before its defeat by the Castilians and Aragonese united under King Ferdinand and Queen Isabella.

The dominant Muslim style in the arts of southern Spain affected artistic production of non-Muslims in many complex ways. From the tenth through the twelfth centuries, i.e. throughout the Romanesque period, in the mountainside principalities of the Christian north, Christian builders built small churches and monasteries in the **mozarab** style, using the horseshoe arches, alternating colored voussoirs, and mosaics of colored stone they had seen in the Muslim south. At the same time, in the northern monasteries, artist monks illustrated manuscripts with paintings that also reflected the dominant Muslim style. Beyond the Pyrenees, along the medieval pilgrimage roads into France, aspects of the Muslim style even influenced French Romanesque art; the twelfth-century wooden doors of Le Puy Cathedral in France bore an elaborate kufic inscription in Arabic: *Mashallah* — "may God protect this place."

Folio of the *Silos Apocalypse*, commentary by Beatus of Liébana illustrated by Prior Petrus, Completed in 1109. Colors, gold and silver leaf on parchment 15″ × 9⅞″ (38 × 25 cm)

We cannot account for the presence of the crossed lions at Moissac in terms of their effectiveness as ornament alone. They belong to an extensive family of savage or monstrous creatures in Romanesque art that retain their demoniacal vitality even as they are forced to perform a supporting function. Their purpose is thus not only decorative but expressive; they embody dark forces that have been domesticated into guardian figures or banished to a position that holds them fixed for all eternity. One medieval bishop argued that seeing animals sculpted in churches would so terrify parishioners that they would be encouraged to refrain from sinful deeds.

A deep porch with lavishly sculptured lateral ends frames the Moissac portal. The messages at Moissac are patently didactic, meant both to command and to enlighten. When visitors on the pilgrim road faced the deep portal of the church they were virtually surrounded by the sculptural program, and this intensified the liminal experience of entering the church (i.e. the experience of crossing the threshold). The journey into the church became a veritable rite of passage, transformative both physically and spiritually.

CATHEDRAL OF SAINT-LAZARE, AUTUN Close to Cluny and dependent on it was the Cathedral of Saint-Lazare at Autun. The tympanum of its west portal (**fig. 10.12**) represents the Last Judgment, the most awe-inspiring scene in Christian art. It depicts Christ after his Second Coming as he separates those who will be eternally saved from those who are damned. His figure, much larger than any other, dominates the tympanum. The sculptor, Gislebertus, whose signature appears immediately under the feet of Christ in the center, treats the subject with extraordinary force. Gislebertus' style is sufficiently individual to enable scholars to posit convincingly that he trained at Cluny before his elevation to master's rank at Autun.

On the left side of the tympanum, apostles observe the weighing of souls, which takes place on the right side. Four angels in the corners sound the trumpets of the Apocalypse. At the bottom, the dead rise from their graves, trembling with fear; some are already beset by snakes or gripped by huge, clawlike hands. Above, their fate quite literally hangs in the balance, with devils yanking at one end of the scales and angels at the other. The saved souls cling like children to the angels for protection before their ascent to the Heavenly Jerusalem (far left), while the condemned, seized by grinning devils, are cast into the mouth of Hell (far right). These nightmarish devils are human in general outline, but they have birdlike legs, furry thighs, tails, pointed ears, and savage mouths. The hierarchical, abstract, and patterned representation of Christ conveys his formidable power more effectively than any naturalistic image could.

The Last Judgment, with its emphasis on retribution, was a standard subject for the tympana of Romanesque churches. It was probably chosen

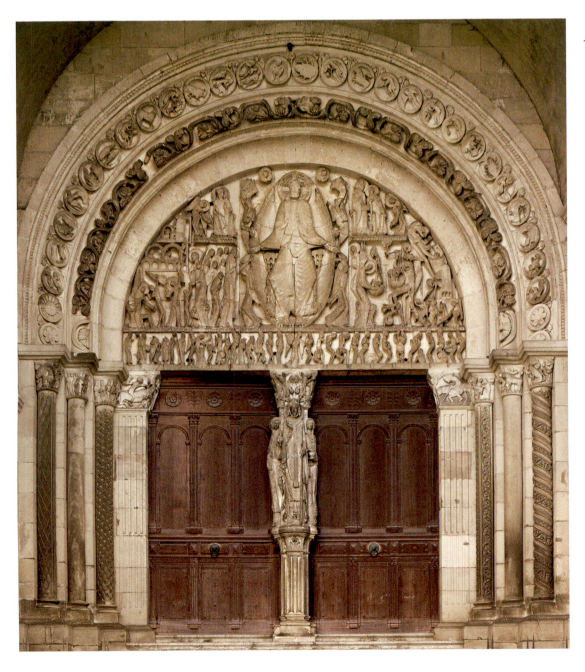

10.12 West portal, with *Last Judgment* by Gislebertus on tympanum, Cathedral of Saint-Lazare. ca. 1120–1135. Autun, France

because medieval judgment was dispensed in front of the church portal, *ante ecclesium*. Thus, actual judicial proceedings paralleled the divine judgment represented here. Trial was by ordeal, whereby the accused established innocence only by withstanding grueling physical tests. The ordeals must, in reality, have been as terrifying as the scenes depicted on the tympanum.

Cistercian Architecture and Art

Cluny's very success meant that it was subject to criticism, particularly by the Cistercians, whose motherhouse was at Cîteaux in Burgundy. The Cistercians were founded in the eleventh century as an ascetic order in opposition to the increasing wealth of the Cluniac Benedictines. In addition to prayer, the Cistercians devoted themselves to hard work, which helped guarantee their own great success. Sound economic planning, skill in agriculture and husbandry, and wealthy benefactors furthered their cause. The Cistercian order and its style spread across Europe, and by the end of the twelfth century the Cistercians controlled nearly 700 monasteries. Cistercian architecture, in its simplicity, contrasts markedly with the architecture of the Cluniac order.

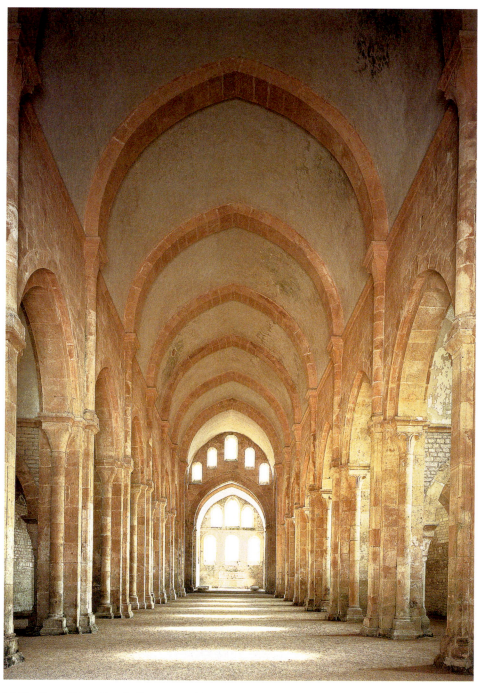

10.13 Nave, Abbey Church, Fontenay. 1139–1147

10.14 *The Building of the Tower of Babel.* Early twelfth century. Detail of painting on the nave vault, Saint-Savin-sur-Gartempe, France

ABBEY CHURCH AT FONTENAY The abbey church at Fontenay, not far from Cîteaux, was begun in 1139. Fontenay exemplifies the Cistercian reliance on simple and unadorned forms, in contrast to the opulence of Cluny. By comparison to the expansive plan of Cluny (see fig. 10.7), where the huge abbey church dominated a sprawling complex, Fontenay is precise, with a pure and tightly controlled equilibrium balancing all of its constituent parts.

The east end of the church is unembellished by apses, and no towers were planned. Since Cistercians permitted neither sculpture nor wall painting, the interior of the church (**fig. 10.13**) lacks applied decoration. Clerestory and gallery are suppressed. However, in their own terms, the clean lines of the pointed transverse arches that define the nave and openings into the side aisles, and the pattern of unframed windows, create an elegant refinement. The simple forms are at once graceful and moving. Once again, the church serves as a safe, tranquil, and spiritual refuge from worldly burdens, although one with a very different effect from the protective enclosures that other Romanesque churches offer (see figs. 10.1 and 10.4).

Wall Painting

Most Romanesque paintings on walls and ceilings, which undoubtedly were numerous, have been destroyed over the centuries. Fortunately, an impressive cycle of wall paintings still survives at the Benedictine abbey church of Saint-Savin-sur-Gartempe. The church was designed particularly to offer a continuous surface for murals. *The Building of the Tower of Babel* (**fig. 10.14**) is part of an extensive cycle of Old Testament scenes on the barrel vault of the nave. It is an intensely dramatic design, crowded with strenuous action. God himself, on the far left, participates directly in the narrative, addressing the builders of the huge structure. He is counterbalanced, on the right, by the giant Nimrod, leader of the project, who frantically hands blocks of stone to the masons atop the tower. The entire scene becomes a great test of strength between God and mortals. The heavy, dark contours and the emphatic gestures make the composition easy to read from the floor below. Elsewhere in the church the viewer can see New Testament episodes and scenes from the lives of local saints.

Book Illustration

As in the early Middle Ages, manuscript production in the Romanesque period continued to be largely the responsibility of monastic scriptoria under the supervision of monks. Manuscripts produced by Cluniac scriptoria are stylistically similar to Cluniac wall painting and often express concerns remarkably akin to those of the period's architects and sculptors. The interrelationship of monastic communities accounts for a consistency of manuscript production across various regions during the Romanesque period.

10.15 *St. Matthew*, from the *Codex Colbertinus*. ca. 1100. Tempera on vellum, 7½ × 4" (19 × 10.16 cm). Bibliothèque Nationale, Paris

THE *CODEX COLBERTINUS* The illustration of *St. Matthew* from the *Codex Colbertinus* (**fig. 10.15**) is similar in concept and pose to a number of Romanesque carvings, particularly the pier reliefs from the Moissac cloister (see fig. 10.9). The manuscript was made at that monastery, or nearby, just when sculptors were at work in the cloister. Matthew appears at the beginning of his Gospel, next to an embellished letter L, the first letter of *Liber*, meaning "book." Figures, animals, foliage, and decorative patterns conform to the shape of the letter, recalling the way Romanesque sculptured figures correspond to their frames (see fig. 10.2).

In contrast to the small, freely disposed figures and animals in the initial, the figure of Matthew confronts us directly. Although he fills the available space of the architectural setting, a number of features deny his solidity. The heavy outlines and bold colors, reminiscent of enamelwork, in combination with a variety of juxtaposed patterns, serve to flatten the image. These devices demonstrate to what extent forms popular during the early Middle Ages remained vital.

THE CORBIE GOSPEL BOOK In its monumentality, the image of *St. Mark* from an early twelfth-century gospel book produced at Corbie (**fig. 10.16**) can similarly be likened to Romanesque sculpture. The active pose and zigzag composition bear comparison with the prophet on the Moissac trumeau (see fig. 10.11). The twisting movement of the lines, not only in the figure of Mark but also in the winged lion, the scroll, and the curtain, recalls Carolingian miniatures of the Reims School as well, such as the *Ebbo Gospels* (see fig. 9.6).

This resemblance helps us see the differences between them, too. In the Romanesque manuscript, every trace of classical illusionism has disappeared. The fluid modeling of the Reims School, with its suggestion of light and space, has been replaced here by firm contours filled in with bright, solid colors. As a result, the three-dimensional aspects of the picture are reduced to overlapping planes. The Romanesque artist has given his work a clarity and precision that had not been possible in Carolingian or Ottonian times. Here, the representational, the symbolic, and the decorative elements of the design are fully integrated.

Regional Variants of the Romanesque Style

Although consistent aesthetic aims expressed across various media link the art of diverse areas of Europe during the Romanesque period, a variety of distinct regional approaches can be identified, apparent in regions of what is now France as well as in other parts of Europe. Regional variety in Romanesque art reflects the political conditions of eleventh- and twelfth-century Western Europe, which was governed by a feudal, though loose, alliance of princes and dukes.

Western France: Poitou

A so-called school of sculptural decoration appears during the Romanesque period in the region of Poitou, part of the Duchy of Aquitaine in southwestern France. A notable example is Notre-Dame-la-Grande in Poitiers, seat of the lords of Aquitaine.

NOTRE-DAME-LA-GRANDE, POITIERS The broad screenlike façade of Notre-Dame-la-Grande (**fig. 10.17**) offers an expanded field for sculptural decoration. Elaborately bordered arcades house large seated or standing figures. Below them a

10.16 *St. Mark*, from a gospel book produced at the Abbey at Corbie. Early twelfth century. Tempera on vellum, 10¾ × 7⅞″ (27.3 cm × 20 cm). Bibliothèque Municipale, Amiens, France

wide band of relief carving stretches across the façade. The Fall of Adam and Eve appears with scenes from the life of Mary, including the Annunciation and Nativity, juxtaposing Eve and Mary. Next to the representation of Adam and Eve, an inscription identifies an enthroned figure as Nebuchadnezzar, the king of Babylon mentioned in the Old Testament. The *Play of Adam*—

a twelfth-century medieval drama of a type that was traditionally performed in churches—probably served as the source for the choice and arrangement of figures at this church. Beside Nebuchadnezzar, centered above the arch on the left of the portal, there are four figures carrying either scrolls or books on which are inscribed lines from the Adam play, in which Adam and Eve figure prominently and Nebuchadnezzar is also mentioned.

Essential to the rich sculptural effect is the deeply recessed doorway, without tympanum but framed by a series of arches with multiple archivolts, decorative moldings or bands that frame the arch. The conical helmets of the towers nearly match the height of the **gable** (the triangular wall section at the top of the façade), which rises above the actual level of the roof behind it. The gable contains a representation of Christ with angels, their height in the composition denoting their heavenly place. The sculptural program spread out over this entire area is a visual exposition of Christian doctrine intended as a feast for the eyes as well as the mind.

Southeastern France: Provence

In the French region of Provence, south of Burgundy, Romanesque art benefited from its proximity to Italy. The name Provence derives from its ancient designation as *Provincia Romana* in recognition of its close political and cultural connections to Rome, and even today considerable vestiges of Roman art and architecture abound in the region.

10.17 West façade, Notre-Dame-la-Grande. Early twelfth century. Poitiers, France

10.18 West façade, Saint-Gilles-du-Gard, France. Mid-twelfth century

SAINT-GILLES-DU-GARD The façade of the abbey church of Saint-Gilles-du-Gard (**fig. 10.18**), like that of Notre-Dame-la-Grande in Poitiers, screens the church. The inspiration for this façade, composed of three arches, can be found in the Roman triumphal arch (see fig. 7.27), connecting ancient triumphal imagery with the important liminal function of entering the church. Given contemporary concerns for Christian victory, in particular the struggle to conquer the Muslims, the formal association between the façade and a Roman triumphal monument must have seemed particularly fitting. The depiction on the lintel supporting the left tympanum of Jesus' triumphal entry into Jerusalem would have had special meaning to contemporary viewers, who were aware that the town of Saint-Gilles on the Rhône River estuary was a principal site of embarkation for French crusaders on their way to the Holy Land.

Tuscany

During the Romanesque period, Tuscany, a region in northwestern Italy divided into several independent city-states, including Pisa and Florence, continued what were basically Early Christian architectural forms. However, they added decorative features inspired by Roman architecture. A deliberate revival of the antique Roman style in Tuscan architecture was the use of a multicolored marble "skin" on the exteriors of churches. Little of this inlay is left today on the ancient monuments of Rome because much of it was literally "lifted" to decorate later buildings. However, the interior of the Pantheon still gives us some idea of what it must have looked like (see fig. 7.18).

BAPTISTERY OF SAN GIOVANNI, FLORENCE In Florence the greatest achievement of the Tuscan Romanesque is the baptistery of San Giovanni (**fig. 10.19**). It is a domed, octagonal building of impressive size, begun in the middle of the eleventh century. The green-and-white marble paneling is typical of the Florentine Romanesque in its severely geometric lines. The triple arches of the second-story blind arcades, with their triumphal-arch design, are extraordinarily classical in proportion and detail.

10.19 Baptistery of San Giovanni, ca. 1060–1150. Florence, Italy

The individual, additive units decorating Tuscan Romanesque buildings have a conceptual parallel in the compartmentalized bays in pilgrimage churches (see fig. 10.4) and also in the way French Romanesque portals (see figs. 10.10, 10.12, 10.17) create a unified composition of individual units. Roman elements in conscious revival—here the use of marble and the repeated arches that rest on columns topped with Corinthian capitals—unite many of these Romanesque works as well.

Normandy and England

In Normandy, Christianity was strongly supported by the Norman dukes and barons. Duke William II of Normandy actively promoted monastic reform and founded numerous abbeys. Normandy soon became a cultural center of international importance. When William invaded Anglo-Saxon England in 1066 and became its king, the country became politically allied to northern France. And for that reason Norman and English art of the Romanesque period share many stylistic traits.

THE BAYEUX TAPESTRY The complex relationship between the Normans and the English is hinted at in the *Bayeux Tapestry* (**fig. 10.20**). In actuality it is not a tapestry at all, since it is not woven but, rather, an embroidered linen frieze 230 feet long. The 50 surviving scenes record the events, culminating in 1066, when WILLIAM THE CONQUEROR crossed the English Channel to claim the throne of England upon the death of King Edward the Confessor. Since a Norman patron presumably commissioned the

10.20 *Crowds Gaze in Awe at a Comet as Harold Is Told of an Omen*. Detail of the *Bayeux Tapestry*. ca. 1066–1083. Wool embroidery on linen. Height 20" (50.7 cm). Centre Guillaume le Conquérant, Bayeux, France

"tapestry," the story is told from the conquerors' perspective, yet its manufacture has generally been credited to English needlewomen, justly famous during the Middle Ages for their skill (see Cultural Context: Women Artists and Patrons: Hildegard of Bingen).

The *Bayeux Tapestry* exhibits a profound interest in narrative that is also apparent in other Romanesque media (see figs. 10.14 and 10.17). The designer of the tapestry has integrated narrative and ornament with complete ease. Two border strips frame the main frieze; while some of the images of these margins are decorative, others offer commentary on the tapestry's continuous narrative. In one scene (see fig. 10.20) an aide announces to a recently crowned Harold the appearance of an amazing natural phenomenon, represented in the upper border as a spinning star leaving its fiery trail. The inscription ISTI MIRANT STELLA ("These men marvel at the star") records the brilliant apparition of Halley's Comet in 1066, during the days immediately following Harold's coronation. To the medieval viewer, the prophetic significance of the natural event would have been clear, especially when viewed after the fact. Beneath Harold, ghostly boats await the Normans, who are preparing to cross the English Channel. The scene foreshadows the violent events to come. Although the *Bayeux Tapestry* does not use the pictorial devices of classical painting, such as foreshortening and overlapping (see fig. 5.33), its account is nonetheless vivid and detailed.

DURHAM CATHEDRAL Norman architecture is responsible for a great breakthrough in structural engineering, which took place in England, where William made donations to build in a Norman style after his conquest of the country. Durham Cathedral, begun in 1093, is among the largest churches of medieval Europe (**fig. 10.21**). Its nave is wider than Santiago de Compostela's, and its overall length (400 feet) is greater. The nave may have been designed to be vaulted from the start. The vault over its eastern end had been completed by 1107, in a remarkably short time, and the rest of the nave was vaulted by 1130.

Women Artists and Patrons: Hildegard of Bingen

THE LATE TENTH through the twelfth century witnessed the unprecedented rise of women as first patrons of art and then as artists. This remarkable development began with the Ottonian dynasty, which forged an alliance with the Church by placing members of the imperial family in prominent positions. Thus Mathilde, Otto I's granddaughter, became abbess of the Holy Trinity convent at Essen in 974. Later, the sister, daughters, and granddaughter of Otto II also served as abbesses of major convents. Hardly less important, though not of royal blood, were Hrosvitha, canoness at the monastery of Gandersheim, who was the first woman dramatist we know of, and the two abbesses of Niedermünster, both named Uota. They paved the way for Herrad of Hohenberg (died 1195), author of *The Garden of Delights*, an encyclopedia of knowledge and history compiled for the education of her nuns.

Most remarkable of all was the Benedictine abbess Hildegard of Bingen (1098–1179). Among the most brilliant women in history, she corresponded with leaders throughout Europe. Hildegard composed almost 80 vocal works that rank with the finest of the day. She also wrote some 13 books on theology, medicine, and science. Hildegard is known above all for her books of visions, which made her one of the great spiritual voices of her day. Although one, *Scivias* (To Know the Ways of God), is now available only in facsimile (it was destroyed in 1945) and the other, *Liber divinorum operum* (The Book of Divine Works), in a later reproduction, it seems likely that the originals were executed under her direct supervision by nuns in her convent on the Rhine.

That there were women artists from the twelfth century on is certain, although we know only a few of their names. In one instance, an initial in a manuscript includes a nun bearing a scroll inscribed in Latin, "Guda, the sinful woman, wrote and illuminated this book"; another book depicts Claricia, evidently a lay artist, swinging as carefree as any child from the letter Q she has decorated. Without these author portraits, we might never suspect the involvement of women illuminators.

Page with self-portrait of the nun, Guda, *Book of Homilies*, from Germany. Early twelfth century. Ink on parchment. Stadt-und Universitäts-Bibliothek, Germany

This vault is of great interest. As the earliest systematic use of a ribbed groin vault over a three-story nave, it marks a fundamental advance in church construction. The groin vault, which had been used so effectively by the Romans (see page 126), efficiently channeled thrust onto four corner points. This allowed for open space under each arch, which could be used for window openings without diminishing the strength of the vault. Looking at the plan of Durham, we see that the aisles consist of the usual almost-square groin-vaulted compartments. The bays of the nave, separated by strong transverse arches, are oblong and also groin-vaulted so that the ribs of each bay form a double-X design. Each vault of the nave is thus divided into seven sections, and they are referred to as septpartite (or seven-part) groin vaults.

Since the nave bays are twice as long as the aisle bays, transverse arches occur only at the odd-numbered piers of the nave arcade. The piers therefore alternate in size. The larger odd-numbered ones are compound, with bundles of column and pilaster shafts attached to a square or oblong core, while the even-numbered ones are thinner and cylindrical.

The ribs were needed to provide a stable skeleton for the groin vault, so that the curved surfaces between them could be filled in with masonry of a minimal thickness. Thus both weight and thrust were reduced. This flexible system resulted in more efficient vault erection and greater economy of construction. The ingenious scheme remains in an experimental stage. While the transverse arches at the crossing are round, those to the west of it are slightly

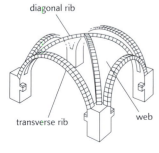

diagonal rib

transverse rib · web

Ribbed groin vault

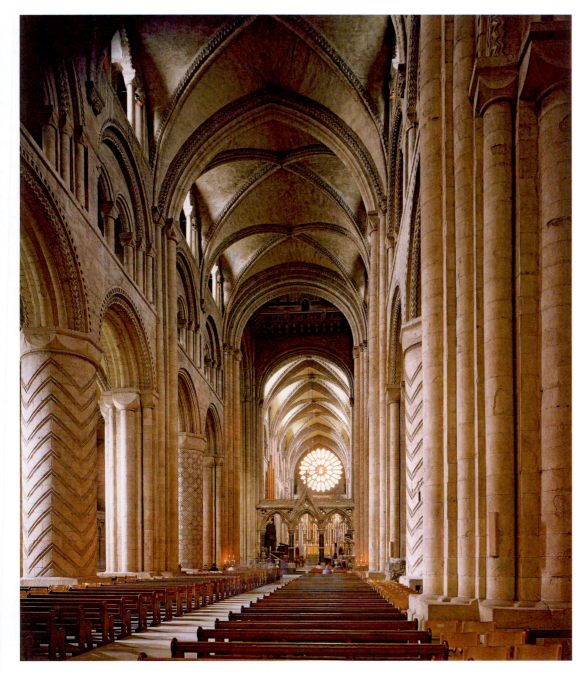

pointed, indicating an ongoing search for improvements.

Durham exhibits great structural strength; even so, the decoration incised in its round piers, each different from the other, and the pattern established by the vault ribs hark back to the Anglo-Saxon love of decoration and interest in surface pattern (see fig. 9.1).

SAINT-ÉTIENNE, CAEN The abbey church of Saint-Étienne at Caen in Normandy was founded by William the Conqueror a year or two after his invasion of England, but it took over a hundred years to complete. Over this period of time the fruits of Durham Cathedral's ribbed groin-vault system matured.

The west façade (**fig. 10.22**) offers a striking contrast with Notre-Dame-la-Grande in Poitiers (see fig. 10.17) and other Romanesque façades (figs. 10.10 and 10.12). The westwork proclaims this an imperial church. Its closest antecedents are Carolingian churches, such as the abbey church at Corvey (see fig. 9.9), built under royal patronage. Like them, it has a minimum of decoration. Four huge buttresses divide the front of the church into three vertical sections. The thrust upward continues in the two towers, the height of which would be impressive even without the tall helmets, added later.

On the interior of Saint-Étienne (**fig. 10.23**), the nave was originally planned to have a wooden ceiling, as well as galleries and a

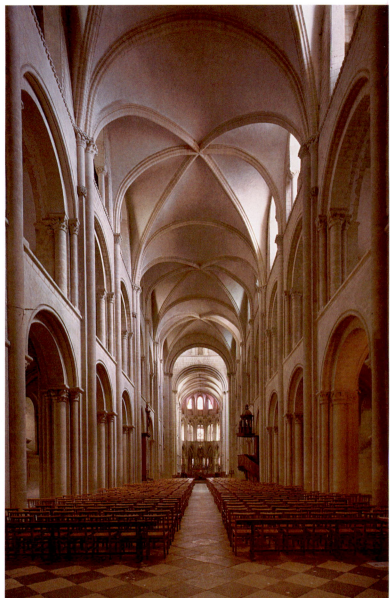

10.22 West façade, Saint-Étienne. Begun 1068. Caen, France

10.23 Nave, Saint-Étienne. Vaulted ca. 1115–1120. Caen, France

clerestory, but after the experience of Durham, it became possible in the early twelfth century to build a groined nave vault, with only slight changes in the wall design. The bays of the nave here are approximately square, whereas at Durham they were oblong. Therefore, the double-X rib pattern could be replaced by a single X with an additional transverse rib, which produced a sexpartite (or six-part) groin vault, with six sections instead of seven. These vaults are no longer separated by heavy transverse arches but instead by simple ribs. The resulting reduction in weight gives a stronger sense of continuity to the nave vault as a whole and produces a less emphatic alternation of piers. Compared with Durham, the nave of Saint-Étienne has an airy lightness.

Durham and Caen mark the culmination of Romanesque architectural experiments. The improved economic conditions and political stability of Europe, outlined at the beginning of this chapter, had their rewards in the secure structures built in the twelfth century. However, the architecture's defensive qualities also suggest a paradox: As much as the stalwart, powerful buildings express a new-found confidence, they also reveal lingering apprehension. The terrifying Last Judgment scenes (see fig. 10.12) and other Romanesque visions of monsters and diabolical beings also attest to this anxiety. The sheltering quality of Romanesque architecture must have been comforting at a time when people yearned for protection from both known and unknown dangers.

SUMMARY

Much of Western European art of the eleventh and twelfth centuries is identified as Romanesque. This term means "in the Roman manner." Indeed, the monumental structures of the period—stone-vaulted constructions decorated with architectural sculptures—were built on a scale that rivaled the achievements of Rome. But Romanesque architects and artists were also influenced by Carolingian, Byzantine, Islamic, and other traditions. Population growth, increased trade and travel, and new settlements all stimulated building activity, much of it for Christian use. Religious fervor, some of it as a result of post-millennium enthusiasm, also contributed to the heightened production of Christian art and architecture and to its dramatic expression.

Romanesque art first appeared in parts of Italy, France, and Spain. An excellent example of early Romanesque architecture is the church of Sant Vincenç in Cardona, Spain, which demonstrates a mastery of stone vaulting techniques. Figurative sculpture—such as the marble lintel at Saint-Genis-des-Fontaines, France—is also a significant achievement of the period.

Buildings of the mature Romanesque style—such as the Cathedral of Santiago de Compostela in Spain, the monastery of Cluny, and the priory of Saint-Pierre at Moissac, France—employed both more sculpture and increasingly sophisticated vaulting techniques. As the Romanesque style matured and developed, it spread throughout Europe. The aesthetic concepts employed by its builders and sculptors are also visible in manuscripts, metalwork, and wall paintings, including those at the church of Saint-Savin-sur-Gartempe.

Regional variety in Romanesque art reflects the political conditions of a continent governed by a loose feudal alliance of princes and dukes. Different regions had different artistic sources available to them, and distinct approaches appeared in parts of France, Italy, Germany, and England.

The secure structures built across Western Europe during the Romanesque period reflect improving economic conditions and political stability. However, they also suggest society's lingering anxieties and yearning for protection.

ART IN TIME

- **1020/21—Carving of marble lintel at Saint-Genis-des-Fontaines, France**

- **1031**—The Caliphate of Córdoba breaks up

- **1040—Consecration of church of Sant Vincenç in Cardona, Spain**

- **ca. 1075–1120—Cathedral built at Santiago de Compostela, Spain**

- **1099**—The First Crusade warriors capture Jerusalem

- By end of **1100s**—Cistercians control nearly 700 monasteries

- **1066**—William the Conqueror invades England

- **ca. 1066–1083—Fabrication of the *Bayeux Tapestry***

- **1088**—Cluny III begun

- **1093—Construction begins on Durham Cathedral, England**

- **1204**—Fall of Constantinople

CHAPTER 11

Gothic Art

W̶e tend to think of history as the unfolding of events in time, yet we are not as aware of their unfolding in terms of place. The Gothic era cannot be defined by means of time alone—we must consider its geographic range as well. At the start, about 1140, this geographical area was small indeed, covering only the province known as the Île-de-France (Paris and vicinity), the royal domain of the French kings (see map 11.1). A hundred years later, most of Europe, from Sicily to Iceland, had adopted the Gothic style, with only a few Romanesque pockets left here and there. By 1400, however, the Gothic area had begun to shrink. It no longer included Italy, and by 1550 it had disappeared almost entirely, except in England.

The term Gothic was used in the sixteenth century to describe a style of building thought to have descended from the Goths, those tribes that occupied northern Europe during the early Middle Ages. Although the ancestry of the style is not as direct as these early writers claimed, they were accurate about its geography, since the style is most recognizable north of the Alps. As Gothic art spread from the Île-de-France to the rest of the country and then through all of Europe, it was referred to in its own time as *opus modernum* (modern work) or *opus francigenum* (French work). These designations are significant, because they tell us that the style was viewed from the beginning as innovative and as having its origins in France. In the course of the thirteenth century, the new style gradually lost its imported flavor, and regional variety began to reassert itself.

For a century—from about 1150 to 1250, during the Age of the Great Cathedrals—architecture played the dominant role in the formation of a coherent Gothic style. Gothic sculpture was at first severely architectural in spirit but became more independent after 1200. Early Gothic sculpture and painting reflect the discipline of their monumental setting, while Late Gothic architecture and sculpture strive for more picturesque effects.

Artistic developments roughly parallel what was happening in the political arena, for the Gothic was a distinctive period not only artistically but politically as well. Aided by advances in cannons and the iron crossbow, princes and kings were able to conquer increasingly large territories, which were administered for them by vassals, who in turn collected taxes to support armies and navies. In France, the Capetian line at first ruled only the fertile territory of the Île-de-France, but by 1300 it had added to this much of the land previously held by the Count of Flanders, and in addition Bourges, Tours, and Amiens—all of which were to become the sites of important Gothic cathedrals—as well as the central province of the Auvergne and the southern province of Languedoc. The French kings also asserted control over various French territories held by England. This gave rise to the conflicting claims over the kingship of France that led to the Hundred Years' War (1337–1453).

Germany remained a collection of independent city-states ruled by electors, who were

Map 11.1 Europe in the Gothic period

responsible for, among other things, choosing kings. Supported by shifting alliances with the papacy, the kings of France and England emerged as the leading powers at the expense of the Germans in the early thirteenth century, which was generally a time of peace and prosperity. After 1290, however, the balance of power quickly broke down.

The growth of urban centers and the increasing importance of cathedrals, the seats of bishops, are formative features of the Gothic period. Universities developed out of cathedral schools as the principal centers of learning, thus taking on the role previously played by monasteries. At the same time literature written in the vernacular (as opposed to Latin) began to emerge, becoming accessible to a broader public. Romanesque art had been predominantly rural and monastic, while Gothic art, by contrast, became increasingly cosmopolitan.

Urban growth was both the result and the cause of economic, social, and demographic changes. Agriculture became more efficient, with increased acreage under cultivation, and surplus production provided commodities for sale and purchase. This produced, in turn, a money economy based on investment, profit, and trade, in place of barter. Consequently a veritable middle class arose, living in cities, which were the centers of trade and commerce. Once out from under the feudal yoke, merchants and artists of this middle class were free to form guilds to control the production and distribution of goods and services. A general and significant increase in population also spurred urban growth.

During the thirteenth century, Catholicism found in St. Thomas Aquinas its greatest intellect since St. Augustine and St. Jerome some 850 years earlier. Aquinas, an Italian theologian, studied in Cologne and taught in Paris. His method of argument, called scholasticism, used reason to understand and explain faith. Gothic builders shared qualities with the Scholastics. They brought the logic and clarity of engineering principles to bear on revelation, using physical forces to create a concord of spiritual experiences in much the same way as the Scholastics used elucidation and clarification to build their well constructed arguments.

Early Gothic Art in France

It is not clear why Gothic art first appeared in the Île-de-France, the area around Paris. Some scholars believe that because this region had not developed a strong local style during the Romanesque period, it was particularly open to innovation and influence from other areas. Others have suggested that it was a result of a concerted effort on the part of the kings of France to aggrandize themselves, since it was here that their domains were located. Certainly the Île-de-France is fortuitously positioned, near the center of France and thus accessible to the south and west, where major sculptural programs flourished during the Romanesque period, and adjacent to Normandy, where many structural innovations, including the ribbed groin vault, had been introduced to France (see pages 237–238).

Saint-Denis: Suger and the Beginnings of Gothic Architecture

The study of Gothic art begins with an examination of the rebuilding of the royal Abbey Church of Saint-Denis just outside the city of Paris. The rebuilding of this historic church was undertaken between 1137 and 1144 by its abbot, Suger. His ambitious building program was designed to emphasize the relationship between the abbey and the French monarchy. The kings of France, who belonged to the Capetian line, derived their authority from a Carolingian tradition. However, they had less power than the nobles who, in theory, were their vassals. The only area that the king ruled directly was the Île-de-France, and even there his authority was often challenged. Not until the early twelfth century did royal power begin to expand, and Suger, as chief adviser to King Louis VI, helped shape this process.

The Abbey Church of Saint-Denis, founded in the late eighth century, enjoyed a dual prestige. It was the shrine of Saint Denis, the Apostle of France and its patron saint, as well as the chief memorial of the Carolingian dynasty. Both Charlemagne and his father, Pepin, were consecrated as kings there. It was also the burial place of the kings Charles Martel, Pepin, and Charles the Bald. Suger aspired to make the abbey the spiritual center of France, a pilgrimage church to outshine all others and to provide a focal point for religious as well as patriotic fervor. To achieve this goal, the old structure had to be rebuilt and enlarged. The great abbot himself wrote two accounts of the church and its rebuilding.

AMBULATORY AND CHOIR The ambulatory and radiating chapels surrounding the arcaded apse (**figs. 11.1** and **11.2**) are familiar elements from the Romanesque pilgrimage choir (compare fig. 10.3), but at Saint-Denis they have been integrated in a new way. The choir is as rationally planned and constructed as any Romanesque church, yet the entire plan is held together by a new kind of geometric order. Seven nearly identical wedge-shaped units fan out from the center of the apse. Instead of being in separate apsidioles, the chapels merge to form, in effect, a second ambulatory. We experience this double ambulatory not as a series of individual compartments but as a continuous space, the shape of which is outlined by the network of slender arches, ribs, and columns that sustains the vaults. Ribbed groin vaulting based on the pointed arch is used throughout. By this date, the pointed arch (which can be "stretched" to reach any desired height regardless of the width of its base) has become an essential part of the ribbed groin vault, which is no longer restricted to square or near-square compartments. It has a new flexibility that allows it to cover areas of almost any shape, such as the trapezoids and pentagons of this ambulatory.

What most distinguishes the interior of Saint-Denis (see fig. 11.2) from earlier church interiors is its lightness, in both senses of the word. The architectural forms seem graceful, almost weightless, compared to the massive solidity of Romanesque architecture. The fluid spaciousness of the choir results from its slim columns, the use of which was made possible by the relative lightness of the vaults they needed to support. In addition, the windows are so large that they are no longer openings cut into a wall but, in effect, translucent walls, filled with stained glass. What

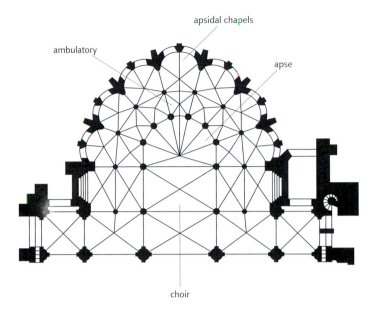

11.1 Plan of the choir and ambulatory, Abbey Church of Saint-Denis, France. 1140–1144 (Peter Kidson)

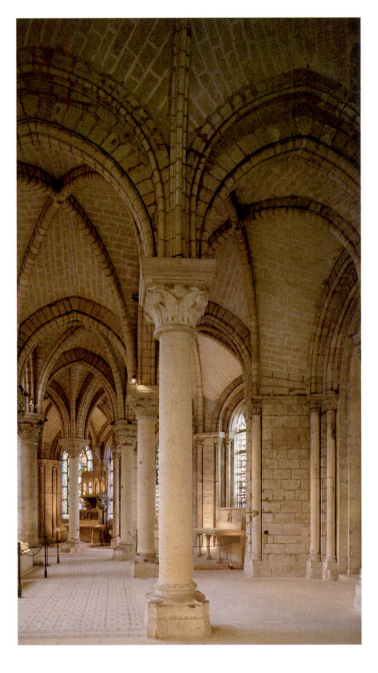

11.2 Ambulatory, Abbey Church of Saint-Denis, France

makes this abundance of light possible are heavy buttresses that jut out between the chapels to contain the outward pressure of the vaults. In the plan (see fig. 11.1), they look like stubby arrows pointing toward the center of the apse. No wonder, then, that the interior appears so airy, since the heaviest parts of the structural skeleton are relegated to the exterior. In describing Suger's ambulatory and choir, we have also described the essentials of Gothic architecture. Yet the elements that make up its design are not really new. The pilgrimage choir plan, the pointed arch, and the ribbed groin vault can be found in regional schools of the French and Anglo-Norman Romanesque. However, they were never combined in the same building until Suger—as he himself tells us—brought together artisans

from many different regions for Saint-Denis. We must not conclude from this, however, that Gothic architecture was merely a synthesis of Romanesque traits. Otherwise we would be hard-pressed to explain the new spirit, particularly the quest for luminosity, that strikes us so forcibly at Saint-Denis. Suger's account of the rebuilding of his church stresses luminosity as the highest value achieved in the new structure. Thus, he suggests, the "miraculous" light that floods the choir through the "most sacred" stained-glass windows becomes the Light Divine, a revelation of the spirit of God. Suger also claims that harmony, the perfect relationship among parts in terms of mathematical proportions or ratios, is the source of all beauty, since it exemplifies the laws by which divine reason made the universe

Dionysian Theology and the Abbey of Saint-Denis

THE INTERPRETATION of light and numerical harmony as reflecting divine reason was well established in Christian thought long before Abbot Suger's time. It derived in part from the writings of a sixth-century Greek theologian who, in the Middle Ages, was mistakenly believed to have been Dionysius the Areopagite, an Athenian disciple of St. Paul, who is mentioned in the New Testament book of Acts of the Apostles. In France,

Dionysius was identified with St. Denis, since that is the saint's name in Latin. Not surprisingly, Suger attached great authority to the writings of Dionysius, which were available to him in the library at Saint-Denis. Dionysian light-and-number symbolism particularly appealed to him and was influential in his thinking about the design and decoration of the abbey church.

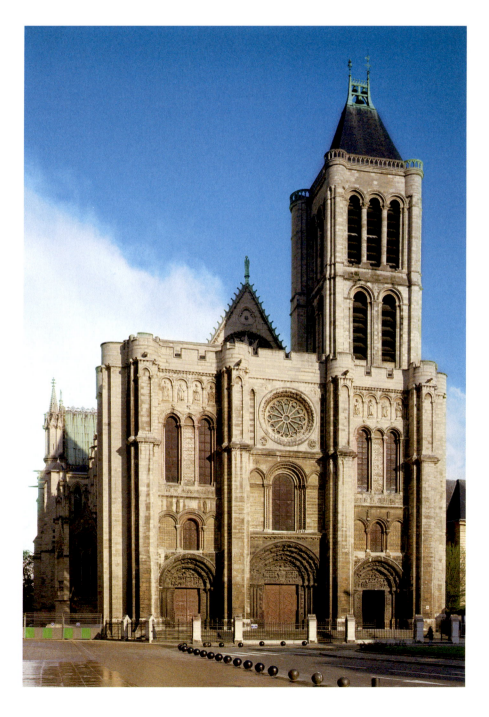

11.3 West façade, Abbey Church of Saint-Denis, France. ca. 1137–1140

(see Cultural Context: Dionysian Theology and the Abbey of Saint-Denis, opposite).

At the heart of Suger's mystical intent for Saint-Denis was the belief that the material realm is the stepping-stone for spiritual contemplation and thus that deep-toned, jewel-like light filtering through the church's stained-glass windows would transport the viewer to "some strange region of the universe which neither exists entirely in the slime of earth nor entirely in the purity of Heaven." The success of the choir design at Saint-Denis, therefore, derives not only from its architectural qualities but also from its extraordinary psychological impact. Visitors, it seems, were overwhelmed by both, and within a few decades the new style had spread far beyond the Île-de-France.

WEST FAÇADE Although Abbot Suger planned to rebuild all of Saint-Denis, the only part that he saw completed, other than the ambulatory and choir, was the west façade. Its overall design (**fig. 11.3**) derived from Norman Romanesque façades. A comparison between Saint-Denis and Saint-Étienne at Caen (see fig. 10.22) reveals a number of shared basic features. These include the pier buttresses that reinforce the corners of the towers and divide the façade vertically into three main parts, the placement of the portals, and the three-story arrangement. However, Saint-Denis's three portals are far larger and more richly carved than those at Saint-Étienne or any other Norman Romanesque church. From this we can conjecture that Abbot Suger attached considerable importance to the sculptural decoration of his church, although his account does not discuss it at length.

The rich sculptural decoration included carved tympana, archivolts, and jambs. The arrangement recalls the façades of southwestern France, such as that at Moissac (see fig. 10.10), and the carved portals of Burgundy, such as that at Autun (see fig. 10.12). These correlations corroborate Suger's claim that his workforce included artists from many regions. Unhappily, the trumeau figure of St. Denis and the statue-columns of the jambs were removed in 1770 and 1771, when the central portal was enlarged. A few years later, during the French Revolution, a mob attacked the heads of the remaining figures and melted down the metal doors. As a result of these ravages and a series of clumsy later restorations, we can gain only a general view of Suger's ideas about the role of sculpture at Saint-Denis. To envision what its west portal originally

looked like we must turn to the Cathedral of Chartres, where some of the Saint-Denis sculptors subsequently worked.

Chartres Cathedral

Toward 1145 the bishop of the town of Chartres, who was a friend of Abbot Suger and shared many of his ideas, began to rebuild a cathedral in the new style, dedicated to Notre-Dame ("Our Lady," the Virgin Mary). Fifty years later a fire destroyed all but the eastern crypt and the west façade.

WEST FAÇADE The surviving west façade (**fig. 11.4**), in many ways reminiscent of Saint-Denis, is divided into units of two and three and is a

11.4 West façade, Cathedral of Notre-Dame. Chartres, France. (Left spire is from the sixteenth century.) ca. 1145–1220

11.5 West portal (Royal Portal), Cathedral of Notre-Dame. Chartres, France. ca. 1145–1150

model of clarity. Yet, because construction proceeded in stages and was never entirely finished, the two west towers, though similar, are by no means identical. Moreover, their **spires**, the tall top sections with tapering roofs, are very different: The spire on the left dates from the early sixteenth century, nearly 300 years later than its mate.

To judge from old drawings of Saint-Denis, the Chartres jambs (**figs. 11.5** and **11.6**) are so similar to those of the original Saint-Denis portals that the same sculptors must have worked on both. Tall figures attached to columns flanked the doorways of both cathedrals. Figures had appeared on the jambs or trumeaux of Romanesque portals (see figs. 10.10–10.12), but they were reliefs carved from the masonry of the doorway. The Chartres jamb figures, in contrast, are essentially statues, each with its own axis. They could, in theory at least, be detached from their supports. That the figures are round gives them a more convincing presence than any we have seen in Romanesque architectural sculpture, and their heads show a gentle, human

quality that indicates a naturalistic trend in Gothic sculpture.

On the west portal of Chartres naturalism appears to spring from a reaction against the fantastic and demoniacal aspects of Romanesque art, a response that may be seen in the solemn spirit of the figures and their increased physical bulk. This is apparent by comparing the Christ of Chartres's center tympanum (see fig. 11.5) with his counterpart in the tympanum at Moissac (see fig. 10.10). It also appears in the discipline of the symbolic program underlying the entire sculptural scheme at Chartres. While an understanding of the subtler aspects of this program requires a knowledge of the theology that would have been taught by leading scholars of the day at the Chartres Cathedral School, its main elements can be readily understood.

The jamb statues form a continuous sequence linking all three portals (see fig. 11.5). Together they represent the prophets, kings, and queens of the Bible. Their purpose is to acclaim the rulers of France as the spiritual descendants of Old Testament royalty and to stress the

the liberal arts as human wisdom pay homage to the divine wisdom of Christ. Finally, in the left-hand tympanum, we see the timeless Heavenly Christ (or perhaps the Christ of the Ascension) framed by the ever-repeating cycle of the year: The signs of the zodiac and their earthly counterparts, the labors of the 12 months.

Laon Cathedral

Because the mid-twelfth-century church that stood behind the west façade of Chartres Cathedral was destroyed by fire in 1194, we must turn to the Cathedral of Notre-Dame at Laon to appreciate an Early Gothic interior. This cathedral was begun just before 1160.

NAVE The interior elevation of Laon Cathedral (**fig. 11.7**) includes a nave arcade, gallery, triforium, and clerestory, all features found in

11.6 Jamb statues, west portal, Cathedral of Notre-Dame, Chartres, France

harmony of spiritual and secular rule, of priests (or bishops) and kings—ideals previously put forward by Abbot Suger. Above the main doorway symbols of the four evangelists flank Christ in Majesty. The apostles are below, while the 24 elders occupy the two outer archivolts. Although the components are similar to those of the Moissac tympanum, the effect at Chartres is calm and comforting, whereas at Moissac it is dramatic and unsettling. The right-hand tympanum at Chartres shows Christ's Incarnation: The Birth, the Presentation in the Temple, and the infant Christ Child on the lap of the Virgin, who symbolizes the Church. The design achieves compositional and thematic unity by elevating Christ in the center of each register: On the manger, on an altar, and on the lap of his mother. In the surrounding archivolts, representations of

11.7 Nave, Cathedral of Notre-Dame, Laon, France. ca. 1160–1210

Romanesque architecture but never together in the same building. The stacking of four levels is a Gothic innovation and lightens the weight of the walls. The elevation develops logically and harmoniously: The single opening of the nave arcade is doubled in the gallery, then triple arches follow in the triforium, while a broad clerestory window balances the single nave arcade opening that began the vertical sequence. The rhythmical arrangement articulates a heightened sense of verticality, while the multiple openings allow increased light to enter the nave, directly from the clerestory and indirectly through galleries and side aisles.

Sexpartite nave vaults over squarish bays at Laon continue the kind of structural experimentation begun by the Norman Romanesque builders of Saint-Étienne at Caen (see pages 237–238) and Durham Cathedral (see pages 235–237). Laon uses the pointed ribbed vaults, pioneered in the western bays of the nave at Durham, throughout the building. Alternating bundles of shafts rising along the wall reflect the nature of the sexpartite vaults above: Clusters of five colonnettes indicate where transverse arches cross the nave, while three colonnettes adorn the intermediate piers. Although the system develops from Romanesque building practice (see pages 217 and 236), the elements seem more delicate in the Gothic building.

A change in program at Laon reveals the evolving objectives of this cathedral's designers. At the east end of the nave, where the building work began, clustered shafts were added to piers as well as to the wall. In the later, more westerly nave bays, the round piers are plain. Instead of the staggered rhythm created by the earlier alternating pier arrangement, the change produced a more flowing effect. However, the price for the increased uniformity of the new arrangement was a loss of structural explicitness. Like uniformity in the plan, the vertical emphasis of the interior is a clear Gothic trait.

High Gothic Art in France

The political and economic stability of France during the thirteenth century encouraged the continued growth of cities, an ideal climate for producing monumental architecture. Some art historians have seen the integration of structure and design in Early Gothic art as a series of experiments that were resolved during the High Gothic period. Thus, High Gothic art is as much

a continuation of Early Gothic experiments as it is their culmination. It is during this time that the names of architects, who previously had been largely anonymous, proliferate, a reflection of the value placed on their achievements and of an increasing interest in personal identity (see Cultural Context: The Architect, the Master, and the Guild, page 250).

The Rebuilding of Chartres Cathedral

The rebuilding of Chartres Cathedral after the fire of 1194 (see page 245) marks the next step in the development of Gothic architecture. The new building was largely completed within the astonishingly brief span of 26 years. Its crypt houses Chartres's most important possession: Remnants of a tunic said to have been worn by the Virgin Mary, to whom the cathedral is dedicated, at the time of Jesus' nativity. The relic, which miraculously survived the great fire of 1194, had drawn pilgrims from all over Europe.

The fire also spared the west façade and portals, and the decision to conserve these architectural features, which, at the time of the fire, were nearly 50 years old and certainly out of fashion, is worth noting. After initial despair at the damage wrought by the fire, civic and ecclesiastical authorities animated their followers by interpreting the fire as an expression of the will of the Virgin herself that a new and more glorious cathedral be built. Since the west end of the church, like the famous relic of the Virgin, had also been spared, it too was treated as a relic worthy of preservation. Recognizing the divine plan in what otherwise would have been disheartening circumstances helped fuel enthusiasm for rebuilding, and accounts for the rapid pace of construction.

To provide room for large numbers of visitors without disturbing worshipers, there is a wide aisle running the length of the nave and around the transept (**fig. 11.8**). It is joined at the choir by a second aisle, forming an ambulatory that connects the apsidal chapels. Worshipers entered the building through the old west portal and passed through a relatively low narthex. It would have taken some time for their eyes to adjust to the darkness of the interior. Once they had recovered from this disorienting effect, they would have become aware of a glimmering light, which guided them into the cavernous church. The transition, both subtle and profound, accentuated the significance of entering the church. As with entries into Romanesque

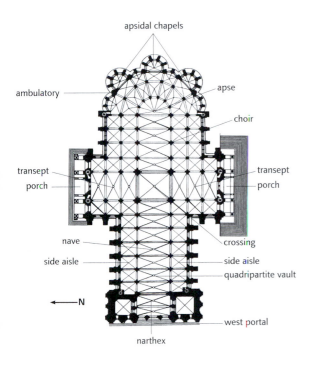

11.8 Plan, Cathedral of Notre-Dame (as rebuilt after 1194), Chartres, France

and Byzantine churches (see pages 171 and 227), a liminal, or transitional, zone signaled that visitors had left the temporal world behind. Patrons, designers, and builders of a religious edifice had again found meaningful physical forms to encourage and sustain powerful spiritual experiences.

NAVE The rebuilt nave of Chartres Cathedral (**fig. 11.9**) is the first masterpiece of the mature, or High Gothic, style. Several features distinguish this style (**fig. 11.10**). By eliminating the gallery, the designers of Chartres imposed a three-part elevation on the wall. Romanesque builders had used tripartite wall divisions (see figs. 10.21 and 10.23, and page 236), but the Chartres solution diminishes horizontality and treats the wall surface as a coherent vertical unit. Shafts attached to the piers stress the continuity of the vertical lines and guide our eye upward to the vaults, which appear as diaphanous webs stretched across the slender ribs. **Quadripartite,**

11.9 Nave and choir, Cathedral of Notre-Dame, Chartres, France. ca. 1194–1220

11.10 Axonometric projection of a High Gothic cathedral (after Acland)

The Architect, the Master, and the Guild

THE WORD "ARCHITECT" derives from the Greek term for "master builder" and was defined in its modern sense of "designer and theoretician" by the Roman writer Vitruvius during the first century BCE. During the Middle Ages, it came to have different meanings. The term could apply not only to masons, carpenters, and even roofers but also to the person who commissioned or supervised a building. Not until about 1260 did Thomas Aquinas revive Aristotle's definition of "architect" as the person of intellect who leads or conducts, as opposed to the artisan who makes. Within a century the term was used by the Italian humanist Petrarch to designate the artist in charge of a project.

In the Middle Ages, the word "master" (Latin, *magister*) was a title conferred by a trade organization, or guild, on a member who had achieved the highest level of skill in the guild's profession or craft. In each city, trade guilds virtually controlled commercial life by establishing quality standards, setting prices, defining the limits of each guild's activity, and overseeing the admission of new members. The earliest guilds were formed in the eleventh century by merchants. Soon, however, craftsmen also organized themselves in similar professional societies, which continued to be powerful well into the sixteenth century. Most guilds admitted only men, but some, such as the painters' guild of Bruges, occasionally admitted women as well. Guild membership established a certain level of social status for townspeople, who were not nobility, clerics (people in religious life), or peasantry.

A boy would begin as an apprentice to a master in his chosen guild and after many years might advance to the rank of journeyman. In most guilds this meant that he was then a full member of the organization, capable of working without direction, and entitled to receive full wages for his work. Once he became a master, the highest rank, he could direct the work of apprentices and manage his own workshop, hiring journeymen to work with him.

In architecture, the master mason, who was sometimes called the master builder, generally designed the building, that is, took the role of architect. In church-building campaigns, there were teams of masons, carpenters (joiners), metalworkers, and glaziers (glassworkers) who labored under the direction of the master builder.

sexpartite vault

quadripartite vault

Comparison of sexpartite and quadripartite vaulting

11.11 Cathedral of Notre-Dame, Chartres, France (from the south)

or four-part, vaults now replace the sexpartite vaults of Early Gothic buildings. Quadripartite vaults cover rectangular bays and, as a result, the builders did not need to concern themselves any longer about an alternating system of supports. The quickened rhythm of shorter, rectangular bays intensifies the perceived pace of propulsion down the nave. The openings of the pointed nave arcade are taller and narrower than before, and the clerestory is larger so that it is the same height as the nave arcade.

BUTTRESSES In Chartres, as in Suger's choir at Saint-Denis, the buttresses (the heavy bones of the structural skeleton) are visible only outside the building (**fig. 11.11**). The plan (see fig. 11.8) shows them as massive blocks of masonry that stick out from the building like a row of teeth. Above the aisles, these piers turn into **flying buttresses**—arched bridges that reach upward to the critical spots between the clerestory windows where the outward thrust of the nave vault is concentrated (see fig. 11.10). The flying buttresses were also designed to resist the considerable wind pressure on the high-pitched roof. This method of anchoring vaults, so characteristic of Gothic architecture, certainly owed its origin to functional considerations. Yet even the flying buttress is an integral aesthetic and expressive feature of the building. Its shape expresses both verticality and support (in addition to actually providing it).

STAINED GLASS Alone among all major Gothic cathedrals, Chartres still retains most of its more than 180 original stained-glass windows (see fig. 11.9). The magic of the jewel-like light from the clerestory is unforgettable to anyone who has experienced it. The windows admit far less light than one might expect. They act mainly as diffusing filters that change the quality of daylight, giving it the poetic and symbolic values so highly praised by Abbot Suger. The sensation of ethereal light dissolves the physical solidity of the church and, hence, the distinction between the temporal and the divine realms. This "miraculous light" creates the intensely mystical experience that lies at the heart of Gothic spirituality.

The majestic *Notre Dame de la Belle Verrière* (literally, "Our Lady of the beautiful window") at Chartres (**fig. 11.12**) appears as a weightless form hovering effortlessly in indeterminate space. This window, the only one apart from those of the west façade to survive the 1194 fire, consists of hundreds of small pieces of tinted

11.12 *Notre Dame de la Belle Verrière* (detail). ca. 1170 (framing panels are thirteenth century). Stained-glass window, height approx. 14′ (4.27 m). Cathedral of Notre-Dame, Chartres, France, north portal, ca. 1210

Stained Glass

A WINDOW SUCH AS *Notre Dame de la Belle Verrière* (fig. 11.12) consists of hundreds of small pieces of tinted glass bound together by strips of lead. The size of these pieces was limited by the methods of medieval glass manufacture. The design was not "painted on glass," rather, the window was painted with glass. The colored glass was produced by creating a molten mixture of silica (basically sand), potash (to lower the temperature at which silica melts), and lime (a stabilizer), plus the addition of metal oxides to color or "stain" the glass: The addition of cobalt oxide produced blue glass, copper oxide, red, and manganese oxide, purple. Hot iron-cutting tools were used to shape or cut the individual pieces to make up a window. It was assembled somewhat as one would put together a mosaic or a jigsaw puzzle, out of odd-shaped fragments cut to fit the contours of the forms. (See diagrams for more detail

about this process.) Only the finer details, such as eyes, hair, and drapery folds, were added by painting—or drawing—in black or gray on the glass surfaces.

Stained-glass production was a costly, time-consuming, and labor-intensive activity with a marked division of labor. The artisans who made the glass supported the work of the glaziers who designed and produced the windows. Although stained glass appears throughout Europe, the most significant achievements were made in northern Europe. To produce stained glass required abundant wood, both for firing the furnaces and kilns and for making potash, and it was in the north that there were sufficient forests to support a glassmaking industry. It was also in the north that the value of light entering a building could best be appreciated. By the late thirteenth century the preference for colored glass had diminished and large areas of clear glass dominated church construction.

1. The stained-glass artist first drew the design on a large, flat surface, then cut pieces of colored glass to match the drawn sections.

2. The individual pieces of glass were enclosed by channeled strips of lead.

3. The lead strips between the individual glass pieces were an important part of the design.

glass held together by strips of lead. Methods of medieval glassmaking limited the maximum size of these pieces. This process encourages an abstract, ornamental style, which tends to resist any attempt at three-dimensional effects. Only in the hands of a great master could the maze of lead strips lead to such monumental forms (see Materials and Techniques: Stained Glass box, above).

Given the way stained glass accentuates pattern and decorative effect, it is not surprising that it was so popular during the Middle Ages. Its brilliant surfaces are like the flat stones and enamel-work so highly prized in northern Europe in earlier periods (see fig. 9.1); enamel is in fact a kind of glass. The intensity with which the viewer engages with the image parallels the direct connection between viewer and object evident in much of the art of the earlier Middle Ages. Worthy comparisons with *Notre Dame de la Belle Verrière* are the Byzantine mosaics from the

Church of the Dormition at Daphni (see figs. 8.20 and 8.21) for the way they command our attention and communicate directly with a viewer. Both use otherworldly light to convey spiritual messages: On the one hand, filtered through stained glass, and on the other, reflected off gold-glass mosaics.

TRANSEPTS AND THEIR SCULPTURE Each of the transept arms of Chartres Cathedral has three deeply recessed and lavishly decorated portals, five **lancets** (tall, narrow windows crowned by a sharply pointed arch), and an immense **rose window**, the large medallion of glass in the center of the façade (see fig 11.11). The walls of these north and south façades have little solidity; they are so heavily pierced as to be nearly skeletal.

The north transept is devoted to the Virgin Mary. She had already appeared over the right portal of the west façade in her traditional role as the Mother of God seated on the Throne of

Divine Wisdom (see fig. 11.5). Her new prominence reflects the growing importance of the cult of the Virgin, which the Church had actively promoted since the Romanesque period. The growth of *Mariology*, as it is known, was linked to a new emphasis on divine love, embraced by the faithful as part of the more human view that increased in popularity during the Gothic era. The cult of the Virgin at Chartres developed special meaning about 1204, when the cathedral received the head of her mother, St. Anne, as a relic. This relic, in combination with the robe of the Virgin that had miraculously survived the fire of a decade earlier, gave Chartres exceptional status among those devoted to Mary.

The jamb statues of the transept portals show a discernible evolution, even among themselves since they were carved at different times. The relationship of statue and column begins to dissolve. The columns are quite literally put in the shade by the greater width of the figures, by the strongly projecting canopies, and by the elaborately carved bases of the statues.

A good instance of the early dissolution of this relationship is seen on one of the south transept portal jambs (**fig. 11.13**). The three saints on the right still echo the cylindrical shape of Early Gothic examples (see fig. 11.6), though the heads are no longer strictly in line with the central axis of the body. By comparison, the knight on the left, St. Theodore, who was carved about ten or fifteen years later than his companions, stands at ease, in a semblance of classical *contrapposto*. His feet rest on a horizontal platform, rather than on a sloping shelf as before, and the axis of his body, instead of being straight, describes a slight but perceptible S-curve. Even more surprising is the wealth of carefully observed detail in his weapons and in the texture of his tunic and chain mail. Above all, there is the organic structure of the body. Not since imperial Roman times have we seen a figure as thoroughly alive as this. Yet the most impressive quality of the St. Theodore statue is not its naturalism but the serene, balanced image that it conveys, an ideal portrait of the Christian soldier.

Reims Cathedral

Reims, as the coronation cathedral of the kings of France, was closely linked to Paris, where the kings held court, and to other cathedrals patronized by the royal family, such as Chartres.

WEST PORTAL SCULPTURE The jamb figures at Reims are not in their original positions because

11.13 Jamb statues, south transept portal, Cathedral of Notre-Dame, Chartres, France. ca. 1215–1220. Left-most figure (St. Theodore) ca. 1230

some sculptures were moved between the west façade and the transept portals. As a result, continuity of style and program is difficult to assess. However, we can study here individual sculptures of distinctive style and high quality. Gothic classicism reached its climax in some of these Reims statues. The most famous of them is the *Visitation* group (**fig. 11.14**), the two figures on the right), which was carved between 1230 and 1233. It depicts the Virgin Mary announcing the news of her pregnancy to her cousin Elizabeth.

For a pair of jamb figures to enact a narrative scene such as this would have been inconceivable in Early Gothic sculpture, where individual figures remained isolated, even within unified programs. That the *Visitation* figures are now free to

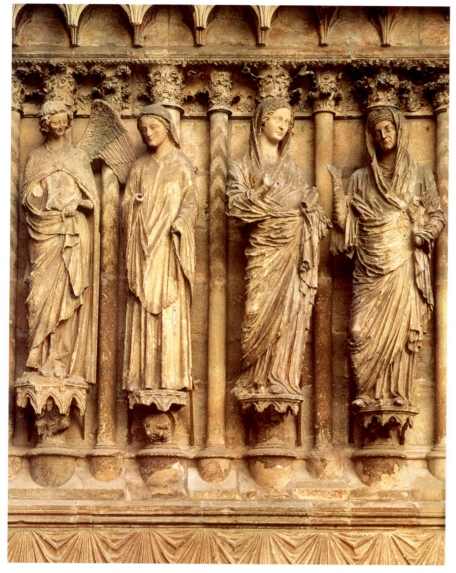

11.14 *Annunciation* and *Visitation*, west portal, Cathedral of Notre-Dame, Reims, France. ca. 1230–1265

interact shows how far the column has receded into the background. The S-curve, resulting from the pronounced *contrapposto*, is much more obvious here than in the St. Theodore from Chartres (see fig. 11.13) and dominates both the side and the front views of the figures. The figures gesture at each other as they communicate across the space that separates them.

Horizontal folds of cloth pulled across the women's abdomens emphasize the physical bulk of their bodies. Mary and Elizabeth remind us so strongly of ancient Roman matrons that we might wonder if the artist was inspired by large-scale Roman sculpture (compare fig. 7.7). A surviving Roman gate attests to the Roman presence in Reims, and excavations during the last century established that the first cathedral on the site was built over Roman baths. That

Roman models might have been available to the Reims sculptors is thus a real possibility.

Because of the vast scale and time frame of the sculptural program at Reims (and at other cathedrals), it was necessary to employ a variety of sculptors working in distinct styles. Two of these styles, both clearly different from the classicism of the *Visitation*, appear in the *Annunciation* group (fig. 11.14, the two figures on the left). The difference in style within a single group derives from the fact that the angel Gabriel and the Virgin were not originally intended as a pair, but at some point were installed next to each other, as we see them today. The Virgin, from between 1240 and 1245, has a rigidly vertical axis, and her garments form straight, tubular folds meeting at sharp angles. The angel, in contrast, is remarkably graceful and was carved at least a decade later than the Virgin of the *Annunciation*, between 1255 and 1265. The tiny, round face framed by curly locks, the emphatic smile, the strong S-curve of the slender body, and the rich drapery of this "elegant style" spread far and wide during the following decades. In fact, it soon became the standard formula for Gothic sculpture. Its effect will be seen for many years to come, not only in France but also abroad.

The High Gothic cathedrals of France represent a concentrated effort rarely seen before or since. The huge cost of these truly national monuments was borne by donations collected from all over the country and from all classes of society. They express the merging of religious and patriotic fervor that had been Abbot Suger's goal. However, the great expense and forced taxation required to construct them did produce vehement objections, and in 1233, for example, construction of Reims Cathedral was suspended as a result of civil unrest directed against the cathedral authorities; it was not resumed for another three years. The cessation of building activity helps explain the variety of styles at Reims. By the middle of the thirteenth century the wave of enthusiasm for large-scale projects had passed. Work on the vast structures now proceeded at a slower pace. New projects were fewer and generally far less ambitious.

Rayonnant or Court Style

One of those who still had the will and means to build on an impressive scale during the mid-thirteenth century was King Louis IX (known as St. Louis following his canonization in 1297, fewer

11.15 Interior of upper chapel, Sainte-Chapelle, Paris. 1241–1248

than 30 years after his death). Under the king's governance and as a result of a treaty with the English that resulted in French control of Normandy, the map of Louis's possessions began to take on the shape of present-day France. The increasing importance of the monarchy and the rising importance of Paris, where the court was located, is reflected in the degree to which Louis was able to define a court style; our sense of Paris as an artistic center effectively begins under St. Louis.

Sainte-Chapelle

St. Louis's mark on the stylistic evolution of Gothic is most dramatically seen in his court chapel, called the Sainte-Chapelle, which was designed by 1241 and completed within seven years (**fig. 11.15**). The two-story building comprises a ground floor, a relatively low chapel for court officials, and an upper floor to which the royal family had direct access from their quarters in the palace. In essence, the building is a type of palatine chapel for which Charlemagne's building at Aachen (see fig. 9.8) serves as an early prototype.

The impetus for the building's construction was Louis's acquisition from his cousin, the emperor of Constantinople, of the Crown of Thorns and other relics of Christ's Passion, including a part of the True Cross, the iron lance, the sponge, and a nail. Such sacred relics required a glorious space for their display. Rich colors, elaborate patterns, and extensive amounts of gold cover the Sainte-Chapelle's walls, vaults, and other structural members. This decoration complements the stained glass that constitutes most of the surface of the chapel. Above the altar, an elevated shrine, destined to frame and display the sacred relics, was left open at the back so that filtered light would bathe the venerated objects on display. The delicate glass cage of a building, jewel-like in the intensity of the colored light that enters it, functions in effect as a monumental reliquary. The tall, thin lancets accentuate verticality to such a degree that the building conveys a sense of monumentality comparable to any cathedral despite its diminutive scale. On entering the building the viewer is virtually immersed within its aura of light, different from any normal experience of the physical world. Thus, as with Hagia Sophia (see pages 172–174), spirituality is made manifest through the materiality of architecture and its decoration.

This phase of Gothic is often referred to as *rayonnant*, from the French *rayonner*, "to radiate

light." The term derives from the prevalence of raylike bar tracery in buildings of the period, which originally appeared in rose windows and later began to appear throughout entire churches. The style, closely associated with the court, spread through the royal domain and then through much of Europe.

Manuscript Illumination

Some scholars have been concerned that the term *rayonnant* is appropriate only for architecture. Recognizing that there were also major achievements in the pictorial arts within Louis IX's court and in the upper echelons of aristocratic society, they prefer the term *court style*, which they use synonymously with *rayonnant* to define the art of this time. In fact, there are many connections between the building arts and the elaborate devotional works with exquisite miniatures produced for the personal enjoyment and education of the royal family and for others who were literate and could afford them. These products of French manuscript workshops disseminated the refined taste that made the court art of Paris the standard for all Europe.

PSALTER OF ST. LOUIS Perhaps the closest parallel between painting and architectural form is the *Psalter of St. Louis*, which was executed about 1260 (**fig. 11.16**). The folio reproduced here illustrates 1 Samuel 11:2, in which Nahash the Ammonite threatens the Jews at Jabesh. The manuscript's painted architecture is modeled directly on the Sainte-Chapelle (see fig. 11.15). The illustration also recalls the canopies above the heads of jamb statues at Chartres (see fig. 11.13). Against the two-dimensional background of the page, the figures stand out in relief by their smooth and skillful modeling. The outer contours are defined by heavy, dark lines, reminiscent of the lead strips in stained-glass windows. The figures themselves display all the features of the elegant style invented by sculptors a few years earlier: Graceful gestures, swaying poses, smiling faces, and neatly waved hair. (Compare the *Annunciation* angel in figure 11.14.) This miniature thus exemplifies the refined court style.

Late Gothic Art in France

Although Late Gothic art builds on earlier Gothic achievements, during this period artists felt free to deviate from previous patterns of

11.16 Nahash the Ammonite Threatening the Jews at Jabesh, from the *Psalter of St. Louis*. 1253–1270. Ink, tempera, and gold leaf on vellum, 5 × 3½" (13.6 × 8.9 cm). Bibliothèque Nationale, Paris

development. Builders showed increased concern for unity of plan, but they also employed curvilinear and elaborate decorative forms that often undermined the clarity of structure so important in earlier Gothic works. Decorations often take the form of undulating curves and reverse curves. Thus a late phase of Gothic architecture is labeled **Flamboyant**, literally meaning "flamelike." Late Gothic manuscripts and sculptures are also highly decorated, with rich surface treatment accentuating their precious qualities.

Manuscript Illumination

Until the thirteenth century, illuminated manuscripts had been produced in monastic scriptoria. Now, along with many other activities that were once the special preserve of the clergy, manuscript production shifted to urban workshops organized by laypeople, the ancestors of the publishing houses of today. Paris was renowned as a center of manuscript production, and it is possible even today to identify the streets on which the workshops were clustered.

11.17 Jean Pucelle. *The Betrayal of Christ* and *Annunciation*, from the Hours of Jeanne d'Évreux. 1325–1328. Tempera and gold leaf on parchment. Each page, 3½ × 2⁷/₁₅″ (8.9 × 6.2 cm). Shown larger than actual size. The Metropolitan Museum of Art, New York. The Cloisters Collection, Purchase, 1954. 54.1.2

HOURS OF JEANNE D'ÉVREUX The interest in depicting sculptural figures represented in depth was of increasing concern during the Late Gothic period and can be seen in the work of the illuminator Jean Pucelle in a tiny, private prayer book—called a BOOK OF HOURS—illuminated in Paris between 1325 and 1328 for Jeanne d'Évreux, queen of France (**fig. 11.17**). The *Annunciation* is represented on the right page and the *Betrayal of Jesus* on the left. The delicate **grisaille** (painting in gray) adds a soft roundness to the forms. This is not Pucelle's only contribution: The architectural interior reveals a spatial recession previously unknown in northern European painting. In the *Annunciation*, Gabriel kneels in an anteroom, while angels appear in the windows of an attic, from which the dove of the Holy Spirit descends.

In representing this new pictorial space, Jean Pucelle had to take into account the special needs of a manuscript page. The Virgin's chamber does not fill the entire picture surface. It is as though it were an airy cage floating on the blank background (note the supporting angel on the right), like the rest of the ornamental framework, so that the entire page forms a harmonious unit. Many of the details are peripheral to the religious purpose of the manuscript. The kneeling queen inside the initial D is surely meant to be Jeanne d'Évreux at her prayers; it is as if her intense devotions have produced a tangible vision of the Annunciation. The identity of the man with the staff next to her is unclear, although he appears to be a courtier listening to the lute player perched on the tendril above him. The combination of scenes is a commentary on experiences that become real even if they lack physical substance: Music is at once actual and ephemeral, as is Jeanne's religious vision.

Other enchanting vignettes fill the page. A rabbit peers from its burrow beneath the girl on the left, and in the foliage leading up to the initial

Developed in the fourteenth century, the BOOK OF HOURS was a prayer book for laypersons that contained psalms and devotional meditations chosen to suit the various seasons, months, days of the week, and hours of the day. Many of these small, portable books are masterpieces of luxurious illumination, especially those made for royal or aristocratic patrons.

we find a monkey and a squirrel. These fanciful marginal designs—or ***drôleries***—are a common feature of Northern Gothic manuscripts. They originated more than a century before Jean Pucelle in the regions along the English Channel. From there they quickly spread to Paris and the other centers of Gothic art. Their subjects include a wide range of motifs, fantasy, fable, and grotesque humor, as well as scenes of everyday life, which appear side by side with religious themes. The essence of *drôlerie* is its playfulness. In this special domain, the artist enjoys an almost unlimited freedom—comparable to a jester's—which accounts for the wide appeal of these little vignettes during the later Middle Ages.

The seeming innocence of Pucelle's *drôleries* nevertheless hides a serious purpose, which is particularly evident in the one at the bottom of the right-hand page, a type of illustration referred to as a ***bas-de-page*** (French for "bottom of the page"). The four figures are playing a game of tag called Froggy in the Middle, a reference to the *Betrayal of Jesus* on the opposite page. Below the *Betrayal of Jesus*, two knights on goats joust at a barrel. This image not only mocks courtly chivalry but also refers to Jesus as a "scapegoat," and to the spear that pierced his side at the Crucifixion.

Sculpture

Sculptors' guilds were now well established. Portal sculpture, the principal interest of the Early and High Gothic periods, is of relatively little consequence during the Late Gothic period. Single figures, carved in the round, many of them cult figures, are now fully detached from any architectural setting. As the individual's importance in society increased, so individual sculpted figures became prominent.

VIRGIN OF PARIS In an early fourteenth-century sculpture of the Virgin, we see how traces of classicism increasingly disappear from Gothic sculpture, while elegance becomes a virtual end in itself. Thus the human figure of the *Virgin of Paris* (**fig. 11.18**) in Notre-Dame Cathedral is now strangely abstract. It consists largely of hollows, and the projections are so reduced that a viewer sees them as lines rather than volumes. The statue is quite literally disembodied—its swaying stance bears little relation to classical *contrapposto*, since it no longer supports the figure. Compared to such unearthly grace, the angel of the Reims *Annunciation* (see fig. 11.14) seems solid indeed; yet it contains the seed of the

11.18. *Virgin of Paris*. Early fourteenth century. Stone. Notre-Dame, Paris

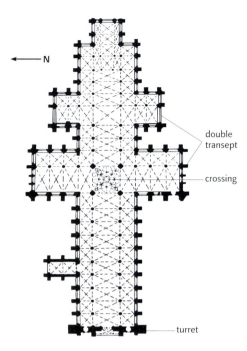

11.19 Plan of Salisbury Cathedral, England. 1220–1265

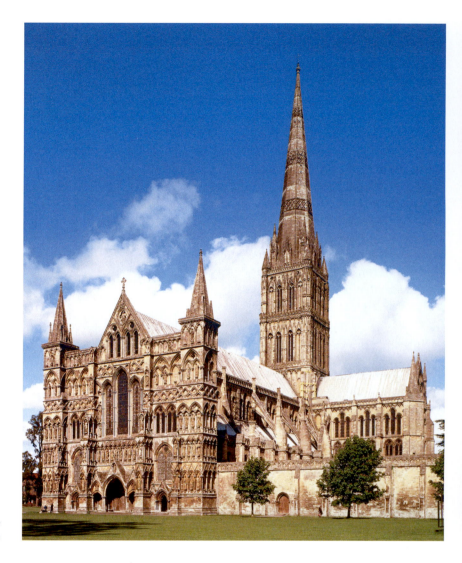

11.20 Salisbury Cathedral, England (from the southwest). (Spire ca. 1320–1330.)

very qualities expressed so strikingly in the *Virgin of Paris*. Earlier instances of Gothic naturalism, which focused on particulars, survive here as a kind of intimate realism in which the infant Christ is no longer a savior-in-miniature facing the viewer but, rather, a human child playing with his mother's veil.

The elegant manner of this new style was encouraged by the royal court of France and thus had special authority. It is this graceful expressive quality, not realism or classicism, that is the essence of later Gothic art.

The Spread of Gothic Art

The royal French style of the Paris region, with its refined taste, was enthusiastically received abroad, where it was adapted to a variety of local conditions. A number of factors contributed to the rapid spread of Gothic art. Among them were the skill of French architects and stone carvers and the prestige of French centers of

learning, such as the Cathedral School of Chartres and the University of Paris. It is debatable whether any of these explanations really go to the heart of the matter: The basic reason for the spread of Gothic art was undoubtedly the persuasive power of the style itself. It kindled the imagination and aroused religious feeling even among people far removed from the cultural climate of the Île-de-France.

England

England was especially receptive to the new style, which developed there as the influence of Gothic forms from the Île-de-France melded with Anglo-Norman Romanesque features. English Gothic, however, developed a well-defined character of its own, known as the Early English style, which dominated the second quarter of the thirteenth century.

SALISBURY CATHEDRAL The exception to the trend of multiple periods and styles in a single English Gothic church is Salisbury Cathedral, in

Wiltshire begun in 1220. One sees immediately how different the exterior of Salisbury (**fig. 11.20**) is from French Gothic churches (see figs. 11.4 and 11.11) and how futile it would be to judge it by the same standards. Compactness and verticality have given way to a long, low, sprawling look. (The crossing tower, which provides a dramatic unifying accent, was built a century later than the rest and is much taller than originally planned.) Since height is not the main goal, flying buttresses are used only as an afterthought, not as integral design elements. The west façade is treated like a screen wall, wider than the church itself and divided into horizontal bands of ornament and statuary. The towers have shrunk to stubby **turrets** (small towers). The plan (**fig. 11.19**), with its double transept, retains the segmented quality of the Romanesque, while the square east end derives from Cistercian architecture (see page 229).

As we enter the nave (**fig. 11.21**), we recognize many elements familiar to us from French interiors of the time, such as Chartres Cathedral (see fig. 11.9). However, the English interpretation produces a very different effect. As on the façade, horizontal divisions dominate at the expense of the vertical. Hence we experience the nave wall not as a succession of vertical bays but as a series of arches and supports, carved of dark stone, which stand out against the rest of the interior. This method of stressing their special function is one of the hallmarks of the Early English style. The use of bands of color also emphasizes horizontality, quite unlike the effect achieved in French Gothic buildings.

Another distinctive feature is the steep curve of the nave vault. The ribs rise all the way from the triforium level. As a result, the clerestory gives the impression of being tucked away among the vaults. At Durham Cathedral, more than a century earlier, the same treatment had been a technical necessity (see fig. 10.21). Now it has become a matter of style, in keeping with the character of Early English Gothic as a whole.

GLOUCESTER CATHEDRAL The change in the English Gothic becomes very clear if we compare the interior of Salisbury with the choir of Gloucester Cathedral, built in the second quarter of the fourteenth century (**fig. 11.22**). Gloucester is an outstanding example of English Late Gothic, also called the **Perpendicular Gothic** style. The name certainly fits, since we now find a dominant vertical accent that was absent in the Early English style. Vertical continuity is most

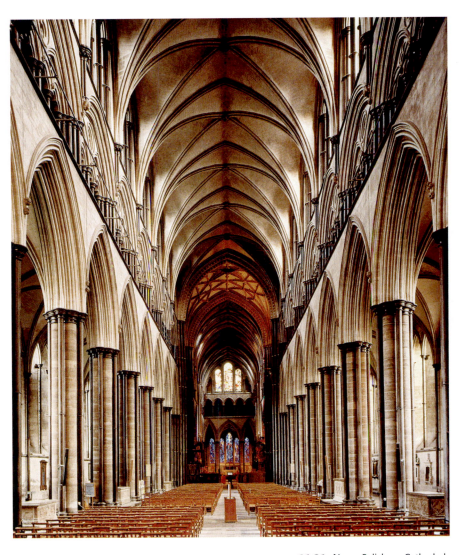

11.21 Nave, Salisbury Cathedral, England

11.22 Choir, Gloucester Cathedral, England. 1332–1357

The ribs of the vaults, on the other hand, have taken on a new role. They have been multiplied until they form an ornamental network that screens the boundaries between the bays so that the entire vault looks like one continuous surface. The ceiling reads as a canopy fluttering above the interior. This effect, in turn, emphasizes the unity of the interior space. Such elaboration of the classic four-part vault is characteristic of the Flamboyant style on the Continent as well, but the English started it earlier and carried it much further.

Germany

In Germany, Gothic architecture took root a good deal more slowly than in England. Until the mid-thirteenth century, the Romanesque tradition, with its persistent Ottonian elements, remained dominant, despite the growing acceptance of Early Gothic features. From about 1250 on, however, the High Gothic of the Île-de-France had a strong impact in the Rhineland. While some German sculptors relied on French models, others pursued a more independent course, unlike German architects. German Gothic sculptures are sometimes dramatic, sometimes poignant, and sometimes lifelike, but they always express deep, if sometimes restrained, emotion.

HEILIGENKREUZ IN SCHWÄBISH-GMÜND Especially characteristic of German Gothic is the hall church, or **Hallenkirche**. This type of church, with aisles and nave of the same height, stems from Romanesque architecture. Although also found in France, it is in Germany where its possibilities were explored fully. Heiligenkreuz (Holy Cross) in Schwäbish-Gmünd (**fig. 11.23**) is one of many examples from central Germany. Heinrich Parler the Elder began Heiligenkreuz in 1317, although it is perhaps his son Peter who is responsible for the enlarged choir of 1351. The space has a fluidity and an expansiveness that enfold us as if we were standing under a huge canopy, reminiscent of the effect at Gloucester Cathedral (see fig. 11.22). There is no clear sense of direction to guide us. And the unbroken lines of the pillars, formed by bundles of shafts that diverge as they turn into lacy ribs covering the vaults, seem to echo the continuous movement that we feel in the space itself.

NAUMBURG CATHEDRAL The growth of Gothic sculpture in Germany can be easily traced. From the 1220s on, German masters who had been

11.23 Heinrich Parler the Elder and Peter Parler (?). Nave and Choir, Heiligenkreuz, Schwäbish-Gmünd, Germany. Begun 1317

evident at Gloucester in the **responds** that run in an unbroken line from the floor to the vault. In this respect, Perpendicular Gothic is much closer to French sources, but it includes so many uniquely English features that it would look out of place on the Continent. The repetition of small uniform tracery panels recalls the bands of statuary on the west façade at Salisbury (see fig. 11.20), and the upward curve of the vault is as steep as in the latter's nave (see fig. 11.21).

11.24 Naumburg Master. *Crucifixion*, on the choir screen, and the *Virgin* and *John the Evangelist*. ca. 1255. Stone. Naumburg Cathedral, Germany

trained in the sculpture workshops of the French cathedrals brought the new style back home. Because German architecture at that time was still mainly Romanesque, however, large statuary cycles like those at Chartres and Reims were not produced on façades, where they would have looked out of place. As a result, German Gothic sculpture tended to be less closely linked with its architectural setting. In fact, the finest work was often done for the interiors of churches.

This independence permitted a greater expressive freedom than in France. It is strikingly evident in the work of the Naumburg Master, an artist whose best-known work is the series of statues and reliefs made around 1255 for Naumburg Cathedral. The *Crucifixion* (**fig. 11.24**) forms the center of the choir screen; flanking it are statues of the *Virgin* and *John the Evangelist*. Enclosed by a deep, gabled porch, the three figures frame the opening that links the nave with the sanctuary. Rather than placing the group above the screen, as was usual, the sculptor brought the subject down to earth physically and emotionally. The suffering of Jesus thus becomes a human reality through the emphasis on the weight and volume of his body. Mary and John,

11.25 *Roettgen Pietà*. Early fourteenth century. Wood, height 34½″ (87.5 cm). Rheinisches Landesmuseum, Bonn

Chapelle (see fig. 11.15), were elaborately painted, as was exterior sculpture; but that paint rarely survives today.

THE *ROETTGEN PIETÀ* Gothic sculpture, as we have come to know it so far, reflects a desire to give a greater emotional appeal to traditional themes of Christian art. Toward the end of the thirteenth century, this tendency gave rise to a new kind of religious image. Originally designed for private devotion, it is often referred to by the German term *Andachtsbild* (contemplation image), since Germany played the leading part in its development. The most widespread type was a representation of the Virgin grieving over the dead Christ. It is called a *Pietà* after an Italian word derived from the Latin *pietas*, the root word for both "pity" and "piety." No such scene occurs in the scriptural accounts of the Passion. We do not know where or when the *Pietà* was invented, but it portrays one of the Seven Sorrows of the Virgin. It thus forms a tragic counterpart to the motif of the Madonna and Child, one of her Seven Joys.

The *Roettgen Pietà* (**fig. 11.25**) is carved of wood and vividly painted. Like most such groups, this large cult statue was meant to be placed on an altar. The style, like the subject, expresses the emotional fervor of lay religiosity, which emphasized a personal relationship with God as part of the tide of mysticism that swept over fourteenth-century Europe. Realism here is purely a means to enhance the work's impact. The faces convey unbearable pain and grief; the wounds are exaggerated grotesquely; and the bodies and limbs are puppetlike in their thinness and rigidity. The purpose of the work clearly is to arouse so overwhelming a sense of horror and pity that the faithful will share in Christ's suffering and identify with the grief-stricken Mother of God. The ultimate goal of this emotional bond is a spiritual transformation that grasps the central mystery of God in human form through compassion (meaning "suffering with").

At first glance, the *Roettgen Pietà* would seem to have little in common with the *Virgin of Paris* (see fig. 11.18), which dates from the same period. Yet they share a lean, "deflated" quality of form and exert a strong emotional appeal to a viewer. Both features characterize the art of northern Europe from the late thirteenth to the mid-fourteenth century. Only after 1350 do we again find an interest in weight and volume, coupled with a renewed desire to explore tangible reality as part of a change in religious outlook.

pleading with the viewer, convey their grief more eloquently than ever before.

The pathos of these figures is heroic and dramatic, compared with the quiet lyricism of the Reims *Visitation* (see fig. 11.14). If the classical High Gothic sculpture of France may be compared with the calm restraint of the Classical Greeks, the Naumburg Master embodies the temperamental counterpart of the strained physicality demonstrated in Hellenistic art (see fig. 5.28).

The paint still visible on Naumburg's interior sculpture helps us appreciate how Gothic sculpture might have looked originally. Gothic interiors, as can be seen in the restored Sainte-

SUMMARY

Gothic style began in the vicinity of Paris in the mid-1100s. Within a hundred years, most of Europe had adopted the style. A general increase in population, expanding urban centers, the appearance of a veritable middle class, and the growing importance of cathedrals are all features of the Gothic period.

Architecture played a dominant role in the formation of a coherent Early Gothic style. At the royal Abbey Church of Saint-Denis, built just outside Paris in the first half of the twelfth century, the graceful architectural forms and large windows mark a contrast with the massive solidity of the Romanesque style.

France's authoritative role in the production of works of art reflected its ambitions in the political realm. French kings acquired control over princely territories and over continental lands previously held by England. The political and economic stability of France during the thirteenth century was an ideal climate for producing monumental architecture with impressive sculptural programs. The rebuilding of Chartres Cathedral after a fire was a crucial step in the development of Gothic architecture, labeled High Gothic. High Gothic French buildings emphasize verticality and translucency.

The increasing importance of the French monarchy and the rising significance of Paris are reflected in King Louis IX's court chapel, the Sainte-Chapelle. This phase of Gothic art is often called *rayonnant*. The style, closely associated with the French court, spread throughout the royal domain and then through much of Europe.

During the period of Late Gothic art, much of it made during the Hundred Years' War (1337–1453), when English monarchs claimed rights to the French throne, artists were able to vary previous patterns and evolve more complex styles. Builders used elaborate arrangements to produce intricate visual displays as seen in the undulating curves of the Flamboyant style. Late Gothic painting—such as that in the *Book of Hours* created for Jeanne d'Évreux by Jean Pucelle—revealed a new interest in representing spatial depth, and in sculpture, individual sculpted figures became prominent.

The royal French style of the Paris region was enthusiastically received abroad, where it was adapted to a variety of local conditions. Its influence in England can be seen in cathedrals built at Salisbury, Gloucester, and elsewhere. In Germany, its effect is apparent in sculptures made for Naumburg Cathedral.

ART IN TIME

- 1137–1144—Rebuilding of Abbey Church of Saint-Denis, outside Paris, by Suger

- ca. 1170—Stained-glass panel of *Notre Dame de la Belle Verrière* created for Chartres Cathedral

- 1180–1223—Reign of French King Philip Augustus

- 1194—A fire destroys much of Chartres Cathedral in France

- 1220—Construction begins on Salisbury Cathedral in England

- 1241—Sainte-Chapelle, Paris, court chapel of King Louis IX, designed

- 1317—Nave and Choir of Heilingenkruez, Schwäbish-Gmünd, begun by Heinrich Parler the Elder and Peter Parler (?)

- 1325–1328—Jean Pucelle illuminates a *Book of Hours* for Jeanne d'Évreux, queen of France

- 1337–1453—The Hundred Years' War between England and France

PART 3

The Renaissance through the Rococo: The Early Modern World

NO SINGLE EVENT marked out the end of the Middle Ages from the beginning of the succeeding era, usually called the Renaissance. Instead, a change of ideas and attitudes accompanied important social, economic, religious and political shifts in the fifteenth and sixteenth centuries. These cultural changes opened the door to further developments in the seventeenth and eighteenth centuries. Ultimately, the character of the Renaissance laid the groundwork for the modern world. This is why many historians refer to the era from 1400 to 1800 as the Early Modern period.

Historians have looked to many moments as indicative of the new era: The fall of Constantinople and the Turkish conquest of southeastern Europe; the journeys of exploration that led to the founding of overseas empires in the New World, in Africa and Asia, with the subsequent rivalry of Spain and England as the foremost colonial powers; and the deep spiritual crises of the Reformation and Counter-Reformation. Yet none of these events, however great their effects, brought about the new era. By the time they happened, the Renaissance was well under way.

One theory holds that the Renaissance began when people realized they were no longer living in the Middle Ages. This is not as simple as it may seem. The Renaissance was the first period in European history to be aware of its own existence and to coin a label for itself. Medieval people did not think they belonged to an age distinct from classical antiquity. The past, to them, consisted simply of "B.C." (before Christ) and "A.D." (*Anno Domini*, in the year of Our Lord), the era "under the Law" (that is, of the Old Testament) and the era "of Grace" (that is, after the birth of Jesus). From their point of view, then, history was made in heaven rather than on earth. The Renaissance, and the Early Modern world, by contrast, divided the past not according to the divine plan of salvation, but on the basis of human achievements.

Humanists of the Renaissance saw classical antiquity as the era when civilization had reached the peak of its creative powers, an era that ended abruptly when barbarian invaders destroyed the Roman Empire. During the thousand-year interval that followed, they believed little was accomplished, but now, at last, this "time in-between" or "Middle Age" had been replaced by a revival of all those arts and sciences that had flourished in antiquity. The present could thus be fittingly labeled a "rebirth"—*rinàscita* in Italian, *renaissance* in French and, by adoption, in English.

We can find this revolutionary view of history as early as the 1330s, in the writings of the Italian poet Francesco Petrarca. Petrarch, as we call him, thought of the new era mainly as a "revival of the classics," limited to the restoration of Latin and Greek to their former purity and the return to the original texts of ancient authors. During the next two centuries, this concept of the rebirth of antiquity grew to embrace almost the entire range of cultural endeavors, including the visual arts. The latter, in fact, came to play a particularly important part in shaping the Renaissance, for reasons that we will explore.

Inspired by a new sense of individualism, Petrarch felt empowered to proclaim, against all established authority, his own conviction that the "age of faith" was actually an era of darkness, whereas the "benighted pagans" of antiquity really represented the most enlightened stage of history. Such readiness to question traditional beliefs and practices was to become profoundly characteristic of the Renaissance as a whole. Humanism, to Petrarch, meant a belief in the importance of what we still call "the humanities" or "humane letters" (rather than divine letters, or the study of scripture): The pursuit of learning in languages, literature, history, and philosophy for its own end, in a secular rather than a religious framework.

Petrarch and his successors did not want to revive classical antiquity in its entirety, however. By suggesting that "a thousand years of darkness" separated themselves and the ancients, they acknowledged (unlike the medieval classicists) that the Graeco-Roman world was irretrievably dead. Its glories could be revived only in the mind, by thinking back across the barrier of time, by rediscovering the secrets of ancient achievements in thought and art, and by trying to compete with these achievements. Yet they lived in a different world from that of the ancients.

When Renaissance writers strove to express themselves as eloquently as the great orators of ancient Rome, they did it in local or vernacular languages, as well as in Latin. Renaissance architects continued to build Christian churches, but they designed them *all'antica*, "in the manner of the ancients," using an architectural vocabulary based on the study of classical structures. And, however great their enthusiasm for classical philosophy, the humanists did not become neo-pagans; instead, they tried to reconcile the heritage of the ancient thinkers with Christianity.

The challenge of antiquity to late medieval thinkers called forth an outpouring of creative energy such as the Western world had never before experienced. Paradoxically, this period's desire to return to the classics brought, not the rebirth of antiquity, but the birth of modern civilization. Unleashing the creative potential of many different kinds of people resulted in a changed world.

Many areas of human activity—science, religion, politics, the economy, to name but a few—were profoundly invigorated by the new freedom to question authority and by a new freedom to innovate.

Those who participated in these changes, the people who lived in the period from 1400 to 1800, are recognizable to us in many ways. Their concerns, fears and goals seem similar to ours. This period fostered the beginning of our modern understanding of the individual, and all that integrates us into our culture. Family, sexuality, gender, identity, work, status, economic fortune, class, education, medicine, religion, and scientific thought began to be viewed in the context of the individual. The visual arts of the Early Modern era give us many glimpses of the people of the period. We can see them in portraits that astonish us by their lifelikeness and in scenes from daily life that touch or amuse us.

We can respond to these images because the artists of the Early Modern era worked in a language we recognize. One of the fundamental gifts of the Renaissance to the modern world, learned from the arts of antiquity, is the emphasis, in the painted and sculptural arts, on representing the world in naturalistic terms. The great Italian writer Boccaccio wrote about 1350 that the Florentine painter Giotto "restored to light this art [of painting] which had been

buried for many centuries." Boccaccio claimed that Giotto depicted every aspect of nature so truthfully that people often mistook his paintings for reality itself. This implies that, for painters, the revival of antiquity inspired close study of the natural world in an effort to reproduce it in their work. Artists in this period created or discovered important new tools, like perspective, to accomplish this goal.

Renaissance artists contributed a great deal to the development of the Early Modern world. As geographic and scientific discovery expanded the universe, artists helped their contemporaries visualize and understand it. As new forms of religious practice developed, artists devised new buildings to accommodate them. As new social structures arose, artists responded with new subjects, such as self-portraits and scenes of everyday life. When we see paintings that depict men and women together, we can begin to grasp not just a couple's relationship with one other; we can also see the connectedness of figures, families, friends, workers, and larger social organizations. Although Early Modern artists often aspired to create ideal and timeless forms based on antiquity, they were members of their own culture, their own social group, and their own time; their products are firmly rooted in the values of that time. When we look at works from this period, it does not seem so long ago.

NORTH SEA

IRELAND

ENGLAND

THE NETHERLANDS

HOLY RO

Oxford
Thames R.
London

Haarlem   Amsterdam
Leyden
The Hague Delft Utrecht
Rotterdam 's Hertogenbosch

Salisbury

Brugge   Antwerp
FLANDERS Ghent
Brussels
Lille   Tournai Liège
Douai   Flémalle

Cologne

Meuse R.

Rhine R.

RHINELAND

English Channel

Caen
NORMANDY

Seine R.

Paris

K

ATLANTIC

OCEAN

Versailles
Fontainebleau

Strasbourg
Colmar
Isenheim
Basel

Consta

Loire R.
Tours

BERRY

Dijon

BURGUNDY

FRANCE

SWITZER

Lake Geneva

SAVOY

Mil
Ca

Rhône R.

Turin

Garonne R.

Avignon

PROVENCE

Loyola

PYRENEES MTS.

PORTUGAL

Duero R.

Ebro R.

COR

SPAIN

Avila

Madrid

Tajo R.

Toledo

Guadiana R.

CORS

Guadalquiver R.

Seville

M   E   D   I   T

ATLANTIC OCEAN

N

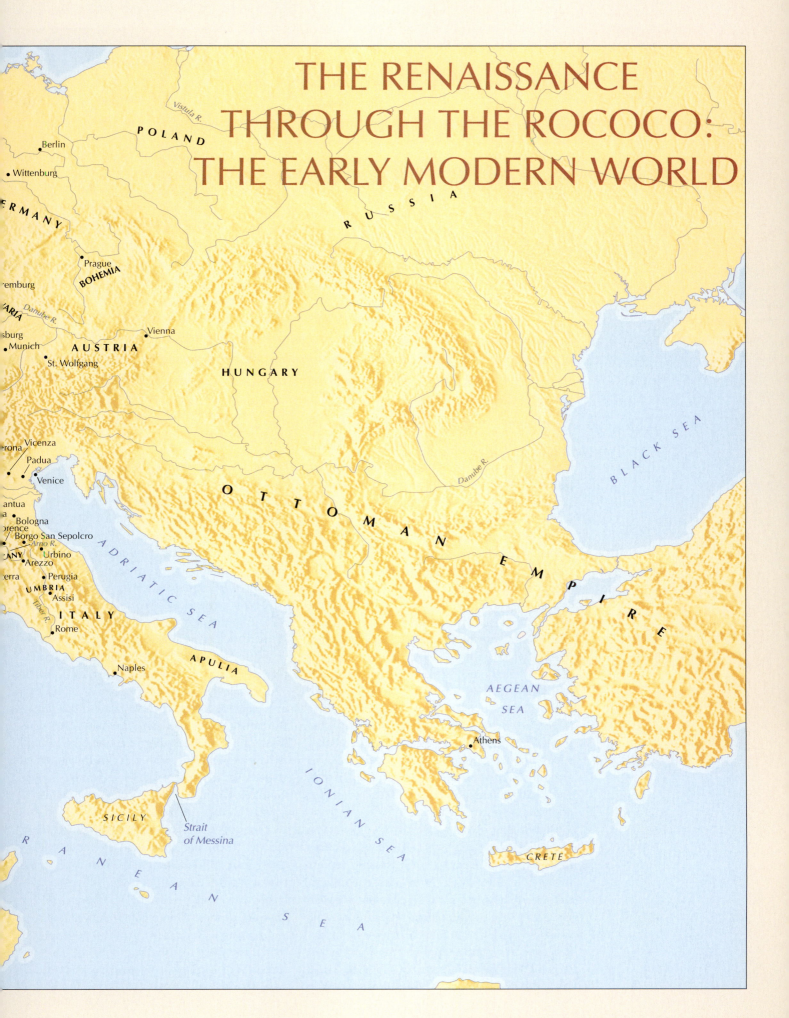

THE RENAISSANCE THROUGH THE ROCOCO: THE EARLY MODERN WORLD

Berlin

Wittenburg

POLAND

GERMANY

Prague
BOHEMIA

remburg

RIA

sburg

Munich

AUSTRIA

St. Wolfgang

Danube R.

Vienna

RUSSIA

HUNGARY

Danube R.

BLACK SEA

rona Vicenza

Padua

Venice

antua

Bologna

rence

Borgo San Sepolcro

Arno R.

ANY

Urbino

Arezzo

erra

Perugia

UMBRIA

Assisi

Tiber R.

ITALY

Rome

ADRIATIC SEA

OTTOMAN EMPIRE

Naples

APULIA

AEGEAN SEA

Athens

SICILY

Strait
of Messina

R

R A N E A N

S E A

IONIAN SEA

CRETE

12 | Art in Thirteenth- and Fourteenth- Century Italy

*A*lthough Italian artists and patrons shared concerns with their contemporaries elsewhere in Europe, for geographic, historical, and economic reasons, the arts in thirteenth- and fourteenth-century Italy struck out in a different direction. Many of the innovations that characterize the Italian Renaissance of the fifteenth and sixteenth centuries have their roots in the developments that took place in this period.

Throughout most of Europe in the thirteenth century, political and cultural power rested with landholding aristocrats. Products from their lands created wealth, and the land passed from one generation to the next. Although hereditary rulers controlled large regions, they usually owed allegiance to a king or to the Holy Roman emperor. But Italy had few viable kingdoms or strong central authorities. During most of the Middle Ages, the two international institutions of the Holy Roman Empire and the papacy dominated Italian politics. However, the emperors generally lived north of the Alps, and sheer distance limited their control in Italy; while for much of the fourteenth century, Rome lacked a pope who could command worldly power, as the papacy had moved to France. While hereditary rulers controlled southern Italy and the area around Milan, much of the rest consisted of individual city-states, competing with each other for political influence and wealth.

Italy's long coastlines on the Mediterranean and Adriatic Seas (see map 12.1) allowed its maritime cities to develop into trading centers throughout the Middle Ages. This encouraged the rise of new groups of merchants and artisans, and also new political institutions. The wealthiest and most influential cities were organized as representative republics; most prominent were the northern city-states of Florence, Siena, Pisa, and Venice. Tensions erupted frequently between aristocratic supporters of the emperor, and supporters of the mercantile parties, who allied themselves with the pope. In these northern cities, power tended to be concentrated in the hands of leading merchant families who had become wealthy through trade, manufacture, or banking. Members of these families would become the foremost patrons of artists in Italy.

Those artists developed their skills in a context that differed from the rest of Europe. Roman and Early Christian art served as an inspiration for medieval Italian architects and sculptors, as is visible in such works as the cathedral of Pisa. Medieval Italy felt the effects of both western imperial forces, such as those of the Holy Roman Emperor Frederick II (1194–1250), who lived for a time in southern Italy, and the eastern Byzantine empire, with whom Italian cities traded. Added to these influences was the French Gothic style, introduced through the travels of artists, scholars, and patrons.

One of those travelers, the churchman, scholar, and poet Francesco Petrarch (1304–1374), exemplifies another aspect of fourteenth-century Italian culture: A growing interest in the creative works of individuals. Petrarch and his contemporaries, Dante Alighieri (1265–1321) and Giovanni Boccaccio (1313–1375), belonged to a generation of thinkers and writers who turned to the study of ancient works of literature, history, and art to seek out beautiful and correct forms. Petrarch also sought to improve the quality of written Latin, and thereby to emulate the works of the Roman authors Vergil and Cicero. This study of ancient thought and art led to a search for moral clarity and models of behavior, a philosophy that came to be known as **humanism**. Humanists valued the works of the ancients, both in the literary and the visual arts, and they looked to the classical past for solutions to modern problems. They particularly admired Roman writers who championed civic and personal virtues, such as service to the State and stoicism in times of trouble.

The study of the art of Rome and Greece would profoundly change the culture and the art of Europe by encouraging artists to look at nature carefully and to consider the human experience as a valid subject for art. These trends found particular encouragement in the ideals and theology of the **mendicant** religious orders, that is, those who lived by collecting alms rather than owning property, such as the Dominicans, who valued classical learning, and the Franciscans, whose founder saw God in the beauty of Nature.

Map 12.1 Italy in the thirteenth and fourteenth centuries

The Cities and the Mendicants

As the lay populations increased in the rapidly growing cities, two major mendicant groups, the Franciscans and the Dominicans, established international "orders" to minister to them. Each order built urban churches where sermons could be preached to crowds of people. The Dominicans, founded by Dominic de Guzmán in 1216, were especially concerned with fighting heresy. The Franciscan order, founded by Francis of Assisi in 1209, worked in the cities to bring deeper spirituality and comfort to the poor. Taking vows of poverty, Franciscans were committed to teaching the laity and to encouraging them to pursue spiritual growth. Toward this goal, they told stories and used images to explain and affirm the teachings of the Church. Characteristically, Franciscans urged the faithful to visualize events such as the Nativity in tangible ways, such as setting up Nativity scenes (*crèches*) in churches as an aid to devotion.

Franciscan Churches and Altarpieces

Franciscan churches began to appear all over Italy as the friars ministered to the spiritual lives of city dwellers. A typical example in Florence is the church of Santa Croce (Holy Cross), begun around 1295 (**fig. 12.1**). The architect was probably the

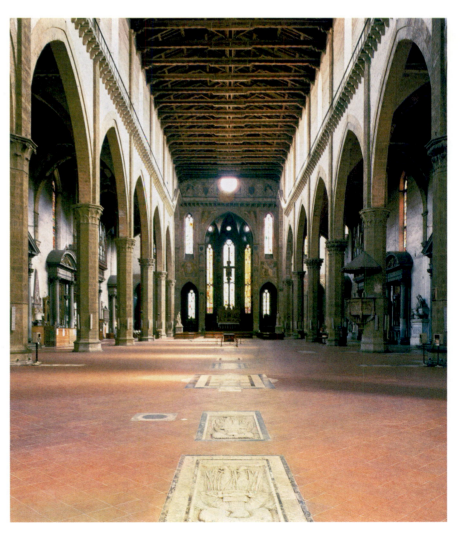

12.1 Nave and choir of Santa Croce. Begun ca. 1295. Florence

Tuscan sculptor Arnolfo di Cambio (ca. 1245–1302). Santa Croce shares some features with Gothic churches in northern Europe, but has some distinctively Italian elements. Its proportions are broad rather than vertical and the nave wall remains fairly unbroken. The nave arcade uses a Gothic pointed arch, while vertical moldings pull the eye up to the ceiling. Where one might expect the moldings to support a vaulted ceiling, however, Santa Croce uses wooden trusses to span the nave. The only vaults are at the apse and several chapels at the ends of the transepts, where Gothic windows pierce the wall. The architect could have covered the entire nave with vaults, so the choice to use wood seems deliberate. Recalling that the nearby Romanesque cathedral of Pisa has a wooden ceiling, we might recognize a regional preference for this kind of roof. Santa Croce's broad nave with high arches also reminds us of Early Christian basilicas, such as Old Saint Peter's (see fig. 8.2). The choice of a wooden ceiling may have sprung from a desire to evoke the simplicity of Early Christian basilicas and thus link Franciscan poverty with the traditions of the early Church.

Somewhat smaller churches were built for use by the female branch of the Franciscans, called Poor Clares, after their founder, St. Clare.

12.2 *Altarpiece of St. Clare.* ca. 1280. Tempera on panel, 9 × 5½' (2.73 × 1.65 m). Convent of Santa Chiara, Assisi, Italy

ALTARS are tables, or sometimes low stones, that are the focal point of religious worship, and are often the site of sacrificial rites. They have been found at most Neolithic sites and are virtually universal. The Christian altar traditionally is a narrow stone "table" that contains bone fragments of a martyr within it (Protestants do not have this requirement) and a prescribed set of liturgical objects used in the rite of Eucharist performed on the top surface (the *mensa*). The altar frontal (*antependium*) may be plain or decorated.

An ALTARPIECE is not an altar, but is placed behind or at the back of the altar table. Early altarpieces were wingless, with painted or carved images in the shrine section and more images in the predella zone below the shrine. Winged altarpieces were developed in the twelfth century: The wings allow the imagery to change according to the Church calendar.

12.3. *Nativity*, detail of the pulpit by Nicola Pisano. 1259–1260. Marble, height of pulpit 15′ (4.6 m). Baptistery, Pisa, Italy

The church and convent she founded are still in service in Assisi in central Italy, where an early example of an ALTARPIECE remains in place (**fig. 12.2**). A tall rectangle of wood, painted in TEMPERA, in which the pigment is bound with egg yolk, the altarpiece was executed around 1280. It is dominated by the figure of St. Clare, dressed in the habit of her order, standing frontally and holding the staff of an abbess. Rather than a portrait with specific features, Clare's face has the large eyes and geometric arrangement of a Byzantine Madonna (see fig. 8.21), while her figure seems to exist in one plane. She is flanked on either side by eight tiny narratives that tell the story of her life, death, and miracles. Sitting on the ALTARS of churches, such images taught viewers about the approved route to salvation and aided devotion.

Urban Churches, Baptisteries, and Civic Buildings

The growing city populations needed churches with large interior spaces and special structures for the baptism of their congregations. For these, churchmen often commissioned monumental pulpits with narrative or symbolic images carved onto them to focus attention during readings of scripture or preaching. A family of sculptors who worked in Pisa, headed by Nicola Pisano (ca. 1220/25–1284), made such large pulpits a

specialty. Having spent time in Naples and in Rome, Nicola had first-hand knowledge of ancient and Early Christian art. For the baptistery of Pisa, he executed an imposing marble pulpit, which was finished around 1260. The hexagonal structure rises to about 15 feet high, and boasts colored marble columns, classically inspired capitals, and small carved figures who represent Virtues. The six rectangular sides contain narratives, carved in relief. One of them is the *Nativity* (**fig. 12.3**), a densely crowded composition that combines the Annunciation with the Birth of Christ. The relief is treated as a shallow box filled with solid convex shapes in the manner of Roman sarcophagi.

Nicola probably knew Byzantine images of the Nativity, for his iconography reflects that tradition. As the largest and most central figure, the reclining Virgin overpowers all the other elements in the composition. Nicola includes many details of the narrative or setting, such as the midwives washing the child and Joseph's wondering gaze, which bring the historical events closer to a viewer's own experience. Yet the classicizing draperies and dignified figures give the scene gravity and significance.

FLORENCE CATHEDRAL Commissioning large and expensive buildings and artistic projects was one means by which Italian cities competed with each other. East of Pisa along the Arno, the

Italian painting of the thirteenth and fourteenth century was dominated by fresco and tempera. Fresco (see page 143) is a wall painting technique that was known in antiquity. Pigment is mixed with water and applied to a surface of wet plaster. The pigment bonds permanently with the plaster. The TEMPERA used in Italy at this period was a mixture of pigment and an emulsion of egg yolk and water. It was applied to wood panels that were first prepared with a coat of gesso (ground plaster or chalk and glue) and underpainted in green or brown.

12.4 Florence Cathedral and Baptistery seen from the air. Cathedral begun 1296

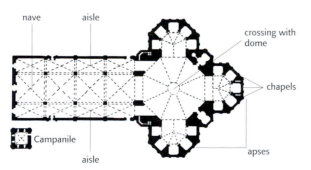

12.5 Plan of Florence Cathedral and campanile

increasing wealth of Florence inspired its citizens to undertake major projects for its cathedral and baptistery (**fig. 12.4**). Arnolfo di Cambio designed a new cathedral for Florence to replace a smaller church that once stood on the site. This project took the skills and energy of several generations. The work, begun in 1296, continued through the fifteenth century as the plan grew larger and more ambitious. The west façade and other portals continued to be adorned with sculpture throughout the Renaissance period, but the marble exterior was not completed until the nineteenth century. Florence's *Duomo* was intended to be a grand structure that would not only serve as the spiritual center of the city, but as a statement of its wealth and importance.

Arnolfo's design was for a broad basilica with a high arcade and trussed wooden roof like Santa Croce. This was later altered to include ribbed groin vaults like northern Gothic buildings. By the mid-fourteenth century the east end of the basilica (see plan, **fig. 12.5**) had been enlarged, to terminate in three faceted arms supporting an octagonal crossing that would be covered by a dome. (This design for the cathedral is depicted in the fresco in fig. 12.13.) The scale of the proposed dome presented engineering difficulties that were not solved until the early fifteenth

century. Instead of tall western towers incorporated into the façade, the cathedral has a freestanding *campanile* or bell tower in the Italian tradition. The Gothic elements of pointed arches and high vaults are tempered by local preference.

BAPTISTERY Opposite the *Duomo* stands the octagonal Baptistery of Florence, built in the eleventh century on older foundations. John the Baptist is the patron saint of Florence, so the Baptistery is a focal point of civic pride. To enhance this important structure, the overseers of the Baptistery commissioned Andrea Pisano (ca. 1295–1348; no relation to Nicola) to create new doors for it. These were finished and installed in 1336 (**fig. 12.6**). Cast in bronze and

12.6 Andrea Pisano. South doors, Baptistery of San Giovanni. 1330–1336. Gilt bronze. Florence

gilded, these expensive doors are adorned by 28 separate panels, mostly representing scenes from the life of the Baptist in clearly laid out narratives. Each vignette is framed by a Gothic quatrefoil, such as those found on the exteriors of French cathedrals, though the overall effect is very symmetrical and more legible than many portals elsewhere in Europe.

PALAZZO DELLA SIGNORIA In addition to churches and baptisteries, Italian cities commissioned buildings to house their governing bodies. In Florence, the Palazzo della Signoria, also known as the Palazzo Vecchio (**fig. 12.7**), served this function. Again the work of Arnolfo di Cambio, it was begun in 1298 and completed in 1310, though it was later expanded and remodeled.

The tall, blocky structure, similar to fortified castles in the region, has walls that are solid at the lowest level, and the surface is **rusticated**, left uneven and rugged, to look even stronger. The three stories of the structure are topped by heavy battlements and surmounted by a tall tower that serves as both a symbol of civic pride and a defensive structure. Boasting the highest tower in the city, the Palazzo della Signoria dominated the skyline of Florence and expressed the power and independence of the city.

New Directions in Tuscan Painting

The stylistic beginnings of Italian painting, like those of other art forms in the thirteenth century, are different from those of the rest of Europe. Painters in Italy had access to models from Rome and Byzantium that were not available elsewhere, and these inspired them to create monumental images and render forms in naturalistic terms. Access to Roman sculpture and relief, if not to Roman painting, provided Italian artists with lessons in creating weighty and solid-looking figures. Many Early Christian and Byzantine mosaics and frescoes survived to supply models for translating Christian narratives into memorable compositions, while architectural traditions provided wall surfaces for fresco painting throughout the Middle Ages. Fresh impetus for the development of Italian painting came from an influx of Byzantine art forms and artists in the thirteenth century, as a result of the Crusades. Indeed, the first historians of Italian art, among them Giorgio Vasari (1511–1574), located the beginning of Italian Renaissance style in the study of the "Greek manner," or Byzantine art. Italian artists were able to absorb the Byzantine tradition far more thoroughly in the thirteenth century than ever before. When Gothic style began to influence artists working in this Byzantinizing tradition, a revolutionary synthesis was accomplished by a generation of innovative and productive painters in Tuscan cities, including Giotto, Duccio and Ambrogio Lorenzetti.

Giotto and the New Florentine Painting

Florentine artists were central to this new synthesis, especially Giotto di Bondone (1267–1336/7). Mentioned in Dante's *Divine Comedy* and honored by his home town, Giotto was famous in his own time, and extremely important to the development of Italian painting. His

12.7 Palazzo della Signoria (Palazzo Vecchio). Begun 1298. Florence innovative style was formed through his knowledge of Byzantine traditions, the Early Christian frescoes of Rome, and the sculptural achievement of Nicola Pisano and his followers. His largest projects were monumental fresco cycles.

THE ARENA CHAPEL The best-preserved example of his work is in the Scrovegni Chapel in Padua, next to the palace of the banker Enrico Scrovegni, which he painted in 1305 and 1306 (**fig. 12.8**). (It is also known as the Arena Chapel because of its proximity to a Roman arena.) The structure itself is a one-room hall covered with a barrel vault (see page 126). Its limited windows left plenty of wall surface, which Giotto and his workshop painted from floor to ceiling in the fresco technique. A blue field with gold stars symbolic of heaven dominates the barrel vault, below which the walls are divided into three registers or horizontal rows. Each register contains rectangular fields for narrative scenes devoted mainly to the life of Christ. The scheme begins at the altar end with the Annunciation and culminates in the Last Judgment at the west end of the chapel. Along the length of the wall, the top register depicts stories of the early life of Mary and her parents; the center register focuses on stories of Christ's public life and miracles; and the lowest register depicts his Passion, Death, and Resurrection. Below the narratives the walls

12.9 Giotto. *The Lamentation*. 1305–1306. Fresco. Arena (Scrovegni) Chapel, Padua, Italy *Northern Renaissance*

are painted to resemble marble panels interspersed with statues symbolizing the virtues and vices.

Giotto turned each of the rectangular fields into a distinct narrative moment; at the same time, the whole program of paintings is a unity expressing a complex theological statement. The frescoes tell the story of salvation, from the incarnation of Christ to his sacrificial death and his predicted return at the end of time. Geometric bands that mimic mosaic frame each scene, while quatrefoils with small narrative scenes in them separate each story. These smaller narratives comment on the main story. One of the most memorable of these paintings depicts the Lamentation, the moment of last farewell between the dead Christ and his mother and friends (**fig. 12.9**). Although this event does not appear in the Gospels, by the end of the Middle Ages versions of it had appeared in both Byzantine and in Western medieval art (see fig. 11.25).

Giotto depicts this moment in truly revolutionary terms. Each figure is conceived as a separate geometric body, rendered as a three-dimensional shape by the light washing over it.

Each naturalistically rendered figure inhabits space as the mourners gather to witness Christ's death. The figures are arranged close to the **picture plane**, so that they dominate the foreground. (The picture plane is the theoretical plane suggested by the actual surface of a painting, drawing or relief.) The bodies overlap each other or stand behind each other and displace so much volume that they create the illusion of space in the painting. Giotto does not suggest a deep space, but a stage on which his actors can move to express the tragic narrative.

Little extraneous detail invades the scene: Even the landscape is reduced to the downward slope of a hill behind the mourners. Nothing allows the viewer's eye to avoid the anguish on the faces of Christ's followers, all of whom look toward the heads of Christ and the Virgin, together the focal point of the scene. The low center of gravity and the hunched figures convey the somber quality of the occasion, as do the cool colors and desolate sky. Giotto boldly contrasts the frozen grief of the human mourners with the frantic movement of the weeping angels among the clouds.

12.10 Giotto. *Madonna Enthroned*. ca. 1310. Tempera on panel, 10'8" × 6'8" (3.3 × 2 m). Galleria degli Uffizi, Florence

The composition is deceptively simple, yet profoundly moving. Even nature seems to participate in the sorrow over Christ's death, as a barren tree stands alone at the crest of the hill. Yet the tree also refers to the Tree of Knowledge of Good and Evil, which the sin of Adam and Eve had caused to wither and which Christians believed would be restored to life through Christ's sacrificial death. Further symbolic enrichment of the narrative appears in the frame element to the left, where the Old Testament prophet Jonah falls into the whale. The juxtaposition of the two themes draws an analogy between Jonah's three days in the body of the whale and Christ's three days in the tomb, as did many Early Christian images (see fig. 8.1).

OGNISSANTI MADONNA Giotto's inventive compositions, combining deeply felt human emotion with strong theological import, established his fame among his contemporaries. Shortly after completing these frescoes he was hired to paint an altarpiece of the *Madonna Enthroned* for the Church of All Saints (*Ognissanti*) in Florence (**fig. 12.10**). Completed by 1310, in tempera (see page 273), the altarpiece depicts the Queen of Heaven and her son enthroned among angels against a gold background. This is a theme depicted in Byzantine paintings and French Gothic sculpture (see fig. 8.21), though once again Giotto gives the figures great weight and solidity. The Virgin's deep blue robe and huge scale bring a viewer's eye directly to her and to the Christ Child on her lap. All the other figures gaze at them, both signaling and heightening their importance. Giotto renders the figures bathed in light, recording a gradual movement from light into dark, so that the figures are molded as three-dimensional objects. Compared to the Byzantine prototypes, Giotto depicts earth-bound figures of the Mother and Child.

The throne itself, based on Italian Gothic architecture, encloses the Madonna on three sides, setting her apart from the golden background. The possibility of space is further suggested by the overlapping figures, who seem to stand behind one another. This celestial assembly offers a glimpse of the court of the Queen of Heaven, for citizens building a new cathedral in her honor. Giotto continued to work in Florence for 30 years after completing this altarpiece, in 1334 being named the architect of the Florentine cathedral, for which he designed the bell tower. His influence over the next generation of painters was inescapable.

Sienese Painting

Giotto's slightly older contemporary, Duccio di Buoninsegna of Siena (ca. 1255–before 1319), directed another busy and influential workshop in the neighboring Tuscan city of Siena. The city competed with Florence on a number of fronts—military, economic, and cultural—and fostered a distinct identity and visual tradition. The Sienese attributed to the Virgin their victory in a key battle; once they established a republic, directed by the *Nove* (the Nine), Siena took the Virgin Mary as its protector and patron, and dedicated its thirteenth-century cathedral to her. The directors of the cathedral honored Duccio by commissioning him to paint a large altarpiece for the high altar, called the *Maestà* as it depicts the Virgin and Child in majesty (**fig. 12.11**). On its back and parts of the front, the altarpiece bears images from the life of Christ and the Virgin, and figures of prophets.

On the front panel of the altarpiece Duccio creates a regal image on a large scale. Members of her court surround the enthroned Virgin and Child in a carefully balanced arrangement of saints and angels. She is by far the largest and most impressive figure, swathed in the rich blue reserved for her by contemporary practice. Siena's other patron saints kneel in the first row, each gesturing and gazing at her. The bodies,

12.11 Duccio. *Madonna Enthroned*, center of the *Maestà Altar*. 1308–1311. Tempera on panel, height 6′10½″ (2.1 m). Museo dell'Opera del Duomo, Siena

12.12 Ambrogio Lorenzetti. *The Allegory of Good Government* (left), *Good Government in the City*, and portion of *Good Government in the Country* (right). 1338–1340. Fresco. Sala della Pace, Palazzo Pubblico, Siena

faces, and hands of the many figures seem to swell with three-dimensional life as the painter explores the fall of light on their forms. Like Giotto, Duccio knew Byzantine painting, with its heritage of Hellenistic–Roman illusionism. Nonetheless, Duccio's work also reflects contemporary Gothic sensibilities in the fluidity of the drapery, the appealing naturalness of the figures, and the glances by which the figures communicate with each other.

Duccio's style is distinct from Giotto's. The drapery worn by Duccio's figures falls in complex, curving patterns, rather than the plain volumes of Giotto's figures; compare the figures of the Christ Child in Duccio's *Maestà* (fig. 12.11) and Giotto's *Madonna Enthroned* (fig. 12.10). Where Giotto strives for a believable spatial context for his figures, Duccio aims for splendor and magnificent color. Commissioned in 1308, the *Maestà* was installed in the cathedral in 1311 amidst processions and celebrations in the city. Duccio's signature at the base of the throne expresses his pride in the work: "Holy Mother of God, be the cause of peace to

Siena, and of life to Duccio because he has painted you thus."

GOOD AND BAD GOVERNMENT Duccio's workshop trained many painters of the next generation. Ambrogio Lorenzetti was a Sienese artist who nonetheless spent time in Florence, where he came under the influence of Giotto. He combined the brilliant color and elegance of Duccio with the robust naturalism of Giotto in a major project for the city hall of Siena, executed between 1338 and 1340. For their meeting hall, the ruling Council of Nine commissioned an allegorical fresco contrasting good and bad government. Members of the council would be inspired by these images, for, as they deliberated, they would see in these frescoes the effects of both (**fig. 12.12**). Although the fresco of Bad Government has been severely damaged, those depicting the positive example of Good Government are remarkably well preserved. On the short wall of the room, Ambrogio depicted *The Allegory of Good Government* as an assembly of virtues who support the large enthroned personification of the city. To the left another enthroned figure personifies Justice, who is inspired by Wisdom. Below the virtues stand 24 Sienese judges under the guidance of Concord. On the long wall, the fresco of *Good Government in the City* bears an inscription praising Justice and the many benefits that derive from her.

To express this idea, Ambrogio paints an architectural portrait of the city of Siena. In his fresco depicting the life of a well ordered citystate, the artist fills the streets and houses with teeming activity. The bustling crowd gives the architectural vista its striking reality by introducing the human scale. On the right, outside the city walls, *Good Government in the Country* provides a view of the Sienese countryside, fringed by distant mountains and overseen by a personification of Security. It is a true landscape—the first since ancient Roman times. The scene is full of sweeping depth, yet differs from classical landscapes in its orderliness, which gives it a domesticated air. The people here have taken full possession of nature: They have terraced the hillsides with vineyards and patterned the valleys with the geometry of fields and pastures. The peasants at their seasonal labors work toward the health and prosperity of Siena.

Late Fourteenth-Century Crises

Ambrogio's ideal vision of the city and its surroundings expresses the way in which the citizens of Siena imagined their government and their city at a moment of peace and prosperity. The first three decades of the fourteenth century in Siena, as in Florence, had been a period of political stability and economic expansion, as well as of great artistic achievement. In the 1340s, however, both cities suffered a series of catastrophes, the effects of which were to be felt for many years.

Upheaval and Plague

Constant warfare led scores of banks and merchants into bankruptcy; internal upheavals shook governments, and there were repeated crop failures and famine. Then, in 1348, the pandemic of bubonic plague—the Black Death—that spread throughout Europe wiped out more than half the population of the two cities. Popular reactions to these events were mixed. Many people saw them as signs of divine wrath, warnings to a sinful humanity to forsake the pleasures of this earth. For them, the Black Death intensified an interest in religion and the promise of heavenly rewards. For others, such as the merry company who entertain each other by telling stories in Boccaccio's *Decameron*, the fear of death intensified the desire to enjoy life while there was still time.

Among the many thousands of people who perished of the Black Death was probably Ambrogio Lorenzetti. The abrupt loss of many promising artists was but one of the effects of the plague. Worried about their mortality, patrons were even more concerned to endow chapels, tombs, and funeral Masses to ensure their souls' eternal health. Many such burials and endowments were made in mendicant churches, such as the Franciscan Santa Croce and the Dominican Santa Maria Novella in Florence.

THE WAY OF SALVATION One Florentine merchant who lived through these difficult times built such a chapel. Buonamico Guidalotti, who died in 1355, paid for a new meeting room for the Dominican community at Santa Maria Novella, which also served as his burial chapel. Because the chapel was used by the friars, it was painted with frescoes articulating their order's role in the struggle for salvation. A fresco on one of the walls, painted by Andrea Bonaiuti (also known as Andrea da Firenze, active 1346–1379) between 1365 and 1367, depicts the actions of Dominicans to assure the access of the faithful to heaven; hence its title, *The Way of Salvation* (**fig. 12.13**). In the lower section of the fresco, spiritual and secular leaders gather in a space identifiable as Florence by the representation of the then unfinished cathedral. Groups of Dominicans preach to the laity and convert heretics, amidst black and white dogs (a punning reference to the order—*Domini canes*, dogs of the Lord). On the upper right some heedless aristocrats enjoy the pleasures of the senses, while, at the center, a Dominican shows the more spiritually minded the path to heaven, whose gate is guarded by St. Peter. Andrea's fresco reveals the influence of Ambrogio Lorenzetti's *Good Government* in its symmetry and sense of order. But where Ambrogio's fresco celebrates the well ordered earthly city, Andrea's fresco shows the viewer the steps to heavenly bliss.

Despite the view shown here, Florence did not complete its cathedral in the fourteenth century. Nor did the city enjoy the calm atmosphere portrayed in Andrea's fresco. The plague

12.13 Andrea da Firenze. *The Way of Salvation*. 1365–1367. Fresco, 38′ (11.6 m) wide. Guidalotti Chapel, Santa Maria Novella, Florence

returned in 1363, the political elite clashed with the papacy, and an uprising among the working classes created social and economic turmoil. Florence overcame these crises to flourish in the fifteenth century as a center of economic energy, political astuteness, and cultural leadership. As the century began, a new generation of Florentine artists would look to the art of Giotto and his contemporaries in their search for new forms of visual expression.

Northern Italy: Milan

Although also wracked by the plague, the other cities of northern Italy experienced a somewhat different situation in the fourteenth century. Unlike Florence, the city of Venice enjoyed a political stability that enhanced its wealth. West of Venice in the rich agricultural region of Lombardy, the city of Milan was ruled by a family with great dynastic ambitions. Having taken

control of Milan, the Visconti positioned themselves among the great families of Europe through marriage ties to members of the Italian and European nobility. By 1395, Giangaleazzo Visconti had been named duke of Milan, had married the daughter of the king of France, and wed his daughter to a French duke.

Giangaleazzo used the visual arts as tools to celebrate his status. Like French aristocrats, he commissioned elaborate illuminated manuscripts with numerous personal references. His *Book of Hours* was painted around 1395 by Giovannino dei Grassi (active ca. 1380–1398). The page in figure **12.14** begins one of the Psalms with an illuminated initial D, wherein King David appears. David is both the author of the Psalms and a good biblical exemplar of a ruler, appropriate for the duke. The page is studded with coats of arms and other Visconti emblems. An unfurling ribbon ornamented with the

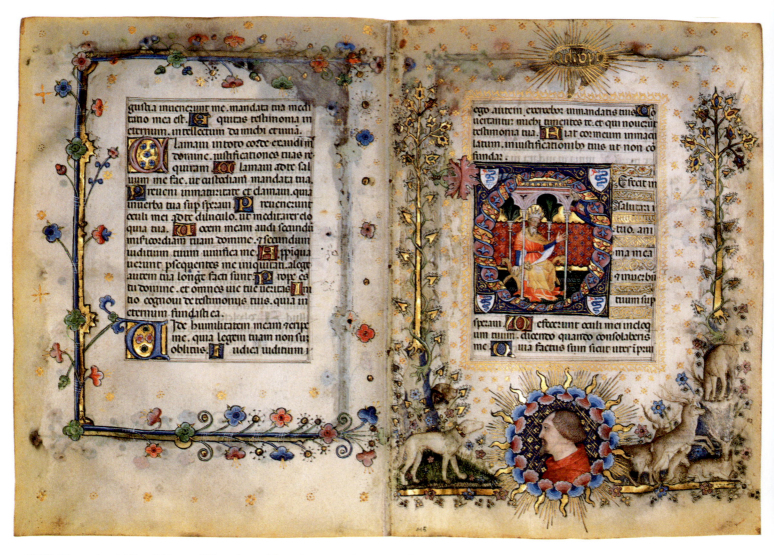

12.14 Giovannino dei Grassi. *Hours of Giangaleazzo Visconti*. ca. 1395. Tempera and gold on parchment, 9¾" × 6⅞" (24.7 × 17.5 cm) Banco Rari, Biblioteca Nazionale, Florence

French *fleur-de-lis* forms the D; shields at the corners bear the Visconti emblem of the viper. Below the text appears a portrait of Giangaleazzo in the profile arrangement familiar from ancient coins. Although this portrait is naturalistic, it is set into an undulating frame that supports the rays of the sun, another Visconti emblem. Around the portrait Giovannino has painted images of stags and a hunting dog, with great attention to the accurate rendering of these natural forms. Such flashes of realism set amidst the splendor of the page reflect both the patron's and the artist's contribution to the developing International Gothic style. Commissioning such lavish books was an expression of the status and power that Giangaleazzo attempted to wield. His ambition to bring most of northern Italy under his control would profoundly affect the arts in Tuscany in the early fifteenth century.

SUMMARY

Thirteenth- and fourteenth-century Italian art had its roots in both Byzantine forms and Italian artists' contacts with Roman and Early Christian precedents. Although its political situation was dominated by contests between the Holy Roman Emperor and the papacy, it was in Italian cities, which were centers for trade, that new wealth accumulated. As a result, Italian art is often the product of commissions by communities of merchants and urban patricians rather than great aristocratic patrons. The activity of the mendicant orders (chiefly the Franciscans and Dominicans) inspired a new spirituality in these urban centers; their vivid preaching accompanied commissions of narrative imagery to speak directly to their lay audience.

One product of the mendicants' mission to preach was the building of large urban churches where sermons could be delivered, such as at Santa Croce in Florence. These structures took advantage of northern Gothic innovations that allowed for large interior spaces and tall proportions. Inside these churches, painted and sculpted forms enhanced worshipers' experience by representing sacred stories in direct and legible terms. In altarpieces and on pulpits, artists in Italy made narrative scenes of holy figures in human situations to stimulate the devotion of city dwellers and teach them their proper doctrine.

As elsewhere, Italian cities like Florence built cathedrals and other ecclesiastical structures, but often these followed local preferences for wooden roofs, solid wall surfaces, and façades without towers. For their citizens, painters developed new techniques to represent the natural world. Fourteenth-century Italian painters explored ways to create images that more closely reflected nature than had earlier medieval art. This generation of artists explored techniques for consistently representing the fall of light on three-dimensional forms and for creating the illusion of space within their paintings, as Giotto did in his Arena Chapel frescoes. These techniques were used to enhance the spiritual impact of the sacred figures they painted and to tell sacred stories more effectively. The innovations of fourteenth-century painters like Giotto and Duccio provided a visual language of naturalism from which artists all over Europe could profit. Municipal patrons commissioned naturalistic imagery to celebrate their accomplishments, and among these commissions was Ambrogio Lorenzetti's *Allegory of Good Government* in Siena.

Changes in the political and economic situation in Italy changed the forms of art produced later in the century. The plague and other catastrophes encouraged patrons to endow burial chapels, and to think about the afterlife. This is the function of the Guidalotti chapel in Florence. The Visconti family in the northern Italian city of Milan commissioned sumptuous books with naturalistic miniatures such as the Hours of Giangaleazzo Visconti to express their new ducal status.

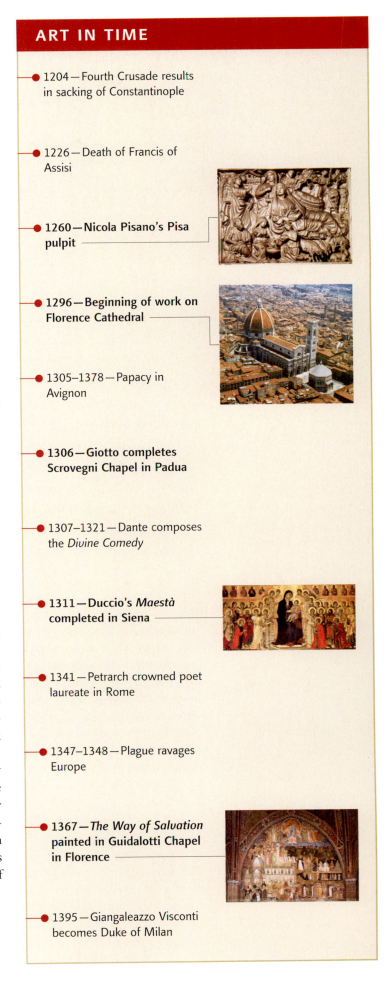

ART IN TIME

- 1204 — Fourth Crusade results in sacking of Constantinople

- 1226 — Death of Francis of Assisi

- **1260 — Nicola Pisano's Pisa pulpit**

- **1296 — Beginning of work on Florence Cathedral**

- 1305–1378 — Papacy in Avignon

- **1306 — Giotto completes Scrovegni Chapel in Padua**

- 1307–1321 — Dante composes the *Divine Comedy*

- **1311 — Duccio's *Maestà* completed in Siena**

- 1341 — Petrarch crowned poet laureate in Rome

- 1347–1348 — Plague ravages Europe

- **1367 — *The Way of Salvation* painted in Guidalotti Chapel in Florence**

- 1395 — Giangaleazzo Visconti becomes Duke of Milan

13 | Artistic Innovations in Fifteenth-Century Northern Europe

*T*he great cathedrals of Europe's Gothic era—the products of collaboration among churchmen, rulers and the laity—were mostly completed by 1400. As monuments of Christian faith, they exemplify the medieval outlook. But cathedrals are also monuments of cities, where major social and economic changes would set the stage for the modern world. As the fourteenth century came to an end, the medieval agrarian economy was giving way to an economy based on manufacturing and trade, enterprises that took place in urban centers. A social shift accompanied this economic change. Many city dwellers belonged to the middle class, whose upper ranks enjoyed literacy, leisure, and disposable income. With these advantages, the middle classes gained greater social influence and cultural significance than they had enjoyed previously. This transformation had a profound effect on European culture, including the development of the visual arts.

Cities such as Paris, London, Prague, Bruges, Barcelona, and Basel (see map 13.1) were home to artisans and merchants as well as aristocrats. Urban economies necessitated bankers, lawyers, and entrepreneurs. Investors seeking new products and markets encouraged technological innovations, such as the printing press, an invention that would change Europe. Trade put more liquid wealth into the hands of merchants and artisans, and thus emboldened them to seek more autonomy from the traditional aristocracy, who themselves sought to maintain the feudal *status quo*.

Two of the most far-reaching changes concerned increased literacy and changes in religious expression. During the fourteenth century, the removal of the papacy to Avignon and the election of two popes had created a schism in the Church that ended only in 1417. The reputation of the institutional Church suffered as a result. Many laypeople turned to religious movements that encouraged them to read and meditate on

sacred texts on their own, and to seek a personal relationship with God. These religious impulses and increasing literacy resulted in a demand for books in vernacular (local) languages, including translations of the scriptures. The printing press made books more readily available, further stimulating the development and spread of knowledge.

Political changes were shaping the modern boundaries of European nations. The end of the Hundred Years' War between France and England in 1453 allowed the French monarchy to recover, but civil war kept England politically unstable until late in the fifteenth century. French kings had to contend with their Burgundian cousins, who controlled the trading hub of northern Europe, the rich lands of Flanders in the Southern Netherlands (present-day Belgium) and the Northern Netherlands (present-day Holland). Indeed, Duke Philip the Good of Burgundy (r. 1419–1467) was one of the most powerful men of the century.

Map 13.1 Europe in the fifteenth century

To the east, in central Europe, the Holy Roman emperor had nominal control, but local rulers within this region often flouted his authority. On the Iberian peninsula, a crucial marriage between Queen Isabella of Castile and King Ferdinand of Aragon created a unified Spanish kingdom that became increasingly important. Competition among the powers of Europe for trade routes led to the exploratory voyages of Columbus, which would change the globe.

A new style of visual art that stressed naturalism accompanied these political and social changes. Aristocrats and churchmen continued to commission works, but the new ranks of society —bureaucrats and merchants—also became art patrons. For merchants and middle-class patrons in urban centers, painters made images in a new medium with a new character. Using oil paints, artists in the Netherlands produced works that still astonish viewers by their close approximation to optical reality. By mid-century, this strongly naturalistic style became the dominant visual language of northern Europe, attracting patrons from all classes and many countries.

This period of transition out of the Middle Ages was gradual and by no means universal. Faced with a growing middle class, the traditional aristocracy attempted to maintain its privileges and status. Among the aristocratic courts of France, the Holy Roman Empire, England, and the Burgundian Netherlands, many of which were linked by treaty or marriage, a preference emerged for a highly refined form of Gothic art. Yet within these courtly images were the seeds of the heightened naturalism that would blossom in the fifteenth century.

Courtly Art: The International Gothic

As the fourteenth century came to an end, aristocratic patrons throughout Europe displayed a taste for objects made of sumptuous materials with elegant forms based on the Gothic style. Cosmopolitan courts such as Avignon and Paris attracted artists from different regions of Europe where they exchanged ideas. These circumstances produced the elegant style termed International Gothic. The chronological limits of this style are somewhat fluid, as its products are dated between the mid-fourteenth and the mid-fifteenth century.

The refined style appeared in France, Flanders, Germany, Spain, Bohemia, Austria, England, and elsewhere. For their elite patrons, artists produced works of exquisite craftsmanship, often with very complex iconographies. Their forms share with the Gothic style a level of idealization and patterns based on geometry, visible in the *Virgin of Paris* (see fig. 11.18). Artists added to these forms touches of directly observed nature, especially in details. Some scholars have seen the detailed naturalism of the International Gothic as a stimulus to the more thoroughgoing naturalism of the early Flemish painters and their followers in the fifteenth century.

Members of the family of King Charles V of France were among the most active patrons of International Gothic. His brother, Philip the Bold, became duke of Burgundy and count of Flanders. The dukes of Burgundy became powerbrokers in the military and economic battles of the fifteenth century.

Artists at the French Courts

Fine works of art enhanced Philip's status, an example that was not lost on his successors. One of his projects was the founding of a Carthusian monastery, the Chartreuse de Champmol, outside Dijon in Burgundy. For the creation of this building, which was almost completely destroyed in the late eighteenth century, Philip assembled a team of artists, many of them from the Netherlands. Chief among them was the sculptor Claus Sluter (ca. 1350–1406) from Brussels.

THE WELL OF MOSES Sluter's work at the Chartreuse de Champmol includes portals, tombs, pulpits, and the so-called *Well of Moses* (**fig. 13.1**). This hexagonal well, surrounded by statues of

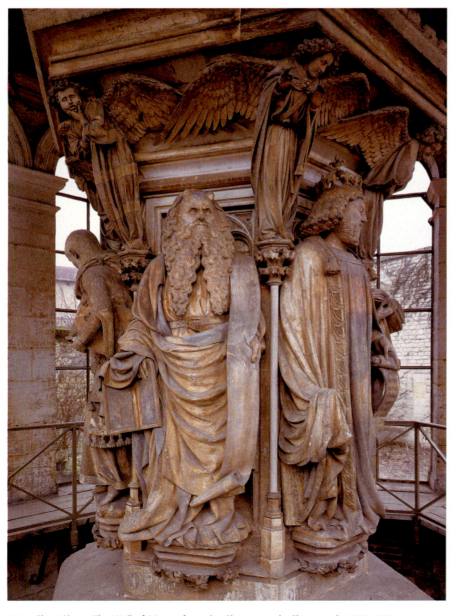

13.1 Claus Sluter. *The Well of Moses*, from the Chartreuse de Champmol. 1395–1406. Stone, height of figures approx. 6′ (1.8 m)

Old Testament prophets, was once topped by a crucifix, which expressed visually the fulfillment by the New Testament of the Old. The majestic Moses has a long, luxuriant beard and flowing drapery; his figure seems to reach out into the surrounding space to interact directly with the viewer. The lifelike quality and naturalistic rendering must have been enhanced greatly by colors added to the stone by the painter Jean Malouel; these have mostly disappeared. To Moses' right stands King David, whose features resemble a portrait. Sluter's naturalistic style is based on specific observations such as the texture of Moses' beard or the wings of the angels and the distinct characterizations of the six prophets.

LES TRÈS RICHES HEURES DU DUC DE BERRY Jean Malouel introduced to Philip his nephews Pol, Herman, and Jean de Limbourg. The crowning achievement of these three brothers is the luxurious Book of Hours known as *Les Très Riches Heures du Duc de Berry* (*The Very Rich Hours of the Duke of Berry*). This lavish book was produced for Jean, duke of Berry, brother of Philip the Bold and the most avid art patron of his day. The brothers shared an appointment as court painters to Duke Jean, reflecting the high regard they enjoyed. Their work reflects not only the idealization inherent in French Gothic art, but the naturalistic experiments of fourteenth-century Italy.

The *Très Riches Heures* was commissioned about 1413 and left unfinished when all three brothers died in 1416. The most famous pages are devoted to the calendar, depicting human activities and the cycles of nature. Such cycles, originally consisting of 12 single figures each performing an appropriate seasonal activity, were an established tradition in medieval art.

The calendar page for July (**fig. 13.2**) demonstrates the Limbourgs' innovative presentation of these themes. Time's passing is noted in several ways on the page. Astrological signs and numbers identify the month, while peasants harvesting wheat and shearing sheep perform the labor of the month. These activities occur below a precisely rendered image of Jean de Berry's Château du Clain (Poitiers), now destroyed. The page depicts the orderly harvesting of a fruitful earth by the peaceful peasantry. This idealized view of the social order of feudalism is achieved by combining the portrait of the castle and naturalistic details of the peasants' work with a space that rises up the picture plane like a tapestry. The

13.2 Limbourg Brothers. *Les Très Riches Heures du Duc de Berry*, calendar miniature for July. 1413–1416. Illumination on vellum, 8⅞ × 5⅜″ (22.5 × 3.7 cm). Musée Condé, Chantilly, France

jewel-like color and splashes of gold leaf in the calendar zone contribute to the sumptuous effect of the page. The prestige of the patron and the sheer innovation of the images, especially the calendar pages, in the *Très Riches Heures* inspired many later copies.

Urban Centers and the New Art

Many of the artists hired by aristocratic patrons for their projects came from the cities of the Southern Netherlands: Bruges, Brussels, Ghent, and Tournai. These towns were centers of international commerce where merchants from all over Europe gathered to do business. The cities were very jealous of their independent status, but their claims to independence often clashed with the aims of overlords who wished to control their inhabitants and their wealth. In addition to these social and economic shifts, the cities of Flanders witnessed the beginnings of an artistic revolution. Working either for courts or for middle-class citizens, artists began to make images in oil painting that represented sacred figures as if they existed in the natural world.

Robert Campin

An early pioneer of this naturalistic revolution was Robert Campin (1378–1444) of Tournai, an important trade center in southwestern Belgium. His most familiar work is the *Mérode Triptych* (**fig. 13.3**), dated to around 1425. The name derives from an early owner of the painting; the subject of the central panel is in fact the Annunciation.

Campin places the Virgin and the angel Gabriel in what appears to be the main room of a bourgeois house. The viewer has the sense of actually looking through the surface of the panel into a world that mimics reality. Campin uses several devices to create this effect. He fits the objects and figures into boxes of space, sometimes uncomfortably. He renders details in such a way as to make every object as concrete as possible in shape, size, color, and texture. He records with great sophistication the fall of light on the painted objects. He uses color to unify all three panels; his bright colors have richness and depth, and he achieves smooth transitions from lights into darks. Campin and his contemporaries expanded the possibilities of using oil paint on panels. Mixing pigments into slow-drying translucent oils allowed them to blend brushstrokes, add layers of color for greater depth and rework forms with great detail. The result is a more thorough illusion of reality than the flashes of natural detail seen in the work of court artists.

Campin catered to the tastes of his fellow citizens, such as the two donors piously kneeling outside the Virgin's chamber. Their identities are not known, but they were wealthy enough to commission this triptych, probably for their own dwelling, as it is too small for installation in a

13.3 Robert Campin. *Mérode Triptych*. ca. 1425–1430. Oil on panel, center 25³⁄₁₆ × 24⅞″ (64.3 × 62.9 cm); each wing approx. 25⅜ × 10⅞″ (64.5 × 27.4 cm). The Metropolitan Museum of Art, New York, The Cloisters Collection, 1956. 56.70

public church. Campin sets the Annunciation in a fully equipped domestic interior with figures that are rendered as real people, with mass and weight. The drapery of their garments falls in deep folds, anchoring the figures to the floor, as in the sculpture of Claus Sluter (see fig. 13.1). Gabriel's position is unclear: Is he standing or kneeling? His gesture and Mary's red dress draw attention to her as she sits on the floor, book in hand. Between them a table supports another book, a vase of lilies, and a candle. On the left wing, the donors kneel in a garden, as though looking through the open door to witness this event. Campin depicts substantial bodies in a recognizably earthly setting for the eyes of the donor couple. The event takes place in their world, not in heaven.

The right wing depicts Joseph, the carpenter, at work, though just what he is making has been a subject of debate. What is the boxlike object on the ledge outside the open window? Scholars have identified it as a mousetrap, an object that the Christian theologian St. Augustine used metaphorically to explain God's plan for salvation when he said, "The Cross of the Lord was the devil's mousetrap." The mousetrap could be a visual clue to the reason for Christ's incarnation, which is about to occur in the central panel. Equally puzzling is the object in Joseph's hand, identified by some scholars as a fire screen (like the one in the central panel) and by others as part of a winepress (with Eucharistic meaning).

Such carefully chosen details have been read as symbols that convey spiritual messages. The flowers, for example, are associated with the Virgin, as emblems of her purity. The smoking candle next to the vase of lilies is more perplexing, and its symbolism obscure. The appearance in Campin's picture of so many carefully delineated objects suggests that these details constitute a symbolic program, which either the artist or the patron conceived. Did Campin consult theologians for these complex symbols? Even if he did, it was he who found the means to express these ideas using forms observed in the visible world.

The Annunciation has important liturgical and theological import, but it is also a story about the conception of a child. From the perspective of the couple in the left wing, the triptych may be a celebration of their own desire for children or their reverence for the Holy Family as a model for their own. Such personalized approaches to holy figures and sacred dramas were an important feature of religious life at the end of the Middle Ages. Believers were encouraged through sermons, by Passion plays, and in written texts to visualize the sacred in terms they could understand and to meditate on events from Christ's life. Artists like Campin may have been responding to the call to see the physical world as a mirror of divine truths and to create moving and pious images of sacred events occurring in everyday environments.

Jan van Eyck

Campin's contemporary Jan van Eyck (ca. 1399–1441) may well have known this picture. Famous in the fifteenth century, he is a figure about whom we know a good deal. He was born in Holland, in Maaseyck, and worked for the count of Holland before establishing his workshop in Bruges. Both a townsman and a court painter, Jan was highly esteemed by the duke of Burgundy, who sent him on several diplomatic errands. Unusually for his time, he signed and dated several surviving pictures.

GHENT ALTARPIECE Jan was working for townsmen when he completed the *Ghent Altarpiece*, which made his reputation as a painter. Large in scale and in a prominent location in the cathedral of Ghent, the altarpiece has drawn a crowd ever since it was installed. An inscription that once appeared on the frame identified Jan van Eyck as the artist who finished this multi-paneled altarpiece in May 1432; the inscription also alluded to the collaboration of his older brother, Hubert, who died in 1426. The basic form of this complex altarpiece is a TRIPTYCH—a central body with two hinged wings—the standard format of altarpieces in the Southern Netherlands, but here each of the three units consists of four panels. Since the wings are painted on both sides, the altarpiece has a total of 20 images of various shapes and sizes. Discontinuities among the many panels suggest that alterations took place as the work progressed. It appears that Jan took over a number of panels left unfinished by Hubert, completed them, added some of his own, and assembled the whole at the request of the wealthy donor, Jodicus Vijd, the mayor of Ghent. Vijd's portrait, with that of his wife, Elizabeth Borluut, appears on the outer panels of the altar when the triptych is closed (**fig. 13.4**).

They are portrayed on the lower tier with two other figures, each in a separate niche framed by Gothic tracery: The patrons of the cathedral, John the Baptist and John the Evangelist, painted in grisaille (a monochrome to imitate the color of statues). The upper tier has two

A TRIPTYCH has three fields for images, a diptych two. They can be fixed panels or wings that fold together and may be of any size.

Diptych

Triptych

pairs of panels of different widths. The artist has combined all four into one interior, whose fore-shortened timber ceiling extends across all four panels. Prophets and Sibyls occupy an upper story, their prophecies written in Gothic script in scrolls above their heads.

When the wings are opened (**fig. 13.5**) the viewer sees a detailed rendering of a celestial assembly. Across the bottom tier, groups of figures converge on a central image of an altar, upon which stands a haloed Lamb (Christ). This assembly includes angels, apostles, popes, theologians, virgin martyrs, hermits, pilgrims, knights, and judges. A verdant landscape provides the setting for this mystic Mass, with towers of numerous churches on the skyline. Above this earthly paradise reigns an imposing Court of Heaven, with the Lord in a bright red robe at the center. Flanking him are Mary and John the Baptist. To the left and right, choirs of angels sing and play musical instruments. At the outer edges of this upper tier stand Adam and Eve, rendered as nudes in shallow niches, below grisaille images of Abel and Cain. The almost life-size nudes are portrayed with careful attention to their anatomy, their forms caressed by a delicate play of light and shade.

The artist breathes life into the forms by rendering the textures and colors of the bodies with great accuracy. Seeing the triptych on the altar of

13.4 Hubert and Jan van Eyck. *Ghent Altarpiece* (closed). Completed 1432. Oil on panel, 11′5″ × 7′6″ (3.4 × 2.25 m). Cathedral of Saint Bavo, Ghent, Belgium

13.5 Hubert and Jan van Eyck. *Ghent Altarpiece* (open). 11′5″ × 15′1″ (3.4 × 4.5 m)

the Vijd Chapel in the Ghent cathedral, a viewer could not fail to be impressed by its scale and setting. The tone and majesty of this ensemble are very different from the domestic intimacy of the *Mérode Triptych*. The function of the altarpiece is to elucidate the liturgy performed in front of it. When open, its subject is the Mass itself, here shown in a paradisiacal setting. Jan's work is large in scale but full of naturally observed details and glowing color. His technique of building up color in layers of glazes gives a highly saturated result, while the slow methodical application of paint blends brushstrokes to a mirrorlike finish. The *Ghent Altarpiece* offers the devout viewer a glimpse into heaven.

THE "ARNOLFINI PORTRAIT" Van Eyck also made purely secular paintings, fulfilling the commissions of the court and of the citizens of Flemish towns. Another of his famous paintings represents a man and a woman standing in the richly furnished main room of a fifteenth-century house, equipped with a brass chandelier, a mirror, and a canopied bed (**fig. 13.6**). Jan signed

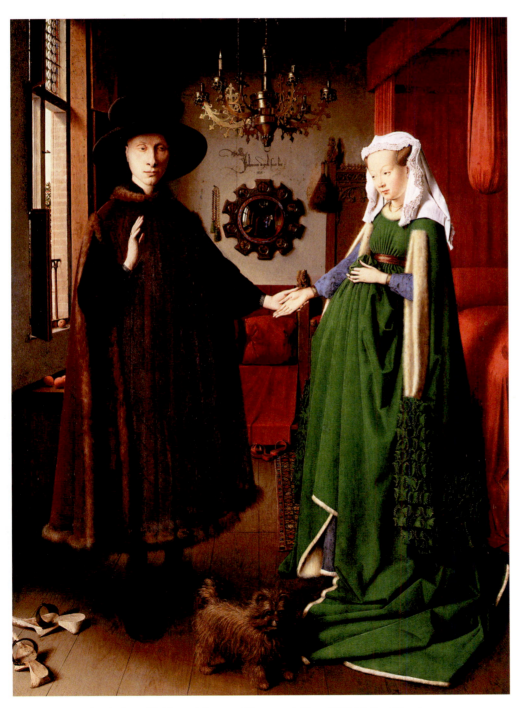

13.6 Jan van Eyck. *The "Arnolfini Portrait."* 1434. Oil on panel, 33 × 22½″ (83.7 × 57 cm). The National Gallery, London. Reproduced by Courtesy of the Trustees **Late Gothic**

the painting, not on the frame, as was his normal practice, but within the panel. Above the painted mirror, in a formal script, the translated signature reads, "Jan van Eyck was here, 1434." The features of the man, if not the lady, are specific enough to be a portrait, and the image is unusual enough for scholars to have used later documents to identify him as Giovanni Arnolfini, an Italian merchant living in Bruges. For many years scholars believed that his companion should be identified as Giovanna Cenami, Arnolfini's wife; recent research, however, makes this doubtful, as that marriage took place much later than 1434.

Whatever their names, the painted couple stand with hands joined, while the man raises his right hand as if in a solemn oath, seemingly quite alone. In the mirror behind them, however, is the reflection of two men who have entered the room. Because the signature appears right above the mirror, many scholars believe that one of these men must be Jan van Eyck himself, perhaps the figure wearing the red headdress. The combination of the signature, with its flourishes and phrasing, and the image of the men in the mirror suggests to some that Jan is acting as a witness to whatever is occurring in the room.

For many years scholars have argued that this panel depicts either the wedding or the engagement of the couple represented, either of which would have required a legal and financial contract between their two families. By this reading, the painting commemorates the union of the couple. If so, the second man in the mirror may be the bride's father, who would have made the contract for the marriage of his daughter. The woman's gesture of lifting her heavy gown may suggest her wish for children, as the bed behind her may suggest the consummation of the marriage. Given the work's secular nature, scholars have debated whether the realistic touches serve simply as an accurate record of an event and its domestic setting, or whether the details of the setting carry more symbolic weight. Is the little dog a beloved pet, or an emblem of fidelity? (*Fides* is Latin for faithfulness, the origin of the traditional dog name Fido.) The other furnishings of the room suggest other questions. Why does a candle in the chandelier burn in broad daylight? Why do pieces of fruit sit on the window sill? What is the function of the mirror? Tiny images of the Passion and Resurrection in the small medallions that surround the mirror sound the only unambiguously religious note. What was Jan's purpose in making this painting? For whom was it made? What function did it serve for the patron? The answers to these questions have become more controversial in recent interpretations, as scholars are now much less certain about the meaning of the image than they once were.

Rogier van der Weyden

As a court painter, Jan van Eyck had been exempt from the restrictions that governed other artists in Flemish towns. The training of artists and the market for works of art were both regulated by the GUILDS, professional organizations of artists established to protect the interests of their members. One illustrious graduate of the guild system was Rogier van der Weyden (1399/1400 –1464), a painter who trained with Robert Campin, but who certainly knew the work of Jan van Eyck. Rogier established a flourishing workshop in Brussels. His most influential work is the *Descent from the Cross* (**fig. 13.7**), which dates from about 1435. It was commissioned as the center of an altarpiece by the crossbowmen's guild of Louvain (near Brussels) for a church there. Rogier depicted the moment when the body of Christ is lowered from the cross, in a composition of mourners crowded into a shallow box. His forms are carefully modeled to suggest sculptural presence, and they are detailed enough to show every nuance of texture.

Rogier's goal is to increase the expressive content of his picture. He emphasizes the emotional impact of the event on its participants. Grief is etched on each figure's face, while their postures express their response to their loss. John the Evangelist on the left and Mary Magdalen on the right are bowed with grief. The Virgin's swoon echoes the pose and expression of her dead son. So intense are her pain and grief that they inspire the same compassion in a viewer. Rogier has staged his scene in a shallow niche or shrine, not against a landscape. This device focuses a viewer's attention on the figures. Furthermore, the emphasis on the body of Christ at the center of the composition alludes to the celebration of the Eucharist, which took place before the altarpiece. The source of these grief-stricken gestures and faces is in sculpture rather than in painting. The figures share the strong emotion of much Gothic sculpture, such as the Naumburg choir screen (fig. 11.24). Rogier's painting inspired many copies, in both painting and sculpture.

Works like Rogier's *Descent from the Cross* offered powerful examples for other artists to follow, in the Netherlands and beyond. As the fifteenth century progressed, the medium of

13.7 Rogier van der Weyden. *Descent from the Cross.* ca. 1435. Oil on panel, 7′2⅝″ × 8′7⅛″ (2.2 × 2.6 m). Museo del Prado, Madrid

painting gained in prestige among both urban and aristocratic patrons. Large-scale sculpture also found a market in the fifteenth-century Netherlands, though little has survived the ravages of war, social upheavals, and changes of taste.

Hugo van der Goes in Ghent

Among the very active patrons of painters in Flanders were international businessmen, who commissioned paintings as acts of piety, but also as markers of their social status. A good example of this phenomenon is a work by Hugo van der Goes (ca. 1440–1482). He was commissioned around 1474 by an agent of the Medici bank in Bruges to paint a huge altarpiece to be shipped to Florence (**fig. 13.8**). The 10-foot-wide central panel represents the Virgin, St. Joseph, and the

Shepherds adoring the newborn Christ Child in Bethlehem. In the wings, members of the donor family, including Tommaso Portinari, his wife, Maria Maddelena Baroncelli, and their children, kneel to face the central image. A spacious landscape unites all three wings as a continuous space, with the bare trees and December sky suggesting Flanders, not the Holy Land. Objects in the distance have turned the blue of the atmosphere; this use of atmospheric perspective infuses the panel with a cool tonality. Hugo fills this setting with figures and objects rendered with precise detail in deeply saturated colors.

Hugo's realistic rendering of both landscape and figures is contradicted by variations in the sizes of the figures. The angels and kneeling members of the Portinari family are dwarfed by the other figures; the patron saints in the wings

13.8 Hugo van der Goes. *The Portinari Altarpiece* (open). ca. 1474–1476. Tempera and oil on panel, center 8′3½″ × 10′ (2.5 × 3.1 m), each wing 8′3½″ × 4′7½″ (2.5 × 1.4 m). Galleria degli Uffizi, Florence

are the same size as Joseph, the Virgin Mary, and the shepherds of the Nativity in the center panel. This change of scale contradicts the pictorial space that the artist has provided for his figures. Another contrast occurs between the raucous intrusion of the shepherds and the ritual solemnity of all the other figures. These fieldhands gaze in breathless wonder at the newborn Christ Child, who is the focus of the gaze of all the figures ranged around him. Mary, however, sits at the physical center of the composition. Such deliberate contrasts between the pictorial and psychological focal points, between the scale of the historical and the contemporary figures, and between their static and kinetic postures contribute to a viewer's unsettled reaction to the work.

The background is populated with narratives that support the main theme. Behind the figures in the left panel, Mary and Joseph travel toward Bethlehem. Behind the saints on the right wing, the Magi progress toward the center. And in the center, the movement of angels flickers across the surface, lit by both natural and supernatural light. Strategically placed at the front of the picture are beautiful still-lifes of flowers and a sheaf of wheat, which have been interpreted as symbolic references. The wheat refers to the bread of the Eucharist and the flowers to the Virgin. Portinari brought the triptych to Florence in 1483 and installed it in the family chapel. There it proclaimed his taste, wealth, and piety. Judging from their imitation of it, Italian painters who

saw the work there especially admired its naturalism and its unidealized representation of the shepherds.

Hieronymus Bosch

Artists of the Northern Netherlands (present-day Holland) also contributed to the development of fifteenth-century painting. Hieronymus Bosch (ca. 1450–1516) spent his life in the town of 's Hertogenbosch, the seat of a ducal residence, from which his name derives. His famous *Garden of Earthly Delights* (**fig. 13.9**) was acquired by King Philip II of Spain in the sixteenth century.

THE GARDEN OF EARTHLY DELIGHTS This large oil painting has the format of a triptych but a subject matter that is surprisingly unorthodox. It represents humans in the natural world. A continuous landscape unites the three sections; the high horizon and atmospheric perspective imply a deep vista of the earth from an omniscient vantage point. Shades of green create an undulating topography marked by thickets of trees and bodies of water. Throughout swarm small creatures, both human and non-human. Strange rock formations and other objects appear at intervals. The left wing appears to represent the Garden of Eden, where the Lord introduces Adam to the newly created Eve. The airy landscape is filled with animals, including such exotic creatures as an elephant and a giraffe, as well as strange hybrid monsters. The central panel reveals a world inhabited by tiny humans who frolic

13.9. Hieronymus Bosch. *The Garden of Earthly Delights*. ca. 1480–1515. Oil on panel, center 7′2½″ × 6′ 4½″ (2.19 × 1.95 m); wings, each 7′2½″ × 3′2″ (2.19 × 0.97 m). Museo del Prado, Madrid *Northern Renaissance*

among giant fruits, birds, and other creatures. In the middle ground, men parade around a circular basin on the backs of all sorts of beasts. Many of the humans interact with huge birds, fruits, flowers, or marine animals. The right wing depicts an infernal zone, which may be hell, where strange hybrid creatures torment the tiny humans with punishments appropriate to their sins. Yet the reverse side of the wings depicts a crystal globe with an image of the earth emerging from a flood, with God watching over the events from above.

Documents record that the painting belonged to Count Henry III of Nassau, in whose palace in Brussels it was reported to be in 1517, though recent research suggests it may have been painted as early as 1480. Many interpretations of it have been offered—that it represents the earth in days of Noah, as shown by the image of a flood on the exterior; that the many swarming nudes express the views of a heretical group that promoted free love; or that the infernal landscape in the right wing demonstrates a moralizing condemnation of carnal sin.

Perhaps the most consistent interpretation of this painting links it to the practice of alchemy as an allegory of redemption. The many strangely shaped and outsized formations refer to the tools

and vessels used in this medieval approach to understanding the earth. The alchemical process required four steps: Conjunction—or mixing, for which the joining of Adam and Eve is a metaphor; child's play—the slow process of cooking diverse ingredients and letting them ferment, for which the central panel would stand; putrefaction—a step in which material is burned, related to the infernal right wing; and the final cleansing of matter—represented by the exterior flood. Bosch, who had married an apothecary's daughter, consciously used the visual symbols of that science to create an unforgettable glimpse of natural processes.

Regional Responses to the Early Netherlandish Style

Artists in many regions of Europe responded to the formal and technical achievements of the artists of Flanders. These regional responses were influenced by local traditions and tastes, but patrons found the naturalism of the new style useful for religious and social purposes. Many regions, including France and Central Europe, produced their own variations on the style.

France

Geographical proximity, trade routes, linguistic links, and political relationships with the Burgundian Netherlands helped to spread the innovations in technique and style throughout France. Artists either traveled to Flemish cities or developed their own brand of naturalism in imitation of the effects that Rogier (see fig. 13.7) or Hugo (see fig. 13.8) had achieved. Yet French art has distinctive features and traditions. In the first half of the fifteenth century, the troubles of the Hundred Years' War limited expenditure on art. Citizens of the war-torn cities commissioned very little, but members of the Church and the court continued earlier forms of patronage.

MELUN DIPTYCH After establishing his rule over France at the close of the Hundred Years' War, King Charles VII appointed Jean Fouquet (ca. 1420–1481) of Tours as his court painter. Both a book illuminator and a panel painter, Fouquet traveled to Italy around 1445, where he learned some of the innovations of contemporary Italian art. His work, however, owes much to Netherlandish style in technique, color, and approach. Around 1450, the royal treasurer, Étienne Chevalier, commissioned Fouquet to paint a **diptych** representing the treasurer and his patron saint, Stephen, in proximity to the Virgin and Child, the so-called *Melun Diptych* (**figs. 13.10** and **13.11**). Like his Flemish contemporaries, Fouquet records the specific physiognomy of the patron in his fur-lined garment. The head of the saint, who carries a book and the stone of his martyrdom, seems as individual as that of the donor.

The two men appear in a room with marbled floors and walls framed by antique-inspired pilasters that recede to suggest space. They gaze across the frame toward an image of the enthroned Virgin and Child. According to tradition, the Madonna is also a portrait: Of Agnès Sorel, Charles VII's mistress. If so, the panel presents an image of courtly beauty, as befits the Queen of Heaven. Fouquet deliberately contrasts the earthly and divine realms. The deep space in the left panel differs markedly from the right panel, organized as a rising triangle, with the cool colors of the Virgin and Child set against the vivid reds and blues of the angels. Unlike his Flemish counterparts, Fouquet is not interested in suggesting specific textures, nor does he provide elaborate details or appeal to the emotions. His images are geometrically ordered and rational rather than expressive.

13.10 Jean Fouquet. *Étienne Chevalier and St. Stephen*, left wing of the *Melun Diptych*. ca. 1450. Oil on panel, 36½ × 33½" (92.7 × 85 cm). Gemäldegalerie, Staatliche Museen zu Berlin

13.11 Jean Fouquet. *Madonna and Child*, right wing of the *Melun Diptych*. ca. 1450. Oil on panel, 36⅝ × 33½" (94.5 × 85 cm). Koninklijk Museum voor Schone Kunsten, Antwerpen, Belgie (Musée Royal des Beaux-Arts, Antwerp, Belgium)

13.12 Michael Pacher. *St. Wolfgang Altarpiece*. 1471–1481. Carved wood. Figures about life-size; wings, oil on panel. Church of Saint Wolfgang, Salzkammergut, Austria

Central Europe

Trade routes and political ties linked the Netherlands to central Europe, where artists and patrons were also receptive to the new style. Here again, painters, illuminators, and sculptors all responded to the naturalism of the Flemish style, but adapted it to local taste. For example, in German-speaking regions, altarpieces were usually made of wood, often large and intricately carved. (In the sixteenth century religious turmoil destroyed many sculpted religious images, so surviving examples are rare.)

MICHAEL PACHER The *St. Wolfgang Altarpiece* (**fig. 13.12**) by the Tyrolean sculptor and painter Michael Pacher (ca. 1435–1498) is impressive both because of its scale and because it remains in its original setting, the pilgrimage church of

Saint Wolfgang. The surviving contract between the abbot who commissioned it and the painter specifies both the subject matter and the quality of the materials and workmanship, which was the normal pattern at this period for contracts given to artists for expensive projects.

Much as Jan van Eyck did in the *Ghent Altarpiece*, Pacher creates a vision of heaven here: The center panel depicts the Coronation of the Virgin as Queen of Heaven, flanked by the patron saints of the monastery. Carved of soft wood that permits the sculptor to create deep folds and sharp edges, the lavishly gilt and colored forms make a dazzling spectacle as they emerge from the shadows under Flamboyant Gothic canopies. The figures and setting in the central panel seem to melt into a pattern of twisting lines that permits only the heads to stand out as separate elements.

The complexity and surface ornamentation that dominate the center contrast with the paintings of scenes from the life of the Virgin on the interior of the wings. Here the artist represents large figures, strongly modeled by clear light, and he suggests a deep space for them. His use of **perspective**, a system for projecting space in a painting, was inspired by developments in contemporary Italian painting. Pacher almost certainly crossed the Alps and visited northern Italy, so he had learned to use the Italian technique for projecting space. (Compare his perspective to

Mantegna's in fig. 14.21.) This perspective appears only in the wings, however, where scenes from the past are set into spaces that look like the Austrian present. The interior of the temple where the circumcision takes place, for example, has a vault much like those in late Gothic churches in the region. Pacher makes the historical scenes in the wings much more down to earth than the spectacle of heaven in the center.

Printing and the Graphic Arts

Along with the new techniques of painting, fifteenth-century Europe saw the development of a new medium: Printmaking. Tradition has credited Johann Gutenberg (ca. 1397–1468) with inventing movable type for printing books, but the roots of printing actually lie in the ancient Near East and China, transmitted to Europe through contact with the Islamic Middle East. This is also true of the technique for manufacturing paper, which gained ground as a cheaper alternative to parchment.

Printing on wood blocks was known in the late Middle Ages, though it was used only for ornamental patterns on cloth. The fifteenth century saw the development of a printing technology capable of producing editions of several hundred copies of relatively inexpensive books. The new technology quickly spread across Europe, spawning the new industry of bookmaking, which was stimulated by a rise in literacy in Western Europe. To compete with illuminated manuscripts, printed books included printed images, which were often hand-colored to imitate the more expensive manuscripts. Ultimately, the printed book almost completely replaced the illuminated manuscript.

The pictorial and the literary aspects of printing were closely linked from the start. The practice of inking pictorial designs carved on wood blocks and then printing those designs on paper began in Europe late in the fourteenth century. Early surviving examples of such prints, called **woodcuts**, come from France, the Netherlands, and Germany. Painters or sculptors supplied designs that were carved onto wood blocks by specialists. (For the various techniques of printing, see Materials and Techniques: Early Printmaking, opposite.)

An early example of a woodcut is the *Buxheim St. Christopher* (**fig. 13.13**), named for the monastery in a German town. This single sheet, hand-colored woodcut bears the date 1423 and

13.13 *Buxheim St. Christopher*. 1423. Hand-colored woodcut, 11⅜ × 8½" (28.8 × 20.6 cm). John Rylands University Library. Courtesy of the Director and the Librarian, Manchester, England

Early Printmaking

PRINTMAKING primarily is used to make multiple copies of an image. In each of the printmaking techniques—woodcuts, engraving, etching—the artist works on a block or plate and then covers the surface with paper to print it. Throughout the process, the artist must keep in mind that the resulting image will be a reverse of the original design. Typically, the artist begins with a drawing and a plan for the project.

Making a woodcut is a fairly simple method for achieving a simple design. The artist cuts away and removes wood that will not be inked. The wood left in high relief receives the ink and becomes the positive image of the print. (Potato cuts or linoleum cuts are made in the same way.) Painters or sculptors probably furnished the designs for early woodcuts. Specially trained artisans actually carved the wood blocks. Early woodcuts, like the *Buxheim St. Christopher*, emphasize contour and offer little detail, but by 1500, artists executed quite intricate woodcuts with this technique. Dürer's *Four Horsemen of the Apocalypse* (fig. 17.6) is an extraordinary example of the fine detail achieved. The white space in the image corresponds to the cut-away areas of the block, and the inked lines and shapes are created by the fine wood ridges. The pressure of the press on the wood block often dulled the ridges and even split the blocks, so the number of examples of a single woodcut was sometimes limited.

Engraving is an example of a process known as **intaglio** (the cutting or incising of an image into a metal plate so that the ink is held below the surface of the plate). Deep cuts are made (engraved) in the metal with a tool called a burin. The

burin

plate is inked, and the ink gathers in the grooves made by the cuts. The artist wipes the surface clean, so the only ink remaining on the plate is in the grooves. A damp sheet of paper is placed over the plate, cushioned with blankets, and then rolled through a press. (The paper is damp so that it is soft and better able to pick up the ink.) Schongauer's *The Temptation of St. Anthony* (fig. 13.14) is an especially accomplished engraving.

Etching also is a form of intaglio printing. In this process the artist uses acid to help make (etch) cuts in the metal plate. To begin, the metal plate is coated with a waxy substance.

drawing on a wax-coated etching plate

Instead of gouging to create grooves directly in the metal, the artist will lightly "draw" on the plate with a stylus, or needle, thereby removing the coating and revealing the metal beneath (see illustration). Next the plate is placed in an acid bath and the revealed metal will react to the acid, which will burn the area deeply. The plate is removed, wiped off, and covered in ink. Then that is wiped off, leaving ink only in the grooves. As for engraving, dampened paper covers the plate and is rolled through a press. Because the acid continues to burn the metal, the etched lines may be uneven, and depending on the

etching needle

drypoint needles

length of time in the bath, the grooves can be very deep. So with etching, the actual creation is much like drawing, but the finished process includes an element of chance.

The range of blacks was explored further by the use of **drypoint**. Drypoint is the process of picking out the metal (see illustration of tool) and leaving the burr, the metal displaced by the needle, on the plate, which will then gather up the ink. This process has the possibility of creating areas of higher black density, as in Rembrandt's *One Hundred Guilder* print (fig. 19.12). Drypoint is often used in combination with etching and engraving.

Another option for creating greater tone is to only partially wipe the plate. This results in an overall dark tone to the print and creates dramatic effects of light and dark. In some cases, Rembrandt seems hardly to have wiped the plate at all, keeping it inked and only selectively wiping it.

In each of the above processes, changes are possible. The initial print is called a state. In each case, after printing one example, the artist can make a change. That second printing, using the same plate or block, is called a second state. There can be many states for a single print. The block or plate is therefore quite valuable and can be used many years later, even after the artist's death, by family members or other owners to provide income. Sometimes the artist will deface the plate (called "striking" it) to prevent anyone else from using it.

13.14 Martin Schongauer. *The Temptation of St. Anthony.* ca. 1480–1490. Engraving, 11½ × 8⅝″ (29.2 × 21.8 cm). The Metropolitan Museum of Art, New York, Rogers Fund, 1920. 20.5.2

two-dimensional, as the landscape forms rise along the picture plane to surround the figures. According to legend, Christopher was a giant who ferried people across a river; he was surprised one day at the weight of a child, who turned out to be Christ. (The saint's name derives from this encounter: "Christ-bearer.") The forms in the print owe a great deal to late Gothic style, but the audiences for prints were not the aristocrats of the Middle Ages. Fifteenth-century woodcuts were popular art. A single wood block yielded thousands of copies, to be sold for pennies apiece, so that for the first time in history almost anyone could own pictures.

From the start, **engravings** appealed to a smaller and more sophisticated public. The oldest surviving examples, from about 1430, already show the influence of Flemish painters. Early engravers were usually trained as goldsmiths, but their prints reflect local painting styles. Their forms are systematically modeled with fine hatched lines, and are often convincingly foreshortened. Engravings in distinctive styles often include initials and dates in the prints. Consequently, we know the names of many engravers of the late fifteenth century. One such artist is Martin Schongauer of Colmar, Germany (ca. 1435/50–1491), a goldsmith and painter familiar with the works of Rogier van der Weyden. The complex designs, spatial depth, and rich textures of his engravings enable them to compete with panel paintings. *The Temptation of St. Anthony* (**fig. 13.14**) is a work by Schongauer that was known and admired in sixteenth-century Italy. The print represents the climax of the hermit St. Anthony's resistance to the devil. Unable to tempt him to sin, the devil sends demons to torment him physically. Schongauer's engraving displays a wide range of tonal values, a rhythmic quality of line, and the rendering of every conceivable kind of surface—spiky, scaly, leathery, furry—achieved by varying the type of mark made on the plate. Without the benefit of color, Schongauer achieves a tonal and textual naturalism on a par with that of contemporary painters.

a prayer to the saint as well as an image. Simple, heavy lines define the forms in the print, including the fall of drapery around the figures and the contours of objects. Thin lines in parallel rows—called **hatching**—denote shadows or textures of objects, but the composition is strictly

SUMMARY

Although it depends on the past, the art of northern Europe in the fifteenth century differs profoundly from that of previous centuries. While the aristocracy preferred to commission objects in a lingering Gothic style, a new form of art in the medium of oil painting appeared in the cities of fifteenth-century Flanders. Made for a new audience of merchant and middle-class artisans, Netherlandish paintings are exceptional not for the expense of their raw materials, but for the skill with which painters recorded the natural world to enhance the spiritual experience of a viewer. The revolution in the visual arts pioneered in Flanders spread all over northern Europe and affected many different media.

Developing out of French Gothic, the International Gothic style appealed to patrons in royal courts. Aristocratic patrons commissioned luxury products based on the traditions of Gothic art, but embellished with naturalistic details, as in *Les Très Riches Heures du Duc de Berry*.

Artists in the urban centers of the Southern Netherlands developed techniques and styles to record the natural world and create religious images that spoke directly to the middle-class patrons who commissioned them. In images made only of wood and oil paint, such as Campin's *Mérode Triptych*, sacred figures resemble earthly people who express emotion vividly. Large paintings like the *Ghent Altarpiece* teach viewers about the sacraments performed in front of them, by presenting glimpses of those rituals in heavenly settings. Portraits record the features of patrons with great accuracy. Details of settings or garments contribute to the realistic effect of these images, while adding symbolic meaning. By the end of the century, these paintings were being commissioned by international merchants, like Tommaso Portinari, and collected in the courts, as was Bosch's *Garden of Earthly Delights*.

Artists throughout Europe adapted the technical and stylistic innovations of the Netherlands. French painters blended this naturalistic style with their tradition of geometric order and clear design to produce stately images of heavenly beauty like Fouquet's *Melun Diptych*. Central European artists extended the naturalistic style to complex sculptural and painted ensembles of great impressiveness, as in the *St. Wolfgang Altarpiece*.

The new technology of printmaking contributed to the spread of Netherlandish naturalism. Inexpensive images could be carried all over Europe. Early prints in woodcut and engraving borrowed motifs and compositions from painters, which they translated into strictly linear elements. By 1500, printmakers like Martin Schongauer were making original compositions with great skill that competed with the naturalism of painting.

ART IN TIME

- 1384 — Philip the Bold of Burgundy inherits Flanders

- ca. 1413 — Limbourg Brothers begin work on *Les Très Riches Heures du Duc de Berry*

- 1417 — Papal Schism ends

- 1419 — Philip the Good becomes Duke of Burgundy

- 1432 — Jan van Eyck finishes the *Ghent Altarpiece*

- ca. 1435 — Rogier van der Weyden's *Descent from the Cross*

- 1453 — End of the Hundred Years' War between England and France

- 1455 — War of the Roses begins in England

- ca. 1455 — Gutenberg prints Bible in Mainz, Germany

- ca. 1480 — Martin Schongauer's *The Temptation of St. Anthony*

- 1483 — Hugo van der Goes' *Portinari Altarpiece* arrives in Florence

- ca. 1480–1515 — Bosch's *The Garden of Earthly Delights*

The Early Renaissance in Fifteenth-Century Italy

*T*here was no single political entity called Italy in the fifteenth century (see map 14.1). Regions of different size and political organization competed with each other economically and often on the battlefield. The Kingdom of Naples in the south was a monarchy. Dukes, princes, and despots carved up northern Italy into city-states, including Milan, Mantua, and Urbino. The pope returned to Rome from Avignon to reclaim control of the Papal States. And the major trading cities of Venice and Florence formed republics, where mercantile elites controlled political power. Though the cultural flowering we call the Renaissance occurred throughout Italy, for many modern scholars the city of Florence was its birthplace.

The Inspiration of Antiquity in Florence

Florence is prominent in histories of the Renaissance, in part because many early humanists were Florentines who patriotically praised their city. Florence was an important manufacturing town, a key point for trade, and a major center for international banking, whose wealth and social dynamism attracted talented individuals. The government of the city was controlled by bankers and merchants, not aristocrats, while groups of merchants and artisans banded together in guilds to strengthen their political positions. The governing council, called the *Signoria*, consisted of officials elected from members of the guilds and prominent mercantile families. The government was a republic, a word that for Florentines signaled their identity as the heirs of the ancient Roman Republic. Florentine politicians and intellectuals celebrated the city's past and urged the model of Rome on the citizenry. Yet Florence was a Christian republic, so its government sponsored many religious projects. In addition, private citizens and guilds gained prestige by paying

for highly visible projects for the community and the Church.

The citizens of Florence undertook programs to beautify the city by building churches and commissioning other artistic projects. A wave of such activity occurred in the opening years of the fifteenth century. Florence had been threatened with invasion by Duke Giangaleazzo Visconti of Milan (see fig. 12.14). His sudden death in 1402 saved Florence from this peril and stimulated patriotic desire to improve the city. The writings of Florentine humanists, such as the Chancellor of the city, Leonardo Bruni, encouraged these efforts. In his *Praise of the City of Florence* of 1402–1403, Bruni compared the city to ancient capitals, like Athens and Rome. He found the virtues of the ancients in the people and institutions of fifteenth-century Florence. The value he placed in the study of the ancients was adopted by many of his countrymen.

As practically minded individuals and businessmen, Florentine patrons were accustomed to competition. They often awarded commissions for artistic projects after holding competitions

Map 14.1 Italy in the Renaissance

SWITZERLAND

Lake Geneva

BAVARIA

Danube R.

Vienna

AUSTRIA

N

A L P S

• Milan

Mantua
•
Padua Venice
•

Bologna • Ferrara

Pisa • Florence •

Borgo San
Sepolcro
Siena

• Urbino
Perugia

CORSICA

ITALY

• Rome

A D R I A T I C   S E A

SARDINIA

• Naples

M E D I T E R R A N E A N
S E A

SICILY

0   150   300 Miles

0   150   300 Kilometers

for them. In this way, they could solicit the best artists to contribute designs for a project and choose among the proposals. This was how the architect for the completion of the cathedral was selected.

Brunelleschi and the Beginnings of Renaissance Architecture

The artist whose design was chosen for the dome of Florence Cathedral was Filippo Brunelleschi (1377–1446), who made significant contributions to Florentine culture through his buildings and technological experiments. He traveled around the Mediterranean studying ancient structures and reportedly taking exact measurements of them. His discovery of linear perspective (discussed later in this chapter, page 327) may well have grown out of his search for an accurate way of recording the appearance of those ancient buildings. His own buildings reflect his study of Gothic, Roman, Byzantine, and maybe even Persian buildings.

THE DOME OF FLORENCE CATHEDRAL In 1419, Brunelleschi won the job of building the dome (see **fig. 14.1**). Such a large project would occupy him for most of the rest of his life. It would come to symbolize Florentine inventiveness, piety, ambition, and skill. When the cathedral, dedicated to Santa Maria del Fiore, was consecrated on March 25, 1436, the city rejoiced. Florence had demonstrated its devotion to the Virgin Mary, as well as its ambition to overawe its neighbors culturally. Florentines were justifiably proud that a native son had so cleverly accomplished what previous generations had not. Brunelleschi's forms would influence architecture far beyond Tuscany.

The basic dimensions and plans for the cathedral of Florence had been established in the fourteenth century (see fig. 12.5). The dome had been planned half a century earlier (see fig. 12.13), so only details could be changed, and its vast size posed a difficult problem of construction. The area it had to cover, and the

14.1 Filippo Brunelleschi. Dome of Florence Cathedral (Santa Maria del Fiore). 1420–1436. 100' high (35.5 m), 459' diameter (140 m)

Early Renaissance

arrangement of the smaller half domes that surround the cathedral's eastern end, both offered challenges to the builders. Brunelleschi decided to lift the dome on a drum above the level of the nave in order to reduce the weight on the walls. He proposed to build the dome in two separate shells: This was a method more common in Islamic than Italian architecture, and one especially employed in Persia. The two shells were supported by a series of ribs, eight of them visible on the exterior but others hidden; the vertical supports were themselves linked by rows of horizontal ribs. This system may have been inspired by the coffered dome of the Pantheon (see fig. 7.18). The dual shells of the dome lighten the whole mass, since their walls are thin relative to their size. Both the use of ribs and the pointed profile of the dome reflect Gothic building practices. The exterior ribs of the dome rise upward dramatically, terminating in a small marble cupola or lantern. Brunelleschi designed this lantern to tie the eight exterior ribs together, but it also marks the climax of that upward movement. Along with these design features, Brunelleschi proposed innovations in the

construction process. Instead of the usual practice of constructing a wooden centering across the span, which required huge pieces of timber, he designed a new system of scaffolding. He devised a way to construct a temporary scaffold that cantilevered out from the walls of the drum, which reduced the amount of timber needed for the project. He also designed new ways to hoist materials to the required height. Brunelleschi's entire scheme reflects a bold, analytical mind that was willing to discard conventional solutions if better ones could be devised.

BRUNELLESCHI AT SAN LORENZO In addition to the cathedral dome, Brunelleschi was commissioned by prominent Florentine families to build chapels and enlarge smaller churches in the city. The church of San Lorenzo was the parish church of the Medici family, who became the most powerful family in the city by mid-century. The family hired Brunelleschi to build a small chapel that would serve as both a burial chapel for its members and the sacristy for the church, but they were so pleased with the result that they asked him to develop a new design for the entire church. Brunelleschi began work in the 1420s, but the nave was not completed until 1469, more than 20 years after his death. (The exterior remains unfinished to this day.) Nevertheless, the building in its present form is essentially what Brunelleschi had envisioned in about 1420, and it represents the first full statement of his architectural aims (**figs. 14.2** and **14.3**).

San Lorenzo recalls Franciscan churches like Santa Croce (see fig. 12.1); it has a square east end, an unvaulted nave and a simple, unadorned elevation. But Brunelleschi placed a new emphasis on symmetry and regularity, accompanied by architectural elements, like the columns of the nave, inspired by the past. In addition to these ancient models, Brunelleschi studied Early Christian and Tuscan Romanesque churches; to him, these exemplified the church architecture of antiquity. They inspired his use of round arches and columns, rather than piers, in the nave arcade. The result is a well-lit space with columns that are lighter and more widely separated than in most medieval buildings.

To achieve this clarity and lightness, Brunelleschi organized his forms according to proportion. As the ground plan shows, he composed with units of space in regular square

blocks, so that each bay of the nave is twice as wide as its side aisles, and the crossing and apse are each four times the size of each unit. Having studied ancient architecture Brunelleschi believed that the secret of good design lay in choosing clear and correct ratios for the major measurements of a building. His theories about proportion and design were probably passed to Leon Battista Alberti (1404–1472), whose buildings we will encounter below. In his *Treatise on Architecture*, Alberti argues that the mathematical ratios determining musical harmony must

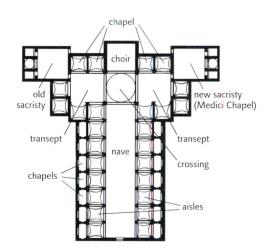

14.3 Plan of San Lorenzo, Florence.

14.2 Filippo Brunelleschi. Nave of San Lorenzo. ca. 1421–1469. Florence

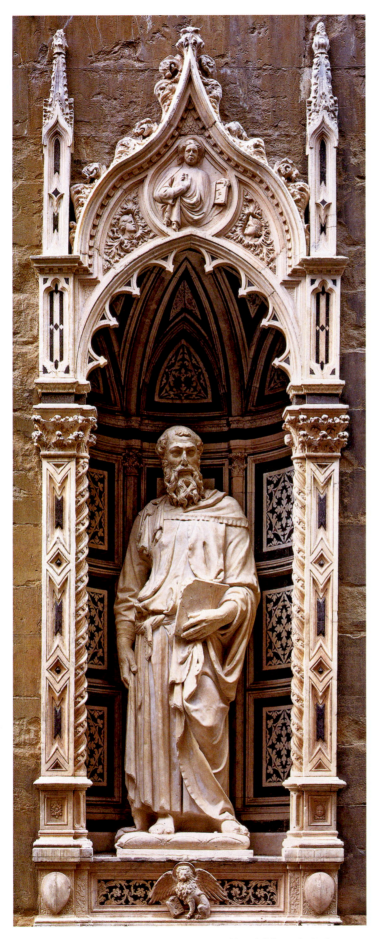

14.4 Donatello. *St. Mark*. ca. 1411–1413. Marble, 7′9″ (2.4 m). Or San Michele, Florence (now Museo di Or San Michele, Florence)

also govern architecture, for they must be divine in origin. Similar ideas, derived from the theories of the Greek philosopher Pythagoras, had been current during the Middle Ages, but they had never before been expressed so directly and simply.

In the revival of classical forms, Renaissance architecture found a standard vocabulary. The theory of harmonious proportions gave architects rules for using those forms that had been mostly absent in medieval architecture. Brunelleschi's achievement applied the lessons of classical antiquity for modern Christian ends. Furthermore, his study of the ancients and his practical application of classical geometric proportions probably stimulated his discovery of a system for rendering forms in three dimensions. This technique became known as linear or scientific perspective (see Materials and Techniques: Perspective, page 327).

DONATELLO AT OR SAN MICHELE The lessons of antiquity that Brunelleschi applied to the dome of Florence Cathedral and San Lorenzo also inspired the sculptors of his time such as Donatello (1389–1466). Just as sculptors had earlier competed to earn the commission to cast the doors of the Baptistery (see fig. 12.6), they vied with one another to fill the exterior niches of the building in central Florence called Or San Michele. Begun in 1337, this structure served as both a granary and a shrine holding a locally venerated image of the Virgin and Child. Each of the guilds of Florence was responsible for a niche on the exterior of the building; the sculptors they hired competed intensely to create impressive statues of the guilds' patron saints.

The Guild of Linen Weavers commissioned Donatello to fill their niche with a figure probably completed in 1413 (**fig. 14.4**). Standing in his niche, their patron, *St. Mark*, is almost eight feet high, but that is only one of the features that make him so imposing. His large, powerful hands grip a book, most probably his Gospel. His body stands in a pose Donatello learned from studying the art of the ancients: One leg is flexed while the other holds the body's weight in a *contrapposto* stance (see fig. 5.14, the *Kritios Boy*). St. Mark's drapery falls in deep folds to reveal and emphasize his posture.

Donatello depicts the human body as capable of movement, and allows the drapery over it to reflect the shapes underneath; this contrasts with the medieval practice of depicting drapery in patterns. Following classical precedents such as the *Doryphoros* (see fig. 5.16), Donatello carefully balances the composition, so that the elements on the left (as a viewer sees it) stress the vertical and the static, while those on the right emphasize the diagonal and kinetic. The deeply carved eyes and undulating beard of the saint maintain control over the whole figure, while the mass of drapery reminds the viewer of the Linen Weavers' products. This work reflects Donatello's deep understanding of the principles that guided the artists of antiquity and his commitment to them. *St. Mark* reveals what the sculptor learned from his studies: An emphasis on naturalistic form, the independence of body and drapery, a balanced but contrasting composition, the potential for movement, and psychological presence.

New Directions in Florentine Painting

Florence was home to a community of artists who knew each other's work and learned from each other. Donatello and Brunelleschi were friends and traveling companions. Both of these men are mentioned by the humanist and architect Leon Battista Alberti, who wrote treatises on architecture and painting, among other topics. Alberti's *On Painting*, finished around 1435, helped to spread Brunelleschi's ideas about perspective. Alberti's treatises codified Florentine innovations in the arts, and because the books were copied, and then printed later in the century, they contributed to the development of Renaissance art in other parts of Italy. Alberti's treatises present the artists of the fifteenth century as learned men; they encouraged patrons and society at large to give more respect to visual artists than had previously been the case. *On Painting* also praised the work of a young Florentine painter named Tommaso di Ser Giovanni di Mone Cassai (1401–1428), called Masaccio. Historians ever since have credited Masaccio with reviving the art of painting in Florence. At both Santa Maria Novella and the Church of Santa Maria delle Carmine, the young Masaccio found employment in painting frescoes for prominent Florentine families in the 1420s.

MASACCIO AT SANTA MARIA NOVELLA Although its date is somewhat uncertain, Masaccio is credited with a fresco in Santa Maria Novella that depicts the Holy Trinity in the company of the Virgin, St. John the Evangelist, and two donors (**fig. 14.5**). The holy characters stand in a painted chapel; God the Father supports the figure of Christ on the Cross, with the dove of the Holy

14.5 Masaccio. *The Holy Trinity with the Virgin, St. John, and Two Donors.* ca. 1425. Fresco, detached from wall, 21'10⅝" × 10'4¾" (6.67 × 3.17 m). Santa Maria Novella, Florence

Spirit between their heads. St. John and the Virgin stand beneath the cross; she looks out to glance at the viewer. Outside this fictive chapel kneel a man and woman, the donors, probably members of the Lenzi family. The lowest section of the fresco depicts a skeleton lying on a sarcophagus. The inscription above the skeleton reads, "What I once was, you are; what I am, you will become." The painting's large scale, balanced composition, and sculptural volume suggest the art of Giotto (see fig. 12.9). Giotto's art was a starting point for Masaccio, though in Giotto's work, body and drapery form a single unit, whereas Masaccio's figures, like Donatello's, are "clothed nudes," whose drapery falls in response to the body wearing it.

The setting reveals the artist's awareness of Brunelleschi's new architecture and of his system of perspective. The tall pilasters next to the painted columns recall the pilasters Brunelleschi designed for San Lorenzo, as do the simple moldings that define the arch and the entablature of this painted chapel. Masaccio uses Brunelleschi's device of perspective to create the illusion of depth. This barrel-vaulted chamber is not a shallow niche, but a deep space in which the figures could move freely. The picture space is independent of the figures; they inhabit the space, but they do not create it. Masaccio used perspective to create an illusion of space where none exists.

In the fresco, Masaccio expresses the theme of the Trinity by the triangular composition that begins with the donors and rises to the halo of God. The composition is carefully balanced by colors, as reds and blues alternate until they meet in the garment worn by God. The whole scene has a tragic air, made more solemn by the calm gesture of the Virgin, as she points to the Crucifixion, and by the understated grief of John the Evangelist. The reality of death but promise of resurrection is appropriate for a funerary monument.

14.6 Left wall of Brancacci Chapel, with frescoes by Masaccio and others. Santa Maria del Carmine, Florence

14.7 Masaccio. *The Tribute Money*. ca. 1425. Fresco, 8'1" × 19'7" (2.46 × 5.96 m). Brancacci Chapel, Santa Maria del Carmine, Florence

MASACCIO AT THE BRANCACCI CHAPEL Even if we are uncertain about the identity of the donors for the *Trinity* fresco, we do know who paid for the largest group of Masaccio's surviving works. To fulfill a bequest from his uncle Pietro, Felice Brancacci paid for the frescoes in the Brancacci Chapel in Santa Maria del Carmine (see **fig. 14.6**). These depict the life of St. Peter, the patron saint of the donor. Work began in the chapel around 1425, when Masaccio collaborated with a slightly older painter named Masolino (1383–ca. 1440). (Some of the work was completed much later in the fifteenth century.) These frescoes transform the space of the chapel into a display of narratives from scripture.

The most famous one is *The Tribute Money* by Masaccio (**fig. 14.7**). The fresco depicts the story in the Gospel of Matthew (17:24–27) by including several episodes in one space. In the center, Christ instructs Peter to catch a fish, whose mouth will contain money for the tax collector. On the far left, in the distance, Peter takes the coin from the fish's mouth, and on the right he gives it to the tax collector. Masaccio uses **linear perspective** to create a deep space for the narrative, but he also models the forms in the picture with light that seems to have its source in the real window of the chapel. Both perspective and this use of light connect the illusory space of the painting to the actual space in which the spectator stands. Masaccio also uses **atmospheric perspective** in the subtle tones of the landscape to make the forms somewhat hazy.

The figures in *The Tribute Money*, even more than those in the *Trinity* fresco, show Masaccio's ability to create forms that have the weight and volume of Giotto's. Yet these figures also have the possibility of movement and power like Donatello's. All the characters stand in balanced *contrapposto*. Instead of employing violent physical movement, Masaccio's figures convey the narrative by their intense glances and a few strong gestures. They express powerful emotion through their sheer physicality. Before he could finish the Brancacci Chapel, Masaccio left for Rome to work on another commission; he died there in 1428 at a very young age, but his work stimulated other painters to experiment with perspective.

Italian Art During the Era of the Medici, 1434–1494

From 1434 to 1494 the Medici family dominated the city of Florence. Across four generations, Medici men were active in government and in business, while Medici women contributed to the social and religious life of the city. The family's wealth came from their mercantile and banking interests and the wise political alliances they struck both within Florence and in other Italian centers. Their status as bankers to the pope helped the Medici become leaders in the Florentine government. Ultimately they became the rulers of the city in all but name.

Plan of floor and ceiling derived from the painting (fig. 14.5)

Masaccio's one-point scientific perspective creates a rational picture space—the illusion that the figures are standing in a coffered, barrel-vaulted niche just above our eye. See fig. 14.5, previous page

The family's rise began at the end of the fourteenth century. By the 1430s, Cosimo de' Medici (1389–1464) became the leader of the Florentine government. Cosimo's sons Piero (1416–1469) and Giovanni followed their father's example; and Piero's son, Lorenzo, called "The Magnificent" (1449–1492), became one of the most celebrated and well-connected men of the century. In addition to creating links to other prominent families in Florence, the Medici family promoted the literary and educational innovations of Florentine humanists, and actively used works of art to express their political and social status.

Many families in Florence either allied themselves with the Medici or competed with them commercially and politically. During this period, the city continued to commission artistic projects to add to its luster. The era of Medici domination saw the continued development of the stylistic innovations of the early fifteenth century along with new themes in art. Brunelleschian forms dominated Florentine architecture, along with the ideas and designs of Leon Battista Alberti. Sculptors of the first part of the century, including Donatello and Lorenzo Ghiberti, were strong presences in mid-century. Religious communities and churches acquired paintings for wall spaces or for altars by painters strongly influenced by the classicism and naturalism of Masaccio and the elegance of Ghiberti. The fame of Florence's new style quickly spread throughout Italy and patrons called these artists to other cities to work for them.

The Baptistery of Florence

Throughout the fifteenth century, the cathedral of Florence and the Baptistery remained the spiritual heart of the city. Although the dome of the cathedral was completed in time for the church to be dedicated in 1436, work continued on the lantern, the façade and the interior. The directors of the Baptistery, members of the Guild of Wool Merchants, had already commissioned a set of bronze doors in 1402 from Lorenzo Ghiberti (1378–1455). These were finally completed in 1424, in a form similar to those by Andrea Pisano (see fig. 12.6). They were so impressive that the sculptor was asked to cast another set of bronze doors for a third portal.

THE *GATES OF PARADISE* These doors, begun in 1425 but not completed until 1452, were ultimately installed in the east entry of the Baptistery, facing the cathedral; this area is called the Paradise, so the doors were termed the *Gates of Paradise*. Each of the two doors contains five large panels in simple square frames; these create a larger field than the 28 small panels in quatrefoil frames of Ghiberti's (and also Pisano's) earlier doors. The panels complete the program of all three sets of doors: The earliest (Pisano's) is devoted to the Life of John the Baptist, the second to the Life of Christ, and this third set to the Old Testament. To achieve a splendid effect, Ghiberti completely gilded the bronze. The selection of themes may have been dictated to him by the chancellor of Florence, but he organized the narratives into memorable and clear images.

In designing these reliefs, Ghiberti drew on the new devices for pictorial imagery that he and his rivals had pioneered, such as the linear perspective developed by Brunelleschi and employed by Masaccio. Ghiberti's figures have more graceful proportions, elegant stances, and fluid drapery than Masaccio's or Donatello's figures. This aspect of the figures reflects Ghiberti's knowledge of the International Gothic style, which had influence in Italy as well as elsewhere in Europe (see fig. 13.1). In telling *The Story of Jacob and Esau* (**fig. 14.8**) Ghiberti has used perspective to create the illusion of a deep space

14.8 Lorenzo Ghiberti. *The Story of Jacob and Esau*, panel of the *Gates of Paradise*. ca. 1435. Gilt bronze, 31¼" (79.5 cm) square. Baptistery of San Giovanni, Florence

14.9 Fra Angelico. *Annunciation.* ca. 1440–1445. Fresco on dormitory level of the Convent of San Marco, 7′1″ × 10′6″ (2.1 × 3.2 m). Museo di San Marco, Florence

defined by the arches of a building planned to accommodate the figures as they appear and reappear throughout the structure. The relief tells the story of Isaac blessing his younger son, Jacob, instead of the elder Esau. The blind Isaac sends Esau off to hunt on the left, but confers his blessing on the disguised Jacob at the right. The story unfolds in a spacious hall, itself a fine example of Early Renaissance architectural design. Using perspective allows Ghiberti to present his story as a continuous narrative with unprecedented coherence, as if all seven episodes of it were taking place simultaneously.

Florentine Churches and Convents at Mid-Century

The work at the cathedral, the Baptistery, and Or San Michele was accompanied by construction and renewal elsewhere in Florence. Throughout the city, churches and convents were rebuilt or enlarged, often with corresponding commissions for their decoration. Renaissance artists and their patrons wished to put the new style to work for their faith. The naturalism and spatial effects now possible could create images that spoke powerfully to believers. Perspective and other devices could connect viewers to religious stories to evoke their empathy. New ideas coming from

the study of the classics inspired artists to create balanced compositions peopled with dignified characters. Yet not all churchmen approved of the increasingly naturalistic and classicizing forms found in religious art in the fifteenth century. The tension between Christian and classical forms erupted at the end of the century with Savonarola's condemnation of "pagan" images (see page 321).

FRA ANGELICO AT SAN MARCO With the support of Cosimo de' Medici, the Dominicans built a second convent for friars in Florence in 1436. Among the members of this community was another talented naturalistic painter, this time from the Florentine countryside, Fra (Brother) Giovanni da Fiesole, called Fra Angelico (ca. 1400–1455). For the friars, Angelico painted altarpieces, books, and many frescoes in their living quarters. His fresco of the *Annunciation*, executed between 1440 and 1445, is placed prominently at the entry to the dormitory (**fig. 14.9**). Angelico sets the two actors in this important event into a vaulted space very similar to the real architecture of the convent. A perspectival scheme defines the space, although the figures are too large to stand comfortably in it. The Virgin and the angel Gabriel glance at each other across the space; they humbly fold their hands, expressing their submission to divine will. The forms are graceful, and the overall scene is spare, rather than extravagant. The colors are pale, the composition has been pared to the minimum, a soft light bathes all the forms. Angelico's composition has the simplicity and spatial sophistication of Masaccio, though his figures are more graceful. An inscription at the base calls on the friars who pass by to say a prayer. The fresco surely enhanced the friars' life of prayer and contemplation, as was the goal of such imagery in religious communities.

DOMENICO VENEZIANO AT SANTA LUCIA DEI MAGNOLI Religious imagery was also needed by the laity to adorn the altars of parish churches. An important shift occurred in the design of altar panels in the 1440s, perhaps at the hands of Fra Angelico, which was soon adopted by many painters. Earlier altarpieces like Giotto's *Madonna Enthroned* (fig. 12.10) were complex

ensembles with elaborately carved frames, but the newer altarpieces, straightforward rectangles, placed less emphasis on gilded carpentry and more emphasis on geometric clarity. For the main altar of the church of Santa Lucia dei Magnoli in Florence, the painter Domenico Veneziano (ca. 1410–1461) executed the *Madonna and Child with Saints* around 1445 (**fig. 14.10**). As his name suggests, Domenico was from Venice, though he came to Florence in search of work in 1439. The altarpiece he painted for Santa Lucia depicts an enthroned Madonna and Child framed by architecture and surrounded by saints, including Zenobius, a patron saint of Florence, and Lucy, an early Christian martyr, who holds a dish containing her eyes.

The theme of the enthroned Madonna surrounded by saints and sometimes angels is often termed a *sacra conversazione* (sacred conversation), which suggests that the image is not a narrative, but a glimpse of a heavenly court peopled by well-behaved courtiers. Domenico depicts

14.10 Domenico Veneziano. *Madonna and Child with Saints.* ca. 1445. Tempera on panel, 6'10" × 7' (2.08 × 2.13 m). Galleria degli Uffizi, Florence

this gathering in a light-filled structure made of pink and green marble. The architecture is clear and convincing, yet the space it defines is an ideal one elevated above the everyday world. Domenico probably knew Masaccio's *Holy Trinity* fresco (fig. 14.5), for his St. John the Baptist (second from left) looks at us while pointing toward the Madonna, repeating the glance and gesture of Masaccio's Virgin. Domenico's perspective setting is worthy of Masaccio's, although his architectural forms look more Gothic than Masaccio's, which emulate Brunelleschi's churches. Donatello's influence appears in the highly individualized faces and solidly rendered figures of the men (see fig. 14.4).

Domenico's *sacra conversazione* is as noteworthy for its color as for its composition. He uses a carefully selected range of blues, reds, greens, and grays in light tones that suggest sunlight streaming into the space. The surfaces reflect the light so strongly that even the shadowed areas glow with color. Color, light, and space come together in this painting to make a heavenly vision in which the faithful may take comfort.

The Spread of Florentine Style

The building of the Florence Cathedral dome, the sculptures on Or San Michele, and the numerous chapels being built and painted in the first half of the fifteenth century made Florence a busy place for artists. The innovative works created by Brunelleschi, Donatello, and Masaccio profoundly impressed visitors from other cities by their power and authority. Through the travels of patrons and artists the new style, born in Florence, spread all over Italy, as artists were called to work for patrons in places as distant as Rome and Venice.

DONATELLO IN PADUA Donatello's successes in Tuscany led to a commission from the republic of Venice in 1443. The commander of the Venetian armies, Erasmo da Narni (nicknamed "Gattamelata"), had recently died, and Venice sought to honor him with a statue. As a result, Donatello produced his largest free-standing work in bronze: The *Equestrian Monument of Gattamelata* (**fig. 14.11**), which still stands in its original position on a tall pedestal near the church of St. Anthony in Padua. Having visited Rome, Donatello certainly knew the tradition of equestrian statues exemplified by the *Marcus Aurelius* (fig. 7.9). Like the Roman work, the *Gattamelata* is impressive in scale and creates

14.11 Donatello. *Equestrian Monument of Gattamelata.* 1445–1450. Bronze, approx. 11 × 13′ (3.35 × 3.96 m). Piazza del Santo, Padua, Italy

a sense of balance and dignity. The horse, a heavy-set animal fit to carry a man in full armor, is so large that the rider must dominate it by force of personality rather than by size. The figure belongs to a tradition of representations of military leaders on horseback as funerary monuments. In this vivid portrait of a general, Donatello reenergizes this tradition by the carefully realistic depiction of the armor and fittings and the powerful characterization of Gattamelata's features.

The Renaissance Palace and its Furnishings, ca. 1440–1490

As their fortunes rose, patrons like Cosimo de' Medici asked artists to create works of art for their families as well as for the Church. Their

Patrician Palaces

Given their status in Florence, the Medici required a lavish palace that would house the family and accommodate political and diplomatic functions as well. The commission went to the architect Michelozzo di Bartolomeo (1396–1472), who had worked as a sculptor with both Ghiberti and Donatello. His design (**fig. 14.12**) recalls the fortress-like Florentine palaces of old. (The windows on the ground floor were added by Michelangelo in 1516–1517, and the whole was extended by the Riccardi family in the seventeenth century.)

Michelozzo borrowed the rustication and some of the window design from the Palazzo della Signoria (compare with fig. 12.7), but the forms are less heavy. The three stories seem to become lighter as they rise. The lowest story features rough-hewn, "rusticated" masonry; the second has smooth-surfaced blocks; and the third has an unbroken surface. On top of the structure rests, like a lid, a strongly projecting cornice such as those found on Roman temples. Inside, the spaces of the palace open to a central courtyard defined by an arcade resting on Brunelleschian classicizing columns. The effect of the whole was to provide a splendid setting for Medici affairs: Familial, social, commercial, and governmental.

Images of Heroes for Florentine Collectors

Creating images for such palaces offered new challenges to Renaissance artists. In sculpture, painting and other media, the artists depicted characters from past or present in clear and powerful ways. Once again, ancient works of art provided examples for the artists.

DONATELLO'S *DAVID* One of the most innovative works of the Renaissance, Donatello's bronze *David* (**fig. 14.13**) once stood on a high pedestal in the courtyard of the Medici palace. The *David* may be the first free-standing, life-sized nude statue since antiquity. The sheer expense of casting a whole figure of this sort in bronze, with parts gilt as well, required a patron with the wealth of the Medici to pay for it. Donatello composed the figure to be seen from every side, as the *contrapposto* stance and high finish of the work demand that the viewer walk around it.

Donatello's depiction of DAVID challenges interpreters. Much in the figure is difficult to square with the biblical story. The young David stands with his left foot atop the severed head of the giant GOLIATH, whom he has miraculously

14.12 Michelozzo di Bartolomeo. Palazzo Medici-Riccardi. Begun 1444. Florence

One of the greatest of Hebrew kings, DAVID (ruled ca. 1012– ca. 972 BCE) was still a boy when, according to the Book of Samuel I, he killed the gigantic Philistine enemy of the Israelites, GOLIATH, with a stone from his slingshot. The story of David and Goliath is a popular one because Jesus' ancestry is traced back to David. He is also the possible author of the Book of Psalms.

palaces needed building or remodeling to provide an appropriate setting for family life and civic display. Furnishings within the home had to express status. Sculptures and paintings proclaimed the ties between families. Works of art depicted new subjects, many of them inspired by ancient art, which displayed the humanist educations of both artists and patrons. In sculpture, the long-lived Donatello continued to innovate, and to inspire other artists. Painters sought the right style to depict imagery drawn from the ancient world. Architects built family homes made more splendid by their use of classical forms. For wealthy patrons with broad cultural and intellectual interests, artists developed new forms and subjects for painting and sculpture.

Instead of depicting David as a full-grown youth like the athletes of Greece, Donatello chose to model an adolescent boy with a softly sensuous torso. David wields Goliath's sword, which is too large for him, and his gaze seems impassive if we consider the terror he has just confronted. An inscription once written on the pedestal may help clarify the statue's meaning; it identified David as the defender of the fatherland. David had long been venerated as a patron of the city of Florence, so the Medici took over this symbol of Florentine civic virtue and placed it in their residence.

Ancient Battles in Prints

Even more questions of meaning surround a print by Donatello's younger colleague Antonio Pollaiuolo (1431–1498), who also made images of nudes. He worked as a sculptor, designer, painter and printmaker in both Florence and Rome. The Medici owned several of his works. Pollaiuolo's most elaborate design is probably his engraving *Battle of the Ten Naked Men* (**fig. 14.14**). Its subject is not known, though scholars have tried to link it to ancient texts. Between 1465 and 1470, when the print must have been produced, depicting the nude in action was still a novel problem. Pollaiuolo realized that a full understanding of movement demands a detailed knowledge of anatomy, down to the last muscle and sinew. These naked men look almost as if their skin had been stripped off to reveal the play of muscles underneath. One purpose the engraving serves is

14.13 Donatello. *David*. ca. 1420s–1460s. Bronze, height 62¼" (1.58 m). Museo Nazionale del Bargello, Florence *Early Renaissance*

defeated. But if David has already defeated his enemy, why does he hold a stone? Most untraditionally, Donatello depicts David nude, which may be intended to suggest his status as a hero in the ancient mode, but then why does he wear the broad-brimmed hat and knee-high boots?

14.14 Antonio Pollaiuolo, *Battle of the Ten Naked Men*. ca. 1465–1470. Engraving, 15'8" × 23'4" (38.3 × 59 cm). Cincinnati Art Museum, Ohio, Bequest of Herbert Greer French, 1943.118

to display the artist's mastery of the nude body in action and thus to advertise his skill. This may account for the prominent signature in the print; he signs it "The Work of Antonio Pollaiuolo of Florence." Pollaiuolo wants to be sure that his name is remembered.

Paintings for Palaces

The interiors of patrician palaces served not only as private quarters and settings for family life, but as public spaces where family members performed civic roles. A visitor would be likely to find paintings and perhaps sculptures, many on religious subjects, in these places. But in addition to religious themes, patrons wanted images that reflected on contemporary history and demonstrated their interest in the culture and art of antiquity.

In addition to acquiring paintings in Florence, the Medici had numerous contacts with northern Europe, not only through diplomatic exchanges, but through their banking business. Medici agents in Bruges sent many works of art to Italy, as did many of the other Italian ruling families, for Flemish art was widely admired in places as disparate as Naples, Venice, Ferrara, and Milan. Through such acquisitions, the Medici palace was filled with panel paintings and tapestries from the North. These objects made a profound impression on Florentine artists.

UCCELLO'S *BATTLE OF SAN ROMANO* Contemporary history, not the ancient past, was the subject of the Florentine artist Paolo Uccello's (1397–1475) painting the *Battle of San Romano* (**fig. 14.15**). This is only one of three panels by the artist depicting a battle that took place in 1432. Recent research reveals that Lionardo Bartolini Salimbeni commissioned the paintings for his townhouse in Florence around 1438, so the events were fresh in his memory. (He had been a member of the governing council of Florence during the battle.) Uccello depicts the charge of the Florentine forces led by Niccolò da Tolentino, the man on the white horse wielding a general's baton at the center of the painting. Uccello's painting looks more like a tournament than a violent battle, though, as the plastic shapes of the figures and horses march across a grid formed by discarded weapons and pieces of armor. These objects form the orthogonals (converging lines) of a perspective scheme that is neatly arranged to include a fallen soldier. Spots of bright color and the lavish use of gold create

14.15 Paolo Uccello. *Battle of San Romano.* ca. 1438. Tempera and silver foil on wood panel, 6′ × 10′5¾″ (1.8 × 3.2 m). The National Gallery, London

14.16 Sandro Botticelli. *The Birth of Venus.* ca. 1485. Tempera on panel, 5'8⅞" × 9'1⅞" (1.8 × 2.8 m). Galleria degli Uffizi, Florence

Early Renaissance

a brilliant surface pattern; its splendor must have been enhanced by the gleam of armor, covered in silver foil that has now tarnished. Uccello's work owes much to International Gothic displays of lavish materials and flashes of natural observation, with the added element of perspectival renderings of forms and space.

The series of paintings by Uccello was described as being in Lorenzo de' Medici's bedroom in a document of 1492. The Medici family came to power as a result of the battle commemorated in these paintings. After the death of the original patron, Lorenzo de' Medici sought to obtain them, first by purchase and, when that failed, by force. The sons of the original owner filed a lawsuit for their return. These circumstances suggest the importance of the paintings for both families. If the image originally celebrated an achievement of government in which Salimbeni took part, for Lorenzo the image marked a turning point in the history of his family.

BOTTICELLI'S *BIRTH OF VENUS* Sandro Botticelli (1445–1510) became one of the favorite painters of the Medici circle—the group of nobles,

scholars, and poets surrounding Lorenzo the Magnificent, the head of the Medici family and, for all practical purposes, the real ruler of the city from 1469 until 1492. Botticelli's most famous image, *The Birth of Venus* (**fig. 14.16**), once hung in a Medici villa. The central figure in the painting is Venus, the Goddess of Love. Born in the sea, she floats slowly toward the shore, where a flower-clad woman waits to enfold her in a flowered robe. Her movement is aided by Zephyr accompanied by Chloris (Flora). The space behind the figures seems to open out into the distance, with the sky and water creating a light, cool tonality for the painting. In the figures, though, the shallow modeling and emphasis on outline produce an effect of low relief rather than of solid, three-dimensional shapes. The bodies seem to be drained of all weight, so that they float even when they touch the ground.

The graceful figures depict a theme from antiquity using ideas that the artist learned from studying ancient art. Botticelli designed the figure of Venus after a Roman version of a statue by Praxiteles (see fig. 5.25). He combines ancient forms with ancient content, in an image that expresses Florentine reverence for both. The subject may derive from the Homeric *Hymn to Aphrodite*, which begins: "I shall sing of beautiful Aphrodite…who is obeyed by the flowery sea-girt land of Cyprus, whither soft Zephyr and the breeze wafted her in soft foam over the waves. Gently the golden-filleted Horae [Hours] received her, and clad her in divine garments." Yet the meaning of the image may owe as much to ancient philosophy as to ancient literature. One of the members of the Medici circle, Marsilio Ficino, based his philosophy on his study of PLATO. The Neo-Platonists like Ficino sought to reconcile platonic thought with Christianity, and drew complex parallels between them. Neo-Platonists believed that Venus exists in two forms: A celestial Venus, the source of divine love, and a worldly Venus, the source of physical love. Ficino described the celestial Venus as "a nymph of excellent comeliness, born of heaven and more than all other beloved by God." In such language, Ficino compares the antique goddess to the Virgin Mary. Botticelli's *Birth of Venus* may be an allegory of the origin of the celestial Venus for an audience attuned to the nuances of Neo-Platonic philosophy. The elegant forms and high finish of the painting, combined with the erudite subject matter based on ancient thought, exemplify the taste of the Medici court.

Portraiture

Images of history, of contemporary events, or of ancient myths demonstrate the expanding interest in secular themes in the art of the Renaissance. Another genre of image in great demand was the portrait. The idea of recording specific likenesses was inspired by the fifteenth century's increasing awareness of the individual, but also by the study of Roman art, where portraits abound. Artists were already making donor portraits, like Masaccio's *Trinity* fresco (fig. 14.5), and commemorations of public figures, like Donatello's *Gattamelata* (fig. 14.11), but new forms of portraiture developed in the fifteenth century. Florentine families who commissioned works of art often included portraits of their political allies as well as themselves to make their political and social networks clear to their neighbors.

The Medici commissioned numerous family likenesses for their palaces and for their friends. They preferred the **portrait bust**, a shoulder-length sculptural likeness, probably to draw parallels between themselves and ancient Roman families, who owned numerous busts of their ancestors. The Florentine busts celebrated the living, however, not the dead, and were made of marble, bronze, or terracotta by some of the leading sculptors of the century. Around 1480, the sculptor Andrea del Verrocchio (1435–1488) and his workshop executed such a bust of Lorenzo de' Medici (**fig. 14.17**). The image captures his physical likeness, but the concentrated gaze and drawn mouth give him an intensity that is meant to express his personality. Lorenzo was young to be the head of the ruling political faction, and the bust portrays him with the dignity and gravitas of a Roman elder as if to compensate for his youth.

The cultivated Lorenzo the Magnificent established what can only be called a court in Florence, despite the claim that Florence was a republic. Lorenzo was the patron of numerous humanists, philosophers, poets, and artists, including the young Michelangelo. Yet this brilliant court did not outlast his death in 1492. His son, Piero de' Medici, did not share his father's diplomatic gifts. Piero also faced an increasingly

14.17 Andrea del Verrocchio and workshop. *Bust of Lorenzo de' Medici.* ca. 1480. Painted terracotta, 25⅞ × 23¼ × 12⅞" (65.8 × 59.1 × 32.7 cm). Samuel H. Kress Collection, National Gallery of Art, Washington, D.C. 1943.4.92

unstable economy (the bank failed in 1494) and invading armies from France and Spain. The Medici family was expelled in 1494, as Florentines sought to restore republican government. A vacuum of power was filled for a time by the Dominican friar Girolamo Savonarola, who attacked the "cult of paganism" and the materialism he saw in Florentine culture. Savonarola's exhortations to repentance and his strong criticism of corruption not only in Florence but in the Church hierarchy made him many enemies, and he was executed in 1498. As the fifteenth century came to an end, Florence was battling for its existence against the stronger powers of the papacy, Spain, and France.

The Renaissance Style Reverberates, 1450–1500

Artists from all over Italy and from other parts of Europe were inspired by the innovative styles and subject matter being created in Florence. Yet, artists outside Florence responded to the new styles as individuals who were steeped in their own regional and personal differences. Additionally, patrons throughout Italy saw the advantages of expressing their authority through visual and textual references to antiquity. By mid-century, linear perspective was in widespread use, and Florentine techniques for rendering form through light were being practiced by many artists. Piero della Francesca blended his own fascination with mathematics, the ancient world, and Flemish painting to create a personal style that found favor in several Italian courts. The Florentine humanist and architect Leon Battista Alberti designed influential buildings in northern Italy, including one for the Marquis of Mantua, who had also attracted the services of the painter-archaeologist Andrea Mantegna. Venetian painters like Giovanni Bellini developed an influential school of Renaissance painting that rivaled the Florentine style. As the papacy regained its control in Rome, Perugino executed projects designed to celebrate papal power.

Piero della Francesca in Central Italy

One of the most distinctive and original artists of the second half of the fifteenth century was Piero della Francesca (ca. 1420–1492), from the town of Borgo San Sepolcro. He worked for patrons throughout central Italy. Piero's early training with Domenico Veneziano (see fig. 14.10) in Florence may be seen in his colors,

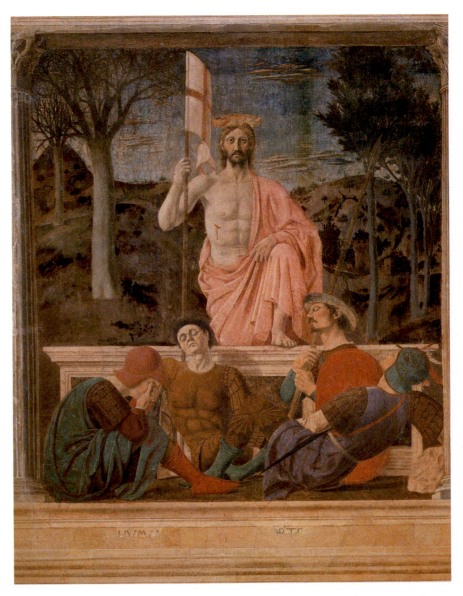

14.18 Piero della Francesca. *Resurrection*. ca. 1463. Fresco, 7′5″ × 6′6½″ (2.25 × 1.99 m). Palazzo Comunale, Borgo San Sepolcro, Italy

while his study of Masaccio is apparent in the solidity and simplicity of his forms and the solemn character of his compositions. The early fifteenth-century systemization of perspective was critical for Piero, who became such an expert at perspective that he wrote a treatise about it. It is likely that he made contact with Leon Battista Alberti, with whom he shared patrons as well as an interest in art theory.

A work that Piero made for his hometown reflects this combination of influences on his art. The city of Borgo San Sepolcro commissioned him to paint a fresco for its town hall, probably around 1463. Befitting the name of the town, which means the "Holy Sepulchre," Piero's theme is *Resurrection*, with Christ stepping out of his tomb (**fig. 14.18**). The figure of Christ dominates the composition: His frontality

14.19 Piero della Francesca. *Double Portrait of Battista Sforza and Federico da Montefeltro*. ca. 1472. Oil and tempera on panel, each panel 18½ × 13″ (47 × 33 cm). Galleria degli Uffizi, Florence

and the triangular composition may derive from the *Trinity* fresco by Masaccio (fig. 14.5), but the light of sunrise and the pale colors reflect the art of Domenico Veneziano. Piero pays special attention to the arrangement of the Roman soldiers asleep in front of the sepulchre; he treats them as variations on a theme of bodies in space. The spectator must look up to see the glorified body of Christ, so perfect in his anatomy and so serene in his aspect as he triumphs over death.

Piero's art brought him to the attention of the cultivated Duke Federico da Montefeltro, who had assembled a team of artists from all over Europe for his court at Urbino. There, Piero came into contact, and perhaps into competition, with artists not only from Italy but also from Spain and Flanders. From them, he learned the new technique of painting with oil glazes and became an early practitioner of this technique in central Italy. Piero's quiet, spatially complex paintings were thus enriched with more brilliant colors and surface textures in the style of Flemish art. The double portrait of Battista Sforza and Federico da Montefeltro that Piero

painted around 1472 (**fig. 14.19**) shows his skill at rendering space and using the rich hues and varied textures made possible by oil painting. This diptych portrays both the count and his wife in profile facing each other in front of a deep continuous landscape. Federico, whose face had been disfigured in a tournament, shows his good side on the viewer's right. His wife, Battista, had recently died from a fever; Piero places her to the viewer's left, the place of honor. Her complicated hairstyle and elegant clothing frame her pale features, while a shadow falls over the landscape behind her. The deep red of his garments and the ruddy features of the duke give him a commanding air, in front of a well lit and busy landscape.

Alberti and Mantegna in Mantua

Mantua, in the northern Po Valley, had been dominated for more than a century by the Gonzaga family. They created a brilliant court, peopled with humanists, educators, and artists. The court was very cosmopolitan and attracted humanists such as Leon Battista Alberti as well as the painter Andrea Mantegna.

SANT'ANDREA Having entered the service of the Gonzaga family, Alberti designed the church of Sant'Andrea in Mantua by 1470 (**fig. 14.20**). Alberti's ultimate goal as an architect was to merge classical temple forms with the traditional basilican church. For this church, Alberti planned only a nave ending in an apse. (The transept, dome, and choir were added in the mid-eighteenth century.) Following the example of the Basilica of Constantine (see fig. 7.30), Alberti replaced the aisles that were usual in basilicas with alternating large and small vaulted chapels, and eliminated the clerestory. These vaulted chapels are opened by large arches flanked by pilasters, like a Roman triumphal arch (see fig. 7.27). A barrel vault of impressive size covers the nave; this has coffers inspired by the dome of the Pantheon (fig. 7.18). The barrel vault rests on an unbroken entablature which is supported by pilasters reaching from floor to vault level; the large pilasters form what is known as a **colossal order**, meaning that it is more than one story high. Alberti used the same colossal order, the same proportions, and the same triumphal-arch motif on the façade of the building.

A comparison with Brunelleschi's San Lorenzo (fig. 14.3) reveals the new direction that Renaissance architecture took through Alberti. Brunelleschi's classicizing columns and contrasting colors create a much lighter and more open space, defined and controlled by the architect's judicious sense of proportion. At Sant'Andrea, Alberti focuses all attention on the nave, eliminating aisles in favor of a huge and imposing hall. Alberti has drawn upon his study of the massive vaulted halls in ancient Roman baths and basilicas, but he interprets these models freely to create a structure that can truly be called a

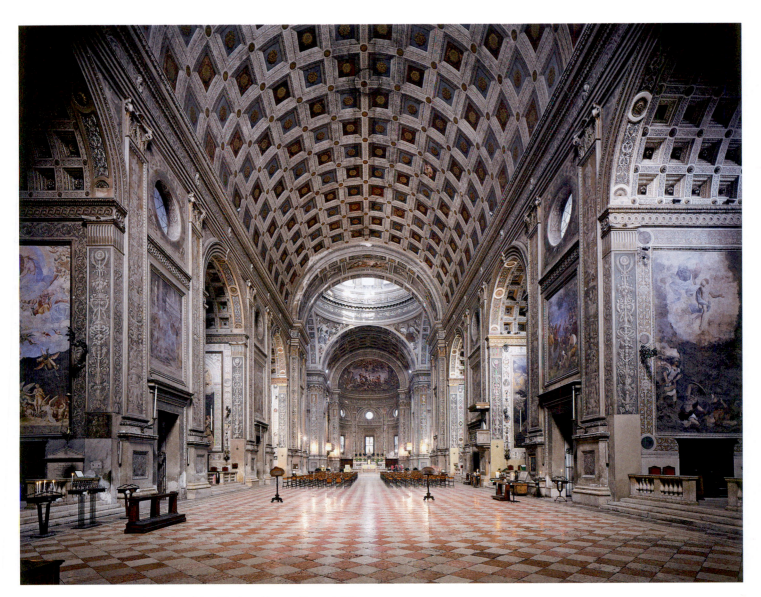

14.20 Leon Battista Alberti. Interior of Sant'Andrea, Mantua. Begun 1470

14.21 Andrea Mantegna. *St. Sebastian*. ca. 1450s. Tempera on panel, 26¼ × 11⅞″ (68 × 30.6 cm). Kunsthistorisches Museum, Vienna

"Christian temple." Such a synthesis of ancient forms and Christian uses was a primary goal of fifteenth-century humanists and their patrician sponsors. Alberti's accomplishment of this goal at Sant'Andrea would inspire many other architects to attempt the same.

MANTEGNA AS COURT ARTIST The humanist court at Mantua played host for many years to one of the most intellectually inclined artists of the century, Andrea Mantegna (1431–1506). Trained in Padua, but aware of artistic currents in Venice, Florence, and Rome, Mantegna became court painter to the Gonzaga in 1460, a position he held until his death at age 75. His interests as a painter, a humanist, and an archaeologist can be seen in the panel depicting *St. Sebastian* (**fig. 14.21**), probably painted in the 1450s. Sebastian was an early Christian martyr who was condemned to be executed by archers, although he recovered from these wounds. Mantegna depicts the anatomically precise and carefully proportioned body of the saint tied to a classical column. These forms are crisply drawn and modeled to resemble sculpture. Architectural and sculptural classical ruins lie at his feet and behind him, and next to him, on the left, is the artist's signature in Greek. A road leads into the distance, traversed by the archers who have just shot the saint; through this device, Mantegna lets the perspectively constructed space denote the passage of time. The scene is bathed in warm late-afternoon sunlight, which creates a melancholy mood. The light-filled landscape shows Mantegna's study of Flemish paintings, which had reached Florence as well as Venice by 1450, where Mantegna would have encountered them.

Mantegna's patron for the *St. Sebastian* is unknown, but as a court painter, he served the Marquis of Mantua by painting his villas and palaces. For the marquis's palace in Mantua, he began painting in 1465 a room that has come to be called the *Camera Picta*, or painted room (**fig. 14.22**). This was a multipurpose vaulted room—sometimes bedroom, sometimes reception hall—that Mantegna finished in 1474. On the walls he painted portraits of the Gonzaga family, their retainers, their children, and their possessions. This room celebrates the marquis's brilliant court, his dynastic accomplishments, and his wealth, all in a witty display that became an attraction for visiting humanists, politicians, artists, and princes. In such ways, princes used art to improve their social and political standing. The *Camera Picta* also celebrates Mantegna's

14.22 Andrea Mantegna. *Camera Picta*. 1465–1474. Fresco. Ducal Palace, Mantua

skill, and brought him fame among his contemporaries.

Mantegna used the actual architecture of the room—the corbels supporting the vaults, the mantel over the fireplace—to create an illusionistic glimpse of the Gonzaga family at home. Through painted pilasters that flank the door, the viewer sees members of the family out of doors; above the mantel, they appear in a more formal setting, surrounded by courtiers. In addition to the specific features of the people and the naturalism of the details, Mantegna's mastery of perspective allows him to connect the painted world to the real world of the spectator. The centerpiece of this illusion occurs at the crown of the vault, where Mantegna paints an illusionistic skylight through which a spectator sees the sky. Mantegna also painted the ceiling vaults with illusionistic reliefs of Roman emperors; he thus advertises his knowledge of history, but also flatters the marquis by including him in this august

company. The brilliance of the court is wonderfully captured by these splendid frescoes.

Venice

While it competed with its neighbors for territory, trade routes, and influence, Venice had a stable republican government throughout the fifteenth century. Ruled by a merchant aristocracy that was firmly established, the city suffered little internal turmoil. Its wealth and influence grew throughout the century; in such conditions, the artists of Venice developed their own form of Renaissance art. Venetian artists like Domenico Veneziano had long explored the intersection of light and color. Added to this visual tradition was an exposure to the new technique of oil painting, in which Venetian artists excelled. Florentine ideas about perspective were exploited by artists such as Mantegna, who also brought to the region his deep study of the art of the ancients.

14.23 Giovanni Bellini. *Madonna and Saints*. 1505. Oil on panel, 16′5⅛″ × 7′9″ (5 × 2.4 m). San Zaccaria, Venice

is the *Madonna and Saints* (**fig. 14.23**), done in 1505 for the venerable Benedictine convent of San Zaccaria. This Queen of Heaven is raised up on a throne with her Child, while saints Peter, Catherine, Lucy, and Jerome stand before her. The placement of the female saints may reflect the interests of the nuns for whom the altarpiece was made. Compared with Domenico Veneziano's *sacra conversazione* of 60 years earlier (fig. 14.10), the setting is simpler but even more impressive. Instead of a Gothic canopy, the saints are gathered below a semidome covered with mosaic like those that appear in numerous Venetian medieval buildings, yet the semidome rests on an antique-inspired entablature supported by Albertian pilasters. Bellini's figures stand comfortably in the space of their apse, though the structure does not appear to be a real church, for its sides are open and the scene is flooded with sunlight. He has arranged the figures in a balanced composition with the Virgin and Child raised above the other figures.

What distinguishes this altar from earlier Florentine examples is not only the spaciousness of the design but its calm, meditative mood. Instead of "conversation," the figures seem deep in thought, so gestures are unnecessary. The silence is enhanced by the way the artist has bathed the scene in a delicate haze. There are no harsh contrasts. Light and shadow blend in almost imperceptible gradations, and colors glow with a new richness. Bellini creates a glimpse into a heavenly court peopled by ideal figures in an ideal space.

Rome and the Papal States

The reinvigoration of the papacy after the end of the schism in 1417 allowed Rome to become a major artistic center by the end of the fifteenth century. As the papacy regained power, the popes began to beautify both the Vatican and the city. They also reasserted their power as rulers over Rome and the Papal States. These popes believed that the monuments of Christian Rome had to outshine those of the pagan past. To achieve this goal, they called many artists from Florence and the surrounding areas to Rome, including Masaccio, Fra Angelico, Piero della Francesca, and Sandro Botticelli. Like the other courts of Italy, the papacy saw the value of spending money on adorning both ecclesiastical and domestic structures.

THE SISTINE CHAPEL Pope Sixtus IV was one of the popes of the late fifteenth century who paid for architectural and artistic projects to beautify

BELLINI AND OIL PAINTING A painter from southern Italy, Antonello da Messina, who may have traveled to Flanders to learn the oil technique, came to Venice in the 1470s and passed this knowledge on to Venetian artists. In the painting of Giovanni Bellini (ca. 1430–1507), Mantegna's brother-in-law and a member of a family of painters, the technique of painting in oil pioneered by the Flemish is combined with Florentine spatial systems and Venetian light and color.

As the foremost artist of Venice, Bellini produced a number of altarpieces of the *sacra conversazione* type. The latest and most monumental

Perspective

PERSPECTIVE is a technique for making a two-dimensional surface appear to be three-dimensional. Artists have used many devices to create this illusion over the centuries, but Italian Renaissance artists systematized the projection of space, using mathematics and geometry. It is useful for paintings, prints, drawings, and relief sculptures. There are two general ways to do this: Through scientific perspective or atmospheric perspective.

Scientific perspective, also called linear or one-point perspective, was probably invented by the Florentine architect and sculptor Brunelleschi, although Leon Battista Alberti was the first to write about it. Alberti compares a painting to a window through which a viewer can see another world. Scientific perspective expects that the viewer of a work has a single, fixed viewpoint. As a viewer's eye looks toward the distance, it can no longer make out forms at a spot on the horizon, known as the **vanishing point**. Artists plot lines that converge and direct our focus to that vanishing point; these are known as **orthogonals**. Sometimes, we can see those orthogonals as drawn by the artist and at other times they are not visible; they may have been used by the artist to establish perspective, but there are no actual drawn lines on the painted or printed surface. We can see the orthogonals in Pietro Perugino's *The Delivery of the Keys* (fig. 14.24). The lines recede from the center foreground to the door of the church in the background. We can imagine similar lines across the walls in Leonardo's *Last Supper* (see fig. 15.2), focusing our attention at their vanishing point, Christ's head.

Atmospheric or aerial perspective is a method of showing depth through the use of color. The decrease in intensity of color (at a horizon line) to a light blue or gray tone suggests a greater depth at the lightest point. We perceive the colors of greater intensity (as a deeper blue in the sky) as closer to us. We see this principle at work at the horizon in Piero's *Double Portrait* (fig. 14.19) and in numerous other examples. Atmospheric perspective is more subtle than scientific. It has been used by artists since Roman times.

Diagram showing the perspective in Pietro Perugino, *The Delivery of the Keys*. Fresco in the Sistine Chapel, Vatican Palace, Vatican City. See fig. 14.24

and improve Rome. One of those improvements was the building at the Vatican of a new chapel for the pope, called the Sistine Chapel, after his name. Around 1481–1482, Sixtus commissioned a cycle of frescoes for the walls of the chapel depicting events from the life of Moses (on the left wall) and Christ (on the right wall), representing the Old and New Testaments. To execute them, he hired most of the important painters of central Italy, among them Pietro Vanucci, called Perugino (ca. 1450–1523). Born near Perugia in Umbria (the region southeast of Tuscany), Perugino maintained close ties with Florence. He completed the fresco of *The Delivery of the Keys* (**fig. 14.24**) in 1482.

The gravely symmetrical design of the fresco conveys the special importance of the subject in this particular setting: The authority of St. Peter as the first pope, as well as of all those who followed him, rests on his having received the keys to the Kingdom of Heaven from Christ himself. Perugino places the main figures at the center of the image with Peter kneeling before Christ. At either side, in a carefully balanced arrangement, the other apostles and a number of bystanders with highly individualized features witness the solemn event. The figures wear heavy drapery that responds to their bodies as it cascades in deep folds to the earth, in forms inspired by Donatello and his followers (see fig. 14.4).

14.24 Pietro Perugino. *The Delivery of the Keys*. 1482. <u>Fresco</u>, 11′5½″ × 18′8½″ (3.5 × 5.7 m). Sistine Chapel, Vatican, Rome

Early Renaissance

In the vast expanse of the background, two further narratives appear: To the left, in the middle distance, is the story of the *Tribute Money* (see fig. 14.7); to the right, the attempted stoning of Christ. The inscriptions on the two Roman triumphal arches (modeled on the Arch of Constantine; see fig. 7.27) favorably compare Sixtus IV to Solomon, who built the Temple in Jerusalem. These arches flank a domed structure seemingly inspired by the ideal church of Alberti's *Treatise on Architecture.* Also Albertian is the mathematically precise perspective, which lends the view its spatial clarity. The symmetry and clear space of the image express the character of the rule of Sixtus IV, not only in spiritual, but in political terms.

SUMMARY

During the dynamic fifteenth century, Italian artists developed new means to depict the world in their images. Starting from a study of Roman art, the sculptors, painters, and architects of Italy created works that united ancient forms with contemporary content. Artists wrote theoretical treatises as if they themselves were scholars, increasing the status of the arts and artists. Their systems for representing the world through perspective, naturalism, and the human form have inspired artists and patrons throughout Europe ever since.

The city of Florence placed great value on commissioning and embellishing public buildings. Competition among artists and among patrons resulted in numerous impressive and innovative monuments, many of them inspired by ancient art. Brunelleschi transformed Florence with his buildings, using Roman forms organized by geometry and proportion to create harmonious spaces, such as the nave of San Lorenzo. Ancient sculpture inspired the young Donatello to give figures like *St. Mark* great naturalism and dignity. Masaccio's frescoes in the Brancacci Chapel display not only his mastery of perspective, but the painter's innovations in modeling forms in light and in the expressive possibilities of the human body.

The rise of the Medici family to political prominence and their skillful use of the visual arts to express their status coincided with important projects commissioned throughout the city. Ghiberti's sculpted doors for the Baptistery used perspective to create pictorial space for his graceful figures. Fra Angelico tempered Masaccio's realism with gentle images of heavenly beings in earthly spaces. Altarpieces, like the *St. Lucy Altarpiece* by Domenico Veneziano, became regular rectangles. Instead of bright gold surfaces, artists strove to depict naturalistic figures in believable settings. Patrons elsewhere, such as in Rome and Venice, sought the talents of Masaccio and Donatello for artistic projects, spreading their innovations throughout Italy.

Florentine families displayed their social rank and civic virtue in private dwellings using classicizing forms. They furnished their homes with paintings and sculptures on religious and secular themes. The Medici populated their palace with images of Florentine civic patrons, such as Donatello's *David*. Themes from history and mythology, like Botticelli's *The Birth of Venus*, were painted for palace walls. Portraiture became an important art form.

The authority of antiquity and the impressiveness of Florentine style inspired artists outside Florence to emulate and adapt it. Piero della Francesca's style was informed by innovations like perspective and the technique of oil painting. Alberti built churches in classicizing styles for rulers in Mantua and elsewhere. Mantegna made paintings influenced by his interest in archaeology and perspective. Venetian painters like Giovanni Bellini also made naturalistic images in which they explored nuances of color and light made possible by oil paints. Rebuilding the city of Rome, popes hired artists to create images that expressed their legitimacy as the heirs of St. Peter. Renaissance Naturalism and Classicism proved adaptable to many needs.

ART IN TIME

- 1401 — Ghiberti wins commission to sculpt northern doors of the baptistery of Florence

- 1420 — Brunelleschi's dome for Florence Cathedral begun

- 1420 — Papacy returns to Rome from Avignon

- ca. 1425 — Masaccio's frescoes in the Brancacci Chapel

- 1445–1450 — Donatello's *Equestrian Monument of Gattamelata*

- 1453 — Constantinople falls to the Ottoman Turks; the Ottoman Empire begins

- 1465 — Mantegna begins the *Camera Picta* in Mantua

- 1469 — Lorenzo de' Medici ascends to power in Florence at the height of the Renaissance

- ca. 1470 — Alberti's Sant'Andrea begun in Mantua

- ca. 1485 — Botticelli's *Birth of Venus*

- 1498 — Girolamo Savonarola executed in Florence

The High Renaissance in Italy, 1495–1520

Painter, architect, and historiographer GIORGIO VASARI (1511–1574) defined Italian Renaissance art with his publication in 1550 of the history of Italian art from Cimabue (ca. 1240–1302?) through Michelangelo; in 1568 he published an expanded and corrected edition of the work. *The Lives of the Most Excellent Italian Architects, Painters, and Sculptors*, known as the *Lives*, gives a mass of anecdotal biographical information about Florentine artists and accords Florence most of the credit for the Renaissance. More significantly, Vasari's view that the goal of art should be the faithful imitation of nature expressed a value judgment favoring classical and Renaissance art that endured for centuries.

*L*ooking back at the artists working around 1500, the artist and art historian Giorgio Vasari wrote in 1550 that these artists had been able to "surpass the age of the ancients." For him, the artists of this generation were paragons of their profession. Following Vasari, artists of subsequent centuries have used the works of this 25-year period between 1495 and 1520, known as the High Renaissance, *as a benchmark against which to measure their own achievements. This brief period saw the creation of what are still some of the most revered works of European art, created by the most celebrated names in the history of art, as chronicled in VASARI's* Lives. *Vasari's book placed the biography of the artist at the center of the study of art, and his* Lives *became a model of art historical writing. The celebrity of artists is a distinctive characteristic of the early sixteenth century.*

Patrons in early sixteenth-century Italy were eager to hire Leonardo, Bramante, Michelangelo, Raphael, Giorgione, and Titian. Michelangelo and Titian were internationally celebrated during their lifetimes. This fame was part of a wholesale change in the status of the artist that had been occurring gradually during the course of the fifteenth century, and which gained impetus with these men. No matter who their families were, or what their personalities, these artists were treated as intellectuals and accorded the same respect as were members of the great royal courts. In some cases, they were called "genius" or "divine." A few were raised to the nobility.

This period saw the coming together of demanding patrons—rulers, popes, princes—and innovative artists. Patrons competed for their output, while the artists' rivalry with each other inspired them to produce innovations in technique and in expression. The prestige of the patrons and the reputations of the artists had a reciprocal effect: As the one developed, it enhanced the other. Although each artist developed a distinctive visual style that grew out of the ideas of the fifteenth century, their works share certain features: A high level of technical skill; an understanding of and reliance on the forms of antiquity; a balance and clarity in their compositions; and great emotional power.

Leonardo and the Florentine High Renaissance

As the fifteenth century came to a close, Florence's reputation as a center for the arts was being challenged by events. The Medici family was expelled in 1494. Many Florentines heeded the warnings of the fiery preacher Girolamo Savonarola (page 321), who encouraged them to reform both their lives and their government. The penitential frenzy that he triggered did not survive his execution in 1498. Florence restored its republican form of government, which lasted only until the next generation of Medici politicians took over in 1512. As a result, Florentine artists often found work elsewhere in Italy, as evidenced by the careers of Michelangelo Buonarroti and Leonardo da Vinci.

Leonardo da Vinci

Leonardo (1452–1519) was at once a scientist, painter, sculptor, musician, architect, and engineer. His works are among the most famous in European art. Born in the small Tuscan town of Vinci, Leonardo trained as a painter in the Florentine workshop of Verrocchio. He left Florence around 1482 to work for Ludovico Sforza, the duke of Milan, primarily as a military engineer and only secondarily as an artist. On Sforza's removal by the French in 1499, Leonardo made his way to Venice, Rome, and Florence, where he executed several commissions between 1503 and 1505. From 1506 through 1516 he worked in Rome and Florence and again in Milan, whose French overlord, Francis I, invited him to retire to a château in the Loire Valley. Leonardo died in France in 1519.

The basis of Leonardo's fame is both his technical skill and his constant investigations of natural and human phenomena. For Leonardo it was not enough to know the rules of perspective; he had to know all the laws of nature. He undertook a broad scientific study of natural phenomena based on careful visual observation; he believed that the eye was the perfect instrument for studying the world. The extraordinary range of his inquiries can be seen in his NOTEBOOKS, preserving the hundreds of drawings and notes that he hoped to turn into an encyclopedic set of treatises. He was fascinated by all elements of nature: Animals, water, anatomy, and the workings of the mind. He made drawing after drawing, invention after invention, his restless mind probing topics that ranged from the musculoskeletal structure of the human body to the character of the sky.

Like other fifteenth-century scholars, he read ancient authorities to further his inquiries. His interest in architecture and engineering led him to the works of the Roman architect Vitruvius, whose treatise had inspired Alberti earlier in the century. A drawing from the late 1480s (**fig. 15.1**) visualizes Vitruvius' notion that the human body may be used to derive the perfect geometrical forms of the circle and the square. This image expresses powerfully the value that humanists and architects placed on these geometric elements, as carriers of meaning as well as visual forms. Like other humanists, Leonardo was interested in the place of man in the world.

15.1 Leonardo da Vinci. *Vitruvian Man.* ca. 1487. Pen and ink, 13½ × 9½″ (34.3 × 24.5 cm). Gallerie dell'Accademia, Venice

THE LAST SUPPER Among the projects Leonardo is most famous for is *The Last Supper* (**fig. 15.2**), executed between 1495 and 1498. Leonardo's patron, Duke Ludovico, commissioned him to decorate the dining hall of the Dominican monastery of Santa Maria delle Grazie in Milan, which housed the duke's family chapel. The resulting painting was instantly famous and copied numerous times by other artists, but a modern viewer can only imagine its original splendor. Dissatisfied with the limitations of the traditional fresco technique, Leonardo experimented with an oil-tempera medium on dry plaster that did not adhere well to the wall. The painting has also been diminished by damage done when the wall was pierced by a doorway.

In the early 1490s, during his stay at the court of Ludovico Sforza in Milan, Leonardo made a meticulous record of his wide-ranging studies in more than 1,000 pages of NOTEBOOKS, today preserved in 31 volumes. Written backward in mirror writing, the notebooks treat four main themes—painting, architecture, mechanics, and human anatomy—and reveal the range and depth of the artist's prodigious mind. Among the devices anticipated by Leonardo but not built until centuries later were flying machines (including the helicopter), bicycles, submarines, missile launchers, and parachutes.

15.2 Leonardo da Vinci. *The Last Supper*. ca. 1495–1498. Oil and tempera on plaster (restored), 15'2" × 28'10" (4.6 × 8.8 m). Santa Maria delle Grazie, Milan

High Renaissance

Despite recent restoration, the image is merely a ghost of itself. Yet what remains is more than adequate to account for its tremendous impact.

Depicting the meal Jesus shared with his disciples on the eve of his Passion and death, the theme of the Last Supper appeared frequently in monastic refectories. Monks or nuns dined before images of the disciples and Jesus at table. In his painting, Leonardo creates a spatial setting that seems like an annex to the real interior of the room. His command of perspective is so thorough that he locates the central vanishing point behind the head of Jesus in the exact middle of the fresco. Thus even the perspective system reflects the import of Jesus' actions. The opening in the wall behind him serves as the architectural equivalent of a halo. All elements of the picture—light, composition, colors, setting—focus the attention on Jesus.

Jesus has presumably just spoken the fateful words, "One of you shall betray me." The disciples ask, "Lord, is it I?" They do not simply react to these words. Each man's response reveals his own personality. In the group to Jesus' right, Peter impulsively grabs a knife; next to him John seems lost in thought; and Judas (the figure leaning on the table) recoils from Jesus into shadow. Leonardo has arranged the men into symmetrically organized groups around Jesus and carefully calculated each pose and expression so that the drama unfolds across the picture plane. The figures exemplify what the artist wrote in one of his notebooks—that the highest and most difficult aim of painting is to depict "the intention of man's soul" through gestures and movements of the limbs.

Leonardo's aim, however, was not merely to tell a story. He condenses the subject, both physically (by the compact, monumental grouping of the figures) and spiritually (by presenting many levels of meaning at one time). Jesus' calm presence at the center of the table suggests that in addition to the drama of the announcement, he is also instituting the Eucharist, in which bread and wine become his body and blood. Such multiple meanings would serve as spiritual food for the Dominican friars who lived in the presence of this image.

MONA LISA After the French invaded Milan, Leonardo returned to Florence. There he painted the portrait of a woman, whom Vasari identified as Lisa di Gherardo, wife of Francesco del Giocondo, the so-called *Mona Lisa* (**fig. 15.3**). If it is indeed the Lady (or Madonna) Lisa, she was about 25 when the portrait was made. For reasons that are unclear, Leonardo kept this painting throughout his life; after his death in France, it entered the collection of Francis I and thence the Louvre. Its history has added to its fame.

But it is also remarkable for its formal qualities, because in it Leonardo reinvented the female portrait. In the fifteenth century, portraits were made of well-off women at their marriages, often in a profile format that stressed the subject's expensive garments over her personality or features. Here, Leonardo adopts the northern European device of the three-quarter pose and represents the woman at half-length, so that her hands are included in the image and her whole face is visible. This allows the entire composition to form a stable pyramid, with the crossed hands establishing a base for the rest of the figure. Light washes over her, drawing attention to her features. This method of modeling is called **chiaroscuro**, the Italian word for "light and dark." Leonardo thinks in terms of three-dimensional bodies, which he renders using dark tones to depict shadows and lighter tones for highlights. Instead of emphatic lines, he softens the contours of his forms in an atmospheric setting. In this painting, the forms are built from layers of glazes so thin that the panel appears to glow with a gentle light from within, despite the dirty varnish that obscures the painting. The lady sits before an evocative landscape, whose mountainous elements emerge from a cool, smoky backdrop, while the rivers and bridges winding through it echo the highlights on her drapery. The landscape and the woman inhabit a moist atmosphere that produces a gentle haze around their forms. This fine haze, called *sfumato* (smokiness), lends an unusual warmth and intimacy to the portrait. Where earlier portraits paid as much attention to a woman's jewels as to her person, Leonardo concentrates on the fashionably plucked high forehead. The skill with which he renders the veil and the hands give the woman as much character as the famous smile. Vasari helped to spread the fame of the painting, for he claimed it exemplified "how faithfully art can imitate nature." For Vasari, this skill was the root of Leonardo's genius.

The High Renaissance in Rome

By the end of the fifteenth century, the papacy had firmly reestablished itself in Rome. Along with their spiritual control of the Church, the

15.3 Leonardo da Vinci. *Mona Lisa*. ca. 1503–1505. Oil on panel, 30¼ × 21″ (77 × 53.5 cm). Musée du Louvre, Paris *High Renaissance*

popes reasserted political and military control over the Papal States in the region around Rome. Although this process took decades, the papacy of Julius II (1503–1513) is marked by his ambition to renew Rome to rival physically the glory of the ancient city. Julius invested vast sums in large-scale projects of architecture, sculpture, and painting, and he invited numerous artists to work for him. Under Julius, Rome became the crucible of the High Renaissance.

Bramante in Rome

The most important architect in Julius's Rome was Donato Bramante (1444–1514). A native of

15.4 Donato Bramante. The *Tempietto*, San Pietro in Montorio. 1502–1511. Rome

of the structure evokes the Early Christian *martyrium*, a special chapel associated with a martyr.

Bramante designed the *Tempietto* as a round, domed chapel sitting on a three-step platform. It is articulated on the exterior with a plain Tuscan Doric order, even simpler and less ornate than the classicizing columns in Alberti's or Brunelleschi's buildings. Like Brunelleschi, Bramante used the proportion of the columns as a tool for designing the details of the façade. For example, the distance between the columns is four times their diameter, and they stand two diameters from the wall. To this simple geometry, Bramante added an almost sculptural treatment of the wall. He placed deeply recessed niches in the upper story to balance the convex shape of the dome. He composed the upper and lower stories as alternating solids and voids, and stressed the intersection of the two stories with strongly projecting moldings and the inventive **balustrade**, or railing. As a result, the building looks much larger and stronger than it is, and recalls Roman buildings much more than any fifteenth-century structure.

SAINT PETER'S Bramante came to the notice of Pope Julius II, whose goal of restoring papal authority over Christendom led him to replace the medieval basilica of Saint Peter's (see fig. 8.2) with a church so magnificent that it would overshadow all the monuments of imperial Rome. He gave the commission to Bramante and laid the cornerstone in 1506. Bramante's original design is known mostly from a plan (**fig. 15.5**) and from the medal commemorating the start of

Urbino, he began his career as a fresco painter. Influenced by Piero della Francesca and Andrea Mantegna, Bramante became skilled at rendering architectural settings in correct perspective. Leonardo may have had some influence on Bramante too, as both men worked at the court of Milan. Bramante's architectural works take Brunelleschi and Alberti as their main points of departure.

After Milan fell to the French in 1499, Bramante went to Rome, where he experienced Roman buildings at first hand. The Spanish rulers, Ferdinand and Isabella, supporters of the Spanish-born pope, Alexander VI, commissioned Bramante around 1500 to build a structure to mark the supposed site of St. Peter's crucifixion, attached to the church of San Pietro in Montorio. Because it looks so much like a Roman temple, it was called the *Tempietto* or little temple (**fig. 15.4**). Yet Bramante was also looking back at Early Christian buildings, for the circular plan

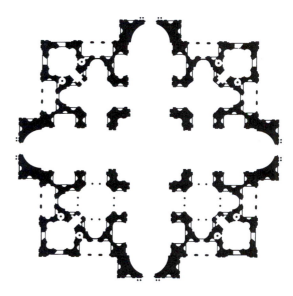

15.5 Donato Bramante. Original plan for Saint Peter's, Rome. 1506 (after Geymuller)

15.6 Cristoforo Foppa Caradosso. Bronze medal showing Bramante's design for Saint Peter's. 1506. The British Museum, London

the building campaign (**fig. 15.6**), which shows the exterior in general terms.

Bramante planned a huge round dome, similar to the Pantheon's (fig. 7.16), to crown the crossing of the barrel-vaulted arms of a Greek cross. He intended to surround the central dome with four smaller domes, each covering a chapel that echoes the main space. As Alberti prescribed, Bramante's plan begins with the circle and the square. Revered by the ancients, these perfect forms became appropriate symbols for Julius's Christian empire. Bramante envisioned four identical façades dominated by classical forms: Domes, half-domes, colonnades, and pediments. The whole façade would have been a unified, symmetrical sculptural form, united by proportion and the interplay of geometric elements.

This logical interlocking of forms went with the structure's huge scale, for Julius's church was intended to be more than 500 feet long. Such a monumental undertaking required large sums of money, and the construction of Saint Peter's progressed so slowly that in 1514, when Bramante died, only the four crossing piers had been built. For the next three decades the project was carried on by architects trained under Bramante, who altered his design in a number of ways. A new and decisive phase in the history of Saint Peter's began in 1546, when Michelangelo took

charge (see fig. 16.6). It was altered again in the seventeenth century (fig. 18.6). Bramante's original plan for Saint Peter's was intended to put Roman imperial and Early Christian forms at the service of a Renaissance pope's spiritual and temporal ambitions.

Michelangelo in Rome and Florence

Julius's ambitions were also the spur for one of the crucial figures in the history of art, Michelangelo di Lodovico Buonarroti Simoni (1475–1564). Acclaimed by his contemporaries, hailed as "divine" by Vasari, Michelangelo is one of the most influential and imitated artists in history. He became the archetype of the genius, whose intellect and talents enabled him to work in many media; he was a sculptor, architect, painter, and poet. In his ambition to outdo the artists of antiquity he was encouraged by Pope Julius II, who gave him the opportunities for some of his most inspired works.

Michelangelo's belief in the human image as the supreme vehicle of expression gave him a sense of kinship with ancient sculpture, more so than with any other Renaissance artist. Among Italian masters, he admired Giotto, Masaccio, and Donatello more than his own contemporaries. His family came from the nobility; and they initially opposed his desire to become an

15.7 Michelangelo. *Pietà*. ca. 1498. Marble, height 5'8½" (1.74 m). Saint Peter's, Rome

artist. Nonetheless he learned techniques of painting from the Florentine painter Ghirlandaio, and studied sculpture with a student of Donatello. He came to the attention of Lorenzo de' Medici, who invited him to study the antique statues in the garden of one of the Medici houses. From the beginning, however, Michelangelo was a carver rather than a modeler. He rarely worked in clay, except for sketches; he preferred harder materials, especially marble, which he shaped with his chisel. He was a sculptor to the core.

PIETÀ Michelangelo left Florence after the Medici were exiled, eventually arriving in Rome, where he was commissioned in 1498 by a French cardinal to carve a *Pietà* for his tomb chapel in Saint Peter's (**fig. 15.7**). The subject of the *Pietà* had appeared in works such as the *Roettgen Pietà* (fig. 11.25), and the theme of the Virgin's Lamentation for her dead son was depicted in Giotto's Arena Chapel frescoes (see fig. 12.9). Michelangelo imagines the farewell between mother and son as a calm and transcendent moment. The composition is very stable; the large figure of the

Virgin in her deeply carved robe easily supports Jesus' weight. She seems too young to be holding her grown son, making the image an echo of the Madonna and Child theme. According to his biographer, Michelangelo himself intended her youth to express her perpetual virginity. He does not merely tell a story, but offers viewers the opportunity to contemplate a central mystery of Christian faith—Christ as God in human form who sacrificed himself to redeem original sin—with the same serenity as Mary herself. To clarify the authorship, Michelangelo carved his name on the Virgin's sash. At 24, his fame was assured.

DAVID Michelangelo was back in Florence in 1501, where the directors of the works for Florence Cathedral commissioned him to execute a figure for one of the buttresses. The 18-foot-high block of marble for this project had been partly carved by an earlier sculptor, but Michelangelo accepted the challenge to create something memorable from it. The result was the gigantic figure of *David* (**fig. 15.8**). When it was completed in 1504, a committee of civic leaders and artists decided instead to put it in front of the Palazzo della Signoria, the seat of the Florentine government, then enjoying a republican phase. They placed a circlet of gilt bronze leaves around the statue's hips and a gilt bronze wreath on his head. The city of Florence claimed the figure as an emblem of its own republican virtues.

Michelangelo treated the biblical figure not as a victorious hero, but as the ever-vigilant guardian of the city. Unlike Donatello in his bronze *David* for the Medici (fig. 14.13), Michelangelo omits the head of Goliath; instead David nervously fingers a slingshot, as his eyes focus on an opponent in the distance. Although both Donatello and Michelangelo rendered David as nudes, the style of the later sculpture proclaims an ideal very different from Donatello's slender youth. Having spent several years in Rome, Michelangelo had been deeply impressed with the emotion-charged, muscular bodies of Hellenistic sculpture. Their heroic scale, their superhuman beauty, and the swelling volume of their forms became part of Michelangelo's own vocabulary and, through him, of Renaissance art in general. In the *David*, Michelangelo competes with antiquity on equal terms and replaces its authority with his own. Instead of the emotionally wrought figures he saw in Hellenistic works, Michelangelo crafted the *David* to be at once calm and tense, active yet static, full of the potential for movement rather than its actual expression.

15.8 Michelangelo. *David*. 1501–1504. Marble, height 13′5″ (4.08 m). Galleria dell'Accademia, Florence

High Renaissance

SISTINE CHAPEL CEILING Julius II summoned Michelangelo to Rome in 1506 to enter his service. Initially commissioned to sculpt Julius's funeral monument, Michelangelo was asked by the pope to paint the ceiling of the Sistine Chapel (see page 327). Michelangelo finished the ceiling in only four years, between 1508 and 1512 (**fig. 15.9**). In this brief period of intense creation in a medium that he never felt was his own, Michelangelo produced a work of truly epochal importance.

The Sistine Chapel is covered by a shallow barrel vault interrupted over the windows by the triangular elements (spandrels) that support it. Michelangelo treated the ceiling's surface as a single entity, with hundreds of figures distributed rhythmically within a painted architectural framework. Several different themes intersect throughout this complex structure (see diagram below). In the center, subdivided by ten illusionistic arches, appear nine scenes from the Book of Genesis, from the Creation of the World (at the altar end) to the Drunkenness of Noah (near the door); large figures of prophets and **sibyls,** ancient Greek prophetesses, flank these narratives. In the triangular spandrels sit the ancestors of Christ, who also appear in the lunettes flanking the windows. Further narrative scenes occur at the corners, focusing on the Old Testament heroes and prophets who prefigured Christ.

Sistine ceiling

End wall with Last Judgment

☐ Scenes from Genesis

1 *Division of Light from Darkness*
2 *Creation of Sun and Moon*
3 *Division of Heaven (Earth) from the Waters*
4 *Creation of Adam*
5 *Creation of Eve*
6 *The Fall and The Expulsion*
7 *Sacrifice of Noah*
8 *The Deluge*
9 *The Drunkenness of Noah*

☐ Sibyls and prophets

☐ Ancestors of Christ

☐ Old Testament scenes

15.9 Interior of the Sistine Chapel showing Michelangelo's ceiling fresco (1508–1512) and the Last Judgment on the end wall (1534–1541); scenes on the side walls by Perugino, Ghirlandaio, Botticelli, and others (1481–1482). Vatican, Rome

High Renaissance

15.10 Michelangelo. *The Creation of Adam*. 1508–1512. Portion of the Sistine Chapel ceiling. Fresco. Vatican, Rome

Scholars are still debating the theological import of the whole program and whether Michelangelo consulted with advisors in its development. Except for the architecture, these themes of creation and salvation are expressed almost entirely by the human figure. The figures convey deep drama and emotion through gesture, scale and their physical beauty.

For example, Michelangelo depicts *The Creation of Adam* (**fig. 15.10**) not as the actual molding of Adam's body, but as the passage of the divine spark—the soul—from God to Man. The design contrasts the beautiful earthbound Adam with the dynamic figure of God rushing through the sky. Adam gazes not only toward his Creator, but toward the figures in the shelter of God's left arm. The identity of these figures has been vigorously debated: The female may be Eve, awaiting her creation in the next panel; another proposal is that she may be Mary, with Jesus at her knee, foreordained to redeem fallen humanity; she has also been identified as a personification of Wisdom. The entire image reflects Michelangelo's view of the human body as a divinely inspired vessel for conveying complex and deeply felt meaning.

Once this project was finished Michelangelo returned to work on the still unfinished tomb for Julius II. The return of the Medici to power in Florence, along with the election of cardinals from this family to the papacy, meant that Michelangelo was back in Florence by the end of this decade, although Rome remained his home for much of the rest of his life.

Raphael

While Michelangelo often conflicted with his patrons and struggled to complete monumental projects such as the Sistine ceiling, his younger contemporary Raphael of Urbino (Raffaello Sanzio, 1483–1520) seems to have avoided such turmoil in his professional life. Because Vasari championed Michelangelo, later generations often venerated him more than Raphael. Where Michelangelo's dramatic conflicts with his art and with his patrons made good stories, Raphael's career seems too much a success story, his work too marked by effortless grace, to match the tragic heroism of the older artist. Raphael succeeded on the strength of his technical brilliance, his intelligent approach to composing pictures, and his dialogue with the other artists of his time. By all accounts, he was also charming and diplomatic with his patrons. During his relatively brief career he created a large body of Renaissance pictorial work and oversaw a lively and large workshop, which fostered many young artists.

ALBA MADONNA Raphael's contribution to the developing High Renaissance may be seen in the *Alba Madonna* (**fig. 15.11**) of about 1510 (so-called after its owners in the seventeenth and eighteenth centuries, the dukes of Alba). It is a

15.11 Raphael. *Alba Madonna*. ca. 1510. Oil on panel, transferred to canvas, 37¼″ (94 cm) diameter. National Gallery of Art, Washington, D.C. Andrew W. Mellon Collection 1937.1.24

good example of the artist's skill at compositional balance, simplicity, serenity, and sculpturesque figures in a **tondo**, or round-format picture. The figures—the Madonna, Christ Child, and the child St. John the Baptist—are arranged in a triangular composition, with the shadow of the group creating an equilateral triangle inscribed in a circle. Like Leonardo, Raphael is a master of *chiaroscuro*, creating the effect of atmosphere surrounding the figures. The large figure of the Virgin owes a debt to Michelangelo. Raphael sets the monumental group outdoors as if they were enjoying a clear spring or summer day, despite the Child Jesus' firm grasp of the crucifix that foretells his fate. Such pleasing paintings brought Raphael many patrons, including Pope Julius II.

SCHOOL OF ATHENS By 1509 Raphael had been called to Rome to paint a series of rooms in the papal apartments; the Stanza della Segnatura was the first of these to be completed. The "Room of the Signature" derives its name from its later function as the place where papal bulls were signed, though originally it housed Julius's personal library. For this room, Raphael painted a cycle of frescoes on the walls and ceiling that refer to the four domains of learning: Theology, philosophy, law, and the arts. In attempting to represent the unity of knowledge in one grand scheme, the frescoes here reflect the ambitions of High Renaissance humanism. The most famous of the frescoes in the Stanza della Segnatura, *The School of Athens* (**fig. 15.12**), demonstrates Raphael's commitment to surpassing antiquity while synthesizing the achievements of his contemporaries. Like Leonardo he crafts a persuasive illusion of space with a composition that is symmetrical and memorable. Like Michelangelo, he gives his figures powerful proportions and complex postures to express their characters. The architecture of the setting seems to reflect the innovations of Bramante. Raphael then sets the whole scene in a clear light that illuminates the complex subject matter.

The title of the fresco was assigned later, but in the scheme of the room the image stands for the study of Philosophy. To embody this branch of knowledge, Raphael arranges a group of famous Greek philosophers in a dramatic architectural setting. Like Leonardo, he organizes the men into carefully composed groups around the two central figures. Inscriptions on the books held by these two men identify them as Plato and Aristotle, the most important Greek philosophers, according to Renaissance humanists. The bearded figure at center stage (whose face resembles Leonardo's) is Plato, holding his book of cosmology and numerology, *Timaeus*; to his right is his pupil Aristotle, grasping a volume of his *Ethics*, which, like his science, is grounded in what is knowable in the material world. The books explain why Plato is pointing rhetorically to the heavens, Aristotle to the earth. On the building behind them, Raphael depicts two sculptures of Greek divinities in niches: Apollo, patron of the arts, with his lyre, on the left, and Athena, in her guise as Minerva, goddess of wisdom, on the right. The other figures have been identified as members of the idealist (Platonic) and empirical (Aristotelian) camps, but in some cases, Raphael's fellow artists play the roles of the philosophers. Euclid, seen drawing or measuring two overlapping triangles with a pair of compasses in the foreground to the lower right, has the features of Bramante. The man wearing a black hat behind these scientists is a self-portrait of Raphael, who places himself in the Aristotelian camp. Raphael added Michelangelo at

15.12 Raphael. *The School of Athens*. 1508–1511. Fresco, 19′ (5.8 m). Stanza della Segnatura, Vatican Palace, Vatican, Rome

High Renaissance

the last minute; he cast the sculptor as Heraclitus, a sixth-century BCE philosopher, shown deep in thought sitting on the steps in the Platonic camp. Not only is this figure a portrait of Michelangelo, it is also rendered in the style of the figures on the nearby Sistine Chapel ceiling. The inclusion of so many artists among, as well as in the guise of, famous philosophers is testimony to their recently acquired—and hard-won—status as members of the learned community.

Raphael's life was cut short in 1520, when he died after a brief illness. Befitting the new status assigned to artists, he was buried in the Pantheon. Significantly, many of the leading artists of the next generation emerged from Raphael's workshop and took his style as their point of departure.

Venice and The High Renaissance

While Florence suffered political instability and Rome became the center of papal patronage, the city of Venice endured threats from its neighbors and invasions from the east. The Republic of Venice was threatened by an international military alliance aimed against it in 1509, with the intention of reducing its territory. Venice also had to fight the invasions of Europe by the Turks. Despite this turmoil, artists there built on the traditions of the fifteenth century and the innovations of Giovanni Bellini to create a distinct visual language that appealed to wealthy patrons. Two artists in particular, Giorgione and Titian, created new subject matter, approaches to images, and techniques.

Giorgione

Giorgione da Castelfranco (1478–1510) left the orbit of Giovanni Bellini (see fig. 14.23) to create some of the most mysterious and beguiling paintings of the Renaissance. He seems to have specialized in smaller-scale paintings on secular themes for the homes of wealthy collectors. His death at a young age, probably from the plague, left the field open for his young colleague, Titian, who worked in his shop. Some of the works traditionally ascribed to Giorgione have, in fact, been reattributed to Titian in recent years.

One such work, the so-called *Fête Champêtre* or *Pastoral Concert* (**fig. 15.13**), has been on display in the Louvre since the nineteenth century. The painting depicts a group of young people gathered in a lush landscape to make music, when a shepherd and his flock come upon them. Attempts to find a narrative subject to link to this image have proven fruitless: No single literary source seems to explain it. Most puzzling are the nude women, one of whom is about to play a recorder, while another takes water from a fountain. They have been identified as the **Muses**, ancient female divinities who inspire the arts. The forms of all figures are rendered in an accomplished *chiaroscuro* technique so that they seem to emerge from the atmospheric landscape as soft round shapes. The landscape moves from dark to light to dark passages, receding into the atmospheric distance. Instead of telling a story, the painting seems designed to evoke a mood. Giorgione initiates what was to become an important new tradition in art, the making of pictorial equivalents to poetry.

Vasari criticized Giorgione for not making drawings as part of his process of painting. Steeped in the Florentine tradition, Vasari argued that drawing or *disegno* was fundamental to good painting. The Venetians, however, valued light and color above all to create their sensual images. Vasari dismissed this as *colore*, or color, which he argued was secondary to the process of drawing. This competition between *disegno* and *colore* provided the grounds for criticizing or praising paintings well beyond the sixteenth century.

Titian

Giorgione's young colleague, Titian (Tiziano Vecellio, 1488/90–1576), who trained with Bellini and Giorgione and even repainted some of their works, would dominate Venetian painting for the next half-century. Fully aware of the innovations of other Renaissance artists, and yet committed to exploring Venetian traditions of subject matter and technique, Titian is one of the most prolific and inventive artists of the period. Throughout his long life, he earned

15.14 Titian. *Madonna with Members of the Pesaro Family*. 1526. Oil on canvas, 16′ × 8′10″ (4.9 × 2.7 m). Santa Maria Gloriosa dei Frari, Venice

commissions from the most illustrious patrons in Europe; he also trained many of the Venetian artists of the sixteenth century.

Titian could transform older traditions even as he respected their conventions. This ability can be seen in his *Madonna with Members of the Pesaro Family* (**fig. 15.14**), commissioned in 1519 and installed in 1526 on the altar of the Immaculate Conception of the Franciscan church of Santa Maria Gloriosa dei Frari. Here he takes a *sacra conversazione* in the tradition of Giovanni

Bellini (fig. 14.23) and re-imagines both the composition and the figures. He sets the Virgin and Child at the apex of a triangular arrangement of figures, but replaces the familiar frontal view with a diagonal composition that is less symmetrical and more dynamic. At the focal point of this rising diagonal stands a pudgy Infant Jesus innocently playing with his mother's veil. More solemnly, the Virgin and St. Peter acknowledge the donor, Jacopo Pesaro, seen kneeling in devotion at the left. This man had commanded the

15.15 Titian, *Man with the Glove*. ca. 1520. Oil on canvas, 39½ × 35″ (100.3 × 89 cm). Musée du Louvre, Paris

papal fleet in a battle against the Turks in 1502, which the Christian forces won. On the other side are the donor's brothers and sons with saints Francis and Anthony. The donors' portraits distinguish the ages and features of all the men gathered to venerate the Virgin.

Titian places the Virgin enthroned on the steps of a monumental church. The elevated columns suggest the character of the setting as the gateway to heaven. This idea is traditionally identified with Mary herself; so the painting celebrates her in her role as the Immaculate Conception, born without original sin. Because the view is diagonal, open sky and clouds fill most of the background. Brilliant sunlight makes every color and texture sparkle, in keeping with the joyous spirit of the altar. The only hint of tragedy is the cross held by the two little angels, which adds a note of poignancy to the scene.

TITIAN AS PORTRAITIST Titian's skill at recording specific features of individuals in a flattering composition made him the most sought-after portraitist of the sixteenth century. We can see this skill in the *Man with the Glove* (**fig. 15.15**). The soft outlines and deep shadows in this portrait reflect Titian's study of the soft *chiaroscuro* of Giorgione. The unidentified man's white collar and cuffs draw attention to his face and hands, while the gloves signal his social status. In this portrait, Titian exploits the possibilities of the oil technique; instead of blending brushstrokes to create a smooth mirror-like finish, he lays the paint on the surface using rich, creamy highlights and deep dark tones that allow the separate brushstrokes, hardly visible before, to become increasingly free. Titian's handling of oil became ever more painterly or loose in his later work, and established yet another tool for artists of future generations to explore.

SUMMARY

For a brief time in the early sixteenth century, highly skilled and insightful artists not only coexisted but competed with each other to excel in their chosen arts. This time, the High Renaissance, has since been seen as a high-water mark for European art. Leonardo's inquisitive mind and insightful handling of light, Bramante's ambitious blending of antique forms with modern uses, Michelangelo's powerful renderings of the human body, Raphael's consummate compositions, Giorgione's sensitive evocation of moods, and Titian's brilliant handling of color and paint have been celebrated ever since.

Their activity occurred in a tumultuous period of intense creativity encouraged by a few key patrons. The loss of the patrons and the death or dispersal of the artists defused the competition. By 1520, Leonardo, Bramante, Giorgione, and Raphael were dead. The Catholic Church, which had been such a munificent patron, found itself challenged by the young Martin Luther in Wittenberg, as the Reformation gathered strength. The two artists who outlived the High Renaissance, Michelangelo and Titian, continued working in the changed conditions after 1520.

The restored Republic of Florence was the birthplace of two of the most influential artists of the Renaissance, Leonardo da Vinci and Michelangelo Buonarroti. Trained in the artistic innovations of the fifteenth century, these two men developed great technical virtuosity in their preferred media of painting and sculpture. Their achievements attracted other artists to Florence, including Raphael of Urbino.

Leonardo da Vinci's mastery of *chiaroscuro* and his restless study of nature led him to create emotionally rich and superbly naturalistic representations of religious and secular subjects. Works like the *Mona Lisa* and *The Last Supper* are among the most famous in the world.

Pope Julius II's commitment to renewing the city of Rome brought Michelangelo, Bramante, Raphael, and others to work there. To rebuild it as a Christian capital, Julius hired Bramante to design the new church of Saint Peter's as a rival to the Pantheon. Michelangelo's deep study of antiquity and dedication to the human figure gave his works, like the *David,* great naturalism and emotional impact. Julius deemed Michelangelo's forms appropriate for his tomb and for the monumental project of the Sistine Chapel ceiling. Raphael's accomplishment was to bring together the innovations of Leonardo in painting with the massive figural style of Michelangelo's sculpture. In *The School of Athens,* he did this by submerging both strains under his own gifts for harmonious composition and depth of meaning.

Despite the uncertain political conditions of Venice in the early sixteenth century, patrons commissioned the painters Giorgione and Titian to produce lively and sumptuous paintings on both religious and secular themes. Working in a technique that stresses color and light, Giorgione created paintings like the *Fête Champêtre* that evoke a mood of poetic reverie. Titian exploited the traditions of Venetian art to create images like the *Pesaro Madonna* that are astonishingly lifelike and sensual.

ART IN TIME

- 1492 — Columbus' first voyage to the Americas

- 1498 — Leonardo completes *The Last Supper*

- 1499 — France conquers Milan

- 1501 — Michelangelo begins the *David*

- ca. 1503 — Leonardo's *Mona Lisa*

- 1503 — Pope Julius II assumes papal throne

- 1506 — Bramante's plan for Saint Peter's

- 1508 — Michelangelo begins painting the ceiling of the Sistine Chapel

- 1517 — Luther posts his Ninety-five Theses, sparking the Reformation

- 1520 — Death of Raphael

- 1526 — Titian's *Madonna with Members of the Pesaro Family*

The Late Renaissance and Mannerism in Sixteenth-Century Italy

The sixteenth century saw many changes in the political and cultural landscape of Italy (see map 16.1). The immense challenge to established Catholicism posed by Martin Luther's protest in 1517 sent shockwaves round Europe (see page 368). The great powers of France, Spain, and Germany warred with each other on the Italian peninsula, while the Turkish expansion into Europe threatened the whole continent. The spiritual challenge of the Protestant Reformation and the rise of powerful courts affected Italian artists, changing the climate in which they worked as well as the nature of patronage. No one style dominated the sixteenth century in Italy, though all the artists working in what is conventionally called the Late Renaissance were profoundly affected by the achievements of the High Renaissance.

The legacy of the High Renaissance would both challenge and nourish later generations of artists. If Leonardo, Raphael, Bramante, and Giorgione did not survive, their works had tremendous authority and influence. Two of the key figures of this generation lived to transform their styles: Michelangelo was active until 1564 and Titian until 1576. In addition to so weighty a visual legacy, the younger generation faced uncertainty in religious, political, and social spheres. Events such as the Sack of Rome by Habsburg troops in 1527 had immediate repercussions for artists, who scattered throughout Italy and indeed Europe. Commissions came mostly from the princely courts, so artists' works reflected the taste and concerns of this powerful elite. The connections among the courts helped to spread a new style, usually labeled Mannerist, which lasted through much of the century. The style was typically used for paintings and sculptures, though some works of architecture exhibit Mannerist tendencies.

Late Renaissance Florence

Because of the connections among courts and the movement of artists, this new style appeared throughout Italy, but some of its most prominent practitioners came from or worked in Florence.

Mannerism

The name of the new style was derived from the word *maniera*, meaning manner or style, used approvingly by contemporaries. Building on the achievements of Raphael and Michelangelo, above all, artists of the 1520s and later developed a style that emphasized technical virtuosity, erudite subject matter, beautiful figures, and deliberately complex compositions that would appeal to sophisticated tastes. Mannerism became a style of utmost refinement, which emphasized grace, variety, and virtuoso display instead of clarity and unity. Mannerist artists self-consciously explored definitions of beauty: Rather than repeat ancient forms, they experimented

Map 16.1 Italy in the sixteenth century

with proportions, ideal figure types, and unusual compositions. Like the artists of the High Renaissance, they aimed for originality and personal expression, which they considered their due as privileged creators.

Under Medici rule, from 1512 to 1527, Florentine artists absorbed the innovations of the High Renaissance as artists came to the city from Rome. Pope Leo X sent Michelangelo to Florence to work on projects for the Medici family. The artistic successors to Raphael came to the city as well. Having contributed so much to the development of the Early and High Renaissance, Florentine artists took a direction that seems to reject the serenity and confidence of High Renaissance art. Using the techniques of naturalism, *chiaroscuro*, and composition learned from Leonardo, Michelangelo, and Raphael, this generation of artists made images that are less balanced and more expressive than those of their immediate predecessors. In works of the 1520s, a group of Florentine artists created

images of deep spiritual power in this new Mannerist style.

In the chaos after the Sack of Rome, the Medici were again ousted and the republic of Florence was reinstated. But the restoration of relations between the pope and the emperor of the Holy Roman Empire allowed the Medici to return to power by 1530. The Medici Pope Clement VII (1523–1534) promoted his family interests, and worked to enhance the power of his family as the rulers of Florence. Although he was an ardent republican, Michelangelo was continually employed by this court, executing works intended to glorify the Medici dynasty in Florence.

Michelangelo in Florence

Michelangelo's activities centered on the Medici church of San Lorenzo. A century after Brunelleschi's design for the sacristy of this church (see the plan of San Lorenzo, fig. 14.3), which held the tombs of an earlier generation of

16.1 Michelangelo. Tomb of Giuliano de' Medici. 1519–1534. Marble, height of central figure 5'11" (1.8 m). New Sacristy, San Lorenzo, Florence

Medici, Pope Leo X decided to build a matching structure, the New Sacristy. It was to house the tombs of Leo's father, Lorenzo the Magnificent, Lorenzo's brother Giuliano, and two younger members of the family, also named Lorenzo and Giuliano. Aided by numerous assistants, Michelangelo worked on the project from 1519 to 1534 and managed to complete the architecture and two of the tombs, those for the later Lorenzo and the later Giuliano (**fig. 16.1**); these tombs are nearly mirror images of each other.

Michelangelo conceived of the New Sacristy as an architectural–sculptural ensemble. The influence of Brunelleschi is clear in the form of the pilasters and the colors of the stone used to articulate the walls. Thereafter, however, Michelangelo took liberties with his model, treating the walls themselves as sculptural forms in a way Brunelleschi never did. Michelangelo's plans for the Medici tombs underwent many changes while the work was underway. Other figures and reliefs for the project were designed but never executed. The present state of the Medici tombs can hardly be what Michelangelo ultimately intended, as the process was halted when the artist permanently left Florence for Rome in 1534.

Despite the chapel's unfinished state, the tomb of Giuliano remains an imposing visual unit, composed of a sarcophagus supporting two sculpted nudes, above which sits an armored figure, all framed by Michelangelo's inventive use of classical architectural elements. He designed the central niche, which barely accommodates the seated figure, to be framed by paired pilasters. These support an entablature that breaks over them. Such architectural forms defy the logic of classical architecture, even while using its vocabulary. Flanking the niche are blank windows topped by curving pediments supported by volutes; the sarcophagus below echoes these forms. The statues form a triangle that is held in place by a network of verticals and horizontals whose slender, sharp-edged forms contrast with the roundness and weight of the sculpture.

The structure has neither Christian imagery nor inscription. Instead of an effigy, two allegorical figures sit atop the sarcophagus—*Day* on the right and *Night* on the left. Some lines that Michelangelo wrote on one of his drawings suggest what these figures mean: "Day and Night speak, and say: We with our swift course have brought the Duke Giuliano to death … It is only just that the Duke takes revenge [for] he has taken the light from us; and with his closed eyes has locked ours shut, which no longer shine on earth." The reclining figures are themselves derived from ancient river gods. The statue of Giuliano, the ideal image of the prince, wears classical military garb and bears no resemblance to the deceased. ("A thousand years from now, nobody will know what he looked like," Michelangelo is said to have remarked.) His beautifully proportioned figure seems ready for action, as he fidgets with his baton. His gaze was to be directed at the tomb of Lorenzo the Magnificent, never completed. Instead of being a commemorative monument that looks retrospectively at the accomplishments of the deceased, the tomb of Giuliano and the New Sacristy as a whole were to express the triumph of the Medici family over time.

Painters and Sculptors in Ducal Florence

Michelangelo's presence brought new energy to artists working in Tuscany. Painters, sculptors and architects there could not fail to be affected by his work. One such artist was Giovanni

Battista di Jacopo, called Rosso Fiorentino (1495–1540). In 1521 a society of lay Catholics called the Company of the Cross of the Day commissioned Rosso to paint *The Descent from the Cross* (**fig. 16.2**) for their chapel in the Tuscan city of Volterra. The theme of the picture is the lowering of the body of Christ from the cross. To reference the name and ideals of the sponsoring

16.2 Rosso Fiorentino. *The Descent from the Cross.* 1521. Oil on panel, 11′ × 6′5½″ (3.4 × 2 m). Pinacoteca Comunale, Volterra, Italy

Established in 1563, the ACADEMY OF DESIGN was sponsored by Duke Cosimo de' Medici in Florence to promote the arts in Tuscany by improving the training of artists. Bronzino and Giorgio Vasari were founding members. The academy stressed drawing and the study of the human figure. Both nature and the ancients were esteemed, and the art of Michelangelo was held to be the highest achievement of the moderns. The academy emphasized the study of history and literature as well as the skills of the artist.

group, Rosso has given a great deal of emphasis to the cross itself and to the emotional reactions of the figures. While the painting looks back in part to earlier Renaissance art, the composition is much less stable than works of that period. Instead of moving slowly and carefully back into space, the forms all appear to exist in the same plane. The muscular bodies of the agitated figures recall Michelangelo, though the draperies have brittle, sharp-edged planes very different from Michelangelo's work. The low horizon line sets the figures against a dark sky, creating a disquieting effect. The colors are not primaries but sharply contrasting, and the brilliant light seems to fall on the bodies irrationally. Rosso creates an unstable composition within a compressed space

staffed by figures that move frantically to lower the body. Only Christ appears serene in the midst of this emotionally charged image. Rosso's rejection of High Renaissance ideals, in this Mannerist style, allows him to create a work that was especially meaningful to the confraternity members who commissioned it. Rosso himself left central Italy after the Sack of Rome in 1527, ultimately being lured to France to work for King Francis I.

BRONZINO Some of Rosso's younger contemporaries remained in Florence to work for the court of the newly named duke of Florence, Cosimo de' Medici. This court was a magnet for artists from all over Europe, because the duke had inherited the Medici habit of underlining power by means of the arts. Duke Cosimo and Duchess Eleonora commissioned works of art of many sorts, including architecture, sculpture, religious and secular paintings, and numerous portraits. In 1563, the duke sponsored the establishment of the ACADEMY OF DESIGN, an educational center for artists, to perfect the arts in his realm. Many of the artists involved in the founding of the Academy, such as Agnolo Bronzino (1503–1572), worked in a Mannerist style of refined technique and complex subject matter. As court portraitist, painter, and poet, Bronzino served the interests of the duke.

Bronzino's *Allegory of Venus* (**fig. 16.3**), which Duke Cosimo presented to Francis I of France, exemplifies the ducal taste. Into a narrow plane close to the surface of the painting, Bronzino crowds a number of figures who have been identified only tentatively: The bald Father Time tears back the curtain from Fraud, the figure in the upper left-hand corner, to reveal Venus and Cupid in an incestuous embrace. This delights the child Folly, who is armed with roses, and dismays the figure tearing his hair, who has been identified as either Jealousy or Pain. On the right, Pleasure, half woman and half snake, offers a honeycomb. The moral of Bronzino's image may be that folly and pleasure blind one to the jealousy and fraud of sensual love, which time reveals.

With its cool tonalities and contorted nudes, Bronzino's painting proclaims a refined eroticism expressed by the marmoreal figures and mirror-like finish. The complexity of the concept matches the intricacy of the composition; the high quality of the technique matches the cleverness of the content. In Bronzino, the Medici found an artist whose technical virtuosity, complex imagery, and inventive compositions perfectly matched their taste and exemplify the Mannerist style. Cosimo's gift of a painting of such erudite imagery and accomplished technique to the king of France demonstrated his realm's achievements in the literary and visual arts.

GIOVANNI BOLOGNA A comparable combination of technical virtuosity and eroticized imagery appears in a sculpted group created by the French-born artist known as Giovanni Bologna (1529–1608). Giovanni came to Florence to study its artistic tradition around 1555. He created the sculpture in **figure 16.4** to demonstrate his skill to his mentors at the Academy of Design. His challenge was to sculpt three contrasting figures united in a single action. When creating the

16.4 Giovanni Bologna. *The Rape of the Sabine Woman*. Completed 1583. Marble, height 13′6″ (4.1 m). Loggia dei Lanzi, Florence

over-life-sized group, the sculptor had no specific theme in mind, but when it was finished the title *The Rape of the Sabine Woman* was suggested and was accepted by him. The duke admired the work so much that he had it installed near the Palazzo della Signoria in Florence.

The subject proposed derives from the legends of ancient Rome. According to the story, the city's founders, who came from across the sea, tried in vain to find wives among their neighbors, the Sabines. Finally, the men resorted to a trick. Having invited the entire Sabine tribe into Rome for a festival, they attacked them, took the women away by force, and thus ensured the future of their tribe. Giovanni Bologna's image sanitizes this act of raw power and violence, as the figures spiral upward in carefully rehearsed movements. He wished to display his virtuosity and saw his task only in formal terms: To carve in marble, on a massive scale, a sculptural composition that was to be seen from all sides. The contrast between form and content that the Mannerist tendency encouraged could not be clearer.

Rome Reformed

The Medici family's efforts to consolidate their power in Florence were aided by their cousins, the Medici popes Leo X and Clement VII. Such papal manipulations of secular power led to conflict between the papacy and the Holy Roman Empire, which resulted in the Sack of Rome in 1527 by the Emperor Charles V's Habsburg troops. On Clement VII's death in 1534, the cardinals turned to a reform-minded member of a distinguished Roman family, Alessandro Farnese, to restore the papacy. As Pope Paul III, he tried to mediate among the great powers of Europe and encourage the emperor's efforts to bring German princes back to the Roman Church in the wake of the Protestant Reformation.

Paul III was deeply concerned with the spiritual crisis presented by the Reformation. Martin Luther had challenged both the doctrine and the authority of the Church, and his reformed version of Christianity had taken wide hold in northern Europe (see Chapter 17). To respond to this challenge, Paul III called the Council of Trent, which began its deliberations in 1545 and issued its regulations in 1564. The council reaffirmed traditional Catholic doctrine and recommended reforms of liturgy, Church practices, and works of art.

The Catholic Church's most far-reaching and powerful weapon for combating what it considered heresy was the Roman INQUISITION, established in Italy in 1542 to investigate unapproved or suspect religious activities. Those found guilty of engaging in such heresy could be imprisoned or executed. To further control the spread of unorthodoxy, the Church compiled the Index of Prohibited Books in 1557. Texts by suspect authors or on subjects deemed unhealthful could be seized or denied publication.

The reformed Catholic Church also found works of art useful to its goals. In large-scale projects in Rome, the papacy and other groups used the artistic vocabulary of the Renaissance to promote their reforms.

Michelangelo in Rome

Paul III summoned Michelangelo to Rome in 1534 to execute several key projects for him, and Rome remained his home for the rest of his life. The new mood of Rome during the Catholic Reformation (sometimes called the Counter-Reformation) may be reflected in the subject chosen for a major painting in the Sistine Chapel. For Paul III, beginning in 1534, Michelangelo painted the powerful vision of *The Last Judgment* (**fig. 16.5**) on the altar wall. The fresco depicts the Catholic view of the end of the world, based on Gospel texts (Matthew 24:29–31), when Christ will return to judge mankind. It took six years to complete this huge painting, which was unveiled in 1541.

The fresco does not follow conventional representations of the theme. Images of the Last Judgment traditionally represent hell as a place of torment; this is the way it is depicted in Giotto's *Last Judgment* at the Arena Chapel (fig. 12.8). Michelangelo's fresco replaces physical torments with spiritual agony, expressed through violent physical contortions of the human body within a turbulent atmosphere. Angelic trumpeters signal the end of time, while the figure of Christ sits at the fulcrum of a wheel of action: As he raises his arm, the dead rise from the earth at the lower left and move toward heaven where the assembly of saints crowds about him. On the right, the damned sink away from heaven toward Charon, who ferries them to the underworld. Throughout the fresco, naked human figures bend, twist, climb, fall, or gaze at Christ, their forms almost superhuman in their muscular power. Their nudity, which expresses Michelangelo's belief in the sanctity of the human body, disturbed his contemporaries, and shortly after

16.5 Michelangelo. *The Last Judgment*. 1534–1541. Fresco. Sistine Chapel, Vatican, Rome

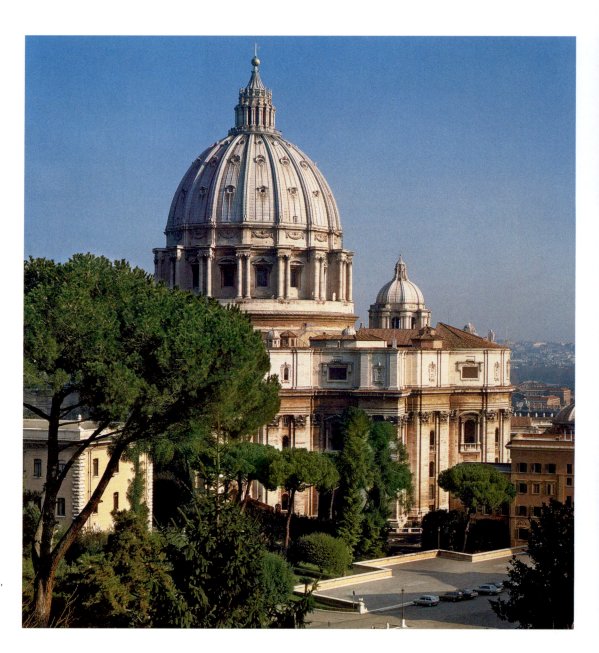

16.6 Michelangelo. Saint Peter's, seen from the west. 1546–1564; dome completed by Giacomo della Porta, 1590. Vatican, Rome

he died in 1564 one of his assistants was commissioned to add bits of clothing to the figures. The fresco was cleaned in 1994, bringing out the brilliant colors, the compressed space, and the dramatic composition. These features link the work to the Mannerist style, though Michelangelo defies such labels.

SAINT PETER'S The pope called on Michelangelo again for another project, the rebuilding of Saint Peter's, left unfinished after Bramante's death. Michelangelo took over the building of the church in 1546, which he designed, following Bramante, as a centrally planned structure topped by a dome (**fig. 16.6**). His plan compressed the interior spaces of the church and gave special focus to the east façade; these elements of Saint Peter's were profoundly altered in the seventeenth century. The dome and western

elevations of the building preserve more of Michelangelo's design.

Where Bramante's plan called for many steps and layers in the elevation (see fig. 15.5), Michelangelo unifies the tall structure by using a colossal order of pilasters across many stories of the exterior. The colossal order supports an entablature and attic story from which spring a high drum and tall dome. Michelangelo's dome has a powerful vertical emphasis that draws energy upward from the vertical pilasters of the elevation. He borrowed not only the double-shell construction but also the high curving profile from Brunelleschi's dome at Florence Cathedral (see fig. 14.1). Where Brunelleschi's dome has smooth planes and flat walls, Michelangelo surrounds his with sculptural forms. The vertical movement of the colossal pilasters is echoed by the double columns of the high drum and then continues upwards over the dome to end in the tall lantern. The logic of this design is so persuasive that almost all domes built between 1600 and 1900 were influenced by it.

The Catholic Reformation and Il Gesù

As the dome for Saint Peter's went up, the Council of Trent was discussing the reform of Roman Catholic Church practices. The centralized plan Michelangelo designed for Saint Peter's presented problems for the Catholic reformers, because the liturgical changes propounded by the council worked best within a basilican structure. The council decreed that believers should see the Elevation of the Host at the heart of the Mass, and this was best accomplished in a long hall as was added to Saint Peter's (see page 393).

A zeal for religious reform in the middle of the sixteenth century, which the Council of Trent exemplified, inspired the creation of a number of reforming religious orders. One of the most ambitious and energetic of these was the Society of Jesus, or Jesuits, founded by Ignatius of Loyola and promoted by Paul III. The order was approved in 1540 and by 1550 their church, Il Gesù in Rome, was in the planning stages. The plan for the church came from one of Michelangelo's assistants, Giacomo Vignola (1507–1573), in 1568. The façade (**fig. 16.7**) was designed by Giacomo della Porta (ca. 1540–1602), but not completed until 1584. As it was the mother church of the Jesuits, its design must have been closely supervised so as to conform to the aims of the order. The Jesuits were at once intellectuals, mystics, and missionaries, whose charge was to fight heresy in Europe and spread Christianity to Asia and America. They required churches that adhered to the precepts of the Council of Trent—churches that would have impressive grandeur while avoiding excessive ornament. Their church of Il Gesù may be seen as the architectural embodiment of the spirit of the Catholic Reformation.

In plan, Il Gesù is a compact basilica dominated by a high nave flanked by chapels, instead of aisles; as a result, the congregation assembles in one large, hall-like space with a clear view of the altar. The façade by Giacomo della Porta is as important as the plan. It is divided into two stories by a strongly projecting entablature supported by paired pilasters that clearly derive from Michelangelo, with whom Della Porta had worked. The same pattern recurs in the upper story on a somewhat smaller scale, with four instead of six pairs of supports. To bridge the

16.7 Giacomo della Porta. Façade of Il Gesù. ca. 1575–1584. Rome

difference in width and hide the roofline, Della Porta inserted two scroll-shaped buttresses. This device forms a graceful transition to the large pediment crowning the façade.

Della Porta has masterfully integrated all the parts of the façade into a single whole: Both stories share the same vertical rhythm, which even the horizontal forms obey. For example, the broken entablature responds to the pilasters, as occurs in Michelangelo's Medici chapel (fig. 16.1). In turn, the horizontal divisions determine the size of the vertical forms, so there is no colossal order. The sculptural treatment of the façade places greater emphasis on the main portal. Its double frame—two pediments resting on coupled pilasters and columns—projects beyond the rest of the façade and gives strong focus to the entire design. This façade and the freedom to add movement and plastic dimension to it were an important precedent for church architecture built by the Jesuits and by others during ensuing centuries.

Cities and Courts in Northern Italy and Venice

Northern Italy was divided into a number of principalities that were smaller than the Grand Duchy of Tuscany or the Papal States. Courts at Mantua, Urbino, Ferrara, and elsewhere competed for imperial titles and territorial gain. Some of the cities of the area tried to maintain their independence from the princely courts, with mixed results. Cities such as Bologna and Parma were fought over and sometimes absorbed by their larger neighbors. Challenged at the opening of the sixteenth century by war and conquest, the republic of Venice succeeded in regaining control of northeastern Italy and reasserting its political and cultural authority.

Mantua

One of the most stable of the north Italian courts was Mantua, where the Gonzaga family retained the title of marquis into the sixteenth century. Mantua had been host to major artists in the fifteenth century such as Alberti and Mantegna. The family's traditions of patronage embraced women as well as men; Isabella d'Este, the wife of Francesco II Gonzaga, was one of the most active patrons of the early sixteenth century. Her son, Federico, became marquis in 1519, a title he held until Charles V created him duke in 1530. Campaigns for such titles were often accompanied by displays of wealth and taste expressed through the arts. As part of his campaign, Federico II Gonzaga commissioned Giulio Romano (ca. 1499–1546) to design and decorate a villa for him outside Mantua, called the Palazzo del Te. There Federico could house his mistress and receive the emperor. Giulio Romano had been Raphael's chief assistant in Rome, but moved to Mantua in 1524.

Inside the Palazzo del Te, Giulio painted a series of rooms with illusionistic frescoes on

16.8 Giulio Romano. *Fall of the Giants from Mount Olympus,* from the Sala dei Giganti. ca. 1530–1532. Palazzo del Te, Mantua, Italy

themes drawn from antiquity. Unlike the frescoes by Mantegna in the *Camera Picta* of the Gonzaga Palace (fig. 14.22) or the frescoes of Raphael in Rome (fig. 15.12), these are not calm images of a dignified court or a distant and beautiful Golden Age, but vivid and dramatic expressions of power. In the Room of the Giants in the palazzo (**fig. 16.8**), Giulio painted a fresco of the gods expelling the giants from Mount Olympus as a cataclysm of falling bodies and columns. The viewer seems to see an entire temple collapsing. The huge figures of the giants are about to be crushed by the falling architectural elements, toppled by the winds, whose personifications appear in the upper corners of the wall. As if witnessing the power of the Olympian gods, the viewer feels drawn into the terror of the event. Of course, the duke himself was imagined as Zeus (Jupiter) in this concept, so the whole illusion speaks to the power of Duke Federico. Giulio uses the impact of Renaissance forms to flatter his patron.

Parma

The city of Parma became part of the Papal States in the sixteenth century, which brought it new wealth and status. The city was the birthplace of a gifted painter, Girolamo Francesco Maria Mazzola (1503–1540), known as Parmigianino. He had made his reputation as a painter in Rome, Florence, and elsewhere before returning to Parma in 1530. A noblewoman there commissioned his most famous work, *The Madonna with the Long Neck* (**fig. 16.9**), in 1535 for a family chapel in the city. Parmigianino had made a deep study of Raphael, but he had a different ideal of beauty. In his painting, he shapes Mary's head as a perfect oval resting on a swanlike neck, while her body swells only to taper to her feet. (Her proportions resemble those of the large amphora offered by the figure at the left.) By contrast, Raphael's *Alba Madonna* (fig. 15.11) seems all circles and cubes. Raphael makes the Virgin's features sweet, while Parmigianino makes them haughty. Parmigianino also replaces Raphael's stable compositions with more dramatic ones. Here, the sleeping Christ Child balances precariously on the Madonna's lap, as she lifts a boneless hand to her breast. The composition is as unbalanced as the postures: Heavily weighted to the left, open and distant to the right. All the figures have elongated limbs and ivory-smooth features, and the space is compressed. In Mannerist fashion, these elements draw attention to the artist's skill and his inversion of Raphael's ideals.

16.9 Parmigianino. *The Madonna with the Long Neck*. ca. 1535. Oil on panel, 7′1″ × 4′4″ (2.2 × 1.3 m). Galleria degli Uffizi, Florence

These choices may also reflect the meaning of the image. The large Christ Child in his mother's lap recalls the theme of the *Pietà* and alludes to his death. Nor is the setting as arbitrary as it may seem. The gigantic column is a symbol often associated with the Madonna as the gateway to heaven and eternal life, as well as with her role as the Immaculate Conception (compare fig. 15.14). *The Madonna with the Long*

Neck is a vision of unearthly perfection, with a cold and memorable elegance.

Bologna

Bologna, an important city north of Florence, was not ruled by a prince, but controlled from Rome in conjunction with a senate composed of local aristocratic families. Its cultural character was also shaped by the presence of its ancient university. These conditions fostered the talents of several women artists during the sixteenth century, including Lavinia Fontana (1552–1614).

The daughter of a painter, Fontana was able through her upbringing to learn an art form that increasingly was being restricted by the new training in the academies. She developed a network of patrons among the noblewomen of the city, for whom she painted religious works and portraits, such as the *Portrait of a Noblewoman*, dated to the 1580s (**fig. 16.10**). The portrait depicts a young woman in her wedding finery, which Fontana rendered with great attention to detail in the dress, the jewelry and the headdress. The young woman averts her eyes from the spectator, as if to demonstrate her modesty. With one hand she caresses a little dog, perhaps a pet, or perhaps a symbol of fidelity; with the other she holds a fur pelt attached by a jewel to her waist, another symbol, this time associated with fertility. Fontana's skill at composing such flattering and

16.10 Lavinia Fontana. *Portrait of a Noblewoman*. ca. 1580. Oil on canvas, 45¼ × 35¼″ (114 × 89.5 cm). National Museum of Women in the Arts, Washington, D.C. Gift of Wallace and Wilhelmina Holladay

sumptuous images made her one of the most sought-after artists of her city.

Venice: The Serene Republic

Despite the attacks it endured at the beginning of the sixteenth century, Venice regained much of its territory and wealth by 1529. Venice remained a nominal republic, controlled by ancient families, who commissioned works for their houses in town and for their villas in the country; artists were therefore able to choose from a wide variety of themes to depict. The painters of Venice built on the achievements of Bellini, Giorgione and Titian, while its architects experimented with classical forms.

TITIAN Titian dominated painting in the city throughout the sixteenth century. Like Michelangelo, he lived a long life, and he had numerous pupils to spread his style and techniques. His fame was such that by the 1530s his work was sought by the most elite patrons of Europe. For example, in 1538, the Duke of Urbino, Guidobaldo II della Rovere, commissioned him to paint the so-called *Venus of Urbino* (**fig. 16.11**). This painting depicts a nude young woman lying on a sumptuous bed in a well-furnished chamber. Gazing out at the viewer, she poses provocatively, her torso and head framed by a deep green curtain. The gentle light illuminates her body, which Titian renders with lush, flowing brushstrokes. In the background, two women search in a large box for something, perhaps for a garment to clothe her. Titian's use of color records the sensuous textures of the woman's body, which has been placed on display for the duke. Though the figure is usually called Venus, the painting may have been intended as an erotic image, not a classical theme, as the duke referred to the image only as "the naked woman." Whether or not this is Venus, the sensuously depicted female nude became a staple product of Titian's workshop, which was supported by the patronage of other powerful men.

16.11 Titian. *Venus of Urbino*. ca. 1538. Oil on canvas, 3′10⅞″ × 5′5″ (119 × 165 cm). Galleria degli Uffizi, Florence

16.12 Paolo Veronese. *The Feast in the House of Levi.* 1573. Oil on canvas, 18'2" × 42' (5.5 × 12.8 m). Galleria dell'Accademia, Venice

Titian's creative output and reputation drew many artists to work in his shop, but he had a tremendous influence even on others. From the island of Crete (then owned by Venice), the young Domenikos Theotokopoulos, called El Greco, came to study in Titian's shop before heading to Spain (see page 367). The two leading painters in Venice after Titian, Veronese and Tintoretto, developed in different directions. Where Veronese made images that depend on early Titian works like the *Pesaro Madonna* (fig. 15.14) and aimed for naturalism, Tintoretto exploited Titian's drama and fluid brushwork to create more dramatic and visionary images.

VERONESE Paolo Cagliari (1528–1588), called Paolo Veronese, made paintings that start from the naturalism inherent in Titian's style, but added grand architectural frameworks and an interest in details of everyday reality, as seen in animals, textiles, and foodstuffs. His huge canvas called *The Feast in the House of Levi* (**fig. 16.12**) exemplifies his style. His symmetrical composition harks back to paintings by Leonardo and Raphael, while the festive mood of the scene reflects examples by Titian of the 1520s, so that at first glance the picture looks like a High Renaissance work born 50 years too late. Veronese, however, is less interested than artists of that period in conveying spiritual or

psychological depth or theological messages. Originally commissioned for the refectory of a Dominican monastery, the painting depicts a sumptuous banquet, but it is unclear which event from the life of Jesus he meant to represent.

As with his contemporaries elsewhere in Italy, Veronese was vague about the subject matter. For this, he was summoned by the religious tribunal of the Inquisition on the charge of filling his picture with "buffoons, drunkards, Germans, dwarfs, and similar vulgarities" unsuited to its theme. The account of the trial shows that the tribunal thought Veronese's representation of *The Last Supper* was irreverent. In the face of their questions, he settled on a different title, which permitted him to leave the offending details in place. In rebuffing the Inquisition, the artist claimed the privilege to "paint pictures as I see fit."

TINTORETTO Veronese's contemporary Jacopo Robusti (1519–1594), called Tintoretto, took a less worldly attitude. Tintoretto reportedly wanted "to paint like Titian and to design like Michelangelo." He did not imitate the High Renaissance phases of those artists' careers, however, but absorbed their later styles, which are more expressive and less realistic in their effects. Tintoretto's final

16.13 Jacopo Tintoretto. *The Last Supper.* 1592–1594. Oil on canvas, 12′ × 18′8″ (3.7 × 5.7 m). San Giorgio Maggiore, Venice

major work, *The Last Supper,* finished in 1594 (**fig. 16.13**), seems to deny in every possible way the balance and clarity of Leonardo's version of the theme painted almost exactly a century before (fig. 15.2). Tintoretto places Jesus at the center of the composition, but his small figure in the middle distance is distinguished mainly by the brilliant halo. The artist barely hints at the human drama of Judas' betrayal; Judas can be seen isolated on the near side of the table across from Jesus, but his role is so insignificant that he could almost be mistaken for an attendant. The table sits at a sharp angle to the picture plane, in exaggerated perspective. This arrangement was designed to relate the scene to the space for which it was commissioned, in the monastic church of San Giorgio Maggiore in Venice. Tintoretto took the viewpoint of the Benedictine monks into account, designing the space as if seen from the choir where they took communion.

The scene is cluttered, with attendants, containers of food and drink, and domestic animals converging upon Jesus just as he offers his body and blood, in the form of bread and wine, to the disciples. The smoke from the blazing oil lamp miraculously turns into clouds of angels, blurring the distinction between the natural and the supernatural and turning the image into a magnificently orchestrated vision. Tintoretto's aim is to make visible the miracle of the Eucharist—the transubstantiation of earthly into divine food. During the Catholic Reformation, the central importance of this sacrament to Catholic doctrine was forcefully reasserted.

PALLADIO AND LATE RENAISSANCE ARCHITECTURE

Like patrons elsewhere in Italy, Venetian aristocrats commissioned works inspired by the ancient world. The field of architecture in Venice was dominated by the figure of Andrea Palladio (1506–1580). Palladio's career centered on his native town of Vicenza, in the Venetian territory, but he achieved worldwide influence through the publication of his *FOUR BOOKS OF ARCHITECTURE,* in 1570. This treatise records his designs and the principles from antiquity that informed them and circulated his ideas around the world.

Andrea Palladio's *Quattro libri dell'architettura (THE FOUR BOOKS OF ARCHITECTURE)* has influenced architects for more than four centuries. Thomas Jefferson, for instance, once referred to it as "the Bible," and the "Palladian" window is still a feature of much of today's architecture. In spectacular detailed drawings, Palladio reconstructed the ruins of classical temples, shrines, basilicas, and arenas, so that they would serve as models for contemporary practitioners.

16.14 Andrea Palladio. Villa Rotonda. ca. 1567–1570. Vicenza, Italy

Much of Palladio's architecture consists of town houses and country villas. The Villa Rotonda (**fig. 16.14**) is a good example of his interpretation of ancient precepts. This country residence, built near Vicenza beginning in 1567, consists of a square block topped by a dome. All four sides of this villa have identical porches in the shape of temple fronts. Compared to the freedom with which Michelangelo treated classical forms, Palladio seems to follow the rules laid down by the Roman architect Vitruvius, whose treatise on architecture he studied and emulated in his own. His structures exhibit the balance and clarity of ancient forms, while serving the needs of his aristocratic patrons. Palladio's use of the temple front here is more than an expression of

his regard for antiquity; he believed that great men required houses that were dignified, beautiful and harmonious. This concept was embedded in the social outlook of the later sixteenth century, which required the display of great wealth and taste to assert social status. Palladio's design also takes advantage of the pleasing views offered in every direction by the site. Beautifully correlated with the walls behind and the surrounding vistas, the porches of the Villa Rotonda give the structure an air of serene dignity and festive grace that is enhanced by the sculptures on the façades. Palladio's approach to architecture was inspired by his study of the ancients, but his practical exploitation of ancient ideals resulted in buildings that express Renaissance values.

SUMMARY

The later sixteenth century saw the growing power of princes and popes over the once independent cities of Italy. Courts were major patrons of the arts, and princes and dukes shared a taste for erudite, complicated, and beautifully executed forms. This tendency has been labeled Mannerist, as it depended so much on the artifice or manner of the highly skilled artist.

The Medici rulers of Florence used art for many purposes: They built palaces, as well as the Medici Chapel, established an academy for training artists, and gave works of art as diplomatic presents, as was the case with Bronzino's *Allegory of Venus*. Artists in Florence made works like *The Rape of the Sabine Woman* that stressed complex compositions and technical virtuosity. The international demand for works from Michelangelo added to the city's reputation as an art center, as did the spread of Florentine-trained artists all over Europe.

Mannerist works made for princes clashed with calls for spiritual and moral renewal coming from the Catholic Church. The challenge of the Protestant Reformation and the shock of the Sack of Rome in 1527 encouraged the popes to commission works that expressed their spiritual authority. In this, many popes turned to Michelangelo. Works like *The Last Judgment* and the Dome of Saint Peter's, steeped in Michelangelo's reverence for antiquity, had gained such authority that his style became the benchmark for others. The ideals of the Catholic Reformation encouraged religious orders such as the Jesuits to commission large basilicas using ancient forms in new patterns inspired by Michelangelo.

Courts throughout Italy hired artists who had trained in Florence or Rome to make visual statements of the local prince's power. Images of Greek and Roman gods stand in for the prince himself in paintings and sculptures of great technical accomplishment, like the *Fall of the Giants from Mount Olympus* by Giulio Romano. In cities where elite families were the key patrons, works reflecting Mannerist innovations, like Parmigianino's *The Madonna with the Long Neck*, coexisted with others exhibiting a style closer to the values of the High Renaissance, like Fontana's *Portrait of a Noblewoman*. Venice clung to local traditions established in the Early and High Renaissance. Titian's long and productive life made his style dominant in the city. His followers expanded the Venetian preference for color and naturalism into large-scale canvases that overwhelm the spectator, such as Veronese's *The Feast in the House of Levi*. The restrained architecture of Palladio placed the forms of antiquity at the service of wealthy patrons and the Church.

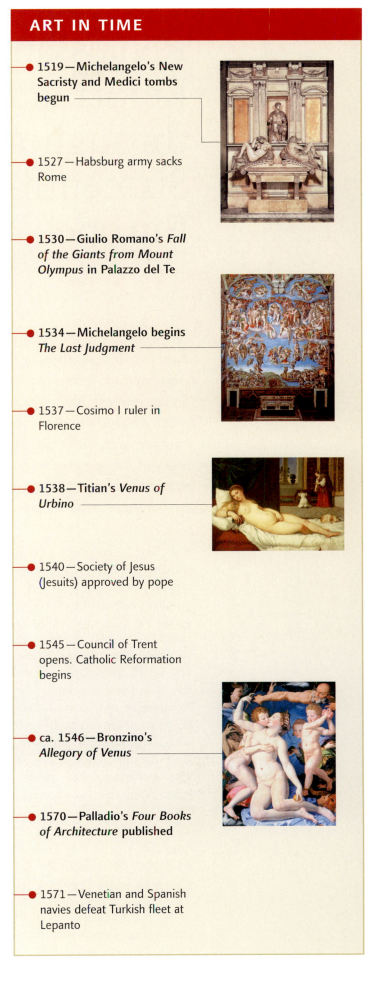

Renaissance and Reformation throughout Sixteenth-Century Europe

In addition to the religious challenge of the Protestant Reformation and the new cultural expressions of the Renaissance, Europeans outside Italy witnessed the growing power of large centralized states in France, England, Spain, and the Holy Roman Empire, and the expansion of Europe's economic reach around the globe. The Reformation changed the map, as whole communities, cities, and even states were converted, fracturing the religious unity of Europe (see map 17.1). While France and Spain remained loyal to the Roman Catholic Church, Germany, England, and the Netherlands were divided by religious sectarianism.

The arts throughout Europe changed in response to these new conditions. The Protestant reformers' suspicion of sculpture meant that the medium of painting increased in importance. As religious patronage waned, artists turned to secular themes, which appealed to patrons in the cities and in the courts. To compete on the open market, artists began to specialize in particular subjects or themes. Italian Renaissance style also challenged artists, who absorbed Italian compositions, ideal figure types, and admiration for antiquity. Patrons in the courts found Italian style particularly useful for emphasizing their power, while Catholic rulers often used Italianate forms to affirm their faith.

France and Spain: Catholic Courts and Italian Influence

France was fertile ground for the importation of Italian ideas. French kings had been intervening in Italy for centuries, and this had given them an

awareness of developments in its art and architecture. Francis I (r. 1515–1547) showed his admiration for Italian art by inviting Leonardo da Vinci to work for him. Francis's generous patronage made his court a magnet for many artists from Italy and from elsewhere in Europe. French traditions were maintained, too, as local architects interpreted Italian ideas.

Italian influence is apparent in the château, or castle, that Francis built south of Paris. In 1528, he decided to expand a medieval hunting lodge amid the forests of Fontainebleau. What began as a modest enlargement soon developed into a sprawling palace. The original design, much altered over the years, was largely the work of the stonemason Gilles Le Breton (d. 1553). The *Cour du Cheval Blanc* (Court of the White Horse) is typical of the project as a whole (**fig. 17.1**). Generations of patrons and architects were needed to build it, yet the façade still preserves an organic unity. (The staircase in the courtyard was built by Jean Androuet Du Cerceau in 1634.) Composed with rectangular pavilions at regular intervals, the façade employs a vocabulary from Italian

Map 17.1 Europe in the sixteenth century

Holy Roman Empire boundary

Empire of Charles V

17.1 Gilles Le Breton. *Cour du Cheval Blanc* (Court of the White Horse), Fontainebleau. 1528–1540

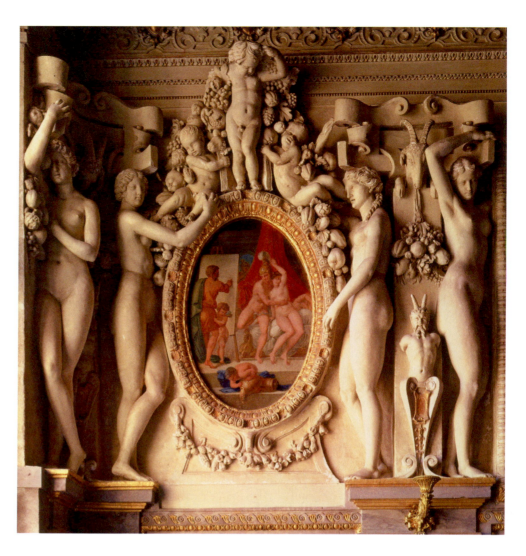

architecture: Pilasters mark each story, entablatures tie the whole façade together horizontally, and the lowest level uses rusticated pilasters. But these elements are blended with vertical proportions, especially in the windows and along the roofline. Such vertical elements distinguish the French interpretation from its Italian models. Fontainebleau set a fashion for French translations of Italianate architecture followed for nearly all French châteaux for the next 250 years.

Francis I's love of Italian art is apparent throughout Fontainebleau. The artists, who came from all over Italy to work on the château, mostly worked in a Mannerist style, creating lavish interiors to flatter the king. For example, Francesco Primaticcio (1504–1570), born in Bologna and trained by Giulio Romano, combined painting and sculpted imagery for the room of the king's mistress, the Duchesse d'Etampes (**fig. 17.2**). Here, Primaticcio surrounds his painting by a frame of stucco nudes, who have the long, elegant proportions of figures by Parmigianino (see fig. 16.9). The four willowy female figures have no specific allegorical significance, although

their role recalls the nudes of the Sistine Chapel ceiling. They enframe paintings devoted to Alexander the Great, executed by assistants from Primaticcio's designs. The one shown depicts the classical artists Apelles painting Alexander with Campaspe. Alexander gave his mistress to Apelles when the painter fell in love with her. Roman texts of this subject characterized this gift as a mark of Alexander's great respect for his court artist. The picture draws a parallel between Alexander and Francis I, and between Campaspe and the duchess, the king's mistress, who had taken Primaticcio under her protection. Such mixtures of violence and eroticism appealed greatly to the courtly audience for which Primaticcio worked.

Spain and Italianate Style

Wealth from the newly colonized Americas and rule over significant portions of Europe made Spain a world power in the sixteenth century. The Spanish ruler Charles V also controlled the Netherlands, most of Central Europe and parts of Italy. When he abdicated in 1556, he split his holdings between his son Philip and his brother

17.3 El Greco. *The Burial of Count Orgaz.* 1586. Oil on canvas, 16′ × 11′10″ (4.9 × 3.6 m). Santo Tomé, Toledo, Spain

Ferdinand. Ferdinand took control of the traditional Habsburg territories in central Europe. Philip reigned as king of Spain, the Netherlands, and New Spain in the Americas from 1556 to 1598. After fending off the Turkish advance into Europe in 1571, the very Catholic Philip took aim at Protestant regions, though less successfully. His attempts to quash the rebellion of the Calvinist Northern Netherlands ultimately produced the independent state of Holland; his attempt to invade England in 1588 strengthened England's stature.

EL GRECO Following Philip's lead, the Spanish court was staunchly Roman Catholic and commissioned churches and church furnishings throughout the century. Italian artists moved to Spain to fulfill such commissions, and Spanish artists went to Italy to study. The best-known painter of sixteenth-century Spain, Domenikos Theotokopoulos (1541–1614), called El Greco, was born in Crete, then under Venetian rule. His style fused the influence of Venetian painters such as Titian and Tintoretto with the influence of Raphael, Michelangelo, and the Italian Mannerists. He arrived in Spain in 1576/77 and settled in Toledo.

Among the most impressive of El Greco's commissions is *The Burial of Count Orgaz,* executed in 1586 in the church of Santo Tomé in Toledo (**fig. 17.3**). This painting sits above the tomb of Count Orgaz, who had died in 1323; he

The Protestant Reformation

I N OCTOBER 1517, Martin Luther, a former Augustinian friar and professor of theology at the University of Wittenberg, issued a public challenge to both the theology and the institutional practices of the Catholic Church. In his famous *Ninety-five Theses*, which he nailed to the church door at Wittenberg Castle, Luther complained about the Catholic practice of selling indulgences—promises of redemption of sins; he argued also against the veneration of Mary and the saints. Fundamental to his critique of Catholicism was Luther's claim that the Bible and natural reason were the sole bases of religious authority, and that the intervention of clerics and saints was unnecessary for salvation, which was freely given by God. It followed, then, that religious authority was transferred from the pope to the individual conscience of each believer. The Catholic Church responded by condemning him in 1521. But many Christians in Europe accepted his critique, the result of which eventually fueled political instability, rebellions, and wars. Many areas of northern Germany converted to the Protestant reform, while southern regions, like Bavaria, remained Catholic. In rethinking these basic issues of faith, Luther was joined by other religious reformers.

The Swiss pastor Ulrich Zwingli stressed access to the scriptures and preaching. His literal reading of the Bible led him to denounce not only the sale of indulgences, but the visual arts as well. Above all, what concerned the reformers were the issues of grace and free will in attaining faith and salvation. By the time of Zwingli's death in 1531, the main elements of Protestant theology had been defined. Around mid-century, John Calvin of Geneva was promoting his vision of a moral life based on a literal reading of scripture.

Studying the Bible required literacy, so now both girls and boys were required to read. The invention of the printing press furthered the spread of Protestantism, by putting the Bible in the hands of many believers. The implications of the Reformation were enormous for the liturgy, for social life, and for art. The Catholic Church would change as well. Luther's complaints spurred reforms beginning in the mid-sixteenth century and continuing into the seventeenth. This Catholic Reformation would have its own effects on European art and life.

was so pious, it was said, that St. Stephen and St. Augustine appeared at his funeral and lowered the body into its grave. El Greco depicts the miracle as a contemporary event and portrays many of the local nobility and clergy of his time among the witnesses to the event. The painting argues the Roman Catholic position that believers must perform good works to achieve salvation and that saints serve as intercessors with heaven.

The display of color and texture in the armor and vestments reflects El Greco's Venetian training. Above, the count's soul (a small, cloud-like figure like the angels in Tintoretto's *Last Supper,* fig. 16.13) is carried to heaven. Where the lower half of the painting seems very concrete, the celestial assembly in the upper half is painted very differently. Every form—clouds, limbs, draperies—takes part in a sweeping, flamelike movement toward the figure of Christ. El Greco's compressed space, unearthly light, and weightless bodies share stylistic features with Italian Mannerist works such as Rosso's *Descent from the Cross* (fig. 16.2). The viewer standing before the actual grave of Count Orgaz sees in El Greco's painting the reenactment of

the miraculous burial, so the space of the painting links directly to the space of the viewer. El Greco directs viewers from their own reality toward a vision of heaven.

Central Europe: The Reformation and Art

While France, Spain, and Italy remained mostly Catholic, elsewhere in Europe the religious and artistic situation was more complex. Emperor Charles V headed the regions that make up modern Germany, Austria, Hungary, and the Czech Republic. These were independent political units, only nominally under the emperor's control. The Reformation fractured their religious unity after 1517 (see Cultural Context: The Protestant Reformation, above). The spread of the reformed faiths led to wars throughout central Europe that finally ended with the Peace of Augsburg in 1555. This compromise allowed the rulers of individual regions to choose the faith for their region's inhabitants, furthering the spread of the reformed faiths and firming up the political divisions. The repercussions for art were equally important. While Luther saw the value of art as a tool for teaching, some of the more radical reformers considered the many forms of medieval and Renaissance religious art as idolatrous, and they encouraged ICONOCLASM, or the destruction of images. As religious commissions dried up, artists had to find new styles, new subjects, and new markets for their work.

Catholic Patrons in Early Sixteenth-Century Germany

Not all regions of central Europe converted to the reformed faiths, and it was not until the 1520s that the Reformation took wide hold, so some religious objects were created in the sixteenth century for Catholic patrons. One memorable example is an altarpiece executed by the painter Matthias Gothart Nithart, who was known for centuries only as Grünewald (ca. 1475–1528). Between 1509/10 and 1515, he painted a transforming triptych called the *Isenheim Altarpiece* for the monastery church of the Order of St. Anthony at Isenheim, in Alsace, France.

This church served the monks of the order and the patients of their hospital, which was for people suffering from a disease called St. Anthony's Fire, caused by eating spoiled rye. The painful symptoms of this disorder include intestinal disorders, gangrenous limbs, and hallucinations. Treatment consisted mostly of soothing baths and sometimes the amputation of limbs. Both monks and patients would have seen Grünewald's altarpiece on the high altar. Its painted panels enclose a carved wooden shrine. Nine panels organized in two sets of movable wings open in three stages or "views." The first of these views, when all the wings are closed, shows *The Crucifixion* in the center panel (**fig. 17.4**). This view was visible on weekdays.

Grünewald depicts Christ's body on the cross on a heroic scale, so that it dominates the other

ICONOCLASM comes from Greek roots that, combined, mean image-breaking. Iconoclasts destroy images for political or religious reasons. While the Byzantine Empire endured a period of Iconoclasm in the seventh and eighth centuries (see chapter 8), several waves of image destruction occurred in the wake of the Reformation in Europe. The more radical reformed faiths deplored the Catholic tradition of religious images and relics and encouraged the destruction of images. This resulted in great loss of works of art from earlier periods.

17.4 Matthias Grünewald. *Isenheim Altarpiece* (closed): *The Crucifixion*; predella: *Lamentation.* ca. 1509/10–1515. Oil on panel, main body 9'9½" × 10'9" (2.97 × 3.28 m); predella 2'5½" × 11'2" (0.75 × 3.4 m). Musée d'Unterlinden, Colmar, France

17.5 Matthias Grünewald. *Isenheim Altarpiece* (open): *The Annunciation; Madonna and Child with Angels; The Resurrection.* ca. 1509/10–1515. Oil on panel, each wing 8′10″ × 4′8″ (2.69 × 1.42 m); center panel 8′10″ × 11′2½″ (2.69 × 3.41 m). Musée d'Unterlinden, Colmar, France

figures and the landscape. The Crucifixion becomes a lonely event silhouetted against a ghostly landscape and a blue-black sky. Despite the darkness of the landscape, an eerie light bathes the foreground figures to heighten awareness of them. On the left, in a white garment, Mary swoons at the sight of her tortured son; St. John's red robe accents her paleness. Below the cross, Mary Magdalen kneels in grief. On the right, John the Baptist points to the crucified Christ with the words, "He must increase, and I must decrease," indicating the significance of Christ's sacrifice. The lamb at his feet bleeds into a chalice, as does the lamb in the central panel of the *Ghent Altarpiece* (fig. 13.5), alluding to the Eucharist. In the predella below, a tomb awaits the tormented body while Christ's mother and friends bid farewell. The predella slides apart at Christ's knees, so victims of amputation may have seen their own suffering reflected in this image.

On Sundays and feast days, the outer wings were opened and the mood of the *Isenheim Altarpiece* changed dramatically (**fig. 17.5**). All three scenes in this view—*The Annunciation*, the *Madonna and Child with Angels*, and *The Resurrection*—celebrate events as jubilant as the Crucifixion is somber. Depicting the cycle of salvation, from the Incarnation to the Resurrection, this view of the altarpiece offered the afflicted a form of spiritual medicine while reminding

them of the promise of heaven. Throughout these panels, Grünewald has depicted forms of therapy recommended for sufferers at the hospital: Music, herbs, baths, and light. The contrast of the body of the dead Jesus in the predella with the Resurrected Christ in the right panel offers consolation to the dying. (The inner wings could also be opened, to reveal sculpted figures.)

Grünewald's color draws the eye through the composition. Reds and pinks in the left panel carry through the central panels to end at the brilliant colors surrounding the Risen Christ on the right. The simple Gothic chapel in which the Annunciation takes place gives way in the next panel to a fantastic tabernacle where choirs of angels play stringed instruments and sing. Beneath that tabernacle appears a figure of the Virgin, crowned and glowing like a lit candle. The central image of the Madonna holding her child in a tender embrace gives way to a vision of heaven, also made of pure light. These elements lead the eye to the right panel, where the body of Christ appears to float above the stone sarcophagus into which it had been placed in the predella. The guards set to watch the tomb are knocked senseless by the miracle. Their figures, carefully arranged in a perspective display, contrast with the weightless and transfigured body of Christ. This figure differs dramatically from the figure on the cross; his body bears no scars and the proportions are closer to the Italian ideal seen in Piero della Francesca's *Resurrection* (fig. 14.18). Grünewald's oil technique, his brilliant use of color, and his detailed rendering of objects derive from northern European art of the fifteenth century, but the *Isenheim Altarpiece* also demonstrates his awareness of Italian perspective. Grünewald's aim is to create an emotional response with the impact of a vision.

Albrecht Dürer as Renaissance Artist

The key figure for the Renaissance in Germany is Grünewald's contemporary, Albrecht Dürer (1471–1528). Dürer's style began in the traditions of northern European realism, but he also delved deeply into the innovations of the Italian Renaissance. Trained as a painter and printmaker in his native Nuremberg, he traveled in northern Europe and Venice in 1494/95; these journeys changed his view of the world and the artist's place in it. Dürer adopted the ideal of the artist as a gentleman and humanistic scholar that had taken hold in Italy. His painting technique owes much to the Flemish masters, but making copies

of Italian works taught him many of the lessons of Italian art. He was able to synthesize these traditions in his paintings and graphic works (prints and drawings). He had wide influence on sixteenth-century art through his prints, which circulated all over Europe.

APOCALYPSE Trained to make both woodcuts and engravings, Dürer expanded the possibilities of each. Prints were not commissioned by individual patrons; they were made for the open market, so Dürer had to invest his own time and materials in these projects. He chose themes that sold well. One of his biggest successes came in 1498. As the year 1500 approached, many people believed that the Second Coming of Christ was imminent, and prepared for the Millennium. With an eye to the market for things pertaining to popular fears about the end of time, Dürer produced a woodcut series illustrating the Apocalypse. This series was his most ambitious graphic work in the years following his return from Italy. The gruesome vision of *The Four Horsemen of the Apocalypse* (**fig. 17.6**) offers the

17.6 Albrecht Dürer. *The Four Horsemen of the Apocalypse.* 1498. Woodcut, 15½ × 11⅛″ (39.3 × 28.3 cm). The Metropolitan Museum of Art, New York. Gift of Junius S. Morgan, 1919. 1919.73.209

17.7 Albrecht Dürer. *Adam and Eve.* 1504. Engraving, 9⅞ × 7⅝″ (25.2 × 19.4 cm). Los Angeles County Museum of Art

viewer a frightening visualization of the text of the Book of Revelation. The woodcut depicts War, Conquest, Famine, and Death overrunning the population of the earth. The physical energy and full-bodied volume of the figures in the Apocalypse woodcuts series is partly owed to Dürer's experience of Italian art, although he eliminates logical space in favor of an otherworldly flatness. Dürer added to the woodcut medium some of the devices of engraving. He replaced the broad contours and occasional hatchings, used to define form in earlier woodcuts, with a wide range of hatching marks, varied width of lines, and strong contrasts of black and white, giving his woodcuts ambitious pictorial effects. (Compare, for example, the Buxheim St. Christopher of 1425 shown in fig. 13.13 with Dürer's woodcuts.) He set a standard that soon transformed the technique of woodcut all over Europe.

ADAM AND EVE Dürer's fusion of northern European and Italian traditions is apparent in his engraving entitled *Adam and Eve* of 1504 (**fig. 17.7**). Here the biblical subject allows him to depict the first parents as two ideal nudes: Apollo and Venus in a densely wooded forest. Carefully detailed animals, trees and foliage accompany the human forms. Dürer enlarged the vocabulary of descriptive marks an engraver could use: The lines taper and swell; they intersect at varying angles; marks start and stop and dissolve into dots. The result is a monochrome image with a great tonal and textural range.

The choice of animals that populate the Garden of Eden is very deliberate: The cat, rabbit, ox, and elk have been interpreted as symbols of the medieval theory that bodily fluids, called humors, controlled personality. The cat represents the choleric humor, quick to anger; the ox

17.8 Albrecht Dürer. *The Four Apostles.* 1523–1526. Oil on panel, each 7′1″ × 2′6″ (216 × 76 cm). Alte Pinakothek, Munich

the phlegmatic humor, lethargic and slow; the elk stands for the melancholic humor, sad and serious; and the rabbit for the sanguine, energetic and sensual. In this moment before the fall, the humors coexist in balance and the humans retain an ideal beauty. The composition itself is balanced and unified by the tonal effects. Dürer's print, which he signed prominently on the plaque by Adam's head, made an enormous impact.

Albrecht Dürer as Reformation Artist

Dürer became an early and enthusiastic follower of Martin Luther. His new faith can be sensed in the growing austerity of style and subject in his religious works after 1520. The climax of this trend is represented by *The Four Apostles* (**fig. 17.8**). Dürer presented these paired panels in 1526 to the city of Nuremberg, which had joined the Lutheran camp. These four men are fundamental to Protestant doctrine. John and Paul, Luther's favorite authors of scripture, face one another in the foreground, with Peter and Mark behind. Quotations from their writings, inscribed below in Luther's translation, warn the city not to mistake human error and pretense for the will of God. The heavily draped apostles have the weight and presence of Raphael's figures. Through the power of his paintings, the portable medium of prints and his workshop, Dürer was the most influential artist of sixteenth-century Germany.

Protestant Courts and New Forms of Art

The realignment of German culture and society produced by the Reformation required most artists to adapt their styles and subject matter for the reformed faiths. This remained a challenge throughout the century. For courtly patrons, artists made images on classicizing themes, in which they used local styles that emphasized detail, texture, and the natural world.

17.9 Lucas Cranach the Elder. *The Judgment of Paris*. 1530. Oil on panel, 13½ × 9½″ (34.3 × 24.2 cm). Staatliche Kunsthalle, Karlsruhe, Germany

Mythologies

One such artist was Lucas Cranach the Elder (1472–1553), a close friend of Martin Luther, who worked mainly for the courts, making portraits and mythological scenes. In *The Judgment of Paris* (**fig. 17.9**) of 1530, Cranach retells a story from Greek mythology in which the Trojan prince Paris selects the most beautiful goddess of Olympus. Cranach depicts Paris as a German knight wearing the fashionable armor of the nobles at the court of Saxony, where he was court artist. The sinewy figures of the goddesses await the judgment of Paris, who confides his choice to Mercury, also dressed in armor. Like Italian artists working for courts, Cranach gives his classical subject an overtly erotic appeal, inviting the viewer to identify with the privileged observer of the weightless female nudes. The lush vegetation of the landscape recalls Dürer's *Adam and Eve* (fig. 17.7), though Cranach exaggerates its foliage into a sensual fantasy of natural beauty.

Landscape

Cranach's and Dürer's influence was deeply felt in southern Germany and Austria in the first half of the sixteenth century among a group of artists who specialized in landscape paintings. The key figure in this group was Albrecht Altdorfer (ca. 1480–1538), who spent most of his career in Bavaria. Altdorfer's work is dominated by his fascination with landscape, evident in *The Battle of Issos* (**fig. 17.10**). The painting, made in 1529, is one of a series of images depicting the exploits of historic heroes for the Munich palace of William IV, duke of Bavaria. In a sweeping landscape, Altdorfer depicts Alexander the Great's victory over Darius of Persia, which took place in 333 BCE at Issos (see fig. 5.33). To make the subject clear, Altdorfer provides an explanatory text on the tablet suspended in the sky, inscriptions on the banners and a label on Darius' fleeing chariot. The artist follows ancient descriptions of the number and kind of combatants in the battle and alludes to the specific locale of the battle.

Altdorfer gives the spectator a viewpoint looking down on the action from a great height. From this omniscient perspective, a viewer hunts for the two leaders lost in the antlike mass of their own armies. The drama of nature is more elaborated than the human actors: One can almost feel the rotation of the globe as the sun sets in the distance and the moon rises. The curve of the earth, the drama of the clouds, the

17.10 Albrecht Altdorfer. *The Battle of Issos*. 1529. Oil on panel, 62 × 47" (157.5 × 119.5 cm). Alte Pinakothek, Munich, Germany

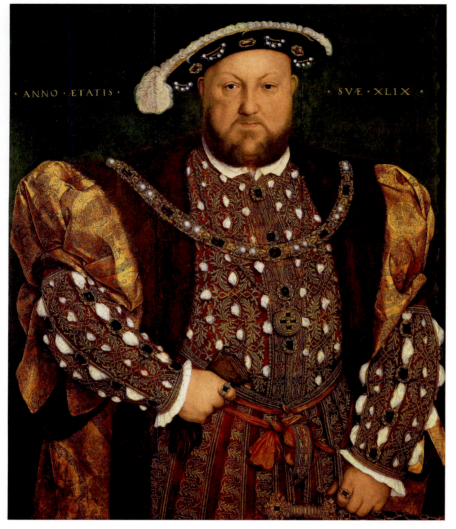

the Catholic Church. He broke away from Catholicism and established himself as the head of the Church of England. Marrying often after this, he had three children, who succeeded him as Edward VI, Mary I, and ELIZABETH I. The latter ruled into the seventeenth century, and oversaw the expansion of England's navy and colonies, when England became a world power.

The Tudor court emphasized portraiture among the arts. Henry VIII appointed a German artist, Hans Holbein the Younger (1497–1543), as his court painter. In this role, Holbein painted numerous portraits of members of Tudor society, as well as the royal family. Holbein took Dürer as his point of departure, but he developed his own distinctive style informed by Netherlandish realism and Italian compositional techniques. His *Henry VIII* (**fig. 17.11**) of 1540 captures the supreme self-confidence of the king. Henry's physical bulk creates an overpowering sense of his ruthless, commanding personality. The frontal pose, assured gaze, and precisely rendered costume and jewels create a memorable public image of strength and power. Holbein's portraits of the king and his courtiers molded British taste in aristocratic portraiture for decades.

17.11 Hans Holbein the Younger. *Henry VIII*. 1540. Oil on panel, 32½ × 29″ (82.6 × 74.5 cm). Galleria Nazionale d'Arte Antica, Rome

ELIZABETH I came to the throne of England in 1558 at the age of 20, and through her shrewdness and some good luck ruled until 1603. She managed to unite a country that had been bitterly divided by religious differences, and increased the wealth and status of England through her diplomacy, her perspicacious choice of advisors and admirals, and her daring. Her most important victory was the defeat of the Spanish Armada, sent to invade England in 1588, but the Elizabethan age is also rightly famous for its music and literary arts. Like her father, she used the visual arts, especially portraits, to create an imposing public image.

craggy mountain peaks overwhelm the human figures. Altdorfer gives the battle an earth-shaking importance, which may well have been the case. However, the soldiers' armor and the fortified town in the distance are unmistakably of the sixteenth century, which encourages us to look for contemporary significance. The work was executed at the moment the Ottoman Turks were threatening to invade Vienna. Altdorfer's image suggests that the contemporary battle between Europeans and Turks has the same global significance as Alexander's battle with Darius had in the fourth century BCE.

Reformation England: The Tudor Portrait

Sixteenth-century England was dominated by the Tudor dynasty. The ambitious Henry VIII, who reigned from 1509 to 1547, wanted England to be a power broker in Europe. Henry sought to annul his marriage to Catherine of Aragon, the aunt of Charles V, but was thwarted by

The Netherlands: World Marketplace

Where the courts of Europe, whether Catholic or Protestant, commissioned visual displays of power, the citizens of the Netherlands had a different taste. This region, present-day Holland and Belgium, had a very turbulent history. When the Reformation began, it was part of the empire under Charles V, who was also king of Spain. Protestantism quickly gained adherents in the Northern Netherlands, and attempts to suppress the spread of its reformed confessions led to a revolt against Spanish rule that resulted in the provinces of the Northern Netherlands declaring their independence in 1579. The city of Amsterdam then became a center of international trade.

The Southern Provinces (roughly corresponding to present-day Belgium) remained in Spanish hands and were committed to Roman Catholicism. The once thriving port of Bruges was replaced as a commercial center by the more strategically located Antwerp, which became the commercial and artistic capital of the Southern Netherlands.

17.12 Gerard David. *Virgin Among Virgins*. ca. 1509. Oil on panel. 48½ × 83½" (119.7 × 212 cm). Musée des Beaux-Arts, Rouen, France

Waves of iconoclasm struck the Netherlands, destroying vast numbers of medieval and Early Renaissance works of art. Painting and other two-dimensional art forms dominated artistic production, and the practice of commissioning large-scale sculpted works of saints or of the Virgin to install in churches was eliminated in reformed regions. In the absence of religious commissions, artists no longer waited for patrons to hire them; they made works of art to sell in the open market. One result was the development of new genres of art that would supplement, and eventually replace, traditional religious subjects. The new Italianate style also challenged Netherlandish artists. Some saw no reason to change the northern European visual tradition they had inherited; some grafted Italianate decorative forms to their traditional compositions and techniques; still others adopted Italian style wholesale.

Bruges

The city of Bruges in the Catholic Southern Netherlands remained an important center for commerce as the sixteenth century began, though much of its trade and prosperity transferred to Antwerp early in the period. Gerard David (ca. 1460–1523) inherited the tradition of

Bruges painting established by Van Eyck. His works give Italianate space, *chiaroscuro*, and stability to themes from the Netherlandish past. A good example of his work is the *Virgin Among Virgins* (**fig. 17.12**), which he gave to the Carmelite nunnery in Bruges in 1509. The painting depicts the Virgin and Child surrounded by female saints. Two angels serenade this assembly, while portraits of David and his wife, Cornelia Cnoop, appear in the corners. In traditional Flemish fashion, the forms exhibit detailed renderings of textures, layers of colors that create brilliant effects, and symbols to enhance the meaning, such as the grapes held by the Child, which refer to the Eucharist and thus to Jesus' ultimate sacrifice. Yet David's cool colors and soft modeling endow these figures with a calm and dignity that are enhanced by the balanced composition and solid forms. These silent virgins gather around the mother and son just as the nuns of the convent would gather for prayer. David and other painters in Bruges continued to make religious images through much of the century.

Antwerp

Where the traditions of Bruges held sway there, Antwerp's rise as a center for commerce brought it great wealth and a dynamic market for art.

Although sculpture was produced in limited quantities, painting and printmaking dominated. The lack of commissions and new market forces stimulated artists to explore new avenues for producing and selling their works. Some artists made images in anticipation of offering them for sale, instead of depending on patrons to commission them. Others developed specialties in specific kinds of painting; these GENRES, or types of art, included landscapes, portraits, still-lifes and scenes of the everyday. Fifteenth-century Netherlandish painting had included these elements in the backgrounds of religious paintings; in the sixteenth century, they become the principal subjects. Such themes allowed painters to sell pictures to clients of any faith.

Although born in the Northern Netherlands, the painter Pieter Aertsen (1507/08–1575) spent his early career in Antwerp. There he made numerous still-life paintings, some of which carry moralizing messages, like *The Meat Stall* (**fig. 17.13**) of 1551. The foreground of this painting is dominated by the products for sale in a butcher's shop, rendered in great detail; some tiny figures in the background are almost hidden by the food. The still-life takes up so much of the picture that the viewer almost misses the religious subject in the background. In the distance appear the Virgin and Child on the Flight into Egypt; they have stopped to give bread to the poor, who are ignored by the worshipers lined up to go to church. A tavern scene appears in the right background, where the products for sale are purely sensual. Confronted with this image, the eye meanders over the objects in the foreground: Some of them are items of gluttony; some, like the pretzels, are eaten during Lent. The two background scenes suggest different choices that the viewer could make: A life of dissipation or a life of almsgiving. The painting seems to argue that Antwerp's principal economic activity must be tempered by spiritual goals.

17.13 Pieter Aertsen. *The Meat Stall*. 1551. Oil on panel, 48½ × 59" (123.3 × 150 cm). University Art Collections, Uppsala University, Sweden

17.14 Pieter Bruegel the Elder. *The Return of the Hunters*. 1565. Oil on panel, 46½ × 63¾″ (117 × 162 cm). Kunsthistorisches Museum, Vienna, Austria

Bruegel and the Everyday

Aertsen's younger contemporary and fellow Antwerp resident, Pieter Bruegel the Elder (1525/30–1569), spent his career in Antwerp and Brussels. We know little of Bruegel's personal life, but, despite a trip to Italy, his style depends on the Netherlandish tradition, in particular the paintings of Hieronymus Bosch (see fig. 13.9). He explored landscape, peasant life, and moral allegory in his work.

As a painter and a designer of prints, he made pictures that demonstrate his interest in folk customs and the daily life of humble people. Bruegel himself was highly educated and the friend of humanists, who, with wealthy merchants, were his main clients. Urban elites collected images of the country and the people who worked the land. He also made images that many scholars have seen as political commentary about the Habsburg rule over the Southern Netherlands. Members of the Habsburg court also collected his work, but during the 1560s,

when Philip II of Spain attempted to quash the Protestant rebellion in the Netherlands, Bruegel became fearful that his politically barbed imagery might cause trouble for his family.

A merchant he knew in Antwerp may have commissioned Bruegel to paint *The Return of the Hunters* (**fig. 17.14**), as part of a series of landscapes symbolizing the months. Such scenes had their origin in medieval calendar illustrations, such as those in the *Très Riches Heures* of Jean de Berry (see fig. 13.2). In Bruegel's work, however, nature is more than a setting for human figures; it is the main subject of the picture. Bruegel organizes the composition of *The Return of the Hunters* with a shelf of snowy space in the foreground on which the hunters appear. The eye moves quickly into the distance toward a snow-covered landscape. The human and canine members of a hunting party return to their village with their skimpy catch in the gray of a northern winter. They move down a hill toward a village, where the water has frozen

17.15 Pieter Bruegel the Elder. *Peasant Wedding*. ca. 1568. Oil on panel, 44⅞ × 64″ (114 × 162.5 cm). Kunsthistorisches Museum, Vienna, Austria

and become a place of recreation and where people rush to get back indoors. Human activity is fully integrated into the natural landscape in Bruegel's image.

The *Peasant Wedding* (**fig. 17.15**), dated around 1568, is one of Bruegel's memorable scenes of rural life. Here he depicts a gathering of peasants in a barn that has been decorated for a wedding. He has totally mastered Italian perspective, so the viewer enters a spacious room dominated by the table at which the wedding guests are gathered. The bride sits before a green curtain to distinguish her, though it is more difficult to locate the groom. Food is being distributed in the foreground, while the many empty jugs in the lower left suggest that much liquid has

already been consumed. Far from the varieties of meats and fish depicted in Aertsen's *The Meat Stall*, the food here is simple porridge. Bagpipers stand ready to play, but the noise level already seems high with so many figures talking amid the clattering of pottery. Bruegel's technique is as precise and detailed as that of his Flemish predecessors; his figures are weighty and solid, which adds to the impression of reality. He treats this country wedding as a serious event, and if he records the peasants' rough manners, he also records their fellowship. He treats the least of the least, like the child licking a bowl in the foreground, as worthy of observation and remembrance. For Bruegel, the common man occupies an important place in the scheme of things.

SUMMARY

Europe in the sixteenth century witnessed the breakdown of traditional certainties in the religious sphere along with the growth of powerful nation-states. As new religious expressions grew, new political and social conditions changed the way artists throughout Europe practiced their art. They made objects for new markets and with new themes, and responded to the new visual language that was developing in Italy.

The Catholic kingdoms of France and Spain quickly adopted the Italian style. French palaces, like Fontainebleau, followed Italian compositions and used ancient forms on their exteriors, though with more vertical proportions. Francis I's court attracted Italian artists whose work emphasized slim, elegant nudes and antique subject matter. Spanish patrons commissioned religious art influenced by Italian models or made by artists trained in Italy. For them, El Greco used the compositions of Mannerist paintings and the brilliant color of Venetian art to create visionary religious paintings, such as *The Burial of Count Orgaz*.

The Reformation changed the art of Central Europe by encouraging the destruction of religious art and reducing commissions for religious subjects. Where Catholicism prevailed, artists made religious images that drew on northern European traditions, but with the added influence of Italian art. Dürer's paintings and prints unite Italian ideas about composition, the human figure, and antiquity with northern techniques and detailed realism. His engraving of *Adam and Eve* exemplifies his style. The lack of Church commissions made the courts important patrons of secular subjects, such as landscapes, classical mythology, and portraits. Portraiture was the dominant art form in the England of Henry VIII and Elizabeth I.

The Reformation resulted in iconoclasm and political division between the Northern and Southern Netherlands. While some artists in the Catholic Southern Netherlands, like Gerard David, continued to make religious art on commission, others created works for the open market. To appeal to a wide clientele, artists explored new subjects, such as landscapes, still lifes, and genre scenes. Pieter Bruegel's paintings of men and women in natural or rural environments depict new themes through the artist's command of Italianate perspective and northern realism.

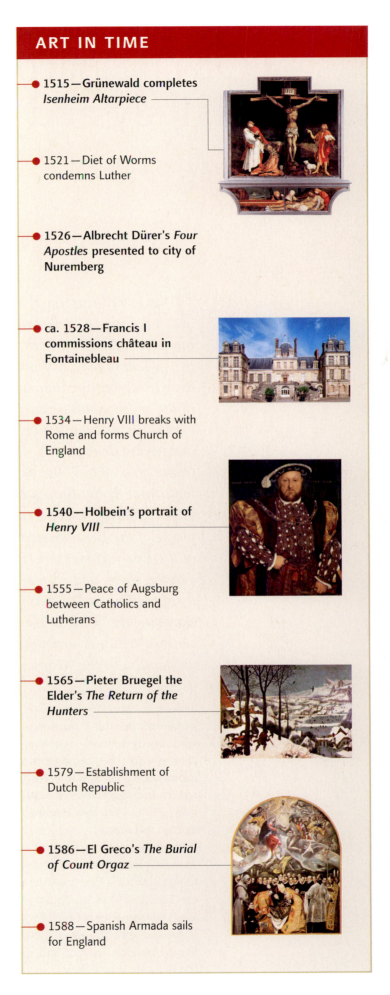

ART IN TIME

- 1515—Grünewald completes *Isenheim Altarpiece*

- 1521—Diet of Worms condemns Luther

- 1526—Albrecht Dürer's *Four Apostles* presented to city of Nuremberg

- ca. 1528—Francis I commissions château in Fontainebleau

- 1534—Henry VIII breaks with Rome and forms Church of England

- 1540—Holbein's portrait of *Henry VIII*

- 1555—Peace of Augsburg between Catholics and Lutherans

- 1565—Pieter Bruegel the Elder's *The Return of the Hunters*

- 1579—Establishment of Dutch Republic

- 1586—El Greco's *The Burial of Count Orgaz*

- 1588—Spanish Armada sails for England

CHAPTER

18 The Baroque in Italy and Spain

*T*he term "Baroque" may come from the Portuguese word Barrocco, referring to an irregular pearl; it means contorted, even grotesque, and was intended as a disparaging description of the grand, turbulent, dynamic, overwhelming style of seventeenth-century art. Art historians remain divided over its definition. Should the term Baroque be used only for the dominant style of the seventeenth century, or should it include other tendencies, such as classicism, to which it bears a complex relationship? (When used to refer to art outside its strict period, it is generally written "baroque.") Should the time frame also include the period 1700 to 1750, known as the Rococo? More important, is the Baroque distinct from both the Renaissance and the Modern eras? Although a good case can be made for viewing the Baroque as the final phase of the Renaissance, we shall treat it as a distinct era. It is the beginning of the Early Modern Period, as so many of the same concerns—issues of gender, class, and sexuality—are explored. The desire to evoke emotional states by appealing to the senses and to persuade, often in dramatic ways, underlies Baroque art. Some of the qualities that characterize the Baroque are grandeur, sensual richness, emotional exuberance, tension, movement, and the successful unification of the various arts.

The expansive, expressive quality of the Baroque paralleled the true expansion of European influence—geographical, political and religious—throughout the seventeenth century. The exploration of the New World that began in the sixteenth century, mobilized primarily by Spain, Portugal, and England (see map 18.1), developed in the seventeenth century into colonization, first of the eastern coasts of North and South America, and then of Polynesia and Asia. The Dutch East India Company developed trade with the East and was headquartered in Indonesia. Jesuit missionaries traveled to Japan, China, and India, and settled in areas of North, Central, and South America. In style and spirit, the reach of the Baroque was global.

The Baroque has been called a style of persuasion, as the Catholic Church attempted to use art to speak to the faithful and to express the spirit of the Counter-Reformation (see Cultural Context: The Counter-Reformation, page 386). The Church celebrated its triumph over the spread of Protestantism. Private influential families, some who would later claim a pope as a member, other private patrons, and ecclesiastical orders all built new and often large churches in Rome in the seventeenth century. And the largest building program of the Renaissance—the rebuilding of Saint Peter's—would finally come to an end and, with its elaborate decoration, profoundly reflect the new glory of the Church.

Map 18.1 Mid-seventeenth century Europe, with emphasis on Italy and Spain

During the first half of the seventeenth century, Europe was torn by almost continual warfare. The Thirty Years' War (1618–1648) was fueled by the ambitions of the kings of France, who sought to dominate Europe, and the Habsburgs, who ruled not only Austria and Spain but also the Southern Netherlands, Bohemia, and Hungary. Although fought largely in Germany, the war eventually engulfed nearly all of Europe. After the Treaty of Westphalia in 1648 ended the war and formally granted their freedom, the United Provinces—or the Dutch Republic, as the independent Netherlands was known—entered into a series of clashes with England and France that lasted until 1679. Yet, other than in Germany, which was fragmented into over 300 little

states, many in financial ruin, there is little correlation between these rivalries and the art of the period. In fact, the seventeenth century has been called the Golden Age of painting in France, Spain, and both the Dutch Republic and the Southern Netherlands.

The Baroque has also been identified as "the style of absolutism," reflecting the centralized state ruled by an autocrat of unlimited powers. Architecture of monumental scale emphasized massiveness, dramatic spaces and lighting, rich interior decoration from floor to ceiling, and luxurious material; and it was meant as a reflection of political and economic power. Absolutism reached its climax during the reign of Louis XIV of France, and is seen in his palace at Versailles, with its grandiose combination of architecture, painting, decoration, and extensive gardens. But we can also associate absolutism with the Vatican, the power of the pope and his claim of authority won and reestablished through the Counter-Reformation. The power of absolutism suggests a style that will overwhelm and inspire awe in the spectator. Yet this would not be a complete definition of the Baroque. A recognition of the subtle relationship between Baroque art and advances in science is essential to an understanding of the age. When scientists placed the sun, not the earth (and humanity) at the center of the universe, they contradicted what our eyes (and common sense) tell us: That the sun revolves around the earth. Not only was the seventeenth century's worldview fundamentally different from that of the Renaissance, but its understanding of visual reality was forever changed by the new science, thanks to developments in optical physics and physiology.

The reality of seventeenth-century life is frequently suggested in genre painting—images from the everyday. These genre paintings include scenes of people drinking, smoking, and playing musical instruments. The paintings are often moralizing; that is, they often warn against the very things they are depicting. Such paintings had already been executed in the sixteenth century (see Bruegel, page 379), but they developed into a major force, along with landscape and still-life painting, in the seventeenth century in nearly every European country. Paintings of foods—plain and exotic—and landscapes of rural, urban, or far-off places were popular. Turkish carpets, African elephants and lions, Brazilian parrots, Ming vases, and peoples from Africa, India, and South America can be found in seventeenth-century art. In part, this list represents "exotica"—but the exotic was a major part of the seventeenth century as people, many of them artists, traveled to faraway places.

In the end, Baroque art was not simply the result of religious, political, intellectual, or social developments: The strengthened Catholic faith, the absolutist state, the new science, and the beginnings of the modern world combined in a volatile mixture that gave the Baroque era its fascinating quality. The interplay of passion, intellect, and spirituality may be seen as forming a dialogue that has never been truly resolved.

Painting in Italy

Around 1600, Rome became the fountainhead of the Baroque, as it had been of the High Renaissance a century before, by attracting artists from other regions. The papacy and many of the new Church orders (Jesuits, Theatines, and Oratorians), as well as numerous private patrons from wealthy and influential families (Farnese, Barberini, and Pamphili), commissioned art on a large scale, with the aim of promoting themselves and making Rome the most beautiful city of the Christian world "for the greater glory of God and the Church." This campaign had begun as early as 1585 (indeed, we may even date this revitalization to the reign of Julius II), and by the opening of the seventeenth century, Rome was attracting ambitious young artists, especially from northern Italy. It was they who created the innovative style.

Caravaggio and the New Style

Foremost among the young artists was the revolutionary painter Michelangelo Merisi (1571–1610), called Caravaggio after his birthplace near Milan. His style of painting, his new subjects, his use of lighting, and his concept of naturalism changed the world of painting. According to contemporary accounts, Caravaggio painted directly onto the canvas, and he worked from a live model. He depicted the world he knew, so that his canvases are filled with ordinary people. They are not idealized as High Renaissance figures, nor given classical bodies, clean clothes, and perfect features. But neither are they distorted, elongated, or overtly elegant as in Mannerism. This was an entirely new concept that was raw, immediate, and palpable.

Caravaggio's first important public commission was a series of three monumental canvases devoted to St. Matthew that he painted for the Contarelli Chapel in San Luigi dei Francesi from 1599 to 1602. Of the three Contarelli paintings, one image is of the angel dictating the Gospel to St. Matthew; another is devoted to his martyrdom. The main image on the left in the chapel illustrates *The Calling of St. Matthew* (**fig. 18.1**), depicting the moment he is chosen by Christ. *The Calling of St. Matthew* displays a naturalism that is both new and radical.

Naturalism was not an end in itself for Caravaggio but a means of conveying profoundly spiritual content. Never before have we seen a sacred subject depicted so entirely in terms of contemporary lowlife. Matthew, the well-dressed

18.1 Caravaggio. *The Calling of St. Matthew.* ca. 1599–1600. Oil on canvas, 11'1" × 11'5" (3.4 × 3.5 m). Contarelli Chapel, San Luigi dei Francesi, Rome

Baroque - Italy

tax collector, sits with some armed men, who must be his agents, in a common, sparse room. Two figures approach from the right. The newcomer's bare feet and simple biblical garb contrast strongly with the colorful costumes of Matthew and his companions.

Why do we sense a religious quality in this scene and not mistake it for an everyday event? What identifies one of the figures on the right as Christ, who has come to Matthew and says "Follow me"? It is surely not his halo, the only supernatural feature in the picture, which is a thin gold band that we might easily overlook. Our eyes fasten instead on his commanding gesture, borrowed from Michelangelo's Adam in *The Creation of Adam* (see fig. 15.10), which bridges the gap between the two groups of people and is echoed by Matthew, who points questioningly at himself.

The men to the right at the table seem not to be engaged in the drama unfolding, while the ones at the left concentrate on the money being counted. In shadows, they are blind to the entrance of Christ—one even wears eyeglasses.

The Counter-Reformation

THE COUNTER-REFORMATION, also known as Catholic Reform, was a movement that began in the mid-sixteenth century and was created specifically to counter the attacks of the Protestant Reformation and to allow the Church of Rome both to reform and reaffirm itself.

These reforms were officially executed through the Council of Trent, which convened between 1545 and 1563 and clarified every aspect of liturgy and doctrine (including the role of art) contested by the Protestant Church. The Council affirmed the role of Mary, the nature of the Eucharist, and other hotly contested points of divergence. It renewed the devotion to martyrs and developed the concept of the guardian angel. (Accordingly, loin-cloths were painted on nude figures of Michelangelo's *Last Judgment*, fig. 16.5).

The Jesuit Order, founded by Ignatius Loyola and recognized by the Church in 1540, had the particular mission of defending and supporting the pope. The Church sought to gain Catholics abroad, having lost so many in Europe to the Protestant Church. Through their missionary work in the East and in the Americas (aimed at converting native peoples to Catholicism), the Jesuits were central to the Reform. Although the Council and the founding of the Jesuits date to the sixteenth century, their impact was greatest in the seventeenth. In 1622, both Loyola and Francis Xavier (also one of the first Jesuits, who was instrumental in carrying Christianity to India and Japan) became saints. In that same year, the mystic Teresa of Ávila (fig. 18.11) and Filippo Neri also achieved sainthood. Charles Borromeo, who was instrumental in the Council of Trent, had already become a saint. With these new seventeenth-century saints, who were nearly contemporary, new imagery, ideas, and a revitalization of the Church were possible. Art, with these exemplary figures as its subject (see fig. 18.11), abounded and was used to spread the teachings of the saints and the Church. The worldly and spiritual splendor of the Church flourished by means of extensive building programs and elaborate commissions to furnish the churches (see fig. 18.7).

Caravaggio uses the piercing light in this scene to announce Christ's presence, as Christ himself brought light: "I am the light of the world; he that followeth me shall not walk in darkness, but shall have the light of life" (John: 8:12).

The beam of sunlight in the darkness above Jesus is most decisive in meaning and style. The select use of light in darkness is known as **tenebrism** (from a Latin word meaning darkness), and Caravaggio was known for his "dark paintings." Caravaggio illuminates Christ's face and hand in the gloomy interior so that we see the actual moment of his calling to Matthew and witness a critical piece of religious history and personal conversion. Without this light, so natural yet so charged with meaning, the picture would lose its power to make us aware of the divine presence. Caravaggio gives direct expression to an attitude shared by certain saints of the Counter-Reformation: That the mysteries of faith are revealed not by speculation but through an inner experience that is open to all people.

Caravaggio's paintings have a quality of "lay Christianity" that spoke powerfully to both Catholics and Protestants. If this work were stripped of its religious context, the men seated at the table would seem like figures in a genre scene. Indeed, Caravaggio's painting would become a source for similar secular scenes. Likewise, fanciful costumes, with slashed sleeves and feathered berets, will appear in the works of his followers. Figures seen in half-length (showing only the upper half of their bodies) will also be a common element in other works by Caravaggio and his followers (see fig. 19.6).

Another aspect of Caravaggio's work is his focus on the sensual and erotic nature of both music and young men, who are depicted as seducing and soliciting. We see these elements in *The Musicians* (**fig. 18.2**), with the four androgynous, semi-nude youths. Actually, it may be two youths seen from two points of view. The musicians are half-length, but life-size; their blushing cheeks and full lips suggest erotic, sensual pleasures, enjoyed with each other and offered to a particular viewer. That viewer (the patron) was Cardinal del Monte, an influential patron who arranged the St. Matthew commission for Caravaggio and who commissioned other homoerotic paintings from him. The lute, the violin, and the music sheets surrounding these half-draped men, and even the grapes being plucked on the side, suggest a contemporary bacchanal. The subject may be disturbing or

18.2 Caravaggio. *The Musicians.* ca. 1595. Oil on canvas, 36¼ × 46⅝″ (92.1 × 118.4 cm). The Metropolitan Museum of Art, New York. Rogers Fund, 1952. 52.81

unsettling, but this is part of the sensuality and passion—both physical and erotic—that will be explored in the Baroque and frequently imitated in later works of art.

An interest in pleasure, in the sensual and erotic, can be discerned in Caravaggio's personality. Highly argumentative, the painter carried a sword and was often in trouble with the law for fighting. When he killed a friend in a duel over a game, he fled Rome and spent the rest of his short life on the run. He went first to Naples, then Malta, then returned briefly to Naples. He died on a journey back to Rome, where he had hoped to gain a pardon. In Italy, Caravaggio's work was praised by artists and connoisseurs—and also criticized. Conservative critics regarded him as lacking decorum: The propriety and reverence that religious subjects demanded. And many who did not like Caravaggio the man were influenced by his work and had to concede that his style was pervasive. The power of his style and imagery lasted into the 1630s, when it was absorbed into other Baroque tendencies.

Artemisia Gentileschi

Most men who were artists had fathers who were also artists, and this applied to most of the few women artists of the seventeenth century as well. Born in Rome, Artemisia Gentileschi (1593–ca. 1653) was the daughter of Caravaggio's friend and follower Orazio Gentileschi, and she became one of the major painters of her day. She took great pride in her work but found the way difficult for a woman artist. In a letter of 1649, she wrote that "people have cheated me" and that she had submitted a drawing to a patron only to have him commission "another painter to do the painting using my work. If I were a man, I can't imagine it would have turned out so. …" Her characteristic subjects are heroines: Bathsheba, the tragic object of King David's passion, and Judith, who saved her people by beheading Holofernes. Both themes were popular during the Baroque era, which delighted in erotic and violent scenes. Artemisia's frequent depictions of these biblical heroines (she often showed herself in the lead role) suggest an ambivalence toward men that was rooted in her turbulent life. (She was raped by her teacher, Agostino Tassi, who was acquitted in a jury trial but expelled from Rome.)

Artemisia's *Judith and Her Maidservant with the Head of Holofernes* (**fig. 18.3**) is a fully mature,

18.3 Artemisia Gentileschi. *Judith and Her Maidservant with the Head of Holofernes*. ca. 1625. Oil on canvas, 6'1½" × 4'7" (1.84 × 1.41 m). The Detroit Institute of Arts. Gift of Mr. Leslie H. Green **Baroque - Italy**

independent, dramatic, and large work, no less powerful for its restraint. The theme is the apocryphal story of the Jewish widow Judith, who saved her people by traveling with her maid to the tent of the Assyrian general Holofernes, made him drunk, and then cut off his head with his own sword; it yields parallels to the story of David and Goliath—might conquered by virtue and innocence. However, with the theme of Judith slaying Holofernes, the victor was not always seen positively, but with some suspicion since her triumph was achieved by deceit: The unspoken promise of a sexual encounter was never realized. Rather than the beheading itself, the artist shows the instant after. Momentarily distracted, Judith gestures theatrically as her servant stuffs Holofernes' head into a sack. The object of their attention remains hidden from view, heightening the air of suspense and intrigue. The hushed, candlelit atmosphere—tenebrism made intimate—creates a mood of mystery that conveys Judith's complex emotions with unsurpassed understanding. Gentileschi's rich palette was to have a strong influence on painting in Naples, where she settled in 1630.

Ceiling Painting and Annibale Carracci

The conservative tastes of many Italian patrons were met by artists who were less radical than Caravaggio, and who continued a more classical tradition steeped in High Renaissance ideals. They took their lead from Annibale Carracci (1560–1609), who arrived in Rome in 1595. Annibale came from Bologna where, in the 1580s, he and two other members of his family formed an "Academy" (see also margin note page 350). He was a reformer rather than a revolutionary. Although we do not know completely what this academy entailed, it seems to have incorporated life-drawing from models and drawing after ancient sculpture. As with Caravaggio, Annibale's experience of Roman classicism transformed his art. He, too, felt that painting must return to nature, but his approach emphasized a revival of the classics, which to him meant the art of antiquity. Annibale also sought to emulate Raphael, Michelangelo, Titian, and Correggio.

Between 1597 and 1601 Annibale produced a ceiling fresco in the GALLERY of the Farnese Palace (**fig. 18.4**): *Loves of the Gods*, his most ambitious work, which soon became so famous that it ranked behind only the murals of Michelangelo and Raphael. Although we have seen ceiling painting in the Renaissance—with works by Mantegna, Correggio, and of course Michelangelo—it is the Baroque period which is most associated with this form of painting.

Executed in chapels, churches, and private residences—in entranceways, hallways, and dining rooms—ceiling painting was meant to convey the power, domination, or even extravagance of the patron. One could not enter such a painted room without a certain feeling of awe. The styles from the beginning of the seventeenth century to the end become increasingly extravagant and contest even the majesty of Michelangelo. The Farnese Palace ceiling, commissioned to celebrate a family wedding, displays a humanist subject, the Loves of the Classical Gods. As on the Sistine Chapel ceiling, the narrative scenes are surrounded by painted architecture, simulated sculpture, and nude youths, which are carefully foreshortened and lit from below so that they appear real. But the fresco does not depend solely on Michelangelo's masterpiece. The main panels are presented as easel pictures. The "framed" painting, "medallions," and "sculpture" on the ceiling all in *trompe l'oeil* (deceiving of the eye) are known as *quadri riportati*, pictures transported to the ceiling (singular is *quadro riportato*). This ceiling reflects the collection of the Farnese that was actually in that room. The figure of Polyphemus, seen on the short wall, hurling the stone in the "easel painting," is based on the "Farnese Hercules," a Hellenistic sculpture owned by the family and displayed in the courtyard. The ceiling is held together by an illusionistic scheme that reflects Annibale's knowledge of the Parma artist Correggio. Each of these levels of reality is handled with consummate skill, and the entire ceiling has an exuberance that sets it apart from both Mannerism and High Renaissance art.

GIOVANNI BATTISTA GAULLI AND IL GESÙ It is a strange fact that few ceiling frescoes were painted after 1635. Ironically, the new style of architecture fostered by Francesco Borromini and others (see page 395) provided few opportunities for decoration. But after 1670 such frescoes enjoyed a revival in older buildings, and this revival reached its peak in the interior of Il Gesù (**fig. 18.5**), the mother church of the Jesuit Order (fig. 16.7). At the suggestion, late in his life, of Gianlorenzo Bernini, the greatest sculptor-architect of the century (see page 393), the commission for the ceiling frescoes went to his young protégé Giovanni Battista Gaulli (1639–1709), known as Il Baciccio. A talented assistant, Antonio Raggi (1624–1686), made the stucco sculpture. The program, which proved extraordinarily influential, shows Bernini's foresight and Gaulli's imaginative daring. As in the Cornaro Chapel (see fig. 18.11), the ceiling is treated as a single unit that evokes a mystical vision. The nave fresco, with its contrasts of light and dark, spills dramatically over its frame, then turns into sculptured figures, combining painting, sculpture, and architecture. Here Baroque illusionism achieves its ultimate expression. The subject of the ceiling painting is the illuminated name of Jesus—the IHS—in the center of the golden light. It is a stirring reference both to the Jesuit Order, dedicated to the Name of Jesus and to the concept that Christ is the Light of the World. The impact of his light and holiness then creates the overflowing turbulence that tumbles out of the sky at the end of days and spreads the word of the Jesuit missionaries: "That at the name of Jesus, every

A GALLERY is a long, rectangular space that usually functions as a passageway or corridor. From the Renaissance onward, galleries in palaces, public buildings, and stately houses would be heavily decorated, frequently with paintings and works of sculpture. From this practice, the word "gallery" came to mean an independent space devoted to the exhibition of works of art. In churches, a gallery is a low story above the nave, often arcaded.

18.4 Annibale Carracci. *Loves of the Gods*. 1597–1601. Ceiling fresco in the Gallery. Farnese Palace, Rome

18.5 Giovanni Battista Gaulli (Il Baciccio). *Triumph of the Name of Jesus.* 1672–1679. Ceiling fresco. Il Gesù, Rome

knee should bow…" (Epistle of St. Paul to the Philippians, 2:10).

Architecture in Italy

The Baroque style in architecture, like that of painting, germinated in Rome, which was a vast construction site from the end of the sixteenth through the middle of the seventeenth century. The goals of the Counter-Reformation caused the Church to embark on a major building campaign. New churches were constructed and the new Saint Peter's was finally completed. Although many of the building projects began during the Renaissance, they developed distinctly different characteristics as they were completed during the Baroque. Some architects continued to use a classical vocabulary but expanded or stretched it, so that the idea of perfection was not considered a circle, but an oval or ellipse (a modern concept that was frequently the object of astronomical discussions). They incorporated domes based on Michelangelo's (fig. 16.6), but which had a steeper profile to suggest greater drama in punctuating the sky; others designed buildings based on amorphous shapes that used the ornamentations but not the principles of classicism.

The Completion of Saint Peter's and Carlo Maderno

Carlo Maderno (ca. 1556–1629) was the most talented young architect to emerge in this vast ecclesiastical building program. In 1603, he was given the task of completing, at long last, the church of Saint Peter's (**fig. 18.6**). Pope Clement VIII had decided to add a nave and narthex to the west end of Michelangelo's building, thereby converting it into a basilica plan. The change of plan, which had already been proposed by Raphael in 1514, made it possible to link Saint Peter's with the Vatican Palace to the right of the church.

Maderno's design for the façade follows the pattern established by Michelangelo for the exterior. It consists of a colossal order supporting an attic, but with a dramatic emphasis on the portals. The total effect can only be described as a crescendo building from the corners toward the center. The spacing of the supports becomes closer, the pilasters turn into columns, and the façade wall projects step by step. This quickened rhythm had been hinted at a generation earlier in Giacomo della Porta's façade of Il Gesù (see fig. 16.7). Recent cleaning of the façade of Saint Peter's revealed it to be of a warm cream color, which emphasizes its sculptural qualities.

18.6 Aerial view of Saint Peter's. Nave and façade by Carlo Maderno, 1607–1612; colonnade by Gianlorenzo Bernini, designed 1657. Rome

architecture   *Baroque – Italy*

Bernini and Saint Peter's

After Maderno's death in 1629, his assistant Gian-lorenzo Bernini (1598–1680) assumed the title "architect of Saint Peter's." Considering himself Michelangelo's successor as both architect and sculptor, Bernini directed the building campaign and coordinated the decoration and sculpture within the church as well. Given these tasks, the enormous size of Saint Peter's posed equal challenges for anyone seeking to integrate architecture and sculpture. How could its vastness be related to the human scale and given a measure of emotional warmth? Once the nave was extended following Maderno's design, Bernini realized that the interior needed an internal focal point in this vast space. His response was to create the monumental sculptural/architectural composite form known as the *Baldacchino* (**fig. 18.7**), the "canopy" for the main altar, at the very crossing of the transept

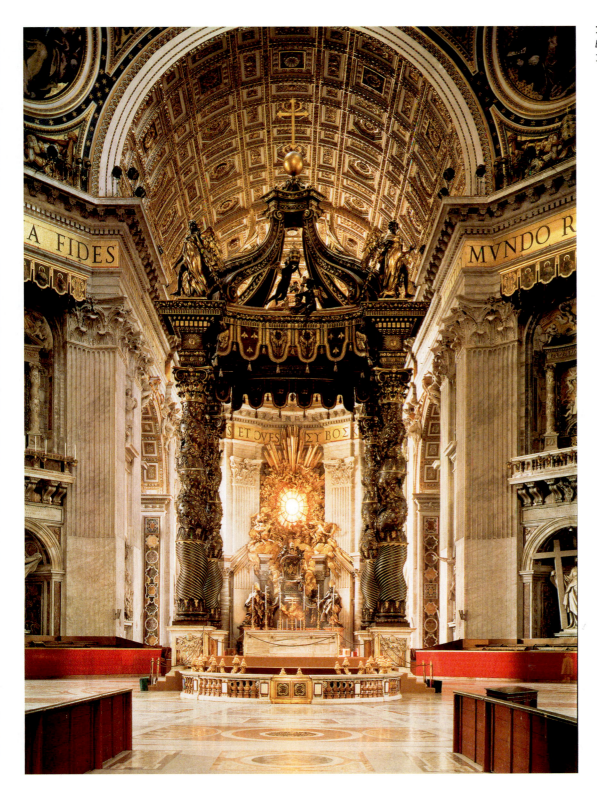

18.7 Gianlorenzo Bernini. *Baldacchino*, at the nave crossing. 1624–1633. Saint Peter's, Rome

and the nave, directly under Michelangelo's dome (see fig. 16.6) and just above the actual crypt of St. Peter where the pope would celebrate Mass. This nearly 100-foot sculptural/architectural piece, created mostly in bronze stripped from the ancient Pantheon (see fig. 7.16), stands on four twisted columns, reminiscent of those from the original Saint Peter's (and thought, too, to replicate those of Solomon's Temple). Rather than an architectural **entablature** (the horizontal members—architrave, frieze, and cornice) mounted between the columns, Bernini inventively suggests fabric hanging between them. The *Baldacchino* is a splendid fusion of sculpture and architecture. At its corners are statues of angels and vigorously curved scrolls, which raise a cross above a golden orb, the symbol of the triumph of Christianity throughout the world. The entire structure is so alive with expressive energy that it may be considered as the epitome of Baroque style. We can see through the columns of the *Baldacchino* to the sculptural reliquary of the throne of St. Peter, the *Cathedra Petri* (the actual encased chair of St. Peter) in the apse of the church, also designed by Bernini.

The papal insignia—the triple crown and crossed keys of St. Peter—and the coat of arms of the pope under whose patronage this structure was created—the Barberini bees of Urban VIII—are significant elements of its decoration. Bernini's *Baldacchino* honors not just the power and majesty of God, but that of his emissary on earth, the pope. Bernini's relationship with the pope was one of the most successful and powerful in the history of patronage.

18.8 Francesco Borromini. Interior view into dome of Sant'Ivo. Begun 1642. Rome

Later, under the patronage of Pope Alexander VII (1655–1667), Bernini orchestrated the main entrance into Saint Peter's. He molded the open space in front of the façade into a magnificent oval piazza that is amazingly sculptural (see fig. 18.6). This "forecourt," which imposed a degree of unity on the sprawling Vatican complex, acts as an immense atrium framed by colonnades, while screening off the surrounding slums. This device, which Bernini himself likened to the motherly, all-embracing arms of the Church, is not new. It had been used by others for private villas, in effect as *belvederes* opening onto formal gardens to the rear. What is novel is the idea of placing it at the main entrance to a building. Also new is the huge scale, creating a grandiose setting. Bernini's one major failure in the visual effect of Saint Peter's was his inability to execute the bell towers that were initially planned by Bramante (see fig. 15.6). He began construction, but they were found to be structurally unsound and physically damaging to the façade; they had to be dismantled. This failure would haunt him, but would provide a competitive resource for other architects.

A Baroque Alternative: Francesco Borromini

Bernini's greatest rival in architecture, Francesco Borromini (1599–1667), was a secretive and emotionally unstable artist who died by suicide. The contrast between these two architects would be evident from their works alone, even without the accounts by their contemporaries. Bernini's church designs are dramatically simple and unified, while Borromini's structures are extravagantly complex. And whereas the surfaces of Bernini's interiors are extremely rich, Borromini's are surprisingly plain, relying on his phenomenal grasp of spatial geometry to achieve their spiritual effects. Bernini himself agreed with those who denounced Borromini for flagrantly disregarding the classical tradition, enshrined in Renaissance theory and practice, that architecture must reflect the proportions of the human body. Surely, of the two, Bernini, even at the height of the Baroque, was the one more tied to a classical vocabulary. But perhaps Bernini's criticism of Borromini simply represented all-too-human rivalries.

SANT'IVO Borromini's church of Sant'Ivo alla Sapienza (**figs. 18.8** and **18.9**) was built at the end of an existing cloister for a university, which soon became the University of Rome. It is compact, but

18.9 Francesco Borromini. Exterior of Sant'Ivo. Begun 1642. Rome

daring. Sant'Ivo is a small, central-plan church based on a star-hexagon. The six-pointed star plan represents *Sapienza* (Wisdom), although as the church was first built under Pope Urban VIII (Barberini) it was suggested by contemporaries that the plan represented the Barberini bee, also seen in Bernini's *Baldacchino* (fig. 18.7). In designing this unique church, Borromini may have been thinking of octagonal structures, such as San Vitale in Ravenna (fig. 8.8), but the result is completely novel. Inside, it is a single, unified, organic experience, as the walls extend the ground plan into the vault, culminating in Borromini's unique, spiral lantern. It continues the star-hexagon pattern of the floor plan up to the circular base of the lantern (see fig. 18.8). The stars on the wall refer to the Chigi family of Pope Alexander VII, who reigned when the building was completed.

Sculpture in Italy

Baroque sculpture, like Baroque painting, was vital, energized, and dynamic, suggesting action and deep emotion. The subject matter was intended to evoke an emotional response in the viewer. The sculpture was usually life-size, but with a sense of grandeur that suggested larger than life-size figures; and many figures were

18.10 Gianlorenzo Bernini. *David.* 1623. Marble, life-size. Galleria Borghese, Rome

Baroque - Italy

indeed monumental. Deeply cut, the facial expressions and clothing caught the light and cast shadows to create not just depth but drama.

The Evolution of the Baroque: Bernini

Bernini was a sculptor as well as an architect, and sculpture and architecture are never far apart in his work, as we have seen in the *Baldacchino* (fig. 18.7). He was trained by his father, Pietro Bernini (1562–1629), a sculptor who worked in Florence, Naples, and Rome, but he was also influenced by Giovanni Bologna (see fig. 16.4). Bernini's style was thus a direct outgrowth of Mannerist sculpture in many ways, but this debt alone does not explain his revolutionary qualities, which emerged early in his career.

DAVID As in the colonnade for Saint Peter's (see fig. 18.6), we can often see a strong relationship between Bernini's sculpture and antiquity. If we compare Bernini's *David* (**fig. 18.10**) with Michelangelo's (see fig. 15.8) and ask which is closer to the Pergamon frieze (see fig. 5.30), our vote must go to Bernini, whose sculpture shares with Hellenistic works that union of body and spirit, of motion and emotion, which Michelangelo so consciously tempers. This does not mean that Michelangelo is more classical than Bernini. It shows, rather, that both the Baroque and the High Renaissance drew different lessons from ancient art.

Bernini's *David* suggests the fierceness of expression, movement, and dynamism of Hellenistic sculpture. In part, what makes it Baroque is the implied presence of Goliath. Unlike earlier statues of David, including Donatello's (see fig. 14.13), Bernini's is conceived not as a self-contained figure but as half of a pair, his entire action focused on his adversary. His *David* tells us clearly enough where he sees the enemy. Consequently, the space between David and his invisible opponent is charged with energy—it "belongs" to the statue.

The *David* shows us the distinctive feature of Baroque sculpture: Its new, active relationship with the surrounding space. But it is meant to be seen, as is most other Baroque sculpture, from one primary point of view. Bernini presents us with "the moment" of action, not just the contemplation of the killing—as in Michelangelo's work—or the aftermath of it, as in Donatello's. Baroque sculpture often suggests a heightened vitality and energy. Because it so often presents an "invisible complement" (like the Goliath of Bernini's *David*), the Baroque statue attempts

pictorial effects that were traditionally outside the realm of monumental sculpture. Such a charging of space with energy is, in fact, a key feature of Baroque art. Caravaggio had achieved it in his *St. Matthew* (fig. 18.1) with the aid of a sharply focused beam of light. And as we have seen in Gaulli's ceiling of Il Gesù (fig. 18.5), both painting and sculpture may even be combined with architecture to form a compound illusion, such as that seen on a stage.

THE CORNARO CHAPEL: *THE ECSTASY OF ST. TERESA* Bernini had a passionate interest in the theater and was an innovative scene designer. A contemporary wrote that he "gave a public opera wherein he painted the scenes, cut the statues, invented the engines, composed the music, writ the comedy, and built the theatre." Thus he was at his best when he could merge architecture, sculpture, and painting. His masterpiece in this vein is the Cornaro Chapel in the church of Santa Maria della Vittoria, containing *The Ecstasy of St. Teresa* (**fig. 18.11**). TERESA OF ÁVILA, one of the great saints of the Counter-Reformation and newly canonized only in 1622, had described how an angel pierced her heart with a flaming golden arrow: "The pain was so great that I screamed aloud; but at the same time I felt such infinite sweetness that I wished the pain to last forever. It was not physical but psychic pain, although it affected the body as well to some degree. It was the sweetest caressing of the soul by God."

Bernini has made Teresa's visionary experience sensuously real, and the saint's rapture is obvious. (In a different context the angel could be Cupid.) The two figures on their floating cloud are lit from a hidden window above, so that they seem almost dematerialized. A viewer thus experiences them as visionary. The "invisible complement" here, less specific than *David's* but equally important, is the force that carries the figures toward heaven and causes the turbulence of their drapery. Its divine nature is suggested by the golden rays (gilt wood), which come from a source high above the altar. In an illusionistic fresco by Guidobaldo Abbatini on the vault of the chapel, the glory of the heavens is revealed as a dazzling burst of light from which tumble clouds of jubilant angels. This celestial explosion gives force to the thrusts of the angel's arrow and makes the ecstasy of the saint fully convincing.

To complete the illusion, Bernini even provides a built-in audience for his "stage." On the sides of the chapel are balconies resembling

ST. TERESA OF ÁVILA (1515–1582) inaugurated reforms in her own Carmelite order that had an immense influence on other congregations of religious women and on the Church as a whole. Her powerful writings include the *Life* (1562–65), a spiritual autobiography; *The Way of Perfection* (after 1565), a discussion of various devotional practices; and *Exclamations of the Soul to God* (1569), meditations that reflect her experiences of mystical union with God. In 1970 Teresa was named the first female Doctor of the Church.

18.11 Gianlorenzo Bernini. *The Ecstasy of St. Teresa* (full chapel view). 1645–1652. Marble, life-size. Cornaro Chapel, Santa Maria della Vittoria, Rome theater boxes that contain marble figures depicting members of the Cornaro family, who also witness the vision. Their space and ours are the same, and thus are part of our reality, while the saint's ecstasy, which is framed in a niche, occupies a space that is real but beyond our reach, as in a divine realm.

It would be easy to dismiss *The Ecstasy of St. Teresa* as a theatrical display, but Bernini was also a devout Catholic who believed (as did Michelangelo) that he was inspired directly by God. Like the *SPIRITUAL EXERCISES* of Ignatius of Loyola, which Bernini practiced, his religious sculpture is intended to help a viewer identify with miraculous events through a vivid appeal to the senses. Theatricality in the service of faith was basic to the Counter-Reformation, which often referred to the Church as the theater of human life: It took the Baroque to bring this ideal about.

Bernini was steeped in Renaissance humanism. Central to his sculpture is the role of gesture and expression in arousing emotion. While these devices were also important to the Renaissance, Bernini uses them with a freedom that seems anti-classical. However, he essentially followed the concept of decorum (which also explains why his *David* is not completely nude), and he planned his effects carefully by varying them in accordance with his subject. Unlike the Frenchman Nicolas Poussin (see page 429), Bernini did this for the sake of expressive impact rather than conceptual clarity. The approaches of the two artists were diametrically opposed as well. For Bernini, antiquity served as no more than a point of departure for his own inventiveness, whereas for Poussin it was a standard of comparison.

Painting in Spain

Politics, art, and a common bond of loyalty to the Catholic Church connected Italy and Spain in the seventeenth century. Spain, still in the throes of the Inquisition (see page 352), was staunchly conservative and unflinching; its king was titled "The Most Catholic Majesty." Spain restricted the Church to only those who professed their unaltering loyalty, and imprisoned, executed, or expelled those who did not, while the Vatican used its resources to bring reformers and the disaffected back to the Church. As we have seen, the Counter-Reformation, or Catholic Reform (see page 384), began in Rome with a new style—Baroque—intended to convince viewers of the dynamism and power of the Catholic Church, its

patrons and defenders. And, at the beginning of the seventeenth century, the largest city on the Italian mainland, Naples, was under the rule of Spain, as were the region around it and the island of Sicily. So the impact of Baroque Roman art on Neapolitan and Spanish art was profound.

At the height of its political and economic power during the sixteenth century, Spain had produced great saints and writers, but no artists of the first rank. The Spanish court and most of the aristocracy held native artists in low esteem, preferring to employ foreign painters whenever possible—above all Titian. Thus the main influences came from Italy and the Netherlands, which was then also ruled by Spain. Jan van Eyck (see page 291) visited Spain and inspired followers there, Titian worked for Charles V of Spain, and in the seventeenth century Rubens visited at least twice, and his work was very much admired. Spanish Baroque art was heavily influenced by the style and subject matter of Caravaggio—directly and via Naples—but with a greater starkness. Spanish naturalism may throw a harsher, stronger light on its subjects, but it is ultimately at least as sympathetic.

Naples and the Impact of Caravaggio: Jusepe de Ribera

Caravaggio's main disciple in Naples was the Spaniard Jusepe de Ribera (1591–1652), who settled there after having seen Caravaggio's paintings in Rome. Especially popular were Ribera's paintings of saints, prophets, and ancient beggar-philosophers. Their asceticism appealed strongly to the otherworldliness of Spanish Catholicism. Such pictures also reflected the learned humanism of the Spanish nobility, who were the artist's main patrons.

His *The Club-Footed Boy* (**fig. 18.12**) smiles openly and endearingly out at us, with a dimpled cheek, although we may be somewhat discomforted by his peasant dress, his begging, and his handicap. The words on the paper he holds state (in translation): "Give me alms for the love of God." In Counter-Reformation theory, this plea for charity indicates that only through good works may the rich hope to attain salvation. The painting, indeed, was made for the Viceroy of Naples, a wealthy collector who would have seen this as a testament to the importance of Christian charity and mercy to the poor. The boy seems almost monumental here as he stands against the broad sky with a low horizon line, like a musketeer; but instead of a weapon across his shoulder, he holds his crutch. His

Ignatius of Loyola (Iñigo de Oñaz y Loyola, 1491–1556) was an influential Catholic teacher, founder of the Jesuit order (see page 384), and eventually a saint and patron of spiritual retreats. His *SPIRITUAL EXERCISES* is a manual for contemplation of the meaning of life as well as a source of pragmatic advice on how to live a spiritual life in the service and honor of God. It is used as a model for many Roman Catholic retreats and missions.

18.12 Jusepe de Ribera. *The Club-Footed Boy*. 1642. Oil on canvas, 64⅛ × 36⅝″ (164 × 93 cm). Musée du Louvre, Paris

deformed foot appears in shadow and the viewer does not quite see it at first, but, as the leg is lit, clearly Ribera is directing our attention to it. The deformity may in fact not be a clubfoot but an indication of cerebral palsy. In either case, in the seventeenth century, such a deformity would have committed the sufferer to a life of begging.

Ribera executed other large paintings of beggars, of the poor, and of the blind, but created with a moral purpose. The boy himself seems an embodiment of joy as he smiles, even laughs. This was considered as a way for the subject to withstand misfortune, for he has the ability to dispense grace: The opportunity for others to do good. Ribera's use of naturalism is a hallmark of Spanish and Neapolitan painting and etching,

and it extends Caravaggio's impact. The impact of which was felt especially in Seville, in southern Spain, the home of the most important Spanish Baroque painter before 1640: Diego Velázquez.

Diego Velázquez: From Seville to Court Painter

Diego Velázquez (1599–1660) painted in a Caravaggesque vein during his early years in Seville. His interests at that time centered on scenes of people eating and drinking rather than religious themes. In the late 1620s, he was appointed court painter to Philip IV, whose reign (1621–1665) was the great age of painting in Spain. Upon moving to Madrid, Velázquez quickly became a skilled courtier and a favorite of the king, whom he served as chamberlain. He spent most of the rest of his life in Madrid, painting mainly portraits of the royal family

Velázquez discovered the beauty of the many Titians in the king's collection with the guidance of the painter Peter Paul Rubens (see pages 408–410) during the Fleming's visit to the Spanish court in 1628 while on a diplomatic mission. Rubens encouraged Velázquez to go to Rome, and some years later he was able to do so when the king dispatched him there in 1648 to purchase paintings and antique sculpture.

THE PORTRAIT OF JUAN DE PAREJA On his mission to Rome, Velázquez took with him Philip's permission to paint Pope Innocent X. But Velázquez's reputation seemed not to have preceded him when he arrived in 1649, and he was left waiting. It was during this interlude that he painted the portrait of his Sevillian assistant and servant of Moorish descent, Juan de Pareja (ca. 1610–1670), who accompanied him to Rome and was an artist himself (**fig. 18.13**). The portrait, stunningly lifelike, was acclaimed when exhibited at an annual art show in the Pantheon in March 1650. It was said that of all the paintings, this one was "truth." Juan de Pareja is shown half-length, in three-quarter view, but facing us— a triangular format developed by Raphael and Titian in the High Renaissance, using, but simplifying, that of the *Mona Lisa* (fig. 15.3) as their point of departure. The same format used here

18.13 Diego Velázquez. *Juan de Pareja*. 1650. Oil on canvas, 32 × 27½″ (81.3 × 69.9 cm). The Metropolitan Museum of Art, New York. Purchase, Fletcher and Rogers Funds, and Bequest of Miss Adelaide Milton de Groot (1876–1967), by exchange, supplemented by gifts from Friends of the Museum, 1971. 1971.86

is a powerful one, riveting our attention to his face. The feathery lace collar, brilliantly painted, picks up the white highlights that create the formidable sculptural visage. A white patch, a tear in his clothing at the elbow, reminds a viewer of his class. The success of this portrait and Velázquez's new fame in Rome may have prompted the pope to sit for him, soon after.

18.14 Diego Velázquez. *The Maids of Honor*. 1656. Oil on canvas, 10′5″ × 9′ (3.2 × 2.7 m). Museo del Prado, Madrid

Baroque - Spain

THE MAIDS OF HONOR Velázquez's mature style is seen at its fullest in *The Maids of Honor* (**fig. 18.14**). Both a group portrait and a genre scene, it might be subtitled "the artist in his studio," for Velázquez depicts himself at work on a huge canvas. In the center is the Princess Margarita, who has just posed for him, among her playmates and maids of honor. The faces of her parents, King Philip IV and Queen Maria Anna, appear in the mirror on the back wall. Their position also suggests a slightly different vantage point from ours, and indeed there are several viewpoints throughout the picture. In this way, the artist perhaps intended to include the viewer in the scene by implication, even though it was clearly painted for the king and hung in the office of his summer quarters at the Alcázar Palace. Antonio Palomino, the first to discuss *The Maids of Honor*, wrote, "the name of Velázquez will live from century to century, as long as that of the most excellent and beautiful Margarita, in whose shadow his image is immortalized." Thanks to Palomino, we know the identity of every person in the painting. Through the presence of the princess and the king and queen, the canvas commemorates Velázquez's position as royal painter and his aspiration to the knighthood in the Order of Santiago—a papal military order to which he gained admission only with great difficulty three years after the painting was executed. In it, he wears the red cross of the order, which was added later, after his death.

Velázquez had struggled for status at court since his arrival. Even though the usual family investigations (almost 150 friends and relatives were interviewed) assisted his claim to nobility, the very nature of his profession worked against him. "Working with his hands" conferred on Velázquez the very antithesis of noble status. Only by papal dispensation was he accepted. *The Maids of Honor*, then, is an expression of personal ambition; it is a claim for both the nobility of the act of painting and that of the artist himself. The presence of the king and queen affirms his status. The Spanish court had already honored Titian and Rubens (although not with the same order), and as these artists were both held in high regard, they served as models for Velázquez. They continued to have a significant impact on him, as men and because of their painterly, lush style.

The painting reveals Velázquez's fascination with light as fundamental to vision. The artist challenges us to match the mirror image against the painting. The glowing colors have a Venetian richness, but the brushwork is even freer and sketchier than Titian's. Velázquez explored the optical qualities of light more fully than any other painter of his time. His aim was to represent the movement of light itself and the infinite range of its effects on form and color. For Velázquez, as for Jan Vermeer in the Netherlands (see pages 423–424), light creates the visible world.

Monastic Orders and Zurbarán

Francisco de Zurbarán (1598–1664) began, as did Velázquez, as a painter from Seville, and he stands out among his contemporaries for his quiet intensity. His most important works, done for monastic orders, are filled with an ascetic piety that is uniquely Spanish. *St. Serapion* (**fig. 18.15**) shows an early member of the Mercedarians (Order of Mercy), who was brutally

18.15 Francisco de Zurbarán. *St. Serapion.* 1628. Oil on canvas, 47⅝ × 41″ (120.7 × 104.1 cm). Wadsworth Atheneum Museum of Art, Hartford, Connecticut. The Ella Gallup Sumner and Mary Catlin Sumner Collection Fund

18.16 Bartolomé Murillo. *The Virgin and Child*. ca. 1675–1680. Oil on canvas, 65¼ × 43″ (165.7 × 109.2 cm). The Metropolitan Museum of Art, New York. Rogers Fund, 1943. 43.13

Zurbarán's painting reminds us of Caravaggio. Shown as a life-size, three-quarter-length figure, St. Serapion fills the picture plane: He is both a hero and a martyr. The contrast between the white habit and the dark background gives the figure a heightened visual and expressive presence, so that the viewer contemplates the slain monk with a mixture of compassion and awe. Here pictorial and spiritual purity become one, and the stillness creates a reverential mood that complements the stark realism. As a result, we identify with the strength of St. Serapion's faith rather than with his physical suffering. The absence of rhetorical pathos is what makes this image deeply moving.

Culmination in Devotion: Bartolomé Esteban Murillo

The work of Bartolomé Esteban Murillo (1617–1682), Zurbarán's successor as the leading painter in Seville, is the most cosmopolitan, as well as the most accessible, of any of the Spanish Baroque artists, and had countless followers. *The Virgin and Child* (**fig. 18.16**) unites the influences of northern European and Italian artists in an image that nevertheless remains unmistakably Spanish in character. His many religious images, especially on the themes of the Virgin and her Immaculate Conception, were hallmarks of the insistence of Spanish art on promoting her into the visual vocabulary of the seventeenth century. The insistence on Virgin imagery defied the Protestant influence in much of Europe. The haunting expressiveness of the faces in his paintings has a gentle pathos that is more emotionally appealing than Zurbarán's austere pietism. This human warmth reflects a basic change in religious outlook. It is also an attempt to inject new life into standard devotional images that had been reduced to formulas in the hands of lesser artists. The extraordinary sophistication of Murillo's brushwork and the subtlety of his color show the influence of Velázquez. He succeeded so well that the vast majority of religious paintings in Spain and its Central and South American colonies were derived from his work for the next 150 years.

murdered by pirates in 1240 but not canonized until a hundred years after this picture was painted. The canvas was placed as a devotional image in the funerary chapel of the order, which was originally dedicated to self-sacrifice.

SUMMARY

The Baroque—the pervasive, dramatic style of the seventeenth century—began in Italy and spread throughout Europe, through the travels of artists, patrons, and missionaries. It conveyed dynamism and strong emotion and was used as the style of the Counter-Reformation, to proclaim the triumph of the Church over Protestantism. Its effects were seen in paintings, sculpture, architecture, the minor arts, and the ornate, complex decorations of the age.

The use of contrast of light and dark, begun with Caravaggio to create tension and emphasize drama or intimacy, continued throughout the century. His followers, such as Artemisia Gentileschi, were so numerous they became known as *Caravaggisti*. Ceiling painting, too, became an important Baroque choice for a variety of wealthy private patrons, and for Church orders that wanted to suggest their dynamic rule over the heavens.

The popularity of painted ceilings owes a debt to Michelangelo, but those of the seventeenth century, such as the Farnese Gallery, were unmistakably Baroque in their complexity and ability to inspire awe. This is even more pronounced later in the century with Cortona's illusionistic ceiling for the Barberini family; and the heavens themselves seem to open up in Gaulli's ceiling for Il Gesù.

The basilica of Saint Peter's (begun at the turn of the sixteenth century) was completed during the Baroque period and became the greatest symbol of the revival and vitality of the Church. Bernini's role as architect and sculptor was pivotal to the age.

Baroque sculpture suggested action, vitality, and emotion—with a single figure or with more complex sculptural and theatrical productions.

Spanish Baroque art was largely influenced by Italian art and Caravaggio, through Spanish-ruled Naples, and noted for its naturalism. Velázquez, the most important artist of the Golden Age of Spain, was court painter to Philip IV in Madrid, but was influenced by both Caravaggio and Titian. The promotion of the Virgin in Spanish art as a significant subject defined Spain's Catholic and conservative art and its role in defying the Reformation of northern Europe.

ART IN TIME

- 1599–1600—Caravaggio's *The Calling of St. Matthew*

- 1605—Miguel de Cervantes Saavedra writes *Don Quixote*

- 1607—First surviving opera still performed, *L'Orfeo* by Claudio Monteverdi

- 1609—Galileo Galilei refines astronomical telescope

- 1622—Ignatius Loyola, founder of the Jesuit Order, Francis Xavier, Theresa of Ávila, Philip Neri all canonized

- 1629—Bernini commissioned to complete Saint Peter's Basilica

- 1633—The Inquisition forces Galileo Galilei to recant

- 1642—Borromini's Sant'Ivo

- 1642—Ribera's *The Club-Footed Boy*

- 1645—Bernini's *The Ecstasy of St. Teresa*

- 1656—Velázquez's *The Maids of Honor*

The Baroque in The Netherlands

*T*he seventeenth century brought a division of the Netherlands into two parts (see map 19.1): The Northern Netherlands (now the Netherlands) and the Southern Netherlands (present-day Belgium and part of France). Each is often known by the name of its most important province: Holland (North) and Flanders (South). The Catholic Spanish Habsburgs had ruled the Netherlands in the sixteenth century, but Philip II's repressive measures against the Protestants and his attempts to curtail their local government led to a rebellion that lasted 15 years. In 1581, the northern provinces of the Netherlands, led by William the Silent, prince of Nassau, of the House of Orange, declared their independence from Spain. Spain soon recovered the Southern Netherlands, and Catholicism remained the official religion there. After a long struggle, the seven major provinces of the North, whose inhabitants were predominantly of the Reformed Church, became the United Provinces and gained their autonomy, which was recognized by the truce declared in 1609. Although hostilities broke out once more in 1621, the freedom of the Dutch was never again seriously in doubt. Their independence was finally ratified by the Treaty of Münster, which ended the Thirty Years' War in 1648; the Dutch Republic then became an independent state.*

The division of the Netherlands had very different consequences for the economy, social structure, culture, and religion of the North and the South. Yet, throughout the seventeenth century, people crossed back and forth between the two regions, ensuring much social and cultural fluidity. After being sacked by Spanish troops in 1576, Antwerp, the leading port of the Southern Netherlands, lost half its population. Many migrated to the North. The city gradually regained its position as Flanders's commercial and artistic capital, although Brussels was the seat of government. As part of the Treaty of Münster, however, the Scheldt River leading to Antwerp's harbor was closed to shipping, thus crippling trade for the next two centuries.

Because Flanders continued to be ruled by Spanish regents, the Habsburgs, who viewed themselves as the defenders of the "true" (i.e. Catholic) faith, its artists relied primarily on commissions from Church and State, but the aristocracy and wealthy merchants were also important patrons.

Holland, in contrast, was proud of its hard-won freedom. Although the predominant religion was the Reformed Church, the Dutch were notable for their religious tolerance. Even Catholicism continued to flourish, and included many artists among its ranks, while Jews, too, found a haven from persecution. Unlike Flanders, where most artistic activity radiated from Antwerp, Holland had a number of local

Map 19.1 Mid-seventeenth-century Europe with emphasis on the Netherlands

schools of painting. Besides Amsterdam, the commercial capital, there were important artists working in Haarlem, Utrecht, Leiden, and Delft.

The new nation was one of merchants, farmers, and seafarers, who may have earned their living from local commerce such as the fishing trade, but who had the opportunity for more distant adventures with the development of the famous Dutch East India Company (known as the VOC from its Dutch initials), established in 1602, and its counterpart, established in 1621, the Dutch West India Company. These companies developed trade in East Asia (China, Japan, and Indonesia), and in the Americas, bringing home exotic wares, strange creatures, and fabulous flora and fauna, as well as engaging in exploration, map-making, and the creation of colonial settlements. Such adventures rippled though the economy: While they were experienced, the merchant sailors also had a direct impact on the directors and governors of the companies, who made their fortunes from these enterprises. Even

the townspeople, who stayed home, were able to purchase or at least see some of the wonders brought back from faraway places. From this time forward, the Dutch—even those who did not travel—would consider themselves worldly.

As the Reformed Church was iconoclastic, Dutch artists rarely had the large-scale church altarpiece commissions that were available throughout the Catholic world. While the House of Orange in The Hague, city governments, and civic bodies such as militias offered a certain amount of art patronage, their demands were limited. As a result, private collectors became the painters' chief source of support. In both regions, North and South, a new class of paron arose—the wealthy merchant.

Flanders

Art in seventeenth-century Flanders was defined by the art of the great painter Peter Paul Rubens

(1577–1640). Rubens brought Flanders, really Antwerp, to international notice and the art of the Western world to Flanders, accomplishing this through his commissions, his own extensive workshop, and his own travels (bringing ideas back).

Baroque art in Flanders thrived on commissions. Its many churches could now, with the Truce of 1609, be rebuilt and redecorated. The Habsburg archduke and archduchess, their family, and private patrons provided these commissions. Rubens's own interests were largely within the realm of painting, but he played a significant role in sculpture and sculptural decoration, architecture, costumes, and illustrated books (published by the famous Plantin Press in Antwerp), all of which were directly affected by him and his art.

The subjects of Flemish art, and the subjects of Rubens's paintings, were primarily religious—they were frequently large altarpieces with life-size figures. But portraits, landscapes, still-lifes, or game pieces, were also popular, and many were executed by other artists in collaboration with Rubens.

19.1 Peter Paul Rubens. *Marchesa Brigida Spinola Doria*. 1606. Oil on canvas, 5′ × 3′2⅞″ (152.2 × 98.7 cm). The National Gallery of Art, Washington, D.C. Samuel H. Kress Collection. 1961.9.60.

Peter Paul Rubens and Defining the Baroque

Although the Baroque style was born in Rome, it soon became international through the work of Rubens. He epitomized the Baroque ideal of the virtuoso artist, acting as diplomat, royal emissary and advisor, with entrée to the courts of Europe—Paris, London, and Madrid. He was widely read and widely traveled, with a knowledge of classical literature, and spoke several languages. He was acclaimed for his intellect, and for a vitality that enabled him to unite the natural and supernatural and to attain a Baroque theatricality and drama that we have also seen in Bernini (see Chapter 18). Trained by local painters, Rubens became a master in 1598, but he developed a personal style only when he went to Italy two years later.

During his eight years in the art and patronage centers of Mantua, Genoa, Florence, and Rome, he absorbed the Italian tradition far more completely than had any northern European before him. He eagerly studied ancient sculpture, the masterpieces of the High Renaissance, and the work of Caravaggio and Annibale Carracci. He obtained major commissions in Italy for both portraits and altarpieces.

RUBENS AS PORTRAITIST Rubens was one of the greatest and most influential portraitists of the seventeenth century, recording the vast wealth and stature of his often noble patrons. He painted several portraits while in Italy and maintained contacts with his Genoese patrons for years after he left. His resplendent portrait of *Marchesa Brigida Spinola Doria* (**fig. 19.1**), a member of the ruling class of Genoese banking families, who invested in trade with Africa and the East, was painted in 1606, probably in celebration of her wedding at age 22.

Although a large painting, it was even more monumental in the seventeenth century—perhaps nine feet high—before it was later cut down on all four sides. Originally the marchesa was shown full-length, striding from the terrace of her palazzo. She is sumptuously dressed in white satin, and bejeweled with gold and gems. Her huge, multilayered ruff, typical of her time and class, frames her face. The vast flowing red cloth, which unfurls behind her, suggests her forward stride. The size, full-length view, elements of movement, and color against her face are just a few of the aspects of a new, dynamic approach to portraiture that were also to influence Rubens's student and assistant Anthony van

Dyck (see fig. 19.4). Later stately portraits of the eighteenth and nineteenth centuries would reflect these influences.

RUBENS AND THE ALTARPIECE Upon Rubens's return to Antwerp in 1609, he was commissioned to paint *The Raising of the Cross* (**fig. 19.2**) as the central panel for the high altar of the Church of Saint Walburga (now destroyed). Its very subject speaks to the dynamism of the Baroque and it shows how much he was indebted to his Italian experience. The muscular figures, modeled to show their physical power and passionate feeling, recall the antique, Hellenistic sculpture that Rubens saw, drew, and collected, and the figures from the Sistine Chapel ceiling that he also copied. These works of art served as models for his heroic figures throughout his life. He also gathered inspiration from the Farnese Gallery (see fig. 18.4), while the lighting

19.2 Peter Paul Rubens. *The Raising of the Cross.* 1610–1611. Center panel of a triptych, 15′1″ × 11′9⅝″ (4.6 × 3.4 m). Antwerp Cathedral, Belgium

Oil   Baroque - Flanders

The term CYCLE refers to a number of scenes, usually painted, that illustrate a story or a series of episodes or events.

suggests Caravaggio's work (see fig. 18.1). The altarpiece's rich color and luminosity are ultimately due to the influence of Titian (compare with fig. 15.14). Thus, it owes much of its success to Rubens's ability to combine Italian influences with Netherlandish ideas such as the realistically indicated foliage, the armor of the soldier, and the curly-haired dog in the foreground. These varied elements are integrated into a composition of tremendous force. The unstable pyramid of bodies, swaying precariously under the strain of the dramatic action, bursts the limits of the frame in a typically Baroque way, making a viewer feel like a participant in the action. Christ is shown parallel to the plane, so that we fully see him being raised to the Crucifixion. The very concept of "the raising" is a Baroque one; it implies movement and action happening at that

moment. The entire scene is dramatic, powerful, and monumental.

The altarpiece would have been 35 feet high in its final form—a triptych (the wings are not shown here). It also included a now lost painting of God the Father above, explaining Christ's heavenward imploring glance. The triptych was placed on the high altar at the top of 19 steps, so the entire altarpiece ensemble would have towered above all else.

Rubens's epic canvases defined the scope and the style of Baroque painting. They possess a seemingly boundless energy and inventiveness, which, like his heroic nudes, express life at its fullest.

MARIE DE' MEDICI CYCLE Rubens exhibited his virtuoso talent in portraits and monumental historical works in the 1620s with a prized commission, his CYCLE of paintings known as the *Marie de' Medici Cycle*. The paintings glorified the career of Queen Marie de' Medici of France, widow of Henry IV and mother of Louis XIII, and were housed in the Luxembourg Palace in Paris. The cycle consists of 21 paintings at least 13 feet high, with some as much as 28 feet wide. Our illustration shows one episode: The young queen landing in Marseilles (**fig. 19.3**). Rubens has turned this uneventful passage into a spectacle of unparalleled splendor, combining both reality and allegory. As Marie de' Medici walks down the gangplank to enter France, having already married Henry IV by proxy in Florence, she has not yet met her husband. (They will meet later in Lyons.) Accompanied by her sister and aunt as Fame flies overhead sounding triumphant blasts, she is welcomed by France, represented allegorically by a figure draped in a *fleur-de-lis* cape. Neptune and his fish-tailed crew, the Nereids, rise from the sea; having guarded the queen's journey, they rejoice at her arrival. Everything flows together here in swirling movement: Heaven and earth, history and allegory.

RUBENS'S WORKSHOP To produce these grand commissions—large paintings, painting cycles, ceilings, and altarpieces—Rubens initially worked on a small scale, with oil sketches, small paintings on wood. He used them to try out ideas and share them with his assistants. Most of the Flemish artists working in the early seventeenth century studied with Rubens in his large workshop. They often traveled where he did, worked on paintings he began or sketched, or started paintings that he completed.

19.3 Peter Paul Rubens. *Marie de' Medici, Queen of France, Landing in Marseilles (3 November 1600).* 1622–1625. Oil on canvas, 12'11½" × 9'7" (3.94 × 2.95 m.). Musée du Louvre, Paris

19.4 Anthony van Dyck. *Portrait of Charles I Hunting.* ca. 1635. Oil on canvas, 8'11" × 6'11½" (2.7 × 2.1 m). Musée du Louvre, Paris. Inv.1236

Anthony van Dyck: History and Portraiture at the English Court

Besides Rubens, only one other Flemish Baroque artist won international stature: Anthony van Dyck (1599–1641). He was that rarity among painters: A child prodigy. Before he was 20 he had become Rubens's most valued assistant. And, like Rubens, he developed his mature style only after a stay in Italy.

Van Dyck's fame rests mainly on the portraits he painted in London between 1632 and 1641. The *Portrait of Charles I Hunting* (**fig. 19.4**) shows the king standing near a horse and two grooms

in a landscape. Representing the sovereign at ease, it is vastly different in effect from Holbein's painting of the earlier English king, *Henry VIII* (fig. 17.11). It is less rigid than a formal state portrait, but hardly less grand, for Charles remains in full command of the state, symbolized by the horse, which bows its head toward its master. The fluid movement of the setting complements the self-conscious elegance of the king's pose. Charles's position, however, was less secure than his confidence suggests. His reign ended in civil war, and he was beheaded in 1649. He was succeeded by the Puritan leader Oliver Cromwell and his

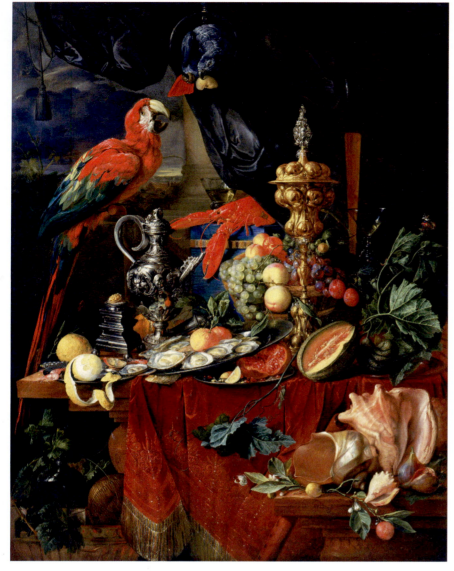

know who commissioned these works and presume they were for the homes of private patrons. At first they were predominantly simple paintings, but by mid-century this genre explores the elaborate and dramatic explosion of objects collected at that time.

THE FLAMBOYANT STILL LIFE: JAN DAVIDSZ. DE HEEM By mid-century, the still-life painting was often a lavish display, known as the *pronk* still life for its visual splendor, as *pronk* means "showy" or "ostentatious." This type reached its peak in the work of Jan Davidsz. de Heem (1606–1684). De Heem began his career in Holland but soon moved to Flanders, where he transformed the still life with his unique, flamboyant style. In *Still Life with Parrots* (**fig. 19.5**), he depicts delicious food, exotic birds, and luxurious goods from around the world: The conch and nautilus shells, the parrots, and the lobsters are probably from the New World, and the Seville oranges, plums, grapes, lemons, melons, pomegranates, and oysters are all imported, commanding high prices in the marketplace.

The food is piled up on pewter platters that are unstable and suggest both abundance and extravagance. De Heem intends this to be theatrical, drawing back a curtain for us to see. Even the column in the background is meant to suggest a heroic work. The result is a stunning display of virtuosity and defines the elements of a *pronk* still life.

19.5 Jan Davidsz. de Heem. *Still Life with Parrots*. Late 1640s. Oil on canvas, 59¼ × 45½" (150.5 × 115.5 cm). Collection of the John and Mable Ringling Museum of Art, the State Art Museum of Florida, Sarasota, Florida. Bequest of John Ringling, 1936. SN289

followers, known as the "Roundheads" in reference to their short cropped hair. In contrast, note that in the painting Charles I's tresses drop below his shoulder in the French (Catholic) manner.

Van Dyck has brought the court portrait up to date by using Rubens and Titian as his points of departure. He died eight years before the beheading of Charles I and so never worked for the subsequent courts. But he created a new aristocratic portrait tradition that continued in England until the late eighteenth century and which had considerable influence on the Continent as well.

Still-Life Painting

Still-life painting in seventeenth-century Flanders took many forms—depictions of flowers, game, food, and precious objects. We usually do not

The Dutch Republic

Art in the Dutch Republic, unlike that of Flanders, was not based largely on Church or State commissions, but was exercised primarily though private patronage and the open art market, as a commodity. Many artists produced for the market rather than for individual patrons. As such, even the greatest masters could not fully support themselves with the money earned from their art. It was not unusual for an artist to keep an inn or run a small business on the side. Yet they survived—less financially secure, but freer as a community of artists.

And there were many artistic communities—in Haarlem, Utrecht, Amsterdam, and Delft, to name but a few. Artists frequently traveled between these cities and may have known each other's work, but most of them are usually associated with only one place—Frans Hals and Judith Leyster worked in Haarlem; Terbrugghen in Utrecht; Rembrandt in Amsterdam; Vermeer in Delft. Some of the paintings were religious in nature, but most were not. There were portraits, group portraits commissioned by civic groups, landscapes, cityscapes, architectural paintings, still lifes, and genre paintings. And the paintings ranged from large to small—small enough to hold in the hand or for ordinary people to hang on the walls of their homes.

The *Caravaggisti* in Holland: Hendrick Terbrugghen

The Baroque style came to Holland from Antwerp through the work of Rubens, and from Rome through contact with the *Caravaggisti*, Caravaggio's followers. Although most Dutch painters did not go to Italy, the majority of those who went in the early years of the century were from Utrecht, a town with strong Catholic traditions. One of these, Hendrick Terbrugghen (1588–1629), worked in Italy for several years and was one of the first of the *Caravaggisti* to return to the North. He adapted Caravaggio's style for religious painting, but also for single-figured genre painting. Terbrugghen's *Singing Lute Player* (**fig. 19.6**) is inspired by Caravaggio's painting of the same subject, his *Musicians* (fig. 18.2), and by others like it, such as the young men in *The Calling of St. Matthew* (fig. 18.1), who wear slashed doublets and feathered berets. Terbrugghen's portrayal of a life-size, half-length figure, filling the entire canvas, became a common one in Utrecht painting, and grew popular elsewhere in Holland. The Utrecht School transmitted the style of Caravaggio to other Dutch masters, such as Frans Hals.

The Haarlem Community and Frans Hals

One of the first to profit from these new ideas permeating the Dutch Republic was the Haarlem artist Frans Hals (ca. 1585–1666), who was born in Antwerp. Hals captured his contemporaries in both portraiture and genre painting, and he excelled at combining both—animating his portraits and setting their poses in somewhat relaxed or even casual stances. He is famed for his six Civic Guard group portraits of life-size figures as well as many individual portraits, none of which repeated the same pose. His genre painting, usually of single figures, portrayed characters that seem to be drawn from real life.

A WEDDING PORTRAIT Hals's only double portrait, *Married Couple in a Garden, Portrait of Isaac Massa and Beatrix van der Laen* (**fig. 19.7**), probably

19.6 Hendrick Terbrugghen. *Singing Lute Player*. 1624. Oil on canvas, 39⅝ × 31″ (100.5 × 78.7 cm). The National Gallery, London

commemorates the couple's wedding in 1622. It combines the relaxed, informal atmosphere of genre painting with the likeness and formal attire of portraiture. This life-size couple modestly display their affection for each other by sitting close together. Ingeniously, Hals set the couple off-center, which adds to the sense of spontaneity, punctuated by the sense that Massa is open-mouthed and speaking to us. Beatrix's arm is looped over his elbow, displaying her ring (customary on the index finger); they smile broadly, their eyes twinkling with enjoyment, as they sit in a garden—an imaginary Garden of Love—surrounded by ivy, a symbol of steadfast love and fidelity. Indeed, they seem to be in love. His right hand touches his chest (his heart) as a show of his intended affection. Isaac Massa (1586–1643), an important and wealthy diplomat, geographer, and a cartographer of Siberia, was active in the fur trade. But his worldliness is only suggested in this wedding portrait set in his own garden.

19.7 Frans Hals. *Married Couple in a Garden, Portrait of Isaac Massa and Beatrix van der Laen.* ca. 1622. Oil on canvas, 55 × 65½" (140 × 166.5 cm). Rijksmuseum, Amsterdam

The painting can be seen in sharp contrast to Jan van Eyck's *The Arnolfini Portrait* (fig. 13.6), and whether we interpret the representation of that earlier couple as a betrothal, wedding, or contract, we can see that the emotional tie between the Arnolfini couple was not Van Eyck's concern. This is more than a difference in personal artistic style; it is the difference between the Renaissance and the Baroque, occurring over the course of 200 years. Between Van Eyck and Hals also stood Rubens, who had executed a wedding portrait of himself and his first wife that may have served as an example to Hals.

HALS AND GENRE PAINTING Hals's mature style is seen in *The Jolly Toper* (**fig. 19.8**), which perhaps represents an allegory of Taste, one of the Five Senses, among the most popular themes in the seventeenth century. The painting combines Rubens's robustness with a focus on the "dramatic moment" that may be derived from

19.8 Frans Hals. *The Jolly Toper.* ca. 1628–1630. Oil on canvas, 31⅞ × 26¼" (81 × 66.6 cm). Rijksmuseum, Amsterdam

Caravaggesque painters in Utrecht. Everything here conveys complete spontaneity: The twinkling eyes and half-open mouth, the raised hand, the teetering wineglass, and—most important of all—the speed with which the painter sets down the forms. Hals worked in dashing brushstrokes, clearly visible. With this open, split-second technique, the completed picture has the immediacy of a sketch.

Hals, like Rembrandt van Rijn and Jan Vermeer whom we will meet later in this chapter, is most closely identified with a period referred to as the Golden Age of Dutch art. Individually these three artists created and developed from their northern heritage the unique style of seventeenth-century Dutch art in Haarlem, Amsterdam, and Delft respectively. None of them traveled to Italy.

The Next Generation in Haarlem: Judith Leyster

The most important follower of Hals was Judith Leyster (1609–1660), who was responsible for a number of works that once passed as Hals's own, although she also painted works most unlike his: Candlelight scenes and paintings that explored the relationship between men and women. She painted portraits and still lifes, but mostly genre paintings. Her *Self-Portrait* (**fig. 19.9**) shows Leyster as both portrait and genre painter and was executed no doubt to show her mastery of both. It was probably her presentation piece to the Guild of St. Luke in Haarlem in 1633, as her master's piece, when she became a master and had her own students. The painting on the easel is a detail of a popular work of hers, and so she is advertising her diverse talents. The portrait reveals her technical skill as she wields numerous brushes and a palette while she sits in her studio, open-mouthed and casually conversing with us. Many women artists, as Leyster does here, showed themselves painting—indicating their new professional status and their unique position. Leyster signed many of her paintings with a monogram, a conjoined J, L, and star, punning on her name,

19.9 Judith Leyster. *Self-Portrait*. ca. 1633. Oil on canvas, 29⅜ × 25⅜″ (72.3 × 65.3 cm). National Gallery of Art, Washington, D.C. Gift of Mr. and Mrs. Robert Woods Bliss. 1949.6.4

which means "leading star." Indeed, she was referred to during her lifetime as a "leading star" in art.

Rembrandt and the Art of Amsterdam

Like Hals and Leyster, Rembrandt Harmensz. van Rijn (1606–1669) was influenced indirectly by Caravaggio through the Utrecht School. While he rivaled Rubens as the most famous artist of his age, Rembrandt is perhaps better known to us today. A painter, draughtsman, and printmaker, he is equally significant in each medium and established himself in the growing and prosperous city of Amsterdam. Rembrandt is known both for the intimacy and poignancy of images that convey personal relationships and emotions—an aspect seldom explored before—as well as for producing individual portraits, large group portraits and history pieces. He had an active workshop for four decades and many of his followers became significant artists in his native Leiden or in Amsterdam.

REMBRANDT'S DRAWINGS The poignancy of his drawings can be seen in many of his studies "from life"—that is, with the model before him. He drew in pen and ink, wash, red or black chalk, silverpoint, and combinations of these. Rembrandt's drawing of his wife in the *Portrait of Saskia van Uylenburgh* (**fig. 19.10**), upon their engagement, is executed on parchment in silverpoint, an unforgiving drawing tool (before the invention of the pencil) that requires precision and a sure hand. It is clearly meant as a very special drawing to commemorate their betrothal. The inscription states (in Dutch): "This is drawn after my wife, when she was 21 years old, the third day of our betrothal, the 8th of June 1633." They were married a year later; the drawing shows a dreamy-eyed Saskia looking very much in love with the artist who catches her likeness. She wears a flowered straw hat, usually associated with shepherdesses and amorous scenes. Saskia came from a well-to-do family and was the niece of Rembrandt's art dealer. Her features appear in many of the paintings and studies for etchings he made before her death at the age of 30 in 1642.

REMBRANDT AND THE CIVIC GUARD By the 1640s, Rembrandt had become Amsterdam's most sought-after portrait painter, and a man of considerable wealth. He executed portraits, mostly life-size, and sometimes full-length, of individuals or couples, as well as history and religious paintings. He painted for the court in The Hague, and for private patrons.

The famous group portrait known as *The Night Watch* (**fig. 19.11**), because of its old darkened varnish (now removed), was painted in 1642. It shows a military group, a Civic Guard Company, possibly assembling for the visit of Marie de' Medici of France to Amsterdam. The Civic Guards, founded in the fourteenth century, were local voluntary militia groups. Although

19.10 Rembrandt van Rijn. *Portrait of Saskia van Uylenburgh*. 1633. Silverpoint on white prepared vellum, arched at the top, 7¼ × 4" (18.5 × 10.7 cm). Staatliche Museen Preussischer Kulturbesitz, Kupferstichkabinett, Berlin. Inv. Kdz 1152

19.11 <u>Rembrandt</u> van Rijn. *<u>The Night Watch</u>* *(The Company of Captain Frans Banning Cocq).* 1642. <u>Oil</u> on canvas, 12'2" × 14'7" (3.8 × 4.4 m). Rijksmuseum, Amsterdam **Baroque - Holland**

they had successfully defended their cities from the Spanish in the 1580s and, indeed, were proud of this accomplishment, with the truce of 1609 the Civic Guards became more like civic fraternities, with civic and religious duties. They began having their portraits painted in the early sixteenth century. Although the members of the company had each contributed toward the cost of this huge canvas (originally it was much larger), Rembrandt did not give them equal weight pictorially. He wanted to avoid the mechanically regular designs of group portraits by many earlier artists. Instead, he made the picture a virtuoso performance filled with move-

ment and lighting, which captures the excitement of the moment and gives the scene unique drama. The focus is on Captain Frans Banning Cocq, whose hand extends toward us and even creates a shadow across the yellow jacket of his lieutenant, while some figures are plunged into shadow and others are hidden by overlapping. Legend has it that the people whose portraits he had obscured were not satisfied with the painting, but there is no evidence for this claim. On the contrary, we know that the work was much admired in its time, and Rembrandt continued to receive some major public commissions in the 1650s and 1660s.

19.12 <u>Rembrandt</u> van Rijn. *The Hundred Guilder Print*. ca. 1647. <u>Etching</u> and dry point, 11 × 12¾" (27.8 × 32.4 cm). The Metropolitan Museum of Art, New York. H.O. Havemeyer Collection, Bequest of Mrs H.O. Havemeyer, 1929. 29.107.35

Baroque - Holland

REMBRANDT AS PRINTMAKER Rembrandt's etchings show a new depth of feeling. His famed *Hundred Guilder Print* (**fig. 19.12**), which derives its name from a story that 100 guilders was the great price paid for it at a contemporary auction, was executed in stages over many years. The etching, which has been interpreted as a depiction of the entire nineteenth chapter of the Gospel of St. Matthew, combines various aspects of Christ's preachings, including the healing of the multitude, and the gathering of children and those who had forsaken all to come to him. The print is poignant and filled with pathos, revealing a humble world of bare feet and ragged clothes. The scene is full of the artist's deep compassion for the poor and outcast, who make up the audience in the print. The setting suggests some corner in Amsterdam where the Jews had found a haven; they are used here to provide an "authentic" background for Christ's teachings. Rembrandt had a special sympathy for them, both as heirs of the biblical past and as victims of persecution, and they were often his models, as well as, occasionally, his patrons. Rembrandt incorporates observations of life from the drawings he made throughout his career. Here, as in Caravaggio's *The Calling of St. Matthew* (see fig. 18.1), it is the magic of light and dark created with the velvety tone of drypoint

(see page 301) that gives *The Hundred Guilder Print* its spiritual significance. And, like Caravaggio, he infuses the story with the same lay Christian spirit that reveals God's ways with his human creations.

SELF-PORTRAITURE Rembrandt painted many self-portraits over his long career. There have been many suggestions as to why—as models for other paintings, as explorations of different expressions, or as possible advertisements for his craft. In our late example (**fig. 19.13**), Rembrandt examines himself with a typically northern European candor. The bold pose and penetrating look bespeak a resigned but firm resolve that suggests princely nobility. A comparison with Holbein's *Henry VIII* (fig. 17.11) suggests a similar expression of power, but Holbein's interest in the detail of fabric and jewels dominates while Rembrandt's display of *chiaroscuro* (light and dark) suggests the mood. There is a marked difference in technique, too, as Rembrandt uses impasto, which is the layering of paints and glazes to achieve textured and atmospheric effects. Rembrandt painted several large self-portraits, including this one, toward the end of his life, and the acquisition of a "large mirror" (its breaking is documented) may have allowed him to do this.

19.13 Rembrandt van Rijn. *Self-Portrait.* 1658. Oil on canvas, 52⅝ × 40⅞" (133.6 × 103.8 cm). The Frick Collection, New York

Baroque - Holland

The Market: Landscape, Still-Life, and Genre Painting

Art in northern Europe was largely made for an open market. Of course, portraits and group portraits, like those for the Civic Guards (Rembrandt's *The Night Watch*), were commissioned works, but a great number of paintings were made "on spec"—that is, with the hope that they would be purchased on the open market from dealers, fairs, stores, and lotteries. With princely patrons in mind, Rubens painted many large works and kept some in stock, but in the Dutch Republic, paintings were often small, cabinet-size, and with subjects suitable for a middle-class home. Most art buyers in Holland preferred subjects within their own experience: Landscapes, architectural views, still-lifes, and genre (everyday) scenes. These subjects, we recall, emerged in the latter half of the sixteenth century (see chapter 17).

The richest of the newly developed "specialties" was landscape, both as a portrayal of familiar views and as an imaginative vision of nature. Landscapes—frequently with only small human figures or none at all—became a staple of seventeenth-century Dutch painting. We can see the beginnings of this in the work of Pieter Bruegel the Elder (see fig. 17.14) and in Italy as well. But in the Netherlands, the sense of reality, almost a "portrait of the land," was a common theme.

Landscape Painting: Jacob van Ruisdael

Identifiable city views—panoramic landscapes with the outlying countryside and picturesque sand dunes, showing Amsterdam, Haarlem, or other cities—became popular throughout the century. In the art of Jacob van Ruisdael (ca. 1628–1682) these views become testaments to the city skyline—and to the sky of this flat, low land. The sky might occupy three-quarters of the

19.14 Jacob van Ruisdael. *Bleaching Grounds Near Haarlem*. ca. 1670. Oil on canvas, 21⅔ × 24½″ (55.5 × 62 cm). Royal Cabinet of Paintings, Mauritshuis, The Hague, the Netherlands

painting, as it does in this work, *Bleaching Grounds Near Haarlem* (**fig. 19.14**). Ruisdael did many paintings of Haarlem, known as *Haarlempjes* (little views of Haarlem). The church spires, windmills, and ruins are all identifiable, as is the major church, the *Grote Kerk* (Great Church), known before the Reformation as Saint Bavo. In the foreground are the bleaching fields, where both domestic and foreign linen was washed and set out to be bleached by the sun. Haarlem water was well known for its purity and so the city was famous for its linen-

bleaching and its beer production. Haarlemmers took pride in their city, in their artists—and in their artists' painted views of the city and its surrounding countryside.

Still-Life Painting: Willem Claesz. Heda

Dutch still-lifes may show the remains of a meal, of food and drink and luxury objects, such as crystal goblets, glasses of different sizes, and silver dishes, chosen for their contrasting shapes, colors, and textures. Flowers, fruits, and sea shells may also be shown.

19.15 Willem Claesz. Heda. *Still Life.* 1634. Oil on panel, 16⅞ × 22⅞" (43 × 57 cm). Museum Boymans-van Beuningen, Rotterdam, the Netherlands

Baroque - Holland

As seen here in his *Still Life* (**fig. 19.15**), the Haarlem artist Willem Claesz. Heda (1594–1680) was fascinated by various surfaces and reflections—the rough edge of the lemon, the liquid, slimy quality of the oysters, the sparkling light on the glass, the multiple reflections of the window in the glass, the *prunts* (glass drops) on the *roemer* (wine glass), and the engraving on the silver. Heda is famous for these light effects, which are heightened by the **tonal** quality (various tones of the same color) of the painting in greens and silvery grays, making it largely **monochromatic** (of one color). These are in marked contrast to the colorful Flemish works of Jan Davidsz. de Heem (fig. 19.5). The table here is set with white wine, lemon, imported pepper in a cone, and oysters, known as an aphrodisiac. Yet the broken glass and overturned silver *tazza* (cup) suggest a hasty departure or some upheaval on a narrative level. Whoever sat at this table was suddenly forced to leave the meal. The

curtain that time has lowered on the scene, as it were, suggests a melancholic air.

Flower Painting and Rachel Ruysch

The independent floral still-life seems to have begun in Flanders, but it developed in both the Northern and the Southern Netherlands. Rachel Ruysch (1664–1750) was one of the leading Dutch flower painters of the day, and was lauded as such in her lifetime. She had a long and prolific career and worked in Amsterdam, The Hague, and Düsseldorf, where she and her husband Juriaen Pool II (1665–1745), a portraitist, became, as a team, court painters to the Elector Palatine until his death. One could even say she was born to be a flower painter, as her father was a professor of anatomy and botany. Ruysch knew every blossom, every butterfly, moth, and snail she put into a piece. We know from the inclusion of flowers in earlier paintings, such as the lilies in a vase in the altarpiece of the *Mérode*

19.16 Rachel Ruysch. *Flower Still Life.* After 1700. Oil on canvas, 29¾ × 23⅞" (75.5 × 60.7 cm). The Toledo Museum of Art, Toledo, Ohio. Purchased with Funds from the Libbey Endowment, Gift of Edward Drummond Libbey. 1956.57

Triptych (fig. 13.3), that they can have meaning beyond their beauty. The flowers in **figure 19.16**, some with stems, wild and impossibly long, are arranged to create an extravaganza of color. Yet the fallen, drooping flowers suggest a theme of the shortness of life, known as **vanitas**, and one that is common in Dutch still-life painting.

Genre Painting: Jan Steen

Genre painting continued throughout the century, but revealed a more complex narrative by mid-century. The human figures are often no longer half-length; they are shown full-length, even when the paintings are small and create a sense of intimacy. Often there are interior scenes of homes and taverns. The paintings of Jan Steen and Jan Vermeer provide a range of subject matter from the comical to the deeply introspective. They suggest a glimpse into the home, family, relationships, and even fashion of the seventeenth century.

A scene of both comical circumstance and family intimacy can be seen in *The Feast of St.*

Nicholas (**fig. 19.17**) by Jan Steen (1626–1679), of a feast still celebrated in much the same way today in Holland. St. Nicholas has just paid his pre-Christmas visit to the household, leaving toys, candy, and cake for the children, who have set their shoes out for gifts. The little girl and boy are delighted with their presents. She holds a doll of St. John the Baptist and a bucket filled with sweets, while he plays with a kolf (a kind of golf) club and ball. Everyone is jolly except their brother, on the left, who has received in his shoe, held by the maidservant, only a birch rod for caning naughty children. Soon his tears will turn to joy, however: His grandmother, in the background, beckons to the bed, where surely a toy is hidden.

Steen tells the story with relish, embroidering it with many delightful details. *The Feast of St. Nicholas* also conveys a serious message as well: The doll of St. John the Baptist is meant as a reminder of the importance of spiritual matters over worldly possessions, no matter how pleasurable. Steen drives his style of storytelling with a moral from the tradition of Pieter Bruegel the Elder (see fig. 17.15).

Intimate Genre Painting and Jan Vermeer

In the genre scenes of the Delft artist Jan Vermeer (1632–1675), by contrast, there is no clear narrative. Single figures, usually women, are seemingly engaged in everyday tasks at secluded, still moments. Vermeer's paintings appear magical, hypnotic, and truly original. In *Woman Holding a Balance* (**fig. 19.18**), a young woman, richly dressed in the at-home wear of the day, is contemplating a balance in her hand, with strings of pearls and gold coins spread out on the table before her. The painting gives a view into this "still-life world"—

with pearls and gold, paintings and fur all magically created to provide an eternal, yet momentary, glance into a private realm where, in fact, our view is not acknowledged. The painting behind her depicts Christ at the Last Judgment, when every soul is weighed. This may be a reference to the soul of her unborn child, and it parallels the woman's own activity, now contemplating the future with the scales she holds. The pans of the balance were once thought to contain gold or pearls but scientific analysis of the painting indicates that they actually contain nothing, only beads of light. The painting is intensely private, quiet, yet also highly sensual, created with optical effects that make the surface shimmer.

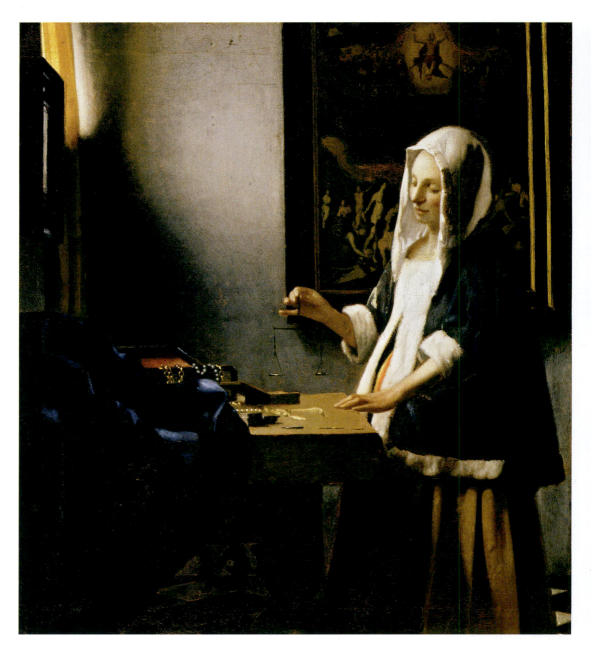

19.18 Jan Vermeer. *Woman Holding a Balance.* ca. 1664. Oil on canvas, 16¾ × 15″ (42.5 × 38.1 cm). National Gallery of Art, Washington, D.C. Widener Collection. 1942.9.97

Vermeer's work is marked with his use of light, frequently from a window at the left, with flecks of light on fabric, and with reflections. To achieve these effects, he seems to have used mechanics that are both old and new. Vermeer may have used a *camera obscura*, an experimental optical device (a forerunner of the photographic camera) that created an image by means of a hole for light on the inside of a dark box. The hole acts as a primitive lens and a scene from outside the box can be seen, inverted, inside it. It is not suggested here that Vermeer copied such scenes, but he may have been inspired by them. They often have a sparkling quality, as seen here in the pearls and in the light on the balance. These sparkling areas are known as "discs of confusion." The *camera obscura* was well known, and there is considerable evidence that it was used by Dutch artists.

This new way of looking is paired with an old way—one-point perspective view with a vanishing point. It has been shown that a hole (for a pin and string) was set in a number of Vermeer's paintings to create a one-point perspective system. The vanishing point in figure 19.18 is just to the left of the little finger of the hand that holds the balance. It sets the balance of all elements of the painting.

Vermeer is a master of the expressive qualities of light. He is concerned with all of light's visual and symbolic possibilities. His paintings reveal a world of introspection. His arrangement of figures, space, and light, while looking incredibly simple, was complex, yet the complexities remained hidden.

SUMMARY

In the seventeenth century, the Southern Netherlands (often known as Flanders, eventually Belgium) and the Northern Netherlands (eventually the Dutch Republic, often called Holland) were separated, even divided, by religion and government, and thus patronage in the two regions differed as well.

Flanders, under Spanish rule, was Catholic, and Catholic church altarpieces, funded by major commissions, were executed in Flanders, frequently by Peter Paul Rubens or members of his large workshop. Rubens's monumental paintings, such as his *Raising of the Cross*, with sculptural figures, sweeping diagonals, brilliant color, and dramatic effects, defined Baroque painting in northern Europe. Rubens traveled to many courts of Europe (Madrid, London, Paris) and had a direct influence on art in these centers. This is true not only for religious painting, but for still life, landscape, and large, life-size portraits that show figures in motion. Rubens's assistant Anthony van Dyck perfected this mode of the ideal court portrait. His paintings for the court of Charles I of England influenced formal portraiture for the next 300 years. The flamboyant style of still life was epitomized by Jan Davidsz. de Heem.

The Dutch Republic predominantly followed the Reformed Church. Topics of a largely non-religious nature, paintings of genre, still life, and landscape, were the dominant themes in Dutch art. These were purchased by the rising middle class, who also commissioned portraits of themselves by Frans Hals and Rembrandt, among others. Group portraits, a form that would become typically Dutch, were also commissioned by Civic Guard organizations. Rembrandt would paint portraits and many self-portraits, religious paintings, and was also known for the contemplative quality of his drawings and etchings. Rembrandt's etchings explored atmospheric effects previously unknown in that medium. The character of Dutch art may be considered distilled in Vermeer's images of women in domestic middle-class settings, such as his *Woman Holding a Balance*.

Despite the seeming differences of the North and South Netherlands, there was much interaction between these two nations and their artists.

ART IN TIME

- 1602 — Dutch East India Company founded

- 1610/11 — Peter Paul Rubens, *The Raising of the Cross*

- 1621 — Philip IV becomes king of Spain

- 1626 — New Amsterdam (New York City) founded by the Dutch West India Company

- 1634 — Willem Claesz. Heda, *Still Life*

- ca. 1635 — Anthony van Dyck, *Portrait of Charles I Hunting*

- 1639 — Japan enforces policy of isolation from Europeans; permits a Dutch trading post

- 1642 — Rembrandt, *The Night Watch*

- 1648 — Treaty of Münster legally recognizes the Dutch Republic

- ca. 1664 — Jan Vermeer, *Woman Holding a Balance*

- ca. 1670 — Jacob van Ruisdael, *Bleaching Grounds Near Haarlem*

- 1676 — Anthony van Leeuwenhoek first to record bacteria under a microscope

The Baroque in France and England

*D*uring the course of the tumultuous seventeenth century, the great monarchies of France and England (see map 20.1)—the former led by an absolute ruler, the latter governed by a king who shared power with Parliament—underwent dramatic change. Devastated by the previous era's religious wars and dynastic struggles, both nations saw their treasuries sorely drained, their populations severely reduced, and their societies bitterly divided, with Catholicism becoming the dominant religion in France and Protestantism in England. Each successive French and English monarch sought to strike a delicate balance between these competing forces. Such was true throughout Europe, where isolated skirmishes eventually coalesced into a conflict that encompassed nearly all its nations—the Thirty Years' War (1618–1648).

England faced still more upheaval and its situation degenerated in 1642 into a civil war that led to the trial of King Charles I, who was convicted of treason and beheaded in 1649. The Puritan Oliver Cromwell was named head of state and Lord Protector. Gradually his rule became a dictatorship with its own monarchical abuses, and upon his death in 1658 his government floundered. Two years later, in 1660, Parliament offered the throne to the son of the beheaded king, Charles II (1649–1685), thus ushering in the period known as the Restoration. Unfortunately, old religious rivalries and economic crises persisted, and the reign of Charles II's successor and brother, James II (r. 1685–1688), was soon in jeopardy. In the so-called Glorious Revolution of 1688, a relatively peaceful and bloodless event, members of the governing classes of Whigs and Tories proclaimed the Prince of Orange, the Stadholder or ruler of the Dutch Republic, as king of England; he and his wife, James's daughter, reigned jointly from 1689 as William III and Mary II (Mary died in 1694, William in 1702). The Bill of Rights (1689) established Parliament's supremacy, thus creating a unique form of

government that would gradually influence nations worldwide, notably the British colonies in North America.

In France, which by mid-century had emerged as Europe's most powerful nation both militarily and culturally, a consolidation of power was most successfully implemented by Louis XIV (1638–1715). Louis evoked the age-old divine right of kings—the idea that the monarch received his authority directly from God. He relied on a form of royal government known as absolutism, which gave full power to the monarch. The ABSOLUTE MONARCHY in France differed from England's constitutional monarchy, which divided power between the ruler and other institutions. In his quest to assert the preeminence of France, Louis XIV embarked on a series of military campaigns from 1688 to 1713 against his rivals, Spain, the Dutch Republic, Germany, and England. Despite eventual defeat, France remained a world power upon Louis's death in 1715.

The wars and social turmoil took perhaps their harshest toll on peasants and commoners, who reeled from continually increasing taxes as

The political system that gives rise to an ABSOLUTE MONARCHY is absolutism, in which full, unlimited, and unchecked power to rule a nation is in the hands of a single individual (an absolute monarch) or a group of rulers (oligarchs). Absolutism emerged in Europe near the end of the fifteenth century and is most clearly embodied by the reign of Louis XIV of France.

Map 20.1 Europe in the seventeenth century

well as from devastating natural disasters and the ensuing food shortages, famine, and rising prices. Yet both England and France reaped enormous profits from investments in their colonial empires, and established trading routes delivering a wide range of goods that enhanced the lifestyles of most Europeans. The development of mercantilism and a worldwide marketplace brought about the rise of a class of increasingly wealthy urban merchants seeking art to furnish and decorate their homes.

The art of these two nations was dominated by **classicism**—the style derived from the ancient Greek and Roman civilizations. And the royal courts in England and France served as the greatest patrons of the arts. In the emerging capital cities of Paris and London, the grandiose style of expanding civic projects, notably architecture, symbolized the wealth of each. Through its use of classical vocabulary—from columns, capitals, and pediments in architecture to styles of dress in painting—classicism represents a response to the ancient world and suggests

authority, order, and enduring tradition in its evocation of the imperial grandeur of Rome. Classicism soon became the hallmark of seventeenth-century French art. It became the official court style of painting between 1660 and 1685, a period corresponding to the climactic phase of Louis XIV's reign. Classical principles also dominated architecture, with the new Louvre and Versailles representing the most visible accomplishments of Baroque Classicism in France.

In England, too, classicism dominated art and architecture, notably the hospitals, churches, and country houses designed by Inigo Jones and Sir Christopher Wren. In the wake of the Great Fire of London in 1666, architecture thrived as massive reconstruction projects were undertaken to rebuild the city. Yet England's lasting artistic successes in the seventeenth century were in literature, with notable works by William Shakespeare, John Donne, and John Milton as well as the royal committee's translation of what would become known as the King James Bible.

France: The Style of Louis XIV

By the late seventeenth century, Paris was vying with Rome as Europe's art center. The French kings Henry IV (r. 1589–1610), Louis XIII (r. 1610–1643), and Louis XIV (r. 1643–1715)—aided by ambitious and able ministers and advisors such as the Duc de Sully, cardinals Richelieu and Mazarin, and Jean-Baptiste Colbert—created the climate for this exciting turn of events. The kings and their officials recognized the power of art to convey the majesty and strength of the monarchy, and they set out to create a massive program of patronage of all the arts and sciences—painting, sculpture, architecture, landscape design, decorative arts, theoretical and applied science, philosophy, and literature. Louis XIV especially manipulated art to serve as propaganda for his absolutist policies. He adopted the symbolic imagery of the sun as manifested by the Greek god Apollo, and came to be called the Sun King. This symbolism provided an ancient lineage for Louis that would serve his principle as absolute ruler. The ideal of *gloire* (glory), seen in the

portraits and architecture he commissioned, reflected his desire to give concrete form to the majesty of his rule, and thus of France.

Scholars often describe the period's art and literature as "classic." In this context, the word has three meanings. It is a synonym for "highest achievement," which suggests that the Louis XIV Style (art created under his reign) is the equivalent of the High Renaissance in Italy or the age of Perikles in ancient Greece. It also refers to the imitation of the forms and subject matter of classical antiquity. Finally, it suggests qualities of balance and restraint shared by ancient art and the Renaissance. Because the Louis XIV Style reflects Italian Baroque art, although in modified form, we may call it Baroque Classicism.

Painting in France

While many foreign artists working in France drew inspiration from that country's styles and traditions, French artists often traveled to Italy and the Netherlands to work. In the hopes of creating a nucleus of artists who would determine the Baroque in France, Louis XIII began officially recalling these artists. That is, those working abroad were required to come home to Paris. Yet the influences of foreign art were significant throughout the century and largely helped define French art. Even indirectly, Caravaggio for some, Carracci for others, Van Dyck and Titian all had an impact on French art.

GEORGES DE LA TOUR AND THE INFLUENCE OF CARAVAGGIO Many French painters in the early seventeenth century were influenced by Caravaggio, although how they were exposed to the Italian artist's style remains unclear. The finest of these was Georges de La Tour (1593–1652), whose importance was recognized only in the nineteenth century. Besides being named a painter to King Louis XIII, he received important commissions from the governor of Lorraine, his home province. He began his career painting picturesque genre figures before turning to religious scenes that appealed to adherents of the Catholic faith, the predominant religion in France. His use of light and his reliance on detailed naturalism derived largely from Caravaggio's northern European followers (see page 413), whom he may have visited in the Dutch Republic.

La Tour's mature religious pictures effectively convey the complex mysteries of the Christian faith. With its carefully observed details and seemingly humble subject, *Joseph the Carpenter* (**fig. 20.1**) might initially be mistaken

20.1 Georges de La Tour. *Joseph the Carpenter*. ca. 1642. Oil on canvas, 51⅛ × 39¾" (130 × 101 cm). Musée du Louvre, Paris

for a genre scene, but its devotional spirit soon overwhelms us. The two figures are set in profile, thus yielding little in their expressions. La Tour lends maximum significance to each gesture, each expression. The boy Jesus holds a candle, a favorite device of the artist, whose flame reinforces the devotional mood and imbues the scene with intimacy and tenderness. The painting has the power of Caravaggio's *Calling of St. Matthew* (fig. 18.1), but the simplified forms, warm palette, and arrested movement are characteristic of La Tour's restrained and focused vision.

NICOLAS POUSSIN AND BAROQUE CLASSICISM

The artist who contributed most to the rise of classicism in France was Nicolas Poussin (1594–1665), one of the most influential French painters of the century. Aside from an ill-fated two-year sojourn in Paris (he was one of the artists Louis XIII "recalled"), Poussin spent his entire career in Rome. There he hosted and taught visiting French artists, absorbing the lessons of Raphael and Carracci. Patrons brought Poussin's paintings back to Paris, where they influenced the royal court. Indeed, when establishing the curriculum of the French ROYAL ACADEMY, Jean-Baptiste Colbert, the king's chief advisor, and the artist Charles Le Brun chose Poussin's classical style to serve as a model for French artists.

POUSSIN AND HISTORY PAINTING: ANCIENT THEMES IN THE GRAND MANNER Arriving in Rome via Venice in early 1624, Poussin studied perspective and anatomy and examined ancient sculpture, the reliefs on ancient sarcophagi and vases, and the paintings of Raphael. His *The Death of Germanicus* (**fig. 20.2**) reflects much of his studies. The work served as a model for artistic depictions of heroic deathbed scenes for the

The ROYAL ACADEMY of Painting and Sculpture was founded in Paris in 1648 to set the standards in art. Charles Le Brun was one of the founders and presented many lectures on the virtues of the painting of Poussin and Raphael.

20.2 Nicolas Poussin. *The Death of Germanicus*. 1627–1628. Oil on canvas, 58¼ × 78" (147.96 × 198.12 cm). Minneapolis Institute of Art, Minneapolis, Minnesota. The William Hood Dunwoody Fund. 58.28

next two centuries and may in fact be the first example of this subject in the history of art.

A typical history painting, the work relates the powerful themes of death, loyalty, and revenge. The story comes from Tacitus and is set in 19 CE. Germanicus was a Roman general who had led campaigns against the Germanic tribes. At the urging of Tiberius, Germanicus' adoptive father, the governor of Syria poisoned the powerful general. Poussin depicts him on his deathbed, flanked on the left by his loyal soldiers swearing revenge and on the right by his mournful family. The promise to avenge is set at the center, commanding attention, as figures gesture their grief, loyalty, and suffering. Framed by the two groups, Germanicus becomes the focus of the composition, which is based on antique death scenes. The architecture sets the stage for the figures, which are arranged horizontally in a rectangular space, as in a classical frieze. The curtain in the rear restricts the action to a shallow space, heightening the drama and creating a more intimate environment.

Poussin believed the highest aim of painting was to represent noble and serious human actions. Emotion is abundantly displayed in the dramatic poses and expressions, but the lack of spontaneity means that the painting fails to touch us. The scene has a theatrical air, and for good reason. Before beginning the painting, Poussin arranged wax figurines on a miniature stagelike setting until he was satisfied with the composition. He believed that the viewer must be able to "read" the emotions of each figure as they relate to the story. Such beliefs later proved influential for his student Charles Le Brun when he was establishing an approved court style for French painting at the Royal Academy of Painting and Sculpture (see page 429). These ideas were not new. Before Poussin, however, no artist had made the analogy between painting and literature so closely or put it into practice so singlemindedly.

POUSSIN AND THE IDEAL LANDSCAPE The "ideal" landscape, serene and balanced, does not represent a particular locale, but rather a

20.3 Nicolas Poussin. *Landscape with St. John on Patmos.* 1640. Oil on canvas, 39½ × 53¾" (100.3 × 136.4 cm). Art Institute of Chicago. A.A. Munger Collection. 1930.500

20.4 Hyacinthe Rigaud. *Portrait of Louis XIV*. 1701. Oil on canvas, 9′2 × 6′3″ (2.8 × 1.9 m). Musée du Louvre, Paris

generalized and often beautiful place. The austere beauty and somber calm of the ideal landscape can be seen in Poussin's *Landscape with St. John on Patmos* (**fig. 20.3**), which continues the classical landscape tradition established by Annibale Carracci. The ancient landscape strewn with architectural ruins suggests both the actual site and the concept of antiquity. Trees on either side balance the composition, and many of the ruins are set parallel to the picture plane. A reclining St. John, who at the end of his life lived on the Greek island of Patmos, is shown in profile facing left. Poussin's pendant (paired) painting, *Landscape with St. Matthew*, shows the saint facing right, yet each work was created independently. Poussin executed both paintings in Rome for the secretary to Pope Urban VIII. The composition suggests the physical, rational arrangement of a spiritual world—a dichotomy truly suited and best explored by Baroque Classicism. Poussin's mythological landscapes show a similar construct of the physical, rational, and mythic.

HYACINTHE RIGAUD AND THE SPLENDOR OF LOUIS XIV The monumental *Portrait of Louis XIV* (**fig. 20.4**) by Hyacinthe Rigaud (1659–1743) conveys the power, drama, and splendor of the absolutist reign. The king is shown life-size and full-length, much like Van Dyck's portrait of Charles I (fig. 19.4). The comparison is intentional. The work follows the then formulaic nature of royal portraiture. It espouses power and authority through the use of the insignia of rulership and the symbols of the opulence of the monarch's reign. Louis is shown draped with his velvet coronation robes lined with ermine and trimmed with gold *fleur-de-lis*. He appears self-assured, powerful, majestic—and also tall, an illusion created by the artist, for his subject measured only five feet four inches. The portrait proudly displays the king's shapely legs (emphasized by the high heels Louis himself designed to increase his height), for they were his pride as a dancer. Indeed, the king actively participated in the ballets of the composer Jean Baptiste Lully (1632–1687) from the 1650s until his coronation. All the arts, from the visual to the performing, fell under royal control—a fact exemplified in Rigaud's painting, which expresses Louis's dominance and unequaled stature as the center of the French State.

French Classical Architecture

Because they were large, ostentatious, and public, building projects, even more than painting,

transmitted the values of the royal court to a wide audience. In French architecture, the classical style expressed the grandeur and authority of imperial Rome and confirmed the ideals of tradition, omnipotence, absolutism (see page 426), strength, and permanence espoused by the monarchy. Mammoth scale and repetition of forms evoke these broad concepts, which were embodied in royal structures erected in the heart of Paris as well as outside the city, in the palace and gardens of Versailles.

In 1655, Louis XIV declared *"L'état, c'est moi"* ("I am the State"). This statement was not just political but represented an artistic and aesthetic intention as well. Louis's projects for his palace and court took on colossal proportions and represented, not a single individual, or even a single monarch, but the entirety of France. He began by renovating the Louvre Palace in Paris, a project begun by his father, but later decided to move his entire royal court to a more isolated location where he could control them more efficiently. And so he began the construction of the palace and gardens of Versailles, located a few miles outside Paris. These complex building projects all share a single style—that of Baroque Classicism.

20.5 Louis Le Vau, Claude Perrault, and Charles Le Brun. East front of the Louvre. 1667–1670. Paris

architecture, The Louvre, France   Baroque- France

THE LOUVRE Work on the palace had proceeded intermittently for more than a century, following Pierre Lescot's original design under Francis I; what remained was to close the square court on the east side with an impressive façade. Bernini was invited to Paris in the hope that the most famous artist of the Roman Baroque would do for the French king what he had done for the popes in Italy. After much argument and intrigue, Louis XIV rejected Bernini's three proposals and turned over the problem to a committee: Charles Le Brun, his court painter; Louis Le Vau (1612–1670), his court architect; and Claude Perrault (1613–1688), a student of ancient architecture. All three men were responsible for the structure (**fig. 20.5**), but Perrault is rightly credited with the major share of the new Louvre.

Perrault based the center pavilion on a Roman temple front—a portico—and the wings look like the sides of the temple folded outward. The colonnade itself was controversial because of its unique use of paired columns, yet this treatment thereafter became a characteristic of French classicism in architecture.

The east front of the Louvre signaled the victory of French classicism over the Italian Baroque as the royal style. It further proclaimed France as the new Rome, both politically and culturally, by linking Louis XIV with the glory of the Caesars. This revitalization of the antique, both in its concept and its details, was Perrault's main contribution.

THE PALACE OF VERSAILLES Louis XIV's largest enterprise was the Palace of Versailles (**fig. 20.6**), located eleven miles from the center of Paris. By forcing the aristocracy to live under royal scrutiny outside the capital, the king hoped to

20.6 Aerial view of the Palace of Versailles, France. Begun 1669

architecture   Baroque - France

prevent a repeat of the civil rebellion known as the Fronde, which had occurred in 1648–1653 during his minority.

The project was begun in 1669 by Le Vau, who designed the elevation of the garden front (**fig. 20.7**), but within a year he died. Under the leadership of Jules Hardouin-Mansart (1646–1708), the structure was greatly expanded to accommodate the ever-growing royal household. The garden front, intended by Le Vau to be the main view of the palace, was stretched to an enormous length but with no change in the architectural elements. As a result Le Vau's original façade design, a less severe variant of the Louvre's east front, looks repetitious and out of scale. The center block contains a single room measuring 240 feet long, the spectacular Galerie des Glaces, or Hall of Mirrors (today still used for ceremonial events, it is where the Treaty of Versailles was signed, ending World War I). The mirrors were placed to reflect the gardens outside, making the room appear larger by day. At night, the myriad reflections of candlelight illuminated the grand space. Whether day or night, the effect was and is impressive.

Baroque features, although not officially acknowledged by the architects, appeared inside the palace. Louis XIV was interested less in architectural theory and monumental classical exteriors than in the lavish interiors that would provide suitable settings for himself and his court.

THE GARDENS OF VERSAILLES Apart from the magnificent interior, the most impressive aspect of Versailles is the park extending west of the garden front (see fig. 20.6). The vast park was designed by André Le Nôtre (1613–1700), who had become director of the gardens of Louis XIII in 1643 and whose family had served as royal gardeners for generations. Le Nôtre transformed an entire natural forest into a controlled park, a massive and expensive enterprise that reflected the grandeur of the king. In concept, the landscape is as significant as the palace—perhaps more so, for it suggests the king's dominion over nature. The gardens form

20.7 Louis Le Vau and Jules Hardouin-Mansart. Garden front of the center block of the Palace of Versailles. 1669–1685

a series of "outdoor rooms" for the splendid fêtes and spectacles that formed an integral part of Louis's court.

The spirit of absolutism is apparent in Le Nôtre's plan, which called for the taming of nature: Forests were thinned to create stately avenues, plants were shaped into manicured hedges, water was pumped into exuberant fountains and serene lakes. The formal gardens consist of a multitude of paths, terraces, basins, and mazes that create a unified geometric whole. An especially important aspect of the landscape design was the program of sculpture, much of which incorporated images of Apollo, the sun god, adopted as the symbol of Louis XIV.

Sculpture: The Impact of Bernini

Sculpture evolved into an official royal style in much the same way as did architecture— through the influence of Rome and the impact of Bernini's visit to the royal court in 1665. While in Paris, Bernini carved a marble bust of Louis XIV. He was also commissioned to create an equestrian statue of the king, which he later executed in Rome and sent back to Paris, where it was reworked. It is now at Versailles.

ANTOINE COYSEVOX Bernini's influence can be seen in the work of Antoine Coysevox (1640–1720), the first of a long line of distinguished French portrait sculptors and one of the artists employed by Charles Le Brun at Versailles. In a vivacious terracotta portrait of Le Brun (**fig. 20.8**), Coysevox shows the artist with slightly parted lips and head turned to the side. The drapery folded over itself below the shoulder line recalls the general outline of Bernini's bust of Louis XIV. Le Brun's face, however, shows a naturalism and subtle characterization that are Coysevox's own.

Baroque Architecture in England

The English gained much from, but contributed little to, the development of Baroque painting and sculpture. Foreign painters, mainly from Italy, Flanders, and the Dutch Republic, including Rubens and Van Dyck, dominated the English royal court throughout the century. During the reign of Charles I, the court painter Anthony van Dyck executed both portraits (see fig. 19.4) and allegorical paintings. After his death many court artists continued his style of portraiture, initiating little in the visual arts until the Restoration of Charles II in 1660. After the Great Fire of London in 1666, the rebuilding of the city gave priority to architecture, which thereafter represented the most important English artistic achievement.

Inigo Jones and the Impact of Palladio

The first significant English architect was Inigo Jones (1573–1652), architect to James I and Charles I as well as the era's leading English theatrical designer. Jones was an affirmed disciple of Antonio Palladio (see page 361), whose classical design principles he admired (Jones visited Italy and Paris) and whose treatises (along with those of Alberti) he owned and annotated. Before Jones, English architecture was a pastiche of medieval and Renaissance forms. He is responsible for introducing Palladio's Renaissance Classicism to England.

The Banqueting House that Jones built at Whitehall Palace in London (**fig. 20.9**) conforms to the principles in Palladio's treatise, although it does not copy any specific Palladian project. Originally intended to be used for court ceremonies and performances called masques

20.9 Inigo Jones. West front of the Banqueting House, Whitehall Palace. 1619–1622. London

20.10 Sir Christopher Wren. Façade of Saint Paul's Cathedral. 1675–1710. London

(spectacles combining dance, theater, and music), evening entertainments were halted after 1635 because smoke from torchlights was damaging Rubens's *Apotheosis of James I*, painted in the recessed compartment of the ceiling. The Banqueting House is more like a Renaissance palazzo than any building north of the Alps designed at that time. Jones uses an ordered, classical vocabulary and the rules of proportion to compose the building with understated elegance. The sculpted garland below the roofline

decoratively and elegantly enhances the overall structure. The building is perhaps starker than originally conceived; it once bore colored stones for each of the stories, but the façade was later resurfaced. Jones's spare style stood as a beacon of classicist orthodoxy in England for 200 years.

Sir Christopher Wren

If it had not been for the destruction caused by the GREAT FIRE OF LONDON of 1666, Sir

Christopher Wren (1632–1723), the most important English architect of the late seventeenth century, might have remained an amateur. Wren may be considered the Baroque counterpart of the Renaissance artist-scientist. An intellectual prodigy, he first studied anatomy and then physics, mathematics, and astronomy, and he was highly esteemed by Sir Isaac Newton, the discoverer of gravity, for his understanding of geometry. Wren held the position of chair in the astronomy department at Oxford University. His technological knowledge may have affected the shape of his buildings; certainly, no previous architect went to such lengths to conceal a building's structural supports.

After the catastrophic fire of 1666, Wren's name was put forward to the short-lived royal commission to reconstruct the city. A few years later he began his designs for the rebuilding of

Saint Paul's Cathedral (**fig. 20.10**), one of many churches destroyed in the conflagration. Wren favored central-plan churches and originally conceived of Saint Paul's as in the shape of a Greek cross with a huge domed crossing, based on Michelangelo's plan of Saint Peter's. This idea was evidently inspired by a previous design by Inigo Jones, who had been involved with the restoration of the original Gothic structure of Saint Paul's earlier in the century. Wren's proposal was rejected by the Church authorities, however, who favored a conventional basilica. In the end, the plan was that of a Latin cross (**fig. 20.11**), the same followed for most Catholic churches including Saint Peter's, an ironic outcome given that the building program could have provided an opportunity to create a new vocabulary for the Protestant Church of England.

On his only journey abroad in 1665–1666, Wren visited France and met Bernini, who was in Paris at the invitation of Louis XIV. The influence of this trip can be seen on the façade of Saint Paul's, where the impact of contemporary architecture in Paris can be discerned—as in the double columns of the Louvre. In contrast to Saint Peter's, Saint Paul's dome rises high above the building and dominates the façade; it looks like a much-enlarged version of Bramante's *Tempietto* (fig. 15.4). Saint Paul's, broad, double-storied and domed, is an up-to-date Baroque design that reflects Wren's thorough knowledge of the Italian and French architecture of the day. Indeed, Wren believed that Paris provided "the best school of architecture in Europe," and he was equally affected by the Roman Baroque.

For Wren, as for Newton (who was appointed a Commissioner of Saint Paul's in 1697), mathematics and geometry were central to the new understanding of the universe and humanity's place in it. The Great Fire of London provided Wren with the opportunity to rebuild and reframe the city and its skyline. Besides Saint Paul's, he worked on 52 of the 87 damaged or destroyed churches. His innovations in this field created English Baroque architecture.

20.11 Plan of Saint Paul's Cathedral, London

SUMMARY

From England's constitutional monarchy to France's absolutism, the royal state reigned supreme. The royal courts of both France and England became the most important patrons of the arts.

Classicism, with its references to the tradition and supremacy of ancient Greece and Rome, became the favored style in painting, sculpture, and architecture. Nicolas Poussin is the painter who best exemplifies this preference. He worked primarily in Rome, but as his paintings representing classical, mythological or religious themes, in relief-like or landscape settings, were sent back to Paris, they continued to influence French art. Poussin introduced the concept of the Grand Manner—suggesting the importance of depicting noble and serious human actions, such as in his painting *The Death of Germanicus*. This work became a model for heroic deathbed scenes over the next 200 years.

In architecture, Baroque Classicism, which suggests enduring absolute power, embodied the ideals of Louis XIV, who moved his court to Versailles. The monumental palace he built there along with its gardens and sculpture, has, ever since, come to represent the concept of absolutism. Grandiose Baroque art and architecture stood as symbols not only of authority, but also of the pride and glory of the nation.

In England, Inigo Jones brought the classical style to London, which was previously rooted in its strong Gothic tradition. Following the treatises of Palladio, he designed the Banqueting House at Whitehall Palace. But later in the century, Christopher Wren created some of the era's most masterful structures, including the renovated Saint Paul's Cathedral, after the Great Fire of London in 1666.

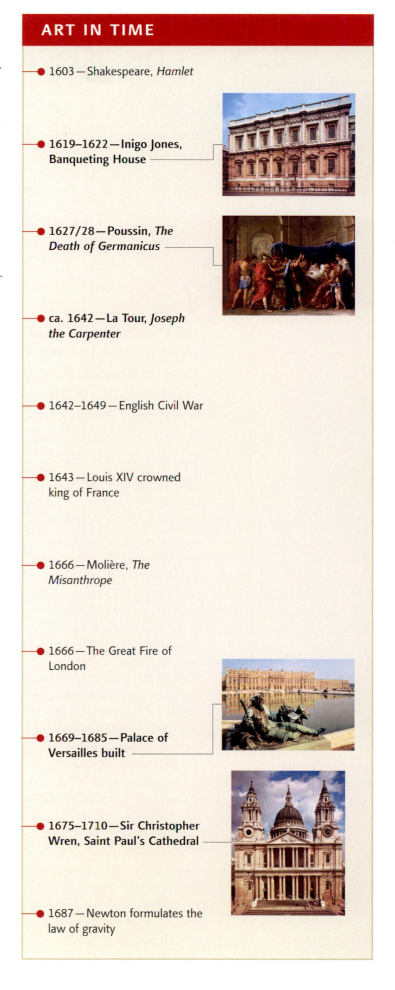

ART IN TIME

- 1603—Shakespeare, *Hamlet*
- 1619–1622—Inigo Jones, **Banqueting House**
- 1627/28—Poussin, *The Death of Germanicus*
- ca. 1642—La Tour, *Joseph the Carpenter*
- 1642–1649—English Civil War
- 1643—Louis XIV crowned king of France
- 1666—Molière, *The Misanthrope*
- 1666—The Great Fire of London
- 1669–1685—**Palace of Versailles built**
- 1675–1710—**Sir Christopher Wren, Saint Paul's Cathedral**
- 1687—Newton formulates the law of gravity

CHAPTER 21 | The Rococo

*I*n France the Rococo style is linked with Louis XV (1710–1774) because it corresponds roughly to his lifetime, although aspects of it extend through to the French Revolution of 1789. Despite similarities between the Baroque and Rococo, a fundamental difference exists between the two styles: In a word, it is fantasy. If the Baroque presents theater on a grand scale, the Rococo stage is smaller and more intimate. Its artifice evokes an enchanted realm that presents a diversion from real life. In some ways the Rococo in France manifests a shift in taste among aristocrats, who reasserted their power as patrons and began to favor stylized motifs from nature and a more domestic art—private rather than public—to decorate their new homes in Paris.

"Rococo" was coined in the nineteenth century as a disparaging term, taken from the French word *rocaille* (meaning "pebble") and the Portuguese *barrocco* ("baroque"), to refer to what was then perceived as the excessive and ornate taste of the early eighteenth century. The word Rococo, then, refers to the playful, irregular pebbles, stones, and shells that decorated the grottoes of Italian gardens and became the principal motifs of French interior designs.

Although sometimes viewed as the final phase of the Baroque, the Rococo asserted its own independent stylistic traits and represents a period of intense creative and intellectual activity. The interest in the poetic genre of the pastoral and subjects of love and loss took on growing importance in the eighteenth century. Patrons were increasingly taken with the notion of "simple man" existing in an idealized nature. The French Academy, still important, even established a new category to reflect this new interest, called the *fête galante*, a type of painting introduced by Jean-Antoine Watteau. The style celebrated eroticism and the tradition of love, and broadened the range of human emotion depicted in art.

Although most directly associated with France, the Rococo cast a wide geographical influence that affected the arts in England as well as most of western and central Europe (see map 21.1). English art, long dominated by foreign artists, saw the development of a distinct school of painting and the establishment of the Royal Academy of Arts in 1768, whose annual exhibitions attracted a fashionable London clientele and the best-known native artists. In western and central Europe, notably in Germany and Austria, the devastation of the Thirty Years' War (1618–1648) was followed in the eighteenth century by a period of rebuilding. Italian artists such as Tiepolo, with his assistants, painted ceiling frescoes in central European churches and palaces in this new elaborate and elegant style; he produced similar works for his native city of Venice as well.

European colonization of the New World continued in the 1700s. Armies battled to secure these distant lands, depleting their nations' treasuries, yet succeeding in sending back to their homelands exotic objects and substances, including the feathers, jewels, and metals that collectors coveted and artists used in the creation of

Map 21.1 Europe in the Rococo period

new art. In the performing arts, the Venetian composer Antonio Vivaldi (1678–1741) produced innumerable operas and the German composer Johann Sebastian Bach (1685–1750) wrote much extraordinary choral music, while London became home to the establishment of legitimate theater, notably in the Haymarket and the Drury Lane–Covent Garden district.

France: The Rise of the Rococo

After the death of Louis XIV in 1715, the nobility, previously attached to the court at Versailles, were now freer from royal control. Louis XV, only five years old at his father's death, would not be crowned until 1723. This early period of the Rococo—between 1715 and 1723—is known as the Regency, so called because France was governed by Louis's cousin Philip, duke of Orléans, acting as regent. With a nobleman as effective king, the aristocracy regained much

power and authority, and abandoned the strict, demanding court life of Versailles. Rather than returning to their châteaux in the provinces, many chose to live in Paris, where they built elegant townhouses or *hôtels* with small, intimate rooms. These were decorated with paintings, porcelain, and small sculpture that created a lavish, light-hearted mood. Paintings, therefore, were just one part of the creation of the ambience of refinement that permeated pre-Revolutionary France. These paintings, as well as interior designs, would influence the decor of western and central Europe throughout the century.

Painting: Poussinistes versus Rubénistes

Toward the end of the seventeenth century, a dispute arose among the members of the French Academy, who then formed two factions named after painters: The **Poussinistes** against the **Rubénistes**. Neither Poussin nor Rubens was still alive during this debate, which focused on the issue of drawing versus color. French artists were familiar with Poussin's paintings, which had been sent from Rome to Paris throughout his career, and they knew Rubens's work from the *Marie de' Medici Cycle* (see fig. 19.3) in the Luxembourg Palace. The conservatives defended Poussin's view that drawing, which appealed to the mind, was superior to color, which appealed to the senses. The Rubénistes (many of whom were of Flemish descent) favored color, rather than drawing, as being truer to nature. They also pointed out that drawing, admittedly based on reason, appeals only to the expert few, whereas color appeals to everyone. This argument had important implications. It suggested that the layperson should be the judge of artistic values and this challenged the Renaissance notion that painting, as a liberal art, could be appreciated only by the educated mind.

JEAN-ANTOINE WATTEAU The greatest of the Rubénistes, who eventually won the day, was Jean-Antoine Watteau (1684–1721). Born in Valenciennes, which had been part of the South Netherlands, Watteau showed an affinity for Rubens, the region's greatest artist. Watteau, who moved to Paris in 1702, was a significant contributor to the new Rococo style as well as to the new subjects associated with it. His painted visions of fantasy show idyllic images of aristocratic life, with elegant figures luxuriously dressed in shimmering pastel colors and set in dreamlike outdoor settings. His carefully posed figures evoke forlorn love, regret, or nostalgia, and imbue his scenes with an air of melancholy. Such works became increasingly sought after by collectors in France, and the popularity of this theme soon spread throughout Europe.

Because Watteau's fantasies had little historical or mythological basis, his paintings broke many academic rules and did not conform to any established category. To admit Watteau as a member, the French Academy created the new classification of painting called *fêtes galantes* (meaning "elegant fêtes" or "outdoor entertainments"). Watteau's "reception piece" for the Academy (the painting he was required to give upon being named a member) was *A Pilgrimage to Cythera* (**fig. 21.1**). The painting is an evocation of love and includes elements of classical mythology. Cythera, which came to be viewed

21.1 Jean-Antoine Watteau. *A Pilgrimage to Cythera*. 1717. Oil on canvas, 4′3″ × 6′4½″ (1.3 × 1.9 m). Musée du Louvre, Paris

21.2 Jean-Antoine Watteau. *Seated Young Woman.* ca. 1716. *Trois crayons* (three-chalk) drawing: Red, black, and white chalks on cream paper, 10 × 6¾″ (25.5 × 17.1 cm). The Pierpont Morgan Library, New York

as an island of love, was one of the settings for the Greek myth of the birth of Aphrodite (Venus), who rose from the foam of the sea.

Watteau has created a delightful yet slightly melancholic setting for love, although is unclear whether the couples are arriving at or leaving the island. The action unfolds in the foreground from right to left like a continuous narrative, which suggests that the figures may be about to board the boat. Two lovers remain engaged in their amorous tryst; behind them, another couple rises to follow a third pair down the hill as the reluctant young woman casts a longing look back at the goddess's sacred grove. Young couples, accompanied by swarms of cupids, pay homage to Venus, whose garlanded sculpture appears on the far right. The delicate colors— pale greens, blues, and pinks—suggest the gentle nature of the lovers' relationship. The subtle gradations of tone showed Watteau's debt to Rubens and helped establish the supremacy of the Rubénistes.

Yet, Watteau's figures are slim, graceful, and small in scale; they appear even more so when compared with most Baroque imagery. The landscape does not overwhelm the scene but echoes its idyllic mood. The nostalgic feeling carries implications of longing and unrealized passion, and is achieved not only with the figures and their gentle touching and hesitancy, but also through the sympathetic parallel found in Watteau's landscape and the sculptures in it.

Watteau's use of color planted him firmly in the Rubéniste camp. However, his innovations and creativity as a draughtsman (which would have implied a Poussiniste status) combined both color and line. Watteau excelled in the technique known as *trois crayons* or three chalks. In *Seated Young Woman* (**fig. 21.2**), he uses the chalks to best effect, so that the red color defining her body suggests a vivacious quality when contrasted against the black and white of her clothing, eyebrows, and upswept hair. The colors enliven and add a spontaneity to this life drawing. In

21.3 Jean-Honoré Fragonard. *The Swing*. 1767. Oil on canvas, 32⅝ × 26″ (82.9 × 66.0 cm). The Wallace Collection, London

Rococo - France

numerous sketches Watteau often worked out poses, movements, gestures, and expressions, many of which (although not this drawing) served as studies for figures in his paintings.

JEAN-HONORÉ FRAGONARD Transforming fantasy into reality in paint was the forte of Jean-Honoré Fragonard (1732–1806)—or at least that was his reputation. A brilliant colorist, an artistic descendant of Watteau, Fragonard won the distinguished Rome Prize in 1752 and spent five years in the city, beginning in 1756. Upon his return to Paris, he worked mostly for private collectors. Fantasy, flirtation, and licentiousness—in short, the spirit of the Rococo, and the continuous tradition beginning with Watteau—coalesce in *The Swing* (**fig. 21.3**). An anecdote provides an interpretation of the painting. According to the story, another artist, Gabriel-François Doyen, was approached by the Baron de Saint-Julien to paint his mistress "on a swing which a bishop is setting in motion. You will place me in a position in which I can see the legs of the lovely child and even more if you wish to enliven the picture." Doyen declined the commission but directed it to Fragonard.

The painting, an example of an "intrigue," suggests a collusion in erotic fantasy between artist and patron, with the clergy as their unwitting dupe. This "boudoir painting" offers the thrill of sexual opportunity and voyeurism, but here in a stagelike outdoor setting. The innocence of the public arena heightens the teasing quality of the motion of the swing toward the patron-viewer. The painted sculpture of a cupid to the left, holding a finger to his lips, suggests the conspiracy at the erotic escapade in which we as viewers are now participants. Fragonard used painted sculpture in many of his works to echo or reinforce their themes. The dense and overgrown landscape, providing secrecy, lit by radiant sunlight, invokes the warmth of spring or summer and overtones of sexuality and fertility. The glowing pastel colors create an otherworldly haze that enhances the sensuality of this fantasy spun by Fragonard.

JEAN-SIMÉON CHARDIN Raised in a bourgeois household, Jean-Siméon Chardin (1699–1779) rose to become Treasurer of the French Academy as well as the member responsible for installing the paintings at its exhibitions. Chardin's expertise was in still life, as well as in genre, and was inspired by the many Dutch and Flemish seventeenth-century paintings then in

21.4 Jean-Siméon Chardin. *Back from the Market*. 1739. Oil on canvas, 18½ × 14¾" (47 × 37.5 cm). Musée du Louvre, Paris

France. Some of his own patrons were important connoisseurs of this art.

To these collectors, members of the rising bourgeoisie in France, such genre scenes and domestic still-lifes proclaimed the virtues of hard work, frugality, honesty, and devotion to family. His quiet household scenes struck a chord with his sophisticated patrons, and demand for them was so high that he often painted copies of his most popular subjects. His paintings were also reproduced as prints, making them affordable to those who lacked the means to buy an original work.

Back from the Market (**fig. 21.4**) shows life in a Parisian bourgeois household. The beauty hidden in everyday life and a clear sense of spatial order beg comparison with the Dutch artist Jan Vermeer (see fig. 19.18). However, Chardin's technique differs significantly from that of any Dutch artist. His brushwork is soft at the edges and

It was in the West in the late eighteenth century, led by the European academies and fueled by the intellectual environment of the Enlightenment, that the **fine arts** (painting, sculpture, drawing, and architecture) were elevated at the expense of the so-called **minor arts**, which include ceramics, textiles and weaving, metalwork and gold- and silversmithery, furniture, glassware and stained glass, and enamel work. **DECORATIVE ARTS** and **applied arts** have been used interchangeably with **minor arts** ever since. Another term, **crafts**, has been in and out of favor for a long time. Until the late Middle Ages in the West, crafts were art; they were art again in Rococo Europe and during the Arts and Crafts Movement at the turn of the twentieth century.

suggests objects rather than defining them. He summarizes forms and subtly alters their appearance and texture, a technique that underlies the appeal of pastel (drawing or painting with colored chalks). Chardin often turned to this medium late in life, when his eyes were failing him.

ÉLISABETH-LOUISE VIGÉE-LEBRUN Portraits allow us to gain the clearest understanding of the French Rococo, for the transformation of the human image lies at the heart of the age. The finest Rococo portraits were those of elaborately garbed women, hardly a surprising fact in a society that idolized love and feminine beauty. Indeed, one of the finest, most accomplished, and most successful portrait painters of the Rococo was a woman, Élisabeth-Louise Vigée-Lebrun (1755–1842). As court painter to Queen Marie-Antoinette, and therefore responsible for glorifying the image of the monarch, Vigée-Lebrun found herself in a dangerous position in the 1780s as the French Revolution approached. Yet she survived, and served as a bridge between the *ancien régime* of Louis XVI and the post-Revolutionary period.

Marie-Antoinette and Her Children (**fig. 21.5**) embodies the vision Vigée-Lebrun chose for the royal mother and the one the queen was eager to incorporate into her life at Versailles. Surrounded by her children, Marie-Antoinette is shown as a "normal," conventional woman. At a time when a high infant mortality was the norm, the image of the empty cradle suggests the death of a child, reinforcing the ordinariness of the royal family. The queen's eldest son, Louis Joseph (known as *le dauphin*; he would die of natural causes just two years later), is pointing to the empty cradle of the infant Sophie. The second son, Louis Charles, sits on his mother's lap while her daughter, Marie Thérèse, stands at her side. This type of imagery, not just of a family scene but specifically of a mother with her children, was in vogue in both painting and literature. Indeed, the concept of motherhood as the epitome of a woman's life became fully developed at this time. A glimpse into the intimate life of the royal family, Vigée-Lebrun's portrait is intended to convey the ordinariness of what was probably the most extraordinary family in eighteenth-century France.

The French Rococo Interior

It is in the intimate spaces of early eighteenth-century interiors that the elegance and charm of the Rococo are shown to their full extent. This fact is manifest—yet disguised—in Vigée-Lebrun's portrait of Marie-Antoinette, which is set in the midst of the magnificence of Versailles. But Versailles is not the only measure of the social world. The Parisian *hôtels*—townhouses of the dispersed nobility—soon developed into social centers. The field of "design for private living" took on new importance at this time. Because these city sites were usually cramped and irregular, they offered few opportunities for impressive exteriors. Hence the layout and decor of the rooms became the architects' main concern. The *hôtels* demanded an intimate style of interior decoration that gave full scope to individual fancy, uninhibited by the classicism seen at Versailles.

Crucial to the development of French decor was the importance assigned to interior designers. They collaborated with architects, who, in turn, became more involved in interior decoration. Along with sculptors, who often created the architectural ornamentation, and painters, whose works were inserted over doors, architects helped to raise the DECORATIVE ARTS to the level of the fine arts, thus establishing a tradition that continues today. The decorative and fine arts were most clearly joined in furniture. Gilt, metals, and enamels were often applied to interior decor to create the feathery ornamentation associated with the Rococo. Many of these artisans came originally from the Netherlands, Germany, and Italy.

The decorative arts played a unique role during the Rococo. *Hôtel* interiors were total environments assembled with extraordinary care by discerning collectors and the talented architects, sculptors, decorators, and dealers who catered to their exacting taste. A room, like an item of furniture, could involve the services of a wide variety of artisans: Cabinetmakers, wood carvers, gold- and silversmiths, upholsterers, and porcelain makers.

NICOLAS PINEAU Few of these Rococo rooms survive intact; the vast majority have been destroyed or greatly changed, or the objects and decorations have been dispersed. Even so, we can get a good idea of their appearance through the reconstruction of one such room (perhaps from the ground floor behind the garden elevation) from the Hôtel de Varengeville, Paris (**fig. 21.6**), designed about 1735 by Nicolas Pineau (1684–1754) for the Duchesse de Villars. His room for the duchess incorporates many contemporary Rococo features. To create a sumptuous

21.5 Élisabeth-Louise Vigée-Lebrun. *Marie-Antoinette and Her Children*. 1787. Oil on canvas, 9′½″ × 7′⅝″ (2.75 × 2.15 m). Musée National du Château de Versailles, Versailles, France effect, the white walls are encrusted with gilded stucco ornamentation in arabesques, C-scallops, S-scrolls, fantastic birds, bat's wings, and acanthus foliage sprays. The elaborately carved furniture is embellished with gilt bronze. Everything swims in a sea of swirling patterns united by the most sophisticated sense of design and materials the world has ever known. No clear distinction exists between decoration and function in the richly designed fireplace and the opulent chandelier. The paintings, too, have been completely integrated into the decorative scheme, and are set over two of the doors.

Porcelain, and especially porcelain by Sèvres, the manufactory established by Louis XV and closely associated with the tastes of his mistress Madame de Pompadour, would have once been one of the prominent decorations within the interior, from the dinner and tea services to containers for playful bowls of pot-pourri.

CLODION AND FRENCH ROCOCO SCULPTURE
Used to adorn interiors, French Rococo sculpture took many forms and was designed to be viewed at close range. A typical example is the miniature *Nymph and Satyr Carousing* (**fig. 21.7**)

21.6 Nicolas Pineau. Varengeville Room in the Hôtel de Varengeville, 217 Boulevard St.-Germain, Paris. ca. 1735. (The chimneypiece on the wall at left is not original to room.) Original paneling probably commissioned by Pineau. Carved, painted, and gilded oak, 18'3¾" × 40'6½" × 23'½" (5.58 × 12.35 × 7.07 m). Photographed about 1995. The Metropolitan Museum of Art, New York. Purchase, Mr. and Mrs. Charles Wrightsman Gift, 1963. 63.228.1

21.7 Claude Michel, known as Clodion. *Nymph and Satyr Carousing.* ca. 1780. Terracotta, height 23¼" (59 cm). The Metropolitan Museum of Art, New York. Bequest of Benjamin Altman, 1913. 14.40.687

by Claude Michel (1738–1814), known as Clodion, a successful sculptor of the Rococo period who later effectively adapted his style to the more austere Neoclassical manner. Clodion began his studies at Versailles and won the prestigious Rome Prize. His greatest contribution to the Rococo was to transform its fantasies into three-dimensional works of coquettish eroticism. The open and airy composition of this sculpture is related to a work by Bernini, but its miniature scale produces a more intimate and sensual effect. Although Clodion undertook several large sculptural cycles in marble, he reigned supreme in the intimate medium of terracotta.

England: Printmaking and Painting

The French Rococo exerted a major influence across the English Channel. Foreign artists—Holbein, Gentileschi, Rubens, Van Dyck—had flourished for generations in England, and the works of Dutch and Italian artists were widely collected. As we have seen with the works of Chardin and Rubens, among others, printmaking was used not just to create new compositions but to disseminate painted works, giving them a larger audience and broader appeal. This task proved most useful for landscapes and genre paintings, areas of great interest to, and increasingly collected by, the British public.

William Hogarth and the Narrative

William Hogarth (1697–1764) was the first major native English artist since the Elizabethan period. He began his career as an engraver and soon took up painting. He made his mark in the 1730s with a new kind of genre painting, which he described as "modern moral subjects…similar to representations on the stage." He created these pictures, and the prints made from them for sale to the public, in series and repeated certain details in each scene to unify the sequence. Hogarth's morality paintings teach, by bad example, solid middle-class virtues and reflect the desire for a return to simpler times and values. They proved enormously popular among the newly prosperous middle class in England.

In the engraving *He Revels (The Orgy)* (**fig. 21.8**), Scene III from *The Rake's Progress*, the artist shows a young man who is overindulging in wine and women. (Later in the series, the rogue is arrested for debt, enters into a marriage of convenience, turns to gambling, enters the debtors' prison, and dies in an insane asylum. Hogarth engraved all the paintings in the series.) The scene is set in a famous London brothel, the Rose Tavern. The girl adjusting her shoe in the foreground is preparing for a vulgar dance involving the silver plate and candle behind her; to the left a chamber pot spills its foul contents over a chicken dish; and in the background a singer holds sheet music for a bawdy song of the day. The scene is full of witty visual clues, which the viewer would discover little by little, adding a comic element to the satire of social evils. Like Jan Steen (see fig. 19.17), Hogarth's moral narratives are so entertaining that viewers enjoy the sermon without being overwhelmed by the stern message.

Thomas Gainsborough and the English Portrait

Portraiture remained the only constant source of income for English painters. Thomas Gainsborough (1727–1788) prospered greatly as the favorite portraitist of British high society, but began by painting landscapes.

Gainsborough spent most of his career working in the provinces, but toward the end of it he moved to London. The splendid portrait (**fig. 21.9**) of the famous tragic actress Sarah Siddons (1755–1831) displays the virtues of the artist's late style: A cool elegance that translates Van Dyck's aristocratic poses into late eighteenth-century terms and a fluid, translucent technique reminiscent of Rubens's that renders the glamorous sitter, with her fashionable attire and coiffure, to ravishing effect. The portrait's unique qualities were summarized most ably by the French nineteenth-century critic Théophile Thoré-Burger (1807–1869) in 1857, more than 70 years after the portrait was painted:

The great tragic actress, who interpreted the passions with such energy and such feeling, and who felt them so strongly herself, is better portrayed in this simple half length, in her day dress, than in allegorical portraits as the Tragic Muse or in character parts. This portrait is so original, so individual, as a poetic expression of character, as a deliberate

21.9 Thomas Gainsborough. *Mrs. Siddons.* 1785. Oil on canvas, 49½ × 39″ (125.7 × 99.1 cm). The National Gallery, London

Siddons as the muse personified seated on her throne, and she is flanked by the allegorical figures of Pity and Terror.

For all their differences, Gainsborough and Reynolds had more in common, artistically and philosophically, than they cared to admit. Each looked back to Van Dyck while drawing different lessons from his example.

selection of pose, as bold color and free handling, that it is a work of no other painter. It is useless to search for parallels, for there are none. Veronese a little—but no, it is a quite personal creation. This is genius.

Joshua Reynolds

As the French critic's pointed remarks suggest, Gainsborough painted Siddons to outdo his great rival on the London scene, Sir Joshua Reynolds (1723–1792), who had portrayed her as the embodiment of the Tragic Muse (**fig. 21.10**). Siddons was one of several well-known English actresses of the era, and she achieved her fame playing tragic roles; she was called "tragedy personified."

For his portrait Reynolds relied on expression and pose, derived from Michelangelo's Prophet Isaiah from the Sistine Chapel ceiling (fig. 15.9), to suggest the aura of the strength of Siddons's moral character. Reynolds, president of the British Royal Academy of Arts since its inception in 1768, championed the academic approach to art (copying the Old Masters), in which he was well versed after having spent two years in Rome. Although he preferred history painting in the grand style (as in the works of Poussin), most of his paintings are portraits that use allegory to ennoble them. Here, Reynolds has shown

21.10 Sir Joshua Reynolds. *Mrs. Siddons as the Tragic Muse.* 1784. Oil on canvas, 7′9″ × 4′9½″ (2.36 × 1.46 m). Henry E. Huntington Library and Art Gallery, San Marino, California

The Rococo in Germany, Austria, and Central Europe

Rococo architecture was a refinement in miniature of the curvilinear, "elastic" Baroque of Borromini. It was readily united with the architecture of central Europe, where the Italian Baroque had firmly taken root. It is not surprising that the Italian style received such a warm response there. In Austria and southern Germany, ravaged by the Thirty Years' War, patronage for the arts was limited and the number of new buildings remained low until near the end of the seventeenth century. By the eighteenth century these countries, especially the Catholic areas, were beginning to rebuild. The Baroque was an imported style, practiced mainly by visiting Italian artists. Not until the 1690s did native architects come to the fore. There followed a period of intense activity that lasted more than 50 years and gave rise to some of the most imaginative creations in the history of architecture. These monuments were built to glorify princes and prelates who are otherwise generally remembered only as lavish patrons of the arts. Rococo architecture in central Europe is larger in scale and more exuberant than that in France. Moreover, painting and sculpture are more closely linked with their settings. Palaces and churches are decorated with ceiling frescoes and sculpture unsuited to domestic interiors, however lavish, although they reflect the same taste that produced the Rococo French *hôtels*.

Balthasar Neumann

The work of Balthasar Neumann (1687–1753), who designed buildings exuding lightness and elegance, is the culmination of the Rococo in central Europe. Trained as a military engineer, he was named a surveyor for the Residenz (Episcopal Palace) in Würzburg after his return from a visit to Milan in 1720. The basic plan was already established and although Neumann greatly modified it, he was required to consult the leading architects of Paris and Vienna in 1723. The final result is a skillful blend of the latest German, French, and Italian ideas. The breathtaking Kaisersaal (**fig. 21.11**) of the Residenz is a great oval hall decorated in the favorite color scheme of the mid-eighteenth century: White, gold, and pastel shades. The structural importance of the columns, pilasters, and architraves has been minimized in favor of their decorative role. Windows and vault segments are framed by continuous, ribbonlike moldings, and

the white surfaces are covered with irregular ornamental designs. These lacy, curling motifs, the hallmark of the French style (see fig. 21.6), are combined with German Rococo architecture. But it is the painted decoration that completes the rich and organic structure. The painting here was executed by the Italian artist Giovanni Battista Tiepolo, whom we will meet below. The abundant daylight, the play of curves and countercurves, and the weightless grace of the stucco sculpture give the Kaisersaal an airy lightness far removed from the Roman Baroque. The vaults and walls seem thin and pliable, like membranes easily punctured by the expansive power of space.

Italy

Just as the new style of architecture invented in Italy achieved its climax north of the Alps, much Italian Rococo painting was created in other countries. The timidity of the Late Baroque style in Italy was transformed during the first decade of the eighteenth century by the rise of the Rococo in Venice, which had stagnated as an artistic backwater for a hundred years. The Italian Rococo is distinguished from the Baroque by a revived appreciation of Veronese's colorism and pageantry, but with an airy sensibility that is new. The Venetians, colorists skilled in Baroque illusionism, were active in every major center throughout Europe, especially in London, Dresden, and Madrid. They were not alone: Many artists from Rome and other parts of Italy also worked abroad.

Giovanni Battista Tiepolo and Illusionistic Ceiling Decoration

The last and most refined stage of Italian illusionistic ceiling decoration can be seen in the works of Giovanni Battista Tiepolo (1696–1770). He spent most of his life in Venice, where his works defined the Rococo style. He lived for two years in Germany, and in the last years of his life he worked for Charles III in Spain. His mastery of light and color, his grace and masterful touch, and his power of invention made him famous far beyond his home territory. When Tiepolo painted the Würzburg frescoes (see fig. 21.11), his powers were at their height. The tissuelike ceiling gives way so often to illusionistic openings, both painted and sculpted, that we no longer feel it to be a spatial boundary. Unlike Baroque ceilings (compare with fig. 18.5), these openings do not reveal avalanches of figures propelled by dramatic bursts of light. Rather, pale blue skies and sunlit clouds are dotted with an occasional winged creature soaring in the limitless expanse. Only along the edges of the ceiling do solid clusters of figures appear.

Tiepolo later became the last in the long line of Italian artists who were invited to work at the Royal Palace in Madrid. There he encountered the German painter Anton Raphael Mengs, a champion of the classical revival, whose presence signaled the end of the Rococo.

21.12 Canaletto. *The Bucintoro at the Molo.* ca. 1732. Oil on canvas, 30½ × 49½" (77 × 126 cm). The Royal Collection. © 2008 Her Majesty Queen Elizabeth II

Canaletto

During the eighteenth century, landscape painting in Italy evolved into a new form in keeping with the character of the Rococo: These paintings were called ***vedute*** (meaning "view" paintings). The new form can be traced back to the seventeenth century, when many foreign artists specialized in depicting the Roman countryside, or to the *Haarlempjes* of Ruisdael (see fig. 19.14). After 1720, however, *vedute* took on a specifically urban identity, focusing more narrowly on buildings or cityscapes. The most famous of the vedutists was Canaletto (Giovanni Antonio Canal, 1697–1768) of Venice. His pictures found great favor with the British, particularly young men on the Grand Tour after their schooling, who brought them home as souvenirs. Canaletto later became one of several Venetian artists to spend long sojourns in London, where he created views of the city's new skyline dotted with the church towers of Wren. *The Bucintoro at the Molo* (**fig. 21.12**) is one of a series of paintings of Venice commissioned by Joseph Smith, an English entrepreneur (later named British Consul to Venice) living there. Smith later issued the paintings as a suite of etchings to meet the demand for mementoes of Venice from those who could not afford an original canvas by the artist. This one shows a favorite subject: The Doge returning on his magnificent barge to the Piazza San Marco from the Lido (the city's island beach) on Ascension Day after celebrating the Marriage of Venice with the Sea. Canaletto has captured the pageantry of this great public celebration, which is presented as a brilliant theatrical display.

Canaletto's landscapes are, for the most part, topographically accurate. However, he usually made very slight adjustments for the sake of the composition. He would sometimes treat scenes with considerable freedom or create composite views. He may have used a mechanical or optical device, perhaps a *camera obscura*, a forerunner of the photographic camera, to render some of his views. The liveliness and sparkle of his pictures, as well as his sure sense of composition, sprang in large part from his training as a scenographer. As in our example, Canaletto often included vignettes of daily life in Venice that lend a human interest to his scenes and make them fascinating cultural documents as well.

SUMMARY

The Rococo style emerged in the eighteenth century partially as a reaction to the large, dynamic, and dark or intensely colored works of the 1600s. The style is characterized by pastel colors, small scale, and delicately rendered figures and settings, and enjoyed by the aristocracy. These wealthy classes indulged in the construction of elaborate *hôtels* (townhouses) in Paris and in their decoration. The charm and appeal of the Rococo style proved popular throughout Europe.

Jean-Antoine Watteau developed the painting type known as the *fête galante*, and helped solidify the supremacy of the Rubénistes over the Poussinistes in the debate about color versus drawing. Jean-Honoré Fragonard continued this tradition in sensual genre scenes within lush landscapes. By contrast, the humble painting categories of still-life and genre scenes were given renewed significance by Jean-Siméon Chardin, whose carefully observed scenes abound with quiet dignity, recalling Dutch and Flemish seventeenth-century traditions. Sculpture, too, embodied the Rococo propensity for intimacy and sensuality, seen especially in the work of Clodion. Yet it was in *hôtel* interiors that the Rococo style was displayed most elaborately, exerting an influence that swept through Europe's aristocracy.

The British public was especially interested in collecting genre paintings and landscapes, and artists responded to this ever-growing demand. William Hogarth executed satirical scenes in paintings and prints of everyday life—in fact thinly disguised moralizing narratives. Gainsborough and Reynolds concentrated on portraiture, working in a refined, elegant style that soon became the height of fashion. Young Englishmen on the Grand Tour of the Continent bought *vedute*, or view paintings, as souvenirs of Venice, by the Venetian painter Canaletto, and brought them back to England.

The Rococo in Germany and Austria exhibited itself primarily in architecture, with paintings and sculptures that are closely linked with their settings. The elaborate, elegant interiors of buildings such as Balthasar Neumann's Kaisersaal, with its illusionistic ceiling paintings by the Venetian Giovanni Battista Tiepolo, embody the culmination of the Rococo in central Europe.

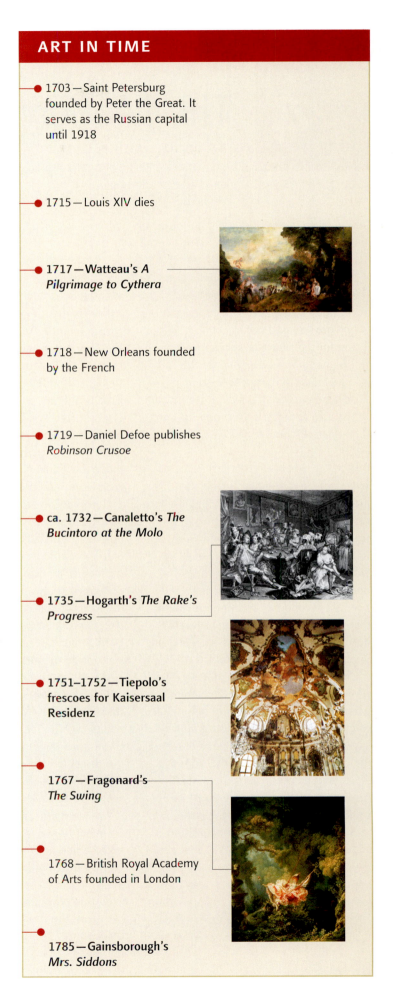

The Modern World

A most remarkable change in our ideas is taking place, one of such rapidity that it seems to promise a greater change still to come. It will be for the future to decide the aim, the nature and the limits of this revolution, the drawbacks and disadvantages of which posterity will be able to judge better than we can.
—Jean d'Alembert (1717–1783)

WHEN THE FRENCH PHILOSOPHER and scientist Jean d'Alembert made this prophetic statement in 1759, the Western world was indeed embarking on a revolution, one that is still unfolding today. This revolution ushered in a radically new way of viewing the world, one that would lead to the social, scientific, economic, and political values that govern our present lives. Little did d'Alembert realize that he was witnessing the birth of the modern world.

This new world was heralded by twin revolutions: The Industrial Revolution, which began first in Britain in the middle of the eighteenth century and gradually spread worldwide in the nineteenth, and the political revolutions of the United States and France in 1776 and 1789, respectively. Democracy, personal liberty, capitalism, socialism, industrialization, technological innovation, urbanization, and the "doctrine of progress," that is, a continuous upward march toward an improved life through science and knowledge, are just some of the many modern concepts that emerged from this period.

The force behind this transformation was the Enlightenment, a term that refers to the modern philosophy that surfaced in Britain, France, Germany, and the United States in the eighteenth century (see map 22.1). The foundation for this new thought lay in late seventeenth-century Britain with the philosopher John Locke (1632–1704) and the physicist and mathematician Isaac Newton (1642–1727), perhaps the two most influential thinkers of their age. Both stressed **empiricism** as the basis for philosophy and science, and they advocated rational thought. For Newton, empiricism meant proceeding from data and observation—not superstition, mysticism, religion, hearsay, or whimsy—and applying this information in a logical fashion. For Locke, empiricism established experience as the only basis for formulating ideas. No longer could ideas be considered innate or ordained by God. Locke upset the fundamental Christian notion of original sin when he declared that all humans are born good and have a natural right to life, liberty, and property. He defined the function of government as the obligation to protect these natural rights; failure to do so granted citizens the license to remove their government, even if that required revolution.

What began as a trickle of influence evolved into a torrent as the basic premises behind the innovative ideas of Locke and Newton produced an explosion of treatises and theories throughout the eighteenth century.

Leading this philosophical charge were the *philosophes*, as the French philosophers are commonly referred to. Among the best-known are Voltaire (the assumed name of François-Marie Arouet, 1694–1778), Jean-Jacques Rousseau (1712–1778), and Denis Diderot (1713–1784), who, along with d'Alembert, edited the 52-volume *Encyclopédie*, the world's first encyclopedia, which in its attempt to document the world and all knowledge epitomizes Enlightenment empiricism.

In addition to establishing basic human rights, logic, and a new moral order, Enlightenment thought also ushered in modern science. Electricity and oxygen were discovered, for example, and chemistry and natural science as we know them today were established. Science helped launch the Industrial Revolution. By mid-century the first mills were churning out yards of fabric at an unimaginable rate in the north of England, and the notion of labor was redefined as the first factory workers, employed at subsistence wages, were tethered to clattering looms in enormous spaces filled with a deafening noise. Miners excavated coal and ore to produce iron, permitting construction of the first metal bridge. Perfection of the steam engine by the Scottish engineer James Watt from 1765 to 1782 aided the mining and textile industries and enabled Robert Fulton, in 1807, to send a steamboat chugging up the Hudson River against the swift current, arriving in

Albany from Manhattan in unimaginably quick time, to public incredulity. Industrialization also gave rise to a new social class, the bourgeoisie or middle class, the group that controlled capital and production and would gradually replace the privileged aristocracy in the nineteenth century.

Not only did industrialization give rise to a new working class, the proletariat, that is workers, generally in factories, who had little if any identification with and pride in their product, but it also produced a new dominant class, the bourgeoisie, the group that controlled capital and production and would gradually rival and replace the privileged aristocracy at the apex of society toward the end of the nineteenth century. The bitter conflict between bourgeoisie and proletariat, between employer and employee, caused Karl Marx and Frederick Engels to publish the *Communist Manifesto* in 1848, a book that argued for communal property in order to rectify the disparity between the classes. The same year a worker's revolution spread across Europe, toppling, if only temporarily, numerous governments.

Also accompanying industrialization was urbanization, the rapid growth of cities as millions of people during the course of the nineteenth century abandoned their agrarian communities and the comfort of millennia-old rural tradition to seek employment in factories in metropolitan areas. Cities were generally unable to accommodate the

rapid growth, resulting in severe dislocation for the country migrants and physical and psychological hardship. Urbanization was so rapid that almost as many people lived in urban centers as not by 1900, and by 1920, city-dwellers outnumbered the remainder of the population in the United States.

The complexion of the Industrial Revolution took on a different face toward the end of the nineteenth century as the Modern Era entered a new phase, generally labeled "modernity." The improved steam engine, the gasoline combustion engine, electricity, and the advent of steel as we know it today elevated Western Civilization to a new technological plane; telephones, electric lights, skyscrapers, the safety elevator, electric trains and subways, airplanes, x-rays, and machines and appliances of all kinds dramatically transformed the world, making it increasingly smaller and life increasingly faster and more harried. The term "rush hour" was coined about the turn of the century, and psychoanalysis, purveyed by great Viennese psychologist Sigmund Freud, emerged to treat the traumas inflicted on the deep recesses of the mind by the stress of civilization. The reliance on machines increased so exponentially in the opening decades of the century that the post-World War I period is often referred to as "The Machine Age." Technological invention further intensified after World War II with the development of jet planes, helicopters, the atomic and hydrogen

bombs, commercial television, transistor radios, satellites, and ultimately spacecraft that launched humankind to space, circling the earth and in 1969 taking astronauts on the moon.

The Modern Era, however, evolved into yet another phase, often called "Post-Industrial." In the closing decades of the twentieth century, microchips, personal computers, the Internet, mobile and camera telephones, text-messaging, barcodes, satellite communication and surveillance, as well as global position satellites have taken humankind into a world long imagined by science fiction. The planet has become a global village, with information and images circling the earth almost instantaneously, connecting people as never before, in effect giving humans a new freedom, and yet paradoxically depriving them of privacy and even identity. Ironically, people now "experience" the world, not first hand, but instead through the media, through television, film, and most importantly the Internet. Today's world would appear incomprehensible to an eighteenth-century European or American colonist and certainly the eighteenth century is like a foreign country to us. Nonetheless, the world we live in, including a worldwide quest for personal liberty, is a continuation of the Modern Era unleashed in the eighteenth century by men who wore gray wigs, powdered their faces, sported calf-length britches with stockings, and dined and read at night by the light of candles.

ARCTIC OCEAN

GREENLAND

BERING SEA

CANADA

Hudson Bay

NORTH
AMERICA

Lake
Superior
Lake
Michigan

NORTH
ATLANTI
OCEAN

Vancouver
Seattle

Montreal

Portland

Mississippi R.

Toronto

Bolton Landing, NY.
Boston

NORTH PACIFIC OCEAN

Great
Salt
Lake

Salt Lake City

Chicago

Pittsburgh

Denver

Cincinnati

New York

Ohio R.

Philadelphia

St. Louis

San Francisco

UNITED STATES

Washington, D.C.
Charlottesville

Los Angeles

San Diego

Dallas

Atlanta

New Orleans

Houston

Gulf of
Mexico

Miami

MEXICO

Havana

CUBA

San Juan

Mexico City

CARIBBEAN SEA

CENTRAL AMERICA

Equator

Amazon R.

SOUTH
AMERICA

TAHITI

SOUTH PACIFIC OCEAN

SOUTH ATL

Paraná R.

NEW
ZEALAND

N

| 0 | 1000 | 2000 Miles |
| 0 | 1000 | 2000 Kilometers |

THE MODERN WORLD

ARCTIC OCEAN

ND

See inset

EUROPE

RUSSIA

A S I A

Ob R.

Yenisey R.

Lena R.

Lake Baikal

SEA OF
OKHOTSK

Volga R.

ARAL
SEA

Lake Balkash

CASPIAN SEA

BLACK SEA

MEDITERRANEAN SEA

Tigris R.

Euphrates R.

*Persian
Gulf*

Indus R.

Ganges R.

Yellow R.

CHINA

Yangtze R.

SEA OF
JAPAN

JAPAN

EAST
CHINA
SEA

PACIFIC
OCEAN

Nile R.

RED SEA

AFRICA

Niger R.

INDIA

ARABIAN
SEA

*Bay of
Bengal*

Hong Kong

VIETNAM

SOUTH
CHINA
SEA

Congo R.

*Lake
Victoria*

Equator

Inset map (Europe)

NORWAY

Oslo

FINLAND

Helsinki

*Lake
Ladoga*

SWEDEN

Stockholm

Leningrad

RUSSIA

SCOTLAND

Glasgow

NORTH
SEA

BALTIC SEA

Moscow

AUSTRALIA

IRELAND

Dublin

UNITED
KINGDOM

THE
NETHERLANDS

Vitebsk

BELARUS

ENGLAND

St. Ives

London

Twickenham

Amsterdam

Utrecht

GERMANY

Berlin

POLAND

English Channel

Brussels

Düsseldorf

Dessau

Warsaw

BELGIUM

Cologne

Rhine R.

Elbe R.

ATLANTIC

OCEAN

Seine R.

Paris

Frankfurt

Stuttgart

Prague

CZECH REP.

Loire R.

*Bay
of
Biscay*

FRANCE

Zürich

SWITZ.

Munich

Vienna

AUSTRIA

Budapest

HUNGARY

Lyons

Rhône R.

Milan

Po R.

Venice

Guernica

Bilbao

Nice

Florence

ITALY

Tiber R.

Danube R.

BLACK
SEA

PORTUGAL

Lisbon

Madrid

SPAIN

Barcelona

Rome

ADRIATIC SEA

Istanbul

TURKEY

MEDITERRANEAN

SEA

GREECE

Athens

| 0 | 250 | 500 Miles |
| 0 | 250 | 500 Kilometers |

22 Art in the Age of the Enlightenment, 1750–1789

The rise of the Enlightenment, which emerged in the mid-eighteenth century, ushered in the Modern Era, and the second half of the eighteenth century was a period of transition as the world moved from the old to the modern, from rule by aristocracy and Church to democracy, from privilege to meritocracy, from agriculture to industry, and from rural life to urban. The art of the period reflects this transformation, for it is often changing and complex, with several almost contradictory attitudes existing in a single work. The dominant style is Neoclassicism, meaning the "New Classicism," which often illustrated what were considered the virtuous actions and deeds of the ancient Greeks and Romans. As we shall see, however, not all works labeled Neoclassical are set in historical antiquity—they may be contemporary genre scenes or contemporary major events that have the look or feel of classical antiquity and that embrace similar moral values.

Neoclassicism was based on the logic and morality of the Enlightenment, which were perhaps best expressed by the *philosophe* Voltaire. In his plays, poems, novels, and tracts, Voltaire used logic to attack what he called "persecuting and privileged orthodoxy," mainly meaning Church and State, but any illogical institution or concept was fair game for his satire. He believed science could advance civilization, and that logic presumed a government that benefited the people, not just the aristocracy. It is from him that we get the "doctrine of progress." The models for Voltaire's new civilization were the republics of ancient Greece and Rome, which in addition to being the first democracies provided the first rationalist philosophers. Neoclassicism took its vocabulary from ancient art, as well as from the classically inspired Renaissance and the great seventeenth-century French painter Nicolas Poussin (see page 429).

Simultaneously, a second and seemingly contrary thread appeared in art: Romanticism. As we shall see in the next chapter, Romanticism came of age about 1800, when the term itself was invented in order to describe the sweeping change in worldview then occurring. Instead of Neoclassicism's logic and its desire to control the forces of nature through science, Romanticism valued emotion and intuition and believed in the supremacy of raw, unrestricted nature. Jean-Jacques Rousseau was the principal proponent of this view, which he articulated in his *Discourse on the Arts and Sciences* (1750). Here he advocated a return to nature, arguing that humans are born good, not in sin, and that they use their innate sense or instincts to distinguish between good and bad, that is, between what makes them happy and what makes them sad. Feeling determines their choices, not rational thought, which is used to explain choices, not to make them. Society, he believed, through its mores, values, and conventions, eventually imposes its own rationalized standards on humans, distracting them from their first true and natural instincts.

Map 22.1 Europe and America in the Age of Enlightenment

Rousseau praised what he called the sincere "noble savage," steeped in nature, and he denounced contemporary civilization for its pretensions, artificiality, and, in general, those social restraints that prevent us from tapping into the power of our basic emotions.

The rational and the emotional survived side by side in art, and sometimes elements of each appeared within the same work, though usually not in equal proportions. Proponents of both attitudes aggressively rejected Rococo art (see Chapter 21), which they perceived as licentious, frivolous, even immoral, and which was generally associated with aristocracy and privilege, the twin evils condemned by the Enlightenment. While there was a call for a new art, one based on classical values, no one was sure what it should look like. Not until the 1780s, with the paintings of Jacques-Louis David, did the Neoclassical style reach full flower. In the meantime, Neoclassicism would appear in many guises, sometimes even containing elements of Rococo elegance, a reminder that the Rococo still persisted. Simultaneously, the Romantic fascination with strong emotions, with the irrational and inexplicable, and with the powerful forces of nature was developing, which ironically would overshadow Neoclassicism by the 1790s, the

decade following David's rise and the French Revolution of 1789. While England and France dominated art in the second half of the century and are the focus of our discussion, Neoclassicism, like the Enlightenment, was an international movement, well represented in Scandinavia, Austria, Germany, and Russia.

Rome Toward 1760: The Font of Neoclassicism

Rome was the center of the art world in the eighteenth century, and virtually anyone aspiring to become a painter, sculptor, or architect felt compelled to study there, experiencing the Roman antiquities and the riches of the Renaissance and Baroque periods at first hand. Not just artists came to Rome, for no gentleman's education was complete without making a "Grand Tour" of Italy, including the north (Florence, Tuscany, Umbria, and Venice, see map 22.1) and Naples, the jumping-off point for Herculaneum and Pompeii, perfectly preserved Roman cities that were excavated beginning in 1738 and 1748, respectively. These archaeological excavations, as well as those in Athens, Palmyra, Baalbek, Split and Ionia, fueled an interest in antiquity and fired the imagination of artists, largely through illustrations published in a large folio format. But the climax of the Grand Tour was Rome, which itself was an enormous archaeological site.

Equally responsible for creating a renewed preoccupation with antiquity were the writings of the German scholar Johann Winckelmann (1717–1768), librarian to the great antiquities collector Cardinal Albani, whose Villa Albani in Rome was one of the antiquities museums— along with the Villa Borghese and the Capitoline Hill—that every gentleman on the Grand Tour had to visit. In 1755, Winckelmann published *Reflections on the Imitation of Greek Art in Painting and Sculpture*, and in 1765, he produced his *magnum opus*, *History of Greek Art*. In both publications, he elevated Greek culture to a position of supremacy that it had never quite held in the classical tradition: An era of perfection that was followed only by imitation and decline in the Roman era. But Winckelmann did not just see beauty in Greek art; he also saw moral qualities that paralleled Enlightenment thought: "The general and predominant mark of Greek masterpieces is *noble simplicity and calm grandeur*, both in gesture and in expression…. The expression of all Greek statues reveals even in the midst of all passions a great and grave soul [italics added]."

He concludes that "the only way for us to become great, and if possible, even inimitable, is through imitation of the ancients." In response to Winckelmann's influence, the rallying cry of Neoclassicism would be the creation of moral works embodying "noble simplicity and calm grandeur."

Artistic Foundations of Neoclassicism: Mengs and Hamilton

Influenced by the revived interest in antiquity, several artists working in Rome, headed especially by Anton Raphael Mengs and Gavin Hamilton, began to lay the foundation for Neoclassicism. Mengs (1728–1779), a German who worked in Rome on and off from 1740 to 1765, gained notoriety when Cardinal Albani, at Winckelmann's urging, commissioned him to paint a ceiling fresco for the Villa Albani. Completed in 1761 and with Winckelmann assisting with the iconography, his *Parnassus* (**fig. 22.1**) depicts the naked cardinal as Apollo surrounded by the female muses, most of whom can be identified as the cardinal's friends. The composition is based on Raphael's Vatican fresco of the same title. Stylistically, Mengs drew on Raphael as well as ancient sources. His painting combines Raphael's **planarity** (objects and figures are

22.1 Anton Raphael Mengs. *Parnassus.* 1761. Ceiling fresco. Villa Albani, Rome

parallel to the picture plane) with **linearity** (objects and figures have crisply drawn contours). The figures themselves are copied from Raphael and from the recently unearthed murals at Herculaneum and Pompeii. Apollo's pose recalls the *Apollo Belvedere*, a work in the Vatican collection made famous by Winckelmann. For the sake of planarity, Mengs dispensed with the Baroque device of an illusionistic ceiling (see fig. 18.4), one that opens up to the sky. Instead he made his ceiling look like a wall painting by Raphael, simply hung on a ceiling. Instead of the lush Rococo brushwork then in style, Mengs daringly used tight brushmarks that dissolve into a smooth, hard surface. All of these elements—planarity and linearity, austere imperceptible brushwork, and classical figures and themes—played a prominent role in the Neoclassical style.

The one element missing from Mengs's painting that would be crucial for the development of Neoclassicism is an austere, moralistic subject. This would be provided by the Scottish painter and antiquities dealer Gavin Hamilton

(1723–1798), who in the early 1760s began making deathbed scenes, such as *Andromache Bewailing the Death of Hector*, a subject taken from Homer and showing the widow Andromache bent over the body of Hector while his generals take an oath to avenge his death. This painting was reproduced in a widely circulated engraving of 1764. The image of mourning shocked eyes accustomed to Rococo gaiety, fantasy, and pleasure. Its moral is matrimonial devotion as opposed to matrimonial indiscretion, unwavering dedication rather than titillating deception, virtue not vice. Hamilton's emphasis on moral virtue would become popular with artists in succeeding decades.

Rome Toward 1760: The Font of Romanticism

The second art current coming out of Rome in the 1750s was an emphasis on evoking powerful emotions in a viewer, a quality that is called

22.2 Giovanni Battista Piranesi. *Tomb of the Metalli*, Plate XV from *Antichità Romane III*. ca. 1756. Etching, 16¾ × 18⅜″ (42.5 × 46.5 cm). The Metropolitan Museum of Art, New York. Rogers Fund, 1941, transferred from library. 41.71.3(15)

Romantic. The source of this current is Giovanni Battista Piranesi (1720–1778), a printmaker who by this time was renowned for his *vedute*, or views, of Rome, which gentlemen on the Grand Tour took home as souvenirs of their visit. (In Venice, they would buy *vedute* by Canaletto and other artists; see page 454). Winckelmann's glorification of the Greeks and belittling of Romans had infuriated Piranesi, and he set out to defend his Roman heritage, which he did by producing *Roman Antiquities*, a four-volume work completed in 1757 and illustrated with several hundred etchings of ruins. These etchings are hardly mere documentation of the sites. Often presenting the structures from a worm's-eye view (**fig. 22.2**), Piranesi transformed them into colossal looming monuments that not only attested to the Herculean engineering feats of the ancient Romans but also the uncontested might and supremacy of Roman civilization. The frightening scale of the monuments dwarfs the wondering tourists who walk among the dramatically lit ruins. These structures seem erected not by mere humans, but by a civilization of towering giants who have mysteriously vanished. Time has taken a toll on their monuments, now crumbling and picturesquely covered by plants.

These images embody Piranesi's own sense of awe in the face of Roman civilization and constitute a melancholic meditation on the destructive ability of time to erode that once great empire. The prints are not intended just to inform; they are also meant to send shivers down a viewer's spine. In them we see the beginning of a sensitivity that is at odds with the noble simplicity and calm grandeur of Neoclassicism.

Before the eighteenth century was out, the sense of awe that Piranesi was trying to evoke would be identified as being caused by what the period called the "sublime." The sublime is not a style, but a quality or attribute. Interestingly, the word became current in 1756, a year before Piranesi's publication, when the British statesman Edmund Burke (1729–1797) published a treatise titled *A Philosophical Inquiry into the Origin of Our Ideas of the Sublime and Beautiful*. Burke's study was directed more toward psychology than aesthetics, but its impact on the world of art was tremendous. He defined beauty as embodying such qualities as smoothness, delicacy, and grace, which produced feelings of joy, pleasure, and love. The sublime, however, was obscurity, darkness, power, vastness, and infinity, anything that generated feelings of fright, terror, being overwhelmed, and awe. The sublime produced "the strongest emotion which the mind is capable of feeling." As the century progressed more and more artists embraced the sublime, catering to viewers' demand to be awed or moved by paintings, sculpture, and architecture.

Neoclassicism in Britain

It almost seems as though the British were predisposed to embracing Neoclassicism, not only because the Enlightenment first developed in Britain but also because the nation already had an intense involvement with antiquity in literature, which dated to the opening decades of the eighteenth century. The Augustan or Classical Age of English poetry was in full bloom by then, with its leading authors, such as John Dryden, Alexander Pope, and Samuel Johnson, emulating the form and content of the writers active during the reign of the first Roman emperor, Augustus (63 BCE–14 CE), many of whom these same British poets translated. Britain at this time was enjoying unprecedented peace and prosperity, which, in part, was responsible for the identification with Augustus' reign, similarly marked by stability, economic prosperity, and the flourishing of culture. The liberal faction of the British aristocracy modeled itself on ancient Rome, relating the British parliamentary government that shared power with the king to the democracy of the Roman Republic that preceded the Caesars. As we shall see, by the 1720s, these liberals, who compared themselves with Roman senators, wanted country homes based on Roman prototypes.

Painting: Historicism, Morality, and Antiquity

The British were particularly receptive to the Neoclassical foundation established by Mengs and Hamilton. Hamilton's moralistic scenes set in antiquity especially had a major impact, and the list of artists inspired by them is extensive, starting with a handful in the 1760s and extending to dozens in the following decades. However, the taste for the classical could also be just that, a taste for a style or look, with little consideration for a moralistic message. This was especially true in the decorative arts.

ANGELICA KAUFFMANN Angelica Kauffmann (1741–1807) was among the most important artists in the development of Neoclassicism in England. She was born in Switzerland, studied in

22.3 Angelica Kauffmann. *Cornelia Presenting Her Children as Her Treasures* (*Mother of the Gracchi*). ca. 1785. Oil on canvas, 3′4″ × 4′2″ (101.6 × 127 cm). Virginia Museum of Fine Arts, Richmond, The Adolph D. and Wilkins C. Williams Fund. 75.22

Rome in the 1760s, and moved to London in 1766. She befriended Joshua Reynolds and was a founding member of the ROYAL ACADEMY in 1768, of which Reynolds was president. Prior to the twentieth century, she was one of only two women admitted into the academy, a statistic that on a negative note reflects male prejudice and on a positive one the high international esteem in which the 27-year-old Kauffmann was held. As a woman, she was denied access to studying the male nude, then considered critical to a history painter's success, and this made her accomplishments all the more remarkable. Of the few eighteenth-century women artists to carve out a successful career in a man's world, Kauffmann was the only one who became a history painter.

Like so many of her contemporaries, Kauffmann raided Greek and Roman literature for her subjects. In 1769 at the first Royal Academy exhibition, she presented *Hector Taking Leave of Andromache*, and three years later she showed *Andromache and Hecuba Weeping over the Ashes of Hector*, two pictures portraying unwavering marital fidelity, both as wife and widow. A classic example of Kauffmann's moralistic pictures is *Cornelia Presenting Her Children as Her Treasures* (*Mother of the Gracchi*) (**fig. 22.3**) of about 1785.

Here she champions child-rearing and family over materialism. While portraying a woman as mother, she counters traditional male stereotyping by presenting her as proactive, deterministic, and controlling. In this second-century BCE story from Roman history, a visiting friend has just shown off her jewelry to Cornelia, wife of Sempronius Gracchus. Instead of displaying her own gems, Cornelia proudly presents her children, two of whom, Tiberius and Gaius, would become great politicians. To prepare her sons for leadership, Cornelia acquired the finest tutors in the world, and it was said that she "weaned" them on conversation, not her breasts. She remained an ally and advisor to both, and in addition to her reputation for virtue and intelligence, she was one of the most powerful women in the history of the Roman Republic. Kauffmann, a woman artist struggling in a man's world, must have identified with the successful Cornelia, whose features resemble the artist's.

In *Cornelia Presenting Her Children*, Kauffmann has created an austere and monumental painting that reinforces the strength and nobility of the mother. Despite the Rococo grace of the gestures and the elegant proportions of the figures, the picture is dominated by the bareness of the floor and walls and the stable composition

The founding in 1768 of Britain's ROYAL ACADEMY OF ART was King George II's way of encouraging painting, sculpture, and architecture in Great Britain. (R.A. after an artist's name or signature indicates membership of the Academy.) Conservative by nature, the Academy is still under the direct patronage of the Crown, which sponsors a large annual show of works by members and non-members.

anchored by a strong, solid triangle culminating in Cornelia. Kauffmann employs the tight paint-handling and linear drawing introduced by Mengs. The Cornelia theme was not unique to Kauffmann, however, and was quite popular with artists. Not only did it illustrate virtue, but it reflected the new interest in the importance of the family unit that stemmed from the Enlightenment teachings of Jean-Jacques Rousseau, who advocated that parents nurture their children at home, rather than sending them off to wet-nurses and nannies until they were adolescents.

The Birth of Contemporary History Painting

Enlightenment empiricism had a major impact on history painting in two ways. One was the strong emphasis on historicism—when portraying a scene set in the historical past, costume, setting, and props all had to be convincing and true to the period. The second impact affected the presentation of major contemporary events that the future would perceive as historically important. Until now, such moments were presented using allegory and symbols, not by portraying the actual scene, or figures were dressed in classical garb in order to give them the sense of decorum and importance that the event apparently required. But with the Enlightenment, paintings had to be logical and real and every bit as convincing to contemporaries as we expect period films to be today. This applied not only to the historical past but to contemporary events as well.

BENJAMIN WEST The artist perhaps most responsible for popularizing contemporary history painting is Benjamin West (1738–1820), one of the most successful British Neoclassical history painters. A Quaker born and raised just outside of Philadelphia, West went to Rome in 1760 where he studied with Mengs, befriended Gavin Hamilton, and immersed himself in antiquity

22.4 Benjamin West. *The Death of General Wolfe*. 1770. Oil on canvas, 59½ × 84″ (1.51 × 2.13 m). National Gallery of Canada, Ottawa. Gift of the Duke of Westminster

and the classically influenced Renaissance masters, especially Raphael. By 1763 he had permanently settled in London, and within three years he was a success, in part because of his innovative Neoclassicism. He was a founding member of the Royal Academy in 1768, and he became its president in 1792 when Joshua Reynolds died. Throughout his life, he was a mentor for many American artists, and always remained proud of his New World heritage, even supporting the American Revolution. (For a discussion of British colonial portraiture and John Singleton Copley, see Introduction, page 2.)

West shocked the London art world in 1770 when he announced that he was working on a contemporary history painting, *The Death of General Wolfe* (**fig. 22.4**), and placing the event in a realistic setting: 1759 Quebec during the FRENCH AND INDIAN WAR. The British general won the Battle of Quebec, which became a turning point in the war, making him a national hero. Upon hearing of West's plan, King George III declared he would never purchase a picture with his soldiers in modern uniforms, and Reynolds frowned on the picture's breach of convention, which required an allegorical apotheosis scene, that is, Wolfe dressed like a saint rising to heaven. But when exhibited at the Royal Academy, the painting was immediately applauded by the public. The scene was so convincing that the audience felt as though it were indeed witnessing its great national hero at the very moment he sacrificed his life for his country in a far-off land, an exotic touch that fascinated the public, which went to look at pictures the way we view movies today. The painting was also successful because West aggrandized and classicized his figures and the event, in effect creating a modern classic. Contemporary viewers recognized that they were in the presence of what amounted to a traditional Lamentation scene (for instance, see fig. 13.7), and that their hero was a modern-day Christ or martyr. The surrounding "apostles" express remorse and concern, but their powerful emotions, worthy of Poussin, are noble and controlled, in keeping with the classical rule of decorum. Figures strike *contrapposto* poses, stand in profile, and have the sculptural quality of an ancient low-relief or Raphael saint, apostle, or Greek philosopher (see fig. 15.12)—they are simultaneously modern and classical. West took the cue for his painting technique from Mengs, for he first drew and then colored in the figures, allowing crisp contours to ennoble them.

Architecture and Interiors: The Palladian Revival

In England a classical revival began much earlier in architecture than it did in painting and sculpture. Its origins date to the architectural treatises of Anthony Ashley Cooper, third Earl of Shaftesbury, and Colen Campbell, published in the 1710s. Both writers argued for a British architecture based on antiquity (see pages 135–139) and Antonio Palladio's classically inspired villas, which not only evoked antiquity but projected a perfect harmony using geometry, mathematics, and logic. Sounding much like Winckelmann did when discussing sculpture some 50 years later, Shaftesbury wrote that the proportions and geometry of ancient architecture reflected the nobility and beauty of the Greek and Roman soul, which have a powerful effect on the enlightened "man of taste." Architecture was beauty and morality, not function.

Both Campbell and Shaftesbury reflect a British antagonism toward Roman Catholicism. In Britain, Baroque architecture was associated with two evils: Papist Rome and French royalty. Shaftesbury, a patron and student of John Locke, was an advocate of individual freedom, and he equated ancient architecture with democracy. He was also a WHIG, a member of the liberal anti-monarchy political party. (The TORIES, the conservative pro-monarchy party, had backed the Roman Catholic Stuart king James II.) In 1714, the Whig party came to power, ending 13 years of political turmoil. Its democratic members especially identified with classical-revival architecture, for they saw themselves as the modern equivalent of Roman senators, who had country villas in addition to their city houses. Campbell, who was virtually unknown prior to the publication of his architectural treatise, could hardly fill single-handedly the demand from Whigs who wanted Palladian-style country houses.

THE COUNTRY VILLA: CHISWICK HOUSE We can see the impact of Campbell's ideas on his patron, Lord Burlington, who after a trip to Italy in 1719 became an amateur architect and eventually supplanted Campbell as the leading Palladian figure. In 1725 Burlington with the landscape painter William Kent (1684–1748) designed Chiswick House (**fig. 22.5**), located on Burlington's estate near London and one of the most famous Palladian-revival houses. This stately home is based on Palladio's *Villa Rotonda* (see fig. 16.14), which Lord Burlington had studied on his Grand Tour.

France and England fought over possession of North America for 150 years. Tension culminated in a nine-year conflict called the FRENCH AND INDIAN WAR. Waged in New York State, New England, and Quebec, it ended in 1763 when Canada was ceded to England.

TORY and WHIG are the terms applied, since the seventeenth century, to Britain's two chief political parties. *Tory* was originally a name for Irish outlaws. Later, it became associated with the political supporters of James II (1633–1701, r. 1685–1688), the Roman Catholic Stuart king. The name *Whig* was used for those who opposed James II's succession to the Crown. Today's Conservative party members are called Tories; Liberal party followers were Whigs, though the term is not applied to the successor party, the Liberal Democrats.

22.5 Lord Burlington and William Kent. Chiswick House. Begun 1725. Chiswick, London

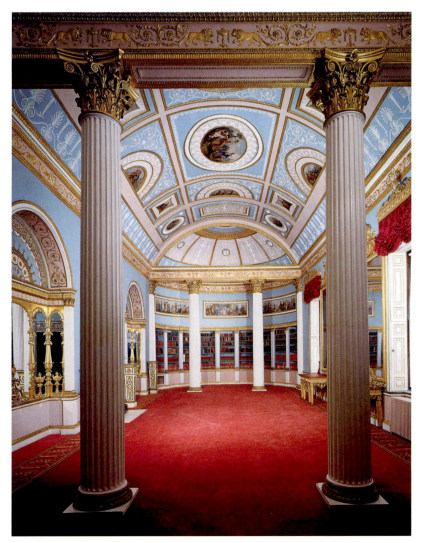

22.6 Robert Adam. The Library. 1767–1769. Kenwood House, London

Chiswick House is distinguished by its simplicity and logic, which make it easy to understand why Lord Burlington was such a success. The building is a cube. Its walls are plain and smooth, allowing for a distinct reading of their geometric shape and the form of the windows. The Greek temple portico protrudes from the wall, again creating a simple and clear form. Even the prominent domed octagonal rotunda is geometric, as are its tripartite semicircular clerestory windows, based on windows in Roman baths. Here we have reason and logic clearly stated, and placed in the service of the ideals of morality, nobility, and republican government. Like Shaftesbury, Burlington believed architecture to be an autonomous art dealing in morality and aesthetics, rather than function.

THE NEOCLASSICAL INTERIOR The British taste for the classical extended to interior design and was largely due to one man, Robert Adam (1728–1792). Adam was a wealthy Scottish architect who undertook the Grand Tour from 1754 to 1758. Upon returning to Great Britain, he began practicing in London and was soon the city's most fashionable architect. Although he designed several houses, his specialty was renovating interiors and designing additions, especially for country houses.

A fine example of his work is the library wing at Kenwood (**fig. 22.6**), on what was then the northern outskirts of London; it was built in

1767–1769. The ceiling of the room is a Roman barrel vault, and at either end is an apse separated from the main room by Corinthian columns. This concept comes largely from Palladio. The decoration is based on classical motifs, which Adam could copy from the many archaeological books then being published. On the one hand, the library is quite classical, not just because of the motifs, but also because it is symmetrical, geometric, and carefully balanced. On the other hand, it is filled with movement, largely because of the wealth of details and shapes that force the eye to jump from one design element to the next. Adam's palette is pastel in color and light in tone; light blues, white, and gold prevail. Curving circles, delicate plant forms, and graceful fluted columns with ornate capitals set a festive, elegant, and refined tone closer to Rococo playfulness than to Neoclassical morality.

22.7 Horace Walpole, with William Robinson and others. Strawberry Hill. 1749–1777. Twickenham, England

Early Romanticism in Britain

Edmund Burke's 1757 treatise on beauty and the sublime marked the beginning of growing interest in horrifying, exotic, or awesome themes that generated powerful emotional responses in viewers. These themes could occur in painting, sculpture, decorative arts, or architecture.

Architecture: Strawberry Hill and the Gothic Revival

An interest in generating strong emotional responses in the viewer first occurred in architecture and landscape design. Instead of planning symmetrical formal gardens for Chiswick, which would have been standard at the time, Kent surrounded the house with a natural-looking landscape of rolling, hilly lawns, irregularly arranged stands of trees and naturalistic serpentine lakes. The British began using the word **picturesque** to describe the irregularity of these designs, which because of their variety provided endless interest for the eye. By the 1740s, Kent was sprinkling his landscapes with classical structures and Gothic ruins, which were meant to evoke a feeling of nostalgia for a distant past, thus adding a hint of the sublime (see page 464) to his designs.

This combination of the picturesque and the sublime can be found in architecture as well, especially in the style known as Gothic Revival. While Roman or Palladian country houses were springing up all over Britain, a Gothic Revival

was taking place as well. An interest in Gothic architecture—which was then perceived as a national architecture because it was believed, wrongly, to have originated in England—was sparked in part by the appearance of some of the first literature on the style. But the style's appeal in large part lay in its sublime qualities. The cathedrals were cold, dark, and gloomy, and contained vast, overwhelming spaces. Gothic ruins, which could be seen everywhere, evoked associations of death, melancholy, and even horror. In 1764, the Gothic novel emerged as a genre with the publication of Horace Walpole's *The Castle of Otranto: A Gothic Story*, set in a haunted castle. The book started a medieval craze that peaked with Victor Hugo's 1831 *Notre-Dame de Paris*, in which the dark, forebidding cathedral is the home of the terrifying hunchbacked recluse Quasimodo.

Horace Walpole (1717–1797) also deserves credit for making the Gothic Revival fashionable when, with a group of friends, he redesigned Strawberry Hill (**fig. 22.7**), his country house in Twickenham, just outside of London. Started in 1749, the renovation took over 25 years to complete. The house is distinctly medieval; the walls are capped with crenellated battlements and pierced by tracery windows. For Walpole, Gothic meant picturesque, and consequently the

22.8 George Stubbs. *Lion Attacking a Horse*. 1770. Oil on canvas, 38 × 49½″ (96.5 × 125.7 cm). Yale University Art Gallery, New Haven, Connecticut. Gift of the Yale University Art Gallery Associates 1955.27.1

L-shaped building is irregular, asymmetrical, and looks like a piling up of additions from different periods, which it actually is because the building was erected piecemeal over a long time, with each section designed by a different person. (The Neoclassical architect Robert Adam, for example, contributed the turret.) But there is little of the sublime on the exterior, which actually has a Rococo delicacy. The crenellations are petite, not massive, and the windows sit near the surface, making the walls look fine and paper-thin, not thick and fortresslike.

Painting: The Coexistence of Reason and Emotion

Just as the Gothic Revival thrived alongside the revival of classicism in Britain, Romantic painting coexisted with the Neoclassical. Romantic undercurrents even appeared in pictures that are essentially classical, a paradox that underscores the limitations of labeling. Like a moth to a flame, the taste of the period was increasingly drawn to the awesome power of nature, the experience of unfettered elemental emotions and instincts, and even the wonder of the irrational. In effect, the Enlightenment at moments could deny its very foundation of logic and empiricism and permit itself to be swept away by the emotional pull of the exotic, wondrous, terrifying, and inexplicable. The thirst for sublime experiences would prevail by the end of the century.

GEORGE STUBBS George Stubbs (1724–1806), who specialized in portraits of horses, is generally described as a Neoclassical painter, in part because his early images had a somewhat hard frozen look, since they were carefully drawn and tightly painted, with the objects aligned parallel to the picture plane. At the same time, he made some of the earliest Romantic pictures, and is one of the first artists who directly responded to Burke's treatise on the sublime and the beautiful. In the early 1760s, Stubbs began a series of approximately 21 paintings of a lion attacking either a horse or a stag, an example of which is the 1770 *Lion Attacking a Horse* (**fig. 22.8**). Stubbs's motivation comes directly from Burke. He was challenged to portray a horrifying natural event that would evoke a sublime emotion in a viewer. Stubbs's protagonists are animals, who, unlike humans, are immersed in nature and at one with it, virtual personifications of unleashed natural forces. We identify with the horse, which is white, a symbol of goodness and purity. Its mouth, eye, mane, and legs are taut with fear and pain. Evil is represented by the lion's dark, powerful legs, which seem almost nonchalant as they rip into the horse's back, pulling the skin to expose a skeletal rib cage. The lion's body disappears into the blackness of the landscape, identifying its evil force with a frightening darkness and elemental powers that surge from the earth. Ominous storm clouds announce the horse's fate as they threaten to cast the entire scene into dark shadow at the moment, we assume, that the doomed horse expires. West, in *The Death of General Wolfe*, similarly harnessed the forces of nature through his dramatic clouds and windswept hair to reinforce the emotional intensity and psychology of his figures.

Neoclassicism in France

As in Britain, the reaction against the Rococo in France first appeared in architecture, but it surfaced in the 1750s and 1760s, rather than the 1710s and 1720s. At first elegant and rational and largely based on seventeenth-century French classical architecture, this new style moved into an austere, awe-inspiring, and even visionary stage by the late 1770s. This "sublime" phase even had a profound impact on painting. Despite repeated appeals from numerous sources, including Enlightenment exponents and the government, painters were slow to meet the challenge to create a new moralistic art based on antiquity. It was not until the late 1770s that large numbers of painters took up the cause, and it was not until the 1780s, with the advent of Jacques-Louis David and his austere brand of

Neoclassicism, that a new style emerged, one that thrived well into the nineteenth century.

Architecture: Rational Classicism

The first phase of French Neoclassical architecture was a reaction to the excesses of the Rococo, which had been about asymmetry, graceful movement, decorative flourishes, and curvilinear elegance. The new architecture was about rational design, and hence was often called "Rational Classicism." All components of a building had to be geometric, symmetrical, and logical in the sense that they were essential to the structure. While this rational phase of Neoclassical architecture was theoretically based on nature, it nonetheless took its lead from seventeenth-century French classical architecture.

THEORETICAL BEGINNINGS Launching the attack on the Rococo was the architect Jacques-François Blondel (1705–1774), who in a speech at the Royal School of Architecture in 1747 condemned the ornate flamboyance of the style. Here, and in his later publications, he called for a return to the classicism of great seventeenth-century architects, such as Claude Perrault. Blondel demanded that buildings be logical, simple, functional, and symmetrical, and that they should be constructed with right angles, not curves. Blondel's rationalism was seconded by the influential writer Abbé Marc-Antoine Laugier (1713–1769), whose aesthetics also accommodated Gothic architecture, for he viewed its soaring stone columns as logical and natural, like a forest of trees, and he loved its spaciousness and light. Buttressing was structural, thus allowed.

JACQUES-GERMAIN SOUFFLOT It was Soufflot (1713–1780), an ardent follower of Blondel, who designed the great rationalist building. Unfortunately, his masterpiece, Sainte-Geneviève (**fig. 22.9**), has been so altered, including its name and function, that its current appearance is quite misleading. Soufflot completed his original design in 1755. It had a clearly stated geometry: An equilateral Greek cross with a six-column portico entrance. The wide square center crossing would have a hemispherical dome (modeled on the Pantheon in Rome) sitting on a drum supported by narrow piers consisting of four triangles, each triangle formed by three columns. Perrault's Louvre was his model. The pedimented section of the Louvre's east façade inspired the portico (see fig. 20.5). The drum for the dome largely derives from the circular

22.9 Jacques-Germain Soufflot. The Pantheon (formerly Sainte-Geneviève). 1757–1790. Paris

peristyle Perrault used for the dome at the Louvre chapel. But Soufflot, following Laugier's vision of combining the clarity and grandeur of the classical with the lightness and space of the Gothic, filled his spacious church with light. Using a daring system of hidden buttresses, he was able to remove the wall mass and open up the building with enormous vertical windows.

Unfortunately the clergy and public attacked Soufflot's 1757 plan, and the church was heavily compromised. An apse was added and the transept extended, destroying the perfect four-sided symmetry of the first design. To adjust to these new proportions, Soufflot had to increase the size of the dome, with the result that it looks more like Christopher Wren's dome on Saint Paul's Cathedral (see fig. 20.10). But the greatest abuses came with the French Revolution. In its ardor to erase religion and honor French heroes, the Directoire government of the new republic in 1793 declared the building a Pantheon to the nation's leaders. To convert the church into a lugubrious mausoleum, the windows were walled in. Additional changes well into the nineteenth century destroyed Soufflot's vision.

The Sublime in Neoclassical Architecture: The Austere and the Visionary

French architecture started to move into a new, more austere phase in the 1770s, one less interested in following the rules of the ancients and more preoccupied with reducing architecture to elemental geometric forms that operated on a monumental scale and created a Piranesian sense

22.10 Claude-Nicolas Ledoux. Barrière de l'Etoile (Etoile Customs House), Paris (now destroyed). 1785–1798. Bibliothèque Nationale, Paris of awe and power. Among the architects largely responsible for this was Claude-Nicolas Ledoux.

CLAUDE-NICOLAS LEDOUX Ledoux (1736–1806) was a student of Blondel, but he was heavily influenced by Piranesi's publications. By the mid-1760s he was a fashionable Parisian architect designing many of the most prestigious *hôtels*, as large private townhouses were called, and by the 1770s he was designing austere Palladian residences, buildings that were stripped down to a geometric essence with austere Tuscan Doric columns, which were unfluted and without bases.

One of Ledoux's greatest public projects was the 50 or more tax gates or customs houses he designed for the new 15-mile (24-kilometer) wall surrounding Paris. Each gate was different, although like the Barrière de l'Etoile, reproduced here (**fig. 22.10**), they were all colossal, severe, and strictly geometric, based on cylinders, cubes, triangles, and circles. While it is classical in its use of pediments and columns, for example, classical proportions and harmony have given way to an exaggerated, imposing scale designed to generate a sense of awe-inspiring power.

Painting and Sculpture: Expressing Enlightenment Values

There was no parallel in French painting and sculpture with the swing toward classicism occurring in French architecture in the 1750s and 1760s. Until the 1780s, the Enlightenment emphasis on reason and morality was best presented not by history painting but by the lower stratum of genre painting.

JEAN-BAPTISTE GREUZE One artist alone virtually created a vogue for genre painting, Jean-Baptiste Greuze (1725–1805), and from 1759 until the 1770s his scenes of everyday life were the sensation of the Paris SALONS. Greuze emerged from a working-class background in the Lyons region and went to Paris in the mid-1750s to make his mark at the Royal Academy. A wealthy collector sponsored a trip to Italy for him from 1755 to 1759, but Greuze left Paris a genre and portrait painter and returned as one as well.

Nonetheless, Greuze became the rage of Paris with *The Village Bride* (**fig. 22.11**), his submission to the Salon of 1761, which shows a Protestant wedding the moment after a father has handed his son-in-law a dowry, dutifully recorded by a notary, seated on the right. The scene seethes with virtue as the various members

of this neat, modest, hardworking religious family express familial love, dedication, and respect. Here is the social gospel of Rousseau: The naïve poor, in contrast to the more cultivated, yet immoral aristocracy, are closer to nature and thus full of "natural" virtue and honest sentiment. Greuze draws a parallel between the family of humans and the family of the hen and her chicks, each with one member separated, thus reinforcing this point about the natural instinct of common folk. Critics and public alike raved about the authenticity of the gestures and emotions, comparing them favorably with those of the noble figures by Poussin (see fig. 20.2).

While Greuze was certainly attempting to match the intensity of emotion and gesture found in history painting, especially in Poussin, he was also inspired by contemporary theater, which accounts for the arrangement of the figures in a *tableau vivant* (a "living painting," when actors onstage freeze as if in a painting to portray a pregnant moment) just when the father is declaiming his poignant speech about the sanctity of marriage. He was particularly influenced by a new realistic form of theater, *drame bourgeois* (middle-class drama), promoted by his good friend DIDEROT. But equally influencing his sense of detail and attention to texture was the increasingly popular seventeenth-century Dutch and Flemish genre and still-life painting, as well as Chardin's down-to-earth imagery (see page 445). Even Greuze's figures are individualized, rather than portrayed as ideal types. They are so real that when Greuze used them again in later paintings, the public decided it was witnessing the continuation of the story of the same family. As we shall see, Greuze's realism and morality as well as his pregnant *tableau vivant* moment will figure prominently in French Neoclassicism when it emerges some 20 years later.

JEAN-ANTOINE HOUDON The French sculptor who perhaps best exemplifies Enlightenment empiricism is Jean-Antoine Houdon (1741–1828). Both Greuze and Houdon used realism in their works, but Houdon, unlike Greuze, incorporated realism into a façade of classicism, instead of the other way round. While a pensioner at the French Academy in Rome from 1765 to 1768, Houdon studied realistic Roman portrait busts, and in 1767 he executed in plaster a life-sized flayed male torso revealing in detail every muscle of the body while it leans against a support in perfect *contrapposto*.

The SALONS of France originated in the seventeenth century as infrequent showings of works by members of the Académie Royal de Peinture et Sculpture. By the early nineteenth century, they had developed into an annual event held in the Salon Carré of the Louvre—hence the name Salon. After 1850, the Salon was held at other sites in Paris. Resentment over abuse of the selection process led Napoleon III to create an alternative exhibition, also "official," in 1863: The Salon des Refusés.

A genius in many fields, including natural science, and a novelist, dramatist, poet, and art critic, Denis DIDEROT (1713–1784) is still best known as the compiler and editor of the great French *Encyclopédie* (1751–1780), a staggering 28-volume compendium of the natural and physical sciences, law, and what would today be called political science. His fellow *philosophe* Jean-Jacques Rousseau was a contributor to the *Encyclopédie*.

22.11 Jean-Baptiste Greuze. *The Village Bride,* or *The Marriage, The Moment When a Father Gives His Son-in-Law a Dowry.* 1761. Oil on canvas, 36 × 46½" (91.4 × 118.1 cm). Musée du Louvre, Paris

As would be expected of such an empirical mentality, Houdon specialized in portraits, and he became the portraitist to the Enlightenment, depicting virtually every major personality, including Diderot, Rousseau, Louis XVI, Catherine II of Russia, and Benjamin Franklin. Houdon's uncanny ability to capture both the look and the personality of his sitter is apparent in *Voltaire Seated* (**fig. 22.12**), here a terracotta cast from the original plaster, which is lost. The sculptor classicizes his sitter by dressing him in a Roman toga and headband, and seating him in an antique-style chair. But he portrays Voltaire realistically by showing the sagging folds of skin on the neck, the sunken toothless mouth, the deep facial wrinkles, and the slumping shoulders, all of which mark the sitter's age and frailty. Houdon has also brilliantly seized the *philosophe*'s sharp intellect and wit: The head is turning and the mouth smiling, and while one hand droops over the arm of the chair, the other grasps it firmly.

The Climax of Neoclassicism: The Paintings of Jacques-Louis David

The reign of genre painting in Enlightenment France was short, with Greuze's popularity peaking by 1765. The tide began to turn toward history painting in 1774 when Charles-Claude d'Angiviller, the new director-general in charge of buildings and art in France and overseer of the FRENCH ACADEMY, made it his personal mission to snuff out what he considered Rococo licentiousness and replace it with moralistic history painting. Beginning in 1777, he regularly commissioned "grand machines," as these enormous oils were called, many based on the noble and virtuous deeds of the ancients as well as exemplary moments from French history. The project triggered a quest, and even a heated competition, among artists to produce *the* great history painting. The fruit of this program appeared in the mid-1780s with the emergence of Jacques-Louis David (1748–1825), whose images were so revolutionary that they have virtually come to epitomize Neoclassicism, thus simplifying a very complex period and a very complicated term that encompasses much more than David's style.

David discovered his mature artistic voice while studying in Rome from 1775 to 1781, and it came as a result of copying a painting of a Last Supper by Valentin de Bologne, a French follower of Caravaggio (see page 385), in 1779. He was especially attracted to de Bologne's powerful naturalism and dramatic lighting, which carved out crisp sculptural figures and objects. D'Angiviller liked David's new style so much that he gave him a major commission.

It took David three years to complete this painting, *The Oath of the Horatii* (**fig. 22.13**), and he finished it in Rome in 1783–1784. When David unveiled *The Oath* in his Rome studio, it instantly became an international sensation, with an endless procession of visitors filing through to see this revolutionary work. *The Oath* arrived in Paris from Rome a few days after the opening of the 1784 Salon, its delayed grand entrance enhancing the public clamor.

The theme for the picture comes from a Roman seventh-century BCE story found in both Livy and Plutarch, recounting how a border dispute between Rome and neighboring Alba was settled by a sword fight by three soldiers from each side. Representing Rome were the three Horatii brothers, for Alba the three Curiatii brothers. Complicating the story, a Horatii sister, Camilla, was engaged to a Curiatii brother, while one of the Horatii brothers was married to a Curiatii sister. Only Horatius of the Horatii brothers survived the violent fight, and David had been instructed to paint the moment when Horatius returns home and slays his sister after she curses him for killing her fiancé. Instead, David painted a scene that does not appear in the literature: The Horatii, led by their father, taking an oath to fight to the death. The composition is quite simple and striking: David contrasts the virile, stoic men, their bodies locked in rigorous determination, with the slack, curvilinear heap of the distressed women, Camilla and the Curiatii wife, who, either way, will lose a brother, husband, or fiancé.

22.12 Jean-Antoine Houdon. *Voltaire Seated*. 1781. Terracotta model for marble original, height 47" (119.3 cm). Institut et Musée Voltaire, Geneva, Switzerland

David was undoubtedly inspired by the many oath-taking paintings that had appeared since Gavin Hamilton made an *Oath of Brutus* in 1764. The dramatic moment, which David made one of the hallmarks of Neoclassical history painting, allowed him to create a *tableau vivant* championing noble and virtuous action dedicated to the supreme but necessary sacrifice of putting State before family. The severity of the Horatii's dedication is reinforced by the severity of the composition. It can be seen in the austerity of the shallow space, and even in David's selection of stark, baseless Tuscan Doric columns, which Ledoux had made fashionable in France the decade before. It also appears in the relentless planarity that aligns figures and architecture parallel to the picture plane and in the harsh geometry of the floor, arches, and grouping of the warriors. It surfaces as well in the sharp linear contours of the figures, making them seem as

Strictly speaking, the FRENCH ACADEMY today is the Institut de France, a cluster of five learned societies brought together during the French Revolution. The original Académie Française began in secret around 1630 under King Louis XIII and was made official in 1635 at the urging of Louis's chief minister, the powerful Cardinal Richelieu (1585–1642). The Académie Royale de Peinture et Sculpture (later, the Académie des Beaux-Arts), established in 1648 to encourage French fine artists and to maintain the aesthetic standards favored by those in power, is sometimes referred to by art historians as the French Academy.

22.13 Jacques-Louis David. *The Oath of the Horatii*. 1783–1784. Oil on canvas, 10′10″ × 13′11″ (3.3 × 4.25 m). Musée du Louvre, Paris

Neoclassicism

solid and frozen as statues. In this planarity and linearity, David is more "Poussiniste" than his idol Poussin, from whom he borrows figures. Line and geometry, the vehicles of reason, now clearly prevail over the sensual color and brushwork of the Rococo.

But it is the Caravaggesque naturalism and intensity that make this image so powerful and distinguish it from Renaissance and Baroque classicism. Sharpening edges and heightening the drama of the painting is a harsh light that casts precise shadows, an effect derived from Caravaggio (see fig. 18.1), as is the attention to textures and such details as chinks in the floor marble. The picture is startlingly lifelike, with the setting and costumes carefully researched to recreate seventh-century BCE Rome.

While *The Oath* is generally perceived as the quintessential Neoclassical picture, one of several

David made that came to define the style, it is filled with undercurrents of Romanticism. It is a horrific scene, one that frightened onlookers, sending chills up their spines. This is not just an image of moral resolve and logic, reflecting Cassius who declares in Voltaire's play *Death of Caesar* that "a true republican's only father and sons are virtue, the gods, law, and country." Under the frozen Neoclassical stillness of this scene lies the tension of the bloodbath soon to come. We see this tension in the father's brightly lit fingers, which echo the stridency of the swords. This enormous 13-foot painting is about the impending violence, from which the nurse in the ominous background shadow tries to shield the children. The picture is a reminder that within 20 years, the Western world will have entered into the Age of Romanticism, as we will see in our next chapter.

SUMMARY

In the last half of the eighteenth century, Western culture entered the modern era, largely due to the Enlightenment. Democracy began to replace monarchy, capitalism and industry to rival agriculture and millennia-old traditions, the new capitalists, or bourgeois, threatened the pre-eminence of the aristocracy, and empiricism and science replaced superstition and religion. Western civilization and its art was becoming increasingly complex. The dominant style, Neoclassicism, emphasized logic and rationality, and often featured moralistic themes borrowed from the ancient Greeks and Romans. Romanticism, a simultaneous thread in art, advocated emotion, imagination, and the supremacy of nature.

Rome, home to treasures from antiquity and the Renaissance, was the place where most artists wanted to study. Fueled by recent archaeological discoveries, notably those of Herculaneum and Pompeii, and the writings of Greek Art by Johann Winckelmann, a renewed interest in antiquity gripped scholars and artists. The austere brushwork, linearity, and planarity of Anton Raphael Mengs, and Gavin Hamilton's moralistic deathbed themes, laid the foundations of the Neoclassical style.

Simultaneously, Romanticism began to emerge. The printmaker Giovanni Battista Piranesi celebrated ancient Roman civilization in dramatic *vedute* (views) of awe-inspiring monumental architecture that embodied the sublime, a term defined by British statesman Edmund Burke in his treatise *A Philosophical Inquiry into the Origin of Our Ideas of the Sublime and Beautiful*.

In Britain, anti-monarchist Whigs and many intellectuals, steeped in the Enlightenment, helped develop Neoclassicism in England, as seen in the paintings of Angelica Kauffmann. Contemporary history painting, first developed by Benjamin West, emerged now as well. Employing Enlightenment logic and attention to authentic costumes and settings, West set recent historic events within classical compositions. The classical revival in architecture, based on ancient buildings and Antonio Palladio's villas, predates Neoclassical painting, appearing in the earliest houses, such as Chiswick House. This revival extended to interiors as well, as seen in the designs of Robert Adam.

In architecture, an equally strong urge for emotion and subjective experiences resulted in part in the Gothic Revival, as seen in Horace Walpole's Strawberry Hill, and in painting, in horrific scenes, such as George Stubbs's *Lion Attacking a Horse*.

Neoclassicism appears later in France than in England, and its first appearance is today called Rational Classicism. The most famous expression of this aesthetic is Soufflot's Pantheon of 1755. Architecture then becomes austere by the 1770s, even sublime, as seen in the hands of Claude-Nicolas Ledoux, who worked with basic geometric shapes, using no ornament, and favoring the undecorated Tuscan order. Enlightenment logic first appears in genre painting, as seen in the realistic moral scenes of Jean-Baptiste Greuze, and in the realistic classical portraits of Jean-Antoine Houdon. Yet the climax of French Neoclassicism is the moralizing history paintings of Jacques-Louis David, notably his *Oath of the Horatii*.

ART IN TIME

- 1725—Burlington and Kent begin constructing Chiswick House

- 1738—Excavation of Herculaneum begins

- 1748—Excavation of Pompeii begins

- 1749—**Walpole begins remodeling Strawberry Hill**

- ca. 1750—Industrial Revolution begins in England

- 1751—Diderot and d'Alembert publish *Encyclopédie*

- 1765–1782—James Watt perfects the steam engine

- 1770—Stubbs, *Lion Attacking a Horse*

- 1775–1784—The American Revolution

- 1783–1784—**David, *Oath of the Horatii***

- 1789—French Revolution begins

Art in the Age of Romanticism, 1789–1848

There is no precise moment when Neoclassicism died and Romanticism was born. Just as Neoclassical and Romantic elements—the rational and the emotional—coexisted in the arts of the Enlightenment era (see Chapter 22) from 1750 to 1789 (and sometimes in the same work), Neoclassicism and Romanticism also thrived side by side from 1789 to 1848, the years bracketed by the French Revolution and the European workers' revolts. If rational Neoclassical components prevailed in the earlier period, then emotional, Romantic components did in the later one. No matter how Neoclassical in look or style, a work produced during this later period is still tinted with Romanticism.

A fundamental change in consciousness in the Western world occurred toward 1800. It was in part triggered by the upheavals accompanying the French Revolution, which resulted in the overthrow of both the monarchy and the Catholic Church and the execution of 17,000 people in France. The Revolution was followed by the Napoleonic Wars, which wreaked havoc throughout Europe until 1814. These momentous events were accompanied by the disorienting rise of industrialization and urbanization, which saw huge migrations from the countryside to the city, where the poor lived in miserable conditions and were forced to work interminable hours for subsistence pay. Complementing the rise of the proletariat, the name given to these workers who were separated from the ownership of their products, was the continued development of the bourgeoisie, as the new wealthy class, which controlled the means of production, was labeled. This group threatened the dominance of the aristocracy. In response to the rise of the proletariat and the bourgeoisie, Karl Marx and Friedrich Engels published their *Communist Manifesto* in 1848, the same year that saw the outbreak of European-wide revolution by the workers.

The Enlightenment seemed to have failed. Instead of social reform and progress, there was turmoil and dislocation. With this seemingly endless succession of crises, the West found a need to believe in something other than the Enlightenment values of logic and scientific empiricism. Thus arose a belief in the subjective emotion of the individual, promoted by Jean-Jacques Rousseau in France (see Chapter 22). What had been a strong undercurrent in the eighteenth century now surfaced as the defining psychology of the Western world. Artists, writers, composers, and intellectuals now placed a premium on powerful emotion, intuition, and unrestrained creative genius. The era itself is often described as being dedicated to the "Cult of the Individual." For the intellectual and cultural elite, total liberation of imagination and creative freedom replaced rules, standards, and logic. As expressed by the French Romantic writer Victor Hugo, "All systems are false; only genius is true." From this perspective, the mind was the conduit of nature, the only means of accessing elemental universal forces, and the goal of the artist was to tap into this reservoir of higher reality and express it. Sincerity and truthfulness were

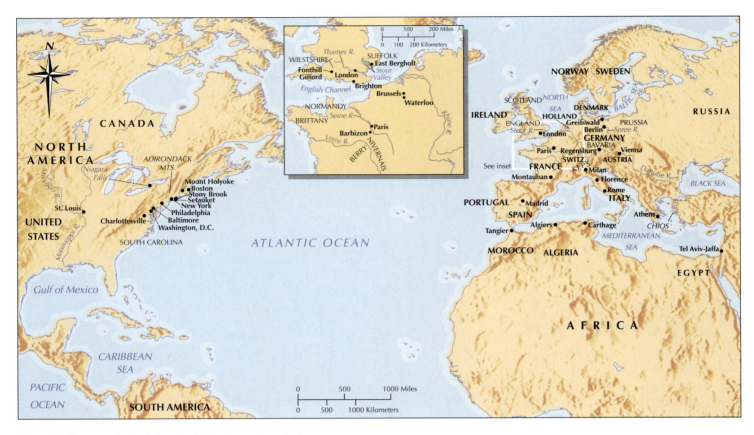

Map 23.1 Europe and North America in the Age of Romanticism

therefore now critical. Enlightenment morality was not applicable. Powerful emotions in response to violence, suffering, chaos, and ugliness, or just the exotic and wondrous, replaced virtuous and noble actions and the perfection associated with ideal beauty. Uniqueness became a strong value in art; copying someone else's genius, originality, or individualism was the manufacture of something false. Consequently, Romanticism was not a style, but an attitude. It was a license to abandon logic and to follow one's genius wherever it led.

Painting

Of all the visual arts, painting is most closely associated in our minds with Romanticism because, unlike sculpture and architecture, it allowed for a spontaneous outpouring of emotion. In fact, many art historians think of the study or sketch, whether painted or drawn, as the quintessential Romantic medium. While some of the most famous examples of Romantic painting are Baroque in their dramatic handling of paint and energetic compositions, Romantic works can just as readily be tightly painted and composed in accordance with Neoclassical

planes, resulting in frozen images that project chilling emotions.

Spain: Francisco Goya

In the opening decades of the nineteenth century, Spanish art was dominated by Francisco Goya y Lucientes (1746–1828), an artist whose work in many ways encapsulates the new psychology and the issues pervading Europe. Charles III (r. 1759–1788) appointed Goya royal painter in 1786, putting him directly in the tradition of Velázquez (see pages 400–403). For Goya, there was not necessarily a conflict between supporting the monarchy and advocating liberal reform. The king recognized the need to bring a stagnant Spain into the eighteenth century and permitted a degree of economic and social development, which gave hope to the progressives. Goya was a member of this progressive group. He was an enlightened Spaniard who admired the French *philosophes*. His social circle, which included many of his aristocratic clients, was like-minded. But the French Revolution terrified heads of state throughout Europe and ushered in reactionary oppression, for now the Enlightenment was associated with revolution, not reform. Both Church and State suppressed the liberal reformers. Spain went to war with

23.1 Francisco Goya. *The Third of May, 1808*. 1814. Oil on canvas, 8'9½" × 11'4½" (2.68 × 3.47 m). Museo del Prado, Madrid

Romanticism

France, forging an alliance with its old enemy England.

We can perceive some idea of Goya's reaction to the political crisis by looking at *The Third of May, 1808* (**fig. 23.1**), painted in 1814 and one of many paintings, drawings, and prints the artist made between 1810 and 1815 in response to the French occupation of Spain in 1808. The corruption of his administration forced Charles IV, the son of Charles III, to abdicate in 1807. He was replaced by his son Ferdinand VII, who was deposed in 1808 when NAPOLEON's troops marched into Madrid and put the emperor's brother, Joseph Bonaparte, on the throne. Enlightened Spaniards were initially optimistic that the enlightened French would reform their nation. But in Madrid a people's uprising spurred by nationalism resulted in vicious fighting and wholesale slaughter on both sides, within days fanning out across the entire country and then

dragging on for six years. Goya's enormous, dramatic picture, painted after Napoleon had been deposed and Ferdinand reinstated, shows the mass execution of Spanish rebels that took place on May 3, 1808, on a hill outside Madrid.

How different this was from Neoclassical history painting, which presented great and famous exemplars of nobleness, morality, and fortitude! Goya presents anonymous nobodies caught up in the powerful forces of history. Here we see the mechanical process of the slaughter. One rebel with raised arms has the pose of Christ in the Garden of Gethsemane when he was surprised by Roman soldiers. His right hand has a wound suggesting the stigmata. But, ironically, Goya denies the rioters status as martyrs. They are consumed by the fear of death, not the ecstasy of sacrifice. No divine light materializes to resurrect them, and the church in the background of this imaginary scene remains dark. When the stable lantern—which in its geometry and light could be construed as an emblem of Enlightenment logic and progress—is extinguished, there will be only eternal night, symbolized by the inert foreground body, whose face is reduced to a gory mass of paint. The faceless executioners, also small cogs in the wheel of history, are indifferent to their victims' fear of death and frantic pleas for mercy. Goya whips up the horror and emotional turmoil of his scene by abandoning Neoclassical tight paint handling, linearity, planarity, and evenly lit scenes, replacing this aesthetic with florid loose brushwork, dramatic contrasts of light and dark, and compositional turmoil on the left and a dramatically receding Baroque line of soldiers on the right.

Goya painted *The Third of May, 1808* at a time when he was desperate for work and wanted to gain royal favor with this picture, hence his scripting of it so that it could be read as being about the sacrifice of the Spanish to the agents of political tyranny. But the real themes of the image are the anonymity of death and the senseless brutality of war. Its power lies in its ability to instill in a viewer an intense sense of terror that makes one confront the inescapable knowledge of one's own mortality.

Britain: The Bond with Nature

Many British painters during the Romantic era followed the lead of such poets as William Wordsworth (1770–1850) and Percy Bysshe Shelley (1792–1822) and steeped themselves in nature, emotionally swept away by its beauties and moods or awed by its sublime power and intimations of the infinite.

JOHN CONSTABLE Landscape gradually became a major vehicle of the search for the truth. This is not surprising considering the importance of nature in Romantic ideology—the need to bond with it and to express its essence as personally experienced. John Constable (1776–1837) is one of two British artists who stand out at this period for their landscapes. Constable was born and raised in the village of East Bergholt, in the Stour Valley of Suffolk, and spent most of his life painting its rich farmland, which until then had been considered too ordinary and thus not suitable subject matter. Instead of working at the family's prosperous farm and mill, Constable, in 1799, was permitted to study at the Royal Academy School in London. He eventually realized that he was just learning to replicate painting conventions, and returned to Bergholt to make

"laborious studies from nature," drawings and oil sketches that he worked up into finished pictures in the studio but that retained the freshness and details of the original source. Constable even considered landscape scientific: "Painting is a science, and should be pursued as an inquiry into the laws of nature. Why, then, may not landscape painting be considered as a branch of natural philosophy, of which pictures are but experiments?" Constable was especially adept at capturing the ephemeral properties of nature— clouds, light, and atmosphere.

Constable's pictures are packed with the emotion that welled within him when experiencing the beauty of the Stour Valley—"Painting is but another word for feeling," he claimed. His pictures were both scientific and subjective, as in *The Haywain (Landscape: Noon)* (**fig. 23.2**) of 1821, shown at the Royal Academy, where he had been exhibiting since 1811. We sense a blue sky pushing out darker clouds, and an atmosphere of moisture that makes everything glisten. Vibrant flecks of paint and color dissolve the material world and make the atmosphere sparkle. The sky is a symphony of subjectivity, presenting a range of emotion, as does the land. It can be dark and undulating, as in the dramatic, energized twisting of tree branches, or bright and placid, as in the horizontal spread of the distant hayfield. Constable fills his picture with detailed anecdote; besides the haywain, there is the dog, the boat, the harvesters in the distant field, and the puffs of smoke coming from the mill. This is no perfect world, representing ideal beauty or a classical Arcadia. Rather, it is a particular site presented in all of its heartfelt specificity. And it is intentionally an English scene, reflecting the welling nationalism that was overtaking all of Europe as artists now painted their own countryside, not classical Italy.

JOSEPH MALLORD WILLIAM TURNER The second major British landscape artist in this period is Joseph Mallord William Turner (1775–1851). In their basic operating premises Constable and Turner could not be further apart. Whereas Constable painted with scientific accuracy the land he knew intimately, Turner aspired to rival great history painting and consequently invested his views with a rich overlay of historical motifs, references to the Old Masters, and metaphorical themes.

Turner began his career in the early 1790s as a topographical watercolorist for hire, and by 1799, at the unheard-of age of 24, he became an associate of the Royal Academy. While he made

A brilliant military strategist with an insatiable appetite for glory, grandeur, and empire, NAPOLEON Bonaparte (1769–1821) dominated European life from about 1802 to 1815. After a decade of astonishing military successes, he came to power in 1799 as first consul of France. In 1804, he had himself crowned Emperor Napoleon I of France. He held that title until his final military defeat at Waterloo (in Belgium) in 1815 at the hands of allied British, Dutch, and German forces and the Prussian army. Napoleon and his first wife, Joséphine de Beauharnais (1763–1814), were ardently fond of the Neoclassical style, which under their influence would come to include Egyptian motifs. Napoleon was, in fact, the first European to direct an archaeological exploration in Egypt.

23.2 John Constable. *The Haywain* (*Landscape: Noon*). 1821. Oil on canvas, 51¼ × 73″ (130 × 185 cm). The National Gallery, London

numerous landscape studies of specific rural scenes as Constable did of the Stour, his drive to artistic greatness led him to take on the great landscape and marine painters of the past—Claude Lorrain and Jacob Ruisdael—whose works his landscapes resemble in composition, subject, and atmosphere. The reason for this mimicry was to outdo them at their own game; his sun was brighter, atmosphere moister, haze hazier, and perspectival space deeper. Like Constable's, his handling of the intangible properties of nature—wind, light, reflections, atmosphere—was magical.

Turner's quest for the grandiose and his rich imagination led him to embed spectacular mythological and historical moments in his landscapes, creating historical landscape on an epic, sublime scale. However, the direct experience of nature became stronger in his late work. Now the image begins to disappear, replaced by an atmospheric blur of paint and color that seems to sit on the surface of the canvas, making the viewer feel immersed in it. Today, Turner is best known for his late, more abstract style, which he developed toward 1838 and which is seen in *The Slave Ship* or *Slavers Throwing Overboard the Dead and Dying—Typhoon Coming On* (**fig. 23.3**) of 1840. These late works were condemned in Turner's own time. His contemporaries thought he had gone mad, for they found the works virtually unreadable, and certainly unintelligible. Furthermore, his epic stories were no longer drawn from mythology or history but from seemingly minor contemporary events. His earlier work may have been atmospheric, but there was always enough drawing to suggest precise objects and legible spatial recession and relationships. Later this readability evaporates in a haze of color and paint that represents the essence of mist, light, and atmosphere.

In *The Slave Ship* Turner shows the sick and dying human cargo thrown into the sea during a typhoon. He was inspired by James Thomson's *The Seasons*, where the poet describes how sharks follow a slave ship during a typhoon, "lured by the scent of steaming crowds, or rank disease, and death." He was also influenced by a recent newspaper account of a ship's captain who jettisoned slaves in order to collect the insurance, which paid for cargo lost at sea but not for death from illness. Turner gives us a close-up of human suffering. Outstretched hands pleading for help, a leg about to disappear into the deep for a last time, the gruesome blackness of flailing chains and manacles, the frenzied predatory fish, and bloodstained water all dominate the immediate foreground. In the background is the slave ship, heading into the fury of the typhoon and its own struggle for survival, its distance and silence a metaphor for the callous indifference of the slavers. The searing brilliance of the sun bathes the sky in a blood-red aura, its seemingly infinite reach complementing the omnipotence of the raging sea.

This is a tragic, horrific scene, painted a few years after Britain banned the slave trade. Turner certainly makes us feel the callous inhumanity of the slavers, encouraging us to despise them. And yet, the picture has a haunting thematic and moral ambiguity: Birds eat fish and human carcasses, fish feed on other fish and discarded humans, and slavers fight for their lives in the face of a storm. The picture is as much about the struggle of daily life and the role of fate as it is about the immorality of the slavers, the only constant being the frightening power of nature.

23.3 Joseph Mallord William Turner. *The Slave Ship* (*Slavers Throwing Overboard the Dead and Dying—Typhoon Coming On*). 1840. Oil on canvas, 35¼ × 48″ (90.8 × 122.6 cm). Museum of Fine Arts, Boston. Henry Lillie Pierce Fund, Purchase. 99.22

Germany: Friedrich's Pantheistic Landscape

Human destiny is treated with a chilling bleakness and unsettling silence in the sublime landscapes of the German artist Caspar David Friedrich (1774–1840). While Turner focuses on the insignificance of all life and endeavors in the face of the all-powerful cosmos, Friedrich's concern is the passage from the physical way-station of earth to the spiritual being of eternity. His landscapes virtually express PANTHEISM, an especially German phenomenon, and he invests his detailed, realistic scenes with metaphysical properties that give them an aura of divine presence.

Friedrich was born into a prosperous bourgeois family of candle and soap manufacturers in the Baltic-coast harbor town of Greifswald, then part of Sweden. Here he found the austere landscape that served as the source material for his drawings, which formed the foundation of many of his paintings. He studied drawing at the Academy of Copenhagen from 1794 to 1797 and then continued his training in Dresden, where he would maintain a studio throughout his life. Until 1807, he worked exclusively in drawing, shunning historical themes and instead making topographical landscapes, including many of the Baltic region. His paintings would retain the hard linear draughtsmanship that he developed in these years.

Gradually, his landscape drawings became metaphorical, often presented in pairs with cyclical themes, such as the times of the day or the seasons. He continued this practice in his early paintings, which include *Monk by the Sea*, paired with *Abbey in an Oak Forest* (**fig. 23.4**), made in 1809–1810. The former, which would be hung on the left and read first, pits the small vertical figure of a standing monk against the vastness of an overwhelming, explosive sky. Traditionally, art historians interpret the funeral depicted in *Abbey* as that of this monk. If the first picture depicts life contemplating death, this second is an image of death, as suggested by a frozen snow-covered cemetery, a lugubrious funeral procession, distraught, barren oak trees, the skeletal remains of a Gothic abbey, and a somber winter sky at twilight. The abbey and oaks, obviously equated, form a gate that the burial cortège will pass under. Religious hope is stated in the Crucifixion mounted on the portal. The oval at the peak of

23.4 Caspar David Friedrich. *Abbey in an Oak Forest*. 1809–1810. Oil on canvas, 43½ × 67⅓″ (110.4 × 171 cm). Nationalgalerie, Staatliche Museen zu Berlin

the tracery window is echoed by the sliver of new moon in the sky, a symbol of resurrection. We sense a rite of passage, a direct connection, between abbey and sky. Just as the moon goes through a cycle as it is reborn, twilight yields to night followed by sunrise and day, and winter gives way to spring, summer, and fall; so also, it is suggested, death will be followed by an afterlife or rebirth. And yet, this is a very gloomy picture that leaves our fate after death in doubt, making us dread the unknown on the other side of the horizon.

America: Landscape as Metaphor and the Popularity of Genre

Art had not been a priority in the struggling British colonies in America during the seventeenth and eighteenth centuries, and the only art market that existed was largely for portraiture. Sculpture was mostly limited to weathervanes and tombstones. This did not change dramatically in the Federalist period (1789–1801) and the opening decades of the nineteenth century, although the first academies and galleries were founded in the first quarter of the century—the Pennsylvania Academy of Fine Arts (1802), the Boston Atheneum (1807), and New York's National Academy of Design (1825). By 1825 New York surpassed Philadelphia as the largest and wealthiest city in the nation, and simultaneously it became the nation's art capital. Consequently, our discussion of American art will center on New York well into the twentieth century.

In the 1820s, landscape painting began to acquire status, and by the 1840s it had eclipsed portraiture as the most esteemed form of American art. A young nation with little history, the United States became preoccupied with a search for its own identity, one that would distinguish it from its Old World roots. Literary figures such as William Cullen Bryant (1794–1878) and Ralph Waldo Emerson (1803–1882) identified the land itself as America's wealth and contrasted its unspoiled virginity to the densely populated, resource-impoverished lands of Europe. America was overflowing with natural resources, a veritable Garden of Eden. These writers also interpreted this pristine land as a manifestation of God, whose presence was to be seen in every blade of grass, ray of sun, and drop of water. To meditate on nature was to commune with God, a theory promoted by American Transcendentalists, such as Emerson in *Nature* (1836) and Henry David Thoreau in *Walden* (1852). The landscape became the symbol of young America.

THOMAS COLE AND THE HUDSON RIVER SCHOOL America's first art movement, based on landscape painting and born in the 1820s, is called the Hudson River School, because the artists, most with studios in New York, were initially centered on the Hudson River Valley before fanning out through all of New England in the 1830s through 1850s. Spring through fall, the artists traveled through New York and New England making studies, generally drawings, of this unique land, which they then developed into large paintings in their New York studios during the winter. The lead figure in this group was Thomas Cole (1801–1848), who produced his first major landscapes after an 1825 summer sketching trip up the Hudson. Initially, his views were filled with the sublime, presenting a wild, primordial nature, often with storms pummeling the forests, dark clouds blackening the earth, and lightning-blasted trees. Despite depicting specific sites, his style relied on European landscape conventions and formulas, with little attention given to detail.

By the 1830s, however, Cole's paint handling became tighter, his pictures less formulaic and more specific, embracing a Romantic truth to nature that we saw in Constable. This is apparent in *The Oxbow* (**fig. 23.5**), made in 1836 for exhibition at the National Academy of Design. In this breathtaking view from atop Mount Holyoke in western Massachusetts, Cole presents the natural wonder of the American landscape. The foreground is sublime wilderness, with blasted, windswept trees and dark storm clouds dumping sheets of rain. Except for the representation of Cole next to his parasol looking up at us (and in effect declaring his preference for primordial nature), there is no sign of humans in the foreground. Far below in the sunlit valley are the Connecticut River and its plain. Closer inspection reveals not just a natural plain but also cultivated fields and settlements. But they are in such harmony with nature that they seem to blend in. Here is the "Garden of Eden," as Americans described their land, blessed by the divine light breaking through the clouds. Cole underscores God's presence in the land by roughly etching, under the guise of cleared forest, the name *Noah* into the distant hill; upside down, these same letters become Hebrew letters for *Shaddai*, meaning "the Almighty." First and foremost, the picture is a paean to the glory of the American land. Cole captures the immense scale of the American landscape and its many moods, from the wild sublimity of the foreground, to the

23.5 Thomas Cole. *The Oxbow (View from Mount Holyoke, Northampton, Massachusetts, after a Thunderstorm).* 1836. Oil on canvas, 51½ × 76" (131 × 194 cm). The Metropolitan Museum of Art, New York. Gift of Mrs. Russell Sage, 1908. 08.228

pastoral tranquility of the valley, to the majestic vastness of the distant hills.

The Oxbow was also a political painting, which viewers at the 1836 exhibition would have recognized. While most Hudson River School painters depicted the glory of God as manifested in the American land, a handful, following Cole's lead, used landscape painting also to comment on the economic and social issues consuming the nation. An 1829–1832 trip to Europe gave Cole first-hand knowledge of Turner's paintings and reinforced his interest in using landscape as a vehicle for themes of historical significance. In 1836, for example, he painted a five-picture series titled *The Course of Empire*, which traced the transformation of the same site from a primitive state, to an agrarian society, to a thriving empire, to a decadent empire, and lastly to a state of ruin. Cole's audience would recognize in *The Course of Empire* a statement reflecting the heated debate about progress then consuming the country. On one side were those Americans arguing for a Jeffersonian agrarian America; on the other were

the advocates of Jacksonian *laissez-faire* ("let it be") economics, which embraced unrestricted industrial, commercial, and financial development—in other words, the development of an empire. Cole, who like the novelist James Fenimore Cooper (1789–1851) was an early environmentalist, found the rapid destruction of the wilderness and disrespect for the land disheartening. His vision of healthy development stopped at Jeffersonian agrarian society, where Americans lived in harmony with the land. He equated Jacksonian politics with empire, which would result not only in the destruction of the land but also the eventual downfall of America.

France: Neoclassical Painting in the Romantic Era

Neoclassicism dominated French art in the late eighteenth and early nineteenth centuries, because of Jacques-Louis David's powerful impact on painting (see pages 474–476). In his lifetime, David had some 400 students, and after 1800 his most gifted followers from the 1790s began to rival him for public attention. Although David convinced the new republican government that they should abolish the French Academy—which was eventually replaced and redefined—the biennial Louvre salon exhibitions were still held during the Directory (1794–1799) and the Napoleonic era (1799–1814) and remained critical to an artist's success.

JEAN-AUGUSTE-DOMINIQUE INGRES The greatest painter to come out of David's studio was Jean-Auguste-Dominique Ingres (1780–1867), who would inherit the mantle of Neoclassicism from David and carry it far into the nineteenth century. Ingres entered David's studio in 1797, and in 1801 he won the Rome Prize, which allowed him to study in Italy. In part because of the Napoleonic wars he could not take advantage of his award until 1806. Once in Rome, Ingres studied ancient art and fell in love with the classicism of Raphael. But as a Romantic, his interests were broad, even exotic, and led him to medieval, Byzantine, and Early Renaissance art. After his four-year stipend expired, Ingres stayed on in Italy at his own expense for an additional 14 years, often impoverished and, like a Romantic artist, painting what he wanted. Periodically, he sent pictures back to Paris for exhibition, where

they were generally met with derision. An example is *Grand Odalisque* (**fig. 23.6**), commissioned in 1814 by Caroline Murat, Napoleon's sister and queen of Naples; it was submitted to the Salon of 1819.

At the time, this was considered a very exotic picture, for it represents a Turkish concubine and is one of the earliest painted examples of ORIENTALISM—as the Western fascination with the culture of the Muslim world of North Africa and the Near East was then called. (Byron's Romantic poem *The Corsair*, also featuring a harem slave, was published the year the painting was commissioned.) Orientalism reflects European imperialism and its accompanying sense of superiority, which viewed non-Christian Arab culture as not only different and exotic but also inferior—backward, immoral, violent, and barbaric. Here, the exotic subject gave Ingres license to paint a female nude who was not a Greek goddess, although she recalls numerous Renaissance and Baroque paintings of a reclining Venus (see fig. 16.11) and sculptures of Ariadne from antiquity. To make his figure more appealing to a Paris audience, Ingres gave his odalisque European features, even a Raphael face and coiffure. Although the figure is alluringly sensual, and the hashish pipe, incense

SPEAKING OF

Oriental

"Oriental" derives from the Latin *oriri*, which means "to rise," and it was thus long employed in the Western world to describe the East, the area in which the sun rises. In the nineteenth century, Europeans responding to ORIENTALISM invested the Middle East with several false stereotypes. It was seen as a sensual paradise, full of mysterious, enticing pleasures but also primitive and ripe for colonization by the "superior" Western nations. Later, the term was extended to include China, Japan, and other East Asian countries. "Oriental" is not an accurate designation of a person or locale; it is always better to cite the specific geographical area being referred to.

23.6 Jean-Auguste-Dominique Ingres. *Grand Odalisque*. 1814. Oil on canvas, 35⅞ × 63″ (91 × 162 cm). Musée du Louvre, Paris

burner, fan, and turban "authenticate" the exotic scene, the painting as a whole projects a soothing sense of cultivated beauty, refinement, and idealization that seems classical.

Ingres's trademark is a beautiful classical line, which we can see as he focuses on the odalisque's flesh. Bathed in a caressing *chiaroscuro*, the body gently swells and recedes with delectable elegance. Its contours languidly undulate with sensuality, the sharply defined edges and tan color contrasting with the objects around it. The opulent color of the objects and the lush fabrics and peacock feathers enhance the sensual aura of the picture. Salon viewers noted that the concubine's back had too many vertebrae and certainly her elbowless right arm is too long; but as far as Ingres was concerned, the sweeping curves of both were essential components of the graceful composition, the line of the right arm even being continued into the folds of the drapery.

In 1821, Ingres received a commission to make an enormous painting of *The Vow of Louis XIII* for the cathedral in Montauban, his home town. Ingres, penniless, otherwise forgotten, and living in Florence, found that this commission turned his life around. He showed the picture at the Salon of 1824 to favorable reviews and was hailed as the great savior of the classical tradition. With the final fall of Napoleon in 1815, David, who had been named painter to the emperor in 1801, was exiled to Brussels, and the careers of all of his students had stalled at the same time, displaced by a new generation of painterly Romantic artists. Almost by default, then, Ingres was crowned the protector of classicism, the champion of line over color, and the savior of the "wholesome traditions of great art" and ideal beauty over the unfettered emotionalism of the Romantics. In 1825, he was elected to the French Academy, and soon became its director. He was also awarded the Legion of Honor. His studio became the destination of choice for aspiring young history painters.

France: Painterly Romanticism and Romantic Landscape

While Ingres was taking Neoclassicism deep into the nineteenth century, Antoine-Jean Gros, a second student of David's, opened up an alternative course, one that would abandon line, order, clear rational space, evenly diffused light, and classical repose for bold brushstrokes, dazzling color, impetuous drama, confused space, irrational lighting, and extreme emotions. In his wake came Théodore Géricault and Eugène Delacroix,

who brought **painterly** (that is, broad paint handling) Romanticism to the fore in the 1820s, with the result that the word Romanticism, previously reserved for literature and music, was now applied also to art. In the 1820s as well, landscape painting in France began to emerge from under the shadow cast by Neoclassicism. French Romantic landscape was never as apocalyptic as its British counterpart nor as pantheistic as in Germany and America. Instead it was more serene and poetic.

ANTOINE-JEAN GROS Gros (1771–1835) entered David's studio in 1785. During the turmoil of the French Revolution, David was able to secure a pass for Gros to go to Rome, although by the time he arrived the city was closed to the antipapist French. Through circumstance, he met Napoleon in Milan, traveled with his army, and impressed the general with his art. Napoleon charged Gros with painting his battles and glorifying his campaigns. Bonaparte, who was as brilliant at propaganda as he was at military strategy, carefully controlled his public image and relied heavily on art to reinforce his political position. He made sure his commissions were shown at the Salons, where they would be seen by everyone and reported in the press.

The Napoleonic era was a catalyst for French Romanticism. The drama, glory, valor, and adventures of the Napoleonic Wars provided endless material for the artistic imagination. The North African campaigns took Europeans into the forbidden Arab world and introduced them to a wondrous, exotic subject matter, which they brought back to Europeans anxious for new experiences. Gros's first commission, *Napoleon in the Pesthouse at Jaffa, 11 March 1799* (**fig. 23.7**), came in 1804 and was exhibited in that year's Salon to huge success. This 23-foot-wide picture was commissioned not only to promote the emperor's bravery and leadership but to reinforce his humanitarian image, which was propagandistically essential considering the enormous human loss tallied in many of his battles, especially in Jaffa, then in Palestine but today a section of Tel Aviv, Israel. During the campaign, bubonic plague broke out among the French ranks. Legend has it that to calm his troops, Napoleon fearlessly entered the pesthouse and walked among the patients. Here we see the general, like Christ healing the sick, courageously touching the open sore of a victim, his presence virtually willing the dying to rise. The painting ignores the fact that Napoleon

23.7 Antoine-Jean Gros. *Napoleon in the Pesthouse at Jaffa, 11 March 1799*. 1804. Oil on canvas, 17'5½" × 23'7½" (5.32 × 7.20 m). Musée du Louvre, Paris

poisoned these same sick troops when he retreated from Jaffa.

While Gros's drawing and brushwork are relatively tight and Davidian, the picture has an overt turbulent drama, created by the dark shadows, bursts of light, splashes of bright red, the rapidly receding perspective of the arcades, and cloud-filled sky. Chaos prevails. Although Napoleon is placed in the center as a compositional anchor, he is momentarily lost in the turmoil of the scene. Our eye goes to the circle of the dead, dying, and sick surrounding him, which includes the Michelangelesque figures in the foreground shadows and the "resurrected" nudes next to him. The male nude is no longer heroic, as in David, but helpless and horrifying. Napoleon's courageous act has to vie for a viewer's attention with the dark mood of psychological and physical suffering and the exoticism, to Western eyes, of the Arab attendants and Islamic architecture. (This picture helped launch the vogue for Oriental subjects that we

saw in Ingres's *Grand Odalisque*.) The monumental arches may pay compositional homage to David's *Oath of the Horatii* (fig. 22.13), but instead of supporting a narrative of Neoclassical stoicism and clarity they contribute to a passionate, Romantic exoticism and a foreboding of horrifying uncertainty.

THÉODORE GÉRICAULT Without the Napoleonic campaigns to feed his imagination, Gros's career soon waned. David's other outstanding students and followers were simultaneously eclipsed. The future was now represented by Théodore Géricault (1791–1824) and those who followed him. Géricault was independently wealthy and largely self-taught, frequenting the Napoleon Museum, where he copied the great colorists: Rubens, Van Dyck, and Titian. Gros, however, was his role model, and Gros and Rubens were clearly the artistic sources for Géricault's submission to the Salon of 1812, *Charging Chasseur*, a work filled with energetic brushwork, sharp diagonal recessions, bold contrasts of light and dark, rippling contours, and flashes of color, all of which could not be further from David or closer to Rubens. Completely gone is the Davidian planarity that structured the turmoil of Gros's pesthouse.

But *Charging Chasseur* revealed Géricault's lack of formal training, namely his inability to draw. Continuing his independent study, he now worked from classical models, copying High Renaissance painters at the Royal Museum, as the Louvre was called after the second fall of Napoleon in 1815 and with the establishment of Louis XVIII's Restoration monarchy. In 1816, Géricault went to Italy, stopping in Florence to draw Michelangelo's Medici tombs (see fig. 16.1), before going to Rome to study the antiquities. Not long after his return to Paris in late 1817, he began thinking about the third and last painting he would exhibit at the Salons, *The Raft of the "Medusa"* (**fig. 23.8**), painted between 1818 and 1819 after many studies. In 1816 the *Medusa*,

a government vessel, foundered off the West African coast with approximately 400 people aboard. The captain commandeered the six lifeboats for government officials and officers, with the remaining 150 passengers set adrift by the crew consigned to a makeshift raft at the mercy of the sea. When the passengers were finally rescued some two weeks later, only a handful had survived. The callous captain was incompetent, an aristocrat who had been politically appointed by the government of Louis XVIII, and the headline-making event was condemned in the press as a reflection of the corruption of Louis's administration.

Géricault decided to paint the moment when the survivors first sight a ship, not the more politically charged moment when the captain sets the raft adrift. The painting is thus about the harrowing mental and physical experience of survival rather than an accusation of injustice. Géricault seems to have latched onto his subject after revisiting Gros's *Napoleon in the Pesthouse*, for the

23.8 Théodore Géricault. *The Raft of the "Medusa"*. 1818–1819. Oil on canvas, 16′1″ × 23′6″ (4.9 × 7.16 m). Musée du Louvre, Paris

foreground is littered with Michelangelesque nudes. From the bodies of the dead and dying in the foreground, the composition recedes in a dramatic Baroque diagonal (see fig. 19.2), climaxing in the group supporting the frantically waving black man. As our eye follows this line of writhing, twisting bodies, we move from death to hope. But this is not a painting just about hope, for there are no heroes, no exemplary moral fortitude. Rather the theme is the human species against nature, and Géricault's goal was to make a viewer feel the trials and tribulations of the castaways. The academic, classically proportioned monumental figures are a catalogue of human misery, reflecting the death, cannibalism, fighting, insanity, sickness, exhaustion, hunger, and thirst that tormented the victims. The stark realism, obtained in part through tight brushwork, heightens our visceral connection to the dramatically lit event; we too are on the crude raft, pitched about in the high seas, and aimlessly buffeted by the wind. Géricault would never exhibit again in a Salon and within six years would be dead at the age of 32.

EUGÈNE DELACROIX In 1822 Eugène Delacroix (1798–1863) emerged as the standard-bearer of painterly Romanticism, the position Géricault so dearly coveted. Delacroix was seven years younger than Géricault and came from a similar background—Parisian and wealthy. Like Géricault, he was essentially independent and self-taught, studying the great masterpieces at the Louvre, especially Rubens, Titian, and Veronese. His greatest excitement came when visiting the studios of Gros and Géricault. He befriended the latter in 1818 and posed for one of the figures in *The Raft of the "Medusa."* His submission to the Salon of 1824, *Scenes from the Massacre at Chios* (**fig. 23.9**), presents a compendium of misery and suffering in the foreground and was obviously inspired by the groupings of the dead and dying in Gros's *Pesthouse at Jaffa* (fig. 23.7) and Gericault's *The Raft of the "Medusa"* (fig. 23.8). In 1820 the Greeks had revolted against the ruling Ottoman (Turkish) Empire, and the following year the Turks raided the Greek island of Chios, destroying villages and either massacring or enslaving virtually the entire populace of 20,000. Delacroix's painting was based upon this event and was, in part, made to show support for Greek independence as well as to express the Romantic passion for democracy and individual freedom.

Burning and slaying take place in a blur of smoke and confusion in the middle- and background of the painting, while the foreground, which focuses on a group of Greeks gathered up for execution or enslavement, is remarkably devoid of violence. Instead, resignation, desperation at the impending loss of loved ones, and hopelessness reign, this pessimism symbolized by the foreboding silhouette of the armed Ottoman guard. Delacroix reinforces the turmoil of the violence in the background through the twisting and turning of the foreground figures and their undulating contours as well as by the chaotic piling up of bodies. The intense colors of the painting have darkened considerably over time, especially the blues and reds, which originally created an optical snap of light and dark that was reinforced by the bravura of the brushwork. Clearly, Rubens is behind these qualities as well as the two asymmetrical compositional pyramids organizing the foreground group and the diagonal recession into deep space. (Delacroix, however, subverts the traditional device of putting a hero at the apex of the pyramids by instead placing villains, the Turkish guards, there.) Delacroix was also influenced by the color and brushwork of Constable, who had three landscapes, including *The Haywain* (see fig. 23.2), in the same Salon. Upon seeing them, Delacroix repainted the sky at the last minute, giving it a brilliant luminosity, and he worked vivid colors into the garments.

This "terrifying hymn in honor of doom and irremediable suffering," as the poet and critic Charles Baudelaire (1821–1867) described the work, established Delacroix as the great Romantic painter. It was the first time the term Romantic was applied to a visual artist, making him the artistic equivalent of the composer Hector Berlioz (1803–1869) and the writer Victor Hugo (1802–1885). And certainly Delacroix shared their Romantic spirit. The year 1824 therefore was a critical one. It was the year Géricault died, Constable was introduced in Paris, and Ingres returned from Italy, unaware that he would be anointed the guardian of the classical tradition.

Romantic Landscape Painting

David's Neoclassicism was so dominant that it even cast its shadow over French landscape painting in the opening decades of the nineteenth century, which was planar and stylized, largely modeled on Poussin and Claude Lorrain. The exhibition of Constable's landscapes at the pivotal Salon of 1824 opened up new possibilities, and a younger generation impressed by his powerful naturalism and Romantic moods made it

23.9 Eugène Delacroix. *Scenes from the Massacre at Chios.* 1824. Oil on canvas, 13′8″ × 11′7″ (4.17 × 3.54 m). Musée du Louvre, Paris

The changeover from a small-scale, agriculturally based economy to one based on the large-scale, mechanized production and sale of manufactured goods is known as the INDUSTRIAL REVOLUTION. This great shift began in England in the late eighteenth century, spread through most of western Europe and the United States in the middle of the nineteenth century, and has continued elsewhere, right up to the present. The most profound effects have been urbanization, the rise of capitalism and the working-class proletariat, and the need for specialization.

the foundation of their work. By the following decades, landscape was established as a viable genre in France, one that could rival history painting in popularity and pave the way for the rise of Impressionism in the 1860s.

THÉODORE ROUSSEAU AND THE BARBIZON SCHOOL A group of academically trained painters known as the Barbizon School took their aesthetic lead directly from Constable, augmenting his direct impression of nature with a study of the great seventeenth-century Dutch landscapists, such as Ruisdael (see fig. 19.14), who were exhibited in the Louvre. The group emerged in the 1830s and took its name from the village of Barbizon, bordering the Forest of

Fontainebleau, where the artists painted and many settled. The forest had been a royal hunting preserve, and as a result it offered nature in a relatively unspoiled state, undisturbed by the INDUSTRIAL REVOLUTION smoldering just 40 miles away in Paris. The best-known Barbizon painter is Pierre-Étienne-Théodore Rousseau (1812–1867). He learned the rudiments of painting from two academically trained artists and by copying landscapes in the Louvre. In the early to mid-1830s, his work was occasionally accepted at the Salons, from which he was banished from 1837 to 1848, his view of nature deemed too unseemly. He led a rather bohemian existence and permanently settled in Barbizon in 1848.

Under the Birches (**fig. 23.10**) of 1842–1843 is a fine example of Rousseau's work, which is perhaps the most diverse of all the Barbizon School. Produced in the studio from studies made on a seven-month trip to the Berry region in central France, the painting, like that of Constable, avoids artificial compositional and stylized motifs and instead captures the essence of nature. We readily sense that this is a specific site; each tree seems individualized, for example, and each wisp of cloud unique. We can feel the onset of twilight and the cool damp atmosphere of autumn. While the blue-green sky and brownish-orange foliage offer a touch of color, Rousseau's palette is somber and earthy, evoking soil, decaying plant and animal matter, and the interior gloom of a thicket. Like Constable, Rousseau's brushwork is stippled, applied in small flecks that make the landscape pulse with energy, reinforced by the nervous outline of trees and bushes. We sense growth and the constant movement of nature. It is little wonder that Rousseau was rejected at the Salons. His dark, honest pictures with their turgid brushwork must have been considered ugly and depressing by conservative taste.

Sculpture

Compared with painting, sculpture was a severely limiting medium for an artist at the opening of the nineteenth century. In its most monumental form, free-standing historical sculpture, it was generally limited to the human figure, and since the Renaissance the sculpted figure had been largely based on antique models. Nineteenth-century sculptors throughout Europe would overwhelmingly follow the classical paradigm of one or two figures that are based on Greek and Roman prototypes and embody some notion of virtue or beauty. Yet in France a dramatic change in the artistic climate toward 1830 allowed a small gap for experimentation. The rise of Delacroix and Romantic painting in the 1820s was followed by the new, more liberal constitutional monarchy of Louis-Philippe (the July Monarchy), which emerged with the 1830

23.10 Pierre-Étienne-Théodore Rousseau. *Under the Birches*. 1842–1843. Oil on wood panel, 16⅝ × 25⅜″ (42.2 × 64.4 cm). Toledo Museum of Art, Ohio. Gift of Arthur J. Secor

Revolution and the abdication of Charles X, Louis' successor. The bourgeoisie had more of a presence in the new government and in society in general, ushering in an era of middle-class taste. These two forces gave a handful of artists the courage to create Romantic sculpture.

Neoclassical Sculpture in the Romantic Era: Antonio Canova

Cementing the dominance of the Neoclassical model in sculpture for 100 years beginning in the 1780s was the preeminence of Antonio Canova (1757–1822). Working in Rome, he became the most famous sculptor in the world, receiving commissions from all over Europe and America. He was the artist whom the majority of sculptors in both the Old and New Worlds emulated and tried to equal.

Canova came from the area near Venice, where his talent was soon recognized and gained him enough financial support to settle in Rome. By the mid-1780s, he was in tremendous demand. One of his commissions came in 1787 from a British tourist, who placed an order for a *Cupid and Psyche* (**fig. 23.11**). Canova first modeled the work in plaster, and assistants roughed it out in marble. Canova then completed the work, which included creating an impressive variety of surface textures, including the remarkable, "cold-perfect" finish for flesh that was never equaled by his many imitators. Nor did anyone match his exquisite compositions of continuous elegant contours, which in *Cupid and Psyche* are visible in the curving pattern of the sensuous arms and legs, as well as in the flowing drapery and the oval mound gently elevating the figures.

Canova delivers more than beautiful, idealized classical models, more than noble simplicity and calm grandeur—he presents an intense emotion that we associate with the Romantic era. Here he portrays the moment when Cupid, who has fallen in love with the human Psyche, gives her a kiss that awakens her from the spell of eternal sleep cast by the jealous Venus. With this kiss,

23.11 Antonio Canova. *Cupid and Psyche*. 1787–1793. Marble, 6′1″ × 6′8″ (1.55 × 1.73 m). Musée du Louvre, Paris

23.12 François Rude. *The Departure of the Volunteers of 1792* ("*La Marseillaise*"). 1833–1836. Stone, approx. 42 × 26′ (12.8 × 7.9 m). Arc de Triomphe, Paris

she is now immortal, like Cupid. Canova captures a tenderness and passion in both expression and gesture that were unthinkable before 1780.

French Romantic Sculpture: Breaking from the Classical Model

It took both daring and considerable imagination for a sculptor to break away from the classical model, which, as just mentioned, in its freestanding form focused on one or two classically inspired figures embodying the virtue of beauty, morality, nobility, or perfection. But a handful of artists, notably François Rude, explored new subjects, feelings, and compositions.

FRANÇOIS RUDE Rude (1784–1855) brought nationalistic fervor to his figurative sculpture and is best remembered for *"La Marseillaise"* (**fig. 23.12**) on the Arc de Triomphe in Paris. Rude enrolled in the École des Beaux-Arts in 1809, studying sculpture, and as a Napoleon sympathizer fled to Brussels when Bonaparte was defeated in 1815. He returned to Paris in 1827, and, with a nationalistic zeal that we associate with the Romantic era, he began studying French sculptural history—first the French Renaissance tradition of the School of Fontainebleau and Giovanni Bologna (see fig. 16.4), and then delving deeper into the past, to Claus Sluter (see fig. 13.1).

It was a perfect match, then, when in 1833 Rude received one of the four sculptural commissions on the Arc de Triomphe, since the works were about patriotic fervor. The arch had been left unfinished when Napoleon was exiled in 1815, and Louis-Philippe and his minister of the interior saw the monument's completion as an opportunity to demonstrate that the new government supported national reconciliation. Hence the sculptural program consisted of four works by different artists, each surrounding the arch opening and offering something to every segment of the French political spectrum. Rude received the assignment based on the success of a rather Neoclassical-looking sculpture of a nude Neapolitan fisherboy playing with a turtle, which he had submitted to the Salon of 1833. The Salon submission hardly anticipated the chaotic explosion we see in *The Departure of the Volunteers of 1792*, the formal title for *"La Marseillaise."*

The scene honors the volunteers who rallied to defend the new French Republic from an Austro-Prussian threat in 1792. A winged allegorical figure representing both France and Liberty leads a collection of soldiers from different periods of the nation's past. Rather than a specific event, Rude evokes an eternal, all-powerful, nationalistic spirit that emanates from the people and arises when called upon. While the figures have a classical anatomy, strike classical poses, and are aligned parallel to the wall in shallow relief, the composition is frenetic, a whirligig of arms, legs, and twisted bodies that energizes the outpouring of patriotism swept along by Liberty above. When unveiled in 1836, *The Departure* was unanimously hailed as the best of the four works on the Arc de Triomphe and was nicknamed *"La Marseillaise"* because it so successfully embodied the national spirit. Rude himself attained no lasting fame from the project, and without commissions, which sculptors, unlike painters, rely on, he had no opportunity to develop further the innovative aesthetic implications of *The Departure*.

Romantic Revivals in Architecture

The social and political turmoil that rocked Europe from 1789 to 1848 resulted in a search for stability and comfort, which in architecture came in the form of revival styles. Instead of developing new forms, architects resurrected the past, its familiarity providing solace and continuity in a world that otherwise seemed fractured, uncertain, and in constant flux. Architects appropriated every known architectural style, selecting

them for their associations, picturesque qualities, or exoticism. Egyptian, Greek, Roman, Romanesque, Gothic, Renaissance, Baroque, Chinese, Turkish, Queen Anne, rustic thatched cottage—everything and anything could be found revived in nineteenth-century European architecture. It was not unusual for an architect to submit several proposals for a single project, each in a different style. Nor was it unusual to find several periods represented in a single building. But by far the most popular revival styles were Gothic and classical.

The Gothic Revival: The Houses of Parliament

Perhaps the most famous Gothic Revival building is the Houses of Parliament in London (**fig. 23.13**) by Sir Charles Barry (1795–1860) and A. W. N. Pugin (1812–1852). It was commissioned in 1836 after the former building burned down, and the competition required the new Houses to be designed in one of two "English" styles, Gothic or Elizabethan—91 of the 97 entries were Gothic. Barry was the head architect and was best known for his work in classical or Renaissance revival styles. Predictably, he laid out the building in a symmetrical, orderly fashion. He wisely hired Pugin, Britain's leading expert on the Gothic, to draw every Gothic detail on both the interior and exterior, which he designed with meticulous historical accuracy in the florid Perpendicular style (see page 261). The picturesque towers are believed to be Pugin's contribution as well. Instead of being sublime, Gothic Revival now is largely picturesque and associational, the style having been specifically selected to conjure up a sense of nationalistic pride.

The Classical Revival

Classical revival was ubiquitous in America, since the new republic modeled itself on the democracies of ancient Greece and Rome. The White House and the nation's Capitol are Neoclassical, and most churches, banks, and government buildings were designed with a Greco-Roman temple façade, although the Gothic was very popular as well for churches.

AN ANCIENT STYLE FOR A NEW REPUBLIC: THOMAS JEFFERSON'S UNIVERSITY OF VIRGINIA In addition to being a politician and farmer, Thomas Jefferson was an amateur architect, who, working in a classical style, designed his home, Monticello (1770–1782), as a Palladian villa, and the Virginia State Capitol (1785) as a

23.13 Sir Charles Barry and A. W. N. Pugin. The Houses of Parliament. Begun 1836. London

version of the Maison Carrée in Nîmes. His best-known project in the Romantic era is the University of Virginia campus in Charlottesville (**fig. 23.14**). Like Monticello and the Virginia State Capitol, the campus is based on antiquity in order to evoke the democratic heritage from Greece and Rome as well as the grandeur of these two great civilizations, which form the bedrock of Western art and culture. Designed between 1804 and 1817, the campus consists of two rows of five Palladian villas connected by a roofed colonnade, off which are rooms for students. Each of the ten villas, which housed the professors and classrooms, was different, symbolizing individualism and aesthetically introducing picturesque variety. Each has a different classical association: One with a Doric order refers to the Baths of Diocletian in Rome, a second with an Ionic order to the Temple of Fortuna Virilis, also in Rome. At one end of the two rows and tying them together is a Pantheon-like Rotunda, the library, suggested by fellow architect Benjamin Latrobe and built in 1823–1826. Lastly, the tree-lined lawn separating the two rows of villas imbues the complex with the naturalism of a picturesque English garden. Jefferson's genius in

23.14 Thomas Jefferson. University of Virginia. Designed 1804–1817, constructed 1817–1828. Charlottesville, Virginia

23.15 Karl Friedrich Schinkel. Altes Museum. 1824–1830. Berlin

Charlottesville was to use Neoclassicism to create a metaphor for the new republic that expresses both the individualism and the unity defining the new nation.

CREATING A NEW ATHENS IN GERMANY: KARL FRIEDRICH SCHINKEL While the Prussian architects were as eclectic as their English, French, and American counterparts, they designed some of the finest classical revival buildings. The most renowned architect is perhaps Karl Friedrich Schinkel, named State architect in 1815 by Friedrich Wilhelm III. Like many architects of the day, Schinkel (1781–1841) worked in every imaginable style—classical, Romanesque, Gothic, and Renaissance. He began as a Neoclassicist, however, as can be seen in the Altes Museum in Berlin (**fig. 23.15**), his second major commission. Designed in 1824, it was modeled on a Greek temple, in part with the intention of endowing the building with the aura of a temple of aesthetic treasures, a place where one came not to worship the gods but to contemplate art. The entrance is on what looks like the side of a temple (the real sides—their edges seen at either end of the colonnaded façade—are plain stone walls with rectangular windows), a brilliant device to suggest a temple without actually copying one, and avoiding the use of the pedimented façade so common in the classical revival. The museum is raised on a high podium and accessed by a centralized staircase, which along with the colossal Grecian order gives the building a serene monumentality and strong sense of axis. The width of the staircase is echoed above by a second-floor attic, which encases a domed room for the display of sculpture. Schinkel is a master of perfect proportions and scale, and the symmetrical and logical interior echoes the exterior harmony.

Prussia emerged as a major political force at the Congress of Vienna, held after the fall of Napoleon in 1815, and the ambitious building program instituted by Friedrich Wilhelm III was designed to reinforce his imperial ambitions. Part of the charisma of the Altes Museum was to link Berlin with the glory and grandeur of ancient Athens.

SUMMARY

The political and social changes spawned by the Enlightenment continued unabated in the first half of the nineteenth century. Instability spread across Europe in the wake of urbanization, industrialization, the French Revolution, and the Napoleonic Wars. Intellectuals and the cultural community saw these crises as a failure of the Enlightenment. Spurning rationalism, logic, empiricism, and science, they now sought what they considered higher truths founded on emotion, imagination, individual genius, and nature. This change in attitude gave rise to the Romantic era of the first half of the nineteenth century.

In Spain, Francisco Goya represented this new Romantic spirit, especially the disturbing psychology that reflected modern doubt about the existence of life after death, and portraying the inherent inhumanity of civilization. In Britain, Romantic painters like John Constable and J. M. W. Turner depicted the English landscape, which they endowed with powerful emotions and viewed as the site of universal forces. In Germany, Caspar David Friedrich similarly invested his landscapes with divine forces, as did American landscape artists, who emerged in the 1820s. The pristine wilderness became the national emblem for Americans.

Neoclassicism survived in France, where Jean-Auguste-Dominique Ingres continued the classical tradition of David. While Ingres championed drawing, planar composition, and ideal beauty, his themes were often Romantic, focusing on such exotic subjects as odalisques. Painterly, rather than Neoclassical, Romanticism prevailed, however, with strong brushwork and color as well as dynamic Baroque compositions creating energetic images, epitomized by Eugène Delacroix. He emerged in the 1820s with exotic scenes set in Greece or inspired by Romantic literature filled with fear, death, and suffering.

Neoclassicism dominated European and American sculpture during the Romantic period, in large part through the powerful influence of an Italian, Antonio Canova. While Canova's figures look classically derived, they nonetheless project powerful emotions that are associated with Romanticism. Only a few sculptors tried to break away from the classical mold to create Romantic sculpture. These include François Rude, whose energetic composition of *"La Marseillaise"* on the Arc de Triomphe in Paris captures the spirit of nationalism.

Revival styles dominated the architecture of the Romantic era and well beyond. In an unstable world dominated by war and the changes brought on by the Industrial Revolution, the architectural styles of the past offered a note of familiarity and stability. They also appealed to the Romantic sensibility for the exotic. Classical and Gothic revivals were perhaps the most common. Among the best examples of the Gothic Revival are the Houses of Parliament by Sir Charles Barry and A. W. N. Pugin, and of the classical revival Thomas Jefferson's University of Virginia campus and Karl Friedrich Schinkel's Altes Museum in Berlin.

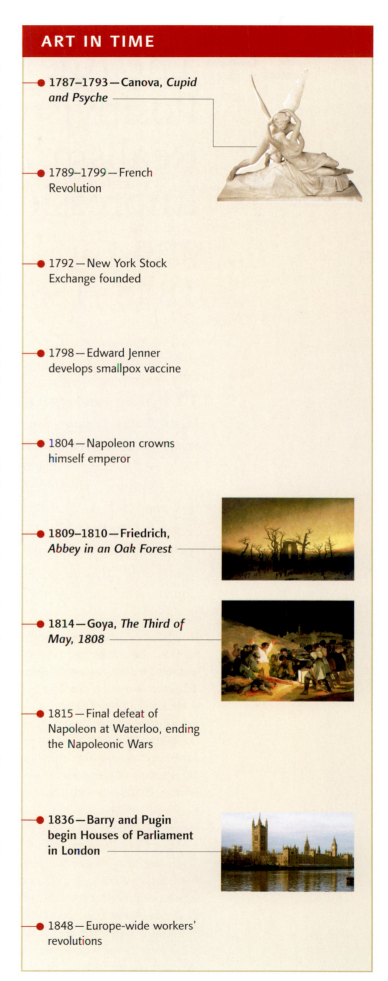

ART IN TIME

- 1787–1793 — Canova, *Cupid and Psyche*

- 1789–1799 — French Revolution

- 1792 — New York Stock Exchange founded

- 1798 — Edward Jenner develops smallpox vaccine

- 1804 — Napoleon crowns himself emperor

- 1809–1810 — Friedrich, *Abbey in an Oak Forest*

- 1814 — Goya, *The Third of May, 1808*

- 1815 — Final defeat of Napoleon at Waterloo, ending the Napoleonic Wars

- 1836 — Barry and Pugin begin Houses of Parliament in London

- 1848 — Europe-wide workers' revolutions

24

The Age of Positivism: Realism, Impressionism, and the Pre-Raphaelites, 1848–1885

*R*omanticism began to dissipate in Europe as an intellectual attitude and stylistic trend after 1848 and was gradually superseded by Realism. Increasingly, people came to rely on the physical, physiological, empirical, and scientific as a way to understand nature, society, and human behavior. Hard facts, not feelings, became the bricks and mortar of knowledge. Positivism is the term often used to describe the new mentality of pragmatism and materialism that emerged in the 1840s. The word was coined by the French philosopher Auguste Comte (1798–1857), who in 1830 began to write a multivolume series called Positive Philosophy. Comte called for social progress to be based on observable fact and tested ideas—in other words, on science. This new scientific approach to studying society came to be called sociology.

Paralleling Comte's sociology was the appearance in the 1830s and 1840s of popular and widely distributed pamphlets called *physiologies*. These were short essays that analyzed in tremendous detail different niches of French society, not just professions and types, such as the Lawyer, the Nun, the Society Woman, but such specific categories as the Suburban Gardener and the Woman of Thirty. In a world undergoing tremendous flux because of rapid industrialization and urbanization, the *physiologies* were a means of understanding the dramatic transformations that were occurring.

In the arts, Positivism resulted in Realism. Now, artists and writers did not idealize life but instead presented it unembellished and unidealized. As early as 1846, the poet and critic Charles Baudelaire called for an art based on modern life. By the 1850s, *réalisme* was the rallying cry of the new art and literature. Instead of valuing

wild flights of imagination, the exotic, and the sublime, Realists planted both feet firmly on the ground and, generally without emotion, bluntly depicted the changes in society. This ranged from the grim existence of country peasants and the downtrodden urban poor to the leisure activities of the rapidly growing metropolitan middle class and *nouveaux riches* (new rich). In landscape painting, this realism evolved into Impressionism, a style that documented the dramatic social changes occurring in the growing suburbs surrounding Paris. The Impressionists empirically captured the world before their very eyes, the shimmering sketchiness of their finished paintings reflecting the impermanence of a constantly changing contemporary world.

While the Impressionists were committed to creating an empirical representational art—a realistic art—a by-product of their stylistic

Map 24.1 Europe and North America in the Age of Positivism

developments was the advent of Modernism. To the following generations, their bright color and broad brushwork, that is, the abstract qualities, seemed to challenge the representational components as the subject matter of their paintings. In the twentieth century, critics and historians would label this shift in art toward abstraction as "Modernism." Impressionism also marked the appearance of the **avant-garde**: The notion that certain artists and ideas are strikingly new or radical for their time. This meant, in effect, that artists began making art that was only understood by a handful of people, namely other avant-garde artists and a few art experts, including collectors. The disconnection between the avant-garde and the general public, including the working class, who felt comfortable attending the highly publicized academy exhibitions, is reflected in the rise of commercial art galleries as the principal venue for the display of new art and the corresponding decline in power of academic salons throughout the Western world. While Realism served as a springboard for the abstraction of Modernism, we must remember that first and foremost it was a movement preoccupied with the dramatic changes occurring in society, and that its birth coincides with the great European-wide Revolution of 1848.

Realism in France

The uprisings began in France. War raged in the streets of Paris as the working class demanded more political representation, and 10,000 people were killed or wounded. This proletarian rebellion produced shockwaves of class revolution that radiated throughout Europe, resulting in similar outbreaks in major cities.

The forces of conservatism ultimately prevailed everywhere. In France, Louis Napoleon Bonaparte (1808–1873), the emperor's nephew, was overwhelmingly elected president of the Second Republic, largely on name recognition. In 1852, however, he dissolved the parliament and arranged to have himself "elected" emperor, becoming Napoleon III and establishing the Second Empire. France prospered under his reign, which ended in 1870 with the Franco-Prussian War. The pace of the Industrial Revolution, which had not gained momentum in France until the 1840s, now increased dramatically, and new financial systems instituted by Louis Napoleon created unprecedented wealth. Dominated by financiers, industrialists, manufacturers, lawyers, and merchants, the bourgeoisie flourished, as did their desire for material possessions. In Paris, the new wealth and increased leisure

24.1 Gustave Courbet. *Burial at Ornans*. 1849–1850. Oil on canvas, 10′3½″ × 21′9½″ (3.13 × 6.64 m). Musée d'Orsay, Paris

Realism

Socialism is the name of an economic and social doctrine that advocates State ownership and control of the basic means of production together with the egalitarian distribution of wealth. A SOCIALIST, therefore, is one who believes in socialism. In France in the mid-nineteenth century, socialism was a sincerely considered alternative to monarchy, empire, and unstable republics, and the goal of ending economic and social oppression by one class or group over another paralleled the impulse that fueled the Revolution of 1848 in Paris.

time gave rise to grand restaurants, cafés, department stores, theaters, clubs, parks, and racetracks, where people, often from different social classes, congregated and shopped.

Realism in the 1840s and 1850s: Painting Contemporary Social Conditions

French Realism developed simultaneously with the Revolution of 1848. Especially in the hands of Gustave Courbet, the self-proclaimed banner carrier of this art movement, Realism was often a highly political style expressing SOCIALIST ideals. It championed laborers and common country folk, groups that challenged the authority and privilege of the Parisian aristocracy and bourgeoisie and that were in part responsible for the upheavals of 1848.

GUSTAVE COURBET Gustave Courbet (1819–1877) came from Ornans, a town at the foot of the Jura Mountains near the Swiss border. He went to Paris in 1839 to study painting, and by the late 1840s became a dominant figure in the cafés on the Left Bank. Courbet met the literary avant-garde, befriending Baudelaire and the critic and writer Champfleury (the pen name of Jules-François-Félix Husson, 1821–1889). It was Champfleury who swayed him toward Realism. Champfleury, who collected folk art and was interested in such nonelitist art forms as popular prints, children's art, and caricature, convinced

Courbet to return to his rural roots and paint the simple world of Ornans.

In the fall of 1849, Courbet returned to his home town, where he painted the 22-foot-wide *Burial at Ornans* (**fig. 24.1**). It was accepted at the Salon of 1850–1851, and was an affront to many viewers. It presented common provincial folk, portrayed in a coarse, heavy form, without a shred of elegance or idealization. The people of Ornans posed for Courbet, and the artist not only documented their clothes and bearing but their distinguishing facial features, which included bulbous noses, grotesquely wrinkled faces, and unkempt hair. Courbet's Realism extends to the democratic presentation of the figures. Despite bold brushwork and a *chiaroscuro* vaguely reminiscent of his favorite artists, Rembrandt and Velázquez, the picture has no Baroque drama and no compositional structure designed to emphasize one figure over another—the dog is as important as the priest or mayor. Nor does it use classical formulas, as Benjamin West did in his pyramidal groupings in *The Death of General Wolfe* (see fig. 22.4). Instead, the image embraces the bold, simple compositions found in such popular art as broadsides, almanacs, and song sheets—the art of the people, not the academy.

The picture seems so matter-of-fact that it is difficult to know what it is about. We see pallbearers and the coffin on the left, then a priest and assistants, followed by small-town patricians, and, to the right, womenfolk. An open grave is in the center foreground. We do not even know whose funeral it is. Nor is it clear that this is a statement about the finality of death, although it is the strongest candidate for the theme. Clearly, the picture is a document of social ritual that accurately observes the distinctions of gender, profession, and class in Ornans. More important, it brazenly elevates provincial bourgeois events to a lofty status equal to historical events. In effect, it was an assault on the highly esteemed genre of history painting.

The Realist Assault on Academic Values and Bourgeois Taste

By presenting provincial bourgeoisie and peasants on a scale reserved for history painting, Courbet launched an assault on the values of the French Academy and bourgeois taste. In effect, he declared contemporary life, and especially contemporary social conditions, just as valid (if not more valid) a subject for painting as historical events, and his emergence signals the death knell of the hierarchy of the genres that can be traced back to the establishment of the academies. Courbet's rejection of academic values in order to depict the social conditions of the modern world was taken up by Édouard Manet (1832–1883) in the early 1860s, followed shortly thereafter by Edgar Degas. Focusing on urban rather than rural life, they depicted musical gatherings in the Bois de Boulogne, the new park on the western outskirts of Paris where the upper classes came to be seen, and showed the fashionable throngs who congregated at Longchamp, the new racetrack, also in the Bois. They painted chic masked balls held at the Opera, courtesans with their clients, and the new leisure activities at the new cafés, dance halls, and restaurants.

ÉDOUARD MANET Manet's pictures are often complex, loaded with references, and densely layered with multiple readings. They are so rich that he could comment on academic values while capturing the energy and psychology of modern society, and the changes occurring in it. What were these academic values? While it is dangerous to characterize any one kind of art as being academic and taught at the École des Beaux-Arts in the 1860s, most of the academicians still believed in the supremacy of history painting, the Greco-Roman tradition, and the highly finished Neoclassical style of paint handling epitomized by Ingres, who was still alive at

the time. Among the more popular subjects was the female nude, and images of nudes plastered the walls of the Salons. However, they were not ordinary nudes, for they were all Venuses, Dianas, bacchantes (followers of Bacchus), or nymphs. In other words, they were noble beings with a classical pedigree. These academic values were especially embraced by the bourgeoisie, who viewed academic art as the epitome of high culture and acquired it in part to gain social status.

Manet's *Luncheon on the Grass* (**fig. 24.2**) was a condemnation of bourgeois values and academic taste as well as a statement of what art should be about—the modern world. Manet himself came from a Parisian bourgeois background, and he studied with a famous academician. His true masters, however, were the painterly artists he copied at the Louvre—Hals, Titian, and the Spaniards Velázquez and Goya. He was a regular at the cafés, especially befriending Courbet, who was his role model.

Out of this background Manet produced the *Luncheon*, which shows two couples picnicking in the Bois de Boulogne. The painting was rejected by the 1863 Salon jurors. But that year they rejected a record number of artists, causing such an uproar that Louis Napoleon decided on a *Salon des refusés* (Salon of the Refused), an exhibition of the rejected artists to be held in conjunction with the official Salon of 1863. Many of these artists preferred not to participate in what was perceived as an inferior exhibition; Manet, however, did.

The public showed up in record numbers to laugh at the rejects, and especially to view Manet's *Luncheon*, which created a scandal by presenting a contemporary scene of a naked woman in a park with two nattily dressed men. The public was outraged, for obviously the nude had to be a prostitute. It did not matter that critics acknowledged that the composition of the painting was based on that of major works by Giorgione and Raphael.

As far as the critics were concerned, referencing these august sources was not enough to overcome Manet's flagrant lack of decorum, a crime he brazenly committed on a roughly seven-by-nine-foot scale. So, why did Manet base his contemporary scene on historical sources? The answer may lie in the artificiality of his figures, who fail to interact convincingly. As pointed out by one art historian, they look like art school students posing to recreate a famous Raphael painting. In effect, Manet is telling us that the present cannot live in the past, which many academicians chose to do. As trumpeted by Baudelaire in 1846,

24.2 Édouard Manet. *Luncheon on the Grass* (*Le Déjeuner sur l'Herbe*). 1863. Oil on canvas, 7' × 8'10" (2.13 × 2.69 m). Musée du Louvre, Paris

Realism

Manet was declaring that artists must find their subject matter, their heroes, in the modern world. Furthermore, he was exposing the disguised eroticism that the tradition of the classical nude had now stooped to. It is possible, as well, that Manet used historical sources as a device to put himself into the long tradition of great art. In effect, he is announcing that his Realism is not only the most valid direction for art to take, but also that it is as important and vital as the great art of the past.

What convinced the jurors and public that Manet was an incompetent sensationalist who deserved to be relegated to the *Salon des refusés* was his style. To their academically focused eye, he could neither model nor create convincing space. The picture looked like a preliminary sketch, not a finished work. The figures are two-dimensional cutouts, flattened by their crisp, silhouetting contours and a flourish of broad brushstrokes that dispenses with the halftones between dark and light needed to mold volume. A shadow indicating a fold on a pants leg, for example, is rendered with one bold, black sweep of the brush. The woman wading in the background is too large for her recessed location and seems to float directly over the seated group. All of the objects—figures, trees, the colorful still life of clothes and basket—hover in space, failing to connect and assemble into a coherent spatial structure.

Manet has undermined the spatial order of the illusionistic Renaissance window and replaced it with a new unifying logic—a sensual sea of brushwork composed of lush, oily, and thickly applied paint that dramatically covers the entire surface of his canvas. Our eyes delight in the lusciousness of his brushwork, the wonderful variety of his Velázquez- and Goya-inspired blacks, the range of greens in the grass, and the deft play of darks next to lights that makes our eyes jump from one light area to another and from one dark patch to the next. These abstract qualities—paint handling and value contrasts, for example—are the new structure of painting, not illusionistic space and modeling. With *Luncheon on the Grass*, Manet began what twentieth-century critics would consider the Modernist tradition, a tradition that emphasized the abstract qualities of art and that would continue for the next hundred years. Manet undoubtedly delighted in how the unfinished, sketchy look of his paintings irreverently countered the slick drawing and modeling of academic tradition and shocked bourgeois taste. Additionally, he used it to create a fleeting, momentary quality that reflected the quickly changing modern world.

EDGAR DEGAS AND JAPONISME Like Manet, Edgar Degas (1834–1917) came from a wealthy background. Initially he aspired to be a history painter. He studied with an Ingres follower and emphasized drawing and modeling in his early work, retaining line even when his art became more painterly. By 1865, Degas entered Manet's and Baudelaire's orbit at the Café Guerbois, and he turned to capturing modern Paris. Degas developed a Manet-inspired painterly approach to his subject, as well as innovative compositional devices that give his images a spontaneous, transitory quality and effectively make a voyeur of the viewer.

A classic work from the 1860s is *The Orchestra of the Paris Opera* (**fig. 24.3**) of 1868–1869. The picture is a genre scene, in which we see not only the members of the orchestra but also the ballet

24.3 Edgar Degas. *The Orchestra of the Paris Opera*. 1868–1869. Oil on canvas, 22¼ × 18³⁄₁₆″ (56.5 × 46.2 cm). Musée d'Orsay, Paris

24.4 Andō Hiroshige. *Plum Estate, Kameido,* from the series *One Hundred Famous Views of Edo.* 1857. Wood block print, 13⅜ × 9″ (34 × 22.8 cm). Brooklyn Museum of Art, New York. Gift of Anna Ferris 30.1478.30

fragment of a complete view. The same is true of the ballet dancers, whose heads and legs are chopped off.

Building on this movement and energy are the planes of the wall, the stage, the front row of the orchestra, and the ballet dancers, all of which are slightly skewed, along with the angular thrust of instruments and the dancers' legs and arms. Space seems compressed, as far and near are dramatically juxtaposed, for example in the dark cello head and brightly colored tutus or ballet skirts. The image seems to climb up the picture plane rather than recede in space, making it appear flattened out. A precise line defines figures and objects, but a sporadic spray of dashing brushwork, best seen in the dancers' tutus, adds spontaneity, giving us a feeling of a passing moment.

Scholars often attribute Degas's innovative compositions to the influence of Japanese prints, which flooded the Parisian market in the late 1850s after Japan was opened up to the West in 1854. The French were especially taken by Japanese culture, and their infatuation was called *japonisme,* a term also used by the English and Americans. Especially intriguing for artists were Japanese prints, works that first arrived in France as packing material for fragile objects but were nonetheless collected by the late 1850s by the artists in Manet's circle, who found them visually fascinating.

As can be seen in *Plum Estate, Kameido* (**fig. 24.4**) by Andō Hiroshige (1797–1858), Japanese image-making was quite foreign to a Western way of seeing. Forms are flat with sharp contours, while space is compressed, the foreground pressed up against the viewer's nose, the background pulled right into the foreground space. There is no transition between near and far. Just the concept of situating a viewer in a tree from which to see the main activity miniaturized in the distance would have been radical to the eye of a Western artist. However, the flat contours, abrupt cropping, and spatial contraction of Japanese prints certainly influenced Degas and Manet, although in a far from obvious manner and never approaching direct copying.

Impressionism: A Different Form of Realism

The label "Impressionism" was coined by a hostile conservative critic in 1874 when reviewing the first exhibition of an artists' collaborative called the *Société anonyme des artistes* (Artists, Inc.), an organization that sought to provide an

dancers onstage. Yet the subject is not just the talented, toiling performers but the intensity, excitement, and fragmentation of contemporary life itself, which is presented in a matter-of-fact way. Degas has put us virtually in the pit, and we feel like unobserved voyeurs. Our view is not head-on but at an angle, which was unusual for a painting at the time but certainly typical for a theatergoer. The cellist is arbitrarily cropped on the right, suggesting that we are only looking at the left side of the orchestra, seeing only a alternative to the Salon. We now refer to that show as the first Impressionist exhibition (there would be eight altogether between 1874 and 1886). Like the general public, the writer found the paintings so sketchy that he felt they were just impressions, not finished paintings.

Impressionism shares with the Realism of Manet and Degas a sketchy unfinished look, a feeling of the moment, and a desire to appear modern. It too presents its subjects matter-of-factly. Many scholars even apply the term Impressionism to the work of Manet and Degas, in part to distinguish their Realism from the earthy, rural Realism of Courbet and to indicate how Impressionism often shares with them a sense of the urbane and the modern. Like Manet and Degas, the Impressionists were interested in recording the transformations occurring in French society, especially the leisure pursuits of the *nouveaux riches*. While they, too, painted city scenes and genre, they focused more on the evolution of the sleepy rural villages surrounding Paris, now easily accessible by train, into bustling suburbs containing, on the one hand, factories, commercial wharves, and railroad trestles, and on the other hand restaurants, regattas, and boating for Parisian weekenders. Rather than the figure, the Impressionists focused more on landscape and cityscape, and instead of constructing their compositions in the studio using models, they worked empirically, out of doors, where they recorded the landscape and weather conditions that they witnessed at a fleeting moment in time. They painted not so much objects as the colored light that bounced off them. In effect, they painted what they saw, not what they knew.

CLAUDE MONET   The leader in developing Impressionism was Claude Monet (1840–1926), who was born and raised in Le Havre in Normandy. He casually studied with an accomplished local landscape painter, who painted outdoors, *en plein air*. But in order to get financial support from his grocer father, he was forced to study in Paris with an academically-minded but liberal painter. In this studio he met Auguste Renoir, who would also become a core member of the Impressionists. Throughout the 1860s, Monet and his friends painted the landscape surrounding Paris, meeting the Barbizon artists, who further encouraged them to paint outdoors. For the Impressionists, however, these paintings were not small studies but large finished products. Painting rapidly in the landscape with bold

brushwork, they sought to capture light, and the color it carried, as it bounced off objects. Monet's extensive use of primary and secondary colors, the principal hues on the traditional color wheel, was also influenced by recent scientific research into color demonstrating that the intensity of complementary colors (for example, blue and orange, red and green, yellow and violet) is increased when they are placed next to one another.

We can see the effectiveness of Monet's palette in *On the Bank of the Seine, Bennecourt* (**fig. 24.5**), painted in 1868 in a small town upriver from Paris, one of the many Seine and Oise river locations that Parisians visited by train on summer weekends, or where they built impressive summer homes. The artist works with glaring sun-drenched whites and bright blues and greens accented with touches of red and yellow. Objects in shadow, such as leaves and grass, retain color and do not go black. Browns are not muddy but a light-filled tan. Monet maintains the strength of his colors by keeping the imagery close to the picture plane, not allowing it to disappear into a dull atmospheric haze to suggest depth. There is no *chiaroscuro* to model forms. The tree foliage is a two-dimensional silhouette, while the blue sky behind is equally flat. The reflection of the house on the water runs up and down the picture plane, reinforcing the two-dimensionality of the broad smears of light and dark blue in the river just below. The solid blue sky is virtually the same shade as the darker blue in the water, a correlation that momentarily pulls the sky to the foreground. Also asserting the surface of the canvas is Monet's bold, variegated brushwork, which changes character from one object to the next and gives the picture a shimmering quality that suggests we are witnessing a fleeting moment in time. The only motif that suggests depth is the rowboat running diagonally back in perspective.

Equally important, contemporaries realized that the brushwork represented the unstable, rapidly changing qualities of modern life. These pictures looked nothing like previous landscapes; they lacked the classical look of Claude Lorrain, the Baroque conventions of the Dutch landscape painters and their earthy palette, and the emotional constructions of the Romantics. Their very look was considered modern, as was their subject matter. We can safely assume that the fashionably dressed woman is not a local, but rather a Parisian, up from the city by train, who has been boating.

24.5 Claude Monet. *On the Bank of the Seine, Bennecourt*. 1868. Oil on canvas, 32⅛ × 39⅝″ (81.5 × 100.7 cm). The Art Institute of Chicago. Mr. and Mrs. Potter Palmer Collection

AUGUSTE RENOIR After meeting Monet and befriending him, Auguste Renoir (1841–1919) also developed an Impressionist style of bright color, bold paint handling, and modern subjects. Often working beside Monet, Renoir painted landscapes. But he was attracted to the figurative tradition as well, and his career straddles the two genres.

Among his best-known figure paintings is *Luncheon of the Boating Party* (**fig. 24.6**) of 1880–1881. The picture's setting is the Restaurant Fournaise on an island in the Seine at Chatou, a small village nine miles by train from Paris. Chatou was especially popular with boaters, and restaurants like this catered to Parisians. In the background, on the river, we can just see sailboats, a rowboat, and a commercial barge. There is also a glimpse of a railroad bridge.

The restaurant party consists of urban types, with the exception of Alphonse Fournaise, the restaurant owner's son, who leans against the railing, his muscular biceps reflecting the time he spends putting rental boats into the water. Renoir portrays a colorful, sundrenched scene of suburban leisure, presenting it as pleasurable, relaxed, and sensuous, qualities enhanced by the lavish spread on the table and the glorious lush brushwork of the tablecloth. The picture has the momentary quality we associate with Realism, achieved in part by the flickering, feathery brushwork and the asymmetrical composition that runs off the right side of the canvas, the picture cropped and fragmented as in Degas's *The Orchestra of the Paris Opera* (fig. 24.3).

24.6 Auguste Renoir. *Luncheon of the Boating Party*. 1880–1881. Oil on canvas, 51 × 69″ (130.2 × 175.6 cm). The Phillips Collection, Washington, D.C. Acquired 1923

MARY CASSATT Another key figure in the Impressionist group was Mary Cassatt (1844–1926), who approached Impressionism from a woman's perspective, her Realism even reflecting the social concerns developing within the women's movement of her time. Cassatt was an American, born into a wealthy family and raised in Pittsburgh. In 1866 she went to Paris and first studied with an artist who offered classes for women. She also studied in Parma and Rome before returning to Paris in 1874, where she befriended Degas and abandoned her academic style for Realism. Invited by Degas, she participated in the fourth Impressionist exhibition in 1879. Now she displayed a bright palette, strong brushwork that hugged the surface, and the Realist compositional devices of asymmetry and cropping.

Like Degas and Manet, Cassatt was a figure painter, and her most famous themes from the late 1870s include women in *loges* (boxes) at the opera, a subject treated by Renoir and Degas as well. She also painted women at home: Reading, visiting, taking tea, sewing, or bathing an infant. She presented the modern woman, sophisticated in dress, manners, and leisure activities. In the 1880s, she abandoned her *loge* theme and focused increasingly on domestic scenes, especially of women and children.

Scholars often attribute Cassatt's subject matter to the restrictions she faced as a female: As a respectable woman, she could not go unattended to the same places as her male counterparts. But more at issue was her belief in the importance of women in society, even if this importance was largely restricted to the home. Her views coincided with developments then occurring in the women's movement. In 1878, the International Congress of Women's Rights was held in Paris, and at the top of its agenda was the need for

24.7 Mary Cassatt. *The Child's Bath*. 1893. Oil on canvas, 39½ × 26″ (100.3 × 66 cm). The Art Institute of Chicago. Robert A. Waller Fund. 1910.2

better education for women, which would not only allow them to become professionals but also to better manage the home and family. The Congress also focused on the important role that women played in nurturing children, advocating that mothers nurse and care for their offspring rather than hiring wet-nurses. This position reflects the increased importance that sociologists placed on the care of children in general in the 1870s, which in part stemmed from a concern about the high infant mortality rate in Europe, especially in France. The path to a healthier society and nation, many argued, began in the home

and was in the hands of the mother who nurtured her children, both physically and emotionally, including attending to hygiene.

Cassatt's many domestic scenes of mothers tending their children, such as *The Child's Bath* (**fig. 24.7**) of 1893, came out of this context. Regular bathing was a modern phenomenon for late nineteenth-century Paris, when people generally bathed only once a week. Not only is the picture about health, but also about intense emotional and physical involvement, as is reflected in the sensual yet tender manner in which the caregiver touches the child.

The picture contains all the ingredients we associate with Realism—the fashionable bourgeois decor, the bright colors, and the sense of spontaneity in the brushwork and skewed composition with its high viewpoint. The style of the picture reflects Cassatt's intense attraction to Japanese prints at this point in her career, an interest that is reflected in the overhead viewpoint as well as in the boldness of her forms and contours. Cassatt was also influenced by her studies of Renaissance art as seen in the strong line-defining contours that have the crispness found in *quattrocento* painting (Italian art of the 1400s). Many of Cassatt's presentations of a mother and child even resemble Renaissance depictions of a Madonna and Child, an allusion that sanctifies the important role of women in creating a better society. But it also reflects the direction that Realism took after 1880, as many of the Impressionists changed course and began to make a more monumental art that recalled the classical art of the past.

British Realism

Realism took a very different form across the English Channel, although the word itself was never applied to art. There Positivism produced a detailed naturalism, an intense truth to nature, and an interest in social types. In Britain, the Industrial Revolution had an almost 100-year headstart over France. Industrialization and urbanization accounted for the poverty and other social ills so familiar to us today from the serialized novels of Charles Dickens (1812–1870), which were set in a cruel, corrupt London suffocated by grime and soot. Materialism and greed were rampant. Cheap, ugly, mass-produced objects replaced the highly refined handmade products that the aristocracy and upper class had once demanded. No longer was the worker a highly trained artisan with pride in his or her product, but a human machine suffering the drudgery of dawn-to-dusk mindless labor to turn out an inferior product without personal identification.

It was the artist, educator, writer, art critic, and environmentalist John Ruskin (1819–1900) who took the lead in attempting to arrest this decline into industrial hell. Among Ruskin's most prominent beliefs was the need for contemporary society to aspire to a new spirituality and moral pride, which required adherence to truth and identification with the divinity of nature. He advocated art education for all social classes, for the working-class producers as well as the bourgeois consumers. He firmly believed that art was a necessity, not a luxury, for it molded people's lives and moral values; great art made great people. And by art, Ruskin meant not only painting, sculpture, and architecture but also the decorative arts, all of which had to be well crafted, beautiful, and honest, as in the Middle Ages.

Ruskin's emphasis on nature and religion marks the beginning of the nineteenth-century search for a simpler life, one that rejected the advances of urbanization and industrialization, and the theme was to dominate the art of the closing decades of the century.

The Pre-Raphaelite Brotherhood

Ruskin championed the Pre-Raphaelite Brotherhood, a society started in 1848 by three students enrolled in the Royal Academy School. Among them were William Holman Hunt and Dante Gabriel Rossetti, the leader and spokesperson. The PRB, as they signed their paintings, denounced the art of the Royal Academy and most painting since the Italian Renaissance after Raphael's early period. They found the work decadent in that it clouded truth and fact with a muddy *chiaroscuro* and placed a premium on such artificial, formal qualities as elegant contours or pleasing compositional patterning. Like Ruskin, the Pre-Raphaelites abhorred bourgeois materialism and taste. Their heroes were the fifteenth-century Italian and Netherlandish "primitives," such as Jan van Eyck (see page 291), whose work they perceived as simpler, more direct, and hence sincere in its attempt to represent nature. They also considered this work more spiritual and moral because it was identified with the intensely religious Late Gothic period.

WILLIAM HOLMAN HUNT The most religious of the Pre-Raphaelite Brotherhood was William

Holman Hunt (1827–1910), who came from a poor working-class family. His work is characterized by a combination of Victorian moral didacticism and intense naturalism. *The Awakening Conscience* (**fig. 24.8**) of 1853–1854 was inspired by a passage in Charles Dickens's *David Copperfield* when David's friend, the simple fisherman Peggoty, goes searching for his beloved Emily, who has run off with an amoral dandy. Hunt tells the tale of one of the thousands of poor women appearing in the Realist literature of the period who perceived prostitution as their only hope of financial security even though it would inevitably lead to ruin. While sitting on her lover's lap and singing a song, a kept woman becomes aware of the lyrics, thinks of her family,

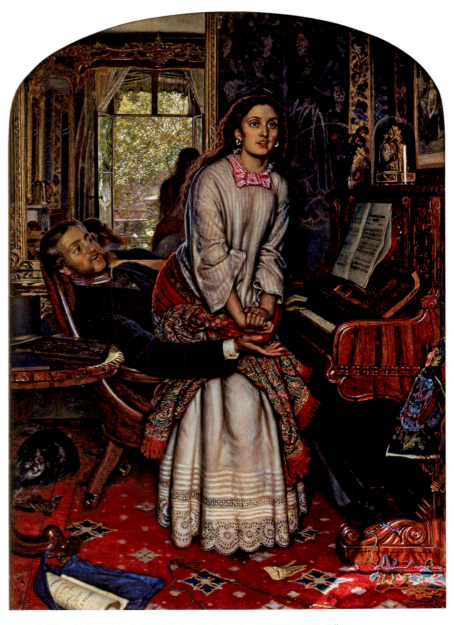

24.8 William Holman Hunt. *The Awakening Conscience*. 1853–1854. Oil on canvas, 29½ × 22″ (76.2 × 55.9 cm). Tate Britain, London

24.9 William Morris (Morris & Co.). Green Dining Room (William Morris Room). 1867. Victoria & Albert Museum, London

and suddenly abhors her sinful situation, from which she must then immediately escape.

Hunt renders the room, cluttered with the shiny, vulgar products of crass consumerism, with a microscopic attention to detail worthy of Jan van Eyck. As in a Van Eyck painting, every object seems to function symbolically. The cat chasing the bird under the table reflects the kept woman's position as prey, and the clock approaching high noon denotes that the time left for decisive action is quickly expiring. The background mirror reflects an open window—freedom—and through it the purity and beauty of sunlit nature beckons, the road to her salvation. The density of objects and figures in the painting eliminates the compositional patterning and pleasing aesthetic contours that the PRB disliked.

WILLIAM MORRIS About 1856, William Morris (1834–1896) became involved with the Pre-Raphaelites. He would dabble in architecture

and become a renowned poet, but his true calling was implementing Ruskin's theories about replacing shoddy mass-produced products with well-designed hand-crafted ones that, as in the Middle Ages, would reconnect workers and their commodities. In 1865 he opened a design company, which eventually was called Morris & Co. It manufactured beautifully crafted fabrics, wallpaper, tapestries, carpets, tiles, furniture, and stained glass, with Morris himself designing most of the wallpaper and fabrics.

The motifs and palette of Morris and his company were organic and Gothic, creating an aura of nature and spirituality. This aesthetic is apparent in the dining room (**fig. 24.9**) that he designed in 1867 for a new applied arts museum in South Kensington, London, known today as the Victoria & Albert Museum. The gold-ground panels represent the 12 months of the year. Morris's wallpaper, laboriously hand-printed from wood blocks, is a flat abstract pattern based on an olive branch. The chest is designed in Late Gothic/early Renaissance style. Morris's impact on the applied arts was far-reaching, launching what is known as the Arts and Crafts Movement, which soon spread to the United States.

The Aesthetic Movement: Personal Psychology and Repressed Eroticism

While William Morris kept the moral and spiritual program of Ruskin alive with his Arts and Crafts Movement, the Pre-Raphaelite group had dissolved by 1860. Rossetti, who had not been very productive in the 1850s, gravitated toward a visionary art set in a medieval guise and expressing his own personal psychology, not social morality. Running through his paintings is an undercurrent of repressed sexuality, a reflection of the strict moral codes of Victorian Britain that did not allow for a display of sexual appeal or even the discussion of sex.

DANTE GABRIEL ROSSETTI Today Rossetti (1828–1882) is best known and most appreciated for his post-PRB work. As the initial leader and spokesperson for the Pre-Raphaelites, his shift from its principles was significant. His *Beata Beatrix* (**fig. 24.10**), begun in 1864, is closer to this later phase of his production, and anticipates the Aesthetic Movement, which we will look at next. The picture is a portrait of his wife and most frequent model, Elizabeth Siddal, who had committed suicide in 1862 by taking an overdose of laudanum, an addictive derivative of opium used to control pain but often abused.

Rossetti depicts Siddal as Beatrice, the elusive, fictitious spiritual lover of his namesake, the Italian poet Dante Alighieri, in Dante's *La Vita Nuova* (ca. 1293), and the style is early Renaissance in its simplicity and linearity (compare fig. 14.7). The sundial in her hand records the hour of nine, when Siddal expired, while a haloed dove, reminiscent of the Holy Spirit, drops the poppy of death in her lap. In the background, Dante and Love walk the streets of Florence, missing each other in the fog, a prefiguration of Beatrice's death before they ever meet. Siddal is dressed in medieval garb, her famous flowing red hair looking very Late Gothic in style. Her head is encased in a "halo" of orange and yellow. She appears in a transitory state between life and death, her expression suggesting prayer, longing, resignation, and even sexuality, all a reflection of Rossetti's state of mind at the loss of his beloved and his own sexual frustration.

24.10 Dante Gabriel Rossetti. *Beata Beatrix*. ca. 1864–1870. Oil on canvas, 34 × 26″ (86.4 × 66 cm). Tate Britain, London

Rippling contours add to the erotic tension. We are now far removed from the Realism and social concerns of the Brotherhood and witnessing the emergence of an art that expresses fantasy and deep psychological urges.

Rossetti's strange, compelling dream anticipated the Aesthetic Movement. The English catalyst for this new attitude was the poet Algernon Charles Swinburne (1837–1909), who in turn was influenced in the 1850s by the French critic Théophile Gautier. Gautier was a leading advocate of "art for art's sake," a theory maintaining that art's function was first and foremost to be beautiful, to appeal to the senses and not project moral values or tell stories. Rossetti came under Swinburne's spell. But the most famous, indeed notorious proponent of the Aesthetic Movement is the American painter James Abbott McNeill Whistler.

24.11 James Abbott McNeill Whistler. *Symphony in White No. II: The Little White Girl.* 1864. Oil on canvas, 30⅛ × 20⅛″ (76.7 × 51.3 cm). Tate Britain, London

JAMES ABBOTT McNEILL WHISTLER Raised in New England and Russia, Whistler (1834–1903) studied painting in Paris from 1855 to 1859, enrolling in the same studio as Monet, whom he met. He also befriended Courbet and initally made his mark as a Realist, painting scenes of contemporary life that captured the underbelly of the city. After moving to London in 1859 (he never returned to America), he continued to spend long periods in Paris, and traveled back and forth between the two cities into the 1860s, maintaining his Parisian connections and friendships and submitting to the Salons. He knew Gautier through Courbet and Manet, and in London he befriended Swinburne.

By 1863, Whistler renounced French Realism to pursue Aestheticism, an example of which is his *Symphony in White No. I: The White Girl*, a title probably inspired by Gautier's poem "Symphony in White Major." Whistler submitted the picture to the 1863 *Salon des refusés*, where it hung not far from Manet's *Luncheon on the Grass* (fig. 24.2). Like Gautier's poem, which is a complex interfacing of different white visions, the painting orchestrates a range of whites, soft yellows, and reds in a full-length portrait of the artist's mistress Jo Hiffernan, who is dressed in white against a largely white ground. While Gautier and Swinburne conceptually influenced Whistler, visually the artist came under the spell of *japonisme*, an influence that is more clearly stated in *Symphony in White No. II: The Little White Girl* (**fig. 24.11**) of 1864. Here, Jo leans on the mantelpiece of Whistler's London home, surrounded by a Japanese blue-and-white vase, fan, and a spray of cherry blossoms, often identified with Japan. At one level, the painting is a sensual display of abstract color, shape, and composition. Using thin, delicate brushstrokes and almost transparent layers of paint, Whistler creates a symphony of whites, yellows, reds, pinks, and blues that gracefully dance across the picture plane. He plays the softness of his paint and such forms as Jo's dress against the rectangular linearity of the mantel, mirror, and reflected picture frames. The flowers entering the composition on the right are another delicate touch, a Japanese compositional device used earlier by Degas to create fragmentation and spontaneity but here to make the petals seem to float magically. Whistler's use of "symphony" in the title reflects how the artist drew a parallel between painting and music, viewing his art as an abstract arrangement of color and form. In the following decade, his work would become increasingly abstract, especially in a series of works entitled *Nocturnes*, a title again reflecting a musical parallel.

Realism in America

The ripple effect of the revolutions of 1848 did not reach America, although it did produce waves of new immigrants. A more defining benchmark for the United States is the Civil War of 1861–1865, which had a devastating physical, psychological, and economic impact on the nation. The Garden of Eden was ravaged. After the war, that metaphor was replaced by the *Gilded Age*, a term coined by Mark Twain and his co-author for an 1871 book of the same title describing the robber barons, the new industrialists and financiers who made vast fortunes, often exploiting workers. The period is also defined by continued Western expansion, fulfilling what the nation saw as its God-given manifest destiny to overrun the North American continent. Survey teams mapped the new territories, and poorly paid workers completed the Transcontinental Railroad, connecting East and West, in 1869. By 1890, the government had subdued the Native American nations, either by containment in restricted territories or by violent annihilation.

Scientific Realism: Thomas Eakins

Thomas Eakins (1844–1916), a Philadelphian, was among the earliest and most powerful Realist painters in America. His scenes of the modern world included not only middle-class leisure activities and the popular sports and pastimes of post-Civil War America but also surgery clinics portraying surgeons as modern heroes and highlighting new scientific techniques such as anesthesia and antiseptic surgery. Eakins even brought a scientific approach to his Realism, which made it quite different from the Realism of Manet and Degas that he witnessed in Paris from 1866 to 1869 while studying with a renowned academician.

Among Eakins's first works upon returning to Philadelphia was a series of sculling pictures, among them *Max Schmitt in a Single Scull* (also called *The Champion Single Sculls*) (**fig. 24.12**), a painting that reflects the rising popularity of the sport and presents Schmitt, the winner of a championship race on the Schuylkill River in Pennsylvania, as a hero of modern life. While

24.12 Thomas Eakins. *Max Schmitt in a Single Scull* (*The Champion Single Sculls*). 1871. Oil on canvas, 32¼ × 46¼" (82 × 117.5 cm). The Metropolitan Museum of Art, New York. Alfred N. Punnett Endowment Fund and George D. Pratt Gift, 1934. 34.92

the picture looks like a *plein-air* painting, we do not see a quickly recorded Impressionist moment but a painstakingly reconstructed event in time. Eakins's paintings are grounded in intense scientific inquiry designed to ensure the accuracy of his Realism. He made numerous perspective studies of the boats and oars, which result in the river receding with breathtaking mathematical precision, firmly locking the boats in place in space. He carefully studied light effects and anatomy. His quest for realism drove him to record minute details, including a steamboat behind the distant bridges, and a train on a railroad bridge, details beyond the reach of normal vision.

Iconic Image: Winslow Homer

Winslow Homer (1836–1910) was in Paris at about the same time as Eakins. He was already disposed toward painting the modern world, for he began his career in 1857 as a magazine illustrator, recording the latest fashions and social activities and later covering the Civil War. He was in Paris in 1866–1867, where he saw the

work of Courbet and Manet, but he was too early to experience the full impact of Impressionism. Upon returning to New York, he made outdoor scenes of the middle class engaged in leisure activities of contemporary life, such as playing croquet, swimming at the newest shore resorts, and taking horseback tours in the White Mountains of New Hampshire, diversions now accessible by train.

Rather than portraying a fleeting moment, however, Homer created iconic symbolic images of American life and issues. We can see this emblematic approach in his *Snap the Whip* (**fig. 24.13**) of 1872. This visual record of a children's game appears at first glance to be an Americanization of Impressionism, for the image is a sun-filled scene rendered with fairly strong color and flashy passages of brushwork. But Homer's color is not as intense as the Impressionists', nor is his brushwork as loose. The picture is not about color and light and empirically capturing a specific scene and transient moment. This image is frozen. The figures are carefully outlined,

24.13 Winslow Homer. *Snap the Whip*. 1872. Oil on canvas, 22¼ × 36½″ (56.5 × 92.7 cm). The Butler Institute of American Art, Youngstown, Ohio

modeled, and monumental, their solidity reinforced by the geometry of the one-room schoolhouse and the bold backdrop of the mountain, which parallels the direction of the boys' movement. The barefoot children in their plain country clothes, like the one-room schoolhouse behind them, are emblems of simplicity and wholesomeness, their youth projecting innocence and future hope for a recently reunified country. At a time when the nation was staggering under the weight of the disillusionment brought on by the Civil War and the turmoil of rampant industrialization, *Snap the Whip* embodied the country's lost innocence and was a nostalgic appeal for values that were quickly fading into memory.

Photography: A Mechanical Medium for Mass-Produced Art

In 1839 the new medium of photography was commercially introduced in both France and England. As a mechanical process that would eventually lend itself to mass-production and popular culture, it was a perfect fit with the Industrial Revolution and seems a natural consequence of it. It was also a perfect tool for the Positivist era, for initially it was largely perceived as a recording device for cataloguing, documenting, and supporting scientific inquiry. It had the appearance of being objective, paralleling the matter-of-fact presentation of much Realism and Impressionism.

First Innovations

In 1838, Louis-Jacques-Mandé Daguerre (1787–1851) unveiled the **daguerreotype**, a photographic process that exposed light on a silver iodide-coated copper plate, and later a glass plate, and allowed for one image, which remained on that plate. Meanwhile, in England, William Henry Fox Talbot (1800–1877) announced in 1839 that he could fix an image on a paper negative, rather than on metal or glass, and in 1841 he took out a patent for the new negative-positive photograph that he called a **calotype**, a salted paper print that allowed for infinite printing of the same image.

Both the daguerreotype and the calotype were displaced in the early 1850s by the simultaneous invention in France and Britain of the **wet-collodion process**, which cut exposure time to under a second and produced a sharp, easily reproducible negative. At about the same time, the **albumen print** was developed, which used salted egg white on paper, creating a smooth, more refined surface that revealed greater detail with less graininess. For the next 30 to 40 years, photographers used wet-collodion plates for recording images and then printed them on albumen paper.

Recording the World

By the 1850s the most prevalent use of photography was for recording the world: People, sights, and objects. These pictures were generally viewed as fact, which is ironic since, as we shall see, photographers could manipulate images in various ways, including the selection of motif and the objects to be included or excluded in a photograph.

PORTRAITURE Among the most celebrated early portraitists of the era was the Parisian Gaspard-Félix Tournachon (1820–1910), known simply as Nadar. He began cashing in on the public infatuation with celebrities by mass-producing albumen prints of the famous, specializing in writers, actors, performers, and artists of bohemian Paris. His background as a caricaturist proved invaluable in setting up his shots, enabling him to create incisive portraits that captured the essence of his sitter's mystique.

We can see this skill in Nadar's 1854–1855 portrait of the art critic Théophile Gautier (**fig. 24.14**), who although in repose has a forceful presence. A low camera angle makes the sitter loom large, a quality reinforced by the stomach protruding through the parted coat. The artistically out-of-focus right side of the figure, anathema in an era of sharp-focus photography, serves as a foil to the in-focus bulk of Gautier's body. Nadar spotlights the writer's forehead and casts the eyes in shadow, suggesting acute mental power and a moody thoughtfulness.

VIEWS Along with portraits, views dominated photography, for they allowed people to travel the world without leaving their living room. Books of photographs of exotic, and not so exotic, places began to appear, such as *Egypt, Nubia, Palestine and Syria*, published in 1852. More popular than such albums, which could be quite expensive, were **stereocards**, which by the 1860s were as prevalent as musical compact disks are today. Stereocards are side-by-side photographs of the same image taken by a camera with two lenses, replicating human binocular vision. When put into a special viewer, the twin flat pictures appear as a single three-dimensional image. To accommodate the tremendous demand for these cards, distributing companies stocked as many as 300,000 different images at one time.

Among the views popular with Americans were those of the frontier. A large contingent of American photographers, like their fellow painters, specialized in landscape, traveling west, often with survey teams, to record the sublime wilderness that symbolized the nation. One of the first and most famous of this group is Carleton Watkins (1829–1916), who beginning in 1861 made hundreds of glass stereographic views of Yosemite along with about a thousand 18- by 22-inch albumen prints.

24.14 Nadar. *Théophile Gautier*. 1854–1855. Albumen salted paper print, mounted on Bristol board, 9⅓ × 7⅓" (23.6 × 18.6 cm). Musée d'Orsay, Paris

24.15 Carleton E. Watkins. *Yosemite Valley from the Best General View*. 1865–1866. Albumen print, 16⅛ × 20½" (85 × 113 cm). Courtesy Janet Lehr Inc., New York / Vered Gallery, East Hampton, New York

The results, as seen in *Yosemite Valley from the Best General View* (**fig. 24.15**), made on a second trip to Yosemite in 1865–1866, were so breathtaking that when shown to President Lincoln they helped convince him to preserve Yosemite as a park. Continuing the romantic tradition of Thomas Cole, Watkins captures the sublime scale of the American wilderness, the mountain peaks dramatically dwarfing Yosemite Falls, one of the highest falls in America. Watkins produced a lush image by working up extremely rich textures in the developing process and a sense of drama by creating powerful value contrasts and a composition of forceful diagonals descending from both right and left. To keep the sky from going a monotonous white, Watkins used a second negative to add clouds.

Reporting the News: Photojournalism

Early photography also recorded famous events, and this was the forerunner of photojournalism. Among the most outstanding examples are images of the Civil War, such as *A Harvest of Death* (**fig. 24.16**) by Timothy O'Sullivan (ca. 1840–1882), who like Watkins became one of the great photographers of the West. Before setting off to document the Civil War, O'Sullivan began his career as an apprentice to Mathew Brady

(1823–1896), owner of the most famous photographic portrait gallery in America, located in New York. (Abraham Lincoln sat for Brady over 30 times and credited Brady's flattering 1860 portrait for helping him win that November's presidential election.) In 1862–1863, O'Sullivan signed up with the photographic team of Alexander Gardner and contributed 44 images to the album *Gardner's Photographic Sketchbook of the War* (1866).

In *A Harvest of Death*, we feel the power of the documentary reality of photography, which a painted image can never have. We see *real* people and *real* death—images of an actual event on a definite date, the Battle of Gettysburg on July 3, 1863—not a fictitious image. Although we know that the war photographers often moved objects and bodies for the sake of their image, we have no evidence that O'Sullivan did so here. In any case, he conveys the grim reality of war. The anonymous corpses are as lifeless as bales of hay waiting to be collected, their dark forms hauntingly contrasted with the void of the overcast sky. The cropped bodies at the right and left add to the brutality of the scene, so convincingly registered with the gaping mouth on the face of the dead soldier in the foreground. The living are pushed deep into the background, shrouded in

24.16 Timothy O'Sullivan. *A Harvest of Death, Gettysburg, Pennsylvania, July 1863*, from Alexander Gardner's *Gardner's Photographic Sketchbook of the War.* 1866. Albumen print (also available as stereocard), 7 × 8¹¹/₁₆″ (17.8 × 22 cm). Library of Congress, Washington, D.C. Brady Civil War Collection

the morning mist, as though life during this seemingly endless national conflict is itself dissolving into just the barest memory.

Photography as Art: Pictorialism and Combination Printing

Not all nineteenth-century photographers saw the new medium as primarily a tool to document reality. Some viewed it as high art and deliberately explored photography's aesthetic potential, confident that it was as valid an art form as painting and sculpture. This attitude, which some critics found threatening, was more prevalent in Europe than America in the first 50 years following the advent of photography.

ENGLISH PICTORIALISM In London, a group of photographers began making composite pictures designed to look like Old Masters or esteemed contemporary painting. They used as many as 30 negatives to make their patchwork images and experimented with cut-and-paste assemblage. The results were heavy-handed photographs that were far from seamless and did not look lifelike. Their style is called Pictorialism, because the staged images were meant to look like paintings.

The most successful Pictorialists to a modern eye were those who did not make composite images and instead manipulated the camera and printing process to meet their needs. Although far less well-known during her lifetime, Julia Margaret Cameron (1815–1879) is perhaps the most celebrated today of the British Pictorialists. Her trademark was an out-of-focus blurring of images to make them seem painterly, as in *Sister Spirits* (**fig. 24.17**) of about 1865. Like the other Pictorialists, she staged scenes using actors, costumes, and sets, and she illustrated such literary sources as the Bible, Shakespeare, and the then poet laureate Alfred, Lord Tennyson (1809–1892). Stylistically, her images recall artists as diverse as Rembrandt and Perugino, Raphael's teacher.

Sister Spirits reflects the impact of the Aesthetic Movement, an example of which is seen in Rossetti's *Beata Beatrix* (fig. 24.10). The scene in Cameron's photograph evokes a spiritual late medieval or early Renaissance past. The women look as though they have stepped out of a *quattrocento* painting and suggest such saints as Mary and Anne; the two children look like angels, and the sleeping child like the Christ Child. One can also view the picture as the three ages of woman, since the title suggests that the baby is most likely female. Cameron's blurred foreground is more than just a gimmick to give the image a painterly touch. It also carries psychological and symbolic meaning, for by dissolving the flowers and baby, leaving them unformed, Cameron makes the focused women consciously aware of the undetermined fate of the sleeping infant. Concern, pensiveness, and questioning are registered on the faces, and we sense a spiritual female bonding in this tight grouping of figures, who are closed off in the background as the image again goes fuzzy. While the image has sensual elements, it does not present women as objects meant for a male viewer, nor as appendages to a male world. Instead it reflects a powerful female vision as it embraces a female spirituality.

Cameron was generally criticized not only for her blurry images, which were attributed to incompetence, but also for just making photographs. As a female photographer in a sexist society, she found it difficult getting men to pose for her. She was criticized for exhibiting, which was a rare event for respectable British women in the Victorian era, and she was admonished for selling her photographs through a major London print dealer because it was deemed inappropriate for women to earn money. By redefining focus, Cameron challenged not only what was becoming the normative approach to photographic vision but also a vocation that was specifically male. Ironically, by the end of the century, men adopted her vision.

24.17 Julia Margaret Cameron. *Sister Spirits*. ca. 1865. Albumen print, 12⁷⁄₁₆ × 10½" (31.6 × 26.6 cm). George Eastman House, Rochester, New York. Gift of Eastman Kodak Company

Architecture and the Industrial Revolution

Iron was another product of the Industrial Revolution, and its relationship to architecture was as nebulous as that of photography to fine art. Initially, in the late eighteenth and early nineteenth centuries, iron was used for civil engineering, in such projects as bridges and factories. Soon, it was used for the columns in textile factories and by 1796–1797 for an entire internal structure. Revival styles continued to dominate architecture up to the closing decades of the nineteenth century, but the use of iron, while quite limited, freed buildings and civic structures from historicism because form (design) was now determined by the material and by engineering principles, thus setting the stage for the advent of modern architecture in Chicago in the 1880s, as we shall see in the next chapter. The pragmatism of iron construction and the blunt presentation of the medium's structural properties parallel the pragmatism and realism of the Age of Positivism.

Ferrovitreous Structures: Train Sheds and Exhibition Palaces

In the early nineteenth century, builders often used cast iron for the columns of Gothic Revival churches, and in the 1830s, with the rise of railroads, they employed it for train sheds as well. The sheds had to span parallel tracks and platforms and be high enough to allow steam and smoke to dissipate. The cast-iron skeleton supported a roof of glass, and this combination of iron and glass is often called ferrovitreous.

Perhaps the most famous ferrovitreous building of the nineteenth century is the Crystal Palace (**fig. 24.18**), built in London in 1851 to house the first great international trade fair, the Great Exhibition of the Works of Industry of All Nations. The exposition was not just a trade fair but a celebration of Western industrialization. England's preeminent greenhouse architect, Sir Joseph Paxton (1801–1865), designed the building and with engineers erected what was essentially a giant greenhouse. While the ferrovitreous

24.18 Sir Joseph Paxton. The Crystal Palace, London. 1851; reerected in Sydenham 1852; destroyed by fire 1936

late 19th Century Art

24.19 Gustave Eiffel. Eiffel Tower. 1887–1889. Paris

late 19th century Art

31 Mars 1889

materials were the same as in Paxton's earlier greenhouses, the form was not, for it resembled an English cathedral, with a long, barrel-vaulted center nave, a lower barrel-vaulted transept, and stepped-down side aisles. (After the exhibition closed, the structure was dismantled and moved to Sydenham in South London, where another transept was added. It was later burnt down.) The building was a cathedral of industry, which had become the new religion.

Announcing the Future: The Eiffel Tower

The most famous iron structure from the period is the Eiffel Tower (**fig. 24.19**), erected by the French engineer Gustave Eiffel (1832–1923) in 1887–1889 as an entrance to the 1889 Paris International Exposition. To create his tower, Eiffel basically appropriated a **trussed pylon** from the many bridges he had already constructed. At 984 feet (300 meters) high, twice the height of any other structure then in the world, it dominated the city, and because its design was largely due to its structural integrity and not to a standard architectural style, it initially affronted the Parisians, who declared it an eyesore. The lacework tower was so thin that it looked fragile and unstable, and Eiffel added arches at the base and organic decoration on the two platforms (removed in the 1930s) to make visitors more comfortable with his radical, visionary structure. The tower anticipated the Modernist architecture of the next century, one that would shed historical references and instead allow style to reflect the nature and geometry of the new building materials.

SUMMARY

Widespread revolutions rocked many countries throughout Europe in 1848, a year that coincided with the rise of a philosophy of materialism and pragmatism, replacing Romantic imagination. Europeans increasingly regarded science and proven facts as the foundation of knowledge. Art in this so-called Age of Positivism became defined by Realism. Rather than idealizing life, artists candidly depicted the realities of the modern era, from the harsh existence of the poor to the leisure pursuits of the well-to-do. In landscape painting this Realism evolved into Impressionism, which documented the transformation of parts of rural France into Parisian suburbs.

With the rise of Louis Napoleon following the Revolution of 1848, French society was greatly transformed. Industrialization and the rise of the bourgeoisie were intensely accelerated and Paris was transformed into its modern-day form. Artists recorded the dramatic societal transformation of France. Gustave Courbet depicted the lifestyle of the provinces and laboring classes. Beginning in the 1860s, painters like Édouard Manet and Edgar Degas shifted Realism's focus to city life, whereas Impressionist artists like Claude Monet relied on careful observation to record the hues of both natural and human-made objects.

In England industrialization and urbanization engendered new wealth for some people but abject poverty for others. Led by John Ruskin, many intellectuals decried the rise of crass materialism and amorality. In art, the era's Positivist mentality resulted in a detailed naturalism, truth to nature, and interest in social issues, as seen in the work of the Pre-Raphaelite Brotherhood. A similar emphasis on spirituality and naturalism surfaced in the decorative arts as well, led by William Morris's design company, which manufactured beautiful hand-crafted objects. In contrast to France, Realism died out early in England, supplanted in the 1860s by the Aesthetic Movement. Led by J. A. M. Whistler, artists embraced an "art for art's sake" aesthetic that also explored private visions and repressed eroticism.

The Civil War rather than the Revolution of 1848 had the greatest impact on the United States during this period. Winslow Homer, for example, produced iconic and naturalist genre scenes incorporating symbolic imagery about the war. Meanwhile, Thomas Eakins applied a scientific Naturalism to his Realist presentations of contemporary America.

The perfect tool for the Positivist era, photography was used initially to record the world and document scientific inquiry. Portraits and places were favorite subjects. However, many photographers thought of their medium as art, not as a mechanical tool. Imitating painting, these photographers, called Pictorialists, staged their motifs and manipulated their images.

Iron helped free architecture from the eclecticism of revival styles. Used mainly for such non-stately buildings as train sheds, and often combined with glass, iron buildings were pragmatically skeletal, with form (that is, design) following function and having no historical references. The Eiffel Tower, built for the 1889 International Exposition in Paris, epitomizes this modern approach to building design.

ART IN TIME

- 1849–1850—Courbet, *Burial at Ornans*

- 1854—Commodore Perry of the United States opens up Japan to trade with the West

- 1854–1855—Nadar, *Théophile Gautier*

- 1859—Charles Darwin publishes *The Origin of Species*, formulating the theory of evolution

- 1861–1865—American Civil War

- 1861—Abolition of serfdom in Russia

- 1864—Whistler, *Symphony in White No. II: The Little White Girl*

- 1876—Alexander Graham Bell patents the telephone

- 1885—Marxist party founded in Russia

- 1887–1889—Eiffel Tower built in Paris

25

Progress and Its Discontents: Post-Impressionism, Symbolism, and Art Nouveau, 1880–1905

The closing decades of the nineteenth century presented a cultural dichotomy. On one side were those who optimistically reveled in the wealth, luxury, and technological progress of the industrialized world. On the other were those who perceived these same qualities as signs of decadence, excess, and moral turpitude. The former experienced exuberance and pride, the latter despair and anxiety. Depending on one's viewpoint, the period was either La Belle Epoque, *"the beautiful era," or* Le Fin de Siècle, *"the end of the century."*

The end of the century, as well as the 14 years leading up to World War I, indeed constituted a period of unprecedented economic growth and prosperity, nurtured by virtually 40 years of peace following the 1870 Franco-Prussian War. National consolidation was largely complete, with many countries functioning as republics. Germany and France joined Britain and Belgium as truly industrialized nations, with Germany producing twice as much steel as Britain by 1914. The United States was included as well in this exclusive group. Spurred by both capitalism and a heated nationalism was a dramatic increase in imperialism, which resulted in the carving up of Africa as well as parts of Asia and the Pacific islands into fiefdoms to be economically exploited.

The modern era, which began in the eighteenth century, now evolved into a new phase called modernity, often labeled the "New Industrial Revolution." The steam engine was refined and improved. Electricity, the telephone, the internal combustion engine, automobiles, submarines, airplanes, oil, moving pictures, and machines increasingly defined modern life, whose pace quickened even as it became more comfortable and efficient. In 1901, Guglielmo

Marconi sent a wireless signal across the Atlantic, further shrinking the globe.

These accomplishments resulted in a dramatic increase in a European sense of superiority. Many cultural anthropologists, however, refused to label any society as better than any other, and found tribal societies to be just as complex as Western civilization. The mores and values of any culture, they argued, were appropriate to its environment and circumstances. Those Europeans who lamented industrialization and who were suspicious of unchecked progress perceived the newly colonized, exploited territories as unspoiled utopias, havens from the materialistic evils of modern civilization. Continuing the tradition launched by Jean-Jacques Rousseau in the eighteenth century, they viewed these so-called primitive societies as still steeped in nature and thus virtuous and pure, as well as connected to universal spiritual forces.

Also arising in the late nineteenth century in reaction to modernity was a renewed search for the spiritual, with a growing number of people fleeing progress by embracing an intense spirituality. People were drawn to orthodox Western religions as well as to Eastern-inspired practices

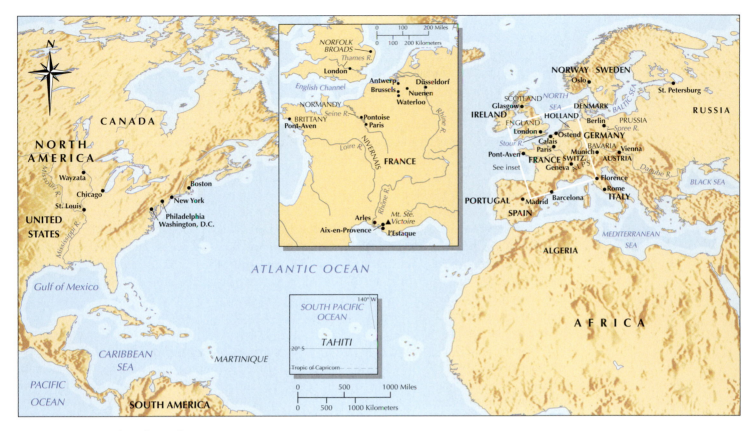

Map 25.1 Europe and North America 1904–1914

such as Theosophy. Many were also drawn to animism and the occult.

The late nineteenth century marks the rise of psychology. The German physiologist Wilhelm Wundt (1832–1920) transformed psychology from a philosophy to a natural science by basing it on scientific method, while the research of the Russian Ivan Pavlov (1849–1936) sparked an intense interest in how human behavior is conditioned by experience and environment. And in Vienna, the neurologist Sigmund Freud began to formulate his theories of the unconscious, publishing his *Interpretation of Dreams* in 1900. This interest in the mind and the elemental forces driving human responses went well beyond science to permeate popular and high culture, and artists as diverse as Auguste Rodin and Edvard Munch increasingly focused on the unseen forces residing deep within the unconscious that produced such outward manifestations as sexual urges and anxiety.

In many respects progress was the watchword of the late nineteenth century, and the force to which some artists responded. The vast majority, however, rejected it, seeking a spiritual, utopian, or primitive alternative. The result was a range of styles or movements, chief among them Post-Impressionism, Symbolism, and Art

Nouveau. Most of the artists built on the brilliant formal innovations of Manet and the Impressionists and created work that was more abstract than representational. Their art was also highly personal, not reflecting a group vision. Consequently many artists, such as Vincent van Gogh and Paul Cézanne, cultivated their own distinctive form of mark-making. Often their work was visionary, depicting fantasies and dreamworlds, and often it was spiritual, as it sought relief from the crass, empty materialism of modernity and a more meaningful explanation for existence. Many artists found their subject matter in the sanctuary of the classical, medieval, and biblical past, which the Realists had so fiercely rejected. Even modern architecture indulged in fantasy and spirituality. While Realism and Impressionism had sought to capture the essence of the modern world, Post-Impressionism, Symbolism, and Art Nouveau largely struggled to escape it and provide an antidote.

Post-Impressionism

The early twentieth-century British art critic Roger Fry coined the term Post-Impressionism to describe the avant-garde art that followed

Impressionism, work that became a springboard to take art in new directions. Each of the four major Post-Impressionist artists—Paul Cézanne, Georges Seurat, Vincent van Gogh, and Paul Gauguin—developed a unique style. Still, there are artistic conditions that unify the period from 1880 to 1904. The Post-Impressionists rejected the empiricism of Realism and Impressionism in order to create art that was more monumental, universal, and even visionary. The Post-Impressionists also rejected a collective way of seeing, which we saw in Impressionism; instead, each artist developed a personal aesthetic. Like the Impressionists, however, many Post-Impressionists continued to mine Japanese art for aesthetic ideas. They also maintained the anti-bourgeois, anti-academic attitude of the Impressionists, similarly turning to artists' cooperatives and private galleries to promote their art.

Paul Cézanne: Toward Abstraction

Actually, Cézanne (1839–1906) is the same generation as the Impressionists, developing his Post-Impressionism in tandem with their art. Born into a wealthy but socially isolated family in Aix-en-Provence in southern France, he went to Paris to study art in 1861. He enrolled at a drawing academy, but was essentially self-taught, copying paintings in the Louvre by Delacroix and Courbet, among others, and developing dark, emotional, painterly work. His mature style began to evolve in 1872, when he started looking at Impressionism. The emotionalism of his early work dissipated, his palette lightened, even becoming colorful, and his compositions took on a powerful structural integrity, which had been suggested in his earlier work but now blossomed. As he would state later in life, he wanted "to make of Impressionism something solid, like the art in the museums."

We can see how Cézanne achieved this goal in a work from the next decade, *Mont Sainte-Victoire* (**fig. 25.1**), painted around 1885–1887 in Provence, where he would spend the remainder of his life. Typical of Impressionism, this canvas presents a light-filled landscape painted with broad brushstrokes and fairly bright color. The picture seems to shimmer at first, then it freezes. Cézanne has locked his image into a subtle network of shapes that echo one another. The curves and bends of the foreground branches can be found in the distant mountain and foothills. The diagonal lines on the edges of the green pastures reverberate in the houses, mountain slopes, and the directionality of the clusters

of parallel dashlike brushstrokes, perhaps best seen in the green pine needles. Just as the building to the right of the tree has a solid cubic presence, combinations of contiguous flat green pastures and ocher fields cause blocklike forms to emerge from the earth, before they dissolve once again in thin planes of color. A fair number of vertical stresses, often quite minute, are tucked into the landscape and play off strong horizontals to suggest an underlying grid.

Many aspects of the picture can be read in two diametrically opposed ways. There is an Impressionistic flicker, but a structurally frozen image. The picture is a deep panoramic view, and yet it is also flat and compressed, for the distant sky sits on the same plane as the foreground tree branches. This conflation is in part due to the tapestry of aligned, off-white brushstrokes that seem simultaneously to encase the pine needles and be woven into the sky. Every brushstroke sits on the canvas as a flat mark asserting the surface; and yet the strokes overlap one another, causing a sense of space or depth to exist between them. Even line has a dual function, for it can be read as shadow, as on the top of the mountain, making depth happen, or it can be seen as flat contour line. There is a conflict between figuration and abstraction, for while the picture obviously depicts a real world, we are never allowed to forget that we are looking at flat paint, lines, and patches of color applied to a flat canvas. We can sense the enormous amount of time that went into resolving all of these conflicts and achieving a balance of two- and three-dimensional space. Most pictures took Cézanne years to paint as he meticulously pondered every mark.

In the succeeding decades, Cézanne's art became increasingly abstract and the space from foreground to background even more compressed. With Cézanne, we meet the painter most responsible for freeing the medium from a representational role and giving artists license to invent images that instead adhered to painting's own inherent laws. The Paris gallery Durand-Ruel began exhibiting Cézanne in the late 1890s, and the public exposure had a powerful influence on other artists, especially Pablo Picasso and Henri Matisse.

Georges Seurat: Seeking Social and Pictorial Harmony

Like Cézanne, Georges Seurat (1859–1891) wanted to make of Impressionism something more like the great art of the past. He studied

25.1 Paul Cézanne. *Mont Sainte-Victoire*. ca. 1885–1887. Oil on canvas, 25½ × 32″ (64.8 × 92.3 cm). Courtauld Institute of Art Gallery, London. The Samuel Courtauld Trust   *Post Impressionism*

briefly in 1878 at the École des Beaux-Arts with a follower of Ingres, and after a year of compulsory military service in Brittany in northwest France returned to Paris, where he spent the rest of his short life. He set up a studio, and in 1884 he unveiled his new style with a large picture called *A Bathing Place, Asnières*, which depicts a group of workers swimming in the Seine in a working-class suburb of Paris, not far from where Seurat grew up. The picture, refused at the Salon, was shown in 1884 at the first exhibition of the Independent Artists, a new artists' cooperative whose shows were unjuried, like those of the Impressionists' Artists, Inc. Seurat next participated in what would be the last Impressionist exhibition, in 1886, submitting *A Sunday Afternoon on the Island of La Grande Jatte* (**fig. 25.2**). The dates of the two shows are significant, for they mark the end of the Impressionist era and the rise of Post-Impressionism.

La Grande Jatte's roots in the realism of Manet and in Monet's impressionistic canvases are obvious, since it is a scene of the lower and middle class taking its Sunday leisure on a sunny, color-filled afternoon. The painting presents a compendium of types that contemporaries would have easily recognized, such as the courtesan, shown walking a monkey, and the boatman, who is the sleeveless man smoking a pipe in the left corner. (Seurat's cataloguing of types extends to the dogs in the foreground and boats on the Seine.) Seurat renders his figures as icons, for each is silhouetted in profile, frontally, or in three-quarter view, following the prescription of the famous Roman architect Vitruvius for the arrangement of sculptural figures on temples. Seurat declared that he wanted "to make the moderns file past like figures on Pheidias' Pan-Athenaic Frieze on the Parthenon, in their essential form.…" And this was no idle claim. The

25.2 Georges Seurat. *A Sunday Afternoon on the Island of La Grande Jatte*. 1884–1886. Oil on canvas, 6'10" × 10'1¼" (2.08 × 3.08 m). The Art Institute of Chicago. Helen Birch Bartlett Memorial Collection. 1926.224

six-by-ten-foot canvas was meant to function on the scale of great history painting and to be seen in the tradition of Poussin and David. Like a history painter, Seurat made detailed studies for every component of his work, even making a painting of the landscape alone, before the insertion of the figures, looking like a stage set.

Despite thematic similarities, Seurat's agenda was quite different from that of Manet, Degas, or Monet, for example. Instead of an objective presentation of his scene, his goal was to create a utopian present, a poetic vision dedicated to showing middle- and working-class tranquility and leisure. His religion was not just classicism, but also science. Familiar with the color theory of the American physicist Ogden Rood, he believed that colors were more intense when mixed optically by the eye rather than on the palette. Consequently, he worked by putting small dots of color next to one another, believing that the eye would then mix these colors together, the color thus stronger than if mixed

on the palette. Actually, this optical mixing was not true. It does not matter, however, that he misinterpreted Rood. Seurat believed his colors were more luminous than the Impressionists', and certainly his technique, which he called "Chromoluminarism" and scholars later labeled "Pointillism" or "Divisionism," created a uniform, if vibrant, surface that was a systematized Impressionism. Like the figures, the regularized dot surface of Seurat's pictures seems mechanical, as though the subjective hand-eye reaction of the Impressionists has been replaced by a machine capable of recording color and light with uniform dots of paint.

In his review of the Impressionist show, the critic Félix Fénéon labeled Seurat's style Neo-Impressionism, the "New Impressionism," and before the decade was out, it had an army of practitioners who were attracted to its scientific approach, monumentality, and modern look. Many of them worked well into the twentieth century. As distinctive as the technique is, it would be a mistake to emphasize it at the expense of the meaning of the art. Seurat was a socialist sympathizer, and his socialist vision of a harmonious, perfect world and belief in science as the force to achieve this characterize his method. This passionate faith in science, technology, and machines as the tools to attain progress and equality will be shared by later generations of artists, as we shall see in the latter chapters.

Vincent van Gogh: Expression through Color and Symbol

Before becoming a painter, the Dutch artist Vincent van Gogh (1853–1890) had tried his hand at preaching and teaching. Drawn to these vocations by his desire for a life both spiritually fulfilling and socially useful, Van Gogh determined that art alone could provide access to the ideal world he sought. After receiving rudimentary art training, he spent the years 1883–1885 painting at the family's vicarage (his father was a pastor) in the village of Nuenen in Holland, where he was deeply affected by the dignity, spirituality, and stolid sturdiness of the impoverished peasants, and made dark, earthy, expressionist paintings heavily influenced by Rembrandt. He then briefly enrolled at the Academy of Fine Arts in Antwerp, where he studied Rubens's paintings and collected Japanese prints. Unhappy in Belgium, Van Gogh went to Paris to be with his brother, Theo, who handled the contemporary painting department at an art gallery. Here, from 1886 to 1888, he experienced Impressionism and Neo-Impressionism at first hand, consuming their lessons with the same fervor that he applied to everything else and developing a bright palette to add to the bold brushwork of his earlier period. He soon started hounding fellow painters to join him in setting up an artists' commune in the sun-drenched south of France, a "Studio of the South" that he envisioned as an Occidental Japan.

Only Paul Gauguin acquiesced in this dream, although he lasted but two months. Alone in Arles, Van Gogh thrived in the Provençal landscape, fiercely generating from 1888 to 1889 his strongest body of work. His intense, uncontrollable emotions took over and his painting became increasingly expressionistic, using color to convey emotion rather than to document reality and employing a personal symbolic vocabulary. The personality that prevailed in the majority of Van Gogh's pictures from this time belongs to the secular evangelist who celebrated all life and longed for universal harmony.

This can be seen in *Starry Night* (**fig. 25.3**). Here we see, snugly ensconced in a valley, the

25.3 Vincent van Gogh. *Starry Night*. 1889. Oil on canvas, 28¾ × 36¼" (73 × 93 cm). Museum of Modern Art, New York. Acquired through the Lillie P. Bliss Bequest (472.1941)

Post Impression

inviting hearth-lit homes of plain rural folk. The yellow glow from their rectangular windows unites them with yellow round stars in the universe above, their contrasting shapes a YIN and YANG of elemental harmony. An upwardly spiraling cypress tree filled with life dominates the foreground. It parallels the church steeple, and both penetrate the fiery, star-filled sky, linking earth with the transcendental. The sky is alight with spectacular cosmic fireworks—haloes of stars and joyous tumbling clouds echo the undulation of the mountains and trees below. Harnessing his expressionistic vocabulary, Van Gogh painted the primitive world and utopia he dreamed of: The peaceful tranquility of simple, unpretentious people, nurtured by nature and in harmony with universal forces. Yet, despite his frenetic output and his humanitarian yearnings, he was a deeply troubled and depressed man. He gradually began to doubt his ability to paint and committed suicide within a year of painting *Starry Night.*

Paul Gauguin: The Flight from Modernity

Paul Gauguin (1848–1903), the fourth of the major Post-Impressionists, shared Van Gogh's distaste for advanced civilization and likewise yearned for a utopian alternative. His abandonment of society, however, was perhaps the most radical of any artist of his time. A stockbroker, he was attracted to art, collected the Impressionists, and by the early 1870s had taken up painting himself. He lost his job in 1882 and began to paint full-time. He studied with his friend, the

Impressionist Camille Pissarro, who introduced him to the work of Cézanne, and participated in the last four Impressionist exhibitions between 1881 and 1886. In the latter year, he abandoned Paris to begin a nomadic search for a more meaningful existence, which he believed could be found in a simpler society steeped in nature. He went first to the village of Pont-Aven, a remote, rural community in Brittany, where locals wore a distinctive regional costume and displayed an intense, charismatic piety.

After briefly leaving Brittany for the Caribbean island of Martinique in 1887, Gauguin returned to Pont-Aven, where he painted with a colleague, Émile Bernard. Together they developed a style they called **Synthetism**, a reference to their synthetic production (i.e. building up) of images based on imagination and emotion as opposed to trying to replicate on canvas what they saw in the real world. In their search to produce an authentic, direct art, as free of civilized influences as possible, they turned to a variety of vernacular and primitive sources, including crude popular illustrations (especially religious) and folk, children's, and medieval art. They were also attracted to such archaic styles as fourteenth-century Italian painting and both Egyptian and Mesopotamian art. Especially appealing were medieval stained-glass windows, because of their spiritual function and saturated colors, and *cloisonné* enamels, which similarly use curvilinear lead dividers to separate areas of flat color.

All of these qualities can be found in Gauguin's Tahitian work. Despite its provincial

25.4 Paul Gauguin. *Where Do We Come From? What Are We? Where Are We Going?* 1897. Oil on canvas, 4′5¾″ × 12′3½″ (1.39 × 3.74 m). Museum of Fine Arts, Boston. Arthur Gordon Tompkins Residuary Collection. 36.270

charm and distance from Paris, Brittany for Gauguin was geographically far too close to modern civilization and its decadent materialism and artificial social conventions. In 1891, he left for the French colony of Tahiti in the South Pacific, convinced that on this remote island he would find Jean-Jacques Rousseau's "noble savage," an elemental, innocent human, a "primitive" steeped in nature and in harmony with the universe. He expected to live in a tropical Garden of Eden, uncovering the most basic truths about human existence. And a Garden of Eden is what he depicts in *Where Do We Come From? What Are We? Where Are We Going?* (**fig. 25.4**) of 1897. Fruit hangs from the trees for the picking, while a statue of a god oversees the welfare of the islanders, bestowing blessings and an intense spirituality on every aspect of daily life, as he points to heaven and the afterlife. The tropical landscape is dense, lush, and sensuous, an abstract tapestry of deeply saturated, flat, curvilinear forms in which everything seems as if gently floating. Here life is languorous and untroubled, and time has stopped.

As the title suggests, the painting represents the three stages of life we have already seen in Renaissance art; birth is pictured on the right, youth in the center, and old age at the far left. The center figure is obviously a Tahitian Eve. The statue of the deity is a composite of the Tahitian goddess Hina, a Javanese Buddha, and an Easter Island megalith. Torsos are twisted so that they resemble Egyptian figures, and the bright gold upper corners with title and signature recall Byzantine and early Renaissance icons. The old woman on the left is derived from a Peruvian mummy that Gauguin saw at a Paris ethnological museum. Pervading the image is the spirituality and look of medieval stained glass and *cloisonné*, as well as the bold forms and colors of Japanese prints. The entire painting is a remarkable synthesis of cultures, religions, and periods, testifying to Gauguin's desire to portray the elemental mythic forces underlying all humanity and his belief that the renewal of Western art and civilization as a whole must come from outside its traditions.

Symbolism

Although Gauguin devised the label Synthetism to describe his art, he was soon heralded as a Symbolist. Symbolism was a literary movement announced in a manifesto issued by the poet Jean Moréas (1856–1910) in the newspaper *Figaro littéraire* in 1886. Another poet, Gustave Kahn, succinctly encapsulated the movement's essence when he wrote shortly after Moréas that the writer's goal was to "objectify the subjective… instead of subjectifying the objective," meaning that the everyday, contemporary world was rejected, replaced by one of dreams that abstractly expressed sensations, moods, and deep-seated fears and desires. The label was soon extended to art, and Gauguin's name always topped anyone's list of important Symbolists. Van Gogh, with his expressionist fantasies, was considered a Symbolist as well.

The Nabis

Gauguin's impact was tremendous, and by the 1890s, flat curvilinear organic patterning was ubiquitous. Gauguin was the formative influence on the Nabis, a secret organization founded in 1888 by young Parisian artists, including Édouard Vuillard and Pierre Bonnard, who were stunned by the novelty and spirituality of Gauguin's Pont-Aven paintings. *Nabis* is Hebrew for "prophet," and as the name suggests, the members immersed themselves in religion, which was perhaps an easier way to flee modernity than by going into voluntary exile in Tahiti.

The group's spiritual interests were extremely broad and included the occult and the supernatural, concerns sweeping Europe and America at the same time as people sought relief from the blunt materialism of modernity. Besides Near and Far Eastern religions, many of the Nabis were taken up by the current craze for THEOSOPHY and Rosicrucianism. Like Gauguin, whose *Where Do We Come From?* attempted to give pictorial form to a synthesis of diverse spiritual and cultural influences, the Nabis sought to convey theosophical mysticism through their art. But instead of seeking transcendent imagery in far-off places, Vuillard and Bonnard turned to scenes of domestic life, leisure activities, and views of their native French landscape.

Although the Nabis fizzled out in the 1890s, Édouard Vuillard (1868–1940) and Pierre Bonnard (1867–1947) developed into prominent artists. Abandoning the group's religious thrust, they retained its emphasis on emotion expressed through abstraction. Reality dissolving into an abstraction of emotion can be seen in Vuillard's small, intimate oil of 1893, *The Suitor* (**fig. 25.5**). Here we see the artist's favorite theme, interiors, which are magical, not mundane. He presents

Nineteenth-century THEOSOPHY originated with the Theosophical Society, founded in New York in 1875 by the Russian *émigrée*, occultist, medium, and mystic, Madame Helena Blavatsky. The Theosophical Society basically claimed that all religions were essentially the same and sought to reveal the mystical connectedness of all things.

25.5 Édouard Vuillard. *The Suitor*. 1893. Oil on millboard panel, 12½ × 14″ (31.8 × 35.6 cm). Smith College Museum of Art, Northampton, Massachusetts. Purchased, Drayton Hillyer Fund, 1938. SC. 1938:15. © ADAGP, Paris and DACS, London 2008

his dressmaker mother, his sister, and her husband, a respected painter and member of the Nabis. The real world disappears into a poetry of paint. Lush, dappled brushwork and a subdued but rich palette create a tranquil, sensuous mood. Tables, chairs, figures, and bolts of fabric are two-dimensional ghosts floating in an enchanting sea of paint, color and form that embodies the sweet intimacy and languid pace of bourgeois domesticity.

Other Symbolist Visions in France

Two artists predating Symbolism were embraced by the movement: Gustave Moreau and Odilon Redon. Moreau emerged in the 1860s, and Redon the following decade. Both gained notoriety when they were featured in Joris-Karl Huysmans's Symbolist novel *À Rebours* (*Against Nature*) of 1884. Huysmans's protagonist is a jaded eccentric who retreats into a strange dream world, a lavish house that is filled with such surreal items as a live turtle with a jewel-encrusted shell, and artworks by Moreau and Redon.

GUSTAVE MOREAU The imagery of Gustave Moreau (1826–1898) combined exotic Romantic motifs with an unsettling, mysterious psychology set in a supernatural world. In his large watercolor *The Apparition* (**fig. 25.6**) of about 1876, the biblical Salome is presented with the head of St. John the Baptist, as she requested. But instead of appearing on a plate, as is traditional, the head, gushing blood and encased in a bright halo, magically levitates. We see a bold confrontation between good and evil and between the sexes, since it was Salome's physical lusting that resulted in John's beheading—if she could not have him in life, then she would in death. The setting and costumes are vaguely Near Eastern, and the vast hall dazzles with imperial opulence. Flowers, clothing, columns, and walls are created with minute, gemlike brushstrokes that are reminiscent of Delacroix and make everything sparkle. In Moreau's hands the story of Salome is not simply illustrated, but becomes a macabre hallucination of sex and death, presented through a dazzling haze of jewel-like marks and a strange, smoldering light.

25.6 Gustave Moreau. *The Apparition* (*Dance of Salomé*). ca. 1876. Watercolor, 41¾ × 28⅜" (106 × 72 cm). Musée du Louvre, Paris

ODILON REDON Perhaps even more visionary and dreamlike are the intense images of another artist claimed by the Symbolists, Odilon Redon (1840–1916). His drawings and prints deliver crepuscular fantasies enveloped in a velvety blurring of black charcoal or lithographic crayon. Redon's style can be seen in the print reproduced here from an 1882 series dedicated to the great American author Edgar Allan Poe (**fig. 25.7**), whose terrifying psychological tales were popular in France. Redon was inspired by Poe's Romantic mood, but his lithographs do not illustrate Poe's text. They are "visual poems" in their own right, evoking the macabre, hallucinatory world of the writer's imagination. In Redon's prints, things float, glide, and hover, and edges are soft, grainy, and indistinct. Everything in Redon's world is in doubt and in some kind of strange evolutionary flux. Here a balloon quietly morphs into a hairy eye and parts the sky as it rises up to heaven

25.7 Odilon Redon. *The Eye Like a Strange Balloon Mounts Toward Infinity*, from the series *Edgar A. Poe*. 1882. Lithograph, 10¼ × 7¹⁄₁₆" (25.9 × 17.8 cm). The Museum of Modern Art, New York. Gift of Peter H. Deitsch

carrying a mysterious cargo, a severed head. A primordial plant with pyrotechnic fronds glows against the forbidding dark sea. Connotations of resurrection, transcendence, a rite of passage, life, death, eternity, and the unknown are embedded in *The Eye*, but the image's narrative meaning remains shrouded in mystery. Instead, what prevails is a troubling psychology and a feeling of frightening uncertainty.

Symbolism Beyond France

Strange dreamlike imagery was not unique to Paris. By the late 1880s, a Symbolist otherworldly aesthetic of fantasy, escapism, and psychology could be found throughout the Western world, including America.

25.8 Edvard Munch. *The Scream*. 1893. Tempera and casein on cardboard, 36 × 29″ (91.4 × 73.7 cm). The National Museum of Art, Architecture and Design, Oslo. © Munch Museum/Munch-Ellingsen Group, BONO, Oslo/DACS, London 2008

Symbolism

EDVARD MUNCH Much Symbolist painting was influenced by Gauguin's mysterious, sinuous patterning and abstraction as well as by a quest to explore visually the most elemental psychological forces underlying modern civilization. Perhaps no one did this better than the Norwegian painter Edvard Munch (1863–1944), whose style matured in the early 1890s after he spent time in Paris. There he experienced at first hand Gauguin's Pont-Aven paintings and the intense brushwork and color of Van Gogh's Arles pictures. Munch's themes were similar to those of his Scandinavian friends, the playwrights Henrik Ibsen and August Strindberg, whose investigations of sexuality and inquiries into the meaning of existence plumbed the deepest recesses of the mind to tap into primordial forces.

Munch crafts an image of horrifying anxiety in *The Scream* (**fig. 25.8**), painted in 1893 after he had moved to Berlin. Clasping hands to a skull-like head, a grotesquely compressed, writhing figure gives voice to a base fear that appears funneled into it from the oozing, hysterical landscape behind. The violent perspective of the uptilted walkway and the Van Gogh-like brushwork elevate the hysteria to a frightening fever-pitch. The scene was perhaps in part prompted by the 1883 eruption of the Indonesian volcano Krakatoa, which was so violent that it generated the loudest sound heard by any human (the soundwaves traveled 1,500 miles) and spewed forth ashes that circled the globe, immersing Europe in frightening blood-red or blue sunsets for some six months. After witnessing such an apocalyptic display of color in Christiania (now Oslo), Munch, already in a melancholic mood, wrote in his diary, "… I sensed a great, infinite scream pass through nature."

AUBREY BEARDSLEY While a morbid, fear-of-the-infinite psychology appears in much of Munch's work, perhaps his most prevalent subject is the uncontrollable yearnings of the libido, along with the sexual conflict it produces, especially as expressed by the *femme fatale* (fatally attractive woman). In part, this theme reflects the increased interest in psychology emerging at the time. But it is also a product of the rise of worldwide movements that appeared toward mid-century demanding greater rights and freedoms for women. In America, for example, it gave rise to the "New Woman," an athletic, independent female who went out in public by herself, attended college, and even went so far as to wear male-style clothing. Most men found these liberated women threatening, set on overturning their male-dominated society. Often, artists and writers alike reflected this fear in the *femme fatale* theme, which became prevalent at the turn of the century.

One of the most famous examples of the theme is Oscar Wilde's French play *Salomé*, which launched a vogue for Salome images. One example (**fig. 25.9**) is by the British illustrator Aubrey Beardsley (1872–1898), which was commissioned for the play's publication in 1894. Salome possessively holds John's severed head, which although dead still projects disdain. His snakelike hair and her octopus coif transform each into an irrational Medusa driven by a base hatred. John's blood drips into a black pool of phallic plants that, like an insidious vine, slither around Salome. Their nightmarish confrontation takes place in an abstract world of curvilinear elegance, one so precious that the line virtually disappears at times as it twists in a sultry rhythm. As we shall shortly see, this tendril-like quality is characteristic of Art Nouveau (see page 538), an architectural and decorative arts style that emerged in the 1890s.

GUSTAV KLIMT A fascination with organic patterns and the psychological meanings they can convey also pervades the work of Gustav Klimt (1862–1918), whose career unfolded primarily in Vienna. Beginning in 1902, Klimt made a series of paintings centering on "the kiss," the best-known version of which dates from 1907–1908 (**fig. 25.10**). Although reflecting Klimt's own personal life (the woman is his lover), the theme is Symbolist-inspired and relates directly to an 1897 painting by Munch of the same title. (In turn, both pictures were inspired by Rodin's sculpture *The Kiss*.) Munch's image presents a couple in a similarly unified form, but they are a simple dark mass, with the lovers' faces frighteningly merging as if consuming one another. Klimt's version of the theme, with its rich surface patterning, shows a faceless, lustful male losing his identity as he is lured by passion and consumed by an enticing but indifferent *femme fatale*, who appears about to pull him over the edge into the abyss below.

Formally inspired by the divine shimmer of Byzantine mosaics, which he studied at first hand in Ravenna, Klimt cloaks his figures in richly patterned gold-leafed robes and encases them in a halo of bright light. In his intricate designs and shifting surfaces, Klimt hints at the instability inherent in individual subjectivity and social relations. Set on a mountain carpet of wild flowers

25.9 Aubrey Beardsley. *Salomé*. 1892. Pen drawing, 11 × 6″ (27.8 × 15.2 cm). Private Collection

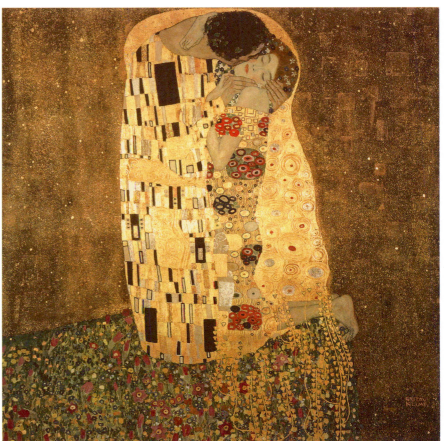

25.10 Gustav Klimt. *The Kiss*. 1907–1908. Oil on canvas, 70⅞ × 70⅞″ (180 × 180 cm). Österreichische Nationalbibliothek, Vienna

WILHELM RICHARD WAGNER (1813–1883) was one of the most influential artistic figures of his era, his operas having an enormous impact on his contemporaries not only in the musical but in other cultural fields. As well as composing the music, he also wrote the scenario and the libretto for all his operas. Most important, however, was his concept of the *Gesamtkunstwerk*, the total artwork, which combined the visual, poetic, musical and dramatic arts and is best represented by his four-opera cycle *Der Ring des Nibelungen* ("The Nibelung's Ring," 1876).

floating high above a celestial neverland, the painting simultaneously suggests the beauty and the spiritual pull of passion as well as its fleeting nature and painful consequences.

Symbolist Currents in American Art

In the 1880s, a significant number of American artists began to make more ethereal, other-worldly pictures. Their imagery was more poetic and music-inspired, in many respects reflecting Whistler's aestheticism. Some Americans are never labeled Symbolists, like Henry O. Tanner, who tends to be associated with the Realism of Thomas Eakins, reflecting his training in Philadelphia. Nonetheless, their art has the dreamlike, visionary, and spiritual qualities found in Symbolist art, and if not Symbolists *per se*, their art is highly influenced by the movement, to the point of sharing its spirit if not its abstract look.

ALBERT PINKHAM RYDER Albert Pinkham Ryder (1847–1917), a somewhat reclusive artist working in New York, abandoned empirical observation to express his emotions abstractly. It was literature that inspired him, in particular works by Chaucer and Poe. He was also influenced by

the Bible, and, as with so many artists on both sides of the Atlantic, by WAGNER's operas. In 1881, Ryder painted *Siegfried and the Rhine Maidens* (**fig. 25.11**), beginning at midnight after attending a performance of *Götterdämmerung*, the final opera of the *Ring* cycle, in New York, and obsessively painting nonstop for 48 hours. He reworked the painting until 1891, when it was exhibited at the Society of American Artists. Here we see again a variant of the *femme fatale* theme, as a sexual struggle is embedded in the legend of the alluring Rhinemaidens who foretell Siegfried's doom for refusing to return to them an all-powerful ring. Echoing the might of Wagner's music, which embodies mythic Nordic forces, the broadly painted, fantastical landscape erupts with seething trees and sky and is lit by the supernatural illumination of a full moon. We sense uncontrollable force, reflecting uncontainable emotions, channeled through every brush-stroke and distorted form.

HENRY O. TANNER The African-American artist Henry O. Tanner (1859–1937) fell under the spell of Symbolism in Paris. He studied in the 1880s under the liberal and supportive Thomas Eakins in Philadelphia, becoming a Realist. With little hope of achieving artistic parity in racist America, he went to Paris in 1892, where he settled permanently. There, his work began to show the influence of Symbolism as he experimented with a more abstract style and pursued new themes, even producing several Salome paintings. Tanner was the son of a preacher, and his work is dominated by religious imagery, such as *Angels Appearing before the Shepherds* (**fig. 25.12**). The composition is ingenious, for Tanner positions the viewer in the sky with the angels. From this vantage point we see the Holy Land, a breathtaking abstraction of lines and marks that nonetheless unmistakably contains hills, terraces, walls, and a city. We can even make out the shepherds' fire, the only note of color in what is otherwise a blue symphony. This spiritual blue pervades earth, sky, and angels, linking them together. Although the paint handling is rich and lush, everything in the image seems ethereal and ephemeral, the material world as transitory and weightless as the transparent angels.

The Sculpture of Rodin

The Symbolist desire to penetrate and portray the innermost essence of being had a parallel in the work of Auguste Rodin (1840–1917), the most influential sculptor of the late nineteenth

25.11 Albert Pinkham Ryder. *Siegfried and the Rhine Maidens*. 1888–1891. Oil on canvas, 19⅞ × 20½" (50.5 × 52.1 cm). National Gallery of Art, Washington, D.C. Andrew W. Mellon Collection. 1946.1.1/886

25.12 Henry Ossawa Tanner. *Angels Appearing before the Shepherds*. ca. 1910. Oil on canvas, 25¾ × 31⅞" (65.3 × 81.1 cm). Smithsonian American Art Museum. Gift of Mr. and Mrs. Norman Robins

century, who single-handedly laid the foundation for twentieth-century sculpture. Rodin's career started slowly: He was rejected at the École des Beaux-Arts, and was forced to attend the Petit Ecole, which specialized in the decorative arts. His big break came in 1880, when he won a prestigious commission to design the bronze doors for a new decorative arts museum. Although the project eventually fell through, Rodin continued to work on it right up to his death. Called *The Gates of Hell* (**fig. 25.13**), the 17-foot-high doors were inspired by Charles Baudelaire's *Flowers of Evil* and Dante's *Inferno* from the *Divine Comedy,* and at one point the thinker sitting in the tympanum contemplating the chaotic, ghoulish scene below was to be Dante. Ultimately, the doors became a metaphor for the futility of life, the inability to satisfactorily fulfill our deepest uncontrollable passions, which is the fate of the sinners in Dante's second circle of hell, the circle that preoccupied Rodin the most. It is the world after the Fall, of eternal suffering, and Adam and Eve are included among the tortured souls below. Despite Rodin's devotion to the project, the work was never cast during his lifetime.

Rodin made independent sculptures from details of the *Gates,* including *The Thinker,* pondering the turmoil below, and *The Three Shades,* the group mounted at the very peak of the *Gates,* which shows the same figure merely turned in three positions. While his figures are based on

25.13 Auguste Rodin. *The Gates of Hell.* 1880–1900. Plaster, height 18′ × 13′ × 3′ (5.52 × 4.0 × 0.94 m). Musée d'Orsay, Paris

familiar models—*The Thinker* (**fig. 25.14**), for example, recalls the work of Michelangelo, his favorite artist—they have an unfamiliar, organic quality. Rodin preferred to mold, not carve, working mostly in plaster or terracotta, which artisans would then cast in bronze. We see where Rodin's hand has worked the malleable plaster with his fingers, for his surfaces undulate. His medium, instead of being smoothed out, remains intentionally rough and uneven, unlike classical sculpture. With Rodin, we are made to feel privy to the creation of the figure, as if watching God making Adam out of clay. This primal quality is reinforced by his figures' nudity, which is less a classical reference than a device to present an elemental figure, a creature that has been stripped down to the very core of its humanity to expose primal fears and passions.

For the sake of expression, Rodin does not hesitate to distort his figures, shattering classical notions of idealized form and beauty. Look, for example, at *The Shades* atop the doors of the *Gates*. Their Michelangelesque musculature has been yanked and twisted, endowing these specters with a form that is at once familiar and unfamiliar. These uncanny messengers have arisen from tombs and now cast their message of eternal gloom on the teeming humanity below. We can even see this distortion to a lesser degree in *The Thinker*. Here, massive hands and feet project a ponderous weight that underscores the thinker's psychological load, while his elongated arm is draped limply over his knee, suggesting inertia and indecision. Clearly, Rodin's preoccupation with expressing elemental fears and passions related him to the Symbolist quest to plumb the depths of the mind, as did his interest in investigating the psychic toll exacted on the individual by civilization.

Art Nouveau and the Search for Modern Design

In 1895, a German entrepreneur, Siegfried Bing, opened a decorative arts shop called *La Maison de l'Art Nouveau* (The House of New Art) in Paris. He had made a fortune importing Japanese art and furnishings, and now sought to promote the Japanese principle of total design: Every detail of an interior space would be integrated into a single style. Aiming to eliminate any distinction between the fine and the decorative arts, he hired famous architects, artists, and designers to develop every detail of entire rooms for his shop, as well as to design individual products, including furniture, vases, tiles, and stained-glass windows. This new style was called Art Nouveau, after Bing's shop. Elsewhere in Europe it took on different names, such as *Jugendstil* (Youth Style) in Germany and the Secession Style in Vienna. Though varying somewhat from one country to the next, the style is usually characterized by organic forms and arabesques.

Art Nouveau can be seen as a response to William Morris's Arts and Crafts Movement, and certainly the emphasis on hand-crafted, finely designed products reflects this. Important differences exist between the Arts and Crafts Movement and Art Nouveau. For instance, many Art Nouveau artists embraced mass-production and new, industrial materials. Also, it is important to note that Art Nouveau designs, though clearly organic, are often purely abstract rather than based on identifiable botanical specimens, as is the case in Morris's designs.

25.14 Auguste Rodin. *The Thinker*. 1879–1887. Bronze, height 27½″ (69.8 cm). Musée Rodin, Paris

late 19th century Art

The Public and Private Spaces of Art Nouveau

Compared with dark, ponderous Victorian interiors, the buoyant naturalism of Art Nouveau was a breath of fresh air, exuding youth, liberation, and modernity. It shared with Symbolism the element of fantasy, in this case a biomorphic fantasy (decoration based on living forms), which can especially be seen in architecture. Art Nouveau designers concerned themselves equally with exterior finish and interior space. The typically complex, animated façades endow Art Nouveau buildings with a sculptural quality that engages viewers on approach. This energetic dialogue continues in the interior, for Art Nouveau spaces pulse with a sense of movement: Interior decoration and furnishings give the impression of having germinated and grown *in situ*. This effect is often enhanced by the admission of sunlight through glass ceilings or skylights, lending the space the fecundity of a greenhouse where everything seems to have grown spontaneously.

VICTOR HORTA The first architectural exponent of the style was the Belgian architect Victor Horta (1861–1947). Born in Ghent, Horta studied drawing, textiles, and architecture there at the Académie des Beaux-Arts, and worked in Paris before returning to Belgium to start his own practice. In 1892, he designed the Tassel House in Brussels. The centerpiece of the design is the ironwork of the stairwell (**fig. 25.15**), malleable wrought-iron columns and railings easily shaped into vines that evolve into whiplash tendrils on the walls, ceiling, and mosaic floor. The supporting columns have been made as slender as possible. In a play on the Corinthian capital, they sprout ribbonlike tendrils that dissolve into arches. The linear patterns extend to the floor and wall, a device that further integrates the space visually. Sunlight filters through the glass ceiling, heightening the organic quality of the stairwell. The curvilinear patterning derives from a variety of sources, including Japanese prints and Gauguin's cloisonnism. Everything has an organic fluidity, a springlike sense of growth and life, which has the effect of destroying the conventional boxlike quality of interior space.

ANTONI GAUDÍ Among the most bizarre Art Nouveau creations are those that sprang from the wild imagination of Antoni Gaudí (1853–1926). Gaudí worked in Barcelona, last major stop for the short-lived style, and his work

25.15 Victor Horta. Interior stairwell of the Tassel House, Brussels. 1892–1893.
© DACS 2008

reflects the fervent nationalism of the period, drawing heavily upon Mediterranean architectural traditions. His remarkable Casa Milá (**fig. 25.16**), a large apartment house, expresses one person's fanatical devotion to the ideal of "natural" form, one quite different from Horta's plantlike designs. The building conjures up the Spanish Baroque, the Plateresque (indigenous Renaissance architecture suggesting elaborate silver plate), and the Moorish mosques of southern Spain. Believing that there are no straight lines in nature, Gaudí created an undulating façade and irregularly shaped interior spaces, in effect destroying the architectural box. With its huge stone blocks, the exterior evokes austere seaside cliffs, while the wrought-iron balconies

25.16 Antoni Gaudí. Casa Milá Apartments. 1905–1910. Barcelona

resemble seaweed and the scalloped cornice mimics ocean waves. The chimneys evoke, among other things, sandcastles. These references to the seashore elicit Barcelona's distinctive geographic, cultural, and economic relationship to the Mediterranean. As the capital of Catalonia, Barcelona held a special significance for Gaudí, who supported Catalan nationalism.

American Architecture: The Chicago School

Little did anyone know that Chicago's devastating Great Fire of 1871 would launch modern architecture and make American architects for the first time the most advanced in the world. Once the flames were extinguished, the issue at hand was not just one of rebuilding. Chicago had been growing rapidly, which put a premium on real estate, and now there was a need to maximize land use by building vertically. This was

made possible by the invention of the safety elevator, perfected in New York in the 1850s and 1860s by Elisha Otis. Ambitious construction was delayed for ten years, however, due to the national financial collapse of 1873, which lasted through the decade. When rebuilding finally proceeded, it was dominated by young designers who were largely trained as engineers with virtually no architectural background. This meant that they were not hampered by strong preconceived notions of what buildings should look like, and were open to allowing their structures to reflect the new technologies and materials they employed. They abandoned the historicism of revival architecture and designed abstract structures as they allowed function to dictate form.

Louis Sullivan and Early Skyscrapers

An important influence on the rise of Chicago architecture was the advent of new technical developments. As the Chicago fire clearly demonstrated, iron is not fire resistant; intense heat makes it soften, bend, and, if hot enough, melt. To avoid towering infernos, it was necessary to fireproof the metal, cladding iron, and shortly thereafter steel (which was developed as we know it today only in the early twentieth century) with terracotta tiles and later with a coating of concrete (modern concrete, called Portland cement, was invented in England in 1825). The insulation also prevented corrosion.

An equally important technological development was the invention of the curtain wall. Unlike a self-supporting wall, a curtain wall hangs from the lip of a horizontal I-beam. Without this innovation, the base of the wall for a tall building would have had to be extremely thick (perhaps six to ten feet for a 15-story building) in order to support the weight of the wall above, severely limiting the number of floors. Furthermore, the curtain wall allowed for entire walls to be made of glass.

The architect generally credited with playing the main role in developing the aesthetic implications of the steel skeleton into powerful architecture is Louis Sullivan (1856–1924). His early masterpiece is the Wainwright Building (**fig. 25.17**), erected in St. Louis in 1890–1891 though since destroyed (most of his major buildings, however, are in Chicago). Using the curtain wall, Sullivan designed a building that reflects the grid structure of the steel skeleton, although for aesthetic purposes he has doubled the number of external piers, with only every other one having a structural beam behind it. The major problem for the early architects of skyscrapers was how to design a building that rose so many floors, while maintaining a visually interesting exterior that did not rely on outmoded revival styles. Sullivan's solution was ingenious. He widened the end piers, thus dramatically framing the building, and he recessed the spandrels (the decorated horizontal panels between piers), giving the building a monumental sculptural quality and a sense of its evolution from a solid block. The seven-story colossal piers and the enormous one-story cornice added to this grandeur.

While the building's exterior presented a compilation of abstract, geometric forms, largely reflecting the substructure, Sullivan did not hesitate to design terracotta panels for the cornice and spandrels featuring a pattern based on an antique *rinceau* motif (an ornamental vine, leaf, or floral design). These biomorphic decorations symbolized his belief that architecture should utilize new technologies to promote

25.17 Louis Sullivan. Wainwright Building, St. Louis, Missouri. 1890–1891. Destroyed

social harmony and progress and to be part of a natural organic evolution of the world. He believed in the mystic and scientist Emanuel Swedenborg's ideas of correspondence—that universal forces flow through and unite all things, each of which is otherwise unique and an individual. The decoration distinguished the various parts of the building, giving each a separate identity (e.g., the upper story, the spandrels); yet at the same time, all of these distinctive parts were tightly woven together into a unified whole. The flowering plant life energized the building, reflected the vitality of the human element within, and related both to the universal current. Although he was down-to-earth, practical, and functional—it was Sullivan who issued the famous dictum that "form ever follows function"—he was also a visionary Symbolist.

Frank Lloyd Wright and the Prairie House

After studying engineering at the University of Wisconsin, Frank Lloyd Wright (1867–1959) worked for Sullivan from 1888 until 1893. His sensitivity and strengths, however, could not have been more different. While Sullivan specialized in commercial buildings, Wright's forte was domestic architecture, although his public buildings are brilliant. Sullivan's innovations were largely in façades, whereas Wright's were in space, including interior space and its relationship to the exterior. Wright's architecture, like Sullivan's, is based on nature, and his reputation was established with what are known as his Prairie Houses, so-called because their strong horizontal sweep echoes the planarity of the Midwest landscape where they were built.

The crowning achievement of Wright's Prairie Houses, which he began designing in the early 1890s, is the Robie House (**fig. 25.18**), designed in Chicago in 1908. The building was so shockingly modern that it would take architects a good 10 to 20 years to understand it and develop its implications. As can be readily seen from the exterior, the house is an abstract play not only of horizontals and verticals, but also of open spaces and enclosed volumes. The dramatic cantilevered roofs (which are not flat as suggested by our reproduction, but slightly sloping) define one space, while the floor of the terrace, or the balcony below, charts another. The interior spaces flow into one another, for the rooms, especially communal rooms, generally do not have doors or four walls.

As abstract and geometric as the Robie House is, it resonates with nature and the organic. The house, constructed of a horizontal brick made to Wright's specifications (the face is 1½ by 5 inches), appears perfectly integrated into the land, its lateral spread paralleling the surrounding plains. The Robie House, like many of his homes, radiates from a large masonry fireplace, which Wright saw as a domestic altar to the "gods of shelter." The rest of the house develops organically from this fulcrum, evolving much as a crystal develops or a tree grows, with one room naturally flowing into another and into the exterior, which in turn is integrated into the surrounding land. This sense of growth can be readily seen from the exterior, where the lateral spread of roofs, terraces, and balconies seems to be in constant movement. The picturesque variety of overhangs and recesses, in part inspired by Japanese buildings, creates a play of light and shadow that we do not normally associate with architecture, but rather with nature. As much as we may want to see early Wright as an abstract, machine-age thinker conceptually playing with spaces and completely breaking with tradition, his theories and sensitivity are very much of the 1890s—he still has one foot planted in the Symbolist nineteenth century that advocated a retreat

25.18 Frank Lloyd Wright. Robie House. 1908–1910. Chicago

architecture   Early 20th Century Art

from modernity into the arms of nature and its rejuvenating spiritual forces.

Photography

The primary preoccupation of photographers at the end of the century was the ongoing debate about whether photography was art. Complicating this was the dramatic increase in non-art photography. The invention of the half-tone printing process was one reason for this upsurge, for it resulted in photographs being directly printed in newspapers, magazines, and books using either lithographic or relief printing. It also brought about the rise of the picture postcard, which during the height of its popularity in 1907–1908 resulted in some 667 million picture postcards being sent through the U.S. mail. Another reason for the proliferation of photographs was the invention of dry plates, which replaced the awkward and impractical wet-plate process. Now photographers could work faster and go anywhere. The process reduced exposure time to one-fiftieth of a second, and hand-held cameras with shutters were invented. Tripods were no longer necessary, and cameras could now record movement. In 1888, the Eastman Dry Plate Company of Rochester, New York, introduced the Kodak camera. It came loaded with a paper roll containing 100 frames which, once exposed, were sent back in the camera to the company for developing and printing. Also appearing about this time was the single-lens reflex camera, which had a mirror that allowed the photographer to see the image in a viewfinder. Suddenly, everyone was taking pictures, and the word "snapshot" came into common parlance. Toward 1890, there were 161 photographic societies worldwide and 60 photographic journals. The medium became so popular that newspapers had an amateur photography column.

Pictorialist Photography and the Photo Secession

To counter the image of photography as a ubiquitous, mindless, popular tool best suited for documenting the visual world, organizations sprang up dedicated to promoting the medium as high art. The first was the Wien Kamera Klub (Vienna Camera Club), founded in 1891, soon followed by the Linked Ring in London and the Photo-Club de Paris (1894). In 1902, Alfred Stieglitz quit the conservative Camera Club of New York to form the Photo Secession. All of these organizations had international membership, often with the same members, and mounted exhibitions and published magazines. And they all promoted a Pictorialist aesthetic, placing a premium on a painterly look, countering the sharp focus that characterized postcard, stereoscope, newspaper, and magazine images and the single fixed focus of the Kodak camera. Photographs by art photographers were taken out of focus, like those of Julia Margaret Cameron, whose work underwent a resurgence of interest. Pictorialist photographs were often highly textured, with gum brushed onto the printing paper before exposure, or the use of a rough, pebbly paper.

GERTRUDE KÄSEBIER The international Pictorialists took their lead from earlier Pictorialist photographers, such as Julia Margaret Cameron, and similarly created painterly, dreamlike images. The New Yorker Gertrude Käsebier (1852–1934) was one of the more prominent figures, becoming a member of the Linked Ring in 1900, less than five years after taking up photography, and one of the founding members of Stieglitz's Photo Secession in 1902. Fleeing a wretched marriage, she enrolled in art classes at Pratt Institute in 1889, and soon took up the camera with the intention of making art, although she supported herself through studio portraiture. In *Blessed Art Thou Among Women* (**fig. 25.19**), an 1899 platinum print on Japanese tissue, we see Käsebier displaying all of the hallmarks of Pictorialism: A soft, grainy image, slightly off focus, with a spectacular range of lush grays that only a platinum print can provide, made all the more delicate by being printed on a gossamerlike Japanese tissue. The mother wears a white Pre-Raphaelite robe and conspicuously stands before an image of the Annunciation on the back wall. The daughter, who is about to cross the threshold to go out into the world, is encased in a **mandorla**-like divine light created by the brilliant white that surrounds her, especially defined by the small gap between her and her mother. The scene has a spiritual quality, set within a sanctum dedicated to maternal protection and nurturing. In a modern urban society becoming increasingly fast, fragmented, and materialistic, Käsebier creates a tranquil domestic sanctuary based on the nurturing care of a mother, as suggested by the title, a quote from the Catholic prayer to the Virgin, *Hail Mary*. Käsebier's image shares with Mary Cassatt's *The Child's Bath* (see fig. 24.7) the late nineteenth-century feminist belief in the important role of women in the development of children, and with Cameron's *Sister Spirits* (see fig. 24.17) a female bonding or spiritual sisterhood designed to protect the rights and future of their gender.

EDWARD STEICHEN Along with Käsebier and Stieglitz, Edward Steichen (1879–1973) helped to found the Photo Secession. Steichen's early contributions to this movement were painterly and moody, with tonalist, mystical qualities. His early style can be seen in his 1902 portrait *Rodin with His Sculptures "Victor Hugo" and "The Thinker"* (**fig. 25.20**), a gum print. Using the painterly effect of the gum combined with the fuzziness of the focus, he created an image that looks more hand-crafted than mechanically reproduced, demonstrating that the photographer made aesthetic decisions profoundly affecting the meaning of the image. Picturing together the brooding silhouettes of Rodin and *The Thinker*, Steichen uses them to frame a brightly lit, phantomlike *Victor Hugo*. Clearly, Steichen identifies Rodin with *The Thinker*. One of the readings of the famous sculpture is that it is meant to represent Rodin and the daunting creative process and mental struggle behind the development of a work of art. This interpretation certainly accounts for this image, as suggested by the light striking Rodin's "brain" and the emergence of Victor Hugo as an apparition, a figment of the sculptor's imagination.

25.19 Gertrude Käsebier. *Blessed Art Thou Among Women*. 1899. Platinum print on Japanese tissue, 9½ × 5⅟₁₆″ (24.2 × 14.8 cm). The Museum of Modern Art, New York. Gift of Mrs. Hermione M. Turner

25.20 Edward Steichen. *Rodin with His Sculptures "Victor Hugo" and "The Thinker."* 1902. Gum print, 14¼ × 12¾″ (36.3 × 32.4 cm). Courtesy George Eastman House. © Joanna T. Steichen

SUMMARY

Although the visual art produced in Europe and the United States from 1880 to 1914 does not cohere around a single style, it can be understood collectively as a response to the development of modernity. Many artists, writers, and intellectuals were appalled by modernity, and instead sought to retreat into a simpler, more primitive and spiritual, pre-industrial world.

United by their responsiveness to the stylistic innovations of Impressionism and their desire to make a distinctly modern art, the Post-Impressionists worked with a variety of styles, subjects, and techniques as they turned away from the Realist premises of Impressionism to create a more abstract art that depicted utopias and private or primitive worlds. Georges Seurat was the only one of the four major Post-Impressionists to continue to present images of modernity. Paul Cézanne, Vincent van Gogh, and Paul Gauguin, finding little solace in science or civilization, sought aesthetic (and often spiritual) authenticity by working outside the rush of Paris.

The Symbolists built on the expressive color and forms of Gauguin and Van Gogh as well as the abstraction of Cézanne to explore the crushing impact of modernity on the psychology of the civilized world. Wild fantasies, strange imaginings, and mysterious narratives characterize the work of many Symbolists, whose works often have a dreamlike quality. Freud's contemporaneous work on dreams and the unconscious parallel this journey by artists into the deep recesses of the mind.

Art Nouveau was conceived as a modern style, the first to turn its back on revival styles and eclecticism and forge a new, fresh look in architecture and design. It especially relied on biomorphic motifs, producing an organic style that broke down the box of conventional architecture and suggested growth and evolution.

Many scholars date the rise of modern architecture to the skyscrapers that went up in Chicago in the 1880s and 1890s. Known as the Chicago School, the architects, who included Louis Sullivan, used new building materials and techniques to design what were considered tall buildings for their time. As important, they allowed form to follow function, making their designs reflect the metal grid skeleton of the building rather than incorporate historical styles. Frank Lloyd Wright also developed innovative interiors, with one space flowing into another and out to the exterior and the surrounding land. Despite developing a modern architecture, Sullivan and Wright invested their structures with universal, spiritual qualities designed to make modernity more meaningful.

The late nineteenth century saw the development of the Kodak camera, which made picture-taking ubiquitous and further challenged the notion that photography could be art. Art photographers increasingly turned to a style called Pictorialism, where photographs were made to look like fine art, such as paintings or drawings. Countering the crisp, sharp images of documentary photography, Pictorialists, such as Gertrude Käsebier and Edward Steichen, worked in soft-focus, even blurry styles that imitated painterly brushwork or dark *chiaroscuro*.

ART IN TIME

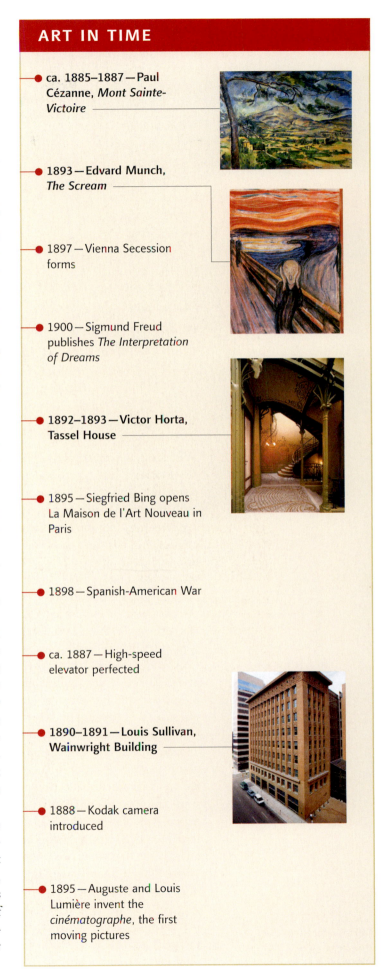

- ca. 1885–1887—Paul Cézanne, *Mont Sainte-Victoire*

- 1893—Edvard Munch, *The Scream*

- 1897—Vienna Secession forms

- 1900—Sigmund Freud publishes *The Interpretation of Dreams*

- 1892–1893—Victor Horta, Tassel House

- 1895—Siegfried Bing opens La Maison de l'Art Nouveau in Paris

- 1898—Spanish-American War

- ca. 1887—High-speed elevator perfected

- 1890–1891—Louis Sullivan, Wainwright Building

- 1888—Kodak camera introduced

- 1895—Auguste and Louis Lumière invent the *cinématographe*, the first moving pictures

Toward Abstraction: The Modernist Revolution, 1904–1914

*T*he opening decades of the twentieth century saw the continued upward march of modernity. But, as in the preceding decades, artists both embraced and fled from progress. In some instances, they even clung to tradition while they purveyed the new, which we will see in the case of Pablo Picasso and Henri Matisse, for example, two artists who successfully knitted together the new and revolutionary in style with the familiar and enduring in subject matter.

The period is marked by landmark scientific developments that artists, like the public at large, could not ignore. Max Planck (1858–1947), in 1900, proved that energy was not distinguishable from matter. He also showed that energy was emitted and absorbed in bundles called quanta, disproving the idea that it existed in a stable, uniform state. Energy and, hence, matter were in constant flux. This concept was fundamental to the discovery of radioactivity in 1902 by Ernest Rutherford (1871–1937). In 1913, the atom itself was further redefined when Niels Bohr (1885–1962) declared that it consisted of protons and neutrons, and was thus in constant movement. But the greatest amendment to classical physics was proposed by Albert Einstein (1879–1955). Einstein's revolutionary concepts appeared in a series of papers published in 1905 and 1916, and they included his theory of relativity, which claimed that time, space, and motion were not fixed but all relative, especially in relation to the observer's own position. The Newtonian world order, based on notions of energy and matter that remained stable, was now supplanted by a more complex and contingent notion of the universe.

Similar ideas emerged in accounts of human behavior by philosophers and psychologists. Henri Bergson (1859–1941), a French philosopher, was so influential in the first years of

the twentieth century that he was well known even to the general public. Bergson postulated that we experience life not as a series of continuous rational moments, but as intuited random memories and perceptions that we then piece together to form ideas. The world, therefore, was complex and fractured, or as expressed by the Harvard philosopher and psychologist William James (1842–1910), whose theories independently paralleled Bergson's, a "booming buzzing confusion." Only intuition transcended this chaos. The mind, according to Bergson, was pure energy, an *élan vital* ("vital force") that penetrated the essence of all things. While Bergson was philosophically redefining consciousness, the Austrian neurologist and founder of psychoanalysis Sigmund Freud (1856–1939) continued to refine his ideas of the unconscious through observations made during clinical practice, an approach that he felt gave his conclusions a scientific basis. Despite taking a different approach, Freud likewise developed a model of human consciousness as fragmented and conflicted.

Artists pursued similar lines of inquiry, testing traditional approaches to art-making against new ideas. Some artists, such as Pablo Picasso and Georges Braque, emulated scientists, treating their studios like laboratories where each creative breakthrough served as a stepping-stone to

Map 26.1 Europe and North America 1904–1914

the next, as they sought to develop a new model of visual perception. Others, such as the Italian Futurists, embraced modernity and used the radical stylistic developments of Picasso and Braque to capture the technological wonders and new psychology of the modern world. Still others, however, like the German Expressionists, sought an antidote for the cold, impersonal tenor and crass materialism of modernity and tried to invest contemporary life with spirituality. Continuing Gauguin's quest to find a spiritual peace in a primitive world that was in tune with nature, many artists turned to the direct, more abstract vocabulary of tribal art as well as children's, folk, and medieval art. Many of these artists were heavily influenced by Theosophy (see page 531) and believed in the mystical interpenetration of all things, which they sought to capture in their art and architecture. For artists attempting to visualize the spiritual, the essence of which is abstract, the new stripped-down vocabulary of art was the perfect vehicle.

Fauvism

The rise of Fauvism, the first major style to emerge in the twentieth century, is part of a colorist tradition that can be traced back through Van Gogh, Gauguin, Monet, and Delacroix to Titian and the Venetians. The Fauves, however,

took the free, expressive use of color to new heights. Van Gogh and Gauguin had the greatest impact on the Fauves, as is readily apparent in the work of Henri Matisse (1869–1954). Matisse was well aware of the aesthetic traditions with which he was wrestling. Trained in the studio of Gustave Moreau (see page 532), Matisse had received an exacting academic education under the auspices of the École des Beaux-Arts. He understood the extent of his participation in and departure from tradition when, in 1905, he presented his latest pictures at the Salon d'Automne, or Autumn Salon, an important venue for vanguard artists. Strongly influenced by the Post-Impressionists' use of color for formal and expressive ends, Matisse pushed even further the independence of color. His experiments proved too radical for some. The art critic Louis Vauxcelles was so shocked by the "orgy of pure colors" he encountered in the work of Matisse and his colleagues at the Salon d'Automne that he declared the pictures *fauves*, or wild beasts.

We can see Matisse's wild Fauve palette in his 1905–1906 painting *Le Bonheur de Vivre* (*The Joy of Life*) (**fig. 26.1**). This work presents intense non-realistic coloring, and in its artificial curvilinear patterning it reflects Matisse's awareness of Gauguin. As innovative as the color, however, is Matisse's daring suspension of logical space and scale, which increases the abstraction of the

26.1 Henri Matisse. *Le Bonheur de Vivre* (*The Joy of Life*). 1905–1906. Oil on canvas, 5′8″ × 7′9¾″ (1.74 × 2.38 m). The Barnes Foundation, Merion, Pennsylvania. © Succession H. Matisse, Paris/DACS, London 2008

Expressionism - Fauv

painting, a move that took him beyond both his own work and that of the Fauves of the year before. No matter how abstract and flat Matisse's earlier Fauvist pictures were, they still projected a rational progression of space. Now, that space is gone, as two enormous reclining nudes in the middle ground are as large if not larger than the pipe player and kissing couple in the foreground. Figures dissolve into one another and so do trees into sky and hills, so that it is nearly impossible to tell which sits in front of which. Reality gives way to a joyous abstract orchestration of colored lines and planes, which takes its hedonistic cue from the classical idyll of dance, passion, and music-making of ancient, Renaissance and Baroque art. But if the theme is traditional, reflecting an escape from modernity, the style is radical, reflecting the groundbreaking scientific investigations making front-page news during the period.

Cubism

The second major style to emerge in the new century was Cubism, largely under the leadership of Pablo Picasso and Georges Braque. Cubism sparked new ways of thinking about the appearance and even the purpose of art. But the journey to Cubism was a long one, starting only after both artists had fully absorbed the lessons offered by Post-Impressionism and Fauvism. Picasso was the first to push further the limits of abstraction developed by Cézanne and Matisse.

Reflecting and Shattering Tradition: *Les Demoiselles d'Avignon*

Pablo Picasso (1881–1973) was born in the Spanish town of Málaga, on the Mediterranean coast, and at age 15 he moved to Barcelona. He was soon a major figure in the art community there, working primarily in a Symbolist style. After roughly four years of shuttling back and forth between Barcelona and Paris and leading a desperate, abject existence, he settled permanently in Paris, living in the bohemian neighborhood of Montmartre, the hill overlooking the city. This was a center for the impoverished cultural avant-garde, and Picasso quickly became part of the group's inner circle. In 1907 he shocked even his closest companions when he unveiled in his studio *Les Demoiselles d'Avignon* (*The Young Ladies of Avignon*) (**fig. 26.2**). The painting's style departed sharply from Picasso's previous work. To his contemporaries, this large, frightening picture seemed to come out of nowhere.

Of course, the painting did not emerge from an aesthetic vacuum. Among Picasso's sources were the great French history paintings of the seventeenth and eighteenth centuries, and its large scale is meant to evoke a serious Salon picture. A more immediate influence was Matisse.

In the case of *Les Demoiselles*, he was responding to the spatial ambiguity of Matisse's *The Joy of Living*, which Picasso felt compelled to upstage.

The title of the painting refers to the "red-light" district in Barcelona. Early studies show a sailor in a brothel, seated before a table with a plate of fruit and surrounded by prostitutes. The sailor is now gone, but the theme remains, for we, the viewers, are seated in his place at the table in front of the fruit, a traditional symbol of lust. Coming through the brothel curtains and staring directly at us are five of the most savage, confrontational nudes ever painted. Thematically, then, the picture began as a typical Symbolist painting about male lust and castrating women.

Instead of relying on conventional forms of pictorial narrative to tell his tale, Picasso allowed the abstract qualities of the medium to speak for him. The formal qualities are threatening and

26.2 Pablo Picasso. *Les Demoiselles d'Avignon (The Young Ladies of Avignon)*. 1907. Oil on canvas, 8′ × 7′8″ (2.44 × 2.34 m). The Museum of Modern Art, New York. Acquired through the Lillie P. Bliss Bequest. © Succession Picasso/DACS, London 2008.

Cubism

violent. The space is incoherent and jarring, virtually unreadable. The entire image is composed of what looks like enormous shards of glass that overlap in no comprehensible way. Instead of receding, they hover on the surface of the picture plane, jostling each other. Sometimes the facets are shaded, as in the diamond-shaped breast of the harlot parting the curtain on the right, but Picasso has reversed the shading, in effect detaching the breast from the body. Even more incomprehensible is the seated figure below her, who has her back to us yet simultaneously faces us. The table with fruit is tilted at such a raking angle that it would shock even Cézanne, who

provided the most immediate model for this spatial distortion.

The use of conflicting styles within a single picture is another disturbing quality. The three nudes to the left with their almond-shaped eyes and severe facial features were inspired by ancient Roman sculptures from the Iberian peninsula (Spain and Portugal), which Picasso collected. But the frightening faces on the right are entirely different. At this point in the creation of the painting, Picasso's Fauve friends took him to the Trocadéro Museum of ethnographic art, where he saw African masks, providing the source for the ski-jump noses, facial scarifications, and

26.3 Georges Braque. *The Portuguese*. 1911. Oil on canvas, 45⅞ × 32⅛″ (116 × 81.6 cm). Kunstmuseum, Basel. Gift of Raoul LaRoche, 1952. © ADAGP, Paris and DACS, London 2008

lopsided eyes. This seems logical enough, for we know that Matisse was already collecting African art, and that Picasso and Matisse had known one another since 1905. Direct sources for Picasso's borrowings can be found in African sculpture, and the abstraction and "barbarism" of the masks must have appealed to the artist's sensibility. Interestingly, however, Picasso, up to his death, denied having been influenced by African art in this picture, and scholars in the 1990s discovered doodles he has made of heads and bodies that anticipated his African-looking figures.

Regardless of his sources, what is most important about *Les Demoiselles* is the new freedom it announced for painting, for now line, plane, color, mass, and void were freed from their representational role to take on a life all their own. The picture laid the foundation for Analytic Cubism.

Analytic Cubism: Picasso and Braque

It may seem incredible that *Les Demoiselles* owes anything to the methodical, highly structured paintings of Cézanne, but Picasso had carefully studied Cézanne's late work and found in his abstract treatment of volume and space the basic units from which to derive the faceted shapes of Analytic Cubism. Picasso did not arrive at this style on his own, however, and even seemed creatively stalled after *Les Demoiselles*. To help him move beyond this point, the emotional Spaniard needed an interlocutor, a steadying force, someone with whom he could discuss his ideas and experiment. This intellectual partner was the French artist Georges Braque (1882–1963), who conveniently lived around the corner from him in Montmartre. From 1908 to 1910 the two fed off each other, their styles developing from a representational picture of fractured forms and space like *Les Demoiselles* to a more geometrically structured, shimmering, evanescent mirage of abstract lines and brushwork like Braque's *The Portuguese* (**fig. 26.3**) of 1911. Picasso and Braque were so intertwined that their styles began to merge by 1910.

The Portuguese is a classic example of the Analytic Cubism that had emerged in 1910. Gone are the emotional terror and chaos of *Les Demoiselles*. Braque arranged a grid of lines following the shape of the canvas and an orderly, geometric pattern of diagonal lines and curves, all recalling Cézanne's vision of a tightly structured world. Despite being abstract, however, these lines and shapes also function as signs. The circle at the lower center is the sound hole of a guitar, and the horizontal lines are the strings, although Braque used the same sign to indicate fingers, a confounding or visual punning of objects that is characteristic of Picasso's and Braque's Cubism. The stenciled letters and numbers are borrowed from a poster that probably read "Grand Bal" and listed the price of admission (10 francs, 40 centimes). The lines and shadows suggest arms, shoulders, and the frontal pose of a figure tapering toward the head. Behind the figure hangs a poster and, in the upper right, we see the harbor from a window. By providing these subtle visual clues, Braque prompts the viewer to recognize that the painting shows a guitar player in a Marseilles bar. Once again, we find a conventional subject—a genre scene—presented with a radical new artistic language. The atmosphere and light that flood the picture and fall on individual facets seem real or naturalistic but fail to create coherent space and volume. Ultimately everything is in a state of flux without absolutes, including a single interpretation of reality. The only reality is the pictorial world of line and paint. In a 1909 review of Braque's earlier work, Louis Vauxcelles, who had named Fauvism, labeled the paintings Cubism, influenced by Matisse's description of earlier Cubist works as appearing to be made of little cubes.

Synthetic Cubism: The Power of Collage

To focus on structure and line, Picasso and Braque painted monochrome images, thus removing the problem of color from their Analytic Cubism. This situation changed in 1912, however, when they began working in collage, pasting flat objects, generally paper, onto the canvas. Picasso made the earliest known example in May 1912, when he glued onto the surface of a painting a sheet of imitation chair caning, a product not unlike contact paper. (These oilcloth sheets with a chair-caning pattern printed on them were normally pasted on wood as an inexpensive way to repair a broken seat.) This device allowed him to complicate notions of the real and the illusionistic, for the chair caning was simultaneously real—a piece of real imitation chair caning—and illusionistic, a picture of chair caning.

Picasso and Braque realized immediately the broader implication of this daring move. The pasted image now literally sat on top of the canvas. Once and for all, the Renaissance conception of the picture plane as a window into an illusionistic world was shattered. Instead of a window,

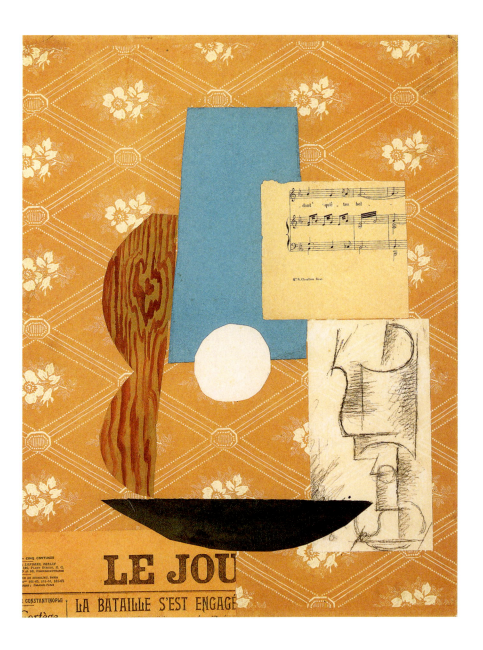

26.4 Pablo Picasso. *Guitar and Wine Glass*. 1912. Charcoal, gouache, and pasted paper, 18⅞ × 14¾″ (45.9 × 37.5 cm). The McNay Art Museum, San Antonio, Texas. Bequest of Marion Koogler McNay. © Succession Picasso/DACS, London 2008

the picture surface became a tray on which art was served. Art occurred in front of, not behind, the canvas, a fact Édouard Manet had implied some 50 years earlier (see pages 503–505).

Collage completely changed the way in which Braque and Picasso made their images. Instead of breaking down or abstracting an object into essential forms, the artists now synthetically constructed it by building it up or arranging it out of cut pieces of paper, hence the name Synthetic Cubism. Constructing the image out of large, flat shapes meant that they could introduce into Cubism a variety of textures and colors, as seen in Picasso's *Guitar and Wine Glass* (**fig. 26.4**) of 1912. Because music is abstract, like their art, it became a favorite theme for the Cubists, who wished to establish parallels between the two art forms. Picasso built his composition on a background of real wallpaper

that, like the imitation chair caning used earlier, serves as a visual pun on illusion and reality.

Picasso puns with solid forms and intangible space as well. The guitar sound hole, an element that should be negative space but appears as a solid circle of paper, contrasts with the wineglass in the drawing, which should be three-dimensional and solid but instead consists of lines on a flat piece of off-white paper that has more physical presence than the drawn glass. Picasso even tells us he is punning, for he has cropped the newspaper collage at the bottom to read LE JOU, a shortening of *Le Journal*, or "newspaper," which in French sounds like the verb *jouer*, meaning "to play," or the noun *jouet*, meaning "toy." The headline for the article is *"La Bataille s'est engagé,"* which translates as "The Battle Has Started," and refers to the violent war then raging in the Balkans, with Greece, Serbia, Bulgaria, and Montenegro fighting for independence against the Ottoman Empire (see map. 26.1). Picasso uses the announcement to signal the friendly rivalry between himself and Braque.

The logical peak of Cubism occurred when Picasso extended Synthetic Cubism to sculpture and created the first **construction**, a three-dimensional assemblage of materials. Although his earliest construction was made in 1912 (and evidence suggests that Braque had made some even earlier), Picasso did not produce a large number of these sculptures until 1914–1915. Most were musical instruments, such as *Violin* (**fig. 26.5**) of 1915. Instead of pasting paper to canvas, he assembled flat or slightly bent sheets of painted metal into a low relief. Just as he had for painting, he now redefined sculpture. Instead of being carved, chiseled, or molded, his sculpture was assembled, and, unlike most sculpture since the Renaissance, it was painted. He used paint perhaps with a bit of irony, since the cross hatching used to represent shading in painting is unnecessary for a sculpture, the three-dimensional form not requiring illusionistic shadow. Again Picasso creates puns about the medium. Without knowing the title, a viewer could not know for certain that this work represents a violin. That is not the issue, however, for Picasso is more concerned with creating a visual equivalent to music—here a staccato rhythm of shape, color, and texture—transforming the individual metal pieces into playful musical notes that we can almost hear.

The outbreak of war in 1914 disrupted daily life, bringing to an end the brilliant visual game between Picasso and Braque. By then, the two artists had completely transformed painting, undermining some 700 years of tradition by destroying notions about what art forms could be. In effect, Braque and Picasso sparked a revolution in the perception of reality as radical as those of Freud and Einstein.

The Impact of Fauvism and Cubism

Matisse's and Picasso's liberation of color and line from illusionistic roles marked important steps in the development of modern art. As innovative as their achievements were, their interests and sensitivity during these years were limited. Their works were rational, intellectual, and pleasurable, and they focused on such traditional subjects as still-life, portraiture, and the figure.

26.5 Pablo Picasso. *Violin*. 1915. Construction of painted metal, 37½ × 25⅝ × 7½″ (94.5 × 65 × 19 cm). Musée Picasso, Paris. © Succession Picasso/DACS, London 2008

Yet they provided a new artistic vocabulary for artists with very different interests and concerns, artists who used this new language to project powerful emotions, spirituality, and the intensity of modernity.

German Expressionism

The long tradition of Expressionism in German art extends back to the grotesque physical and psychological tensions of such Renaissance artists as Matthias Grünewald (see fig. 17.4) and Albrecht Dürer (see fig. 17.6). German Expressionism surfaced as a cohesive movement, however, toward 1905, and although it encompassed a range of issues and styles, it can be characterized as tortured, anguished, and brutally primitive on the one hand, or passionately spiritual, reflecting elemental cosmic forces on the other.

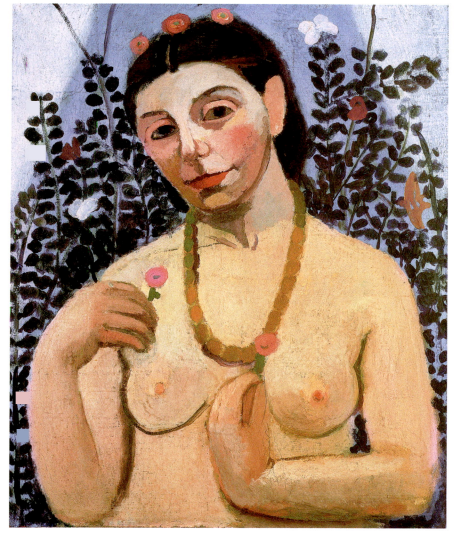

26.6 Paula Modersohn-Becker. *Self-Portrait.* 1906. Oil on canvas, 24 × 19¾″ (61 × 50.2 cm). Öffentliche Kunstsammlung Basel, Kunstmuseum, Basel, Switzerland. © Estate of Paula Modersohn-Becker

A precursor of the first German Expressionist movement is Paula Modersohn-Becker (1876–1907), whose career was cut short by her early death. Her artistic activity was limited to two mature years, during which she produced remarkable pictures that promised a brilliant future. In 1898, she settled in the commune of Worpswede, a haven for artists and intellectuals seeking escape from modern urban life, just outside Bremen in north Germany. There, she befriended two major Symbolist writers who urged her to seek the spiritual in her art and to reject the naturalistic. Modersohn-Becker visited Paris regularly, and in 1905–1906 she was especially influenced by exhibitions of works by Gauguin and Cézanne.

The emergence of her individual style is represented by her 1906 *Self-Portrait* (**fig. 26.6**). In this revolutionary work, the artist presents herself nude and as an emblem of fertility, an earth

goddess. Showing herself frontally, like an icon, she reduces her contours to a Gauguin-like curvilinear simplicity. Her awkward yet charming pose suggests the primitive, recalling especially Gauguin's Tahitian women (see fig. 25.4). Her amber necklace even resembles a *lei* (a Tahitian flower necklace). She poignantly displays two small flowers, symbols of fertility, which she has colored and shaped like her nipples. Also symbolic of fecundity is the garden in which she depicts herself. A celestial blue halo deifies her and reinforces her elemental presence.

What is revealing about the image is Modersohn-Becker's German primitivism, which differs radically from that of Gauguin or Picasso. There is a cultivated crudeness throughout the picture, reflected in the pasty application of paint, particularly in the masklike face and neck, and the awkward gestures, especially of her left hand. It appears as well in the ungainly flat ear and coarse fingers of the right hand. Despite the beautiful, colorful palette, we sense a raw, primal energy and an earthiness, characteristics of much German Expressionism.

DIE BRÜCKE Scholars generally assert that German Expressionism began with *Die Brücke* (The Bridge), a group conceived in 1903 when four Dresden architecture students, including Ernst Ludwig Kirchner (1880–1938), decided to form an art alliance "to clear a path for the new German art." In 1905, the group officially formed and went public with no artistic program other than to oppose "older well-established powers" and create a "bridge" to the future.

The initial problem confronting these largely self-taught artists, who shared a communal studio in a former butcher shop, was to find subject matter and a way to express it. Initially they focused on the unsettling psychology of modern Germany and turned to intense color to express it. Kirchner, the leader of *Die Brücke*, was among the first to mature artistically, about 1907, as seen in his *Street, Dresden* (**fig. 26.7**) of 1908. The group's love of Van Gogh and their recent discovery of Matisse are reflected in the intense Fauvist color liberated from a representational role. As important is the impact of Edvard Munch (see fig. 25.8), who exhibited throughout Germany and often resided in Berlin after 1892. The disturbing psychological undertones and arabesque patterning are decidedly Munch-like, and Kirchner's crowded street evokes a claustrophobic anxiety worthy of the Norwegian artist. Like most Munch images, this one focuses on

26.7 Ernst Ludwig Kirchner. *Street, Dresden.* 1908 (dated 1907 on painting). Oil on canvas, 4'11¼" × 6'6⅞" (1.51 × 2 m). The Museum of Modern Art, New York. © Ingeborg and Dr. Wolfgang Henze-Ketter, Wichtrach/Bern, Switzerland

sexual confrontation. Wraithlike women stare out. One, dressed in yellow, lifts her dress to reveal her petticoat. Searing pinks, yellows, and oranges contrast with electrifying blues and greens, creating a disturbing dissonance and sexual excitement. This unsettling picture could never be mistaken for one by Matisse.

DER BLAUE REITER The second major German Expressionist group, *Der Blaue Reiter* (The Blue Rider), developed in Munich, in southern Germany. It lasted but four months, from December 1910 to March 1911. Like their *Brücke* counterparts, the artists associated with *Der Blaue Reiter* drew on art forms from Western art history as well as non-Western and folk art traditions to create images that reveal their skepticism toward modern, industrial life. The group focused on visually expressing a spirituality they believed resided beneath the surface of the visual world.

The key figure in *Der Blaue Reiter* was the Russian artist Vasily Kandinsky (1866–1944). He left Moscow in 1896 to study art in Munich and took with him Russian influences, namely the spirituality of native religious icons and the robust, emotional colors of folk art. His interest in folk culture was rekindled when, in 1908, he moved to Murnau, just south of Munich in the Bavarian Alps. There he immersed himself in folk culture and was deeply affected by the

powerful colors and the simple directness of paintings on glass, a medium that he adopted. He also lived in the Schwabing neighborhood of Munich, a bohemian enclave of cafés and liberalism. The area was a breeding ground for explorations of spirituality and the occult, where Theosophy was in daily conversation (see page 531). Inspired in part by Theosophy, Kandinsky in 1910 wrote *Concerning the Spiritual in Art*, published the next year and read worldwide. He proclaimed the need to paint one's connectedness with the universe and to use an abstract vocabulary, one that functioned much like music, to portray the abstract qualities of spirituality.

It was not until 1911 that Kandinsky began making totally abstract pictures, as seen in *Sketch I for "Composition VII"* (**fig. 26.8**). Painted in 1913, this was one of numerous preliminary studies for a large final version that retains some of the same compositional elements but has a very different palette. Drawing a parallel with music, Kandinsky titled many of his works "composition," "improvisation," and "concert." He was especially influenced by Richard Wagner (see page 536) in his conjuring of universal forces and a sense of musical abstraction. These qualities differ greatly from the lyrical, refined imagery of James Abbott McNeill Whistler, who similarly aspired to create visual music (see page 515). In *Sketch for "Composition VII,"* the references to

26.8 Vasily Kandinsky. *Sketch I for "Composition VII."* 1913. Oil on canvas, 30¾ × 39⅜" (78 × 100 cm). Private Collection.
© ADAGP, Paris and DACS, London 2008

German Expressionism

horses, riders, figures, buildings, and specific landscape motifs that had appeared in *Compositions I* and *II* of 1910 are now gone, these motifs yielding to an abstract play of color and painted line and form that still nonetheless recalls the deep saturated colors of medieval stained-glass windows, reverse glass painting and Russian folk art. The image may appear apocalyptic and chaotic, but these dynamic qualities are meant to capture the relentlessness of universal forces, not to portend a catastrophic future.

Austrian Expressionism

Another major center for German Expressionism was Vienna. Home of Sigmund Freud, it was an especially repressive city, socially and culturally dominated by a conservative bourgeoisie and a decadent aristocracy resistant to change. Not surprisingly, Viennese artists generated some of the era's most neurotic and disturbing visual imagery.

OSKAR KOKOSCHKA Perhaps the most prominent Viennese artist is Oskar Kokoschka (1886–1980), who initially specialized in portraiture. In 1908 he exhibited with avant-garde artists at the Vienna *Kunstschau*, an exhibition for cutting-edge art, where his violent portraits, inspired by Van Gogh, generated so much controversy that he was expelled from art school. Kokoschka called his expressionistic portraits "black portraits," and the sitters appeared to be so troubled that he became known as "the Freud of painting" who "paints the dirt of one's soul."

We can get a sense of how expressionistic these portraits looked from the figures in *The Bride of the Wind* (**fig. 26.9**), Kokoschka's 1914 self-portrait with his lover Alma Mahler, the notoriously beautiful and sophisticated widow of the famous Austrian composer Gustav Mahler (1860–1911). By 1914, their passionate relationship was threatened, and it ended the following year. *The Bride of the Wind* visually encapsulates the artist's distress. Originally, Kokoschka intended to disguise this personal dilemma as *Tristan and Isolde*, based on Wagner's opera about tragic lovers. Kokoschka expresses his anxiety through coarse, violent brushstrokes and a seething, swirling composition. Oblivious to this turmoil, Mahler is shown peacefully sleeping, while Kokoschka restlessly worries, his body transformed into a flayed corpse, his hands grotesquely gnarled. The couple is cradled in a monstrous shell-like berth adrift in a landscape that is bleak, uncontrollable, and subject to cosmic forces, as suggested by the gravitational pull of a distant moon.

Cubism in Paris after Picasso and Braque

In France, Cubism was thoroughly entrenched by 1911–1912, expanding well beyond Picasso and Braque. A handful of individual painters had closely followed Picasso's and Braque's developments in 1909–1910, and in late 1910 they began exhibiting together at the large Paris salons and at a private gallery, calling themselves the *Section d'Or* (Golden Section). In 1912, two Cubists in the group, Albert Gleizes and Jean Metzinger published *Du Cubisme* (On Cubism), the first book on the style.

26.9 Oskar Kokoschka. *The Bride of the Wind*. 1914. Oil on canvas, 5′11¼″ × 7′2⅝″ (1.81 × 2.20 m). Öffentliche Kunstsammlung Basel, Kunstmuseum, Basel, Switzerland. © Foundation Oskar Kokoschka/2008 DACS

26.10 Robert Delaunay. *Homage to Blériot*. 1914. Tempera on canvas, 8'2½" × 8'3" (2.5 × 2.51 m). Öffentliche Kunstsammlung Basel, Kunstmuseum, Basel, Switzerland. Emanuel Hoffman Foundation. © Robert Delaunay/L&M Services B. V. Amsterdam

ROBERT DELAUNAY Of the *Section d'Or*, Robert Delaunay (1885–1941) was among the most influential. Unlike concurrent Analytic Cubist works by Braque and Picasso, Delaunay's 1910 Cubist paintings of the Eiffel Tower, an icon of modern technology, incorporated color. They also differed in their subject: The movement and energy of modernity and the constant flux of the contemporary world.

Delaunay's preoccupation with the dynamism of the modern world is evident in his 1914 *Homage to Blériot* (**fig. 26.10**), honoring the French aviator Louis Blériot (1872–1936), inventor of the modern single-wing airplane and the first pilot to fly across the English Channel. Delaunay integrates emblems of modernity—airplanes, propellers, and the Eiffel Tower—into a kaleidoscope of floating balls and rotating disks suggesting whirling propellers and blazing suns. He creates movement not only through the ambiguity of Cubist space but also through the use of what Delaunay called "simultaneous contrasts," the placement of flat planes of primary and secondary colors next to one another, not only creating movement but also light and space,

none of which is illusionistic. Two years before, Delaunay had even exhibited total abstractions called *Simultaneous Disks* or *Simultaneous Contrasts*, paintings consisting entirely of the multi-hued circles seen in *Homage to Blériot*. While Delaunay's color theory was derived from the same nineteenth-century color theorists who had influenced Seurat, his move into total abstraction was prompted by his contact with Kandinsky. (Delaunay had been included in the first *Blaue Reiter* exhibition.) In his 1913 review of the Salon des Indépendants, the art critic Guillaume Apollinaire labeled Delaunay's abstract work Orphism, a reference to the mythological lyre player Orpheus and evocative of the parallel between abstract art and music.

Italian Futurism: Activism and Art

In January 1909, Filippo Tommaso Marinetti (1876–1944), a free-verse poet based in Milan, launched the Futurist movement when he published his *Manifesto of Futurism*, a pamphlet sent to thousands of artists and poets. On February 20, it appeared on the front page of the Parisian newspaper *Le Figaro*. Marinetti called for a rebirth of Italy, a country he saw as mired in the dusty, anachronistic classical past. He advocated an uncompromising acceptance of modernity in all its manifestations, including electricity, automobiles, and machines, writing that "all subjects previously used must be swept aside in order to express our whirling life of steel, of pride, of fever and of speed."

For Marinetti, Futurism was a continual process, a permanent revolution. Toward this end, he arranged Futurist evenings, where from a stage he expounded upon his theories, often provoking, if not insulting, the audience in his attempt to incite them to action or even violence, which he perceived as socially cleansing and productive. Marinetti was intent on generating constant activism, which he saw as the conduit for a cultural *Risorgimento*, or rebirth, of Italy.

After a 1909 lecture in Milan presented to the avant-garde art group *Famiglia Artistica* (Artistic Family), Marinetti enlisted a handful of its members, including Umberto Boccioni (1882–1916), to become Futurists. In 1909, these artists were mostly Neo-Impressionists (see page 528), who transformed the color and energy of Divisionism to portray contemporary dynamism. Their manifesto claimed that "Motion and light destroy the materiality of bodies" and that their concern would be the visualization of movement and energy. For their visual vocabulary, they rejected anything redolent of classical Italian culture and instead turned to science: The sequences taken by late nineteenth-century photographers that served as motion studies, the physicist and philosopher Ernst Mach's (1838–1916) graphic representations of shockwaves, and the physicist Wilhelm Konrad Röntgen's (1845–1923) X-rays, which proved the dematerialization of all things.

By the end of 1911, the group had turned from Neo-Impressionism to Cubism. Their interest in Cubism, however, departed from the concerns of Braque and Picasso because the Futurists wanted to convey motion, dynamic energy, and social progress. After visiting Paris and seeing Cubist works in 1911, Boccioni painted *States of Mind I: Farewells* (**fig. 26.11**). Embedded in a fractured world of Cubist facets is an eruption of steam, sound, moving objects, and psychic energy. The white curving lines over

the locomotive reflect Mach's lines of thrust, whereas the repetition of the vaguely rendered green-tinted embracing couple is inspired by nineteenth-century motion sequences, multiple pictures taken within one second of, for example, a horse running. Boccioni is championing not just modern technology, as represented by the train, electric railroad signals, and trussed steel towers, but the perpetual movement of all objects and energy. In a May 1911 lecture in Rome, he proclaimed that painting had to capture the energy in all matter, energy in perpetual motion that dissolves the object while fusing it with surrounding space, an effect he called "plastic dynamism."

In *States of Mind I: Farewells*, we sense not only the dematerialization of the train and figures through time and movement, in part created by Boccioni's application of Divisionism, but also the simultaneous presence of space as something plastic and as vital as form. Also

26.11 Umberto Boccioni. *States of Mind I: Farewells*. 1911 (second version). Oil on canvas, 28 × 37⅞″ (70.7 × 96 cm). Museum of Modern Art, New York. Gift of Nelson A. Rockefeller. © Estate of Umberto Boccioni

swirling throughout the chaotic image is an emotional energy—a sense of painful separation and disappearance—which the title reveals as a theme of the work.

Cubo-Futurism and Suprematism in Russia

Of the major European countries in the 1910s, Russia was the least industrialized. Nevertheless, it became an important center for avant-garde art. Most of the population were serfs ruled by an indifferent czar and dominated by the Orthodox Church. Despite a rush to modernize, Russia in some respects remained trapped in the Middle Ages. In a culture dominated by folk art and icon-painting traditions, how did radical art emerge? Part of the explanation may lie in the country's

desperate need for reform. In 1917 the October (or Bolshevik) Revolution, led by Vladimir Ilyich Lenin (1870–1924), overthrew the regime and established a Communist state, finally bringing about improvements; but change was far more radical than it had been in eighteenth-century America or France. The transformation in Russia was so revolutionary that it even embraced equality for women, who had proved integral to developing the radical art of the preceding years.

THE RUSSIAN AVANT-GARDE In Moscow, Sergey Shchukin and Ivan Morozov, two of the greatest collectors of contemporary art, made available to Russian artists their extraordinary holdings of works by Matisse and Picasso. In response to these works and to growing ties with the

26.12 Lyubov Popova. *The Traveler*. 1915. Oil on canvas, 56 × 41½″ (142.2 × 105.4 cm). Norton Simon Art Foundation, Pasadena, California

Western European avant-garde, Russian artists began to explore Cubism and other approaches to abstraction, and by 1912 they were heavily influenced by Futurism. These groups embraced the modern, emphasizing the machine and industry, both critical to bringing Russia into the twentieth century.

One of the outstanding painters in this avant-garde circle was Lyubov Popova (1889–1924), who studied in Paris in 1912 and in Italy in 1914, experiencing at first hand the latest developments in Cubism and Futurism. These influences are reflected in *The Traveler* (**fig. 26.12**) of 1915. In this depiction of a woman wearing a yellow necklace and holding a green umbrella, Popova combines the fracturing of Cubism with the energy and movement of Futurism.

KAZIMIR MALEVICH By 1913 many of the Russian artists were calling themselves *Cubo-Futurists*, a term coined by Kazimir Malevich (1878–1935) that reflects the dual origins of the style. In 1913 Malevich designed Cubo-Futurist costumes and sets for what was cited as the "First Futurist Opera" and titled *Victory over the Sun*. Presented in St. Petersburg, this radical "opera" embraced the principle of **zaum**, a term invented by progressive Russian poets. Essentially, *zaum* was a language based on invented words and syntax, the meaning of which was supposedly implicit in the basic sounds and patterns of speech. The intention was to return to the nonrational and primitive base of language that, unencumbered by conventional meaning, expressed the essence of human experience. In *Victory over the Sun*, performers read from non-narrative texts often consisting of invented words while accompanied by the clatter of an out-of-tune piano. Malevich's geometric costumes and sets were equally abstract. A stack of triangles ran up and down the legs of one costume, while one backdrop was a square divided in half to form two triangles, one white, the other black.

It took Malevich two years to realize the implications of *zaum* for his art. In 1915, after working in a Cubo-Futurist style similar to Popova's, Malevich presented 39 non-objective geometric paintings in a St. Petersburg exhibition entitled *0, 10 (Zero–Ten): The Last Futurist Exhibition*. The best-known work in the show was *Black Square*, simply a large black square floating on a white ground. In his 1920s Suprematist treatise *The Non-Objective World*, Malevich explained that Suprematism is the supremacy of feeling. This feeling is not just personal or emotional but

26.13 Kazimir Malevich. *Suprematist Composition: Airplane Flying*. 1915 (dated 1914). Oil on canvas, 22⅞ × 19″ (58 × 48.3 cm). Museum of Modern Art, New York. Purchase. Acquisition confirmed in 1999 by agreement with the Estate of Kazimir Malevich and made possible with the funds from the Mrs. John Hay Whitney Bequest (by exchange). 248.1935

revelatory, for the abstract essence of the world is translated into painting using an entirely new abstract language, stripped of any vestiges of realism. Like his fellow Russian Kandinsky, Malevich was a mystic, searching for cosmic unity, even a utopian world, as would supporters of the Bolshevik Revolution of 1917. *Black Square* embodies both the legacy of simple, otherworldly Russian icons and the mysticism of folk art.

Malevich's abstract language included different geometric shapes and colors. In *Suprematist Composition: Airplane Flying* (**fig. 26.13**), also painted in 1915, he used red, yellow, and blue shapes in addition to black to create a sensation of movement and floating. Color, size, and shape produce a unique rhythm against the white ground. From one composition to the next, Malevich altered the rhythm by changing these characteristics.

Although the title includes the word airplane and suggests an infatuation with technology, the image itself relates to the experience of air travel and the new relationship to the universe brought about by this mode of transportation.

Unfortunately, reproductions of Malevich's paintings almost never show their organic quality. The shapes in *Airplane Flying* may appear to be hard-edged and geometric, but on the actual painting one can see that their boundaries waver ever so slightly and a degree of brushwork is present. Malevich's paintings contain the same human presence evident in the work of Kandinsky. Like Kandinsky, Malevich powerfully projects a serene mystical connection with the universe, which he accomplishes through the use of the white ground extending beyond the canvas into infinity.

Cubism and Fantasy: Giorgio de Chirico

In his abstract compositions, Malevich stripped down Cubist geometry to the point that Cubist structure itself virtually disappeared. Other artists, such as Giorgio de Chirico (1888–1978),

took the linear structure and spatial convolutions of Cubism and adapted them to a distinctly representational format, using the distortions of the style to create dreamlike fantasy imagery.

The Italian De Chirico arrived in Paris in 1910. While studying in Munich from 1905 to 1909, he was heavily influenced by German Romantic and Symbolist artists and the philosophy of Friedrich Nietzsche, who described life as a "foreboding that underneath this reality in which we live and have our being, another and altogether different reality lies concealed." Like Kandinsky, De Chirico was steeped in the theosophical debates swirling around Munich. Upon arriving in Paris, he abandoned his painterly style for crisply drawn scenes with multiple vanishing points. His reliance on diagonal line and disjointed space vaguely echoes Cubism, which surely must have influenced his sudden and dramatic change in style. He set many of his scenes in an empty town square resembling a stage, such as that in *Mystery and Melancholy of a Street* (**fig. 26.14**), made in Ferrara in 1914 after he returned permanently to Italy.

26.14 Giorgio de Chirico. *Mystery and Melancholy of a Street*. 1914. Oil on canvas, 34¼ × 28½″ (87 × 72.4 cm). Private collection. © DACS 2008

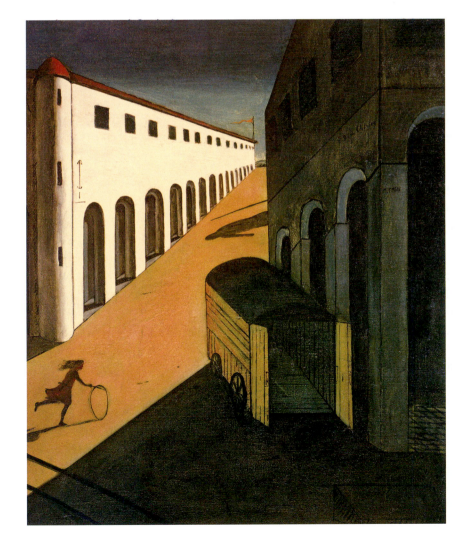

Unlike his Futurist compatriots, De Chirico idolized rather than rejected the classical past, although he subverted its austere authority by evoking a Romantic melancholy, using ominous shadows, intense light, and skewed perspective to create an unsettling eeriness. In *Mystery and Melancholy of a Street*, railroad tracks, darkened windows and arches, the empty moving van, and the girl with the hoop seem to be symbols, but De Chirico provides no clues about their meaning, insisting that none existed. Instead, the painting offers a dreamscape that can be interpreted uniquely by each viewer, just as individuals respond differently to the symbolic narratives of their dreams. De Chirico called his works metaphysical paintings, and his psychologically disturbing poetic reveries would serve as a springboard for representational Surrealism in the next decade.

Modernist Sculpture: Constantin Brancusi

The sculptures of Constantin Brancusi (1876–1957) were among the most innovative artworks being produced before World War I. Indeed, Brancusi's work is so minimal-looking and abstract that it has come to symbolize modern sculpture itself. Ironically, Brancusi's background could not have been more removed from the modern world. The son of Romanian peasants, he grew up herding sheep in the remote village of Tîrju-Jiu in the Carpathian Mountains. The region had a long tradition of ornate folk carving, in which Brancusi excelled. After studying art in Bucharest and passing through Munich in 1903, he settled in Paris and became an assistant to Auguste Rodin. Declaring that "Nothing can grow under big trees," he struck out on his own.

Escaping the far-reaching shadow of Rodin and his strong ties to nineteenth-century art, Brancusi steered a radical course that, aesthetically if not thematically, broke with sculptural tradition and laid a foundation for much twentieth-century sculpture. Brancusi's mature style began to evolve with *The Kiss* of 1907, here represented by the 1909 version (**fig. 26.15**). As we have seen, this Symbolist subject had also appeared in works by Rodin, Munch, and Klimt (see fig. 25.10). Brancusi's treatment of the theme is unique. The two nude figures are clenched together as one, forming a primordial block with minimal details etched in low relief.

26.15 Constantin Brancusi. *The Kiss*. 1909. Stone, height 35¼″ (89.5 cm). Tomb of T. Rachevaskaia, Montparnasse Cemetery, Paris. © ADAGP, Paris and DACS, London 2008

Rather than psychological conflict or Symbolist passion, Brancusi presents a tribute to the highest ideals, the universal need to create life. The stone's geometric severity recalls prehistoric monuments such as Stonehenge or austere Egyptian sculpture. Through its simplicity, *The Kiss* has shed the clutter of visual reality to pursue invisible essential truths, the very core of existence and the life force. As Brancusi explained, "Simplicity is not an end in art, but one arrives at simplicity in spite of oneself in approaching the real sense of things."

In the early 1910s, Brancusi began to simplify his works further. In *The Newborn* (**fig. 26.16**), he reduced his subject to an ovoid suggesting an egg. The form also resembles a head, with the concave depression as the mouth releasing its first cry and the narrow triangle as the nose. Yet the whole is so abstract that we are left with a sense of the elemental power of the marble, which seems to harbor the hidden mysteries

26.16 Constantin Brancusi. *The Newborn*. 1915. Marble, 5¾ × 8¼ × 5⅞" (14.6 × 20.9 × 14.9 cm). Philadelphia Museum of Art. Louise and Walter Arensberg Collection. 1950–134-10. © ADAGP, Paris and DACS, London 2008

of life. The work has the appeal of Cycladic (early Greek) sculpture and the types of simplified, geometric African masks that Brancusi knew well.

American Art

Modernism did not come to America until the second decade of the twentieth century, when it first appeared in New York at the Little Galleries of the Photo Secession, commonly referred to as "291" after its Fifth Avenue street number and owned by Alfred Stieglitz (see page 543). Beginning in 1909, Stieglitz started featuring such seminal Modernists as Picasso, Matisse, Henri Rousseau, Rodin, and Brancusi as well as African art and children's art. The momentous Modernist event in New York was the 1913 International Exhibition of Modern Art, known as the Armory Show after the 26th Street armory where it was held. Exhibited were over 400 European works, mostly French, from Delacroix through Courbet, Monet, Gauguin, Van Gogh, and Cézanne to Picasso, Brancusi, and Matisse. Three times as many American artists were represented, but by comparison their work looked provincial and was largely ignored.

Ruthless newspaper reviews lambasted the radical contemporary French art, and the public came out in droves—75,000 people attended the four-week show. The exhibition's slogan was "The New Spirit," and its symbol was the pine tree flag of Revolutionary Massachusetts. The American organizers intentionally set out to create their own revolution to jolt conventional bourgeois taste and bring about an awareness and appreciation for contemporary art. Despite the public's derision, the show spawned several modern art galleries and collectors adventurous enough to dedicate themselves to supporting radical art.

America's First Modernists: Arthur Dove and Abstraction

American artists digested European Modernism almost as quickly as it was made, but those in Europe, especially in Paris, absorbed most rapidly the new movements of Fauvism and Cubism. In 1908 a young Arthur Dove (1880–1946) was in Paris, where he saw work by Matisse and the Fauves. When he returned to New York, he met Stieglitz and began showing at "291."

While remaining involved in the New York art world throughout his life, Dove lived in rural areas in New York State and Connecticut, even spending several years on a houseboat anchored off Long Island. His art focused on nature, not modernity, and on capturing universal forces. By 1910 he was painting complete abstractions, two years before Kandinsky. In *Plant Forms* (**fig. 26.17**), from a series of pastels titled *The Ten Commandments*, Dove has supplied all the components of nature without painting it illusionistically.

As with Cubism, the composition of *Plant Forms* is made up of abstract components, although they overlap in a logical, consistent fashion to suggest continuous recession in space. The work has light and atmosphere as well as an organic quality, largely due to the elliptical, oval, and round forms and the biomorphic shapes suggestive of plants and trees. The curved white and yellow forms evoke suns, moons, and hills, and although the frondlike shapes recall plants and trees, they are also symbols of an unidentifiable burst of energy. We feel the powerful surge of nature and an elemental life force, and because each form suggests many different objects, Dove is able to convey the universal interconnectedness of all things. The picture is cosmic in its scope yet provides an intimate view of nature. Dove's preoccupation with portraying potent natural forces will become a

26.17 Arthur Dove. *Plant Forms.* ca. 1912. Pastel on canvas, 17¼ × 23⅞" (43.8 × 60.6 cm). Whitney Museum of American Art, New York. Collection of the Whitney Museum of American Art. Purchase. Purchase with Funds from Mr. and Mrs. Roy R. Neuberger 51.20

major theme in American art and, as we shall see, one of the major issues for artists in Stieglitz's circle.

Early Modern Architecture in Europe

In the last chapter, we saw the emergence of two distinct approaches to modern architecture, one in the United States and another in Europe. American architects like Louis Sullivan and Frank Lloyd Wright challenged historicism and conventional revivalism when they eliminated the distinction between the form of a building and its proposed function. In Europe, we also saw a rejection of revival styles when Art Nouveau defined modern architecture as an organic style of growth and movement. Throughout the twentieth century, modern architecture followed these opposite poles set by the Chicago School and Art Nouveau—the rational, geometric and functional versus the personal, referential, organic, and expressive.

German Modernist Architecture

Germany played a major role in shaping architectural developments in the opening decades of the century, largely because the German government and industry nurtured Modernist architecture. In 1896, government officials sent the architect Hermann Muthesius to London, then the world leader in quality mass-production, to study British industry and design. Upon returning in 1904, Muthesius was appointed to the Prussian Trade Commission and given the task of restructuring education in the applied arts. To dominate world markets, he advocated mass-production of functional objects executed in a well-designed machine style. In 1907, he was instrumental in establishing the Deutsche Werkbund, an association of architects, designers, writers, and industrialists whose goal was "selecting the best representatives of art, industry, crafts, and trades, of combining all efforts toward high quality in industrial work." In architecture he called for a new monumental style based on Schinkel's classicism (see fig. 23.15), but reflecting modern industrial values. More important, this industrial architectural style had to be a machine style—one that was based on a *Typisierung*, meaning a type or a basic unit, which permitted the development of a mass-produced modular building usable by all architects.

WALTER GROPIUS The Werkbund architect who fulfilled Muthesius's goal was Walter Gropius (1882–1969). With his associate Adolf Meyer, he was commissioned in 1911 to design the Fagus Factory (**fig. 26.18**), a shoe plant in Alfeld-an-der-Leine, Germany. In this building, Gropius reached back to the Chicago School architects and utilized their steel-grid skeleton, sheathed in a ferro-vitreous curtain wall. The factory's glass façade appears to be magically suspended from the brick-faced entablature above. It even turns corners unobstructed, making it appear to float. The building feels light and transparent, the window mullions thin and elegant. Horizontal opaque panels, the exact size and shape of the glass, indicate each of the three floors and continue the modular composition of the windows. Here was the machine style Muthesius was seeking: An unadorned building that adheres to a grid skeleton. This building type was sufficiently efficient and reproducible to serve as the prototype for the glass-box structures that would dominate world architecture in the second half of the century.

26.19 Bruno Taut. Glass Pavilion, Werkbund Exhibition. 1914. Cologne

German Expressionist Architecture

Not all German architects embraced technology, the machine age, and Muthesius's concept of the *Typisierung*. Others instead designed expressive spiritual structures meant to counter the cold, impersonal impact of modernity.

BRUNO TAUT An overt spiritual contribution to the 1914 Werkbund Exhibition was the Glass Pavilion (**fig. 26.19**) built by Bruno Taut (1880–1928) for the glass industry and reflecting his belief in the mystical properties of crystal. The guru of glass was the poet Paul Scheerbart, whose 1914 essay *Glasarchitektur* (Glass Architecture) had a tremendous impact on artists and architects. The entablature of Taut's Glass Pavilion is even etched with Scheerbart's sayings about the power of glass.

Scheerbart claimed that only a glass architecture that opened all rooms to light could raise German culture to a new spiritual level. Consequently, Taut used glass brick for the walls and floors. The bulbous dome, which resembles a giant crystal, is made of two layers of glass; the outer one reflective, the inner a myriad of colored-glass pieces resembling medieval stained glass. Taut also considered his cupola to be Gothic, its facets evoking the vital force of Flamboyant ribbing (see Chapter 11). The ceiling of the main space had a central oculus that emitted a shower of mystical colored light.

SUMMARY

The social and cultural conditions of the early twentieth century were a crucible for the continuing development of modern art in the West. Scientific breakthroughs revised centuries-old beliefs about the fundamental nature of matter and energy, leading artists to reconsider the basic principles of composition, some even finding the essence of humanity in pure abstraction.

When seen at the Salon d'Automne of 1905, the brilliant works of Matisse and his colleagues struck viewers as so shocking and unconventional that the group was labeled fauves, wild beasts. While Fauvist art abandoned representational color and conventional systems of perspective, the themes were far from radical: Idyllic pastoral views, portraits, still lifes.

Picasso deliberately engaged French academicism as well when he painted his radical *Les Demoiselles d'Avignon* in 1907. The picture, which shattered conventional pictoral space, led to Cubism, which Picasso developed with Georges Braque. The two artists built on Cézanne's solidly structured meditations on nature, making images with multiple viewpoints and deconstructing objects into a web of abstract line and form

The emotional restraint of Fauvism and Cubism gave way to Expressionism. Tapping into elemental, often difficult emotions, the German and Austrian Expressionists sought a visual language that could convey the raw intensity of their feelings, both toward contemporary life and universal forces.

Meanwhile, Giorgio de Chirico developed the new Cubist reconfigurations of space to represent fantastical landscapes of dream, myth, and memory that evoke ancient Rome. His Italian contemporaries, the Futurists, shunned the past, instead embracing what they believed were the hallmarks of modernity: Industrialization, speed, factories, and even mechanized warfare. They used the fractured world of Cubism to convey the movement and dynamic energy of modernity.

The Modernist Constantin Brancusi reduced sculpture to a minimal essence of abstract form that captured elemental truths about life and experience.

Alfred Stieglitz's gallery "291" and the 1913 Armory Show sought to introduce Modernism to America and succeeded in generating a handful of galleries and collectors dedicated to supporting modern art. The most advanced art was created by those American artists who went to Europe, including Arthur Dove, who made abstract paintings as early as 1910.

Modern European architecture first appeared in Germany, among other countries, and followed one of two paths. Either it was mechanomorphic, adhering to the form-follows-function concept of the Chicago School, a path taken by Walter Gropius, who viewed a building as a steel-grid skeleton clad in a skin of glass. Or it was personal, expressionistic, and fantastic, following the model established by Art Nouveau, and advocated by a group of German architects, especially Bruno Taut, who made buildings out of glass, allowing mystical light to permeate the interior.

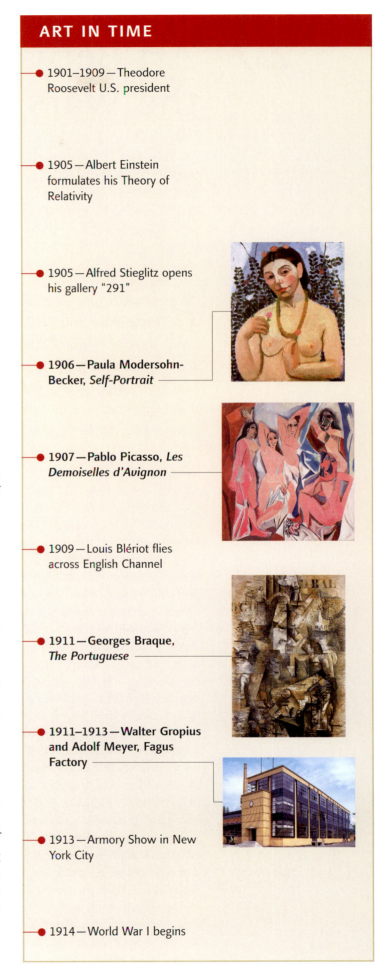

ART IN TIME

- 1901–1909 — Theodore Roosevelt U.S. president

- 1905 — Albert Einstein formulates his Theory of Relativity

- 1905 — Alfred Stieglitz opens his gallery "291"

- 1906 — Paula Modersohn-Becker, *Self-Portrait*

- 1907 — Pablo Picasso, *Les Demoiselles d'Avignon*

- 1909 — Louis Blériot flies across English Channel

- 1911 — Georges Braque, *The Portuguese*

- 1911–1913 — Walter Gropius and Adolf Meyer, Fagus Factory

- 1913 — Armory Show in New York City

- 1914 — World War I begins

27 | Art Between the Wars

*P*hysically and psychologically, World War I devastated Western civilization. The destruction and loss of life were staggering, with hundreds of thousands of soldiers dying in single battles. The Enlightenment-based logic, science, and technology that many thought would bring about a better world had gone horribly awry. Instead of a better world, the advancements of the nineteenth century had produced such high-tech weapons as machine guns, long-range artillery, tanks, submarines, fighter planes, and mustard gas.

To many, the very concept of nationalism now seemed destructive, and the rise of the first Communist government in Russia in 1917 offered the hope of salvation. Around the world, branches of the Communist Party sprang up, with the goal of creating a nationless world united by the proletariat, the working class that provided the labor force for the capitalist system. Others maintained that a new world order could not be attained without first destroying the old; they advocated anarchy (a complete lack of any form of government or control), which remained a constant threat in the postwar decades. Despite this drive to create a nationless and classless world, by the 1930s it was fascism that dominated European politics. Fascism, a totalitarian political system that exalts the nation over the individual and demands allegiance to a single leader, held a special appeal for nations defeated in World War I. Germans gradually became enthralled by Adolf Hitler (1889–1945) and his Nazi party, who skillfully used economic crises and anti-Semitism (anti-Jewish sentiment and practices) to consolidate power. In Italy and Japan as well, fascists, under the command of charismatic leaders, took control. Armed with new technological tools of destruction, these nations would plunge the world into another great war by 1939.

While fascism, Communism, anarchy, and democracy jockeyed for dominance in Europe, America enjoyed unprecedented prosperity in the 1920s. Historians have called the economic and cultural exuberance of the postwar years the Roaring Twenties; it was a time of jazz, speakeasies (illicit drinking clubs), radio, and film. The 1920s also saw the rise of the city as the emblem of the nation. Technology and machines were king in America, where the world's largest skyscrapers could be erected in a year. This economic exhilaration came to a screeching halt with the stockmarket crash of October 1929, which sent the entire world into a downward economic spiral known as the Great Depression, lasting throughout the 1930s. A reactionary backlash then occurred in both Europe and America (see map 27.1): Fascism in the former, and a conservative regionalism and isolationism in the latter. Nonetheless, the 1930s marked the advent in America of liberal social and economic programs, instituted by Franklin Delano Roosevelt's administration (1932–1944). Believing that economic markets were inherently unstable, Roosevelt advocated the New Deal, which created millions of government-sponsored jobs, including many for artists.

Perhaps the strongest defining influence for artists between the wars was the Great War itself

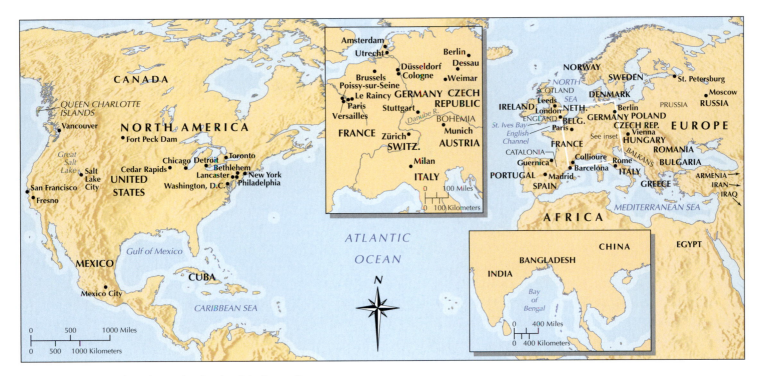

Map 27.1 Europe and North America showing Asia (inserted)

and the technology, science, and Enlightenment rationalism that enabled it to be so devastating. A direct result of the war was Dada, a movement that created a nonsensical nihilistic art attacking bourgeois values and conventions, including faith in technology. The Dadaists aimed to wipe the philosophical slate clean, leading the way to a new world order. Other artists embraced the modernity of the Machine Age (as this interwar period is sometimes called), seeing it as a means to create classless utopias; still others rejected it, seeking higher truths or a meaningful spirituality in an increasingly materialistic, soulless world. Both groups often turned to abstraction to implement their vision. Those supporting technology embraced the geometry and mechanical look of the Machine Age, while those who rejected it sought higher truths using an organic or biomorphic vocabulary.

A second major force was Sigmund Freud (see page 546), whose theories about the unconscious and dreams were a formative influence on Surrealism, a prevailing movement in the 1920s and 1930s. Like many abstract artists, the Surrealists sought to reveal invisible, not spiritual realities, but nonetheless the elemental universal forces that drive all humans. These unseen realities are deeply embedded in the mind and symbolically revealed in dreams. Freud maintained that the conventions of civilization had repressed the elemental needs and desires shared by all people, and that this suppressed, invisible world

of desires and sexual energy was fundamental to human behavior. For Surrealist artists, as well as writers and intellectuals, Freud's theory of the unconscious confirmed the existence of realities unseen by the eye or not perceived by the conscious mind, and they served as the springboard for the development of Surrealist imagery and style.

Politics also strongly shaped the art of the period. Many if not most avant-garde artists were socialists and Communists, or at least sympathizers, and their utopian dreams and aesthetic visions stemmed in part from these political ideologies. The narrative, representational murals of the great Mexican artists directly champion Communism, especially when paired with science, as the vehicle for creating a classless utopian society. With the rise to power of Hitler and his National Socialist (Nazi) Party, some avant-garde artists turned their attention to making anti-fascist imagery and exposing the insane thinking and sadistic brutality of the new German government.

This era also saw a growing interest in racial and ethnic identity, which was expressed in Mexican as well African-American art. The Mexican muralists were preoccupied with national identity, which they associated with the indigenous population, not the Euro-Mexicans, while African Americans looked to uncover their heritage and culture. Just as Mary Cassatt and Julia Margaret Cameron sought to present women from a female as opposed to a male viewpoint, obtaining very different results, so the Mexicans and African Americans did the same for their own societies. These artists presented a very different image of and attitude toward non-European cultures.

Dada

The Great War halted much art-making, as many artists were enlisted in their country's military service and a great number were killed. But the conflict also produced one art movement: Dada. Its name was chosen at random, the story goes, when two German poets, Richard Huelsenbeck and Hugo Ball, plunged a knife into a French-German dictionary and its point landed on *dada*, the French word for "hobbyhorse." The word's association with childishness as well as the random violence of the poets' act of word choice fit the postwar spirit of the movement perfectly. As the birth story of Dada suggests, the foundations of the movement lay in chance occurrences and the absurd. Reason, the Dada artists concluded, had led only to war. For them the nonsensical and the absurd became tools to jolt their audience out of their bourgeois complacency and conventional thinking. The movement was profoundly committed to challenging the *status quo* in politics as well as in culture.

27.1 Jean (Hans) Arp. *The Entombment of the Birds and Butterflies (Head of Tzara).* 1916–1917. Painted wooden relief, 15¾ × 12¾" (40 × 32.5 cm). Kunsthaus, Zurich. © DACS, 2008

Dada began in 1916 in Zurich, in neutral Switzerland, where a large number of writers and artists had sought refuge from the war.

Zurich Dada: Jean (Hans) Arp

In Zurich, the poet Hugo Ball founded the Cabaret Voltaire in 1916 as a performance center where writers and artists could protest at the absurdity and wastefulness of the Great War. Ball was soon joined by the Romanian poet Tristan Tzara, who became Dada's most vociferous proponent. Through absurd art, literature, and performances, they hoped to produce anarchy, a *tabula rasa* or clean slate, that would provide a new, fresh foundation for an understanding of the world.

The Zurich Dadaists exhibited a broad range of avant-garde art, such as paintings by De Chirico (see fig. 26.14)—as long as it undermined bourgeois taste and standards. Most of the art was abstract. Among the strongest visual artists in the group was Jean ("Hans" in German) Arp (1886–1966), whose abstract collages hung on the walls of the Cabaret Voltaire on opening night. Arp made his collages by dropping pieces of torn rectangular paper on the floor; where they fell determined the composition. Although he claimed that chance alone arranged the papers, Arp probably manipulated them.

Arp believed that chance itself replicated nature. For him, life, despite the best-laid plans, was pure happenstance. Arp had been in Munich with Kandinsky (see pages 555–556), and there he adopted a mystical view of the world that envisioned a life force running through all things, binding them together in no particular order. Like Kandinsky, Arp sought to capture abstract universal forces. This spiritual outlook can be seen in the low-relief sculptures that he began making at about this time, such as *The Entombment of the Birds and Butterflies (Head of Tzara)* (**fig. 27.1**). The different shapes were determined by doodling on paper. He then had the shapes cut out of wood, which he painted and assembled into abstract compositions evoking plant and animal forms as well as clouds, cosmic gases, and celestial bodies. The title came last, and, as it suggests, the image can also be seen as a head, suggesting an elemental connection between humans and nature.

New York Dada: Marcel Duchamp

In New York, Dada was centered on Marcel Duchamp. The New York artists had no Café Voltaire, no manifestos, and no performances.

The word Dada was never used at the time to describe their art; it was applied only in retrospect because their spirit was similar to that found in Zurich. Similarly they used chance processes and the absurd and outrageous to challenge bourgeois sensitivity and the *status quo*.

Perhaps the highlight of New York Dada is Duchamp's *Fountain* (**fig. 27.2**). The artist submitted his sculpture to the 1917 exhibition of the Society of Independent Artists, an organization set up several decades earlier to provide exhibition opportunities for artists who did not conform to the conservative standards of New York's National Academy of Design, which had been the primary exhibition venue. Duchamp labeled his *Fountain* an "assisted Readymade." He took the term from American readymade clothing, and applied it to sculptures that simply re-presented a found object, such as a snow shovel, which he hung from the ceiling and entitled *In Advance of a Broken Arm*. Duchamp called "assisted Readymades" those objects that he "assisted," by combining two found items, as in *Bicycle Wheel* of 1913, in which he mounted a bike wheel on a bar stool, or by signing, as in *Fountain*.

Fountain was, in fact, a urinal manufactured by J. L. Mott Iron Works in New York. Duchamp selected it, purchased it, turned it ninety degrees, set it on a pedestal, and crudely signed it with the fictitious name of "R. Mutt"—a reference not only to the manufacturer but also to the character in the popular *Mutt and Jeff* comic strip. The work was submitted to the society's exhibition under Mutt's name, not Duchamp's. According to the society's rules, those paying the $6 admission fee would have their work accepted. But Duchamp knew the hanging committee would not allow Mutt's *Fountain* to go on view, and when it was removed at the opening, his friends formed a rowdy removal procession that drew attention to its rejection.

Duchamp continued the hoax of R. Mutt's authorship of the piece when he wrote an article about it in his small newspaper, *The Blind Man*. The article was illustrated by a Stieglitz photograph of it placed before a painting by the American artist Marsden Hartley, thus asserting that the proper context for *Fountain* was the art world. The article defended Mutt's right to create a Readymade: "Whether Mr. Mutt with his own hands made the fountain or not has no importance. He chose. He took an ordinary article of life, placed it so that its useful significance disappeared under a new title and point of view …[creating] a new thought for that object."

27.2 Marcel Duchamp. *Fountain*. 1917. Photograph by Alfred Stieglitz, from *The Blind Man*. May 1917. Philadelphia Museum of Art, Louise and Walter Arensberg Collection. © Succession Marcel Duchamp/ADAGP, Paris and DACS, London 2008

Like all of Duchamp's works, *Fountain* is rich in ideas, and it stands as one of the seminal works of twentieth-century art, although the original has disappeared. The sculpture is all about idea. A viewer of *Fountain* must ask, what is the work of art? Is it the urinal, the provocation of submitting it to the exhibition, the flamboyant parade when it was removed from the show, or the article in *The Blind Man*? Obviously, it is all of these things. Even the title is essential to the work, since it is an essential part of the sculpture, allowing Duchamp to make it clear that he is attacking a revered art form, the fountain, the centerpiece of many European towns and city squares and, in some respects, a symbol for the tradition of fine art. The satirical title also reinforces the humor of the piece, an ingredient found in much of Duchamp's work. He is telling us that art can defy conventional notions of beauty, and while intellectually engaging us in a most serious manner, can also make us smile or laugh. He challenges the notion of what is art and the importance of technique or craft, as well as the artist's signature. He also asks how a work of art takes on meaning. Here, Duchamp emphasizes the relationship between context and meaning: By taking a urinal out of its normal context he has changed its meaning. (For a more extensive discussion of Duchamp, see the Introduction, pages 9–11.) He even allows a viewer to assign meaning to the work, underscoring how this is a reality for all art. Duchamp declared that, unlike all art before him, his Readymades have no aesthetic value and theoretically no intended meaning. They are merely a device to launch ideas.

Because *Fountain* is industrially manufactured and can be easily replaced if broken or lost, Duchamp also questions the significance attached to the uniqueness of a work of art. As we shall see, in the second half of the twentieth century, Duchamp will become the dominant figure in art as artists worldwide make what will be called Conceptual Art. For those artists, an idea or conceptual premise is an important component of their work, often the most important.

Berlin Dada

With the end of the war, the Dada poet Richard Huelsenbeck (1892–1974) left Zurich for Berlin. There he found a moribund city, which like all of Germany was without food, money, medicine, or a future. Germans, especially the working class, loathed the military-industrial machine, which they felt had betrayed their interests by leading them into war. With the surrender, conditions worsened as Germany was punished by harsh and, some thought, unrealistic reparation

demands. Inflation was rampant, and the value of the German mark plunged. Open class conflict in 1919 resulted in Communist-led worker uprisings in Berlin and Munich that were brutally repressed by right-wing armed units. The Weimar Republic government, which had replaced the emperor and represented Germany's first experience with democracy, failed to revive the economy.

For many, hope lay in the East, in Russia, where the Bolshevik Revolution established the prospect for a nationless world governed by the proletariat. The artists and writers in Berlin Dada looked to international worker solidarity as Germany's salvation. Here was a situation where Dada anarchy and nihilism could be put to practical use. Almost without exception, the Berlin Dada contingent made political art and were political activists, with some members joining the Communist Party.

RAOUL HAUSMANN Raoul Hausmann (1886–1971) quickly became the leader of the Berlin Dadaists, and was perhaps the most visually inventive, as can be seen in his 1920 assemblage *Mechanical Head (Spirit of the Age)* (**fig. 27.3**). He used found objects, which at the time were so foreign to the art world that they were considered junk: A mannequin's head, a collapsible cup, a wallet, labels, nails, and rulers. But now we see a new approach to making sculpture: The found objects are assembled together, for the purpose of making a statement condemning materialism and the loss of individuality and personal identity.

HANNAH HÖCH Hausmann, however, is best known for his use of language, in Dada poems and in collage, which he called photomontages and which evoke a machine-made, massproduced, anti-art aesthetic. Some of the most elaborate and powerful Dada collages from the period were created by Hannah Höch (1889–1978). They mimic manipulated photographic portraits made for the German military. Individuals or entire battalions hired photographers to create fictitious portraits by photographing the patron or patrons, then cutting out their heads and pasting them onto pre-existing pictures of, for example, mounted militia.

Cut with the Kitchen Knife Dada Through the Last Weimar Beer Belly Cultural Epoch of Germany (**fig. 27.4**) speaks volumes about the agenda of Berlin Dada. Using a chaotic, cramped composition of crowds, words, machinery, and lettering of different sizes and styles, Höch captures the

27.3 Raoul Hausmann. *Mechanical Head (Spirit of the Age)*. ca. 1920. Assemblage, height 12¾" (32.5 cm). Musée National d'Art Moderne, Centre Georges Pompidou, Paris. © ADAGP, Paris and DACS, London 2008

27.4 Hannah Höch. *Cut with the Kitchen Knife Dada Through the Last Weimar Beer Belly Cultural Epoch of Germany.* ca. 1919. Collage, 44⅞ × 35⅛″ (114 × 90.2 cm). Staatliche Museen, Berlin. © DACS 2008

hectic social, political, and economic intensity of the Weimar Republic. Her photomontage represents the reality captured by photographers for the popular press. To Höch and her Dada colleagues, the camera was another machine, related to the technological advances that had led to the war. With her "kitchen knife," she rearranged the imagery to create a handmade photograph, thus forcing the machine to be subject to the human rather than vice versa. The result is a spinning, gearlike composition with a portrait of the radical antiwar female artist Käthe Kollwitz at the center. German masses and the new leaders of their government, the

Weimar Republic, are pushed to the sides and villainously labeled as the "anti-Dada," meaning against Dada and leftist politics.

Cologne Dada

In the city of Cologne, Dada initially took its lead from Berlin, but it was never as overtly political. Dada artists here were intrigued by Freud's theory of the unconscious and favored figures that combined mechanical and human forms (sometimes called **mechanomorphic** art), reminiscent of the work of Duchamp and Picabia. The key Cologne Dada artist was Max Ernst (1891–1976), who appropriated the Berlin artists' collage technique.

Typical of Ernst's work from this very productive period is *1 Copper Plate 1 Zinc Plate 1 Rubber Cloth 2 Calipers 1 Drainpipe Telescope 1 Piping Man* (**fig. 27.5**), a collage with gouache, ink, and pencil made on an illustration from a 1914 book about chemistry equipment. With a line here and a dab of paint there, Ernst transformed the picture of laboratory utensils into bizarre robotic figures set in a stark symbol-filled landscape. Perhaps we should say dreamscape, for the glazed-over stares, and the skewed De Chirico-like perspective that culminates in a mystifying square, give this little collage an elemental power suggesting some otherworldly sphere—one of the imagination. The dreamlike quality of Ernst's image endows his figures with heavy psychological overtones. Not surprisingly, Ernst was fascinated by Freud's theories about the unconscious and the importance of dreams.

Through Arp, Ernst was put in contact with two leaders of the Paris Dada movement, the poets André Breton and Paul Eluard, both of whom had also come under Freud's spell, entranced by the idea that the unconscious contained realities suppressed by civilization. In 1922, Ernst emigrated to Paris, and in 1924 Breton issued a Surrealist Manifesto, anointing a 1921 Paris show of Ernst's collages as the first Surrealist exhibition.

Paris Dada: Man Ray

The transition from Dada to Surrealism was well underway by 1922, and it occurred in Paris. Dada had established a foothold in the French capital with the return of Duchamp at the end of 1918.

One of the artists who moved in and out of the Paris Dada circle and would soon be labeled a major Surrealist was the American Man Ray (1890–1976). He had befriended Duchamp in

27.5 Max Ernst. *1 Copper Plate 1 Zinc Plate 1 Rubber Cloth 2 Calipers 1 Drainpipe Telescope 1 Piping Man*. 1920. Collage, 12 × 9" (30.5 × 22.9 cm). Estate of Hans Arp.
© ADAGP, Paris and DACS, London 2008

New York, participated in New York Dada, and followed Duchamp to Paris in 1921. Best known as a photographer, Man Ray was extraordinarily inventive and worked in many media, some, such as airbrush painting, being quite innovative. Most important, Man Ray was the first artist to use photography consistently within a Dada context, and helped establish it, at least within Dada and Surrealist circles, as a medium on a par with painting and sculpture.

In 1922, Man Ray had a major impact on the development of photography, as well as on Dada and abstract art, when he popularized the photogram—a one-of-a-kind cameraless photograph made by putting objects directly on photographic paper and then exposing both object and paper to light (**fig. 27.6**). Solid objects block light from striking the white paper, so they appear white in the image, while the spaces between and around them become black, since there is nothing to prevent the light from exposing the paper. Tzara dubbed Man Ray's print a "rayograph."

Reproduced here is a photograph of one of these first rayographs, *Champs délicieux* (Delightful Field), which contains the silhouettes of a brush and comb, a sewing pin, a coil of paper, and a strip of fabric, among the identifiable items. The image, like much of Man Ray's work, helps demonstrate the close relationship between the random and defiant art of Dada and the evocative, often sensual, art of Surrealism. The objects appear ghostlike and mysterious, in a strange environment where darks and lights have been reversed and where a haunting overall darkness prevails. Shapes and lines move in and out of dark shadows, sometimes vibrating, as with the brush and comb silhouette, at other times crisply stated, as in the center oval. Man Ray's photograms, as with the Surrealistic art that would follow, have a magical blend of the real and nonreal. We feel the presence of a real comb and sewing pin, and yet they seem to exist in a dream world. Just as impossible to explain is the relationship of these objects and shapes to one another.

Surrealism

Surrealism had existed in spirit, if not in name, well before 1924, but the movement was formally launched by Breton that year when he issued his Surrealist Manifesto. Surrealism, Breton wrote, is "pure psychic automatism, by which it is intended to express, either verbally, or

27.6 Man Ray. *Champs délicieux*. 1922. Rayograph gelatin silver print. © Man Ray Trust/ADAGP, Paris and DACS, London 2008

in writing, or in any other way, the true functioning of thought. Thought expressed in the absence of any control exerted by reason, and outside all moral and aesthetic considerations." Banished was the Neoclassical god of reason, the sureness of logic, and the need to portray an observable reality. Also gone was Dada nihilism, replaced by an intensive, positive exploration of the unconscious.

Surrealists argued that we see only a surface reality. More important was uncovering the reality that, as Freud maintained, resided in the deep-seated secrets and desires of the unconscious mind. Breton's manifesto proposed several ways to tap into the unconscious. He encouraged the use of dreamlike images, the juxtaposition of unrelated objects, and, for writers, stream-of-consciousness writing. He emphasized the concept of creating "the marvelous," images, either verbal or visual, that are mysterious, chance, and poetic, and jolt the audience into a new, unknown plane of reality, a surreality. But visual art had little place in Breton's manifesto, and artists were mentioned only as a footnote, appearing in a single sentence. Among those listed were Ernst, Man Ray, De Chirico, and Picasso. Perhaps the most surprising name on Breton's list is Picasso's, but Breton saw Picasso's Cubism as the first step toward loosening the grip of reality on the artistic imagination, and he especially admired *Les Demoiselles d'Avignon*.

Surrealism in Paris

In 1924, Breton, like everyone, had doubts about the possibility that there could even be Surrealist art. Many argued that the visual arts, unlike writing, did not allow for a stream of consciousness. The imagery could seem surreal, but the method was not. Initially, many of the visual artists championed by Breton relied on automatic drawing and chance to produce their images. The Parisian André Masson is best known for developing automatic drawing, producing a wiry automatic line while in a trancelike state. He then allowed the initial chance drawing to spur his imagination, fleshing out the composition from there. Not to be outdone, Max Ernst developed the technique of *frottage*, which consisted of placing paper on top of an object, say, a piece of wood, and then rubbing graphite or charcoal over the surface to obtain an image, which like Masson's automatic drawing would spur his imagination to create a fantasy world.

Another artist championed as a Surrealist by Breton was Joan Miró (1893–1983), born in Catalonia, who came to Paris in 1920. He adopted Masson's wiry line to make abstractions of biomorphic and geometric forms set against a minimal color field that suggested a landscape or watery environment. Miró's paintings became increasingly abstract, as seen in *Composition* (**fig. 27.7**), a 1933 oil. The work was one in a series based on collages on cardboard made from images cut out of product catalogues, with the idea that the shape and even details of the objects would fire his imagination. The setting of *Composition* is a hazy atmospheric environment of washes, suggesting a kind of primeval landscape. This eerie world is populated by strange curvilinear floating forms that suggest prehistoric and microscopic creatures, as well as spirits, ghosts, or souls. We can even find a story in places, such as two figures playing with or fighting over a ball in the upper left corner. Or are they? Regardless, they suggest play or fighting, as other features in the painting express sex, struggle, and fear. Miró uses a minimal vocabulary, which includes color as well as form, to create a mythic image evoking primal conditions.

Representational Surrealism: Salvador Dalí

Initially, Breton's strongest support was for an abstract Surrealism based on chance, spontaneity, and trance. Over the next decade, however, artists with all kinds of styles would move in and out of the movement, and representational Surrealism in particular became popular.

One of the major Surrealists working in a representational style was Salvador Dalí (1904–1989). He came to Paris from Madrid, where he had already developed a meticulously detailed realist style heavily based on the psychological complexes that Freud described in his writings. Dalí made his paintings using a process he called "paranoiac-critical"—"[a] spontaneous method of irrational knowledge based upon the interpretative-critical association of delirious phenomena." He created in a frenzy, a self-induced paranoid state where he would begin a painting with a single object in mind. Then, he would respond to that object and so on, developing a mysterious image reflecting an irrational process that released the unconscious. *The Persistence of Memory* (**fig. 27.8**) began with the strange amorphous head with an elongated trailing neck lying on the ground. Looking at a plate of soft Camembert cheese at dinner, he was then

27.7 Joan Miró. *Composition*. 1933. Oil on canvas, 51⅜ × 64⅛″ (130.5 × 162.9 cm). Wadsworth Atheneum, Hartford, Connecticut. The Ella Gallup Sumner and Mary Catlin Sumner Collection Fund. © Succession Miró/ADAGP, Paris and DACS, London 2008

27.8 Salvador Dalí. *The Persistence of Memory*. 1931. Oil on canvas, 9½ × 13″ (24.1 × 33 cm). The Museum of Modern Art, New York. Given anonymously (162.1934). © Salvador Dalí, Gala-Salvador Dalí Foundation/DACS, London 2008 *Surrealism*

inspired to paint the soft pocket watches. While allowing no certain reading, the picture evokes a host of associations, such as male impotency, and most obviously the crippling passage of time that leads to inevitable deterioration and death. Dalí has created a provocative image of mysterious objects that can be read as metaphors for the deepest desires, fears, and anxieties, especially sexual, of the mind, and that can unleash multiple interpretations from a viewer's own unconscious.

The Surrealist Object

When Miró began work on his *Composition*, he started with an image that, like a dream, took him on a journey of psychological exploration and formal invention. Surrealists also created objects that would initiate such journeys for viewers as well as for themselves. In fact some of the most succinct Surrealist artworks were fetishistic objects, mysterious poetic things that were found or created, and had no narrative, but jolted the unconscious and spawned infinite associations, mostly sexual and often violent.

Probably the most famous Surrealist object was made by Meret Oppenheim (1913–1985). Born in Germany, she went to Paris as an 18-year-old in 1932. Inspired by an off-hand comment she made when lunching with Picasso in 1936, she covered a teacup, saucer, and spoon

with gazelle fur and called it *Object* (**fig. 27.9**), although Breton, when he included it in a Surrealist exhibition, retitled it *Luncheon in Fur*, punning on Manet's sexually fraught *Luncheon on the Grass* (see fig. 24.2). Oppenheim presents us with eroticism offered and eroticism denied, for

27.9 Meret Oppenheim. *Object (Luncheon in Fur)*. 1936. Fur-covered teacup, saucer, and spoon; diameter of cup 4¼″ (12.1 cm); diameter of saucer 9⅜″ (23.8 cm); length of spoon 8″ (20.3 cm). The Museum of Modern Art, New York. © DACS 2008

individually, fur and beverage are sensual, but juxtaposed as they are, they are disconcerting, if not outright repulsive. The fur anthropomorphizes the porcelain and spoon, and suggests pubic hair. The work is designed to trigger the unconscious, to evoke infinite associations that deal with the repressed realities of eroticism, sensuality, desire, and anxiety. Using minimal means, Oppenheim created the "marvelous" that takes a viewer into the realm of the surreal.

Organic Sculpture

The abstract Surrealism of Miró and Arp inspired many artists to search for universal truths beneath the surface of things. As did the Romantic landscape painters of the previous century, they focused on nature, trying to pry loose the unseen pulse of the cosmos that coursed through the natural world. To reveal these higher truths and realities, a number of artists, including Alexander Calder in Paris and Henry Moore in England, turned to working with abstract organic forms. Often, they showed in Surrealist exhibitions and were occasionally labeled Surrealists, especially since their work dealt with hidden realities. But despite many parallels, their interests were quite different from Breton's as they evolved in the 1930s. Breton was more concerned with the psychology of anxiety, desire, and sex; the artists working with abstract organic forms were interested in the powerful forces of the universe.

Alexander Calder in Paris

The American Alexander Calder (1898–1976) went to Paris in 1926, where he befriended Miró and the abstract Dutch painter Piet Mondrian. In the early 1930s he started making **mobiles**, a name that Duchamp gave his kinetic sculpture (work involving movement). Each mobile was constructed of painted sheet metal attached to wires that were hinged together and perfectly balanced. With the slightest gust of air, the mobile seems to glide, tilting and turning in space. The mobiles vary in size from tabletop models to others with a 30-foot span that hang from a ceiling.

27.10 Alexander Calder. *Lobster Trap and Fish Tail*. 1939. Painted steel wire and sheet aluminum, approx. 8′6″ × 9′6″ (2.59 × 2.89 m). The Museum of Modern Art, New York, Commissioned by the Advisory Committee for the Stairwell of the Museum. © Calder Foundation, New York/DACS, London 2008

27.11 Henry Moore. *Recumbent Figure*. 1938. Green Hornton stone, length approx. 54″ (137.2 cm). The Tate Britain, London. © The Henry Moore Foundation

Taking his lead from Miró and Arp, Calder generally used organic shapes, as seen in *Lobster Trap and Fish Tail* (**fig. 27.10**) of 1939. The forms suggest marine life, but generally they are abstract, and like Miró's paintings, simultaneously suggest the microscopic and macroscopic. The black forms in *Lobster Trap* can be seen as a school of fish, but viewed together they can suggest something skeletal, even primeval. Calder was inspired to develop kinetic sculpture to suggest growth and cosmic energy. He kept his colors basic, generally using primary and secondary colors, as well as black and white. All colors stem from these, so Calder's palette symbolized the basic building blocks of life, a notion that he took from Mondrian, whose Paris studio he visited in 1930.

Henry Moore in England

The organic abstract style favored by Miró jumped the English Channel in the 1930s, surfacing in the work of Henry Moore (1898–1986). Moore's mature style emerged by the early 1930s, represented here by *Recumbent Figure* (**fig. 27.11**), made in 1938. The work is reminiscent of a classical reclining river goddess, although based more directly on Pre-Columbian figures. Moore is more interested in projecting the elemental and universal than in classical antiquity as he explores the associations between the forms of nature and the shapes of the figure. We see a woman, but the stone retains its identity as stone, looking like a rock that has been eroded by the elements for millions of years. Moore ingeniously suggests that figure and rock are one and the same, even making the female form harmonize with the striations of the stone. The universal forces present in the rock are transferred to the figure, which becomes an earth goddess or fertility figure. The undulation of her abstract body virtually transforms her into a landscape. Adding to the mystical aura is Moore's brilliant interplay between solid and void, each having the same weight in the composition and evoking the womblike mystery of caves or tidal pools embedded in seashore rocks.

Creating Utopias

While Dada and Surrealism constituted a major force for the period between the wars, there were other major movements. Many twentieth-century artists remained committed to exploring abstract art. Surrealists and abstract artists often shared similar social goals: Both groups championed individual freedom, and both wished to undermine bourgeois values, to eradicate nationalism, to destroy capitalism, and to create a classless society. Many Dadaists and Surrealists were socialists who also participated in Communist Party activities, as were many abstract artists. Many of the latter, however, viewed abstract art itself as a vehicle for creating a utopian society.

Two major centers of geometric abstraction emerged simultaneously: Constructivism, which appeared with the Russian Revolution in 1917, and De Stijl (The Style), which appeared in Amsterdam. A third center was the Bauhaus in Germany, an art school founded in 1919 that succeeded as a significant force in the following decade and was often influenced by Constructivist refugees from Russia and De Stijl artists.

Russian Constructivism: Productivism and Utilitarianism

The most direct connection between abstract art and radical politics came in the revolutionary society that developed in Russia. There, before and after the October Revolution of 1917, artists committed themselves to developing new art forms that they hoped would bring about a new utopian society. Building on the innovations of Malevich's Suprematism (see page 561), several movements followed, each attempting to put art at the service of the new revolutionary society.

VLADIMIR TATLIN As Malevich was developing his Suprematist painting in Moscow, a fellow Russian, Vladimir Tatlin (1885–1953), was working in Berlin and Paris. In 1914, Tatlin visited Picasso's Paris studio and saw his constructions (see pages 551–553). Upon returning to Russia, he then made his own constructed reliefs. Like Malevich's Suprematism, these were entirely abstract, and eventually his geometric abstract style, which had many Russian followers, became known as Constructivism.

With the Bolshevik Revolution in 1917, Tatlin's attitude toward his art changed. He embraced Communism and focused his effort on supporting the party's goal of creating a utopian society. He worked for the Soviet Education Commissariat and turned his attention to architecture and engineering. A major component of his teachings was his passionate belief in the utility of modern machinery, the democratic quality of mass-produced objects, and the efficiency of industrial materials. Technological modernity was the future and the new religion, and industrial efficiency and materials had to be incorporated into art, design, and architecture, where they would produce a new, better, classless world. In other words, the social revolution had to be complemented with an aesthetic revolution. According to Tatlin's theory called Constructivist Productivism, everything—from appliances to clothing, from living space to theater—now had to be machinelike and streamlined. Form must follow function and objects were to be stripped of all ornamentation, which was associated with bourgeois values and aristocratic ostentation.

Tatlin's most famous work is his *Project for "Monument to the Third International"* (**fig. 27.12**), begun in 1919 and exhibited in Petrograd (St.

27.12 Vladimir Tatlin. *Project for "Monument to the Third International."* 1919–1920. Wood, iron, and glass, height 20′ (6.10 m). Destroyed; contemporary photograph

Petersburg) and Moscow in December 1920. The "monument" was to be 1,300 feet high, which would have made it the tallest structure in the world at that time. It was to have a metal spiral frame tilted at an angle and encompassing a glass cube, cylinder, and cone. These steel and glass units, housing conferences and meetings, were to revolve, making a complete revolution once a year, month, and day, respectively. The industrial materials of steel and glass and the dynamic, kinetic nature of the work symbolized the new machine age and the dynamism of the Bolshevik Revolution. The tower was to function as a propaganda center for the Communist Third International, an organization devoted to world revolution, and its rotating, ascending spiral symbolized the aspirations of Communism.

De Stijl and Universal Order

In 1917 in Amsterdam, the artist Piet Mondrian (1872–1944) founded a movement called De Stijl (The Style) with several other artists and architects, and they were joined by the architect Gerrit Rietveld (1888–1964) in 1919. Though not backed by a revolutionary government, as were the Russian artists, their goal was every bit as radical and utopian, for De Stijl artists sought to create, through abstraction, total environments so perfect that they embodied a universal harmony. Unlike their Russian counterparts, their mission was actually spiritual. Driven by Mondrian's intense commitment to Theosophy (page 531), De Stijl, like the Communists, sought a universal order that would make nationalism obsolete. They called their style the International Style, applying it most often to a new architecture of glass and steel that was modern, pure, and universal, with no national identification.

PIET MONDRIAN In the magazine *De Stijl*, the group's publication, Mondrian published his theory of art in a series of articles. His philosophy was based on Theosophy, which he was interested in before his move to Paris in late 1911. After returning to neutral Amsterdam during the Great War, he was further influenced by the ideas of the mystical lay philosopher and his close acquaintance M. H. J. Schoenmaekers. Schoenmaekers argued that there was an underlying mathematical structure to the universe that constituted true reality and that an artist could access and present this structure through the rational manipulations of geometric forms. Mondrian developed an art based on such geometry, which he called Neo-Plasticism, meaning

27.13 Piet Mondrian. *Composition No.II/Composition I//Composition with Red, Blue, and Yellow.* 1930. Oil on canvas, 20⅛ × 20⅛″ (51 × 51 cm). The Fukuoka City Bank Ltd, Japan © 2008 Mondrian/Holtzman Trust. c/o HCR International, Warrenton VA

"new plasticism." By "plastic" in painting, he meant that the world of the painting had a plastic, or three-dimensional, reality of its own corresponding to the harmonious plastic reality of the universe. In other words, he sought to replicate in his art the unseen, underlying structure of the universe.

Beginning in 1917, Mondrian struggled to achieve this using total geometric abstraction, and only succeeded upon returning to Paris in 1919. Once having established his style, he pretty much retained it for the rest of his life, as seen in the *Composition* of 1930 above (**fig. 27.13**). His paintings, which are always asymmetrical, are remarkable for their perfect harmony. Mondrian very precisely gives every element equal weight. Each line and rectangle in this square canvas is assigned its own identity; every line exists in its own right, not as a means of defining the color rectangles. (The thickness of the lines often varies in his paintings, a function of individual identity.) Each component sits on the same plane on the surface—there is no foreground or background, no one object sitting on top of another. Despite this perfectly interlocking surface, the

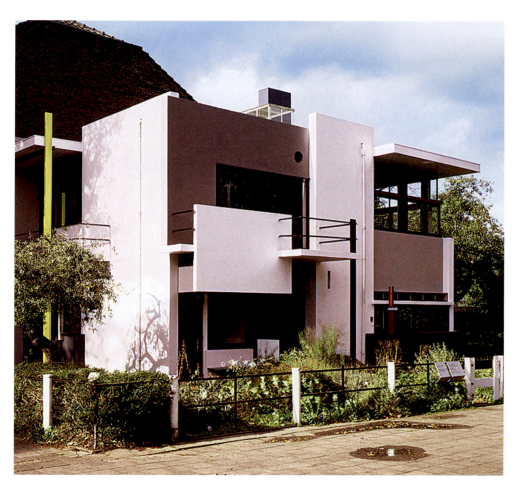

27.14 Gerrit Rietveld. Schröder House, Utrecht, Holland. 1924

painting has a feeling of tremendous space, even of infinity, largely because the rectangles expand off the edge of the canvas. Space and mass have merged into a harmonious whole of what Mondrian called "dynamic equilibrium," where everything is energized yet balanced. Mondrian has attempted to capture the complexity of the universe—the individuality of its infinite components and the harmony that holds everything together.

Mondrian made endless variations of these motifs. Even the color did not change, since these elementary hues, from which all colors are derived, are symbolic of the building blocks of the cosmos. But in principle, painting was not the end product of Mondrian's aesthetic program. He considered it just a stop-gap measure until perfect abstract environments of architecture, furniture, and objects embodying all of these same principles could be achieved.

GERRIT RIETVELD Mondrian's De Stijl colleagues sought to implement his theories in architecture and interior design. Once they discovered and understood Frank Lloyd Wright (see page 542),

they were able to apply architectural solutions to the theoretical ideas of Neo-Plasticism. They recognized that Wright had destroyed "the box," and declared "the new architecture will be anti-cubic." Combining the color and floating planes of Mondrian and the fluid spaces of Wright, Rietveld produced the definitive De Stijl building in 1924, the Schröder House in Utrecht (**fig. 27.14**), which was built onto the end of existing row houses. On the façade, we can find Mondrian's "floating" rectangles and lines. Even the Wright-like cantilevered roof appears to float. The interior is designed along the same principles, with wall-to-ceiling sliding panels allowing for a restructuring of the interior space. Both inside and out, the Schröder House is ethereal, buoyant, and harmonious, embodying dynamic equilibrium.

The Bauhaus: Creating the "New Man"

As we have seen, most Dadaists, Surrealists, and abstract artists were socialists or Communists who believed that the Bolshevik Revolution in Russia would save the world from bourgeois materialism and decadence and would establish a worldwide utopian society. Left-wing artists regularly held conferences in Germany, attempting to commit to a social program that would put art at the service of restructuring society. All of these attempts came to naught. Instead, it was the Bauhaus, an art and design school, that gradually emerged as the strongest center for advocating social progress through art.

The Bauhaus was founded in Weimar, Germany, in 1919 by Walter Gropius. In many respects, the Bauhaus School was the embodiment of Muthesius's German Werkbund (see page 565), since the goal of the workshops was to design modern high-quality production-line products. Its guiding principle, however, was more utopian and less commercial, for the Bauhaus (meaning House of Building) was dedicated to the creation of utilitarian design for "the new man" through the marriage of art and technology. The school was formed by the merger of two Weimar arts and crafts schools, and was designed to combine the fine and applied arts, giving each equal weight. The artists were called artisan/craftspeople, and their mission was to create an abstract environment of the most progressive modernity. Their design ethic was based on "the living environment of machines and vehicles." Only "primary forms and colors" could be used, all in the service of creating "standard types for all practical

commodities of everyday use as a social necessity." Like De Stijl, this was a philosophy oriented toward environments, not just painting and sculpture, and the Bauhaus is often more associated with the work that came out of the textile, metal, and ceramic workshops, such as Marcel Breuer's 1927 aluminum tubular chairs and Anni Albers's abstract textiles, than the paintings of Kandinsky, who also taught at the school.

MARCEL BREUER We can see the Bauhaus machine aesthetic at work in the living room of a Gropius house built in 1927 for a Werkbund housing development in Stuttgart (**fig. 27.15**). The furniture and lighting were designed by Marcel Breuer (1902–1981), a former Bauhaus student who became a faculty member in 1925, heading the furniture workshop. All of Breuer's objects are geometric, made of modern materials, and easily mass-produced. On the far right is perhaps his most famous product, the "Wassily" armchair, made of polished, nickel-plated tubular steel and cotton fabric. In its planarity, the design was clearly influenced by De Stijl aesthetics. But now the heavy wood favored by De Stijl has been replaced by a strong but light metal tube that is geometrically structured in an airy, open pattern. The feeling that results echoes the transparency and weightlessness of Suprematist

27.15 Walter Gropius. Living Room, two houses for the Werkbund housing development Am Weissenhof, Stuttgart, with furniture by Marcel Breuer. 1927. © DACS 2008

painting and Constructivist sculpture, qualities that can even be seen in Tatlin's *Project for "Monument to the Third International"* (see fig. 27.13).

WALTER GROPIUS Many scholars consider the crowning aesthetic achievement of the Bauhaus to be the building itself, designed by Gropius in 1925 when the school moved from Weimar to Dessau. The building consists of three L-shaped wings coming off a central hub, one of which is the Shop Block, a workshop wing (**fig. 27.16**). The entire complex is dominated by a clearly articulated geometry. The workshop wing looks like an empty glass box, the glass curtain wall on two sides continuing around corners and flush with the stuccoed parapet above and socle (the projecting molding under the wall) below. Instead of mass, we feel a weightless volume as defined by the metal and glass wall. And because the building projects over a setback half-basement, it appears suspended.

Gropius's Bauhaus came to epitomize High Modernist architecture—the architecture that evolved out of early Modernism (see pages 565–566) in the period between the two wars. With High Modernism, buildings became more severely geometric and so light that they seemed to float. Their unadorned geometric shapes represented volume, not mass. Their walls were thin membranes of a taut veneer that encased the building, and, as with the Bauhaus Workshop, often this veneer was a curtain of glass. But

High Modernism was more than just a style; it was a social movement predicated on utopian socialist philosophy and a rationalist belief in progress. Life could be improved, the theory went, by creating a machine-age environment. Ultimately, the movement was reduced to a style in 1932 when the architect Philip Johnson and the historian Henry-Russell Hitchcock organized an exhibition entitled "The International Style" at the newly opened Museum of Modern Art in New York. Their concern was with the look of the architecture, not its social premises. The exhibition brought the style to the attention of Americans, and resulted in the label "International Style" being used to describe High Modernist architecture.

The Machine Aesthetic

The machine aesthetic and the utopian dream that accompanied it also made their way to Paris, where they found a rather different voice in the architecture of Charles-Edouard Jeanneret, called Le Corbusier (1886–1965). Unlike Moscow, Amsterdam, and Dessau, Paris had no art schools or major artistic movements pushing for a utopian vision. Instead, the cause there was undertaken by individuals.

LE CORBUSIER'S IDEAL HOME Le Corbusier was Swiss, and settled in Paris after briefly working in 1910 with Walter Gropius in the Berlin office of a leading German architect. With a third

Modernist architect, Mies van der Rohe (see page 616), they talked about creating a machine-based, easily reproduced architecture.

In 1922, Le Corbusier opened an architectural firm with his cousin, and by 1923 he had developed the principles for his ideal home, which he published in an article entitled "Five Points of a New Architecture." His five points were as follows: (1) No ground floor, with the house raised on columns called *pilotis*; (2) a flat roof, which would be used as a garden terrace; (3) an open floor plan, with partitions slotted between supports; (4) free composition of the exterior curtain walls; and (5) preferably ribbon (horizontal) windows. The raised house allowed for privacy and light and made the outdoors accessible by putting a garden on the roof. Much later, Le Corbusier remarked that "a house is a machine for living in," which suggested—wrongly—to many critics that he advocated a brutal functionalism that was not concerned with beauty and comfort. In fact, Le Corbusier wanted to create a classical purity based on geometry and a machine-age look. His emphasis was on the human being and "living." Machine-age values and technology were meant to serve humans: His houses would have a machine-age look and efficiency, using the latest technology. And they would be filled with light.

The 1928 Villa Savoye (**fig. 27.17**) in Poissy-sur-Seine, outside Paris, is Le Corbusier's best-known house, and here we can see most of the elements called for in his "Five Points": The *pilotis*, the raised living space, the ribbon windows, and the flat-roof terrace, which is protected behind the enormous cylindrical windscreens that look like ocean-liner smokestacks. The main floor, the second, has an open-space plan using partition walls, and it faces into a court, from which a ramp leads up to the roof. Everywhere we look we see a beautiful classicizing geometry, the building blocks of Le Corbusier's design aesthetic. The building is a perfect square box precisely defined by its taut skin of concrete; the *pilotis* are cylinders, and the windbreakers are enormous arcs. Like the Bauhaus and Schröder House, the house appears light, virtually floating on its *pilotis*.

27.17 Le Corbusier. Villa Savoye. 1928–1929. Poissy-sur-Seine, France

Art in America: Modernity, Spirituality, and Regionalism

Perhaps more than Europe, the United States could embrace the machine as the emblem of progress, for after World War I, America was the undisputed technological leader of the world. In contrast to the European avant-garde, and its search for a classless, nationless world, Americans were preoccupied with national identity. American artists, living in a politically stable country, generally did not have a utopian vision. Instead they viewed skyscrapers, factories, and machines as symbols of the nation's technological superiority. But not everyone embraced modernity. As the economy boomed in the post-war years, culminating in the dizzying exuberance of the Roaring Twenties, many artists rejected materialism and sought the spiritual. While some artists turned to nature in search of universal truths, others sought strength in old-fashioned American values that could be found in the country's heartland, especially in the lifestyle of its hearty, hard-working, God-fearing farmers.

The City and Industry

Arriving in New York harbor for the first time in 1915, Marcel Duchamp marveled at the towering skyscrapers and pronounced them the epitome of modernity. He saw in America the future of art. The skyscraper and modern industry did indeed become the emblems of America in art, replacing landscape, which had dominated painting in the previous century. The symbol of the nation for many artists and intellectuals was New York, and its defining feature the skyscraper, often described as the "cathedral of capitalism" or "commerce."

27.18 Joseph Stella. *The Voice of the City, New York Interpreted*. 1920–1922. Oil and tempera on canvas, five panels, 8′3¾″ × 22′6″ (2.53 × 6.86 m). The Newark Museum, Newark, New Jersey. 37.288 a–e. © Joseph Stella

JOSEPH STELLA Perhaps the greatest single visual icon of the city was made by the Italian immigrant Joseph Stella (1877–1946). Entitled *The Voice of the City, New York Interpreted* (**fig. 27.18**) and completed in 1922, it is an 8-foot-high, five-panel work that features in the center panel an abstraction of the city's towers, with the famous Flat Iron building in the foreground, surrounded by both actual and fictitious buildings. The panels flanking the center panel represent the "Great White Way," Broadway's theater district, which has been reduced to an abstraction of color and light. The far left panel presents the harbor on the Hudson River on the west side of lower Manhattan, while the right panel shows the Brooklyn Bridge on the east side. Every image features the technological wonders of Manhattan. We see communication towers, air venting systems, and elevated trains in the harbor picture. The Great White Way panels present the dazzling illumination of Times Square at night, which at the time had no equivalent anywhere else in the world. In effect, these two panels are an homage to electricity and the energy of the city. And even 35 years after opening, the Brooklyn Bridge still remained one of the world's great feats of engineering.

Stella moved to America in 1896, but returned to Italy to study in 1910, where he met the Futurists (see pages 558–560). Through the Stieglitz "291" gallery and his friendship with Duchamp and Man Ray, among others, he kept in touch with European trends, with Cubism becoming his primary artistic language in the 1910s. The Great White Way panels especially reflect the tenets of Futurism, for here we see the soundwaves and Mach-like indications of motion that we saw in Boccioni's *States of Mind* (see fig. 26.11). Their dizzying kaleidoscope of color powerfully captures the intense visual experience of Times Square at night. But in the skyscraper and Brooklyn Bridge panels, Stella is not only representational, he is iconic, centering his motifs and transforming them into emblems of modernity. His palette is deeply saturated and color is often encased in heavy black-line drawing, in effect transforming his image into a "stained-glass window." He reinforces the religious motif by adding a **predella** at the bottom (see page 370), which itemizes the different tunnels and utility tubes running beneath the city. Stella is declaring technology and modernity to be the religion of the twentieth century.

PAUL STRAND Photography, it turns out, was especially well suited to capturing the triumphs of the machine age. But first the medium had to break away from Pictorialism (see pages 520–521). This occurred when the young Paul Strand (1890–1976) between 1915 and 1917 made a large body of work of sharply focused, high-contrast photographs. Stieglitz immediately recognized their importance and showed a selection of them at "291." *Wire Wheel* (**fig. 27.19**) is from this period. Its abstracted subject is a Model T Ford, an icon of the machine age since it marked the advent of the assembly line. The picture rejects the "painterliness" of turn-of-the-century pictorial photography. In its place is a new compositional style based on the Cubism that Strand saw displayed at Stieglitz's "291" gallery and the Armory Show. By taking a close-up of the car, Strand created a skewed perspective and tight cropping, resulting in a difficult-to-read image with a flattened and complicated space.

MARGARET BOURKE-WHITE Strand's hard-edged aesthetic transformed photography, not only in America, but eventually throughout the world. His style was especially appropriate for techno-logical and industrial images, reinforcing the

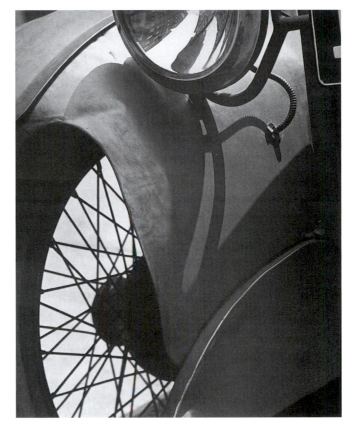

27.19 Paul Strand. *Wire Wheel*. New York. 1920. Platinum print from enlarged negative, 12⅝ × 10¼" (32.4 × 25.8 cm). George Eastman House, Rochester, New York. © Estate of Paul Strand

27.20 Margaret Bourke-White. *Fort Peck Dam, Montana*. 1936

27.21 Georgia O'Keeffe. *Black Iris III*. 1926. Oil on canvas, 36 × 29⅞"
(91.4 × 75.9 cm). The Metropolitan Museum of Art, New York. The Alfred
Stieglitz Collection, 1949. 60.278.1

*Realism in
America*

machine-made precision of the subject. The pho-
tojournalist Margaret Bourke-White especially
embraced this new aesthetic and was drawn to
technological imagery, as seen in *Fort Peck Dam,
Montana* (**fig. 27.20**), the cover image for the very
first issue of *Life*, a picture-essay magazine published on November 23, 1936. The photograph's
power lies in its severe austerity, which reinforces
the mammoth scale of the dam, dwarfing the
antlike workers below. Each of the dam's pylons
is identical, looking as though they were pressed
out of an enormous machine mold, and because
the photograph of the dam is cropped on either
side, these gigantic assembly-line towers seem
endless as well. But they take on the grandeur of
ancient Assyrian or Egyptian monuments, and
again we find an artist declaring modern technology to be the new classicism.

Seeking the Spiritual

In the 1910s, much of the American creative
community turned its attention to producing an
American art. Writers, musicians, artists, and
poets all felt that American culture was derived
from Europe; now they would seek to discover
what was unique about the American experience
and try to express it in an indigenous way. For
some artists, like Stella in *The Voice of the City,
New York Interpreted*, the answer lay in American
modernity. Others looked to nature, going back
to the pantheistic Romanticism of the Hudson
River School and its successors. Stieglitz became
preoccupied with this issue of an American art,
deciding in the 1920s to represent only American
artists and naming his last gallery, which he
opened in 1928, "An American Place." The artists
that Stieglitz showed from the early 1920s until
his death in 1946 were generally, but not always,
preoccupied with finding a higher meaning in
life within a materialistic modern world, often
focusing on nature. One of them was Georgia
O'Keeffe (1887–1986).

GEORGIA O'KEEFFE When Stieglitz first showed
her work in 1916, Georgia O'Keeffe was making
small, abstract, minimalist watercolors that
evoked sublime landscape. Toward 1920, her
presentation of nature evolved into close-ups of
flowers, as seen in *Black Iris III* (**fig. 27.21**) of
1926, where the image is so magnified that it virtually becomes abstract. We do not have to look
far to find the pictorial source for O'Keeffe: Paul
Strand. O'Keeffe briefly fell in love with the
young, handsome Strand in 1917 and was smit-
ten as well by the power of his photography,

especially the use of the close-up image. This compositional device, she wrote, forced a viewer to see flowers with the same intensity that she did. But by abstracting the close-up, O'Keeffe accomplished much more: The forms of the flowers morph into the parts of a woman's body, and the iris is redolent of female sexuality. The petals ethereally dissolve into their surroundings, seeming to become one with the rest of nature.

Partly because of Stieglitz's marketing, art critics described O'Keeffe's flowers as overtly erotic and sexual. This interpretation outraged O'Keeffe, who denied that her pictures were about sexuality *per se*. And they are not. As with the banned, sexually explicit novels of her friend the English author D. H. Lawrence, her paintings were not about lust but the uncontainable surging force of nature, which includes the urge to procreate. Sexuality was portrayed as being natural, beautiful, and as essential as a flower blossoming, disseminating pollen, and reproducing. And if her wonderful organic flower, which seems to be growing before our very eyes, begins to take on the look of other objects, such as clouds, smoke, buttocks, and flesh, it only increases the sense of universal equivalence that she believed ran through all things. In this microcosm of an iris, O'Keeffe presents a macrocosm so large that it encompasses the entire universe.

Regionalism and National Identity

While the New York avant-garde sought a national identity and spirituality using either images of modernity or compact abstract styles, a group of Midwest artists, headed by Grant Wood, Thomas Hart Benton, and John Stewart Curry, turned to "old-fashioned" representational art and regional imagery. Although trained in modern art centers (Benton and Wood studied in Europe as well as in New York and Chicago), they generally preferred to work in the Midwest, where they came from and with which they identified.

The most famous image produced by this group is *American Gothic* (**fig. 27.22**) by Grant Wood (1891–1942) of Cedar Rapids, Iowa. The picture was shown at the Art Institute of Chicago in 1930, where it caused a stir and brought Wood to national attention. It was intended as a window into the Midwest world in which the artist grew up and lived. A fictitious father and spinster daughter are presented as the God-fearing descendants of stalwart pioneers who first worked the soil. They are dressed in traditional, even old-fashioned, clothes and stand

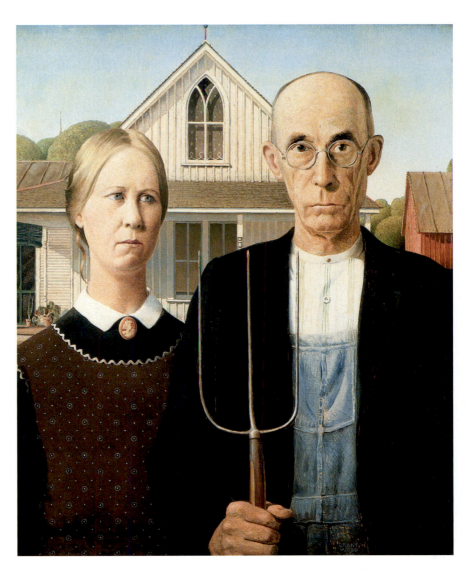

27.22 Grant Wood. *American Gothic*. 1930. Oil on board, 30¹¹⁄₁₆ × 25¹¹⁄₁₆″ (78 × 65.3 cm). The Art Institute of Chicago. Friends of American Art Collection. All rights reserved by the estate of Nan Wood Graham/Licensed by VAGA, New York

firmly against the march of progress. The style of their house, from which the title of the painting is taken, is called Carpenter Gothic, a nineteenth-century style evoking both the humble modesty and old-fashioned ways of the residents as well as their religious intensity, which parallels the fervor of the medieval period, when Gothic cathedrals were built. The characters' faith is emphasized by the numerous crosses embedded within the façade, and by putting a church steeple in the distant background.

Wood tells us his figures are orderly and clean, as suggested by the crisp drawing and severe horizontal and vertical composition. This propriety also stems from the primness of the woman's conservative dress and hair and the suggestions that she carefully tends to the house, as she does to the plants on the front porch. The figures' harsh frontality, the man's firm grasp on his pitchfork, and his overalls suggest that they are hardworking and strong. There is no hint of modernity, and the simplicity and the austerity of the setting suggest that they are frugal. Nonetheless, many critics viewed Wood as ridiculing his sitters and their lifestyle, and indeed the picture does contain humor, such as the woman warily looking off to the side as if to make sure nothing untoward is occurring. But, regardless of the interpretation, no one seemed to deny that it appeared to capture something fundamentally American, and especially Midwestern.

The Harlem Renaissance

In the 1910s and 1920s, hundreds of thousands of African Americans fled the racism and poverty of the rural South for the cities of the industrial North, where they hoped to find jobs, justice and equality. This confluence of blacks in New York's Harlem and Chicago's South Side resulted in a cultural flourishing devoted to self-discovery and to establishing a black identity, something white America had methodically denied African Americans. The movement was then called the New Negro Movement, although today it is generally known as the Harlem Renaissance, after its primary center, often described as its "capital."

Leading this movement in literature, music, theater, and art was the Howard University philosopher Alain Locke (1886–1954), who called for a distinctive style that evoked a black sensibility and perspective. He advocated recapturing the African past and its art and encouraged representations of African Americans and their lives as well as a portrayal of the distinctive physical qualities of the race, just as African masks often stressed black physiognomy. In effect, he was advocating that artists and writers declare "black is beautiful." In his promotion of a black aesthetic, he encouraged artists to depict a distinct African-American culture, one that departed from the Euro-American tradition and reflected the enormous contributions Americans of African descent had made to American life and identity.

JACOB LAWRENCE One of the most famous painters to emerge from the Harlem Renaissance was Jacob Lawrence (1917–2000), who received his training as a teenager in the 1930s at the federally sponsored Harlem Art Workshop and Harlem Community Art Center. Lawrence regularly went to midtown to take in all the art the city had to offer, from a Primitive Art show at the Museum of Modern Art, to Mexican textiles, to all of the latest European styles. In the late 1930s, he began making large narrative series dedicated to black leaders, including the slavery abolitionist Harriet Tubman (1820–1913), the Haitian revolutionary Toussaint L'Ouverture (1745–1803), and the abolitionist Frederick Douglass (ca. 1817–1895). The images were small and modest, made of poster paint on cardboard or posterboard.

27.23 Jacob Lawrence. *The Migration of the Negro* Series, number 58: *In the North the Negro Had Better Educational Facilities*. 1940–1941. Casein tempera on hardboard, 12 × 18″ (30.5 × 45.7 cm). Museum of Modern Art, New York. Gift of Mrs. David M. Levy. © ARS, New York and DACS, London 2008

Lawrence is best known for his *Migration Series*, begun in 1940. In 60 images, he presented the black migration and the African-American experiences in both North and South. While the series is anecdotal, the images did much of the talking through their abstraction, as seen in no. 58, *In the North the Negro Had Better Educational Facilities* (**fig. 27.23**). Three girls write numbers on a blackboard, but we do not see their faces, which would make them individual. Instead they represent the race and human vitality. We see numbers and arms rising higher, suggesting elevation through education, and we see a clean slate for a clean start. The girls' brightly colored dresses affirm life and happiness, while the jagged and pointed edges in their hair and skirts impart an energy and a quality of striving. Lawrence's sparse and beautifully colored pictures embody a remarkable psychology, which is often reinforced by the Modernist space of his pictures. Here a flat field pushes the figures to the surface, prominently displaying them.

Mexican Art: Seeking a National Identity

The Mexican Revolution, which began in 1910 with the overthrow of the dictatorship of General Porfirio Dîaz and ended in 1921 with the formation of the reformist government of Alvaro Obregón, triggered a wave of nationalism within the cultural community, one that focused on indigenous traditions while rejecting European influences. A government building campaign resulted in a large number of impressive mural commissions, which in turn gave rise to a school of muralists headed by Diego Rivera, among others. Either socialists or Communists, the muralists proclaimed murals as the true art of the people. The Mexican muralists gained international renown and were especially popular in the United States, where they received enormous commissions, ironically from major capitalists, such as the Rockefeller family.

Diego Rivera

Diego Rivera (1886–1957) is perhaps the best-known muralist. He lived in Europe, primarily in Paris, from 1907 to 1921, and was an accomplished Cubist. By the late 1910s, Rivera was consumed by the idea of creating a nationalistic revolutionary art through mural painting, and he traveled to Italy to study Renaissance murals. Upon returning to Mexico, he jettisoned his elite esoteric Cubism for the straightforward representational art of the *quattrocento*, giving it a monumentality that also echoed the strong simple forms of Aztec and Mayan art. Furthermore, he shunned easel painting, declaring it a bourgeois capitalistic art form, a commodity for the rich. He viewed his fresco murals as a public art, an art for the masses. He also felt his art should be about the indigenous people, not the Mexicans of European blood and their European customs. Consequently, many of his mural commissions are about national identity and the uniqueness of Mexican customs and tradition.

Rivera was a Communist, and his politics, especially his championing of the common folk and labor, appear in his murals. From 1930 to 1934, he received numerous commissions in the United States, and his representational art had a tremendous impact on American mural painting, proliferating thanks to support from Franklin Roosevelt's New Deal administration, which provided artists with work. One major project was the lobby of the RCA building in Rockefeller Center. Entitled *Man at the Crossroads Looking with Hope and High Vision to a New and Better Future*, it included a portrait of the Communist leader Lenin, and this outraged the Rockefellers, who had commissioned the mural. The Rockefellers paid Rivera and then destroyed the mural. Rivera remade it as *Man, Controller of the Universe* (**fig. 27.24**) at the Museo del Palacio de Bellas Artes in Mexico City in 1934. The painting praises science and Communism, which, for Rivera, were the twin tools of progress. In the center of the composition we see Man, positioned under a telescope and with a microscope to his right (our left), signaling that humankind will control the future through science. Two criss-crossing ellipses of light seem to emanate from Man, one depicting a microscopic world, the other the cosmos. Below him is the Earth, and the superior agricultural products generated by scientific discovery. To Man's left (our right), we see, sandwiched between the healthy microorganisms and a harmonious cosmos, Lenin holding hands with workers of different races. Beyond is a scene of healthy unified labor. To Man's right (our left) are the evils of capitalism. Between the ellipses showing diseased organisms and a clashing cosmos is a decadent bar scene depicting the well-heeled bourgeoisie, which includes John D. Rockefeller, Jr. Beyond are frightening soldiers and discontented, protesting laborers.

27.24 Diego Rivera. *Man, Controller of the Universe.* 1934. Fresco, 15'11" × 37'6" (4.85 × 11.45 m). Museo del Palacio de Bellas Artes, Mexico City. © 2008 Banco de Mexico Diego Rivera and Frida Kahlo Museums̀ Trust, Mexico D. F./DACS

The Eve of World War II

In October 1929, the New York stockmarket crashed, unleashing the Great Depression that fanned out around the globe. The deprivation it inflicted lasted an excruciating 16 years. Meanwhile, Europe was threatened by fascism as Germany, Italy and Spain came under the rule of charismatic totalitarian leaders, who brought about a politics of repression, ruthlessly imprisoning and often executing anyone perceived as unfriendly to their regimes. A dark cloud was cast over the Western world, which was reflected in art.

America: The Failure of Modernity

The avant-garde continued to work in abstraction through the 1930s, but, in an era dominated by the terrible social ills of the Great Depression, it grew increasingly difficult for artists not to be socially concerned. Many avant-garde artists became involved by becoming socialists or Communists and by supporting the labor movement, even forming their own unionlike organizations. But for many artists, political activity was not enough. Now, more and more artists worked in a style called Social Realism, a representational format that focused on such pervasive problems as poverty, labor oppression, the suffering of migrant workers, alienation resulting from increased urbanization and industrialization, and racism, especially as seen in the Ku Klux Klan lynchings.

EDWARD HOPPER One of the most powerful representational painters of the period was Edward Hopper (1882–1967), who was based in New York. His pictures are saturated with the alienation associated with life in the big city, and more generally with modern America. A classic Hopper is *Early Sunday Morning* (**fig. 27.25**) of 1930. The image is frightening in its uncanny quiet and emptiness, qualities reinforced by the severe, frozen geometry of the composition. The second-floor windows suggest a different story for each apartment, but none is forthcoming as their inhabitants remain secreted behind curtains and shades. A strange relationship exists among the fire hydrant, the barbershop pole, and the void of the square awning-framed window between them. The harsh morning light has a theatrical intensity. Hopper's only love outside of art was film and theater, and his paintings have a cinematic or staged quality that intimates that something is about to happen. His pictures are shrouded in mystery, and because their settings are distinctly American, the troubling psychology he portrays becomes distinctly American as well.

DOROTHEA LANGE The largest art patron during the Great Depression was the United States government, which put tens of thousands of unemployed artists to work through the Works Project Administration and Federal Art Project, important components of Franklin Delano Roosevelt's New Deal. What was so remarkable about these

27.25 Edward Hopper. *Early Sunday Morning*. 1930. Oil on canvas, 35 × 60″ (88.9 × 152.4 cm). Whitney Museum of American Art, New York. Purchase with funds from Gertrude Vanderbilt Whitney. 31.426

programs was their lack of racial, ethnic, or gender discrimination, and the result was financial support for women and minorities. One especially influential project, the Farm Security Administration (FAS), was designed to document the suffering and poverty of both rural and urban Americans. It hired about 20 photographers to record the desperate conditions of the poor. These images were then distributed to the media.

One of the most famous images from the FSA project is Dorothea Lange's *Migrant Mother, California* (**fig. 27.26**). Using the sharp-focus photography that had become commonplace by the 1930s, Lange created a powerful image that in its details captures the sitter's destitution, and in its complex composition of hands, arms, and turned heads, the family's emotional distress. Because of this photograph and an accompanying news story, the government rushed food to California, and eventually opened relief camps for migrant workers. The immediate impact of this poignant photograph testifies to the overpowering credibility projected by the medium of photography.

27.26 Dorothea Lange. *Migrant Mother, California*. 1936. Gelatin silver print, Library of Congress, Washington, D.C.

27.27 Pablo Picasso. *Guernica*. 1937. Oil on canvas, 11′6″ × 25′8″ (3.51 × 7.82 m). Museo Nacional Centro de Arte Reina Sofia, Madrid. On permanent loan from the Museo del Prado, Madrid. © Succession Picasso/DACS 2008

Europe and Fascism

While some of the most powerful anti-fascist works came from the German Expressionists and Dada artists, the single most famous such work was made by the Parisian-based Spaniard Pablo Picasso.

PABLO PICASSO In 1936 civil war broke out in Spain when conservatives loyal to the king and under the leadership of Franco (the Nationalists) tried to overthrow the popularly elected, leftist, republican government (the Republicans or Loyalists). In some ways, this conflict was a rehearsal for World War II. Hitler and Mussolini provided military and political support for the Nationalists, while the Loyalists consisted of Communists, socialists, and Catalan and Basque separatists, as well as the International Brigade, made up of volunteers from all over the world. On April 26, 1937, Hitler's Nazi pilots used saturation bombing to attack the undefended Basque town of Guernica, killing thousands of civilians. Picasso, like most of the free world, was outraged, and responded by painting *Guernica* (**fig. 27.27**), an enormous black, white, and gray mural that he exhibited as a protest at the Spanish Republican Pavilion of the 1937 Paris International Exposition. He pulled every artistic device

out of his Cubist and Surrealist arsenal to create a nightmarish scene of pain, suffering, grief, and death. We see no airplanes and no bombs, and the electric light bulb is the only sign of the modernity that made the bombing possible.

The symbolism of the scene resists exact interpretation, despite several traditional elements: The mother and her dead child are descendants of the *Pietà*, the woman with the lamp who vaguely recalls the Statue of Liberty suggests enlightenment, and the dead fighter clutching a broken sword is a familiar emblem of heroic resistance. We also sense the contrast between the menacing, human-faced bull, which we know Picasso intended to represent the forces of brutality and darkness, and the dying horse, which stands for the people. The figure resembling a Mary Magdalene at the cross also brings to mind Goya's supplicating rebel in *The Third of May, 1808* (see fig. 23.1).

Picasso denied that this was an anti-fascist picture, and he may very well have meant in part that this monumental mural was more than just mundane propaganda against Franco and his ilk. Instead, this horrifying image is meant to portray the psychology of a world in perpetual conflict and misery, capturing the mood of the black cloud hanging over Europe.

SUMMARY

World War I had an incalculable impact on Western civilization, both in physical and psychological terms. In Europe, many artists now sought to undermine the nationalism and bourgeois values, particularly capitalism, that brought about the war. Many artists favored creating utopian societies. In contrast to Europe, America entered a period of unprecedented prosperity that climaxed with the Roaring Twenties. Politically stable, America had no interest in creating a nationless, classless society.

Dada was the one style directly produced by World War I. Originating in Zurich in the war, it was based on chance and nonsense and designed to undermine the bourgeois logic that—its creators believed—had produced the conflict destroying Europe. In Berlin, the movement was highly expressionistic and political and relied heavily on photomontage, in Cologne, it was more dreamlike and psychological, and in Paris, it was witty and analytic, taking its cue from Marcel Duchamp, Francis Picabia, and Man Ray, also key figures in wartime New York Dada.

Dada evolved into Surrealism, a style officially declared in Paris in 1924 by the poet André Breton. Largely based on the theories of Sigmund Freud, Surrealism was dedicated to revealing the higher realities, especially repressed sexual urges, that lay deep within the unconscious. Like Dada artists, Surrealists relied on chance, dreamlike images and the juxtaposition of disparate objects to plumb the depths of the mind.

In Russia, the first Communist nation, artists led by Vladimir Tatlin developed an abstract, geometric aesthetic based on Malevich's Suprematism. In sculpture, this style was called Constructivism, in design, Productivism. In Germany, the cause of Productivism was embraced by a new art school, the Bauhaus, headed by Walter Gropius. The most famous product of the school was the building itself. Designed by Gropius, the Bauhaus was the climax of High Modernist architecture, an abstract, mechanomorphic style based on utopian ideals. In Paris, utopian High Modernist architecture was purveyed by Le Corbusier, and in Amsterdam, it was championed by a movement called De Stijl, represented in a painting by Piet Mondrian. De Stijl, however, was also deeply spiritual, for it was heavily influenced by Theosophy.

Many artists in America, including Georgia O'Keeffe, sought relief from the cold, impersonal technology of the machine age and crass consumerism, and instead created a spiritual art. Other artists, such as Grant Wood, favored a return to pre-twentieth-century values, and painted representational images of the rural Midwest. The interwar period also saw the rise of African-American art, which focused on racial identity, providing an alternative to Modernism, and the Mexican Revolution brought about a wave of nationalism that was dominated by mural painters, led by Diego Rivera.

The Great Depression that began in 1929 and the rise of fascism in Italy, Germany, and Spain in the 1930s cast a dark shadow over the Western world, reflected in Pablo Picasso's *Guernica*, the disturbing urban scenes of Edward Hopper, and FSA photographers like Dorothea Lange.

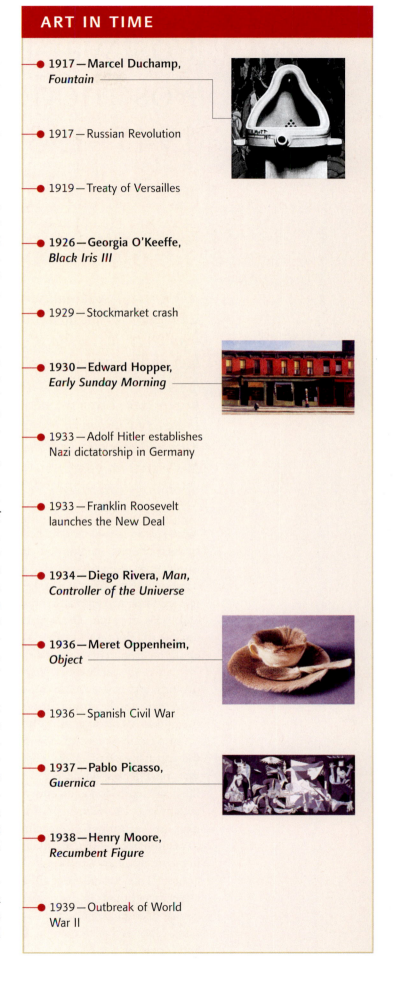

ART IN TIME

- 1917—Marcel Duchamp, *Fountain*
- 1917—Russian Revolution
- 1919—Treaty of Versailles
- 1926—Georgia O'Keeffe, *Black Iris III*
- 1929—Stockmarket crash
- 1930—Edward Hopper, *Early Sunday Morning*
- 1933—Adolf Hitler establishes Nazi dictatorship in Germany
- 1933—Franklin Roosevelt launches the New Deal
- 1934—Diego Rivera, *Man, Controller of the Universe*
- 1936—Meret Oppenheim, *Object*
- 1936—Spanish Civil War
- 1937—Pablo Picasso, *Guernica*
- 1938—Henry Moore, *Recumbent Figure*
- 1939—Outbreak of World War II

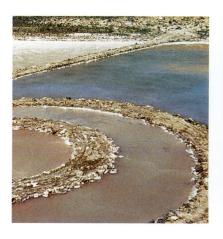

CHAPTER 28

Postwar to Postmodern, 1945–1980

Scholars traditionally view World War II (1939–1945) as a turning point for the art world, the time when its focus shifted from Paris to New York (see map 28.1). In fact, the 1950s, not the 1940s, were the watershed for the second half of the century. Now Duchamp's preoccupation with how art functions and his questioning of the importance of craft became a driving force as the decade progressed. Likewise, many artists became obsessed with the concept, rooted in the early Cubism of Picasso and Braque, that art- and image-making were a form of language, and they dedicated their work to revealing the structure of this visual language and the complex ways it could be used to present ideas and opinions, even to deceive and manipulate.

Artists also realized that art need not be limited to the traditional mediums, such as oil on canvas, cast bronze, or chiseled marble. It did not have to hang on a wall or sit on a pedestal. Artists could use anything to make art, and by the late 1950s and 1960s, they did. They used televisions, film, junk, earth, fluorescent lights, steel tiles, acrylics, entire environments, postcards, and words. Performance Art, earthworks, Conceptual Art, happenings, and video art are just a handful of the movements and concepts that sprang up from the mid-1950s through the 1970s.

In part, this burst of new mediums reflects the expansive spirit of the period, especially in the United States. World War II ended 16 years of financial depression and deprivation in America, and by the 1950s, the country had become a nation of consumers. Returning soldiers, eager to resume normal life, married and had children in record numbers, creating the baby-boom generation. They moved from cities to new cookie-cutter tract houses in the suburbs. And, as never before, Americans shopped—for cars, televisions, labor-saving household appliances, boats, and movie cameras. Americans were fascinated

by everything technological, symbolized by the Cold War space race.

The new postwar American lifestyle, however, was not equally available to all. Magazines, newspapers, and television depicted a distinct hierarchy within American democracy, with white males heading up a patriarchal society that viewed women and people of color as second-class citizens. In response, Beatniks, Zen Buddhists, underground improvisational jazz musicians, bikers, and urban gangs of juvenile delinquents established alternative lifestyles in the late 1940s and 1950s.

But it was the civil rights movement that first seriously challenged accepted norms in the second half of the 1950s, gaining tremendous momentum in the following decade. Spurred also by the Vietnam War (1964–1973), which generated persistent anti-war protests, the mid-1960s saw the start of a period of social upheaval that produced the feminist movement, Gay Pride, Black Power, Gray Power, and environmental groups such as Greenpeace. It was an age of liberation aimed at shattering the *status quo* and questioning the validity of any claim to

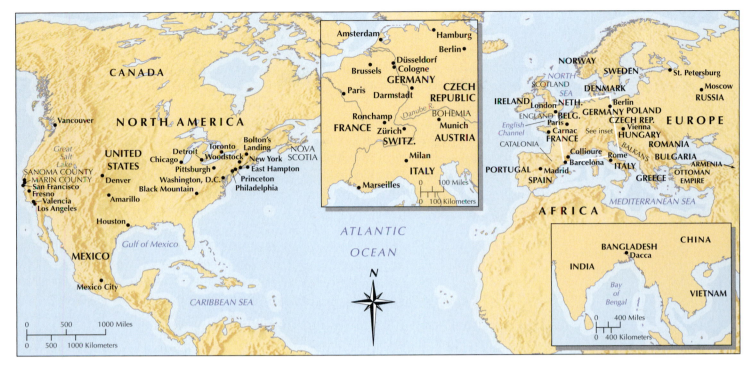

Map 28.1 Europe and North America showing Asia (inserted)

superiority or fixed truth. And in the forefront was art. But before this artistic revolution could occur, the center of the art world had to move from Paris to New York. This "coup," often referred to as the "Triumph of New York Painting," coincided with the rise of Abstract Expressionism in the late 1940s.

Existentialism in New York: Abstract Expressionism

Abstract Expressionism grew out of Surrealism, which traced its roots to the Dada movement of the 1910s (see pages 570–575). Like the Surrealists, the Abstract Expressionists were preoccupied with a quest to uncover universal truths. In this sense, their heritage goes back to Kandinsky (see page 555), Malevich (see page 561), and Mondrian (see page 581). In many respects, Abstract Expressionism is the culmination of artists' concerns in the first half of the twentieth century. But the Abstract Expressionists were also driven by a deep-seated belief in Existentialism, a philosophy that came to the fore following the devastation caused by World War II. The war shattered not only faith in science and logic, but even the very concept of progress, the belief in the possibility of creating a better world.

Existentialism maintained that there were no absolute truths—no ultimate knowledge, explanations, or answers—and that life was a continuous series of subjective experiences from which each individual learned and then responded to in a personal way. Essential to this learning process was facing the direst aspects of human existence—fear of death, the absurdity of life, and alienation from individuals, society, and nature—and taking responsibility for acts of free will without any certain knowledge of what is right or wrong, good or bad. The Abstract Expressionists, like so many intellectuals after the war, embraced this subjective view of the world. Their art was a personal confrontation with the moment, reflecting upon their physical, psychological, and social being.

Abstract Expressionism: Action Painting

Just as Dada developed into Surrealism, New York Surrealism seamlessly evolved into Abstract Expressionism. The transformation occurred when all of the symbols and suggestions of myths and primordial conditions disappeared, and images dissolved into a complete abstraction containing no obvious references to the visible world. Two artists are largely responsible. One is Jackson Pollock, who, in 1947, made the physical act of energetically applied paint—the gesture—the undisputed focus of painting, and the second is Willem de Kooning.

JACKSON POLLOCK Through the 1930s, Jackson Pollock (1912–1956) was a marginal figure in the New York art world. In the early 1940s, just when he started Jungian psychoanalysis, he became a hardcore Surrealist, making crude but powerful paintings filled with slapdash hieroglyphs ("letter-pictures"), totems, and references to primitive myth, whipped about in a swirling sea of paint.

In 1947, he unveiled at Peggy Guggenheim's "Art of This Century" gallery his first **gesture** or **action paintings**. The latter term was coined in the 1950s by the art critic Harold Rosenberg (1906–1978) and is represented here by *Autumn Rhythm: Number 30* (**fig. 28.1**) of 1950, an 8- × 17-foot wall of house paint applied by dripping, hurling, and splattering when the unstretched canvas was on the floor. Pollock had worked on it from all four sides, and he claimed that its source was his unconscious. Despite the apparent looseness of his style, Pollock exerted great control of his medium by changing the viscosity of the paint, the size of the brush or stick he used to apply it, and the speed, size, and direction of his own movements, and he rejected many paintings when he did not like the results. The energy of the painting is overwhelming, and when hanging on the wall the work looms above us like a frozen wave about to crash, although unlike a wave, the picture really does not have a sense of gravity, since it had been painted on from four sides. Our eye jumps from one stress to another—from a white blob, to a black splash, to a Surrealistic automatic line, and so on. There is no focus upon which the eye can rest. Because of these even stresses throughout the image, Pollock's compositions are often described as **allover paintings**.

Pollock constructed his picture as he went along, with each new move playing off the previous one, and emotional intuition dictating the next gesture. The resulting image is not just a record of the physical self, but also of the psychological being. Because the artist must face the challenge of the bare canvas and the risk-taking responsibility of making each mark, painting becomes a metaphor for the challenges of the human condition and the risks inherent in taking responsibility for one's actions, particularly in an Existentialist world. World War II dashed the blind belief in the superiority of science, progress, and utopian societies. The one thing that could be trusted and believed in was the self, and *that* became the sole subject of Abstract Expressionist painting.

WILLEM DE KOONING Pollock's style was too personal to spawn significant followers. The gesture painter who launched an entire generation of artists was Willem de Kooning (1904–1997), a Dutch immigrant, who quietly struggled at his

28.1 Jackson Pollock. *Autumn Rhythm: Number 30.* 1950. Enamel on canvas, 8'8" × 17'3" (2.64 × 5.26 m). The Metropolitan Museum of Art, New York, George A. Hearn Fund, 1957 (57.92). © ARS, New York and DACS, London 2008

Abstract Expressionism Action

art for decades in New York's Greenwich Village. De Kooning made Picasso-inspired Cubist-Surrealist paintings in the 1940s, mostly of women. He finally obtained a one-person show in 1948, at the Egan Gallery, when he was 44. The radical works that he presented appeared to be total abstractions of dramatically painted curving lines and shapes, entirely covering the canvas with the same evenness as in Pollock's allover paintings.

Despite the spontaneity implied by the bravura paint handling, the pictures were laboriously crafted, often using methods similar to those of the Surrealists. For example, De Kooning fired his imagination by pinning line drawings on his canvas, not only at the beginning but throughout the process. He jump-started other paintings by inscribing large letters across the canvas. Like Pollock, he constructed the paintings through a continuous process of gestural reactions based on intuition and emotion, with the resulting marks reflecting his presence, feeling, and uncontrollable urges.

De Kooning shocked the art world with his second exhibition, held at the Sidney Janis Gallery in 1953. He did the unthinkable for an Abstract Expressionist: He made representational paintings, depicting women, as seen in *Woman I* (**fig. 28.2**), a work he struggled with from 1950 to 1952. It now became clear that the curvilinear patterning of the earlier abstractions was as sexual as everyone had suspected it was. De Kooning reportedly painted and completely repainted *Woman I* hundreds of times on the same canvas, and he made numerous other paintings of women in the summer of 1952. The other paintings in the Women series show a compendium of female types, not just the hostile-looking creature of our picture. The process of making the painting was almost as important as the final product, as though it were a ritualistic catharsis of sorts. *Woman I* is by far the most violent and threatening of the series, with the others that followed having a neutral appearance and embodying a broad range of attributes.

Woman I was meant to be as unfixed in meaning, or as open to interpretation, as the other women in the series. De Kooning was surprised that viewers did not see the humor in his threatening, wide-eyed, snarling figure, which was based as much on contemporary advertisements of models smoking Camel cigarettes as on primitive fertility goddesses, such as the Paleolithic *Woman of Willendorf* (see fig. 1.7), both of which the artist cited as sources. In the Women series,

28.2 Willem de Kooning. *Woman I*. 1950–1952. Oil on canvas, 75⅞ × 58″ (1.93 × 1.47 m). The Museum of Modern Art, New York. Purchase. © The Willem de Kooning Foundation, New York/ARS, NY and DACS, London 2008

as in all of his paintings, De Kooning played out his own emotions, which, because they constantly changed, allowed him to keep repainting his figure.

Abstract Expressionism: Color-Field Painting

Abstract Expressionism had a flip side. If one side was gestural painting, then the other was **color-field painting**. Instead of bombastic brushstrokes and the overt drama of paint, these painters used large, meditative planes of color to express the innermost primal qualities that linked them to universal forces. The objective of the color-field painters, like that of their gestural counterparts, was to project the sublime human condition as they themselves felt it. The principal color-field painters all started out by making myth-inspired abstract Surrealist paintings in the 1940s and were close friends until 1952.

28.3 Mark Rothko. *No. 62 (Rust and Blue)* [61] (also known as *Brown, Blue, Brown on Blue*). 1953. Oil on canvas, 9²⁄₃ × 7²⁄₃″ (2.94 × 2.32 m). The Museum of Contemporary Art, Los Angeles. The Panza Collection. © 1998 Kate Rothko Prizel and Christopher Rothko. ARS, NY and DACS, London 2008

Abstract Expressionism - Color Field

MARK ROTHKO Mark Rothko (1903–1970) ranks among the best-known color-field painters. His work in the 1940s drew heavily on Greek tragedy, such as Aeschylus' *Agamemnon Trilogy*, and on Christ's Passion cycle and death—scenes with a harrowing psychology where the lone individual faces ultimate truths about existence, death, and spirituality. But all suggestion of figuration disappeared in 1947. In 1949, Rothko arrived at his mature style, from which he did not deviate for the remainder of his life.

Beginning in 1949, Rothko's paintings consisted of flat planes of color stacked directly on top of one another, as in the 10-foot-high 1953 work *No. 62 (Rust and Blue)* (**fig. 28.3**). There is no longer any storytelling, nor any hieroglyphics or symbols, not even in the title. The artist has

painted what he himself has confronted, the inevitable void of our common future and our sense of mystical oneness with unseen cosmic forces, a theme reminiscent of Caspar David Friedrich's in *Abbey in an Oak Forest* (see fig. 23.4). Rothko's subject, he explained, was "tragedy, ecstasy, doom, and so on." His ethereal planes are so thin that color glimmers through from behind and below, creating a shimmering spiritual light. Their edges are ragged, and like clouds dissipating in the sky, they seem precariously fragile. Although the painting is not about gesture, we feel Rothko's hand building up the planes with individual marks, giving the work a poignant organic quality. Space is paradoxically claustrophobic and infinite. On the one hand, the planes literally crowd the picture to the edges and hover at the very front of the picture plane, while on the other hand, the pervasive blue ground seems to continue forever, uncontained by the edge of the canvas and suggesting infinity. Enormous shifts in scale give a sense of the sublime. Note, for instance, the tiny, thin wisp of soft white on the bottom of the middle plane, which seems so insignificant in comparison to the enormous planes and the vast size of the canvas.

Regardless of the palette, whether bright yellows and oranges or the more moody blues and browns in *No. 61*, the colors in a Rothko painting have a smoldering resonance that makes the image seem to glow from within and evoke a spiritual aura. Rothko wanted viewers to stand close to his enormous iconic images, which would tower over them, and where they would be immersed in this mystical void of the unknown future, as if standing on the precipice of infinity and death.

Rejecting Abstract Expressionism: American Art of the 1950s and 1960s

By the mid-1950s other styles were already beginning to overshadow Abstract Expressionism. The 1950s planted the seeds of a cultural revolution, producing a thirst for freedom of expression that required the invention of radically new art forms. Combines, environments, happenings, Minimal art, and Conceptual Art took art into uncharted territory, breaking down the barriers that had narrowly restricted it to certain standard media.

Re-Presenting Life and Dissecting Painting

No one person or event triggered the dramatic change that occurred in art in the 1950s, but Robert Rauschenberg and Jasper Johns certainly played major roles. While both artists created paintings that had the gestural mark-making of the Abstract Expressionists, these works were an intellectual, impersonal analysis of art rather than an explosion of feelings and primal urges. both artists sought to escape the hold that Abstract Expressionism had on the art world.

ROBERT RAUSCHENBERG Rauschenberg (b. 1925) was a Texan from a working-class family who ended up in New York studying painting by 1947. A critical component of his development was attending the avant-garde Black Mountain College in North Carolina in the fall of 1948, and again in 1951 and 1952. The art department at the small liberal arts school encouraged experimentation, which turned Rauschenberg away from pure painting toward an analysis of the very concept of art. At Black Mountain in 1951, he made, for example, a series of White Paintings. These were large canvases painted a solid white, with no evidence of brushwork. Viewers wondered what they were supposed to see. Themselves for one thing, for their shadows were cast on the canvases, which also caught reflected colored light and accumulated dust and dirt. These canvases captured real life, which was presented without comment or meaning. Viewers could read anything into them that they wanted. Like Duchamp, Rauschenberg was making conceptual art, determined by chance, and aimed at capturing the world without attaching any firm meaning to the art. He was also trying to incorporate life into art directly.

In 1955 Rauschenberg actively incorporated the real world into his artwork when he began making what he called "**combines**," innovative works that combined painting, sculpture, collage, and found objects, as in his *Odalisk* (**fig. 28.4**) of 1955–1958. This four-sided "lamp"—there is an electric light inside—is crowded with collaged material culled from contemporary magazines and newspapers as well as detritus from the street and thrift shops. Even the title is part of this busy collage, for it has to be considered when we try to construct a narrative for the work. But is there a narrative in this poetic collage of disparate material? Obviously, *Odalisk* has a subject, for it is filled with sexual innuendo: The phallic pole jammed into the pillow on the

28.4 Robert Rauschenberg, *Odalisk*. 1955–1958. Mixed media, 6'9" × 2'1" × 2'1" (205.7 × 63.5 × 63.5 cm). Museum Ludwig, Cologne. Art © DACS, London/VAGA, New York 2008

Abstract Combines

bottom, the cock mounted above the nude pinup while the dog howls at her from below, the comic strip of a woman in bed being surprised by a man (on a side of the sculpture not pictured here). Even the title, which is a pun on *odalisque* (see fig. 23.6) and *obelisk*, can be interpreted sexually. But the artist places no value on material, suggests no interpretation, makes no grand statement. The work just is. It is our content, our time, our life. Rauschenberg re-presents it with extraordinary formal powers and with a poetry of paint and collage. In its energy and fragmentation, the work powerfully captures the spirit of the constantly changing world and the fractured way we experience it.

JASPER JOHNS In 1954 Rauschenberg met Jasper Johns (b. 1930) and moved into a loft in the same run-down building in lower Manhattan. Johns is primarily a painter, and his works are literally about painting. This can be seen in *Three Flags*, a work of 1958 (**fig. 28.5**). Because of the Americana theme, many writers talk about this painting as Pop Art, a style that in New York emerges in the early 1960s and derives its imagery from popular culture. *Three Flags*, however, is not about popular culture, for it is part of a series in which the artist repeatedly painted flat objects, such as numbers, targets, and maps, with the intention of eliminating the need to paint illusionistic depth. Here he has painted a flat object (a flag) on a flat surface (the canvas), so we are not tempted to read, for example, a white star as sitting on top of a blue field because we know it does not. Furthermore, Johns does not place the flag in any context that allows us to read specific meaning or emotion into it. His flag is a sign to which he has attached no specific meaning or emotion. In other words, he has created a non-illusionistic, impersonal image. What we are left to look at is *how* the picture was made. Johns's very beautiful and methodical application of wax-based encaustic paint reminds us that a painting consists of paint on canvas. And, of course, painting can be about color, here red, white, and blue. Lest we forget that a painting is a three-dimensional object, Johns has stacked three flag paintings one atop another. We see their sides and hence their depth. Lastly, he reminds us that painting can produce an image. However, he does not give us an illusionistic image; we would never mistake Johns's flag for an illusion of a real flag. In this way, Johns tells us that an image is a sign, that painting is an abstract language, just like verbal language. Just as a word is a sign, standing for something else and not the real thing, so too is painting; it signifies something else, just as numbers and maps are signs for something else.

While the intellectual gymnastics in Johns's paintings are complex and rigorous, the works themselves are objective, devoid of any emotion. Like Rauschenberg, Johns paved a way for artists to break away from the subjectivity and vocabulary of Abstract Expressionism. His powerful assertion of the properties of painting and its inherent flatness would inspire numerous artists in the following decade.

Environments and Performance Art

Rauschenberg's combines played a major role in setting off a chain reaction that caused an explosion of art-making redefining art entirely. Art was no longer just painting, sculpture, and work

28.5 Jasper Johns. *Three Flags*. 1958. Encaustic on canvas, 30⅞ × 45½ × 5″ (78.4 × 115.6 × 12.7 cm). Whitney Museum of American Art, New York 50th Anniversary Gift of the Gilman Foundation, A. Alfred Taubman, an anonymous donor and purchase. 80.32. Art © Jasper Johns/VAGA, New York/DACS, London 2008 on paper; now it took on the form of limitless media and moved out of galleries and museums into the real world, sometimes interacting with daily life, at other times taking place in locations so remote that few people ever got to see it. Art was often no longer an object; rather, it could be temporary and ephemeral, something that could not be bought and sold.

ALLAN KAPROW   In 1958, influenced by Rauschenberg's use of found objects and the enormous scale of Jackson Pollock's paintings, Allan Kaprow (b. 1927), a painter teaching at Rutgers University, began to make what he called **environments**. These were constructed installations that a viewer can enter. His most famous environment, *Yard* (**fig. 28.6**), came in 1961. Filled mostly with used tires, the work had the allover look and energy of a Pollock painting, but visitors to the townhouse garden where it was installed were expected to walk through it, experiencing it physically, including the smells. Like Rauschenberg in his combines, Kaprow attached no firm meaning to his works, although the discarded synthetic materials suggested a modern industrial urban environment, as well as a sense of waste, even death.

Kaprow soon added the live human figure to his environments, which initially were made of a variety of collaged non-art materials that ran from floor to ceiling, vaguely resembling a Rauschenberg combine. He unveiled the result to the New York art world in 1959 at the Reuben Gallery as *18 Happenings in 6 Parts*. Kaprow divided his collaged environment into three rooms, in which seated spectators watched, listened, and smelled as performers carried out such tasks as painting (Rauschenberg and Johns participated), playing records, squeezing orange juice, and speaking fragments of sentences, all determined by chance. In a sense the work was like a Rauschenberg combine that took place in time and space and with human activity. Because of the title of Kaprow's innovative work, a **happening** became the term for this new visual art form in which many of the major artists of the day, including Rauschenberg, started working. While many artists accepted this term, others used different labels, all of which can be grouped under the umbrella term **Performance Art**, distinguished from theater in that it takes place in an art context.

GEORGE SEGAL   Living down the road from Kaprow in rural New Jersey was George Segal (1924–2000), who responded to his friend's

28.6 Allan Kaprow. *Yard*. 1961. Environment of used tires, tar paper, and barrels, as installed at the Martha Jackson Gallery, New York. Life-size. Destroyed. Photo © Robert McElroy/Licensed by VAGA, New York

environments and happenings by creating representational, not abstract, environments out of real objects and populated by plaster figures, as in *The Gas Station* (**fig. 28.7**) of 1963. Now the performers are frozen, reduced to ghost-white mannequins. To create them, Segal used real people, making castings of them by using medical plaster bandages. Like Rauschenberg and Kaprow, he was breaking down the barrier between art and life. But his art is far from neutral; it is emotional and makes a statement. Segal's work condemns the alienation he perceived in contemporary life. This alienation can be seen in his figures, which are left white, as though drained of life. Generally they are lethargic, exhausted, and alone, and seem trapped by a harsh geometry of the horizontals and verticals of their setting.

The works even contain symbols used in more traditional art. *Gas Station*, for example, is dominated by a Bulova clock, a *memento mori* ("reminder of death") motif, which floats in a 10-foot expanse of darkness. Its shape mysteriously resonates with the tire on the floor. The vending machine, tires, cans of high-performance oil, and the gas station itself suggest modernity, technology, and fast, efficient living. Missing from this materiality, however, is something meaningful—human interaction and spirituality. Segal retains the Existential angst of his Abstract Expressionist background by questioning the meaning of modern existence. Although he often used contemporary branded objects, such as Coke bottles, to give his environments the look of reality and modernity, Segal never celebrated the products of consumer culture, nor questioned how mass-media imagery, including advertising, manipulates its audience. His sculpture is closer in spirit and style to the paintings of Edward Hopper (see fig. 27.25) than to Pop Art, with which he has been mistakenly associated.

Pop Art: Consumer Culture as Subject

Pop Art is a style that emerged in New York in the early 1960s, although it had appeared in a very different guise in Britain a decade earlier. The style earned its name because it derives its imagery from popular or vernacular culture. Like Rauschenberg and Kaprow, Pop artists represented the artifacts of the world they lived in, namely the imagery of the mass media, although they did it using conventional painting rather than new media. Unlike Johns and Segal, both of whom occasionally used popular imagery, Pop artists focused on the products of popular culture by taking what art historians often describe as a *low* art form, that is, commercial art, and incorporating it into one that is considered *high*, meaning fine art. By doing so, however, they subversively revealed the manipulative impact of the mass media. Among the best-known Pop artists are the Americans Roy Lichtenstein and Andy Warhol.

ROY LICHTENSTEIN   Another close friend of Kaprow's, Roy Lichtenstein (1923–1997), came to Rutgers University to teach in 1960. When he arrived he was an Abstract Expressionist painter. Within a year, however, he was making what would be considered Pop paintings, in part influenced by Kaprow's dictum: To make art that did not look like art.

The contemporary life that Lichtenstein scavenged and represented was not that in the urban streets, as was the case with Kaprow, Rauschenberg, and Segal, but the crude black-and-white advertisements in telephone books and newspapers and the prosaic drawings in comic books. These he cropped and adjusted into visually riveting images, like *Drowning Girl* (**fig. 28.8**). Traditionally, Lichtenstein is appreciated for seeing the beauty of "low art" and elevating it to "high art," in effect celebrating popular culture, and in particular American culture.

Lichtenstein's work does more than just blur the distinctions between fine art and mass culture. Like Johns, whose *Flag* paintings had a profound impact on him, Lichtenstein was interested in the language of art, particularly in regard to issues of perception. He does not just imitate the comic strip, he also plays with that genre's technique of making an image out of benday dots, the small dots that when massed together create color and shading in printed material. He was intrigued by how an illusion of three-dimensional volume could be made using flat dots and flat black lines. When viewed from close up, Lichtenstein's large images dissolve into a flat abstract pattern, virtually becoming Abstract Expressionist compositions.

The images that Lichtenstein selected for his paintings from 1961 to 1964 fall into a distinct pattern: Men are portrayed as strong, virile soldiers and fighter pilots, whereas women are shown as emotionally distraught, dependent on men, and happily slaving around the house doing domestic work. With deadpan brilliance, Lichtenstein made his paintings a mirror of contemporary society, revealing the stereotyping deeply embedded in the media. But the paintings themselves appear objective and unemotional, giving little suggestion of a polemical agenda or a sense of the artist's presence, whether his hand (brushwork) or emotions.

ANDY WARHOL Andy Warhol (1928–1987) was making art based on comic books at exactly the same time as Lichtenstein, and when the dealer Leo Castelli decided to represent Lichtenstein and not him, he turned to other kinds of popular imagery, namely product design and newspaper photographs. Among his most famous motifs are Campbell's soup cans, as seen in *32 Campbell's Soup Cans* (**fig. 28.9**), begun in 1961. Warhol produced 32 soup can images for his first exhibition, held at the Ferus Gallery in Los Angeles in 1962. Campbell's offered 32 soup varieties at the time, hence 32 paintings, which Warhol hand-painted himself. He installed the works as monotonously as possible, evenly spacing them and placing them on a shelf, as soup cans would be in a supermarket. Just as the soup came off a mass-production assembly line, Warhol, soon after his Ferus Gallery exhibition, began mass-

28.8 Roy Lichtenstein. *Drowning Girl*. 1963. Oil on canvas, 5'7⅝" × 5'6¾" (1.72 × 1.69 m). The Museum of Modern Art, New York. Philip Johnson Fund and Gift of Mr. and Mrs. Bagley Wright. © The Estate of Roy Lichtenstein, DACS 2008

producing his paintings in his studio, which he called "the Factory." Assistants made the works to his specifications using a silkscreen process to print a photographic image onto canvas, or onto paper, as he did to make prints. While he was intensely involved in the entire process, the works nonetheless appeared to be factory-produced, with Warhol simply signing the back. With a Duchampian gesture, he tells us that paintings are commodities, that people are buying a name product—that is, a Warhol—and that art is about idea, not necessarily about technique or craftsmanship. But he also comments on the camouflaging function of product design, on how it tells us nothing about the mass-produced commodity it promotes and how the packaging lures us into buying it. Warhol's message is that Campbell's soups are everywhere, having penetrated to the farthest reaches of the country, and that mass-production uniformity and consumerism dominate American society. In effect, these soup cans are a portrait of modern America. As with Lichtenstein, Warhol neither praises nor condemns. (For a further discussion

28.9 Andy Warhol. *32 Campbell's Soup Cans*. 1961–1962. Acrylic on canvas, 32 works, each 20 × 16″ (50.8 × 40.6 cm). Museum of Modern Art, New York. Gift of Irving Blum; Nelson A. Rockefeller Bequest, gift of Mr. and Mrs. William A.M. Burden, Abby Aldrich Rockefeller Foundation. © 2008 Andy Warhol Foundation for the Visual Arts/ARS, New York/DACS, London

Pop Art

of Warhol, please see the Introduction, pages 3–4 and 8.)

Formalist Abstraction of the 1950s and 1960s

The most influential art critic in the 1940s and well into the 1960s was Clement Greenberg (1909–1994). He began by championing Pollock's formalism, but as the 1940s progressed he increasingly promoted an art that was totally abstract and dealt with just those qualities inherent in the medium, that is color, texture, shape of field (meaning shape of the picture), and composition. This work, which emphasized the formalist or abstract qualities of the medium, could make no reference beyond itself. Greenberg's theories had an enormous impact on the way painters, sculptors, and critics thought about art. His criticism helped lay a foundation for the Hard-Edge painting and Minimalist art that emerged in the 1950s and 1960s.

Formalist Painting and Sculpture

Formalist painting emerged in the heyday of Abstract Expressionism, the early 1950s, and in large part was a reaction to it. Just as Rauschenberg, Johns, Kaprow, and the Pop artists rejected the subjective components of Pollock and De Kooning, the formalist painters sought to make unemotional art. They replaced bold, gestural brushwork with smooth surfaces that gave no hint of the artist's hand or feelings. Instead of the push-pull Cubist space of De Kooning's style of Abstract Expressionism, they powerfully asserted the flatness of the canvas, virtually eliminating any sense of space. Led by Greenberg, they were attracted to the formalist implications of Abstract Expressionism, not its emotional content. They also embraced the style's enormous scale. Among the formalist abstraction styles of the period are Hard-Edge Abstraction, typified by Ellsworth Kelly, and Minimalism, exemplified by Donald Judd.

ELLSWORTH KELLY Ellsworth Kelly (b. 1923) developed a distinctly American brand of abstract painting in Paris between 1948 and 1954. During those years, he began to reduce painting to a bare-bones simplicity, which some critics called Hard-Edge Abstraction. To free his mind

28.10 Ellsworth Kelly. *Red Blue Green*. 1963. Oil on canvas, 6'11⅝" × 11'3⅞" (2.12 × 3.45 m). Collection of the Museum of Contemporary Art San Diego. Gift of Dr. and Mrs. Jack M. Farris. © Ellsworth Kelly 1963

from earlier art, he based his abstractions on the shapes that he saw in the world around him, especially negative spaces, such as the opening under a bridge, a shadow, or a window. His paintings use just a handful of geometric shapes in solid primary and secondary colors, and with these explore how forms move through space, colors interact, and "figure" relates to "ground," that is, how image relates to background. Kelly generally locks his figure and ground so tightly into a single unit that they seem to coexist on the same spatial plane.

In *Red Blue Green* (**fig. 28.10**), a 1963 work, Kelly plays a red rectangle and a blue curved shape off against a green ground. The left side of the painting appears fixed, whereas the right has movement. When standing in front of this enormous work, which is more than 11 feet wide, a viewer can feel at one moment the green ground consuming the blue and at the next moment the blue plunging down into the green. In other words, the figure–ground relationship is reversed. But never to be forgotten is the sheer intensity of the color, especially as presented on such a large scale. Kelly's genius is his simple gesture: He strips everything else away, including any sense of himself, to make a painting that is about color—in this case red, blue, and green—and movement.

Formalist Sculpture: Minimal Art

A group of sculptors emerged in the early 1960s who generally composed their work using a mathematical or conceptual premise. The reliance upon geometry in this new work emphasized conceptual rather than emotional content and favored the means and materials of mass-production. Their sculpture came to be known as Minimal art. The artists generally did not make their objects themselves, preferring to send specifications to an artisan, or more likely a factory, for production. Like Pop paintings, Minimal sculpture lacks the evidence of the artist's touch that traditionally served as the sign of personal emotion and expression as well as proof of the artist's technical accomplishment. There is no sign of the artist at all. Furthermore, the artists used unconventional non-art materials to make art—Plexiglas, fluorescent tubes, galvanized steel, magnesium tiles—continuing the exploration of new materials that characterized so much of the art-making of the late 1950s and 1960s. Similarly, one of their concerns was to make art that did not look like art. They wanted their artworks to be perceived as independent objects, having no reference to anything beyond themselves.

DONALD JUDD The characteristics of Minimalism are apparent in *Untitled*, a 1969 sculpture of copper boxes (**fig. 28.11**) by Donald Judd (1928–1994), one of the leading Minimalists. The sculptor determined the shape and spacing of the boxes by mathematical premise (each box is 9 × 40 × 31 inches, with 9 inches between boxes), not by intuition or artistic sensitivity. Judd's work was constructed by serial repetition of elements, so there is no hierarchy of composition and no

28.11 Donald Judd. *Untitled*. 1969. Copper, ten units, 9 × 40 × 31″ (22.8 × 101.6 × 78.7 cm) each, with 9″ (22.8 cm) intervals; 14′2″ × 40″ × 31″ (4.32 m × 101.6 cm × 106.7 cm) overall. Solomon R. Guggenheim Museum, New York. Panza Collection. 91.37.13. Art © Judd Foundation/VAGA, New York/DACS, London 2008

evocation of emotion. A viewer can take in and readily understand his composition at a glance. The sculpture is a real object, a "specific object" as Judd called it to distinguish Minimalism from traditional art, and critics admired it for its precision, consistency, color, texture, and scale.

In addition to possessing the properties of a well-made "real thing," Judd's boxes occupy space like ordinary things as well. They are not presented on a base, and there is no glass case to protect them. By relinquishing the props that announce an object to be a work of art, Minimalism heightens our awareness of the spaces in which we view art. In other words, the actual space around the object becomes an integral part of the work and of the art experience.

The Pluralist 1970s: Post-Minimalism

The cold objectivity of Minimalism and formalist abstraction dominated contemporary art in the mid-1960s, overshadowing styles that focused on subjectivity and the human figure. Even Pop Art seemed unemotional and machine-made. But as the 1960s progressed, so did an interest in an art based on emotion, the human being, and referential and representational subject matter. In the midst of the Vietnam War and the civil rights-led social revolution that challenged the *status quo*, artists began to view formalist abstraction as an escapist indulgence. With Minimalism, the Modernist avant-garde seemed to many in the art world to have completely lost touch with society, retreating into a hermetic world of its own. By the mid-1960s, artists could no longer remain removed from their emotions and the hotly contested social and political issues of the day. By the late 1960s, American artists began to put the human component back into art, and many addressed the issues tearing the nation apart. The responses were diverse, with artists using what seems like an endless array of media to deal with an endless array of issues. Now, many artists made art that was temporary or conceptual and could not be collected, in effect, dematerializing the art object.

While often driven by aesthetic premises, these artists nonetheless reflected the antimaterialistic stance of the 1960s social revolution and its anti-capitalist stance. Led by women, African Americans, and Latinos, minority groups, generally ignored by the white-male-dominated art establishment, protested at their exclusion from the art world. They picketed museums, denouncing the prejudices of those organizations, and made art that dealt with issues not considered mainstream or valid aesthetic concerns by museum curators and directors—issues such as gender, ethnic and racial identity, and sexual orientation. Disenfranchised artists, like the Impressionists 100 years earlier, began opening their own galleries to provide an alternative to museums. Because the pluralism of the 1970s came on the heels of Minimalism, and in many respects is a response to its hermetic (closed-off) aesthetics, the art from this decade is often called Post-Minimalism.

Post-Minimal Sculpture: Geometry and Emotion

Some of the first Post-Minimal sculptors retained the geometry of Minimalism, but they were hardly creating insular objects. To the contrary, their geometric forms were loaded with powerful emotional issues.

EVA HESSE One of the outstanding Post-Minimalists in the 1960s was Eva Hesse (1936–1970). Her accomplishment is astonishing when one considers that her career was cut short by her death from a brain tumor at age 34. Born in Hamburg, Germany, she was raised in New York after her Jewish parents fled Nazi persecution. Hesse worked with a variety of unusual materials, such as acrylic paint on papier-mâché over balloons. Her works were abstract and had a basis in geometry. Because her sculptures reveal the dripping, pooling, flowing, stretching, and drying by which they took shape, they suggest organic forms and processes, as well as growth and sexuality. In 1968 she began using fiberglass, which became her trademark material and was perhaps responsible for her brain cancer.

A classic work is *Untitled* (**fig. 28.12**), which has as its starting point the geometric form of Minimalism. The four rectangular units of which it is composed imply boxes or framed paintings because of their curled edges. Contradicting their geometry are the uneven, rippling surfaces and sides, which transform the fiberglass into an organic substance, recalling especially skin. The strange ropelike latex appendages eccentrically flopping from either side of center suggest arms or legs, although they ultimately are nothing more than abstract elements, like the rectangular units. The work is full of contradictions: It is simultaneously funny and morbid, geometric and organic, erotic and repulsive, abstract and

28.12 Eva Hesse. *Untitled*. 1970. Fiberglass over wire mesh, latex over cloth and wire (four units), 7'6⅞" × 12'3⅝" × 3'6½" (2.31 × 3.75 × 1.08 m), overall. Des Moines Art Center, Des Moines, IA. Purchased with Funds from the Coffin Fine Arts Trust, Nathan Emory Coffin, Collection of the Des Moines Art Center, 1988 (1988.6.a-d). © Estate of Eva Hesse, Hauser & Wirth, Zürich/London

referential. Perhaps the most powerful quality in Hesse's sculptures is the sense of frailty, wear, decay, and aging—best expressed in *Untitled* by the wobbly "legs."

Earthworks and Site-Specific Art

By the late 1960s, the Post-Minimal aesthetic operated on an enormous scale, not only far beyond the confines of the gallery but far away from the art world, and in many instances in uninhabited, remote areas. Several artists began sculpting with earth, snow, volcanoes, lightning, and deep-sea sites, their work by definition often temporary and existing today only in photographs and drawings. Usually the work had a strong geometric component, reflecting the influence of Minimal art and Hard-Edge Abstraction. But in contrast, this sculpture generally was filled with references, including environmental, ontological (concerned with the nature of being), and political issues, as we can see in the work of Robert Smithson.

ROBERT SMITHSON One of the most famous **earthworks**, works of art created by manipulating the natural environment, is *Spiral Jetty* (**fig. 28.13**), made by Robert Smithson in 1970. Smithson became a prominent figure in the New York art world in the mid- to late 1960s because

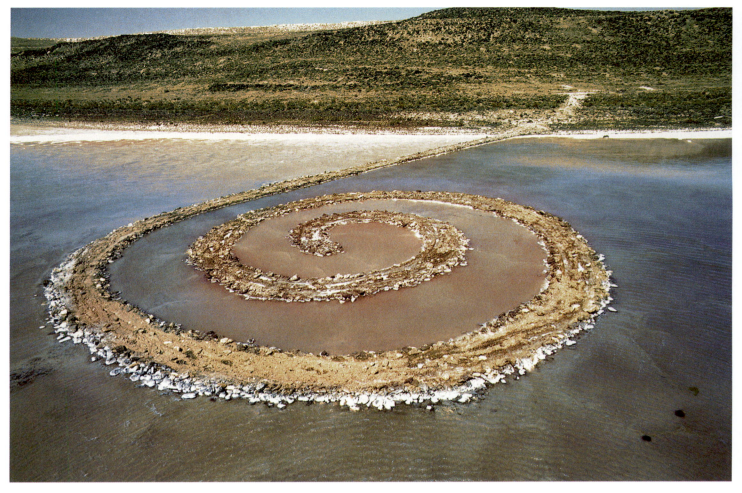

28.13 Robert Smithson. *Spiral Jetty*. 1970. Black rock, salt crystals, earth, red water (algae). Total length 1,500' (457.2 m); width of jetty 15' (4.57 m). Great Salt Lake, Utah. Art Courtesy James Cohan Gallery, New York. Collection DIA Center for the Arts, New York. Photo by Gianfranco Gorgoni

Mix media   *Earthworks – Site Specific Art*

of his articles on art, which often took an environmental approach to discussing land and nature.

Like Hesse's sculpture, Smithson's Minimalist-looking work is full of references and issues, which is apparent in *Spiral Jetty*. The work is 1,500 feet long, 15 feet wide, and involved moving 6,650 tons of mud and black basalt. It is located at Rozel Point, a remote area of Utah's Great Salt Lake that looks like an industrial wasteland because of the rusting, discarded mining equipment littering the surrounding area. Just as time consumes civilization, and all things for that matter, so too will the jetty eventually disappear as it erodes into the lake. The spiral form, as it wraps around itself, going nowhere, and trapping microorganisms that turn the water red, seems like the relic of a prehistoric civilization. Rather than just a minimal geometric shape to be admired for its own sake, *Spiral Jetty* is a powerful sculpture that utilizes time as a major component to speak about the entropy of all things.

Conceptual Art: Art as Idea

Although the Frenchman Marcel Duchamp had made ideas the focus of art beginning in the 1910s (see Chapter 27), the term Conceptual Art did not become commonplace until the 1960s, when a large number of artists started producing art that emphasized ideas rather than the aesthetics of style. Of course, ideas appear in all art, but the ideas are closely tied to the formal qualities of the art and cannot exist without them. In Conceptual Art, the art generally exists solely as an idea, with no visual manifestation other than words. Or the idea or information can appear as a graph, chart, map, or documentary photograph.

JOSEPH KOSUTH By the late 1960s, more and more artists were making art based on ideas, and one of the leading figures in this movement was Joseph Kosuth (b. 1945). Characteristic of Kosuth's work is *One and Three Chairs* (**fig. 28.14**) of 1965, in which he combined a large gelatin-silver print of a folding chair with the real chair and a photograph of a dictionary definition of a chair. By using words instead of just an image, Kosuth tells us how cerebral and nonaesthetic his intentions are.

The work appears to be a textbook study in semiotics, the science of signs—a popular topic in universities and in a small segment of the art community at the time. In the language of semiotics, the real chair is the "signified," the photograph is the "signifier," signifying that particular chair, and the dictionary definition is the idealized nonspecific chair. By arranging three versions of a chair in this particular way, Kosuth has determined their context, which leads a viewer to consider issues of language and meaning, rather than such typical art issues as beauty and expression. Reading the definition, we tend to think of the real chair next to it. If it were not present, we would probably think of some other chair from our own experience. If we look only at the photograph of a chair, we may even think that the subject of the photograph is not necessarily the chair but the absence of a person sitting in the chair. The title is an important part of the work, for it too provides context, suggesting that we can view the chairs as the same chair (one chair) or as three different chairs with very different stories. In other words, this work is about ideas as much as it is about the aesthetics of the visual presentation, which is as unemotional and straightforward as Minimalism. Ultimately, the task of establishing meaning is the viewer's.

One and Three Chairs also reflects a new approach to photography that appeared in the mid-1960s: The medium was no longer the sacred preserve of professional photographers, who worked on a modest scale, carefully took their own photographs, and often slaved over their prints. Now photographs were used by installation, earthwork, Performance, and Conceptual artists, who in their primary medium often worked on a large scale. They now made photographs based on their work that functioned at a similar size, even rivaling painting. Generally, they did not take their own pictures, and few if any did their own printing. Most shocking to traditional photographers, they often integrated photography into other media, as Kosuth did in *One and Three Chairs*, thus violating the time-honored integrity of the medium.

JOSEPH BEUYS Joseph Beuys (1921–1986) was a German Conceptual artist who produced work so complex and rich in ideas that it is nearly

28.14 Joseph Kosuth. *One and Three Chairs*. 1965. Wooden folding chair, photographic copy of chair, and photographic enlargement of dictionary definition of chair; chair, 32⅜ × 14⅞ × 20⅞″ (82.2 × 37.8 × 53 cm); photo panel, 36 × 24⅛″ (91.5 × 61 cm); text panel, 24 × 24⅛″ (61 × 61.2 cm). The Museum of Modern Art, New York. Larry Aldrich Foundation Fund. © ARS, New York and DACS, London 2008

impossible to pin down exactly what his art is. His objects, diagrams, photographs, and performances interrelate so tightly that no one piece can comfortably stand on its own. He was based in Düsseldorf, a city that by the 1970s was home to many of the world's leading artists, its art scene perhaps second only to New York's. Beuys played a major role in developing this artistic climate. His impact included spurring German artists to confront their Nazi past, to rediscover the German Romantic tradition, and to invest their art with spirituality, much as the German Expressionists had done in the early twentieth century.

Two key factors in Beuys's development were his experiences in World War II as a fighter pilot in Hitler's Luftwaffe and the 1963 arrival in Düsseldorf of the Fluxus artists, highly Conceptual artists noted for, among other things, their Performance art, which had been influenced by Kaprow. Beuys propagated a myth that his plane was shot down in 1943 in a snowstorm over the Crimea, and that nomadic Tartars saved him from freezing to death by covering him in animal fat and layers of felt, materials that became a foundation for much of his sculptural work.

In 1961 Beuys was teaching at the Düsseldorf Art Academy, and two years later he was introduced to Fluxus, joining them for a segment of their European performance tour. In 1965 he performed *How to Explain Pictures to a Dead Hare* (**fig. 28.15**). For three hours he moved his lips as if silently lecturing the dead hare cradled in his arm about the pictures surrounding him on the walls. Attached to his left sole was felt, and to his right, steel, the one representing "spiritual warmth," the other "hard reason." Honey and gold paint covered Beuys's head, transforming him into a shaman, a high priest who uses magic to cure ills. The honey represented a life force. This mysterious ritualistic performance was about the meaninglessness of conventional picture-making—art that had to be explained—and about the need to replace it with a more spiritual and natural form of communication, an art the meaning of which could be felt or intuited by a viewer rather than understood intellectually. The performance was designed to create a magical art that would cause people to invest their own lives with spirituality. Anyone who watched the performance found it riveting and unforgettable, even if they did not understand it. His objects, too, such as a worn wooden chair with a pile of fat on its seat, affected people similarly.

Television Art: Nam June Paik

Another artist who participated in Fluxus activities in Düsseldorf in the early 1960s was the Korean-born musician, Performance artist, and sculptor Nam June Paik (b. 1932). Living in Düsseldorf in 1963 and performing in the Fluxus program, he began making art using television monitors. He called television the "electronic superhighway" and declared it the medium of the future, dedicating his life to working with it. The following year he moved to New York, and with the launch of the first affordable video camera by Sony, he often used video as well. As a result, he is often labeled a "video artist."

Paik's work in the 1970s became increasingly grand and complex. Typical of the more elaborate structure of the later work is a piece from 1995, *Electronic Superhighway: Continental U.S.* (**fig. 28.16**). Fed by numerous computer-controlled video channels, this installation consists of dozens of monitors inserted in a neon map of the 48 continental states. The rapidly changing images generally relate to the respective states, except for New York, which was fed from a live camera in the New York Holly Solomon Gallery, where the work was shown and from where our reproduction originates.

In the *Electronic Superhighway*, Paik reaffirms the prevalence of television in American society, presenting it with the fast-paced continuous stream of information characteristic of broadcast television. The work celebrates American vernacular culture, both in its use of neon and television as media and in the Americana presented on the videos. Television is America, Paik tells us. It is, in effect, real life, because most Americans experience the world through their television screens.

Art with a Social Agenda

Most of the postwar artists discussed thus far did not have a social agenda. Even some who did, such as Lichtenstein and Warhol, subversively buried their message so that it was not readily visible, especially to the groups they criticized. While an atmosphere of counterculture dominated the vanguard art world paralleling the social revolution that was occurring not only in America but also worldwide by the late 1960s, few artists made political art. By the 1970s the

28.15 Joseph Beuys. *How to Explain Pictures to a Dead Hare.* 1965. Performed at Galerie Schmela, Düsseldorf, Germany. © DACS 2008

28.16 Nam June Paik. *Electronic Superhighway: Continental U.S.* 1995. Installation: Forty-seven-channel closed-circuit video installation with 313 monitors, laser disk images with sound, steel structure and neon, 15 × 32 × 4′ (4.57 × 9.75 × 1.2 m). Courtesy of the Artist and Holly Solomon Gallery, New York. © Estate of Nam June Paik

trickle of artists making work that dealt with social issues began to swell into a torrent. So great was its influence that we think of social issues playing a major role in avant-garde art for the last 35 years. An art with a social agenda became a key component of 1970s Post-Minimalism.

African-American Art: Ethnic Identity

In the 1960s, a handful of artists began doing what had been unthinkable in the art world: Turning their backs on both Minimalism and abstraction in general and instead making art about the nation's problems and issues, particularly those concerning race, ethnic background, gender, and sexual orientation. Because of the civil rights movement, African-American artists were challenged to make art about their heritage. At university and in art school, they were trained like everyone else to make abstract art. But their communities pressured them to do the exact opposite: Make narrative art and take up the black cause. To balance both claims was a challenge.

ROMARE BEARDEN In New York in 1963, a number of African-American artists formed a loose group called Spiral, dedicated to supporting the civil rights movement. They met in the studio of Romare Bearden (1911–1988), a New York University-educated mathematician and philosopher who in the 1940s increasingly became a committed artist. Influenced by Martin Luther King, Jr.'s 1963 March on Washington, D.C., Bearden suggested a collaborative project for Spiral that involved the members all contributing to a large photo collage about black identity. When no one turned up, Bearden undertook the project by himself, cutting up newspapers and magazines to make collages, for which he became famous.

The composition of Bearden's collages is based on Cubism, as seen in *The Prevalence of Ritual: Baptism* (**fig. 28.17**), created in 1964, but the subject matter is distinctly African-American. Bearden grew up in Charlotte, North Carolina, before moving to New York City's Harlem, and the fractured image shows a baptism, reflecting the importance of religion in black culture. The faces not only express the African physiognomy but in some instances also suggest African masks. This work has the effect of tracing American culture back to its African roots and reinforcing the continuous importance of ritual and community. The collage composition has a wild syncopation, and even a sense of improvisation, that seem to relate to the black jazz musicians of the period,

28.17 Romare Bearden. *The Prevalence of Ritual: Baptism.* 1964. Collage of photochemical reproduction, synthetic polymer, and pencil on paperboard, 9⅛ × 12″ (23.2 × 30.5 cm). Hirshhorn Museum and Sculpture Garden, Smithsonian Institution, Washington, D.C. Gift of Joseph H. Hirshhorn, 1966. Art © Romare Bearden Foundation/DACS, London/ VAGA, New York 2008

such as Charlie Parker or John Coltrane. The power of Bearden's work lies in the artist's ability to pack so much information and energy into a single image that it overflows with the vitality and essence of the African-American experience.

Feminist Art: Judy Chicago and Gender Identity

Betty Friedan's 1963 book *The Feminine Mystique* signaled the start of the feminist movement. Almost simultaneously a number of women artists began making work that dealt with women's issues. Nancy Spero (b. 1926), for example, made simple but powerful expressionistic drawings depicting violence toward women.

The most famous work emerging from the women's movement is *The Dinner Party* (**fig. 28.18**), orchestrated by Judy Chicago (b. 1939) and made by over 400 women between 1974 and 1979. By the late 1960s, Chicago was a dedicated feminist, who in the early 1970s established a Feminist Art Program, the first of its kind, at California State University at Fresno. Shortly thereafter, with the artist Miriam Schapiro (b. 1923), she started a second similar program at the California Institute of the Arts in Valencia. The thrust of these courses was to encourage women to make art and deal with gender issues, which the art world, including

university and art school faculties, said she could not do because the work did not conform to the aesthetic norms of Modernist formalism that signified serious art. The Feminist Art Program was designed to provide support for women artists and to redefine aesthetic values in contemporary art.

The Dinner Party reflects Chicago's shift from a maker of abstract Minimalist objects and paintings to works on feminist themes in alternative media and installations. It pays homage to the many women who, she felt, were ignored, underrated, or omitted from the history books. Chicago laboriously researched these lost figures. She then designed a triangular table with 39 place settings, 13 to a side, each honoring a significant woman, ranging from ancient goddesses to such twentieth-century icons as Georgia O'Keeffe. In addition, 919 other women's names are inscribed on the white floor tiles lying in the triangular intersection of the tables. Each place setting included a hand-painted ceramic plate that pictured a vagina executed in a period style. The American poet Emily Dickinson's reproductive organ, for example, is surrounded by lace, and the medieval queen Eleanor of Aquitaine's is encased in a *fleur-de-lis*. Under each place setting is an embroidered runner, often elaborate and again in period style.

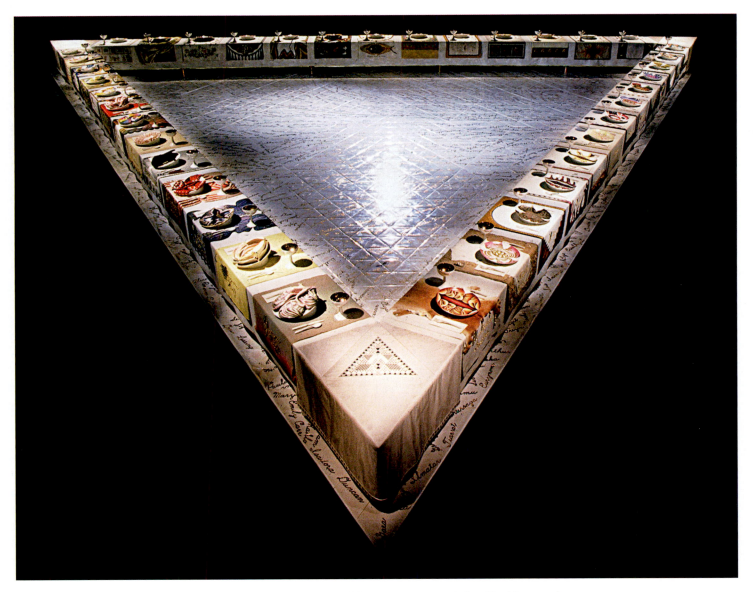

28.18 Judy Chicago. *The Dinner Party*. 1979. Mixed media, 3 × 48 × 42' (0.9 × 17.6 × 12.8 m). Brooklyn Museum of Art, New York. Gift of the Elizabeth A. Sackler Foundation © ARS, New York and DACS, London 2008

Instead of using bulldozers, chain saws, hoists, and welding equipment as men did for their environments, Chicago intentionally turned to media associated with women—painted china, ceramics, and embroidery—and created an elegant, beautiful work that subtly operates on an epic scale, spanning millennia. Also present is a sense of community and ritual, for we feel as though Chicago has appropriated and transformed the Christian male theme of the Last Supper into a spiritual communion of women.

Late Modernist Architecture

Modernist architecture thrived after World War II, especially in America, which previously preferred traditionalist architecture (skyscrapers, for example, in a Gothic style). But now Modernist architecture was only a look or style. It no longer had the utopian vision and revolutionary zeal to improve the world that we saw in the High Modernism of De Stijl and the Bauhaus (see pages 581–584), and in the art and design of Constructivist Productivism (see pages 580–581). However, some of the most influential buildings of the period continued to be designed by the great Early and High Modernist architects: Wright, Le Corbusier, and Mies van der Rohe, not discussed in the last chapter. While Mies continued the International Style aesthetic of light, floating geometric buildings with taut, thin glass walls, Frank Lloyd Wright and Le Corbusier developed a sculptural architecture that emphasized mass and the physical presence of a building, and they were not afraid to be referential.

28.19 Ludwig Mies van der Rohe and Philip Johnson. Seagram Building, New York. 1954–1958

architecture   20th century Art

Continuing the International Style: Ludwig Mies van der Rohe

Postwar Late Modernism resulted in glass boxes sprouting up in urban centers and dotting the beltways that circled American cities, especially beginning in the 1960s and 1970s. The glass box became the required image for corporate headquarters, as seen the Seagram Building (**fig. 28.19**) in New York by Ludwig Mies van der Rohe (1886–1969), built from 1954 to 1958, with interiors by Philip Johnson (1906–2005). If one were to choose a single building to epitomize the Late Modernist skyscraper, it would be this tower. This is the building that was imitated worldwide. But rarely did the imitations begin to approach the perfection that Mies achieved with his aesthetic of "Less is more," which he developed in the 1920s when stripping buildings down to a pure, simple geometric essence that projected an image of breathtaking elegance.

We can see these minimal gestures in the Seagram Building. Mies began by removing the building from its urban environment, placing his 38-story tower on a plaza elevated above street level. The plaza is simple but sumptuous; it is made of pink granite, has two shallow pools placed symmetrically on either side of the building, and is surrounded by a low, serpentine marble wall. The weightless, tinted glass-and-bronze tower sits on a colonnade of *pilotis*, or pillars, that leaves the first floor open, and every detail, including the paving stones, is carefully proportioned to create a sense of perfection and elegance. With the rise of Hitler in Germany, Mies had joined the new Bauhaus in Chicago, and in the Seagram Building we can see the influence of the nineteenth-century Chicago School in the emphasis on its skeletal grid. To acknowledge the functionalism of the grid, Mies used thin I-beams for the mullions, or solid spaces, between windows. They provide the vertical accent that the proportions of the horizontal spandrels so perfectly counterbalance with their thin ridges at top and bottom. Inside and out, lavish, beautifully harmonized materials embellish the building's exquisite proportions.

Sculptural Architecture: Referential Mass

Mies's architecture was essentially nonreferential, just like Minimalist sculpture. However, his contemporaries Frank Lloyd Wright (see page 542) and Le Corbusier (see page 584) took Late Modernist architecture in a different direction. Their buildings contain historic references and are organic, if not outright expressionistic. Made of poured concrete, they are massive monumental buildings that have a powerful sculptural presence. For a discussion of Frank Lloyd Wright's Solomon R. Guggenheim Museum, built at virtually the same time as the Seagram Building and some 60 blocks north of it in Manhattan, please see the Introduction, pages 14–15.

SUMMARY

The focus of the art world shifted from Paris to New York after World War II. But the watershed for the remainder of the century occurred in the 1950s, when art was totally redefined. In the United States, the civil rights movement of the 1950s and 1960s challenged the status quo, and with the Vietnam War of the 1960s a period of social upheaval began. Artists issued similar challenges, accepting nothing at face value.

Abstract Expressionism, the first important postwar style, surfaced in New York in the late 1940s, with the existential gestural paintings of Jackson Pollock and Willem de Kooning. A flip side of Abstract Expressionism was color-field painting, as represented by Mark Rothko, in which large planes of color express primal qualities linked to universal forces.

In the 1950s, radically new art forms appeared like Robert Rauschenberg's combines, which joined painting, sculpture, and found objects in a single work, Jasper Johns's unemotional paintings of common flat objects, and Allan Kaprow's environments and happenings. Pop Art emerged in America in 1961 when Roy Lichtenstein and Andy Warhol began incorporating into their work commercial, mass-media imagery. These artists blurred the distinction between fine art and popular art, and highlighted the subtle yet pervasive impact of the media on culture.

In the 1940s the influential art critic Clement Greenberg developed a critical approach that advocated an art based solely on a work's formal qualities. During the next two decades, formalist painters, such as Ellsworth Kelly, sought to create completely abstract art that was devoid of emotion or references. Formalist abstraction in sculpture took the form of Minimalism.

By the late 1960s, many artists began putting the human element back into art, addressing political, social, and environmental problems. Because it followed Minimalism, the art of the 1970s is often called Post-Minimalism. The sculptures of Eva Hesse retain the geometry of Minimalism but are loaded it with powerful emotional content. Others made art that was not only temporary but far removed from traditional gallery or museum settings—for example, the earthworks of Robert Smithson. Another trend was Conceptual Art, an art based on ideas.

The social agenda played a key role in 1970s Post-Minimalism. The 1960s social revolution had been led by groups generally ignored by the white-male-dominated establishment. Many artists, like Romare Bearden and Judy Chicago, now dealt with issues of gender, ethnicity, racial identity, and sexual orientation.

Modernist architecture flourished in America in the 1950s. Ludwig Mies van der Rohe continued the International Style aesthetic of light, seemingly weightless geometric buildings encased in thin glass walls. Moving in a different direction were architects like Frank Lloyd Wright, who chose to instill their structures with historic references, emphasizing mass and their actual physical presence.

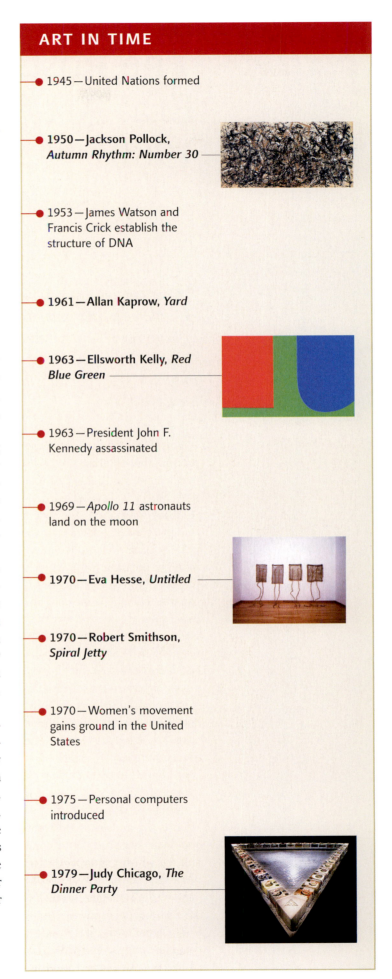

ART IN TIME

- 1945—United Nations formed
- 1950—Jackson Pollock, *Autumn Rhythm: Number 30*
- 1953—James Watson and Francis Crick establish the structure of DNA
- 1961—Allan Kaprow, *Yard*
- 1963—Ellsworth Kelly, *Red Blue Green*
- 1963—President John F. Kennedy assassinated
- 1969—*Apollo 11* astronauts land on the moon
- 1970—Eva Hesse, *Untitled*
- 1970—Robert Smithson, *Spiral Jetty*
- 1970—Women's movement gains ground in the United States
- 1975—Personal computers introduced
- 1979—Judy Chicago, *The Dinner Party*

The Postmodern Era: Art Since 1980

*T*he art that came to the art world's attention toward 1980 is generally
known as Postmodern. The term was coined in the mid-1960s by a circle
of European literary critics that included the French philosophers Jacques
Derrida (1930–2004) and Jean Baudrillard (b. 1929), and was first applied to
literature. (The group's theories are also called Deconstructionism or Post-
Structuralism.)

At the heart of European Postmodernism is the
premise that all literature and art is an elaborate
construction of signs, and that the meaning of
these signs is determined by their context. A
Raphael altarpiece, for example, meant one
thing to a sixteenth-century Catholic viewing it
in its original context, a church, but it conveys a
different message today when it is presented as a
fine art object in a prestigious museum. Context
can also change as viewers bring their personal
experiences to the work. Postmodernists
claimed that there can be no fixed meaning, and
thus no fixed truths. By the late 1970s, artists and
critics had digested this theory and applied it to
art. Postmodern theory now became the driving
force behind much art-making and art criticism,
and a self-consciousness about entering a new
era arose in the art world in the late 1970s. Now
a large number of artists and critics asked more
overtly and persistently: How do signs acquire
meaning? What is the message? Who originates
it? What—and whose—purpose does it serve?
Who is the audience and what does this tell us
about the message? Who controls the media—
and for whom? More and more artists, such as
the American Cindy Sherman and the German
Sigmar Polke, began using familiar images in
new contexts, revealing—or deconstructing—
their deeper social, political, economic, and aesthetic meanings. The preferred media for many
of these artists were those of the mass media,
namely photography, electronic signs, billboards,
and video.

While this Postmodernist attitude signified a
major thrust in art toward 1980, it has been only
one of numerous issues that have preoccupied
the art world in the last 25 years. The period is
characterized by pluralism, in effect continuing
the pluralism associated with 1970s Post-Minimalism. Now, however, it had a philosophical
foundation in Postmodern theory. By denying
any one system, reading, interpretation, or truth,
Postmodern theory destroyed the credibility of
the authoritarian hierarchies of styles, media,
issues, and themes, and it opened the door for
everything and everyone.

In effect, Postmodernism marked the end of
the Modernist era. Modernism viewed modern
art as a linear progression of one style building
upon the last, continuously advancing art
toward the "new." By the 1980s, artists had
license *not* to be new. Not only did they appropriate art in every imaginable style and medium
from the history of civilization and combine it
as they saw fit, many of the leading artists,
such as Felix Gonzalez-Torres and Kiki Smith,
did not even concern themselves with cultivating a distinguishable style as they jumped
from one medium to the next, relying on a
theme rather than a look to tie their work
together. Message was more important than
having a readily identifiable, single style, a

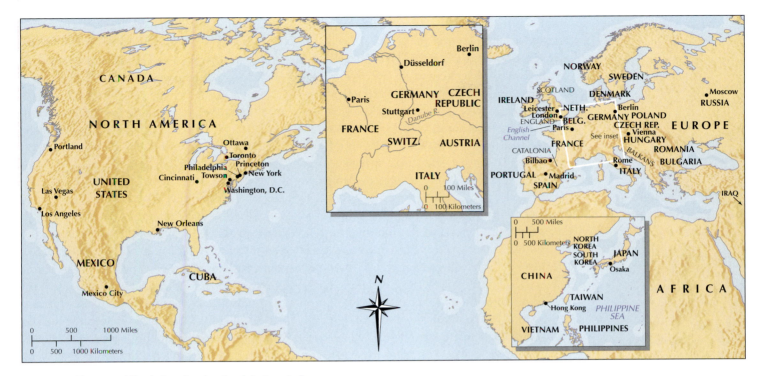

Map 29.1 Europe and North America showing Asia (inserted)

quality that had been one of the hallmarks of Modernism.

The Postmodern era also redefined the nature of the art world itself. The art establishment widened to embrace artists of all ethnicities and races, accepting all kinds of media, styles, and issues without placing a value on one over another. In this new multicultural environment, artists who had been marginalized in the 1970s became mainstream. Furthermore, artists from all over the world, not just America and Europe, molded contemporary art. The acceptance of artists worldwide mirrors the global restructuring of the last 25 years. Political and economic realignments resulted as first the U.S.S.R. and then China abandoned a strict adherence to Communism, experimented with capitalism, and opened up to foreign trade and investment. In the 1990s, Europe formed the European Union, and the United States, Mexico, and Canada signed the North American Free Trade Agreement (see map 29.1). Barriers were falling everywhere, with people crossing borders more readily than ever before. Another important force behind the creation of a world art is the long-term impact of the American civil rights movement and the independence movements, especially in Africa and Asia, of the post-colonial 1950s and 1960s. These movements asserted their cultural traditions as viable and valuable alternatives to mainstream culture, and in the last 25 years they have increasingly been woven

into the fabric of a world culture. But perhaps the communications field more than anything else has been responsible for the creation of the "Global Village." Television, cellular phones, satellites, computers, and the Internet have linked the world. The Post-Industrial era is also the Information Age. Today, the world's leading artists come from countries as varied as Lebanon, Iran, Israel, Cambodia, Thailand, Korea, Japan, China, South Africa, Mali, Russia, Colombia, Brazil, Cuba, and Iceland.

In this world of complex media and changing interpretations, scholars do not always agree on the meaning of Postmodernism. While the term initially was applied specifically to the European philosophy that emerged in the 1960s, today scholars and historians use the term quite loosely, to encompass all of the art made since 1980. In effect, they use it to mean art made after Modernism. We will use it in the same way.

Architecture

Postmodernism appeared in architecture in the 1960s and was accompanied by a manifesto of sorts, a book titled *Complexity and Contradiction*, by the Philadelphia architect Robert Venturi. In it, Venturi called for a new architecture, one that rejected the cold, abstract Modernist International Style. The new architecture would be referential, that is, buildings would recall earlier architectural styles, or contain motifs that referred to the past and present. Furthermore, architects would be free to design buildings without following a set of rules or principles. They were free, too, to be entertaining and witty. Venturi's message was gradually absorbed by the architectural community, and by the 1980s, an architecture that it labeled "Postmodern" emerged. The term was used specifically to describe work that made references to earlier periods and styles.

Since fundamental to European Postmodernism is the concept that no one authoritative style or set of principles can prevail, architecture since the 1980s reflects a broad range of issues and interests going well beyond just designing referential buildings. Among them is a revised Modernism, one strain of which we can call Hi-Tech because of its highly technological appearance. Another strain is Deconstructivism, a concept relating to Derrida's theories of Deconstruction and embracing the notion that architecture should not have a fixed structure or logic, thus being wide open to interpretation.

Postmodern Architecture

Robert Venturi (b. 1925) upset the architectural establishment by attacking Modernist architecture in *Complexity and Contradiction*. He challenged Mies van der Rohe's dictum "Less is more" with "Less is a bore" and argued that

architecture could be whatever the architect wanted it to be. By the late 1970s his writing triggered the rise of a referential architecture, an architecture often referred to as "Postmodern."

ROBERT VENTURI Venturi practiced what he preached. In 1962, he designed a house for his mother in Chestnut Hill, Philadelphia (**fig. 29.1**). The structure resembles a Modernist abstraction of flat planes, strict geometry, clean lines, and a play of forms and spaces, notably in the enormous cleft in the center of the façade. But the house is also referential, for it is a parody of a conventional American home, complete with a slanted gable (the roof is much lower), a front porch, and behind that a large rectangular block that looks like a chimney. (It is a false chimney; the real chimney is dwarfed in front of it.) Venturi then complicates the house with endless architectural references—the "lintel" that seems to support the two halves of the façade and the interrupted "segmental arch," floating over and framing the entrance, recall an Egyptian pylon. Venturi has imbued the over-scaled house with humor, irony, and allusions, transforming the traditional American home into a rich architectural statement.

MICHAEL GRAVES Postmodern architecture did not become prevalent until the late 1970s. A fine example is the Public Services Building (**fig. 29.2**)

29.1 Robert Venturi. Vanna Venturi House. 1962. Chestnut Hill, Philadelphia. Venturi, Scott Brown and Associates, Inc.

29.2 Michael Graves. Public Services Building. 1980–1982. Portland, Oregon

of 1980–1982 in Portland, Oregon, designed by the Princeton, New Jersey architect Michael Graves (b. 1934). The building is complex and quite difficult to interpret, and furthermore, it is filled with paradox, as every design on its surface begs to be seen in several ways: Flat and sculptural, representational and abstract, historical and modern. The form of the building is a Palladian cube sitting atop a platform, with the square or near-square motif echoed in the outline of the façade and in additional squares within (for example, the enormous mirror-glass window, which encases a square defined by the maroon vertical piers). The individual windows are each four feet square. The wall can be read as a flat mural, a thin Modernist membrane stretched over the metal skeleton; but suddenly it becomes three-dimensional and sculptural, an effect heightened by the maroon-colored vertical shafts in front of the large mirror window. These mullionlike shafts become the fluting of pilasters, topped with bracket capitals, which support an enormous keystone above. Yet, if we read the keystone with the beige-colored wall, it becomes part of a flat arch framing the mirror window. The façade can even be described as anthropomorphic, for the pilasters and keystone can be read as a huge face, the capitals as eyes, and the pilasters as legs. The building has a whimsical sense of play, but it is also serious, recalling such great historical models as Palladio and Mannerism.

New Modernisms: Hi-Tech Architecture

Major Postmodern architecture in the vein of Venturi faded in the 1990s, superseded by an exhilarating diversity that expanded architecture to a true Postmodernism, that is, a pluralism that is the term Postmodernism generally refers to. Many architects began to revisit Modernism,

29.3 Richard Rogers and Renzo Piano. Centre National d'Art et Culture Georges Pompidou. 1971–1977. Paris

reinvigorating it with the new artistic license that had emerged during the late 1970s. An extreme version of this New Modernism is Hi-Tech, a style whose buildings resemble powerful industrial machines. Perhaps the most famous prototype for the Hi-Tech Modernism that became fashionable in the following decades is the 1971–1977 Pompidou Center (**fig. 29.3**) in Paris. Its architects, Richard Rogers (b. 1933) and Renzo Piano (b. 1937), exposed the building's utilities—instead of being buried within the interior, they are displayed on scaffolding around the perimeter of what is otherwise a classical Modernist glass box. Elevators and escalators, plumbing, electrical, and ventilation ducts are all prominently displayed as exterior "ornament." Besides challenging architectural aesthetics, this device has the advantage of completely opening up the interior space, allowing for any necessary configuration.

Deconstructivism: Countering Modernist Authority

In 1988 the Museum of Modern Art in New York mounted an exhibition titled *Deconstructivism*. The show included seven architects whose work displayed a Constructivist geometry and planarity that created an architecture of "disruption, dislocation, deviation, and distortion," as the curators for the show wrote. The term Deconstruction caught on, and a major trend emerged in the 1980s challenging the idea that architecture had to adhere to any single concept or ideal and the notion that architecture had to aspire to some kind of perfection, order, or logic.

FRANK GEHRY Frank Gehry (b. 1929) was one of the seven architects included in the *Deconstructivism* show, but he views himself as an independent, refusing to be associated with any style or group. Nevertheless, his projects share with those of the other artists in the exhibition a sense of disorder, fragmentation, and energy, as seen in his most famous building, the Guggenheim Museum, Bilbao (**fig. 29.4**). Its unique forms and vocabulary make it impossible to establish any specific meaning or architectural references, although people have described its forms as a boat, a fish, and a blossoming flower (Gehry's own description). Ultimately the structure is an exploration of the abstract sculptural play of enormous volumes, and it shows

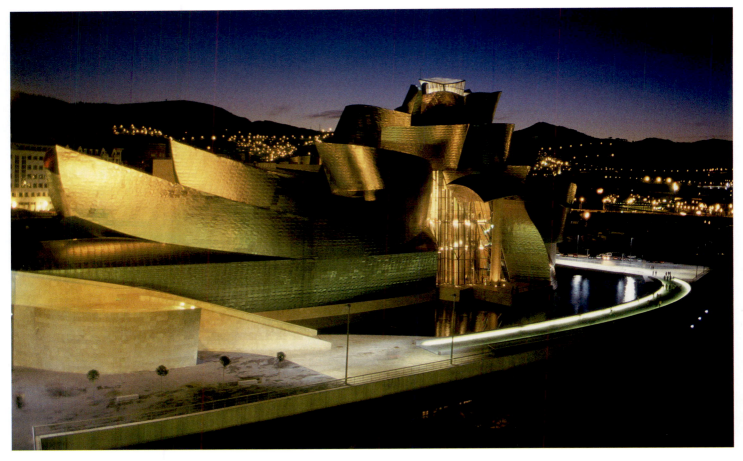

29.4 Frank Gehry. Guggenheim Museum. 1992–1997. Bilbao, Spain

architecture

clearly the architect's pure delight in architectural freedom.

The building's curvilinear masses are contrary to orthodox Deconstructivism, which emphasizes flat planes and angularity. Gehry designed the complex forms using computer technology, an integral tool in the fabrication of the building as well. The museum even feels Hi-Tech, for covering the steel skeleton is a thin skin made up of thousands of tiny titanium shingles. These shimmer in the light, changing color—silver, blue, gold—according to the time of day or the weather.

The Guggenheim, Bilbao is an example of the architectural diversity that had emerged by the end of the twentieth century, when all rules about design were suspended. As important, it reflects how architecture has moved beyond just being about designing buildings. Architects have, once again, begun to create prominent symbols for a city. From its conception, the museum was intended to be more than just a museum; it was meant to change the image of this Spanish industrial port, giving it cultural cachet and transforming it into a tourist destination. And that is precisely what happened.

Postmodernism

Post-Minimalism and Pluralism: Limitless Possibilities

Beginning in the late 1960s, the Post-Minimalists had rejected the austerity of Minimalism (see pages 607–608) and once again returned the human figure, the artist's hand, subjectivity, and references back into art. The reaction to Minimalism was accompanied by the rise of a broad range of issues, styles, and media in the 1970s. During the 1980s this pluralism began to gain widespread acceptance as it moved from marginalized art to the mainstream. At the same time, Postmodern theory provided a philosophical basis for pluralism, as it argued against all authoritative aesthetics and philosophical positions. The Modernist notion that one and only one style was correct and could move art forward at any given moment was dead. Indeed, if a single word could encapsulate the art made since the 1980s, it would be "diverse."

Among the many developments of the last 25 years are a revival of interest in painting, the popularity of installation art, and the ascendance of photography and video as leading media.

Among the more popular themes are racial, ethnic, and gender identity, a preoccupation with the body and death, and a Postmodern analysis, or Deconstruction, of how images and art take on meaning. But if there is anything that unites this period, it is the belief that Modernism and its authoritarian posturing is dead, and that the possibilities of what art can be and be about are limitless.

The Return of Painting

Painting was back by 1980. Not that it had disappeared, but in the late 1960s and 1970s it had been overshadowed by Conceptual, video, Performance, and earth art. The Derrida-influenced art critics of the late 1970s associated painting with Modernism and were talking about "the death of painting," even though a stream of shows featuring the medium opened in London, New York, Germany, and Italy in the late 1970s and the 1980s.

The new type of painting that emerged came to be known as Neo-Expressionism, an appropriate label for works that are both painterly and expressionistic. Neo-Expressionism appeared first in Germany and Italy in the 1970s and then migrated to New York. In Germany, painters self-consciously recalled the northern Romanticism and Expressionism so deeply ingrained in that nation's culture. Joseph Beuys, through his mystical performances, was the catalyst for this resurrection of the German past. Among the themes he and other artists began to explore was the legacy of Hitler's Third Reich.

ANSELM KIEFER Among Beuys's students at the Düsseldorf Art Academy was Anselm Kiefer (b. 1945). Kiefer created images of mythical themes and epic scope that evoke centuries of German history. His enormous painting *To the Unknown Painter* (**fig. 29.5**) explodes with the energy of flailed paint and the dramatic perspective of crop

29.5 Anselm Kiefer. *To the Unknown Painter*. 1983. Oil, emulsions, woodcut, shellac, latex, and straw on canvas, 9'2" × 9' × 2" (2.79 × 2.74 m × 5 cm). The Carnegie Museum of Art, Pittsburgh. Richard M. Scaife Fund; A. W. Mellon Acquisition Endowment Fund. © Anselm Kiefer

furrows rushing toward an eerie monumental tomb. Cold, bleak, and lifeless, the neutral-colored image seems to exude an atmosphere of death. Or does it? Crops lying fallow in the winter will be reborn in the spring; the cycle of life continues. Kiefer's expressive use of paint and dramatic composition can be interpreted as a metaphor for the constant movement and force of nature. Inspired by Beuys's use of symbolic objects, Kiefer often incorporated real materials into his paintings, imbuing them with a similar ritualistic magic. In this work, he embedded straw into the paint, and viewers could smell its scent for years. Nature is not just illustrated in this work, it is physically present. Yet unlike crops in a field that are continually rejuvenated, the straw in this painting will eventually disintegrate.

How does the tomb fit into this image? As the title suggests, the mausoleum is for painters. We deduce that they are German because the tomb is not painted but rendered by a large woodcut, a medium associated with German art since being widely used by northern European artists during the Renaissance as well as by Expressionists such as Kirchner (see page 554) in the early twentieth century. The bunkerlike shape suggests a shelter, and the isolated but well-anchored monument seems to be surrounded by the swirling forces of nature, representing not only the German mythical past but also the Romantic spirit that has driven German artists for centuries. We know from other works by Kiefer that these destructive forces are meant to symbolize Hitler's perversion of the German Romantic tradition, which he manipulated to serve his racist agenda.

In a painting about national identity, Kiefer's Expressionistic style and his use of Romantic themes proclaim his place within the northern European Romantic tradition. He assures us that this tradition is once again in safe hands. With its wealth of symbols, metaphors, and overlapping and interlocking interpretations, the resulting image is varied and complex, reflecting the epic scale Kiefer covers and the mythical themes he evokes.

JEAN-MICHEL BASQUIAT Of the many American Neo-Expressionists to emerge in the 1980s, among the most exciting was Jean-Michel Basquiat (1960–1988), born in New York to a middle-class family. Basquiat's father was Haitian and his mother was of Puerto Rican descent. He dropped out of school at age 17, first writing poetry and then becoming a street artist. By studying art books, he became knowledgeable

about art history and began painting. By the time he was 22, he had achieved international stardom. He died of a drug overdose at age 27.

In *Horn Players* (**fig. 29.6**) of 1983, Basquiat combines both poetry and graffiti. More important, he draws upon the lessons of the pluralistic 1970s by brilliantly incorporating the era's strategies of using texts, making process art, working with narratives, and dealing with social politics, here racial identity. Basquiat also owes a debt to Abstract Expressionism, seen in his dynamic handling of paint, and to Pop Art, visible in his cartoonlike imagery and popular-culture references.

Basquiat was prolific, working quickly and with the stream-of-consciousness intensity sensed here. We can feel him painting, writing, crossing out. He draws us into the canvas by forcing us to read and piece it together. He makes us

29.6 Jean-Michel Basquiat. *Horn Players*. 1983. Acrylic and oil paintstick on canvas, three panels, overall 8' × 6'5" (2.44 × 1.91 m). Broad Art Foundation, Santa Monica, California. © ADAGP, Paris and DACS, London 2008

experience the sounds coming out of the saxophone, think about the repetition of words and the rhythms they make, and analyze his masterful use of color—a brilliant pink and blue here, yellow and green there. Because they are so powerfully presented, we cannot dismiss Basquiat's use of the words, such as *alchemy* (a reference to the alchemy of jazz), *ornithology* (a nod to the jazz musician Charlie Parker, nicknamed "Bird"), and *ear* (an allusion to musical instinct). His works evoke the raw energy of the 1950s: Beat poetry, improvisational jazz, and Abstract Expressionism. But 1980s hip-hop also comes to mind. Basquiat creates a powerful, sensuous experience as he shares his passionate feelings about the black musicians Dizzy Gillespie and Charlie Parker, with whom he clearly identifies. Much of his work features African-American musicians, singers, and athletes, and is a reflection of the importance artists were now giving to racial, ethnic, and gender identity.

Sculpture

The Post-Minimal aesthetic in sculpture, the combination of the geometry of Minimalism with references and emotion that we saw in the

work of Eva Hesse (see fig. 28.12), continued unabated into the 1980s and 1990s.

MAYA LIN One of the great Post-Minimal sculptures of the 1980s is the *Vietnam Veterans Memorial* (**fig. 29.7**) by Maya Lin (b. 1959). Lin received the commission while still a student in the architecture program at Yale University. This was a daunting project because of the strong emotions and opinions surrounding the Vietnam War, but Lin's solution proved beautiful in its simplicity, ingenious in its neutrality, and sublime in its emotional impact. She presents the names of the dead and missing in action in a chronological list from 1959 to 1975. The names are etched into slabs of black granite that together carve out a V-shaped gash in the earth. Viewers start reading from the left, representing the year 1959, where the first killed are listed and the granite rises out of the ground. The name-laden stone gradually rises along its 247-foot length as more and more Americans die. The names keep coming, and the viewer soon becomes emotionally overwhelmed by their number.

At its 10-foot peak, the granite turns at a 130-degree angle and then descends along another

29.7 Maya Lin. *Vietnam Veterans Memorial.* 1982. Black granite, length 493′6″ (150.42 m). The Mall, Washington, D.C.

247-foot length, with fewer soldiers listed as the 1973 withdrawal from Vietnam approaches. At the end, as the granite again disappears into the ground, many viewers are left with a feeling of existential nothingness. Adding to this sense of loss is the impact of the granite's polished surface, which acts like a mirror, casting reflections of the living onto the names of the dead. This memorial is a sharp departure from traditional representational monuments to heroism, like Rude's *La Marseillaise* (see fig. 23.12), which glorified nationalistic spirit and dedication. In a sense, the granite wall acts as an enormous tombstone. While the structure takes the form of Minimal sculpture, it has been transformed through references into a brilliant Postmodern monument of powerful emotions.

Deconstructing Art: Context as Meaning

By 1980 many artists were making art that analyzed how images functioned. We saw Warhol and Lichtenstein doing this in the 1960s (see Chapter 28), by appropriating mass-media images to comment on how they influence public perception. Now, influenced by Postmodern Deconstruction theory, even more artists were exploring how images function and how context affects meaning. They were also influenced by the Post-Structuralist philosopher Jean Baudrillard, and especially by his theory of simulacrum. Baudrillard wrote that contemporary American culture was based on a notion of hyperreality—that Americans, especially through the mass media, including films and television, had constructed an artificial, perfect, timeless world that was more "real" than reality itself. In effect, the copy had replaced authenticity, and looking at images and experiencing the world through images had become a simulacrum, or visual substitute, for real experience. Artists now began representing this simulacrum, borrowing images from the mass media—a process often referred to as appropriating—and analyzing the effect of context on meaning.

In effect, their art was about deconstructing images as used in the social environment. Often they recontexualized and layered the appropriated images and designs with the intention of exposing, or deconstructing, the social, aesthetic, political, and economic systems that the original images presented.

SIGMAR POLKE During the 1960s and 1970s, the art world was focused so precisely on New York that other art centers, especially those in Europe, were all but ignored. Particularly in Germany, artists in the city of Düsseldorf were producing some of the most important work of the period, yet only Joseph Beuys was well known internationally. It was not until the 1980s that the New York art world discovered Sigmar Polke (b. 1941) and other major Düsseldorf artists, who conquered the New York, London, and Paris art scenes in the closing decades of the twentieth century. Their paintings were such eye-openers because they powerfully reflected Derrida's theory of Postmodern Deconstruction. But instead of Postmodern theory, they were influenced by Robert Rauschenberg and Pop Art, especially the works of Lichtenstein and Warhol, which they knew from magazines. Their work also reflects the impact of the spirituality of Beuys, who taught at the art academy where they were students.

Armed with this background, Polke made paintings that combined appropriated images, patterns, and designs from various sources, as seen in *Alice in Wonderland* (**fig. 29.8**) of 1971. On top of fabrics with designs of soccer players or polka dots, Polke, like Warhol, mechanically reproduced images taken from other media. In this painting, the white image of a basketball player came from a magazine. Alice and the caterpillar with his hookah is an illustration lifted directly from the original *Alice in Wonderland*. Hard to see in our reproduction are the 1950s-style outlined heads of a man and woman, hand-stamped repeatedly in yellow and red. Polke borrowed all this imagery from popular culture and re-presented it in this enormous painting, which is not on canvas but on store-bought printed fabric. Viewed separately and in a different context, each of these images would be interpreted differently from the interpretation when they are experienced together in this work. In other words, their relationship here creates a context that influences and changes their meaning. Polke avoids assigning a fixed meaning; instead he allows us to weave any story we like from this kaleidoscope of motifs.

Polke is concerned with the way in which the popular imagery we confront daily structures our world. He explores how what we see becomes what we know and, by extension, what we believe in. He examines how images structure our thinking, feelings, and attitudes. In *Alice in Wonderland*, he fashions a Pollyanna vision of childhood—the naive innocence that believes in perfect romance, wholesome sports, and charming fairy tales—all propagated by the mass media

29.8 Sigmar Polke. *Alice in Wonderland.* 1971. Mixed media on fabric strips, 10′6″ × 8′6¾″ (3.2 × 1.6 m). Private collection, Cologne. © Sigmar Polke

and interior design. But unlike the works of the American Pop artists, Polke's paintings have an emotional content. The ghost-white silhouettes hovering over the fabric and the stamped 1950s heads immersed in the patterns of dots and soccer players create a sad, ethereal feeling, even a romantic quality. A sense of absence and loss, of the fleeting nature of life and things, lends a startling spiritual quality to Polke's paintings.

PHOTOGRAPHY: CINDY SHERMAN The art community's excitement over painting lasted through the 1980s, but the same period also saw the rise of photography, video, and installation as principal art forms. The first to challenge the painters were a group of New York Postmodern photographers, which included Cindy Sherman. Although initially unsuccessful commercially, by the time the decade was over the photographers

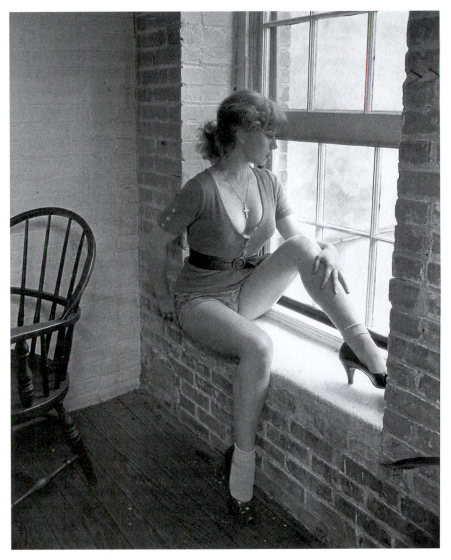

29.9 Cindy Sherman. *Untitled Film Still #15*. 1978. Gelatin silver print, 10 × 8″ (25.4 × 20.3 cm). Courtesy of the artist and Metro Pictures, New York. © Cindy Sherman

had rivaled, if not dethroned, the painters. Their art now seemed more relevant than painting, for it presented the world, as Baudrillard pointed out, as we actually experience much of it—through the lens of a camera. As was the case with Joseph Kosuth and the many other vanguard artists who started using the camera in the 1960s and 1970s (see pages 610–611), most are not interested in the mechanics of taking and processing pictures. Some of them do not handle the camera, and almost none do their own printing. What interests these artists is revealing how the context of an image determines its meaning, and how the mass media subversively structure content to manipulate viewers.

Cindy Sherman (b. 1954) takes this position in her work, although in addition to the power of the mass media, especially movies, she is also interested in revealing a viewer's participation in determining meaning. Beginning in 1977,

Sherman began a series called *Film Stills*, in which she photographed herself in situations that resemble a still from a B-grade movie. For each, she created a set and a female character that she played herself, wearing different clothes, wigs, and accoutrements so that she is unrecognizable as the same person from one still to the next. That she is always the actress is conceptually important, for her metamorphosis represents the transformation women undergo subliminally as they conform to societal stereotypes reinforced, if not actually determined, by the mass media. In *Untitled Film Still #15*, Sherman plays the "sexy babe" who seems to be anxiously awaiting the arrival of a date or lover (**fig. 29.9**). But is this really what is happening? Sherman leaves the viewer guessing. She may suggest a narrative, but she never provides enough information to determine one securely. In effect, the story viewers imagine tells more about their own backgrounds, experiences, and attitudes than it does about the picture itself, which remains ambiguous. Her "babe" could very well be dressed for a costume party instead of a date, and her look of concern could be for something occurring on the street below. Innumerable stories can be spun from this image, taking into account such details as her cross pendant or the old-fashioned spindle-back chair and brick wall. Remove any one of these motifs, and the story would change.

The Power of Installation and Video Art

Installation art had existed since the late 1950s (when the work was called environments), but its popularity surged dramatically in the 1980s, when it became a featured medium, just as

29.10 Ilya Kabakov. *The Man Who Flew into Space from His Apartment*, from *Ten Characters*. 1985. Mixed-media installation, life-size. Centre Pompidou, Paris © DACS 2008

photography had. As we saw in Kiefer's incorporation of actual materials into his canvases, a thirst for the real figures prominently in much art since 1980.

ILYA KABAKOV Of the legions of installation artists who emerged in the 1980s, one of the most engaging is the Russian Ilya Kabakov (b. 1933), who emigrated from Moscow to New York in 1988. In Russia between 1981 and 1988 he made a series of rooms called *Ten Characters* that replicated the types of seedy communal apartments assigned to people by the Russian state under the Communist regime. Each was inhabited by an imaginary person with an "unusual idea, one all-absorbing passion belonging to him alone." One spectacular cubicle was *The Man Who Flew into Space from His Apartment* (**fig. 29.10**). We see the room after its occupant has achieved his dream of flying into space, hurled through the ceiling from a catapult suspended by springs, an allusion to the space race between the U.S. and Russia. Like the other rooms, this one is accompanied by a grim story, worthy of the Russian novelist Fyodor Dostoevsky. The text, the collapsed ceiling, limp sling, and clutter become a tableau of life in Communist Russia, where claustrophobic squalor has brought about a hopeless delusional state, and flights of fantasy are the only escape from the drudgery of daily life. The ruin we are witnessing in *The Man Who Flew into Space* is not just the devastation of one man's life, but rather the shattered dream of the utopia in which Tatlin, the Constructivists, the Dadaists, and the Communist world in general had so firmly believed (see Chapter 27). Kabakov's installation is presented as a relic of an actual event, and like any relic, it possesses a powerful aura, almost impossible to achieve in conventional painting and sculpture.

BILL VIOLA An especially popular form of installation is video or film installation, which had its roots in the film and video installations of the 1960s. Among its best-known practitioners is Bill Viola (b. 1951), who was also one of the first major artists to specialize in video. He started working with the medium in the 1970s after graduating from Syracuse University and by the early 1980s was incorporating it into installations or environments containing real objects. Although Viola's work does not always have a clear sequential narrative, it always has a theme, usually an unsettling, intense questioning of the meaning of existence.

One of Viola's best-known—and simpler—works is *The Crossing* (**fig. 29.11**). In two simultaneous, approximately ten-minute projections, shown side by side, or on either side of a single screen, a plainly dressed man approaches from the distance, passing through an empty, darkened space and stopping when his body, now nearly 12 feet tall, fills the screen. In one projection, water begins to drip on him, eventually becoming a deluge that washes him away. In the other, a small fire erupts at his feet, increasingly swelling into a bonfire that ultimately consumes him. The projections end with water hauntingly dripping in one, and a fire mysteriously smoldering in the other. Both videos are accompanied by a deafening soundtrack of pouring water and crackling fire, which intensifies the force of the imagery and heightens its visceral impact. Viola's elemental symbols of fire and water seem to have destroyed the figure. Or perhaps the two forces have brought about a transformative process, as the body dissolves into a spiritual state, crossing into a higher reality and becoming one with the unseen universal forces. The video relentlessly instills a sense of the physical and sensory and then suddenly leaves us in an existential void. In an era when technology and science were and still are extending life and providing hope for cures for deadly diseases, artists such as Bill Viola were returning to the early twentieth-century quest for the spiritual. Others, as we shall now see, bypassed the spiritual and instead were preoccupied only with death.

Many Styles, One Artist: Felix Gonzalez-Torres

By rejecting traditional hierarchies in medium, style, and content, Postmodern artists gained the freedom to work in a variety of media and styles. Cultivating an easily recognizable "look" or identity was not important. Felix Gonzalez-Torres (1957–1996) is a classic example of this attitude, also found in the work of Kiki Smith and Cai Guo-Qiang, discussed later in this chapter. While he covered a wide range of media and social issues, Gonzalez-Torres is often discussed for his work focusing on the psychological impact of AIDS and the attitudes toward this epidemic. Gonzalez-Torres, who was born in Cuba and came to America in the 1981 Mariel boatlift (a mass exodus to Florida), can best be described as a Conceptual artist working in a Minimalist mode. He presents an idea using simple materials and forms. Despite his spare vocabulary the

29.11 Bill Viola. *The Crossing*. 1996. (Video still.) Video/sound installation. First exhibited at the West Bank Gallery, Savannah College of Art and Design, Savannah, Georgia. Courtesy of Bill Viola Studio. Photo Kira Perov

emotional impact is significant, and the content and implications are far-reaching.

Gonzalez-Torres's media stretch from jigsaw puzzles and mirrors to strings of light bulbs, candy, and stacks of paper. Like many artists in the 1980s, he took his work out of an art context and into the public domain. In 1991, as an exhibition at the Museum of Modern Art in New York, he had a black and white photograph of an empty, unmade bed installed on 24 billboards around the city (**fig. 29.12**). Unlike traditional advertising billboards, this one was enigmatic and forced people to question who made it and why. Most viewers never even knew it was art. The quintessential Postmodern picture, it was highly suggestive and subject to broad interpretation. Even devoid of text, the simple image of an unmade bed spoke volumes. It conjured thoughts of intimacy, relationships, and love as well as loss, absence, and death. For some viewers, the image of the empty bed evoked realizations of the thousands of men, women, and children who had become victims of the AIDS epidemic, creating public awareness and discussion of the disease. Gonzalez-Torres died of AIDS at the age of 38.

Preoccupation with the Body

Gonzalez-Torres is one example of the tremendous impact that the AIDS crisis had on artists during the Postmodern era, and their concern with drawing public attention to this disease, which pervaded all segments of American society and was tragically ignored by the administration of Ronald Reagan. His brave and powerful foray into this theme encouraged many other artists to follow suit. His work reflects a new interest in the body, in human strength and frailty, an awareness brought about by the death and suffering of AIDS victims.

KIKI SMITH One artist to explore the vulnerability of the body and the brevity of life was the New Yorker Kiki Smith (b. 1954). In the 1980s, she created a work consisting of eight identical jars of blood, and another presenting silver-coated water-cooler bottles etched with the names of such bodily fluids as tears, milk, saliva, vomit, semen, urine, and sweat, which a viewer is led to believe are in the jars. Because these works contain repeated elements, they resemble Minimal art. Yet the conceptual component—the thoughts we have when confronting the blood, for example—packs a strong visceral response and the emotional punch of Baroque art or German Expressionism. By reducing the human being to bodily fluids, ones that carry viruses and are subject to attack, Smith denies individuality and uniqueness. She reveals an elemental essence linking all humans that courses through the body and out of it.

Toward 1990, Smith began constructing entire figures, usually using such impermanent materials as paper, papier-mâché, and wax, which served as a metaphor for the fragility of the body and the transience of life. In the 1990 untitled work reproduced here (**fig. 29.13**), she cleverly revives the classical tradition of the nude figure. However, we are viewing neither Greek gods and goddesses nor heroic athletes and soldiers. Rather, she portrays flesh-and-blood mortals. The woman oozes milk from her breast and the man semen from his penis, attributes of nourishment, procreation, and life. But death dominates, in the form of the limp figures slumped on their poles and the jarring discoloration of the skin. Smith presents the entire life cycle, but it is the sadness of deterioration and our ultimate fate of death that prevails.

A World Art: Cai Guo-Qiang

The closing decades of the twentieth century have marked the rise of a world art, although this phenomenon has its roots in the 1950s. With the Internet and satellite communications and jet

29.12 Felix Gonzalez-Torres. *"Untitled."* 1991. Billboard, overall dimensions vary with installation. The Felix Gonzalez-Torres Foundation. Courtesy of Andrea Rosen Gallery, New York. © The Felix Gonzalez-Torres Foundation

29.13 Kiki Smith. *Untitled.* 1990. Beeswax and micro-crystalline wax figures on metal stands, female figure installed height 6′4¹⁵⁄₁₆″ (195 cm). Collection Whitney Museum of American Art, New York. Purchase, with funds from the Painting and Sculpture committee. 91.13 (a–d). © Kiki Smith

travel, the entire world is artistically bound together, transforming it into one large art gallery and making it nearly impossible to talk about art in one hemisphere without talking about developments occurring everywhere else. Now, artists worldwide use the same art language, deal with similar issues, and avidly follow each other's work.

It seems only fitting to end this book with Cai Guo-Qiang (b. 1957), a Chinese artist living in New York since 1995. Among the most visible artists today, Cai brings to this new global art a Chinese background and perspective, enriching the world's visual language. Like Gonzalez-Torres, Cai is primarily a Conceptual artist working in a broad range of media. His oeuvre is dominated by installation art and the use of explosions, namely fireworks, which have become his signature style. Explosives, including fireworks, are a Chinese invention, and through his use of this medium, Cai highlights his cultural identity. Yet his choice of explosives is motivated by other aesthetic and conceptual concerns. As the artist explains: "Explosions make you feel something intense at the very core of your being because, while you can arrange explosives as you please, you cannot control the explosion itself. And this fills you with a great deal of freedom." Cai "draws" with the explosives, sometimes evoking Chinese calligraphy. And like the work of the Abstract Expressionists, his drawing contains sublime references or represents an attempt to tap into universal forces. He even discusses the yin and yang of the explosions, the way in which the work, in a split second, presents both creation and destruction.

In 2003 Cai was commissioned by New York City and the Central Park Conservancy to create an explosion piece in Central Park. Titled *Light Cycle: Explosion Project for Central Park* (**fig. 29.14**), the work lasted four minutes and was divided into three parts: "Signal towers" (pillars of light), "The Light Cycle" (a series of haloes), and "White Night" (small-shell explosions of brilliant white light). The degree to which Cai controls the explosions is remarkable. He draws and paints with the medium. Through his work, Cai seeks to capture a spiritual essence. He has said that his work is for extraterrestrials, and he has subtitled many of his explosions "Project for Extraterrestrials." Just as the art world has become global, so Cai, perhaps with a little wink, is looking beyond Earth, seeking to create art for the universe.

29.14 Cai Guo-Qiang. *Light Cycle: Explosion Project for Central Park*. New York. 2003. Fireworks: tiger tail, titanium solutes fitted with computer chips, shells with descending stars. © Cai Guo-Qiang. Commissioned by Creative Time in conjunction with the city of New York and Central Park Conservancy for the 150th Anniversary of the creation of Central Park

SUMMARY

Art historians have labeled the period since 1980 as Postmodern. The term comes from the European Deconstruction or Post-Structural philosophy of the 1960s, and is generally used to describe the recognition by many intellectuals that context determines meaning, including personal experience, and that it constantly changes; they therefore believe that there are no absolute meanings or truths. The result is that pluralism has characterized Postmodern art, in contrast to the Modernist position that believed that one and only one style at any given moment best moved art forward. Postmodernism also undermines Modernism's emphasis on style, uniqueness, and authorship, with artists now working in multiple styles and even in groups.

In architecture the break with Modernism had occurred in the 1960s and was promoted by the architect Robert Venturi, who advocated that buildings incorporate not only traditional references to architecture's past but also contemporary imagery, elements, or materials, resulting in an eclectic mix of old and new that many architects readily embraced. But it was not until the 1980s that Postmodern buildings, such as Michael Graves's Public Services Building in Portland, Oregon, appeared in cities worldwide. Some architects revisited Modernism, reinvigorating it through the use of an industrial style known as Hi-Tech, which was anticipated by Renzo Piano and Richard Rogers's Pompidou Center in Paris. Others, such as Frank Ghery in his Guggenheim, Bilbao, developed a Deconstructivist idiom, which disrupted viewers' preconceived notions of architecture.

The pluralism of the 1970s became widespread in the 1980s as artists explored a wide spectrum of subjects, styles, and media. Painting made a comeback in the 1980s, strengthened by the emergence of Neo-Expressionism in works by Anselm Kiefer and Jean-Michel Basquiat. The Post-Minimal aesthetic continued in sculpture in the 1980s and 1990s, as seen in the powerful and moving Vietnam War memorial by Maya Lin. Artists in varied media also created works exploring how the function and meaning of images change in different contexts. In photography, video, and installation art, as well as painting, artists analyzed popular symbols, imagery, and even the medium itself to expose issues related to gender, sexuality, and race, to name just a few.

ART IN TIME

- 1978—Cindy Sherman, *Untitled Film Still #15*

- 1980–1982—Michael Graves, Public Services Building

- 1982—Maya Lin, Vietnam Veterans Memorial

- 1989—Berlin Wall is torn down

- 1991—European Union formed

- 1991—Soviet Union collapses

- 1991—World Wide Web launched

- 1991–1992—Republic of South Africa repeals apartheid

- 1992–1997—Frank Gehry, Guggenheim, Bilbao

- 1996—Bill Viola, *The Crossing*

- 2001—Al Qaeda terrorists attack U.S.

- 2003—Cai Guo-Qiang, *Light Cycle*

Glossary

Cross-references are indicated by words in SMALL CAPITALS.

ACTION PAINTING See GESTURE PAINTING.

ALBUMEN PRINT A process in photography that uses the proteins found in eggs to produce a photographic plate.

ALLOVER PAINTING Painting that has even stresses throughout the image.

ALTAR A mound or structure on which sacrifices or offerings are made in the worship of a deity. In a Catholic church, a tablelike structure used in celebrating the Mass.

AMBULATORY A passageway to the outside of the NAVE that forms a walkway around the APSE of a church.

ANDACHTSBILD German for "devotional image." A late medieval image, either painted, engraved, or carved, that was designed to inspire pious feelings in the viewer as he or she contemplated it.

APSE A large architectural niche facing the NAVE of a BASILICA or church, usually at the east end. In a church with a TRANSEPT, the apse begins beyond the crossing.

APSIDIOLE A small apse or chapel connected to the main apse of a church.

ARABESQUE A type of linear ornamentation characterized by flowing, organic shapes, often in the form of interlaced vegetal, floral, and animal motifs.

ARCADE A series of arches and their supports.

ASHLAR MASONRY Carefully finished stone that is set in fine joints to create an even surface.

ATMOSPHERIC PERSPECTIVE Means of showing distance or depth in a painting by lightening the tones of objects that are far away from the PICTURE PLANE and by reducing in gradual stages the contrast between lights and darks.

ATRIUM In ancient architecture, a room or courtyard with an open roof; or the vestibule, usually roofed, in an Early Christian church.

AVANT-GARDE Meaning "advance force" in French, the artists of the avant-garde in nineteenth- and twentieth-century Europe led the way in innovation in both subject matter and technique, rebelling against the established conventions of the art world.

BALUSTRADE (1) A railing supported by short pillars called balusters. (2) Occasionally applied to any low parapet.

BARREL VAULT A semicylindrical vault.

BAS-DE-PAGE Literally "bottom of the page." An illustration or decoration that is placed below a block of text in an illuminated manuscript.

BASILICA During the Roman period, a large meeting hall, its exact form varying according to its specific use as an official public building. The term was used by the Early Christians to refer to their churches. An Early Christian basilica had an oblong plan, a flat timber ceiling, a trussed roof, a NAVE, and an APSE. The entrance was on one short side, and the apse projected from the opposite side, at the far end of the building.

BAYS Compartments into which a building may be subdivided, usually formed by the space between consecutive architectural supports.

BUTTRESS A masonry support that counteracts the thrust exerted by an arch or a vault. See FLYING BUTTRESS.

CALOTYPE Invented in the 1830s, calotype was the first photographic process to use negatives and positive prints on paper.

CENTRAL-PLAN CHURCH The standard design used for churches in Eastern Orthodox Christianity, in which symmetrical chambers radiate from a central primary space.

CHIAROSCURO Italian for "light and dark." In painting, a method of MODELING form primarily by the use of light and shade.

CLASSICISM Art or architecture that harkens back to and relies upon the style and canons of the art and architecture of ancient Greece or Rome, which emphasize certain standards of balance, order, and beauty.

CLERESTORY A row of windows piercing the NAVE walls of a BASILICA or church above the level of the side aisles.

CODEX (pl. **CODICES**) A manuscript in book form made possible by the use of parchment instead of papyrus. During the first to fourth centuries CE it gradually replaced the *rotulus*, or "scroll," previously used for written documents.

COLONNETTE A small, often decorative, column that is connected to a wall or pier.

COLOR-FIELD PAINTING A technique of Abstract painting in which thinned paints are spread onto an unprimed canvas and allowed to soak in with minimal control by the artist.

COMBINES A term applied to the three-dimensional work of Robert Rauschenberg that combines painting and sculpture.

COMPOUND PIER A pier with columns, pilasters, or shafts attached.

CONSTRUCTION A sculpture constructed by adding one element to another, as opposed to carving, chiseling, or casting.

CONTINUOUS NARRATION Portrayal of the same figure or character at different stages in a story that is depicted in a single artistic space.

CONTRAPPOSTO Italian for "set against." The disposition of the parts of the body so that the weight-bearing, or engaged, leg is distinguished from the raised, or free, leg resulting in a shift in the axis between the hips and shoulders. Used first by Greek sculptors as a means of showing movement in a figure.

CORBELING A space-spanning technique in which each layer of stone increasingly tapers inward to form an arch or a vault.

DAGUERREOTYPE Originally, a photograph on a silver-plated sheet of copper that had been treated with fumes of iodine to form silver iodide on its surface and, after exposure, was developed by fumes of mercury. The process, invented by L.-J.-M. Daguerre and made public in 1839, was modified and accelerated as daguerreotypes gained worldwide popularity.

DRÔLERIES French word for "jests." Used to describe the lively animals and small figures in the margins of late medieval manuscripts and in wood carvings on furniture.

DRUM Cylindrical wall supporting a dome; one of several sections composing the shaft of a column.

DRYPOINT A type of INTAGLIO printmaking in which a sharp metal needle is used to carve lines and a design into a (usually) copper plate. The act of drawing pushes up a burr of metal filings, and so, when the plate is inked, ink will be retained by the burr to create a soft and deep tone that will be unique to each print. The burr can only last for a few printings. Both the print and the process are called drypoint.

EARTHWORKS Using very large scale, outdoor artwork that is produced by altering the natural environment.

ENCAUSTIC Method of painting in colors mixed with wax and applied with a brush, usually while the mixture is hot. The technique was practiced in ancient times and in the Early Christian period, and has been revived by some modern painters.

ENGRAVING A graphic-arts process in which a design is INCISED in reverse on a copper plate; this is coated with printer's ink, which remains in the incised lines when the plate is wiped off. Damp paper is placed on the plate, and both are put into a press; the paper soaks up the ink and produces a print of the original. Also, a print made by this process.

ENVIRONMENTS In art, environment refers to the Earth itself as a stage for Environmental art, works that can be enormously large yet very minimal and abstract. These works can be permanent or transitory. The term Earth art is also used to describe these artworks.

ETCHING (1) A print made by coating a copperplate with an acid-resistant resin and drawing through this ground, exposing the metal with a sharp instrument called a *stylus*. The plate is bathed in acid, which eats into the lines; it is then heated to remove the resin and finally inked and printed on paper. (2) The technique itself is also called etching. Like ENGRAVING, etching is an INCISING graphic-arts process. However, the design is drawn in reverse with a needle on a plate thinly coated with wax or resin. The plate is placed in a bath of nitric acid, which etches the lines to receive ink. The coating is then removed, and the prints are made as in engraving. Also, a print made by this process.

FAIENCE (1) A glass paste fired to a shiny opaque finish, used in Egypt and the Aegean. (2) A type of earthenware that is covered with a colorful opaque glaze and is often decorated with elaborate designs.

FLAMBOYANT GOTHIC A style of late Gothic architecture in which the bar tracery supporting the stained glass windows is formed into elaborate pointed, often flame-like, shapes.

FLYING BUTTRESS An arch that springs from the upper part of the pier buttress of a Gothic church, spans the aisle roof, and abuts the upper NAVE wall to receive the thrust from the nave vaults; it transmits this thrust to the solid pier buttresses.

FOLIO A leaf of a manuscript or a book, identified so that the front and the back have the same number, the front being labeled *recto* and the back *verso*.

FRONTALITY Representation of a subject in a full frontal view.

GABLE Triangular part of a wall, enclosed by the lines of a sloping roof.

GESTURE PAINTING A technique in painting and drawing where the actual physical movement of the artist is reflected in the brush stroke or line as it is seen in the artwork. The artist Jackson Pollock is particularly associated with this technique. Also called ACTION PAINTING.

GRISAILLE Monochromatic painting in greys that simulate sculpture (often used on the outer wings of altarpieces).

GROIN VAULT vault formed by the intersection at right angles of two BARREL VAULTS of equal height and diameter so that the groins form a diagonal cross.

HALLENKIRCHE German word for "hall church." A church in which the nave and the side aisles are of the same height. The type was developed in Romanesque architecture and occurs especially frequently in German Gothic churches.

HAPPENING A type of art that involves visual images, audience participation, and improvised performance, usually in a public setting and under the loose direction of an artist.

HATCHING A series of parallel lines used as shading in prints and drawings. When two sets of crossing parallel lines are used, it is called *crosshatching*.

HERALDIC Relating to a system of elaborate symbols used to designate family membership. Heraldic symbols were often employed to decorate the homes and armor of noble families.

HIERATIC SCALE An artistic technique in which the importance of figures is indicated by size, so that the most important figure is depicted as the largest.

HUMANISM A philosophy emphasizing the worth of the individual, the rational abilities of humankind, and the human potential for good. During the Italian Renaissance, humanism was part of a movement that encouraged study of the classical cultures of Greece and Rome; often it came into conflict with the doctrines of the Catholic church.

HYPOSTYLE A hall whose roof is supported by columns.

ICON A panel painting of Christ, the Virgin, or saints; regarded as sacred, especially by Eastern Christians.

ILLUMINATION A painting technique combining rich pigments, gold, and other precious metals to produce dazzling color effects. A term used generally for describing painting in manuscripts. Illuminated manuscripts may contain separate ornamental pages, marginal illustrations, ornament within the text, entire miniature paintings, or any combination of these.

INCISING Technique of cutting into a hard surface with a sharp instrument to create a linear image.

INTAGLIO A printing process using the principle of cutting into a plate (ex. Engraving).

JAMB Side of a doorway or window frame.

KORE Archaic-period Greek statue of a draped maiden.

KOUROS Archaic-period Greek statue of a standing nude youth.

LAMASSU An ancient Near Eastern guardian of a palace; often shown in sculpture as a human-headed bull or lion with wings.

LANCET A tall, pointed window common in Gothic architecture.

LINEAR PERSPECTIVE Also known as scientific perspective. See PERSPECTIVE.

LINEARITY The use of obvious line to define forms.

LUNETTE A semicircular zone, either painted or sculpted, usually above a window or doorway.

MANDORLA Italian for "almond." An almond-shaped radiance of light surrounding a holy figure.

MARTYRIUM A church, chapel, or shrine built over the grave of a martyr or upon the site of a great miracle.

MASTABA Aboveground tomb building with a flat roof and inward-sloping walls, linked by a deep shaft to an underground burial chamber. A tomb form popular in ancient Egypt.

MECHANOMORPHIC   A mechanical form made to look human, or a human made to look mechanical.

MENDICANT   For a Latin word for begging, having to do with late medieval religious groups which lived on charitable donations. The two most important mendicant groups were the Franciscans and the Dominicans.

MIHRAB   A niche in the center of the qibla wall.

MINARET   A tower on or near a mosque, varying extensively in form throughout the Islamic world, from which the faithful are called to prayer five times a day.

MINBAR   A type of staircase pulpit, found in more important mosques to the right of the mihrab, from which the Sabbath sermon is given on Fridays after the noonday prayer.

MODELING   An additive sculptural process in which a malleable material is molded into a three-dimensional form. In painting or DRAWING, the means by which the three-dimensionality of a form is suggested on a two-dimensional surface, usually through variations of color and the play of lights and darks.

MONOCHROMATIC   Term used to describe a painting or drawing created by shades of black and white or values of a single color.

MORTISE AND TENON JOINT   A joining technique used primarily in stonemasonry and carpentry, where a projection (the tenon) on one piece of stone or board is inserted into a hole (the mortise) in a second piece.

MOSQUE   A building used as a center for community prayers in Islamic worship; it often serves other functions including religious education and public assembly.

MOZARAB   Term used for the Spanish Christian culture of the Middle Ages that developed while Muslims were the dominant culture and political power on the Iberian peninsula.

MUSES   In Greek mythology, the nine goddesses who presided over various arts and sciences. They are led by Apollo as god of music and poetry and usually include Calliope, muse of epic poetry; Clio, muse of history; Erato, muse of love poetry; Euterpe, muse of music; Melpomene, muse of tragedy; Polyhymnia, muse of sacred music; Terpsichore, muse of dancing; Thalia, muse of comedy; and Urania, muse of astronomy.

NARTHEX   The vestibule at the main entrance of a BASILICA or church.

NATURALISM   A style of art that aims to depict the natural world as it appears.

NAVE   The central aisle of a BASILICA or church; also, the section of a church between the main entrance and the CHOIR.

NECROPOLIS   Greek for "city of the dead." A burial ground or cemetery.

OBELISK   A tall, tapering four-sided stone shaft with a pyramidal top. First constructed as *megaliths* in ancient Egypt, certain examples have since been exported to other countries.

ORANT   A standing figure with arms upraised in a gesture of prayer.

ORTHOSTAT   An upright slab of stone constituting or lining the lowest courses of a wall, often in order to protect a vulnerable material such as mud-brick.

PAINTERLY   The use of strong or obvious brushwork.

PARCHMENT   From Pergamon, the name of a Greek city in Asia Minor where parchment was invented in the second century BCE. (1) A paperlike material made from bleached animal hides used extensively in the Middle Ages for manuscripts. Vellum is a superior type of parchment made from calfskin. (2) A document or miniature on this material.

PENDENTIVES   Among the supports for a dome, the triangular segments of a wall leading from the square base to the circular DRUM.

PERFORMANCE ART   A type of art in which performance by actors or artists, often interacting with the audience in an improvisational manner, is the primary aim over a certain time period. These artworks are transitory, perhaps with only a photographic record of some of the events.

PERISTYLE   Colonnade (or ARCADE) around a building or open court.

PERPENDICULAR GOTHIC   The third style of English Gothic architecture, in which the bar tracery uses predominantly vertical lines. The fan vault is also used extensively in this style.

PERSPECTIVE   A system for representing spatial relationships and three-dimensional objects on a flat two-dimensional surface so as to produce an effect similar to that perceived by the human eye. In atmospheric or aerial perspective, this is accomplished by a gradual decrease in the intensity of color and value and in the contrast of light and dark as objects are depicted as farther and farther away in the picture. In color art-

work, as objects recede into the distance, all colors tend toward a light bluish-gray tone. In scientific or LINEAR PERSPECTIVE, developed in Italy in the fifteenth century, a mathematical system is used based on orthogonals receding to vanishing points on the horizon. Transversals intersect the orthogonals at right angles at distances derived mathematically. Since this presupposes an absolutely stationary viewer and imposes rigid restrictions on the artist, it is seldom applied with complete consistency. Although traditionally ascribed to Brunelleschi, the first theoretical text on perspective was Leon Battista Alberti's *On Painting* (1435).

PICTURE PLANE   The imaginary plane suggested by the actual surface of a painting, drawing, or relief.

PICTURESQUE   Visually interesting or pleasing, as if resembling a picture.

PIETÀ   In painting or sculpture, a representation of the Virgin Mary mourning the dead Jesus, whom she holds.

PILGRIMAGE PLAN   The general design used in Christian churches that were stops on the pilgrimage routes throughout medieval Europe, characterized by having side aisles that allowed pilgrims to ambulate around the church.

PLANARITY   The arrangement of objects so that they run parallel to the picture plane.

POLYCHROMY   The decoration of architecture or sculpture in multiple colors.

PORTRAIT BUST   A sculpted representation of an individual, usually encompassing the head and shoulders, though sometimes more of the upper torso. It was a Hellenistic and Roman art form revived during the Renaissance.

POST-AND-LINTEL CONSTRUCTION   A space-spanning technique in which two or more vertical beams (posts) support a horizontal beam (lintel).

PREFIGURATION   The representation of Old Testament figures and stories as forerunners and foreshadowers of those in the New Testament.

PROVENANCE   The place of origin of a work of art and related information.

PYLON   In Egyptian architecture, the entranceway set between two broad, oblong towers with sloping sides.

QIBLA   The direction Muslims face when praying. A wall in each mosque marks this direction (toward Mecca).

QUADRIPARTITE   A quadripartite vault is one whose ribs divide the vault into four compartments.

QUADRO RIPORTATO (pl. *quadri riportati*) Meaning "a painting taken somewhere else" in Italian. The illusion of a framed painted scene arranged in a ceiling vault.

RED-FIGURE A type of Greek vase painting in which the design is outlined in black and the background painted in black, leaving the figures and the reddish color of the baked clay after firing. This style replaced the black-figure style toward the end of the sixth century BC.

REGISTER A horizontal band containing decoration, such as a relief sculpture or a fresco painting. When multiple horizontal layers are used, registers are useful in distinguishing between different visual planes and different time periods in visual narration.

RESPOND A projecting and supporting architectural element, often a pier, that is bonded with another support, usually a wall, to carry one end of an arch.

ROSE WINDOW Round windows decorated with stained glass and tracery, frequently incorporated into façades and TRANSEPTS of Gothic churches.

SARCOPHAGUS (pl. sarcophagi) A coffin made of stone, marble or terracotta, and less frequently, of metal. Sarcophagi are often decorated with paintings or reliefs.

SCRIPTORIUM (pl. **SCRIPTORIA**) A workroom in a monastery reserved for copying and illustrating manuscripts.

SIBYL In Greek and Roman mythology, any of numerous women who were thought to possess powers of divination and prophecy. They appear on Christian representations, notably in Michelangelo's Sistine ceiling, because they were believed to have foretold the coming of Christ.

SPIRE A tall tower that rises high above a roof. Spires are commonly associated with church architecture and are frequently found on Gothic structures.

STELE (pl. stelae) A vertical stone slab decorated with a combination of images in relief and inscriptions; often used as a grave marker.

STEREOCARDS A single card with side-by-side photographs of the same image taken by a camera with two lens, replicating human binocular vision. When put into a special viewer, the twin flat pictures appear as a single three-dimensional image.

SYNTHETISM A style associated with Paul Gauguin when he was working in Pont-Aven, France. The word is a reference to the synthetic production of images based on imagination and emotion as oppposed to a mimetic, empirical replication of reality.

TABLINUM The Latin word meaning "writing tablet" or "written record." In a Roman house, a room at the far end of the atrium and the second courtyard, used for keeping family records.

TENEBRISM Meaning "dark/darkness" in Italian and refers to the intense darkness and its contrast in painting.

TONDO A circular painting or relief sculpture.

TONE A reference to the color, darkness, depth, or brightness of a pigment.

TRANSEPT In a cross-shaped church, the arm forming a right angle with the NAVE, usually inserted between the latter and the choir or APSE.

TRIFORIUM An ARCADE running along the walls of a church above the NAVE, and usually pierced by three openings per BAY.

TRIUMPHAL ARCH A massive, freestanding ornamental gateway; originally developed by the ancient Romans to honor a military victory. Also, a monumental arch inside a structure.

TROMPE L'OEIL Meaning "trick of the eye" in French, it is a work of art designed to deceive a viewer into believing that the work of art is reality, an actual three-dimensional object or scene in space.

TRUMEAU A central post supporting the lintel of a large doorway, as in a Romanesque or Gothic portal, where it was frequently decorated with sculpture.

TRUSSED PYLON A steel pylon composed of trusses.

TURRET (1) A small tower that is part of a larger structure. (2) A small tower at a corner of a building, often beginning some distance from the ground.

TYMPANUM The semicircular panel between the lintel and arch of a medieval portal or doorway; a church tympanum frequently contains relief sculpture.

VEDUTA (pl. **VEDUTE**) A painting, drawing, or print of an actual city.

VELLUM Thin, bleached calfskin that can be written, printed, or painted upon.

VERISTIC From the Latin *verus*, meaning "true." Describes a hyperrealistic style of portraiture that emphasizes individual characteristics.

VOUSSOIRS Wedge-shaped stones forming an arch.

WET-COLLODION PROCESS A photographic technique that involves coating a plate in a collodion, a very sensitive material consisting of gun-cotton dissolved in alcohol ether. This process, invented shortly after 1850, resulted in camera exposure times being reduced to under a second, as opposed to the daguerreotype, which required minutes.

WOODCUT A printing process in which a design or lettering is carved in relief on a wooden block; the areas intended not to print are hollowed out.

ZAUM A term invented by progressive Russian poets in the early twentieth century to refer to a language based on invented words and syntax, the meaning of which was supposedly implicit in the basic sounds and patterns of speech. The poets' intention was to return to the non-rational and primitive base of language that, unencumbered by conventional meaning, expressed the essence of human experience.

ZIGGURAT An elevated platform, varying in height from several feet to the size of an artificial mountain, built by the Sumerians to support their shrines.

Books for Further Reading

This list includes standard works and the most recent and comprehensive books in English. Books with material relevant to several chapters are cited only under the first heading.

Introduction

Broude, Norma, and Mary D. Garrard, eds. *Feminism and Art History: Questioning the Litany*. Harper & Row, New York, 1982.

Holt, Elizabeth Gilmore, ed. *A Documentary History of Art*. 3 vols. Vols. 1–2, Princeton University Press, Princeton, 1981–86; vol. 3, Yale University Press, New Haven, 1986.

Kostof, Spiro. *A History of Architecture: Settings and Rituals*. 2nd ed. Oxford University Press, New York, 1995.

Panofsky, Erwin. *Meaning in the Visual Arts*. Reprint of 1955 ed. University of Chicago Press, Chicago, 1982.

Taylor, Joshua C. *Learning to Look: A Handbook for the Visual Arts*. 2nd ed. University of Chicago Press, Chicago, 1981.

Trachtenberg, Marvin, and Isabelle Hyman. *Architecture: From Prehistory to Post-Modernism*. Harry N. Abrams, New York, 1986.

PART ONE
THE ANCIENT WORLD

1 Prehistoric Art

Chauvet, Jean-Marie, Éliette Brunel Deschamps, and Christian Hillaire. *Dawn of Art: The Chauvet Cave*. Trans. Paul Bahn. Harry N. Abrams, New York, 1996.

Clottes, Jean. *Chauvet Cave: The Art of Earliest Times*. Trans. Paul Bahn. University of Utah Press, Salt Lake City, 2003.

———. *The Shamans of Prehistory: Trance and Magic in the Painted Caves*. Harry N. Abrams, New York, 1998.

Cunliffe, Barry, ed. *The Oxford Illustrated Prehistory of Europe*. Oxford University Press, New York, 1994.

Fowler, Peter. *Images of Prehistory*. Cambridge University Press, New York, 1990.

Ruspoli, Mario. *The Cave of Lascaux: The Final Photographs*. Harry N. Abrams, New York, 1987.

Sandars, Nancy K. *Prehistoric Art in Europe*. Reprint of 1985 2nd integrated ed. Pelican History of Art. Yale University Press, New Haven, 1992.

Saura Ramos, Pedro A. *The Cave of Altamira*. Harry N. Abrams, New York, 1999.

White, Randall. *Prehistoric Art: The Symbolic Journey of Humankind*. Harry N. Abrams, New York, 2003.

2 Ancient Near Eastern Art

Amiet, Pierre. *Art of the Ancient Near East*. Harry N. Abrams, New York, 1980.

Aruz, Joan, ed. *Art of the First Cities: The Third Millennium BC from the Mediterranean to the Indus*. Exh. cat. Metropolitan Museum of Art New York; Yale University Press, New Haven, 2003.

Collon, Dominique. *Ancient Near Eastern Art*. University of California Press, Berkeley, 1995.

Curtis, John, and Nigel Tallis. *Forgotten Empire: The World of Ancient Persia*. Exh. cat. British Museum Press, London, 2005.

Feldman, Marian. *Diplomacy by Design: Luxury Arts and an "International Style" in the Ancient Near East, 1400–1200 BCE*. Chicago: University of Chicago Press, 2006

Frankfort, Henri. *The Art and Architecture of the Ancient Orient*. 5th ed. Pelican History of Art. Yale University Press, New Haven, 1997.

Leick, Gwendolyn. *A Dictionary of Ancient Near Eastern Architecture*. Routledge, New York, 1988.

Lloyd, Seton. *The Archaeology of Mesopotamia: From the Old Stone Age to the Persian Conquest*. Rev. ed. Thames & Hudson, New York, 1984.

Reade, Julian. *Mesopotamia*. 2nd ed. Published for the Trustees of the British Museum by the British Museum Press, London, 2000.

Zettler, Richard, and Lee Horne, eds. *Treasures from the Royal Tombs of Ur*. Exh. cat. University of Pennsylvania, Museum of Archaeology and Anthropology, Philadelphia, 1998.

3 Egyptian Art

Arnold, Dieter. *Building in Egypt: Pharaonic Stone Masonry*. Oxford University Press, New York, 1991.

———. *Egyptian Art in the Age of the Pyramids*. New York: Harry N. Abrams, 1999.

Davis, Whitney. *The Canonical Tradition in Ancient Egyptian Art*. New York: Cambridge University Press, 1989.

El Mahdy, Christine, ed. *The World of the Pharaohs*. Thames & Hudson, London, 1990.

Málek, Jaromir. *Egypt: 4000 Years of Art*. Phaidon, London, 2003.

Parry, Dick. *Engineering the Pyramids*. Sutton, Stroud, England, 2004.

Robins, Gay. *The Art of Ancient Egypt*. Harvard University Press, Cambridge, MA, 1997.

Schulz, Regine, and Matthias Seidel. *Egypt: The World of the Pharaohs*. Könemann, Cologne, 1998.

Smith, William Stevenson. *The Art and Architecture of Ancient Egypt*. Rev. ed. Pelican History of Art. Yale University Press, New Haven, 1999.

Tiradritti, Francesco. *Ancient Egypt: Art, Architecture and History*. British Museum Press, London, 2002.

Wilkinson, Richard. *Reading Egyptian Art: A Hieroglyphic Guide to Ancient Egyptian Painting and Sculpture*. Thames & Hudson, New York, 1992.

4 Aegean Art

Akurgal, Ekrem. *The Aegean, Birthplace of Western Civilization: History of East Greek Art and Culture, 1050–333 BC*. Metropolitan Municipality of Izmir, Izmir, Turkey, 2000.

Dickinson, Oliver T. P. K. *The Aegean Bronze Age*. Cambridge University Press, New York, 1994.

Elytis, Odysseas. *The Aegean: The Epicenter of Greek Civilization*. Melissa, Athens, 1997.

German, Senta C. *Performance, Power and the Art of the Aegean Bronze Age*. Archaeopress, Oxford, 2005.

Getz-Preziosi, Pat. *Sculptors of the Cyclades: Individual and Tradition in the Third Millennium BC*. University of Michigan Press, Ann Arbor, 1987.

Hood, Sinclair. *The Arts in Prehistoric Greece*. Pelican History of Art. Yale University Press, New Haven, 1992.

Preziosi, Donald, and Louise Hitchcock. *Aegean Art and Architecture*. Oxford University Press, New York, 1999.

Renfrew, Colin. *The Cycladic Spirit: Masterpieces from the Nicholas P. Goulandris Collection*. Thames & Hudson, London, 1991.

5 Greek Art

Beard, Mary. *The Parthenon*. Harvard University Press, Cambridge, MA, 2003.

Boardman, John. *Greek Art*. 4th ed., rev. and expanded. The World of Art. Thames & Hudson, New York, 1996.

———. *The History of Greek Vases: Potters, Painters, and Pictures*. Thames & Hudson, New York, 2001.

Carratelli, Giovanni P., ed. *The Greek World: Art and Civilization in Magna Graecia and Sicily*. Exh. cat. Rizzoli, New York, 1996.

Fullerton, Mark D. *Greek Art*. Cambridge University Press, New York, 2000.

Haynes, Denys E. L. *The Technique of Greek Bronze Statuary*. P. von Zabern, Mainz am Rhein, 1992.

Hurwit, Jeffrey M. *The Acropolis in the Age of Pericles*. Cambridge University Press, New York, 2004.

———. *The Art & Culture of Early Greece, 1100–480 BC*. Cornell University Press, Ithaca, NY, 1985.

Lawrence, Arnold W. *Greek Architecture*. Rev. 5th ed. Pelican History of Art. Yale University Press, New Haven, 1996.

Osborne, Robin. *Archaic and Classical Greek Art*. Oxford University Press, New York, 1998.

Pedley, John G. *Greek Art and Archaeology*. 2nd ed. Harry N. Abrams, New York, 1997.

Pollitt, Jerome J. *Art and Experience in Classical Greece*. Cambridge University Press, New York, 1972.

———. *Art in the Hellenistic Age*. Cambridge University Press, New York, 1986.

Ridgway, Brunilde S. *Hellenistic Sculpture: Vols. I–III*. University of Wisconsin Press, Madison, Wisconsin, 1990–2002.

Stafford, Emma. *Life, Myth, and Art in Ancient Greece*. J. Paul Getty Museum, Los Angeles, 2004.

6 Etruscan Art

Boëthius, Axel. *Etruscan and Early Roman Architecture*. 2nd ed. Pelican History of Art. Yale University Press, New Haven, 1992.

Bonfante, Larissa, ed. *Etruscan Life and Afterlife: A Handbook of Etruscan Studies*. Wayne State University, Detroit, MI, 1986.

Brendel, Otto. *Etruscan Art*. Pelican History of Art. Yale University Press, New Haven, 1995.

Haynes, Sybille. *Etruscan Civilization: A Cultural History*. J. Paul Getty Museum, Los Angeles, 2000.

Spivey, Nigel. *Etruscan Art*. The World of Art. Thames & Hudson, New York, 1997.

Steingräber, Stephan, ed. *Etruscan Painting: Catalogue Raisonné of Etruscan Wall Paintings*. Johnson Reprint, New York, 1986.

Torelli, Mario, ed. *The Etruscans*. Exh. cat. Bompiani, Milan, 2000.

7 Roman Art

Beard, Mary, and John Henderson. *Classical Art: From Greece to Rome*. Oxford University Press, New York, 2001.

Claridge, Amanda. *Rome: An Oxford Archaeological Guide*. Oxford University Press, New York, 1998.

Clarke, John R. *The Houses of Roman Italy, 100BC – AD 250. Ritual, Space and Decoration*. University of California Press, Berkeley, 1991.

Elsner, Jas. *Imperial Rome and Christian Triumph: The Art of the Roman Empire, AD 100–450*. New York: Oxford University Press, 1998.

Kleiner, Diana. *Roman Sculpture*. Yale University Press, New Haven, 1992.

———, and Susan B. Matheson, eds. *I, Claudia: Women in Ancient Rome*. Yale University Art Gallery, New Haven, 1996.

Ling, Roger. *Ancient Mosaics*. British Museum Press, London, 1998.

———. *Roman Painting*. Cambridge University Press, New York, 1991.

Pollitt, Jerome J. *The Art of Rome, c. 753 BC – AD 337: Sources and Documents*. Cambridge University Press, New York, 1983.

Ramage, Nancy H., and Andrew Ramage. *Roman Art: Romulus to Constantine*. 4th ed. Pearson Prentice Hall, Upper Saddle River, NJ, 2005.

Richardson, Lawrence. *A New Topographical Dictionary of Ancient Rome*. Johns Hopkins University Press, Baltimore, MD, 1992.

Vitruvius. *The Ten Books on Architecture*. Trans. I. Rowland. Cambridge: Cambridge University Press, 1999.

Ward-Perkins, John B. *Roman Imperial Architecture*. Reprint of 1981 ed. Pelican History of Art. Penguin, New York, 1992.

Zanker, Paul. *The Power of Images in the Age of Augustus*. University of Michigan Press, Ann Arbor, 1988.

PART TWO
THE MIDDLE AGES

Alexander, Jonathon J. G. *Medieval Illuminators and Their Methods of Work*. Yale University Press, New Haven, 1994.

Calkins, Robert G. *Medieval Architecture in Western Europe: From A.D.300–1500*. Oxford University Press, New York, 1998.

Coldstream, Nicola. *Medieval Architecture*. Oxford History of Art. Oxford University Press, New York, 2002.

Luttikhuizen, Henry and Dorothy Verkerk. *Snyder's Medieval Art*. 2nd ed. Prentice Hall, Upper Saddle River, 2006.

Stokstad, Marilyn. *Medieval Art*. Westview Press, Boulder, 2004.

8 Early Christian, Byzantine, and Early Islamic Art

Blair, Sheila S., and Jonathan M. Bloom. *The Art and Architecture of Islam 1250–1800*. Pelican History of Art. Yale University Press, New Haven, 1996.

Cormack, Robin. *Byzantine Art*. Oxford History of Art. Oxford University Press, New York, 2000.

——. *Icons*. British Museum Press, London, 2007.

Dodds, Jerrilynn D. *al-Andalus: The Art of Islamic Spain*. Metropolitan Museum of Art, New York, 1992.

Ettinghausen, Richard, Oleg Grabar, and Marilyn Jenkins-Madina. *Islamic Art and Architecture, 650–1250*. 2nd ed. Pelican History of Art. Yale University Press, New Haven, 2003.

Evans, Helen C., ed. *Byzantium: Faith and Power, 1261–1557*. Metropolitan Museum of Art, New York, 2004.

Evans, Helen C., and William D. Wixom, eds. *The Glory of Byzantium: Art and Culture of the Middle Byzantine Era, A.D. 843–1261*. Metropolitan Museum of Art, New York, 1997.

Grabar, Oleg. *The Formation of Islamic Art*. Rev. and enl. edition. Yale University Press, New Haven, 1987.

Hilldenbrand, Robert. *Islamic Architecture: Form, Function and Meaning*. New ed. Columbia University Press, New York, 2004.

Kitzinger, Ernst. *Byzantine Art in the Making: Main Lines of Stylistic Development in Mediterranean Art, 3rd–7th Century*. Harvard University Press, Cambridge, 1995.

Krautheimer, Richard, and Slobodan Curcic. *Early Christian and Byzantine Architecture*. 4th ed. Pelican History of Art. Yale University Press, New Haven, 1992.

Lowden, John. *Early Christian and Byzantine Art*. Phaidon, London, 1997.

Mango, Cyril. *The Art of the Byzantine Empire, 312–1453: Sources and Documents*. Reprint of 1972 ed. University of Toronto Press, Toronto, 1986.

Mathews, Thomas F. *The Clash of the Gods: A Reinterpretation of Early Christian Art*. Princeton University Press, Princeton, 1993.

——. *Byzantium from Antiquity to the Renaissance. Perspectives*. Harry N. Abrams, New York, 1998.

9 Early Medieval Art

Barral i Altet, Xavier. *The Early Middle Ages: From Late Antiquity to A.D. 1000*. Taschen, Cologne, 1997.

Conant, Kenneth J. *Carolingian and Romanesque Architecture, 800–1200*. 4th ed. Pelican History of Art. Yale University Press, New Haven, 1993.

Davis-Weyer, Caecilia, ed. *Early Medieval Art, 300–1150: Sources and Documents*. Reprint of 1971 ed. University of Toronto, Toronto, 1986.

Dodwell, C. R. *The Pictorial Arts of the West, 800–1200*. New ed. Pelican History of Art. Yale University Press, New Haven, 1993.

Kitzinger, Ernst. *Early Medieval Art, with Illustrations from the British Museum*. Rev. ed. Indiana University Press, 1983.

Lasko, Peter. *Ars Sacra, 800–1200*. 2nd ed. Pelican History of Art. Yale University Press, New Haven, 1995.

Mayr-Harting, Henry. *Ottonian Book Illumination: An Historical Study*. 2 vols. Oxford University Press, New York, 1991–93.

Nees, Lawrence. *Early Medieval Art*. Oxford History of Art. Oxford University Press, New York, 2002.

Sekules, Veronica. *Medieval Art*. Oxford History of Art. Oxford University Press, New York, 2001.

Stalley, Roger, A. *Early Medieval Architecture*. Oxford History of Art. Oxford University Press, New York, 1999.

10 Romanesque Art

Barral i Altet, Xavier. *The Romanesque: Towns, Cathedrals, and Monasteries*. Taschen, Cologne, 1998.

Bowie, Fiona, and Oliver Davies, eds. *Hildegard of Bingen: Mystical Writings*. Crossroad, New York, 1990.

Focillon, Henri. *The Art of the West in the Middle Ages*. Ed. Jean Bony. 2 vols. Reprint of 1963 ed. Cornell University Press, Ithaca, 1980.

Hearn, M. F. *Romanesque Sculpture: The Revival of Monumental Stone Sculpture in the Eleventh and Twelfth Centuries*. Cornell University Press, Ithaca, 1981.

Petzold, Andreas. *Romanesque Art*. Perspectives. Prentice Hall, Upper Saddle River, 2003.

Schapiro, Meyer. *Romanesque Art*. Braziller, New York, 1993.

Stones, Alison, Jeanne Krochalis, Paula Gerson, and Annie Shaver-Crandell. *The Pilgrim's Guide: A Critical Edition*. 2 vols. Harvey Miller, London, 1998.

Toman, Rolf and Achim Bednorz. *Romanesque: Architecture, Sculpture, Painting*. Könemann, Cologne, 2008.

11 Gothic Art

Bony, Jean. *French Gothic Architecture of the Twelfth and Thirteenth Centuries*. California Studies in the History of Art. University of California Press, Berkeley, 1983.

Camille, Michael. *Gothic Art*. Perspectives. Prentice Hall, Upper Saddle River, 2003.

Frisch, Teresa G. *Gothic Art, 1140–c. 1450: Sources and Documents*. Reprint of 1971 ed. University of Toronto Press, Toronto, 1987.

Toman, Rolf, and Achim Bednorz. *The Art of Gothic: Architecture, Sculpture, Painting*. Könemann, Cologne, 1999.

Williamson, Paul. *Gothic Sculpture, 1140–1300*. Pelican History of Art. Yale University Press, New Haven, 1995.

Wilson, Christopher. *The Gothic Cathedral: the Architecture of the Great Church, 1130–1530*. 2nd rev. ed. Thames and Hudson, London, 2005.

PART THREE
THE RENAISSANCE THROUGH THE ROCOCO: THE EARLY MODERN WORLD

Campbell, Lorne. *Renaissance Portraits: European Portrait-Painting in the 14th, 15th, and 16th Centuries*. Yale University Press, New Haven, 1990.

Harbison, Craig. *The Mirror of the Artist: Northern Renaissance Art in its Historical Context*. Harry N. Abrams, New York, 1995.

Hartt, Frederick and David G. Wilkins. *History of Italian Renaissance Art: Painting, Sculpture, Architecture*. 5th ed. Harry N. Abrams, New York, 2003.

Hults, Linda C. *The Print in the Western World: An Introductory History*. University of Wisconsin Press, Madison, Wisconsin, 1996.

Wittkower, Rudolf. *Architectural Principles in the Age of Humanism*. 5th ed. St. Martin's Press, New York, 1998.

Paoletti, John T., and Gary M. Radke. *Art in Renaissance Italy*. 3rd ed. Pearson Prentice Hall, Upper Saddle River, 2006.

Pope-Hennessy, J. *An Introduction to Italian Sculpture: Vol. 1, Italian Gothic Sculpture. Vol. 2, Italian Renaissance Sculpture. Vol. 3, Italian High Renaissance and Baroque Sculpture*. 4th ed. Phaidon Press, London, 1996.

Smith, Jeffrey Chipps. *The Northern Renaissance*. Art & Ideas. Phaidon, London and New York, 2004.

Snyder, James. *Northern Renaissance Art: Painting, Sculpture, the Graphic Arts, from 1350 to 1575*. 2nd edition. Harry N. Abrams, New York, 2005.

Welch, Evelyn S. *Art in Renaissance Italy, 1350–1500*. New ed. Oxford University Press, Oxford, 2000.

12 Art in Thirteenth- and Fourteenth-Century Italy

Meiss, Millard. *Painting in Florence and Siena After the Black Death: The Arts, Religion, and Society in the Mid-Fourteenth Century*. Princeton University Press, Princeton, 1978, © 1951.

Norman, Diana, ed. *Siena, Florence and Padua: Art Society and Religion 1280–1400*. Yale University Press, New Haven, 1995.

Stubblebine, James H. *Assisi and the Rise of Vernacular Art*. Harper & Row, New York, 1985.

Vasari, Giorgio. *The Lives of the Artists*. Trans. with an introduction and notes by J. C. Bondanella and P. Bondanella. Oxford University Press, New York, 1998.

White, John. *Art and Architecture in Italy, 1250–1400*. 3rd ed. Pelican History of Art. Yale University Press, New Haven, 1993.

13 Artistic Innovations in Fifteenth-Century Northern Europe

Cuttler, Charles D. *Northern Painting from Pucelle to Bruegel: Fourteenth, Fifteenth, and Sixteenth Centuries*. Rev. and updated printing. Holt, Rinehart, and Winston, New York, 1972.

Dixon, Laurinda. *Bosch*. Art & Ideas. Phaidon, London, 2003.

Friedländer, Max J. *Early Netherlandish Painting*. 14 vols. Praeger, New York, 1967–1973.

Nuttall, Paula. *From Flanders to Florence: The Impact of Netherlandish Painting, 1400–1500*. Yale University Press, New Haven, 2004.

Panofsky, Erwin. *Early Netherlandish Painting*. 2 vols. Harvard University Press, Cambridge, 1971.

Stechow, Wolfgang. *Northern Renaissance Art, 1400–1600: Sources and Documents*. Northwestern University Press, Evanston, Ill., 1989.

14 The Early Renaissance in Fifteenth-Century Italy

Baxandall, Michael. *Painting and Experience in Fifteenth Century Italy: A Primer in the Social History of Pictorial Style*. Oxford University Press, New York, 1988.

Borsook, Eve. *The Mural Painters of Tuscany: From Cimabue to Andrea del Sarto*. 2nd ed., rev. and enl. Oxford University Press, New York, 1980.

Burckhardt, Jacob C. *The Civilization of the Renaissance in Italy*. Penguin Classics. Penguin, Harmondsworth, England, 1990.

Cole, Bruce. *The Renaissance Artist at Work: From Pisano to Titian*. Harper & Row, New York, © 1983.

Gilbert, Creighton E. *Italian Art, 1400–1500: Sources and Documents*. Reprint of 1980 ed. Northwestern University Press, Evanston, Ill., 1992.

Gombrich, E. H. *Norm and Form: Studies in the Art of the Renaissance*. 4th ed. University of Chicago Press, Chicago, 1985.

Heydenreich, Ludwig Heinrich and Wolfgang Lotz. *Architecture in Italy, 1400–1500*. Rev. ed. Pelican History of Art. Yale University Press, New Haven, 1996.

Huse, Norbert, and W. Wolters. *The Art of Renaissance Venice: Architecture, Sculpture, and Painting, 1460–1590*. University of Chicago Press, Chicago, 1990.

Janson, H. W. *The Sculpture of Donatello*. 2 vols. Princeton University Press, Princeton, 1979.

Kent, Dale. *Cosimo de' Medici and the Florentine Renaissance*. Yale University Press, New Haven, 2000.

Seymour, Charles, Jr. *Sculpture in Italy, 1400–1500*. Pelican History of Art. Penguin, Harmondsworth, England, 1966.

15 The High Renaissance in Italy, 1495–1520

Brown, Patricia Fortini. *Art and Life in Renaissance Venice*. Prentice Hall, Upper Saddle River, N.J., 1997.

Cole, Alison. *Virtue and Magnificence: Art of the Italian Renaissance Courts*. Perspectives. Harry N. Abrams, New York, 1995.

Freedberg, Sydney J. *Painting of the High Renaissance in Rome and Florence*. New rev. ed. 2 vols. Hacker Art Books, New York, 1985.

Hall, Marcia B. *The Cambridge Companion to Raphael*. Cambridge University Press, New York, 2005.

Kemp, Martin. *Leonardo da Vinci: Experience, Experiment and Design*. Princeton University Press, Princeton, 2006.

Partridge, Loren W. *The Art of Renaissance Rome*. Perspectives. Harry N. Abrams, New York, 1996.

Pope-Hennessy, John. *Italian High Renaissance and Baroque Sculpture*. 3 vols. 3rd ed. Oxford University Press, New York, 1986.

Rowland, Ingrid D. *The Culture of the High Renaissance: Ancients and Moderns in Sixteenth Century Rome*. Cambridge University Press, New York, 1998.

Steinberg, Leo. *Leonardo's Incessant Last Supper*. Zone Books, New York, 2001.

Wallace, William E. *Michelangelo: The Complete Sculpture, Painting, Architecture*. Hugh Lauter Levin, Southport, 1998.

16 The Late Renaissance and Mannerism in Sixteenth-Century Italy

Ackerman, James S. *Palladio*. Penguin, Harmondsworth, England, 1977.

Barkan, Leonard. *Unearthing the Past: Archaeology and Aesthetics in the Making of Renaissance Culture*. Yale University Press, New Haven, 1999.

Freedberg, Sydney J. *Painting in Italy, 1500–1600*. 3rd ed. Pelican History of Art. Yale University Press, New Haven, 1993.

Klein, Robert, and Henri Zerner. *Italian Art, 1500–1600: Sources and Documents*. Reprint of 1966 ed. Northwestern University Press, Evanston, Ill., 1989.

Murphy, Caroline. *Lavinia Fontana: A Painter and her Patrons in Sixteenth Century Bologna*. Yale University Press, New Haven, 2003.

Partridge, Loren W. *Michelangelo—The Last Judgment: A Glorious Restoration*. Harry N. Abrams, New York, 1997.

Rosand, David. *Painting in Sixteenth-Century Venice: Titian, Veronese, Tintoretto*. Cambridge University Press, New York, 1997.

Smyth, Craig Hugh. *Mannerism and Maniera*. 2nd ed. Bibliotheca artibus et historiae. IRSA, Vienna, 1992.

Shearman, John K. G. *Mannerism*. Reprint of 1967 ed. Style and Civilization. Penguin, Harmondsworth, England, 1986.

17 Renaissance and Reformation Throughout Sixteenth-Century Europe

Baxandall, Michael. *The Limewood Sculptors of Renaissance Germany.* Yale University Press, New Haven, 1980.

Eichberger, Dagmar, ed. *Durer and His Culture.* Cambridge University Press, New York, 1998.

Foister, Susan. *Holbein and England.* Yale University Press, New Haven, 2005.

Hayum, Andrée. *The Isenheim Altarpiece: God's Medicine and the Painter's Vision.* Princeton University Press, Princeton, 1989.

Kavaler, Ethan Matt. *Pieter Bruegel: Parables of Order and Enterprise.* Cambridge University Press, New York, 1999.

Koerner, Joseph Leo. *The Moment of Self Portraiture in German Renaissance Art.* University of Chicago Press, Chicago, 1993.

———. *The Reformation of the Image.* University of Chicago Press, Chicago, 2004.

Mann, Richard G. *El Greco and His Patrons: Three Major Projects.* Cambridge University Press, New York, 1986.

Osten, Gert von der and Horst Vey. *Painting and Sculpture in Germany and the Netherlands, 1500–1600.* Pelican History of Art. Penguin, Harmondsworth, England, 1969.

Panofsky, Erwin. *The Life and Art of Albrecht Dürer.* 4th ed. Princeton University Press, Princeton, 1971.

Wood, Christopher S. *Albrecht Altdorfer and the Origins of Landscape.* University of Chicago Press, Chicago, 1993.

Zerner, Henri. *Renaissance Art in France: The Invention of Classicism.* Flammarion, France, 2003.

18 The Baroque in Italy and Spain

Bissell, R. Ward. *Masters of Italian Baroque Painting.* Detroit Institute of Art in association with D. Giles Ltd., Detroit, MI; London, 2005

Blunt, Anthony. *Borromini.* Harvard University Press, Cambridge, MA, 1979.

Brown, Beverly L., ed. *The Genius of Rome, 1592–1623.* Exh. cat. Royal Academy of Arts, London; Dist. in the United States and Canada by Harry N. Abrams, New York.

Brown, Jonathan. *Painting in Spain, 1500–1700.* Pelican History of Art. Yale University Press, New Haven, 1998.

———. *Velázquez: The Technique of Genius.* Yale University Press, New Haven, 1998.

Dempsey, Charles. *Annibale Carracci and the Beginnings of Baroque Style.* 2nd. ed. Cadmo, Fiesole, Italy, 2000.

Enggass, Robert, and Jonathan Brown. *Italy and Spain, 1600–1750: Sources and Documents.* Reprint of 1970 ed. Northwestern University Press, Evanston, Ill., 1992.

Garrard, Mary D. *Artemisia Gentileschi: The Image of the Female Hero in Italian Baroque Art.* Princeton University Press, Princeton, NJ, 1989.

Marder, Tod A. *Bernini and the Art of Architecture.* Abbeville Press, New York, 1998.

Montagu, Jennifer. *Roman Baroque Sculpture: The Industry of Art.* Yale University Press, New Haven, 1989.

Varriano, John. *Italian Baroque and Rococo Architecture.* Oxford University Press, New York, 1986.

Wittkower, Rudolf. *Art and Architecture in Italy, 1600–1750.* 4th ed. Pelican History of Art. Yale University Press, New Haven, 2000.

19 The Baroque in The Netherlands

Alpers, Svetlana. *The Art of Describing: Dutch Art in the Seventeenth Century.* University of Chicago Press, Chicago, 1983.

Chapman, H. Perry. *Rembrandt's Self-Portraits: A Study in Seventeenth-Century Identity.* Princeton University Press, Princeton, NJ, 1990.

Franits, Wayne E. *Dutch Seventeenth-Century Genre Painting: Its Stylistic and Thematic Evolution.* Yale University Press, New Haven, 2004.

Kiers, Judikje, and Epco Runia, eds. *The Glory of the Golden Age: Dutch Art of the 17th Century.* 2 vols. Exh. cat. Waanders, Rijksmuseum, Amsterdam, 2000.

Salvesen, Sally, ed. *Rembrandt: The Master and his Workshop.* 2 vols. Exh. cat. Yale University Press, New Haven, 1991.

Schama, Simon. *The Embarrassment of Riches: An Interpretation of Dutch Culture in the Golden Age.* University of California Press, Berkeley, 1988.

Slive, Seymour. *Dutch Painting. 1600–1800.* Pelican History of Art. Yale University Press, New Haven, 1995.

Sutton, Peter. *The Age of Rubens.* Exh. cat. Museum of Fine Arts, Boston, 1993.

Vlieghe, Hans. *Flemish Art and Architecture, 1585–1700.* Pelican History of Art. Yale University Press, New Haven, © 1998.

Westermann, Mariët. *Art and Home: Dutch Interiors in the Age of Rembrandt.* Exh. cat. Waanders, Zwolle, 2001.

———. *Rembrandt.* Art & Ideas. Phaidon, London, 2000.

———. *A Worldly Art: The Dutch Republic 1585–1718.* Perspective. Harry N. Abrams, New York, 1996.

Wheelock, Arthur K., ed. *Johannes Vermeer.* Exh. cat. Yale University Press, New Haven, 1995.

20 The Baroque in France and England

Blunt, Anthony. *Art and Architecture in France, 1500–1700.* 5th ed. Pelican History of Art. Yale University Press, New Haven, 1999.

Downes, Kerry. *The Architecture of Wren.* Rev. ed. Redhedge, Reading, England, 1988.

Lagerlöf, Margaretha Rossholm. *Ideal Landscape: Annibale Carracci, Nicolas Poussin, and Claude Lorrain.* Yale University Press, New Haven, 1990.

Liechtenstein, J. *The Eloquence of Color: Rhetoric and Painting in the French Classical Age.* University of California Press, Berkeley, 1993.

Mérot, Alain. *French Painting in the Seventeenth Century.* tr. Caroline Beamish. Yale University Press, New Haven, 1995.

Summerson, John. *Architecture in Britain, 1530–1830.* Rev. 9th ed. Pelican History of Art. Yale University Press, New Haven, 1993.

Tinniswood, Adrian. *His Invention So Fertile: A Life of Christopher Wren.* Oxford University Press, New York, 2001.

Verdi, Richard. *Nicolas Poussin 1594–1665.* Zwemmer in association with the Royal Academy of Arts, London, 1995.

Whinney, Margaret D. *Wren.* World of Art. Thames & Hudson, New York, 1998.

21 The Rococo

Bailey, Colin B. *The Age of Watteau, Chardin, and Fragonard: Masterpieces of French Genre Painting.* Yale University Press, New Haven, in association with the National Gallery of Canada, 2003

Gaunt, William. *The Great Century of British Painting: Hogarth to Turner.* 2nd ed. Phaidon, London, 1978.

Kalnein, Wend von. *Architecture in France in the Eighteenth Century.* Pelican History of Art. Yale University Press, New Haven, 1995.

Levey, Michael. *Painting and Sculpture in France, 1700–1789.* New ed. Pelican History of Art. Yale University Press, New Haven, 1993.

———. *Painting in Eighteenth-Century Venice.* 3rd ed. Pelican History of Art. Yale University Press, New Haven, 1993.

Rosenberg, Pierre. *Chardin.* Exh. cat. Royal Academy of Art, London; Metropolitan Museum of Art, New York, 2000.

Scott, Katie. *The Rococo Interior: Decoration and Social Spaces in Early Eighteenth-Century Paris.* Yale University Press, New Haven, 1995.

Sheriff, Mary D. *The Exceptional Woman: Elisabeth Vigée Lebrun and the Cultural Politics of Art.* University of Chicago Press, Chicago, 1996.

Wintermute, Alan. *Watteau and His World: French Drawing from 1700–1750.* Exh. cat. Merrell Holberton, London; American Federation of Arts, New York, 1999.

PART FOUR
THE MODERN WORLD

Arnason, H. Harvard, and Marla Prather. *History of Modern Art.* 4th ed., rev. and enl. Harry N. Abrams, New York, 1998.

Bergdoll, Barry. *European Architecture 1750–1890.* Oxford History of Art. Oxford University Press, New York, 2000.

Chipp, Herschel B., ed. *Theories of Modern Art: A Source Book by Artists and Critics.* University of California Press, Berkeley, 1968.

Colquhoun, Alan. *Modern Architecture.* Oxford University Press, New York, 2002.

Documents of Modern Art. 14 vols. Wittenborn, New York, 1944–1961.

McCoubrey, John. *American Art, 1700–1960: Sources and Documents.* Prentice Hall, Engelwood Cliffs, NJ, 1965.

Newhall, Beaumont. *The History of Photography from 1830 to the Present Day.* Rev. and enl. 5th ed. Museum of Modern Art, New York; Dist. by Bullfinch Press/Little, Brown, 1999.

Patton, Sharon F. *African-American Art.* Oxford History of Art. Oxford University Press, New York, 1998.

Robinson, Hilary. *Feminism-Art-Theory: An Anthology 1968–2000.* Blackwell, Oxford and Malden, MA, 2001.

Stiles, Kristine, and Peter Selz. *Theories and Documents of Contemporary Art.* University of California Press, Berkeley, 1996.

22 Art in the Age of Enlightenment, 1750–1789

Crow, Thomas. *Painters and Public Life in Eighteenth-Century Paris.* Yale University Press, New Haven, 1985.

Eitner, Lorenz. *Neoclassicism and Romanticism, 1750–1850: Sources and Documents.* Reprint of 1970 ed. Harper & Row, New York, 1989.

Honour, Hugh. *Neoclassicism.* Reprint of 1968 ed. Penguin, London, 1991.

Irwin, David G. *Neoclassicism.* Art & Ideas. Phaidon, London, 1997.

Miles, Ellen G., ed. *The Portrait in Eighteenth-Century America.* University of Delaware Press, Newark, 1993.

Ottani Cavina, Anna. *Geometries of Silence: Three Approaches to Neoclassical Art.* Columbia University Press, New York, 2004.

Rosenblum, Robert. *Transformations in Late Eighteenth Century Art.* Princeton University Press, Princeton, NJ, 1967.

Saisselin, Rémy G. *The Enlightenment Against the Baroque: Economics and Aesthetics in the Eighteenth Century.* University of California Press, Berkeley, 1992.

Solkin, David. *Painting for Money: The Visual Arts and the Public Sphere in Eighteenth-Century England.* Yale University Press, New Haven, 1993.

23 Art in the Age of Romanticism, 1789–1848

Boime, Albert. *The Academy and French Painting in the Nineteenth Century.* New ed. Yale University Press, New Haven, 1986.

Brown, David B. *Romanticism.* Art & Ideas. Phaidon, New York, 2001.

Chu, Petra ten-Doesschate. *Nineteenth-Century European Art.* Pearson Prentice Hall, Upper Saddle River, NJ, 2002.

Hartley, Keith. *The Romantic Spirit in German Art, 1790–1990.* Exh. cat. South Bank Centre, London © 1994.

Herrmann, Luke. *Nineteenth Century British Painting.* Giles de la Mare, London, 2000.

Honour, Hugh. *Romanticism.* Harper & Row, New York, 1979.

Middleton, Robin. *Architecture of the Nineteenth Century.* Electa, Milan, © 2003.

Noon, Patrick J. *Crossing the Channel: British and French Painting in the Age of Romanticism.* Exh. cat. Tate, London, 2003.

Novak, Barbara. *Nature and Culture: American Landscape and Painting, 1825–1875.* Rev. ed. Oxford University Press, New York, 1995.

24 The Age of Positivism: Realism, Impressionism, and the Pre-Raphaelites, 1848–1885

Broude, Norma. *Impressionism: A Feminist Reading.* Rizzoli, New York, 1991.

Clark, Timothy J. *The Painting of Modern Life: Paris in the Art of Manet and His Followers.* Rev. ed. Princeton University Press, Princeton, NJ, 1999.

Herbert, Robert. *Impressionism: Art, Leisure, and Parisian Society.* Yale University Press, New Haven, 1988.

House, John. *Impressionism: Paint and Politics.* Yale University Press, New Haven, 2004.

Jenkyns, Richard. *Dignity and Decadence: Victorian Art and the Classical Inheritance.* Harvard University Press, Cambridge, MA, 1991.

Mainardi, Patricia. *The End of the Salon: Art and the State in the Early Third Republic.* Cambridge University Press, Cambridge, 1993.

Nochlin, Linda, ed. *Impressionism and Post-Impressionism, 1874–1904: Sources and Documents.* Prentice Hall, Englewood Cliffs, NJ, 1976.

———. *Realism and Tradition in Art, 1848–1900: Sources and Documents.* Prentice Hall, Englewood Cliffs, NJ, 1966.

Novak, Barbara. *Nature and Culture: American Landscape and Painting, 1825–1875.* Oxford University Press, New York, 1995.

Prettejohn, Elizabeth. *The Art of the Pre-Raphaelites.* Princeton University Press, Princeton, NJ, 2000.

Rewald, John. *Studies in Impressionism.* Harry N. Abrams, New York, 1986, © 1985.

Werner, Marcia. *Pre-Raphaelite Painting and Nineteenth-Century Realism.* Cambridge University Press, New York, 2005.

25 Progress and Its Discontents: Post-Impressionism, Symbolism, and Art Nouveau, 1880–1905

Denvir, Bernard. *Post-Impressionism.* The World of Art. Thames & Hudson, New York, 1992.

Dorra, Henri, ed. *Symbolist Art Theories: A Critical Anthology.* University of California Press, Berkeley, 1994.

Gibson, Michael. *The Symbolists.* Harry N. Abrams, New York, 1988.

Herbert, Robert L. *Georges Seurat, 1859–1891*. Metropolitan Museum of Art; Dist. by Harry N. Abrams, New York, 1991.

Silverman, Debora. *Art Nouveau in Fin-de-Siècle France*. University of California Press, Berkeley, 1989.

Troy, Nancy J. *Modernism and the Decorative Arts in France: Art Nouveau to Le Corbusier*. Yale University Press, New Haven, 1991.

26 Toward Abstraction: The Modernist Revolution, 1904–1914

Behr, Shulamith. *Expressionism*. Movements in Modern Art. Cambridge University Press, Cambridge, 1999.

Bowlt, John E., ed. *Russian Art of the Avant-Garde: Theory and Criticism, 1902–1934*. New York: Thames & Hudson, 1988.

Edwards, Steve. *Art of the Avant-Gardes*. Yale University Press in association with the Open University, New Haven, 2004.

Golding, John. *Cubism: A History and an Analysis, 1907–1914*. 3rd ed. Harvard University Press, Cambridge, MA, 1988.

Herbert, James. *Fauve Painting: The Making of Cultural Politics*. Yale University Press, New Haven, 1992.

Rosenblum, Robert. *Cubism and Twentieth-Century Art*. New York: Harry N. Abrams, 2001.

Taylor, Brandon. *Collage: The Making of Modern Art*. Thames & Hudson, London, 2004.

Washton, Rose-Carol, ed. *German Expressionism: Documents from the End of the Wilhelmine Empire to the Rise of National Socialism*. The Documents of Twentieth-Century Art. G. K. Hall, Boston, 1993.

Weiss, Julie. *The Popular Culture of Modern Art: Picasso, Duchamp and Avant Gardism*. Yale University Press, New Haven, 1994.

27 Art Between The Wars

Corn, Wanda. *The Great American Thing: Modern Art and National Identity, 1915–1935*. University of California Press, Berkeley, 2001.

Durozoi, Gerard. *History of the Surrealist Movement*. University of Chicago Press, Chicago, 2002.

Fer, Briony, et al. *Realism, Rationalism, Surrealism: Art Between the Wars*. Modern Art—Practices and Debates. Yale University Press, New Haven, 1993.

Gale, Matthew. *Dada & Surrealism*. Art & Ideas. Phaidon, London, 1997.

Gössel, Peter, and Gabriele Leuthäuser. *Architecture in the Twentieth Century*. Taschen, Cologne, 1991. 1999.

Haskell, Barbara. *The American Century: Art & Culture, 1900–1950*. W. W. Norton, New York, 1999.

Hochman, Elaine S. *Bauhaus: Crucible of Modernism*. New York: Fromm International, © 1997.

Hopkins, David. *Dada and Surrealism: A Very Short Introduction*. Oxford University Press, New York, 2004.

Lane, Barbara. *Architecture and Politics in Germany, 1918–1945*. New ed. Harvard University Press, Cambridge, MA, 1985.

Lodder, Christina. *Russian Constructivism*. Yale University Press, New Haven, 1983.

Silver, Kenneth E. *Esprit de Corps: The Art of the Parisian Avant-Garde and the First World War, 1914–1925*. Princeton University Press, Princeton, NJ, 1989.

28 Postwar to Postmodern, 1945–1980

Archer, Michael. *Art Since 1960*. World of Art. Thames & Hudson, New York, 2002.

Beardsley, John. *Earthworks and Beyond: Contemporary Art in the Landscape*. 3rd ed. Abbeville Press, New York, 1998.

Carlson, Marvin A. *Performance: A Critical Introduction*. 2nd ed. Routledge, New York, 2004.

Causey, Andrew. *Sculpture Since 1945*. Oxford History of Art. Oxford University Press, New York, 1998.

Crow, Thomas. *The Rise of the Sixties: American and European Art in the Era of Dissent*. Laurence King, London, 2005, © 1996.

Hopkins, David. *After Modern Art: 1945–2000*. Oxford University Press, New York, 2000.

Sandler, Irving. *Art of the Postmodern Era: From the Late 1960s to the Early 1990s*. Icon Editions, New York, 1996.

29 The Postmodern Era: Art Since 1980

Belting, Hans. *Art History After Modernism*. Chicago: University of Chicago Press, 2003.

Broude, Norma, and Mary Garrard., eds. *Reclaiming Female Agency: Feminist Art History After Postmodernism*. University of California Press, Berkeley, 2005.

Brunette, Peter, and David Wills, eds. *Deconstruction and the Visual Arts: Art, Media, Architecture*. Cambridge University Press, New York, 1994.

Foster, Hal, ed. *The Anti-Aesthetic: Essays on Postmodern Culture*. New Press; Dist. by W. W. Norton, New York, 1998.

Harris, Jonathan. *The New Art History: A Critical Introduction*. Routledge, New York, 2001.

Jencks, Charles. *What Is Post-Modernism?* 4th rev. ed. Academy Editions, London, 1996.

Wallis, Brian, ed. *Art After Modernism: Rethinking Representation*. Documentary Sources in Contemporary Art, 1. Godine, Boston, 1984.

Picture Credits

Introduction

I-1 © 2005 The Newark Museum/Art Resource/Scala, Florence; I-2 © 2007. The Museum of Modern Art, New York/Scala, Florence; I-3 Alinari; I-4 Dallas & John Heaton/Free Agents Ltd/Corbis; I-5 Photograph © The Art Institute of Chicago; I-6 Diane Bondareff/AP Photo; I-7 Image © 2005 The Board of Trustees, National Gallery of Art, Washington; I-9 © 2003. Photo Scala, Florence/John Bigelow Taylor; I-10 O'Hara Gallery, NY; I-11 © Lee Friedlander, Courtesy Fraenkel Gallery, San Francisco; I-12 IKONA; I-13 RMN/© Droits réservés; I-14 David Heald © The Solomon R. Guggenheim Foundation, New York; I-15 Ben Mangor/SuperStock; I-16 Image © 2004 The Board of Trustees, National Gallery of Art, Washington. Photo Jose A. Naranjo; I-17 Peter Willi/SuperStock; p19l Philippe Berthe © CMN, Paris; p19cl Boltin Picture Library/Bridgeman Art Library; p19cr © Vatican Museums; p19r © Pubbli Aer Foto

Chapter 1

p22 Erich Lessing/akg-images; 1.1 Jean Vertut Collection, Courtesy Yvonne Vertut; 1.2 French Ministry of Culture and Communication, Regional Direction for Cultural Affairs – Rhone Alpes, Regional Department of Archaeology; 1.3 Philippe Berthe © CMN, Paris; 1.5 Jean Vertut Collection, Courtesy Yvonne Vertut; 1.6 Thomas Stephan, © Ulmer Museum; 1.7 Erich Lessing/akg-images; 1.8a&b Erich Lessing/akg-images; 1.9 English Heritage. NMR (Aerofilms Collection); p31t Erich Lessing/akg-images; p31ct Jean Vertut Collection, Courtesy Yvonne Vertut; p31c Erich Lessing/akg-images; p31b English Heritage. NMR (Aerofilms Collection); p32t © The Trustees of the British Museum; p32b © The Trustees of the British Museum, London

Chapter 2

p34t The Art and Architecture of the Ancient Orient, Yale University Press (1997) fig 3.2; 2.1 World Tourism Organization, Iraq, scanned from 6E, 03-01, p.71; 2.2 Courtesy of the Oriental Institute of the University of Chicago; 2.3a&b © The Trustees of the British Museum; 2.4 Gianni Dagli Orti/ Corbis; 2.5 RMN/© Les frères Chuzeville; 2.6 © Michael S. Yamashita/ CORBIS; 2.7 RMN/© Hervé Lewandowski; 2.8 World Tourism Organization, Iraq; 2.9 © The Trustees of the British Museum; 2.10 © 2005. Photo Scala, Florence/Bildarchiv Preussischer Kulturbesitz, Berlin; 2.12 Gerard Degeorge/Corbis; p45t © The Trustees of the British Museum; p45ct © The Trustees of the British Museum; p45c © 2005. Photo Scala, Florence/Bildarchiv Preussischer Kulturbesitz, Berlin; p45b Gerard Degeorge/Corbis

Chapter 3

p46 Dagli Orti/Art Archive; 3.1a&b Werner Forman Archive, London; 3.2 Gianni Dagli Orti/Art Archive; 3.3 Photo Peter Clayton; 3.5 Dallas & John Heaton/Free Agents Ltd/Corbis; 3.6 Peter Clayton; 3.7 Araldo de Luca/INDEX, Florence; 3.8 RMN/© Hervé Lewandowski; 3.9 Foto Marburg/Art Resource, NY; 3.10 © 2007 The Metropolitan Museum of Art/Art Resource/Scala, Florence; 3.11 Woodfin Camp & Associates/Robert Frerck; 3.12 Dagli Orti/Art Archive; 3.13 © 2005. Photo Scala, Florence/Bildarchiv Preussischer Kulturbesitz, Berlin; 3.14 © 2005. Photo Scala, Florence/Bildarchiv Preussischer Kulturbesitz, Berlin; 3.15 Boltin Picture Library/Bridgeman Art Library; p63t Werner Forman Archive, London; p63ct Dallas & John Heaton/Free Agents Ltd/Corbis; p63c © 2007 The Metropolitan Museum of Art/Art Resource/Scala, Florence; p63b © 2005. Photo Scala, Florence/Bildarchiv Preussischer Kulturbesitz, Berlin

Chapter 4

p64 © 1990. Photo Scala, Florence; 4.1 John Bigelow Taylor; 4.2 from John Griffiths Pedley, *Greek Art and Archaeology*, 2/e, Prentice Hall, 1998, fig 3.1, p.65; 4.3 Courtesy McRae Books Srl, Florence; 4.4 © Studio Kontos/Photostock; 4.5 © Studio Kontos/Photostock; 4.6 © 1990. Photo Scala, Florence; 4.7 Erich Lessing/akg-images; 4.8 Studio Kontos/Photostock; 4.9 © Studio Kontos/Photostock; 4.10 © Studio Kontos/Photostock; p73br from John Griffiths Pedley, Greek Art and Archaeology, 2/e, Prentice Hall, 1998, fig 3.40, p.95; 4.11 Dagli Orti/Art Archive; 4.12 Hirmer Verlag, Munich; p75t John Bigelow Taylor; p75ct © Studio Kontos/Photostock; p75c © 1990. Photo Scala, Florence; p75cb Hirmer Verlag, Munich; p75b © Studio Kontos/Photostock

Chapter 5

p76 Nimatallah/akg-images; 5.1 Nimatallah/akg-images; 5.2 © The Trustees of the British Museum; 5.5 Marco Cristofori/Corbis; 5.6 © The Trustees of the British Museum; 5.7 © 2007. The Metropolitan Museum of Art/Art Resource/Scala, Florence; 5.8 Dagli Orti/Acropolis Museum, Athens/Art Archive; 5.9 © Studio Kontos/Photostock; 5.10 Photo Studio Koppermann; 5.12 © Vatican Museums; 5.14 Nimatallah/akg-images; 5.15 National Archaeological Museum, Athens © Ministry of Culture Archaeological Receipts Fund; 5.16 INDEX, Florence; 5.18 © Studio Kontos/Photostock; 5.19 © The Trustees of the British Museum; 5.20 © Studio Kontos/Photostock; 5.21 © Studio Kontos/Photostock; 5.22 Ruggero Vanni/Corbis; 5.23 From Howard Colvin, Architecture and the After Life, Yale University Press, 1991, fig 31, p.35; p102t From Howard Colvin, *Architecture and the After Life*, Yale University Press, 1991, fig 31, p.35; 5.24 Hirmer Fotoarchiv; 5.25 © Vatican Museums; 5.26 From Jerome Pollitt, *Art in the Hellenistic Age*, Cambridge University Press, 1986, fig 31, p.35; 5.27 © Georg Gerster/Panos; 5.28 From Jerome Pollitt, *Art in the Hellenistic Age*, Cambridge University Press, 1986, fig 31, p.35; 5.29 RMN/© Hervé Lewandowski; 5.30 © Araldo de Luca/Ikona; 5.31 © Photo Scala, Florence/Bildarchiv Preussischer Kulturbesitz, Berlin.; 5.32 © 2005. Photo Scala, Florence/Bildarchiv Preussischer Kulturbesitz, Berlin; 5.33 Photo Studio Koppermann; 5.34 © Studio Kontos/Photostock; 5.35 © 2003. Photo Scala, Florence – courtesy of the Ministero Beni e Att. Culturali; p113t © Vatican Museums; p113ct Nimatallah/akg-images; p113c © Studio Kontos/Photostock; p113b © Georg Gerster/Panos

Chapter 6

p114 Erich Lessing/akg-images; 6.1 Pubbli Aer Foto; 6.2 © Soprintendenza Etruria Meridionale/Ikona; 6.4 Photo Scala, Florence; 6.5 Museo delle Antichita Etrusche e Italiche, Universita di Roma "La Sapienza"; 6.6 Canali Photobank; 6.7 Erich Lessing/akg-images; p121t © Soprintendenza Etruria Meridionale/Ikona; p121c Museo delle Antichita Etrusche e Italiche, Universita di Roma "La Sapienza"; p121b Erich Lessing/akg-images

Chapter 7

p122 SuperStock; 7.1 Anna Mura Sommella, from "La Grande Roma dei Tarquini, Alterne vicende di una felice intuizione". Bullcom (2000), fig 7-26, p.25; 7.2 Canali Photobank; 7.3 © Vanni/Art Resource; 7.5ab&c Foto Marburg/Art Resource, NY; 7.5d RMN/© Les frères Chuzeville; 7.6 Penelope Davies; 7.7 SuperStock; 7.8 San Antonio Museum of Art, gift of Gilbert M. Denman, Jr.; 7.9 Canali Photobank; 7.10 Canali Photobank; 7.11 Canali Photobank; 7.12 Robert Frerck/Woodfin Camp & Associates; 7.13 Photo Scala, Florence; 7.15a © Pubbli Aer Foto; 7.15b From Frank Sear, *Roman Architecture*, diagram 78, p.136 © 1982 by Frank Sear. Used by permission of the publisher, Cornell University Press.; 7.16 Canali Photobank; 7.17 From William L. McDonald, *Architecture of the Roman Empire*, An Introductory Study, Volume 1, Yale University Press, p.96; 7.18 © JUPITERIMAGES/ABLESTOCK/Alamy; 7.19 Oronoz; 7.20 Penelope Davies; 7.21 © Trustees of the National Museum of Scotland; 7.22 akg-images/Bildarchiv Steffens/Henri Stierlin; p143t From Mary Beard and John Henderson, *Classical Art: From Greece to Rome*, Oxford History of Art, Oxford University Press, 2001, p.39. By permission of Oxford University Press; 7.23 Canali Photobank; 7.24 Canali Photobank; 7.25 © Vatican Museums; 7.26 Canali Photobank; 7.27 © Araldo De Luca Archives, Rome; 7.28 INDEX/Vasari, Florence; 7.29 Photo Scala, Florence; 7.31 From Jas Elsner, *Imperial Rome and Christian Triumph: The Art of the Roman Empire AD 100-400*, Oxford University Press, 1998, fig. 90, p. 131; 7.32 © Achim Bednorz, Cologne; p151t Canali Photobank; p151ct Canali Photobank; p151c Canali Photobank; p151cb © Trustees of the National Museum of Scotland; p151 © Araldo De Luca Archives, Rome; p153l © Fabbrica di San Pietro/Ikona; p153cl © Achim Bednorz, Cologne; p153r Giraudon/Bridgeman Art Library

Chapter 8

p156 Canali Photobank; 8.1 Canali Photobank; 8.2 © Biblioteca Apostolica Vatican; MN (after Frazer); MN From Krautheimer, *Early Christian and Byzantine Architecture*, Yale University Press, 1984, image 34; 8.3 Scala; 8.4 Canali Photobank; 8.5 Canali Photobank; 8.6 © Photo. Scala, Florence/Bildarchiv Preussischer Kulturbesitz, Berlin; 8.7 © Fabbrica di San Pietro/Ikona; 8.9 Canali Photobank; 8.10 Canali Photobank; 8.11 Canali Photobank; 8.12 Canali Photobank; 8.14 © Achim Bednorz, Cologne; 8.15 Marvin Trachtenbeg; 8.16 © Trustees of the British Museum; 8.17 Bildarchiv der ONB, Vienna; 8.18 Jean Luc Manaud/ Rapho/Hachette; 8.20 Erich Lessing/akg-images; MN From John Lowden, *Early Christian and Byzantine Art*, Phaidon, 1997, fig. 149, p. 260; 8.21 © Studio Kontos/Photostock; 8.22 Image © 2004 The Board of Trustees, National Gallery of Art, Washington; 8.23 Dagli Orti/Art Archive; 8.24 Annie Griffiths Belt/Corbis; 8.25 "Full Interior from Qibla Door, Aubbat as-Sakhra/Dome of the Rock. Masjid al-Aqsa, Jerusalem" © 1992, Said Nuseibeh; Cultural Context box Photo Katya Kallsen © 2004 President and Fellows of Harvard College; 187t © Biblioteca Apostolica Vatican; 187ct © Fabbrica di San Pietro/Ikona; 187c Canali Photobank; 187cb Marvin Trachtenbeg

Chapter 9

p188 Bayerische Staatsbibliothek, Munchen; 9.1 © The Trustees of the British Museum; 9.2 © The Board of Trinity College Dublin; 9.3 The British Library, London; 9.4 Erich Lessing/akg-images; 9.5 Kunsthistorisches Museum, Wien; 9.6 Bibliothèque Municipale Epernay; 9.7 ©

2004. Photo Pierpont Morgan Library/Art Resource/Scala, Florence; 9.8 © Achim Bednorz, Cologne; 9.9 © Achim Bednorz, Cologne; p202 (after Beseler); 9.10 © Achim Bednorz, Cologne; 9.11 © Dom-Museum, Hildesheim/ Frank Tomio; 9.12 © Erich Lessing/AKG-images; 9.13a&b Bayerische Staatsbibliothek, Munchen; 9.14 Bayerische Staatsbibliothek, Munchen; 9.15 © Rheinisches Bildarchiv, Museen der Stadt, Cologne; 9.16 Roger Wood/Corbis; 9.17 © Achim Bednorz, Cologne; 9.18 © Achim Bednorz, Cologne; 9.19 Walter B. Denny; 9.21 Photograph © 1980 The Metropolitan Museum of Art; p213t © The Trustees of the British Museum; p213ct The British Library, London; p213c © Achim Bednorz, Cologne; p213b Bibliothèque Municipale Epernay

Chapter 10

p214 Bibliothèque Municipale, Amiens/Lauros/Giraudon/Bridgeman Art Library; 10.1 Oronoz; 10.2 © Achim Bednorz, Cologne; 10.4 Oronoz; 10.5 Photograph © 1995 The Metropolitan Museum of Art; 10.6 © 2006. Photo Scala, Florence; 10.8 From Kenneth John Conant, *Carolingian and Romanesque Architecture, 800–1200*, The Pelican History of Art, Penguin, 1959, plate 66; 10.9 © David Peter Adams; 10.10 © Achim Bednorz, Cologne; 10.11 © Achim Bednorz, Cologne; p226 The British Library, London; 10.12 © Achim Bednorz, Cologne; 10.13 © Achim Bednorz, Cologne; 10.14 Abbey Church, Saint-Savin-sur-Gartempe/Lauros /Giraudon/Bridgeman Art Library; 10.16 Bibliothèque Municipale, Amiens/Lauros/Giraudon/ Bridgeman Art Library; 10.17 © Achim Bednorz, Cologne; 10.18 © Achim Bednorz, Cologne; 10.19 © 2002. Photo Scala, Florence; 10.20 Erich Lessing/akg-images; p236t Universitätsbibliothek Johann Christian Senckenberg Frankfurt am Main; 10.21 A. F. Kersting; 10.22 © Achim Bednorz, Cologne; 10.23 © Achim Bednorz, Cologne; p239t © Achim Bednorz, Cologne; p239ct Oronoz; p239c Erich Lessing/akg-images; p239b A. F. Kersting

Chapter 11

p240 © Photo Josse, Paris; 11.2 © Achim Bednorz, Cologne; 11.3 © Achim Bednorz, Cologne; 11.4 © Achim Bednorz, Cologne; 11.5 © Achim Bednorz, Cologne; 11.6 © Achim Bednorz, Cologne; 11.7 © Achim Bednorz, Cologne; 11.9 © Achim Bednorz, Cologne; p250bl From James Snyder, *Medieval Art*, Prentice Hall, fig 453, p. 354; 11.11 © Achim Bednorz, Cologne; 11.12 © Photo Josse, Paris; 11.13 © Achim Bednorz, Cologne; 11.14 © 1990. Scala, Florence; 11.15 © Achim Bednorz, Cologne; 11.17 Photograph © 1991 The Metropolitan Museum of Art; 11.18 Giraudon/Bridgeman Art Library; 11.20 A. F. Kersting; 11.21 A. F. Kersting; 11.22 A. F. Kersting; 11.23 © Achim Bednorz, Cologne; 11.24 .© Achim Bednorz, Cologne. Reproduction forbidden. Copyright by Dom Kapitel, Naumberg; 11.25 Landschaftsverband Rheinland/ Rheinisches Lanesmuseum, Bonn; p265t © Achim Bednorz, Cologne; p265ct A. F. Kersting; p265c © Achim Bednorz, Cologne; p265b Photograph © 1991 The Metropolitan Museum of Art; p267l Canali Photobank; p267cl © Vanni Archive/CORBIS; p267cr Rijksmuseum, Amsterdam; p267r © 2007. The Metropolitan Museum of Art/Art Resource/Scala, Florence

Chapter 12

p270 © Studio Quattrone, Florence; 12.1 © 1990. Photo Scala, Florence/Fondo Edifici di Culto-Min. dell' Interno; 12.2 © 2004. Photo Scala, Florence; 12.3 © 1990 Scala, Florence; 12.4 © Achim Bednorz, Cologne; 12.6 Tosi/Index, Florence; 12.7 © Achim Bednorz, Cologne; 12.8 Scala; 12.9 Canali Photobank; 12.10 © Studio Quattrone, Florence; 12.11 Canali Photobank; 12.12 © 1990. Photo Scala, Florence; 12.13 Canali Photobank; 12.14 Biblioteca Nazionale, Florence/Microfot/ Ikona; p285t © 1990 Scala, Florence; p285ct © Achim Bednorz, Cologne; p285c Canali Photobank; p285b Canali Photobank

Chapter 13

p286 Oronoz/Museo Nacional del Prado, Madrid; 13.1 Erich Lessing/akg-images; 13.2 RMN/© R. G. Ojeda; 13.3 Photograph © 1996 The Metropolitan Museum of Art; 13.4 Erich Lessing/akg-images; 13.5 © 1994. Photo Scala, Florence; 13.6 Photo © The National Gallery, London; 13.7 Erich Lessing/akg-images; 13.8 © 1990. Photo Scala, Florence – courtesy of the Ministero Beni e Att. Culturali; 13.9 Oronoz; 13.10 © 2005. Photo Scala, Florence/Bildarchiv Preussischer Kulturbesitz, Berlin; 13.11 © Koninklijk Museum voor Schone Kunsten, Antwerp/Lukas; 13.12 Erich Lessing/akg-images; 13.13 Reproduced by courtesy of The University Librarian and Director, The John Rylands University Library, The University of Manchester; 13.14 © 1999. Photo Scala, Florence; p303t RMN/© R. G. Ojeda; p303ct Erich Lessing/akg-images; p303c Oronoz; p303b © 1999. Photo Scala, Florence

Chapter 14

p304 Canali Photobank; 14.1 © Vanni Archive/CORBIS; 14.2 Photo Scala, Florence; 14.4 Canali Photobank; 14.5 Canali Photobank; 14.6 © Studio Studio Quattrone, Florence; 14.7 © Studio Quattrone, Florence; 14.8 Museo dell' Opera del Duomo, Florence/Bridgeman Art Library; 14.9 Erich Lessing/akg-images; 14.10 © 1990. Photo Scala, Florence – courtesy of the Ministero Beni e Att. Culturali; 14.11 Codato/Canali Photobank; 14.12 ©1998.Photo Scala, Florence; 14.13 Nimatallah/akg-images; 14.15 Photo © The National Gallery, London; 14.16 Canali Photobank; 14.17 Image © 2008 The Board of Trustees, National Gallery of Art, Washington; 14.18 Canali Photobank; 14.19 © 2001. Photo Scala, Florence – courtesy of the Ministero Beni e Att. Culturali; 14.20 Canali Photobank; 14.21 Erich Lessing/akg-images; 14.22 © 1990. Photo Scala, Florence – courtesy of the Ministero Beni e Att. Culturali; 14.23 Canali Photobank; 14.24 Canali Photobank; p329t Vanni/Art Resource, NY; p329ct Codato/Canali Photobank; p329c © 1990. Photo Scala, Florence – courtesy of the Ministero Beni e Att. Culturali; p329cb Canali Photobank; p329b Canali Photobank

Chapter 15

p330 Canali Photobank; 15.1 Photo Scala, Florence; 15.2 Ghigo Roli/Index, Florence; 15.3 RMN/© Hervé Lewandowski; 15.4 © Foto Pirozzi, Rome; 15.6 © Trustees of The British Museum; 15.7 Canali Photobank; 15.8 © 2005. Photo Scala, Florence – courtesy of the Ministero Beni e Att. Culturali; 15.9 Musei Vaticani/IKONA; 15.10 Canali Photobank; 15.11 Image © The Board of Trustees, National Gallery of Art, Washington; 15.12 Vatican Museums and Galleries, Vatican City/Giraudon/Bridgeman Art Library; 15.13 © 1990. Photo Scala, Florence; 15.14 Canali Photobank; 15.15 RMN/© Thierry Le Mage; p345t Ghigo Roli/Index, Florence; p345ct © 2005. Photo Scala, Florence – courtesy of the Ministero Beni e Att. Culturali; p345c RMN/© Hervé Lewandowski; p345b Canali Photobank

Chapter 16

p346 Photo © The National Gallery, London; 16.1 © 1992. Photo Scala, Florence – courtesy of the Ministero Beni e Att. Culturali; 16.2 akg-images/Erich Lessing; 16.3 Photo © The National Gallery, London; 16.4 Canali Photobank; 16.5 © Vatican Museums; 16.6 Canali Photobank; 16.7 © 1990. Scala, Florence; 16.8 © 2004. Photo Scala, Florence; 16.9 © Studio Quattrone, Florence; 16.10 National Museum of Women in the Arts, Washington, D.C. Gift of Wallace and Wilhelmina Holladay; 16.11 © 1996. Photo Scala, Florence – courtesy of the Ministero Beni e Att. Culturali; 16.12 © 1990. Photo Scala, Florence – courtesy of the Ministero Beni e Att. Culturali; 16.13 © Cameraphoto Arte, Venice; 16.14 Achim Bednorz, Cologne; p363t © 1992. Photo Scala, Florence – courtesy of the Ministero Beni e Att. Culturali; p363ct © Vatican Museums; p363c © 1996. Photo Scala, Florence – courtesy of the Ministero Beni e Att. Culturali; p363b Photo © The National Gallery, London

Chapter 17

p364 Photograph © The Metropolitan Museum of Art; 17.1 Age Fotostock/SuperStock; 17.2 Patrick Muller © CMN, Paris; 17.3 © 1995. Photo Scala, Florence; 17.4 © Musée d'Unterlinden, Colmar; 17.5 © Musée d'Unterlinden, Colmar; 17.6 Image © The Metropolitan Museum of Art; 17.7 Getty Images/Hulton Archive; 17.8 Bayerische Staatsgemaldesammlungen, Alte Pinakothek Munich; 17.9 Staatliche Kunsthalle, Karlsruhe, Germany; 17.10 © 1990. Photo Scala, Florence; 17.11 Canali Photobank; 17.12 Musée des Beaux-Arts, Rouen/Lauros/Giraudon/Bridgeman Art Library; 17.13 Bo Gyllander; 17.14 Erich Lessing/akg-images; 17.15 Erich Lessing/akg-images; p381t Photo by O. Zimmermann/© Musée d'Unterlinden, Colmar; p381ct Age Fotostock/SuperStock; p381c Canali Photobank; p381cb Erich Lessing/akg-images; p381b © 1995. Photo Scala, Florence

Chapter 18

p382 © Achim Bednorz, Cologne; 18.1 Canali Photobank; 18.2 © 2007 The Metroplitan Museum of Art/Art Resource/Scala, Florence; 18.3 Photograph © 1984 The Detroit Institue of Arts; 18.4 Canali Photobank; 18.5 © 2007. Photo Scala, Florence/Fondo Edifici di Culto-Min. dell' Interno; 18.6 Aerocentro Varesino/IKONA; 18.7 © 1990. Photo Scala, Florence; 18.8 INDEX, Florence; 18.9 © Achim Bednorz, Cologne; 18.10 © 2000. Photo Scala, Florence – courtesy of the Ministero Beni e Att. Culturali; 18.11 IKONA; 18.12 Erich Lessing/akg-images; 18.13 Photograph © 1981 The Metropolitan Museum of Art; 18.14 Erich Lessing/akg-images; 18.16 Photograph © 1982 The Metropolitan Museum of Art; p405t Canali Photobank; p405ct © Achim Bednorz, Cologne; p405c © 1990. Photo Scala, Florence; p405b Erich Lessing/akg-images

Chapter 19

p406 Erich Lessing/akg-images; 19.1 Image © 2005 The Board of Trustees, National Gallery of Art, Washington; 19.2 Peter Willi/SuperStock; 19.3 Erich Lessing/akg-images; 19.4 RMN/© Christian Jean; 19.5 The John and Mable Ringling Museum of Art; 19.6 Photo © The National Gallery, London; 19.9 Image © The Board of Trustees, National Gallery of Art, Washington; 19.10 © 2005. Photo Scala, Florence/Bildarchiv Preussischer Kulturbestitz; 19.12 Image © The Metropolitan Museum of Art; 19.13 © Photo The Frick Collection, New York; 19.18 Image © The Board of Trustees, National Gallery of Art, Washington. Photo Richard Carafelli; p425t Peter Willi/SuperStock; p425ct RMN/© Christian Jean; p425c Image © The Board of Trustees, National Gallery of Art, Washington. Photo Richard Carafelli

Chapter 20

p426 Getty Research Institute for the History of Art and the Humanities/Wim Swaan; 20.1 RMN © Gérard Blot; 20.3 Photograph © The Art Institute of Chicago; 20.4 RMN/© Hervé Lewandowski; 20.5 © Achim Bednorz, Cologne; 20.6 © Yann Arthus-Bertrand/Altitude; 20.7 Getty Research Institute for the History of Art and the Humanities/Wim Swaan; 20.8 Wallace Collection, London/Bridgeman Art Library; 20.9 A. F. Kersting; 20.10 A. F. Kersting; p439t A. F. Kersting; p439ct Minneapolis Institute of Arts, The William Hood Dunwoody Fund; p439c Getty Research Institute for the History of Art and the Humanities/Wim Swaan; p439b A. F. Kersting

Chapter 21

p440 Wallace Collection, London/Bridgeman Art Library; 21.1 RMN © Gérard Blot; 21.2 © 2000 Pierpont Morgan Library/Art Resource/Scala, Florence; 21.3 Wallace Collection, London/Bridgeman Art Library; 21.4 RMN/© Hervé Lewandowski; 21.5 RMN/© Hervé

Lewandowski; 21.6 © 2007. The Metropolitan Museum of Art/Art Resource/Scala, Florence; 21.7 © 2007. The Metropolitan Museum of Art/Art Resource/Scala, Florence; 21.8 © 2003. Photo Scala, Florence/HIP; 21.9 Photo © The National Gallery, London; 21.10 Courtesy of the Huntington Library Art Collections, and Botanical Gardens, San Marino, CA; 21.11 Bayerische Verwaltung der Staadlichen Schloesser; 21.12 The Royal Collection. © 2008 Her Majesty Queen Elizabeth II; p455t RMN/© Hervé Lewandowski; p455ct © 2003. Photo Scala, Florence/HIP; p455c Bayerische Verwaltung der Staadlichen Schloesser; p455b Wallace Collection, London/Bridgeman Art Library; p457l Erich Lessing/akg-images; p457cl The Samuel Courtauld Trust, The Courtauld Gallery, London; p457cr © 2008. Digital image, The Museum of Modern Art, New York/Scala, Florence; p457r Superstock

Chapter 22

p460 © 2007. Yale University Art Gallery/Art Resource, NY/Scala, Florence; 22.1 © Photoservice Electa/Ikona; 22.2 Image © The Metropolitan Museum of Art; 22.3 Photo Kathernine Wetzel/The Virginia Museum of Fine Arts; 22.4 Photo © National Gallery of Canada, Ottawa. Transfer from the Canadian War Memorials, 1921; 22.5 © Achim Bednorz, Cologne; 22.6 © 2003. Photo Scala, Florence/HIP; 22.7 © Crown copyright. NMR; 22.8 © 2007. Yale University Art Gallery/Art Resource, NY/Scala, Florence; 22.9 French Government Tourist Office; 22.11 Erich Lessing/akg-images; 22.12 Erich Lessing/akg-images; 22.13 RMN © Gérard Blot/Christian Jean; p477t © Achim Bednorz, Cologne; p477ct © Crown copyright. NMR; p477c © 2007. Yale University Art Gallery/Art Resource, NY/Scala, Florence; p477b RMN © Gérard Blot/Christian Jean

Chapter 23

p478 RMN © Thierry Le Mage; 23.1 Oronoz; 23.2 National Gallery, London/Bridgeman Art Library; 23.3 Photograph © 2008 Museum of Fine Arts, Boston; 23.4 © 2005. Photo Scala, Florence/Bildarchiv Preussischer Kulturbesitz, Berlin; 23.5 © 2007 The Metropolitan Museum of Art/Art Resource/Scala, Florence; 23.6 RMN/© Hervé Lewandowski; 23.7 RMN/© Thierry Le Mage; 23.8 RMN/© Daniel Arnaudet; 23.9 RMN/© Thierry Le Mage; 23.11 RMN/© Christian Jean; 23.12 © Bernard Boutrit/Woodfin Camp & Associates; 23.13 © Stewart McKnight/Alamy; 23.14 © Peter Aaron/Esto; 23.15 © Achim Bednorz, Cologne; p499t RMN/© Christian Jean; p499ct © 2005. Photo Scala, Florence/Bildarchiv Preussischer Kulturbesitz, Berlin; p499c Oronoz; p499b © Stewart McKnight/Alamy

Chapter 24

p500 The Phillips Collection, Washington, D.C.; 24.1 RMN © Gérard Blot/Hervé Lewandowski; 24.2 RMN/© Hervé Lewandowski; 24.3 RMN/© Hervé Lewandowski; 24.4 © Brooklyn Museum; 24.5 Photograph © The Art Institute of Chicago; 24.6 The Phillips Collection, Washington, D.C.; 24.7 Photograph © The Art Institute of Chicago; 24.8 Tate Gallery, London/Art Resource, NY; 24.9 V&A Images/Victoria and Albert Museum; 24.10 Tate Gallery, London/Art Resource, NY; 24.11 Tate Gallery, London/Art Resource, NY; 24.12 © 2007 The Metropolitan Museum of Art/Art Resource/Scala, Florence; 24.13 © Butler Institute of American Art, Youngstown, OH. Museum Purchase 1918/Bridgeman Art Library; 24.14 RMN/© Patrice Schmidt; 24.16 Library of Congress, Prints and Photographs Division, Washington, D.C; 24.17 Courtesy George Eastman House; 24.18 Art Archive; 24.19 Getty Images/Hulton Archive; p523t RMN/© Gérard Blot/Hervé Lewandowski; p523ct RMN/© Patrice Schmidt; p523c Tate Gallery, London/Art Resource, NY; p523b Getty Images/Hulton Archive

Chapter 25

p524 © 2008. The Museum of Modern Art, New York/Scala, Florence; 25.1 The Samuel Courtauld Trust, The Courtauld Gallery, London/Bridgeman Art Library; 25.2 © The Art Institute of Chicago; 25.3 © 2008. The Museum of Modern Art, New York/Scala, Florence; 25.4 Photograph © 2008 Museum of Fine Arts, Boston; 25.6 RMN/© Jean-Gilles Berizzi; 25.7 © 2008. The Museum of Modern Art, New York/Scala, Florence; 25.8 Art Archive/Nasjonal Galleriet, Oslo/Joseph Martin. © Munch Museum/Munch – Ellingsen Group, BONO, Oslo/DACS, London 2008; 25.9 Stapleton Collection/Bridgeman Art Library; 25.10 Bildarchiv der ONB, Vienna; 25.11 Image © The Board of Trustees, National Gallery of Art, Washington; 25.12 © 2004. Smithsonian American Art Museum/Art Resource/Scala, Florence; 25.13 RMN/© Droits réservés; 25.14 Musée Rodin, Paris/Bridgeman Art Library; 25.15 Société Multimedia des Auteurs de Arts Visuels; 25.16 Gala/SuperStock; 25.17 © Art on File/Corbis; 25.18 © Robert Frerck/Woodfin Camp & Associates; 25.19 Photo Bruce M. White. © 1998 Photo: Trustees of Princeton University.; 25.20 Courtesy George Eastman House © Joanna T. Steichen; p545t The Samuel Courtauld Trust, The Courtauld Gallery, London; p545ct Art Archive/Nasjonal Galleriet, Oslo/Joseph Martin; p545c Société Multimedia des Auteurs de Arts Visuels

Chapter 26

p545b © Art on File/Corbis; 26.1 Photograph reproduced with the permission of The Barnes Foundation; 26.2 © 2008. Digital image, The Museum of Modern Art, New York/Scala, Florence; 26.3 Photo Martin Buhler/Kunstmuseum, Basel; 26.4 The McNay Art Museum, San Antonio, Texas. Bequest of Marion Koogler McNay; 26.5 RMN/© Béatrice Hatala; 26.6 Photo Martin Buhler/Kunstmuseum, Basel; 26.7 © 2008. Digital image, The Museum of Modern Art, New York/Scala, Florence; 26.9 Hans Hinz/ARTOTHEK; 26.10 Colorphoto Hinz, Allschwil-Basel, Switzerland. © Robert Delaunay/L&M Services B.V. The Hague, 20080506; 26.11 © 2008. Digital image, The Museum of Modern Art, New York/Scala, Florence; 26.12 Norton Simon Foundation; 26.13 © 2008. Digital image, The Museum of Modern Art, New York/Scala, Florence; 26.15 French Government Tourist Office; 26.16 Philadelpia Museum of Art: The Louise and Walter Arensberg Collection, 1950; 26.17 Photograph Geoffrey Clements/Whitney Museum of American Art; 26.18 © Vanni Archive/CORBIS; 26.19 French Government Tourist Office; p567t Photo Martin Buhler/Kunstmuseum, Basel; p567ct © 2008. Digital image, The Museum of Modern Art, New York/Scala, Florence; p567c Photo Martin Buhler/Kunstmuseum, Basel; p567b © Vanni Archive/CORBIS

Chapter 27

p568 © 2004. The Newark Museum/Art Resource/Scala, Florence; 27.3 Photo CNAC/MNAM/RMN/© Droits réservés; 27.4 Erich Lessing/akg-images; 27.6 Telimage, 2004; 27.8 © 2008. Digital image, The Museum of Modern Art, New York/Scala, Florence; 27.9 © 2008. Digital image, The Museum of Modern Art, New York/Scala, Florence; 27.10 © 2008. Digital image, The Museum of Modern Art, New York/Scala, Florence; 27.11 The Tate Gallery, London/Art Resource, NY; 27.12 Moderna Museet, Stockholm; 27.14 © Bildarchiv Monheim GmbH/Alamy; 27.15 Bauhausarchiv-Museum fur Gestaltung, Berlin; 27.16 © Vanni/Art Resource, NY; 27.17 © 2007. Digital image, The Museum of Modern Art, New York/Scala, Florence; 27.18 © 2004. The Newark Museum/Art Resource/Scala, Florence; 27.19 Courtesy George Eastman House © Aperture Foundation, Inc., Paul Strand Archive; 27.20 Margaret Bourke-White/Time-Life Pictures/Getty Images; 27.21 © 2007 The Metropolitan Museum of Art/Art Resource/Scala, Florence. Photo Malcolm Varon, NY; 27.22 Photograph © The Art Institute of Chicago.; 27.23 © 2007. Digital image, The Museum of Modern Art, New York/Scala, Florence; 27.24 © 2005. Art Resource/Scala, Florence; 27.25 Photograph by Geoffrey Clements/Whitney Museum of American Art; 27.27 © 2003. Photo Scala, Florence/John Bigelow Taylor; p595t Philadelphia Museum of Art: Gift (by exchange) of Mrs Herbert Cameron Morris, 1998; p595ct Photograph by Geoffrey Clements/Whitney Museum of American Art; p595c © 2008. Digital image, The Museum of Modern Art, New York/Scala, Florence; p595b © 2003. Photo Scala, Florence/John Bigelow Taylor

Chapter 28

p596 Courtesy James Cohan Gallery, New York. Collection DIA Center for the Arts, New York. Photo by Gianfranco Gorgoni; 28.1 © 2007. The Metropolitan Museum of Art/Art Resource/Scala, Florence; 28.2 © 2007. Digital image, The Museum of Modern Art, New York/Scala, Florence; 28.4 Museum Ludwig, Rheinisches Bildarchiv, Museen der Stadt, Cologne; 28.5 Photograph by Geoffrey Clements/Whitney Museum of American Art; 28.6 Photo © Robert McElroy and Getty Research Institute for History and Humanities. Courtesy Allan Kaprow Estate Hauser & Wirth Zürich London; 28.8 © 2007. Digital image, The Museum of Modern Art, New York/Scala, Florence; 28.9 © 2008. Digital image, The Museum of Modern Art, New York/Scala, Florence; 28.10 Photograph by Philipp Scholz Ritterman; 28.11 Photograph by David Heald/ Solomon R. Guggenheim Museum; 28.12 © The Estate of Eva Hesse. Hauser & Wirth Zürich London; 28.14 © 2007. Digital image, The Museum of Modern Art, New York/Scala, Florence; 28.15 © Ute Klophaus, D-Wuppertal; 28.17 © Hirshhorn Museum and Sculpture Garden, Smithsonian Institution, Washington, DC. Gift of Joseph H. Hirshhorn, 1966 Photographer: Lee Stalsworth; 28.18 Photograph © Donald Woodman; 28.19 © Ezra Stoller/Esto; p617t © 2007. The Metropolitan Museum of Art/Art Resource/Scala, Florence; p617ct Photograph by Philipp Scholz Ritterman; p617b Photograph © Donald Woodman

Chapter 29

p618 © Peter Aaron/Esto; 29.1 © Matt Wargo for VSBA; 29.2 © Peter Aaron/Esto; 29.3 Centre Pompidou, Musée National d'Art Moderne; 29.4 SuperStock; 29.5 Photograph © 2007 Carnegie Museum of Art, Pittsburgh; 29.7 © Frank Fournier; 29.8 © Galerie Michael Werner; 29.9 Courtesy of the Artist and Metro Pictures; 29.10 Photo James Dee; 29.11 Courtesy of Bill Viola Studio, Photo: Kira Perov; 29.12 Photograph by Peter Muscato; 29.13 Photograph by Jerry L. Thompson/Whitney Museum of American Art; 29.14 Photo by Hiro Ihara, courtesy Cai Studio; 29.9 Courtesy of the Artist and Metro Pictures; 29.2 © Peter Aaron/Esto; 29.4 SuperStock; 29.14 Photo by Hiro Ihara, courtesy Cai Studio

Index

Boldface names refer to artists. Pages in italics refer to illustrations.

Dadaim, 572–574, *572*, *573*

Bernini, Gianlorenzo, 13, 389, 435
Baldacchino, 393–394, *393*
David, 396, *397*
The Ecstasy of St. Teresa, 397, *398*, *399*

Beuys, Joseph, 612, 624
How to Explain Pictures to a Dead Hare, 612, *612*

Bible *see also* Christianity; Reformation
King James Bible, 427
versions of 166

Bing, Siegfried, 538

Birth of Venus, The (Botticelli), 319–320, *319*

Black Death *see* plague

Black Iris III (O'Keeffe), 588–589, *588*

Blaue Reiter, Der, 555–556, *556*

Bleaching Grounds Near Haarlem (Ruisdael), 420, *420*

Blessed Art Thou Among Women (Käsebier), 543–544, *544*

Blue Rider *see* Blaue Reiter

Boccaccio, Giovanni, 267
Decameron, 282

Boccioni, Umberto, 558
States of Mind I: Farewells, 559–560, *559*

Bologna, Giovanni, *The Rape of the Sabine Woman,* 351–352, *351*

Bonheur de Vivre, Le (The Joy of Life) (Matisse), 547–548, *548*

Book of Durrow (Symbol of St. Matthew), 192, *193*

Book of Homilies (Guda), 236, *236*

Book of Hours, 258, 283

Borromini, Francesco, 389
Sant'Ivo alla Sapienza, Rome, 394, 395–396, *395*

Bosch, Hieronymus, *The Garden of Earthly Delights,* 296–297, *297*

Boston Atheneum, 485

Botticelli, Sandro, *The Birth of Venus,* 319–320, *319*

Bourke-White, Margaret, *Fort Peck Dam, Montana,* 588, *588*

Brady, Mathew, 519

Bramante, Donato, 333–335, 340
Tempietto, 334, *334*
Saint Peter's Basilica, 334–335, *335*, 354

Brancacci Chapel (Masaccio frescoes), Santa Maria del Carmine, Florence, 311

Brancusi, Constantin
The Kiss, 563, *563*
The Newborn, 563–564, *564*

Braque, Georges, *The Portuguese,* 550, *551*

Breton, André, 574–576, 578

Breuer, Marcel, Living Room, Werkbund housing development, Stuttgart, 583, *583*

Bride of the Wind, The (Kokoschka), 556–557, *557*

Bronze Age, 19
Aegean, 64, 66, 72

bronze work, 92, 120
Baptistery of San Giovanni, doors (Pisano), Florence, 275–276, *275*
Baptistery of San Giovanni, doors *Gates of Paradise* (Ghiberti), 312–313, *312*
David (Donatello), 316–317, *317*
Equestrian Monument of Gattamelata (Donatello), 315, *315*
Equestrian Statue of a Carolingian Ruler, 195–196, *195*
Equestrian Statue of Marcus Aurelius, 131, *131*
She-Wolf, 120, *120*
Zeus or Poseidon, 92–93, *93*

Bronzino, Agnolo, *Allegory of Venus,* 350–351, *350*

Brücke, Die, 554–555, *555*

Bruegel the Elder, Pieter
Peasant Wedding, 380, *380*
The Return of the Hunters, 379–380, *379*

Brunelleschi, Filippo
Florence Cathedral dome, 305–306, *306*
San Lorenzo, Florence, 306–307, *307*, 347–348

Brussels, Tassel House (Horta), 539, *539*

Bryant, William Cullen, 485

Bucintoro at the Molo, The (Canaletto), 454, *454*

Buddhism, 43

building and construction
arches, 124, 139, *139*, 150, 209, 217, 219, 229, 232–233, *232*, *233*, 307; corbel, 73, *73*; horseshoe, 226; pointed, 224, 242–243, 272; Roman, 126, *126*; transverse, 236, 238; triumphal, 133, 162, 165, 233, 323
ashlar masonry, 66, 73–74
buttresses, 38, 126, 172, 219, 237, 243, 355, 471–472; flying, 249, 251, 261
concrete, 124–126, 136, 138, 148; Portland cement, 541
curtain wall, 541, 565
masonry techniques, 216
mortise and tenon joint, 30
mud bricks, 33, 38, 50, 66, 118–119
orthostats, 41
piers 211–212, 236–237, 248, 249, 541, 621; compound, 217, 219, *249*
post-and-lintel construction, 29, 59, *59*, 73, 125, 148
pylons, 59; trussed, 522
steel, 541
vaults, 73, 172, 211, 235, *250*, 249, 251, 262, 272, 452; barrel, 126, *126*, 148, 220, *277*, 310–311, 323, 338, 522; corbel, *73*; groin, 126, *126*, 149, *236*, 236–238, 242–243, 275; ribbed, 248; Romanesque stone, 223
voussoirs, 126, 209, 226

Building of the Tower of Babel, The (Romanesque wall painting), 229, *229*

Burial at Ornans (Courbet), 502–503, *502*

Burial of Count Orgaz, The (El Greco), 367–368, *367*

Burke, Edmund, 464, 469, 471

Burlington, Lord, Chiswick House (with William Kent), London, 467–468, *468*

Bust of Lorenzo de' Medici (Verrocchio), 320, *320*

buttresses *see* building and construction

Buxheim St. Christopher (woodcut), 300, *300*

Byzantine art
origins, 157

Byzantine art, early
architecture, 169–174, *169–170*, *172*, *173*
icons, 176–177, *177*
illustrated manuscripts, 175–176, *176*
mosaics, 171–172, *171*, 174–175
San Vitale church, Ravenna, 169–172, *169–172*
sculpture, 174–175, *175*

Byzantine art, late
icons, 180–181
mosaics and murals, 181–182, *182*

Byzantine art, middle
architecture, 179, *179–180*
iconoclasm, 178
illustrated manuscripts, 178, *178–179*
mosaics, 179–180, *179*, *180*

Byzantium *see* Constantinople

C

Caen, Normandy, Saint-Étienne church at, 237–238, *238*

Caesar, Julius, 123, 135

Cai Guo-Qiang, 632–634
Light Cycle: Explosion Project for Central Park, 634, *634*

Calder, Alexander, *Lobster Trap and Fish Tail,* 578, *579*

caliphs, 159

Calling of St. Matthew, The (Caravaggio), 384–386, *385*

Camera Club of New York, 543

camera obscura, 424, 454

Camera Picta (Mantegna), 324–325, *325*

Cameron, Julia Margaret, 543
Sister Spirits, 520–521, *521*

campanile, Florence, 275

Campbell's Soup Cans (Warhol), 605, *606*

Campin, Robert, *Mérode Triptych,* 290–291, *290*

Canaletto (Giovanni Antonio Canal), *The Bucintoro at the Molo,* 454, *454*

canon, 92

"canon" of proportions, Egyptian, 54; Aegean, 65

Canova, Antonio, *Cupid and Psyche,* 494, *494*

capital *see also* columns; 81

Cappadocia, 18

Caravaggio, 399, 413, 428
The Calling of St. Matthew, 384–386, *385*
The Musicians, 386–387, *387*

Cardona, Spain, Church of Sant Vincenç, 216, 217

Carolingian art
architecture, 199–201, *199*, *200*
illustrated manuscripts, 196–199, *196–198*
sculpture, 195, *195*, 196

Carracci, Annibale, *Loves of the Gods,* 389, *390*